MW00824072

THE
OLD COVENANTS

THE OLD TESTAMENT
2 CHRONICLES–MALACHI

from the Joseph Smith New Translation
of the Holy Bible

RESTORATION EDITION

© 2019 Restoration Scriptures Foundation. All rights reserved.
Restoration Scriptures Foundation is a trademark of Restoration Archive LLC.

First Edition

ISBN 978-1-951168-55-1

TEXT V1.241 - 2020.09.10

CONTENTS

FOREWORD

JOSEPH SMITH warned in 1831 that "except the church [receive] the fullness of the Scriptures that they would yet fall." The "fullness" was defined as the Book of Mormon, the revelations, and the new, inspired Bible revisions (*see* Teachings and Commandments 105:13–14). Less than one year later, in September 1832, the saints of God were condemned by the Lord and commanded to *repent and remember the new covenant, even the Book of Mormon and the former commandments which I have given them, not only to say, but to do according to that which I have written* (T&C 82:20). This is often interpreted as the Lord rebuking the saints for failing to *do* according to that which He had written, while the assumption is made that the saints had been correctly *saying* what He had written. But the saints did not *say;* they failed to accurately preserve the revelations that God provided to them, and their texts became corrupted.

This volume of scripture is one of three that together constitute a unified effort to recover what the scriptures originally said and to prune away the uninspired alterations of man. This endeavor began with individuals who were separately directed by God to begin this work and were then inspired to find one another. Eventually two groups were formed, each unknown to the other. As they faced the completion of their respective projects in mid-December of 2016, they became aware of one another, and on December 31, 2016, Denver Snuffer Jr. facilitated a meeting between the two groups, in which they determined to unify their efforts. Each group brought different components to the endeavor that provided for a greater outcome than either project had possessed alone. Moving forward, the united team worked closely with one another, with the Lord, and with the Lord's servant, and produced a record that is more accurate and more true to the Lord's intent and to the Restoration.

This edition of scripture stands as a witness to the whole world; it is the sign that the moment has arrived when the things that have been prophesied of in scripture will now occur in a single generation. Mankind doesn't have to accept the witness, they don't even have to notice the witness; it's only required that God send the witness. If He sends the witness, God has done His part. These scriptures are a new witness of Him and a sign of His invitation to renew communication with mankind.

Although commonly referred to as the Old Testament, this volume has been renamed *The Old Covenants* because it includes the covenants that were established with Adam, Enoch, Noah, Abraham, and Moses. This new title more accurately reflects the nature of the material contained within it and places it in juxtaposition with the volume called *The New Covenants*.

The hand of the Lord has been present in the process of preparing these scriptures. May His Spirit guide you and testify to you as you receive them.

CANONIZATION

On Saturday, September 2, 2017, during the Covenant of Christ Conference held in Boise, Idaho, this volume was canonized as scripture by affirmative vote of the general assembly of the body of believers, both assembled there and participating by video stream throughout the world. This marked the first and only time, to that point in history, that the Book of Mormon had ever been formally voted upon and accepted as a canon of scripture by any group of believers. Further, with the adoption of The Old Covenants, The New Covenants, and Teachings and Commandments (T&C) as "a standard for governing ourselves, as a law, and as a covenant, to establish a rule for our faith, and as the expression of our religion," those professing to believe in the Doctrine of Christ formally received the Book of Mormon not only as a canon of scripture, but also as a covenant from God. This fulfilled the last prerequisite necessary in obtaining a new covenant from Him that would commence the grafting of the gentiles into the house of Israel to be numbered among His people (*see* Jacob 3; also *Answer and Covenant*). The following morning, the Lord offered His grafting covenant to the world, which was authoritatively administered by his servant Denver Snuffer Jr. and continues to be available to all who will receive it (*see* T&C 158).

What follows is a transcript of the canonization proceedings, held at Eagle Island State Park in Eagle, Idaho on Saturday, September 2, 2017:

SPEAKER: "The scriptures to this point have been the result of thousands of hours of labor by dozens of volunteers. They were prayerfully presented to the Lord, who was asked to accept the labor as our best attempt to preserve and recover the scriptures provided to us in the Restoration through Joseph Smith. We asked the Lord to continue the work of the Restoration and allow his revelations, work, covenant, and blessings to roll forth with us, and the things kept hidden be uncovered, and a fullness be given to us as a people. The prayer said this:

> It is written that those who will not harden their hearts will receive a greater portion of your word, until they know the mysteries of God in full (see Prayer for Covenant, T&C 156:14).

"We seek to leave behind a hard heart and to be as open to receiving a greater portion of your word and to know of your mysteries and obtain your grace for us as a people that we may become yours. We have added only things to the scriptures as we have understood to also have come from you and would be pleasing to you. We ask that you accept these books as yours, so that people of faith may then rely upon this work as your word to this generation, as a standard for governing ourselves as a law, and as a covenant to establish a rule for our faith, and as the expression of our religion so we may have correct faith and be enabled to worship you in truth.

"In his *Answer to Prayer for Covenant*, the Lord stated this:

> I commend your diligent labor, and your desire to repent and recover the scriptures containing the covenant I offer for the last days. For this purpose I caused the Book of Mormon to come forth. I commend those who have participated, as well as those who have offered words of caution, for I weigh the hearts of men and many have intended well...
>
> There is great reason to rejoice because of the work that has been done...the records in the form you have of The Old Covenants given from Adam until Moses and from Moses to

John are of great worth and can serve my purposes, and are acceptable for this time...

As you have labored with the records you have witnessed the alterations and insertions, and your effort to recover them pleases me and is of great worth...

I, the Lord, say to you...what you have gathered as scriptures are acceptable to me for this time, and contain many plain and precious things. Nevertheless, whoso is enlightened by the spirit shall obtain the greater benefit, because you need not think they contain all my words nor that more will not be given, for there are many things yet to be restored unto my people...

And now I will accept what you have produced...

(T&C 157:4, 6, 15, 44–45)

"We now invite all of you — as a body of believers assembled in this conference and those who are viewing from at home — to also accept the content of the scriptures project as our new Restoration scriptures, not only as our best effort to recover what has already been given, but also as an expression of our willingness to receive more. All those who choose to accept the scriptures as a rule for our faith and as the expression of our religion, please stand.

"Let me read that one more time: All those who choose to accept the scriptures as a rule for our faith and as the expression of our religion, please say, 'Yes.'

"Thank you. Please be seated."

PREFACE

This edition of the Old Testament is drawn from Joseph Smith's *New Translation of the Holy Bible*, commonly known as the *Inspired Version*. During talks that Joseph Smith gave in the Nauvoo era, there were several times when he said, "The Bible reads this way, but it ought to read that way," or "This is what it says, but a plainer meaning or plainer translation would be this." In 1867, the Reorganized Church of Jesus Christ of Latter Day Saints (RLDS) first published Joseph's *New Translation* under the title *The Holy Scriptures, Translated and Corrected by the Spirit of Revelation*. When the Joseph Smith Translation (JST) was first published by the RLDS Church, the publishing committee made a number of editorial changes. Additionally, Joseph Smith made changes that did not get incorporated into their version. This Restoration Edition of the Old Testament encompasses every change Joseph Smith made, whether they were in the version published by the RLDS Church or not; also, all of the editorial changes that were inserted by their committee have been eliminated. Great effort has been taken to gather and correctly reflect exactly what Joseph Smith intended. However, Joseph's labor to recover and restore the text of the Bible was never completed, hindering this current effort to fully reflect his intentions.

All available sources of the Joseph Smith *Inspired Version* of the Bible have been used to align the text with Joseph's efforts to improve the text. In addition to the written edits made by Joseph, a number of other textual adjustments have been made; these adjustments were things that Joseph stated in public discourses that never became part of his written New Translation.

The following is a simple list of the updates and changes made to the Old Testament for this Restoration Edition of the scriptures:

- For the first time, the entire Book of Moses will be contained within the Book of Genesis, where it rightfully belongs, as Genesis 1:1–Genesis 5:12. Joseph's work of translation and revision of the Bible commenced with this particular book, and he received it by revelation, starting in June of 1830. Chapters of the Book of Moses were originally published in *The Evening and Morning Star* and the *Times and Seasons*. Later, portions of the book were published in the 1851 edition of the LDS Pearl of Great Price, with a more complete edition printed in 1878. The RLDS Church included the Book of Moses in its 1864 edition of the Doctrine and Covenants and placed portions in its 1867 edition of the JST. The Book of Moses contains accounts of Adam, Noah, and Moses, as well as the Book of Enoch.

- The Song of Solomon has been removed, as Joseph declared that it was not an inspired writing.
- Archaic language updates to the Bible were approved by the Lord and have been restricted to updating words, phrases, and grammar that are no longer used in modern speech (*see* Teachings & Commandments 157:15).
- Some phrases and sentences have been modified in consequence of these word updates or when current wording made the meaning unclear. This was only permitted when the intent of the meaning was retained, as directed by the Lord (ibid.). Whenever meaning was questionable, the text was left alone. This meant that odd-sounding or incorrect text was not necessarily good justification for change. For example: *For in their anger they slew a man, and in their self-will they digged down a wall* (Genesis 12:21); *digged* has been updated to *dug*, but a more correct translation of *digged down a wall* would be an understanding that Simeon and Levi amused themselves by ham-stringing or laming cattle. That correction was not made.
- Particular attention has been paid to how words are used and their structure. For example, *first born* refers to birth order, whereas *firstborn* is titular and refers to the birthright; *every one* refers to all of the parts of a subset, whereas *everyone* refers to all people.
- The distinction of LORD/Lord and GOD/God have been let go and standardized to Lord and God.
- Name spellings have been standardized.
- Some old grammatical structures have been updated to make reading significantly easier, such as Verb>Noun>Object was changed to Noun>Verb>Object; for example: *Then answered they him* became *Then they answered him* (John 5:2). Some exceptions were made when the text needed to be respected more than it

needed to be updated, for example...*created I him; ...created I them* (Genesis 3:14).

- Chapters have been set by context rather than tradition, and verses have been expanded to paragraphs to allow the context to influence the reading of the text. This diminishes the divorcing of statements from their greater context, which often occurs when a scriptural text is poorly divided into smaller chapters and verses.
- Punctuation has been reduced, whenever possible, to allow multiple interpretations where the text suggests that possibility. Otherwise, modern grammatical rules have been applied.
- Some literary tools have been used to invite new or particular perspectives to be considered. For example, when referring to God, pronouns have all been rendered in lowercase to help reduce the historically-perceived distance between God and man. Words that can convey multiple meanings are largely rendered in lowercase, even when one of the meanings would demand capitalization, such as *earth*. Also, a significant number of titles have been rendered in lowercase to avoid elevating some men and positions above others.

Great effort has been put into honoring the work of Joseph Smith in this collection. Because numerous changes indicated in the Bible that Joseph used for his translation have never been included in any prior version of the JST, this should be considered the *most complete* JST currently available.

EDITOR'S NOTE

In the world of English language publishing, books typically start on a right-hand page. In the complete volume of The Old Covenants, however, 2 Chronicles falls on a left-hand page. To match the layout in this book with that of the complete Old Covenants, this book begins on a left-hand page as well. Thank you.

THE SECOND BOOK OF THE CHRONICLES

AND Solomon the son of David was strengthened in his kingdom, and the Lord his God was with him and magnified him exceedingly. Then Solomon spoke unto all Israel, to the captains of thousands and of hundreds, and to the judges, and to every governor in all Israel — the chief of the fathers. So Solomon and all the congregation with him went to the high place that was at Gibeon, for there was the tabernacle of the congregation of God which Moses the servant of the Lord had made in the wilderness. But the ark of God, David had brought up from Kiriath-Jearim to the place which David had prepared for it; for he had pitched a tent for it at Jerusalem. Moreover, the brazen altar that Bezalel the son of Uri, the son of Hur, had made, he put before the tabernacle of the Lord; and Solomon and the congregation sought unto it. And Solomon went up there, to the brazen altar before the Lord which was at the tabernacle of the congregation, and offered a thousand burnt offerings upon it.

2 In that night did God appear unto Solomon, and said unto him, Ask what I shall give you. And Solomon said unto God, You have shown great mercy unto David my father, and have made me to reign in his stead. Now, O Lord God, let your promise unto David my father be established, for you have made me king over a people like the dust of the earth in multitude. Give me now wisdom and knowledge, that I may go out and come in before this people; for who can judge this your people that is so great?

3 And God said to Solomon, Because this was in your heart, and you have not asked riches, wealth, or honor, nor the life of your enemies, neither yet have asked long life, but have asked wisdom and knowledge for yourself, that you may judge my people over whom I have made you king, wisdom and knowledge is granted unto you. And I will give you riches, and wealth, and honor, such as none of the kings have had that have been before you, neither shall there any after you have the like.

4 Then Solomon came from his journey to the high place that was at Gibeon to Jerusalem, from before the tabernacle of the congregation, and reigned over Israel. And Solomon gathered chariots and horsemen, and he had a thousand and four hundred chariots and twelve thousand horsemen, which he placed in the chariot cities and with the king at

Jerusalem. And the king made silver and gold at Jerusalem as plenteous as stones, and cedar trees made he as the sycamore trees that are in the vale for abundance. And Solomon had horses brought out of Egypt, and linen yarn — the king's merchants received the linen yarn at a price. And they fetched up and brought forth out of Egypt a chariot for six hundred shekels of silver, and a horse for a hundred fifty. And so brought they out horses for all the kings of the Hittites, and for the kings of Syria, by their means.

5 And Solomon determined to build a house for the name of the Lord, and a house for his kingdom. And Solomon counted out seventy thousand men to bear burdens, and eighty thousand to hew in the mountain, and three thousand six hundred to oversee them.

6 And Solomon sent to Hiram the king of Tyre, saying, As you did deal with David my father, and did send him cedars to build him a house to dwell therein, therefore behold, I build a house to the name of the Lord my God, to dedicate to him — to burn before him sweet incense, and for the continual showbread, and for the burnt offerings, morning and evening, on the Sabbaths, and on the new moons, and on the solemn feasts of the Lord our God. And this ordinance shall be kept in Israel for ever. And the house which I build shall be a great house, for great is the Lord our God above all gods. But who is able to build him a house, seeing the heaven and Heaven of heavens cannot contain him? Who am I then that I should build him a house, save only to burn sacrifice before him?

7 Send me now therefore a man skilled to work in gold, and in silver, and in brass, and in iron, and in purple, and crimson, and blue, and that have skill to engrave with the expert men that are with me in Judah and in Jerusalem, whom David my father did provide. Send me also cedar trees, fir trees, and algum trees out of Lebanon, for I know that your servants have skill to cut timber in Lebanon.

8 And behold, my servants I will send with your servants, even to prepare for me timber in abundance, for the house which I am about to build shall be wonderful, great. And behold, I will give to your servants, the hewers that cut timber, twenty thousand measures of beaten wheat, and twenty thousand measures of barley, and twenty thousand baths of wine, and twenty thousand baths of oil.

⁹ Then Hiram the king of Tyre answered in writing, which he sent to Solomon: Because the Lord has loved his people, he has made you king over them. Hiram said moreover, Blessed be the Lord God of Israel that made heaven and earth, who has given to David the king a wise son, endowed with prudence and understanding, that might build a house for the Lord and a house for his kingdom.

¹⁰ And now I have sent a skilled man, endowed with understanding, of Huram my father's — the son of a woman of the daughters of Dan, and his father was a man of Tyre — skillful to work in gold, and in silver, in brass, in iron, in stone, and in timber, in purple, in blue, and in fine linen, and in crimson, also to engrave any manner of engraving, and to find out every device which shall be put to him, with your expert men and with the expert men of my lord, David your father.

¹¹ Now therefore, the wheat and the barley, the oil and the wine which my lord has spoken of, let him send unto his servants. And we will cut wood out of Lebanon, as much as you shall need, and we will bring it to you in floats by sea to Joppa, and you shall carry it up to Jerusalem.

¹² And Solomon numbered all the strangers that were in the land of Israel, after the numbering by which David his father had numbered them, and they were found a hundred fifty-three thousand six hundred. And he set seventy thousand of them to be bearers of burdens, and eighty thousand to be hewers in the mountain, and three thousand six hundred overseers to set the people to work.

¹³ Then Solomon began to build the house of the Lord at Jerusalem in Mount Moriah, where the Lord appeared unto David his father, in the place that David had prepared in the threshing floor of Ornan the Jebusite. And he began to build in the second day of the second month, in the fourth year of his reign.

¹⁴ Now these are the things wherein Solomon was instructed for the building of the house of God: the length by cubits after the first measure was sixty cubits, and the breadth twenty cubits. And the porch that was in the front of the house, the length of it was according to the breadth of the house, twenty cubits, and the height was a hundred twenty. And he overlaid it within with pure gold. And the greater house he paneled with fir tree, which he overlaid with fine gold, and set thereon palm trees and chains. And he garnished the house with

precious stones for beauty, and the gold was gold of Parvaim. He overlaid also the house, the beams, the thresholds, and the walls thereof, and the doors thereof with gold, and engraved cherubim on the walls.

15 And he made the most holy house, the length whereof was according to the breadth of the house, twenty cubits, and the breadth thereof twenty cubits; and he overlaid it with fine gold amounting to six hundred talents. And the weight of the nails was fifty shekels of gold. And he overlaid the upper chambers with gold.

16 And in the most holy house, he made two cherubim of image work, and overlaid them with gold. And the wings of the cherubim were twenty cubits long: one wing five cubits, reaching to the wall of the house, and the other wing five cubits, reaching to the wing of the other cherub; and one wing of the other cherub was five cubits, reaching to the wall of the house, and the other wing was five cubits also, joining to the wing of the other cherub. The wings of these cherubim spread themselves forth twenty cubits, and they stood on their feet, and their faces were inward.

17 And he made the veil of blue, and purple, and crimson, and fine linen, and wrought cherubim thereon.

18 Also, he made before the house two pillars of thirty-five cubits high, and the chapiter that was on the top of each of them was five cubits. And he made chains, as in the Holy of Holies, and put them on the heads of the pillars, and made a hundred pomegranates and put them on the chains. And he reared up the pillars before the temple, one on the right hand and the other on the left, and called the name of that on the right hand Jachin, and the name of that on the left Boaz.

19 Moreover, he made an altar of brass: twenty cubits the length thereof, and twenty cubits the breadth thereof, and ten cubits the height thereof.

20 Also, he made a molten sea of ten cubits from brim to brim, round in shape, and five cubits the height thereof; and a line of thirty cubits did encompass it round about. And under it was the similitude of oxen, which did encompass it round about—ten in a cubit, encompassing the sea round about. Two rows of oxen were cast when it was cast. It stood upon twelve oxen: three looking toward the north, and three looking toward the west, and three looking toward the south, and three looking toward the east. And the sea was set above upon them,

and all their hindquarters were inward. And the thickness of it was a handbreadth, and the brim of it like the work of the brim of a cup, with flowers of lilies. And it received and held three thousand baths.

21 He made also ten basins, and put five on the right hand and five on the left, to wash in them. Such things as they offered for the burnt offering they washed in them, but the sea was for the priests to wash in. And he made ten candlesticks of gold, according to their form, and set them in the temple — five on the right hand and five on the left. He made also ten tables and placed them in the temple — five on the right side and five on the left. And he made a hundred basins of gold.

22 Furthermore, he made the court of the priests, and the great court, and doors for the court, and overlaid the doors of them with brass. And he set the sea on the right side of the east end, toward the south.

23 And Huram made the pots, and the shovels, and the basins. And Huram finished the work that he was to make for king Solomon for the house of God — that is, the two pillars, and the finials, and the chapiters which were on the top of the two pillars, and the two wreaths to cover the two finials of the chapiters which were on the top of the pillars; and four hundred pomegranates on the two wreaths — two rows of pomegranates on each wreath — to cover the two finials of the chapiters which were upon the pillars. He made also bases, and basins made he upon the bases; one sea, and twelve oxen under it; the pots also, and the shovels, and the forks, and all their instruments did Huram his father make to king Solomon for the house of the Lord of bright brass. In the plain of Jordan did the king cast them, in the clay ground between Succoth and Zeredathah.

24 Thus, Solomon made all these vessels in great abundance, for the weight of the brass could not be found out. And Solomon made all the vessels that were for the house of God: the golden altar also, and the tables on which the showbread was set; moreover, the candlesticks with their lamps, that they should burn after the manner before the Holy of Holies, of pure gold; and the flowers, and the lamps, and the tongs made he of gold, and that perfect gold; and the snuffers, and the basins, and the spoons, and the censers of pure gold; and the entry of the house, the inner doors thereof for the most holy place, and the doors of the house of the temple, were of gold.

25 Thus, all the work that Solomon made for the house of the Lord was finished, and Solomon brought in all the things that David his father had dedicated. And the silver, and the gold, and all the instruments put he among the treasures of the house of God.

2 Then Solomon assembled the elders of Israel and all the heads of the tribes — the chief of the fathers of the children of Israel — unto Jerusalem, to bring up the ark of the covenant of the Lord out of the city of David, which is Zion. Wherefore, all the men of Israel assembled themselves unto the king in the feast which was in the seventh month.

2 And all the elders of Israel came, and the Levites took up the ark. And they brought up the ark, and the tabernacle of the congregation, and all the holy vessels that were in the tabernacle — these did the priests and the Levites bring up. Also, king Solomon and all the congregation of Israel that were assembled unto him before the ark sacrificed sheep and oxen, which could not be told nor numbered for multitude.

3 And the priests brought in the ark of the covenant of the Lord unto his place, to the Holy of Holies of the house, into the most holy place, even under the wings of the cherubim; for the cherubim spread forth their wings over the place of the ark, and the cherubim covered the ark and the staves thereof above. And they drew out the staves of the ark, that the ends of the staves were seen from the ark before the Holy of Holies, but they were not seen outside. And there it is unto this day. There was nothing in the ark save the two tablets which Moses put therein at Horeb when the Lord made a covenant with the children of Israel, when they came out of Egypt.

4 And it came to pass, when the priests had come out of the holy place (for all the priests that were present were sanctified and did not then wait by course), also the Levites who were the singers (all of them of Asaph, of Heman, of Jeduthun, with their sons and their brethren — being arrayed in white linen, having cymbals and psalteries and harps — stood at the east end of the altar, and with them a hundred twenty priests sounding with trumpets), it came even to pass as the trumpeters and singers were as one, to make one sound to be heard in praising and thanking the Lord — and when they lifted up their voice with the trumpets, and cymbals, and instruments of music, and praised

the Lord, saying, For he is good, for his mercy endures for ever — that then the house was filled with a cloud, even the house of the Lord, so that the priests could not stand to minister by reason of the cloud; for the glory of the Lord had filled the house of God.

5 Then said Solomon, The Lord has said that he would dwell in the thick darkness; but I have built a house of habitation for you, and a place for your dwelling for ever. And the king turned his face, and blessed the whole congregation of Israel. And all the congregation of Israel stood. And he said, Blessed be the Lord God of Israel who has with his hands fulfilled that which he spoke with his mouth to my father David, saying, Since the day that I brought forth my people out of the land of Egypt, I chose no city among all the tribes of Israel to build a house in, that my name might be there. Neither chose I any man to be a ruler over my people Israel. But I have chosen Jerusalem, that my name might be there, and have chosen David to be over my people Israel.

6 Now it was in the heart of David my father to build a house for the name of the Lord God of Israel. But the Lord said to David my father, Forasmuch as it was in your heart to build a house for my name, you did well in that it was in your heart. Notwithstanding, you shall not build the house, but your son who shall come forth out of your loins, he shall build the house for my name.

7 The Lord therefore has performed his word that he has spoken, for I am risen up in the place of David my father and am set on the throne of Israel, as the Lord promised, and have built the house for the name of the Lord God of Israel. And in it have I put the ark wherein is the covenant of the Lord that he made with the children of Israel.

8 And he stood before the altar of the Lord, in the presence of all the congregation of Israel, and spread forth his hands; for Solomon had made a brazen scaffold of five cubits long, and five cubits broad, and three cubits high, and had set it in the middle of the court. And upon it he stood, and kneeled down upon his knees before all the congregation of Israel, and spread forth his hands toward Heaven, and said:

9 O Lord God of Israel, there is no God like you in the heaven nor in the earth, who keeps covenant and shows mercy unto your servants that walk before you with all their hearts. You who have kept with your

servant, David my father, that which you have promised him and spoke with your mouth, and have fulfilled it with your hand as it is this day.

10 Now therefore, O Lord God of Israel, keep with your servant, David my father, that which you have promised him, saying, There shall not fail you a man in my sight to sit upon the throne of Israel, if only your children take heed to their way, to walk in my law as you have walked before me. Now then, O Lord God of Israel, let your word be verified which you have spoken unto your servant David.

11 But will God in very deed dwell with men on the earth? Behold, Heaven and the Heaven of heavens cannot contain you. How much less this house which I have built? Have respect therefore to the prayer of your servant and to his supplication, O Lord my God, to listen unto the cry and the prayer which your servant prays before you, that your eyes may be open upon this house day and night, upon the place whereof you have said that you would put your name there, to listen unto the prayer which your servant prays toward this place. Listen therefore unto the supplications of your servant and of your people Israel which they shall make toward this place. Hear from your dwelling place, even from Heaven; and when you hear, forgive.

12 If a man sin against his neighbor, and an oath be laid upon him to make him swear, and the oath come before your altar in this house, then hear from Heaven and do, and judge your servants — by repaying the wicked, by recompensing his way upon his own head, and by justifying the righteous, by giving him according to his righteousness.

13 And if your people Israel be put to the worse before the enemy because they have sinned against you, and shall return and confess your name, and pray and make supplication before you in this house, then hear from the Heavens and forgive the sin of your people Israel, and bring them again unto the land which you gave to them and to their fathers.

14 When the heaven is shut up and there is no rain because they have sinned against you, yet if they pray toward this place, and confess your name, and turn from their sin when you do afflict them, then hear from Heaven and forgive the sin of your servants and of your people Israel when you have taught them the good way wherein they should walk; and send rain upon your land which you have given unto your people for an inheritance.

15 If there is dearth in the land, if there is pestilence, if there is blasting, or mildew, locusts, or caterpillars, if their enemies besiege them in the cities of their land, whatever sore or whatever sickness there be, then whatever prayer or supplication shall be made of any man or of all your people Israel — when everyone shall know his own sore and his own grief, and shall spread forth his hands in this house — then hear from Heaven, your dwelling place, and forgive, and render unto every man according unto all his ways, whose heart you know — for you only know the hearts of the children of men — that they may fear you, to walk in your ways so long as they live in the land which you gave unto our fathers.

16 Moreover, concerning the stranger who is not of your people Israel, but has come from a far country for your great name's sake, and your mighty hand, and your stretched out arm — if they come and pray in this house, then hear from the Heavens, even from your dwelling place, and do according to all that the stranger calls to you for, that all people of the earth may know your name and fear you, as does your people Israel, and may know that this house which I have built is called by your name.

17 If your people go out to war against their enemies by the way that you shall send them, and they pray unto you toward this city which you have chosen and the house which I have built for your name, then hear from the Heavens their prayer and their supplication, and maintain their cause.

18 If they sin against you — for there is no man who does not sin — and you are angry with them and deliver them over before their enemies, and they carry them away captives unto a land far off or near, yet if they reconsider themselves in the land where they are carried captive, and turn and pray unto you in the land of their captivity, saying, We have sinned, we have done amiss, and have dealt wickedly — if they return to you with all their heart and with all their soul in the land of their captivity where they have carried them captives, and pray toward their land which you gave unto their fathers, and toward the city which you have chosen, and toward the house which I have built for your name — then hear from the Heavens, even from your dwelling place, their prayer and their supplications, and maintain their cause, and forgive your people who have sinned against you.

19 Now, my God, let, I implore you, your eyes be open, and let your ears be attentive unto the prayer that is made in this place. Now therefore arise, O Lord God, into your resting place — you, and the ark of your strength. Let your priests, O Lord God, be clothed with salvation, and let your saints rejoice in goodness. O Lord God, turn not away the face of your anointed. Remember the mercies of David your servant.

20 Now when Solomon had made an end of praying, the fire came down from Heaven and consumed the burnt offering and the sacrifices, and the glory of the Lord filled the house. And the priests could not enter into the house of the Lord because the glory of the Lord had filled the Lord's house. And when all the children of Israel saw how the fire came down, and the glory of the Lord upon the house, they bowed themselves with their faces to the ground upon the pavement, and worshipped and praised the Lord, saying, For he is good, for his mercy endures for ever.

21 Then the king and all the people offered sacrifices before the Lord. And king Solomon offered a sacrifice of twenty-two thousand oxen, and a hundred and twenty thousand sheep. So the king and all the people dedicated the house of God. And the priests waited on their offices, the Levites also, with instruments of music of the Lord which David the king had made to praise the Lord, because his mercy endures for ever, when David praised by their ministry. And the priests sounded trumpets before them, and all Israel stood.

22 Moreover, Solomon hallowed the middle of the court that was before the house of the Lord, for there he offered burnt offerings and the fat of the peace offerings, because the brazen altar which Solomon had made was not able to receive the burnt offerings, and the meal offerings, and the fat.

23 Also at the same time, Solomon kept the feast seven days, and all Israel with him, a very great congregation, from the entering in of Hamath unto the river of Egypt. And in the eighth day, they made a solemn assembly, for they kept the Dedication of the Altar seven days and the feast seven days. And on the twenty-third day of the seventh month, he sent the people away into their tents, glad and merry in heart for the goodness that the Lord had shown unto David, and to Solomon, and to Israel his people.

24 Thus, Solomon finished the house of the Lord and the king's house. And all that came into Solomon's heart to make in the house of the Lord, and in his own house, he prosperously effected.

25 And the Lord appeared to Solomon by night, and said unto him, I have heard your prayer and have chosen this place to myself for a house of sacrifice. If I shut up heaven that there is no rain, or if I command the locusts to devour the land, or if I send pestilence among my people, if my people who are called by my name shall humble themselves, and pray, and seek my face, and turn from their wicked ways, then will I hear from Heaven, and will forgive their sin, and will heal their land. Now my eyes shall be open, and my ears attentive unto the prayer that is made in this place; for now have I chosen and sanctified this house, that my name may be there for ever, and my eyes and my heart shall be there perpetually.

26 And as for you, if you will walk before me, as David your father walked, and do according to all that I have commanded you, and shall observe my statutes and my judgments, then will I establish the throne of your kingdom according as I have covenanted with David your father, saying, There shall not fail you a man to be ruler in Israel.

27 But if you turn away, and forsake my statutes and my commandments which I have set before you, and shall go and serve other gods and worship them, then will I pluck them up by the roots out of my land which I have given them. And this house which I have sanctified for my name will I cast out of my sight, and will make it to be a proverb and a byword among all nations. And this house which is high shall be an astonishment to everyone that passes by it, so that he shall say, Why has the Lord done thus unto this land and unto this house? And it shall be answered, Because they forsook the Lord God of their fathers who brought them forth out of the land of Egypt, and laid hold on other gods, and worshipped them, and served them. Therefore, he has brought all this evil upon them.

3 And it came to pass at the end of twenty years, wherein Solomon had built the house of the Lord and his own house, that the cities which Hiram had restored to Solomon, Solomon built them and caused the children of Israel to dwell there. And Solomon went to Hamath-Zobah and prevailed against it. And he built Tadmor in the

wilderness, and all the store cities which he built in Hamath. Also, he built Bethhoron the upper and Bethhoron the lower, fortified cities with walls, gates, and bars; and Baalath, and all the store cities that Solomon had, and all the chariot cities, and the cities of the horsemen, and all that Solomon desired to build in Jerusalem, and in Lebanon, and throughout all the land of his dominion.

2 As for all the people that were left of the Hittites, and the Amorites, and the Perizzites, and the Hivites, and the Jebusites — who were not of Israel, but of their children who were left after them in the land, whom the children of Israel consumed not — them did Solomon make to pay tribute until this day. But of the children of Israel did Solomon make no servants for his work. But they were men of war, and chief of his captains, and captains of his chariots and horsemen. And these were the chief of king Solomon's officers, even two hundred fifty that bore rule over the people.

3 And Solomon brought up the daughter of Pharaoh out of the city of David unto the house that he had built for her; for he said, My wife shall not dwell in the house of David king of Israel, because the places are holy unto which the ark of the Lord has come.

4 Then Solomon offered burnt offerings unto the Lord on the altar of the Lord which he had built before the porch, even after a certain rate every day, offering according to the commandment of Moses on the Sabbaths, and on the new moons, and on the solemn feasts three times in the year — even in the Feast of Unleavened Bread, and in the Feast of Weeks, and in the Feast of Tabernacles. And he appointed, according to the order of David his father, the courses of the priests to their service, and the Levites to their charges to praise and minister before the priests, as the duty of every day required, the porters also by their courses at every gate; for so had David the man of God commanded. And they departed not from the commandment of the king unto the priests and Levites concerning any matter, or concerning the treasures.

5 Now all the work of Solomon was prepared unto the day of the foundation of the house of the Lord and until it was finished. So the house of the Lord was perfected.

6 Then went Solomon to Ezion-Geber and to Eloth at the seaside in the land of Edom. And Hiram sent him, by the hands of his servants, ships, and servants that had knowledge of the sea. And they went with

the servants of Solomon to Ophir, and took from there four hundred fifty talents of gold, and brought them to king Solomon.

7 And when the queen of Sheba heard of the fame of Solomon, she came to prove Solomon with hard questions at Jerusalem with a very great company, and camels that bore spices, and gold in abundance, and precious stones. And when she came to Solomon, she spoke with him of all that was in her heart. And Solomon told her all her questions, and there was nothing hidden from Solomon which he told her not. And when the queen of Sheba had seen the wisdom of Solomon, and the house that he had built, and the food of his table, and the sitting of his servants, and the attendance of his ministers and their apparel, his cupbearers also and their apparel, and his ascent by which he went up into the house of the Lord, there was no more spirit in her.

8 And she said to the king, It was a true report which I heard in my own land of your acts and of your wisdom. Nevertheless, I believed not their words until I came and my eyes had seen it. And behold, the one half of the greatness of your wisdom was not told me, for you exceed the fame that I heard. Happy are your men and happy are these your servants who stand continually before you and hear your wisdom. Blessed be the Lord your God, who delighted in you to set you on his throne, to be king for the Lord your God. Because your God loved Israel, to establish them for ever, therefore he made you king over them, to do judgment and justice.

9 And she gave the king a hundred twenty talents of gold, and of spices great abundance, and precious stones. Neither was there any such spice as the queen of Sheba gave king Solomon. And the servants also of Hiram and the servants of Solomon who brought gold from Ophir brought algum trees and precious stones. And the king made of the algum trees terraces to the house of the Lord and to the king's palace, and harps and psalteries for singers. And there were none such seen before in the land of Judah. And king Solomon gave to the queen of Sheba all her desire, whatever she asked, besides that which she had brought unto the king. So she turned and went away to her own land, she and her servants.

10 Now the weight of gold that came to Solomon in one year was six hundred sixty-six talents of gold, besides that which peddlers and merchants brought. And all the kings of Arabia and governors of the

country brought gold and silver to Solomon. And king Solomon made two hundred shields of beaten gold — six hundred shekels of beaten gold went to one shield. And three hundred shields made he of beaten gold — three hundred shekels of gold went to one shield. And the king put them in the house of the forest of Lebanon.

11 Moreover, the king made a great throne of ivory and overlaid it with pure gold. And there were six steps to the throne, with a footstool of gold, which were fastened to the throne, and armrests on each side of the sitting place, and two lions standing by the armrests. And twelve lions stood there on the one side and on the other upon the six steps. There was not the like made in any kingdom.

12 And all the drinking vessels of king Solomon were of gold, and all the vessels of the house of the forest of Lebanon were of pure gold; none were of silver. It was not anything accounted of in the days of Solomon, for the king's ships went to Tarshish with the servants of Hiram; every three years, once came the ships of Tarshish bringing gold, and silver, ivory, and apes, and peacocks.

13 And king Solomon passed all the kings of the earth in riches and wisdom. And all the kings of the earth sought the presence of Solomon, to hear his wisdom that God had put in his heart. And they brought every man his present: vessels of silver, and vessels of gold, and raiment, harness, and spices, horses and mules, a rate year by year. And Solomon had four thousand stalls for horses and chariots, and twelve thousand horsemen whom he bestowed in the chariot cities and with the king at Jerusalem. And he reigned over all the kings, from the river even unto the land of the Philistines and to the border of Egypt. And the king made silver in Jerusalem as stones, and cedar trees made he as the sycamore trees that are in the low plains in abundance. And they brought unto Solomon horses out of Egypt, and out of all lands.

14 Now the rest of the acts of Solomon, first and last, are they not written in the book of Nathan the prophet? And in the prophecy of Ahijah the Shilonite? And in the visions of Iddo the seer against Jeroboam the son of Nebat? And Solomon reigned in Jerusalem over all Israel forty years. And Solomon slept with his fathers, and he was buried in the city of David his father. And Rehoboam his son reigned in his stead.

4 And Rehoboam went to Shechem, for to Shechem had all Israel come to make him king. And it came to pass, when Jeroboam the son of Nebat—who was in Egypt, where he had fled from the presence of Solomon the king—heard it, that Jeroboam returned out of Egypt. And they sent and called him. So Jeroboam and all Israel came and spoke to Rehoboam, saying, Your father made our yoke grievous. Now therefore ease somewhat the grievous servitude of your father and his heavy yoke that he put upon us, and we will serve you. And he said unto them, Come again unto me after three days. And the people departed.

2 And king Rehoboam took counsel with the old men that had stood before Solomon his father while he yet lived, saying, What counsel do you give me to return answer to this people? And they spoke unto him, saying, If you be kind to this people, and please them, and speak good words to them, they will be your servants for ever. But he forsook the counsel which the old men gave him, and took counsel with the young men that were brought up with him, that stood before him.

3 And he said unto them, What advice do you give that we may return answer to this people who have spoken to me, saying, Ease somewhat the yoke that your father did put upon us? And the young men that were brought up with him spoke unto him, saying, Thus shall you answer the people that spoke unto you, saying, Your father made our yoke heavy, but make it somewhat lighter for us—thus shall you say unto them: My little finger shall be thicker than my father's loins, for whereas my father put a heavy yoke upon you, I will put more to your yoke. My father chastised you with whips, but I will chastise you with scorpions.

4 So Jeroboam and all the people came to Rehoboam on the third day, as the king bid, saying, Come again to me on the third day. And the king answered them roughly. And king Rehoboam forsook the counsel of the old men and answered them after the advice of the young men, saying, My father made your yoke heavy, but I will add unto it. My father chastised you with whips, but I will chastise you with scorpions. So the king listened not unto the people; for the cause was of God, that the Lord might perform his word which he spoke by the hand of Ahijah the Shilonite to Jeroboam the son of Nebat.

5 And when all Israel saw that the king would not listen unto them, the people answered the king, saying, What portion have we in David?

And we have no inheritance in the son of Jesse. Every man to your tents, O Israel. And now, David, see to your own house. So all Israel went to their tents.

6 But as for the children of Israel that dwelled in the cities of Judah, Rehoboam reigned over them. Then king Rehoboam sent Hadoram that was over the tribute, and the children of Israel stoned him with stones, that he died. But king Rehoboam made speed to get him up to his chariot, to flee to Jerusalem. And Israel rebelled against the house of David unto this day.

7 And when Rehoboam had come to Jerusalem, he gathered of the house of Judah and Benjamin a hundred eighty thousand chosen men who were warriors, to fight against Israel, that he might bring the kingdom again to Rehoboam. But the word of the Lord came to Shemaiah the man of God, saying, Speak unto Rehoboam the son of Solomon, king of Judah, and to all Israel in Judah and Benjamin, saying, Thus says the Lord: You shall not go up, nor fight against your brethren. Return every man to his house, for this thing is done of me. And they obeyed the words of the Lord and returned from going against Jeroboam.

8 And Rehoboam dwelled in Jerusalem, and built cities for defense in Judah. He built even Bethlehem, and Etam, and Tekoa, and Bethzur, and Soco, and Adullam, and Gath, and Mareshah, and Ziph, and Adoraim, and Lachish, and Azekah, and Zorah, and Aijalon, and Hebron which are in Judah and in Benjamin, fortified cities. And he fortified the strongholds and put captains in them, and store of provisions, and of oil and wine. And in every single city he put shields and spears and made them exceedingly strong, having Judah and Benjamin on his side.

9 And the priests and the Levites that were in all Israel gathered to him out of all their regions; for the Levites left their suburbs and their possession, and came to Judah and Jerusalem (for Jeroboam and his sons had cast them off from executing the priest's office unto the Lord, and he ordained himself priests for the high places, and for the devils, and for the calves which he had made). And after them, out of all the tribes of Israel, such as set their hearts to seek the Lord God of Israel came to Jerusalem, to sacrifice unto the Lord God of their fathers. So they strengthened the kingdom of Judah, and made Rehoboam the

son of Solomon strong three years; for three years they walked in the way of David and Solomon.

¹⁰ And Rehoboam took him Mahalath, the daughter of Jerimoth the son of David, to wife, and Abihail, the daughter of Eliab the son of Jesse, who bore him children: Jeush, and Shamariah, and Zaham. And after her, he took Maacah the daughter of Absalom, who bore him Abijah, and Attai, and Ziza, and Shelomith. And Rehoboam loved Maacah the daughter of Absalom above all his wives and his concubines (for he took eighteen wives and sixty concubines, and begot twenty-eight sons and sixty daughters).

¹¹ And Rehoboam made Abijah the son of Maacah the chief, to be ruler among his brethren, for he thought to make him king. And he dealt wisely, and dispersed of all his children throughout all the countries of Judah and Benjamin, unto every fortified city; and he gave them provisions in abundance. And he desired many wives.

¹² And it came to pass, when Rehoboam had established the kingdom and had strengthened himself, he forsook the law of the Lord, and all Israel with him. And it came to pass that in the fifth year of king Rehoboam, Shishak king of Egypt came up against Jerusalem (because they had transgressed against the Lord) with twelve hundred chariots and sixty thousand horsemen. And the people were without number that came with him out of Egypt — the Lubim, the Sukkiim, and the Ethiopians. And he took the fortified cities which pertained to Judah, and came to Jerusalem.

¹³ Then came Shemaiah the prophet to Rehoboam, and to the princes of Judah that were gathered together to Jerusalem because of Shishak, and said unto them, Thus says the Lord: You have forsaken me, and therefore have I also left you in the hand of Shishak — whereupon the princes of Israel and the king humbled themselves, and they said, The Lord is righteous.

¹⁴ And when the Lord saw that they humbled themselves, the word of the Lord came to Shemaiah, saying, They have humbled themselves, therefore I will not destroy them, but I will grant them some deliverance. And my wrath shall not be poured out upon Jerusalem by the hand of Shishak; nevertheless, they shall be his servants, that they may know my service and the service of the kingdoms of the countries.

¹⁵ So Shishak king of Egypt came up against Jerusalem and took away the treasures of the house of the Lord and the treasures of the king's house; he took all. He carried away also the shields of gold which Solomon had made, instead of which king Rehoboam made shields of brass and committed them to the hands of the chief of the guard that kept the entrance of the king's house. And when the king entered into the house of the Lord, the guard came and fetched them, and brought them again into the guard chamber.

¹⁶ And when he humbled himself, the wrath of the Lord turned from him, that he would not destroy him altogether. And also in Judah things went well.

¹⁷ So king Rehoboam strengthened himself in Jerusalem and reigned. For Rehoboam was forty-one years old when he began to reign, and he reigned seventeen years in Jerusalem, the city which the Lord had chosen out of all the tribes of Israel, to put his name there. And his mother's name was Naamah, an Ammonitess. And he did evil because he prepared not his heart to seek the Lord.

¹⁸ Now the acts of Rehoboam, first and last, are they not written in the book of Shemaiah the prophet? And of Iddo the seer concerning genealogies? And there were wars between Rehoboam and Jeroboam continually. And Rehoboam slept with his fathers, and was buried in the city of David. And Abijah his son reigned in his stead.

5 Now in the eighteenth year of king Jeroboam began Abijah to reign over Judah. He reigned three years in Jerusalem. His mother's name also was Maacah, the daughter of Uriel of Gibeah. And there was war between Abijah and Jeroboam. And Abijah set the battle in array with an army of valiant men of war, even four hundred thousand chosen men. Jeroboam also set the battle in array against him with eight hundred thousand chosen men, being mighty men of valor.

² And Abijah stood up upon Mount Zemaraim, which is in Mount Ephraim, and said, Hear me Jeroboam, and all Israel. Ought you not to know that the Lord God of Israel gave the kingdom over Israel to David for ever? Even to him and to his sons by a covenant of salt? Yet Jeroboam the son of Nebat, the servant of Solomon the son of David, is risen up, and has rebelled against his lord. And there are gathered unto him vain men, the children of Belial, and have strengthened

themselves against Rehoboam the son of Solomon, when Rehoboam was young and tender-hearted and could not withstand them.

3 And now you think to withstand the kingdom of the Lord in the hand of the sons of David. And you are a great multitude, and there are with you golden calves, which Jeroboam made you for gods. Have you not cast out the priests of the Lord, the sons of Aaron and the Levites? And have made you priests after the manner of the nations of other lands? So that whoever comes to consecrate himself with a young bullock and seven rams, the same may be a priest of them that are no gods?

4 But as for us, the Lord is our God, and we have not forsaken him. And the priests who minister unto the Lord are the sons of Aaron, and the Levites wait upon their business. And they burn unto the Lord every morning and every evening burnt sacrifices and sweet incense. The showbread also set they in order upon the pure table, and the candlestick of gold with the lamps thereof, to burn every evening. For we keep the charge of the Lord our God, but you have forsaken him. And behold, God himself is with us for our captain, and his priests with sounding trumpets to cry alarm against you. O children of Israel, fight not against the Lord God of your fathers, for you shall not prosper.

5 But Jeroboam caused an ambush to come about behind them, so they were before Judah and the ambush was behind them. And when Judah looked back, behold, the battle was before and behind. And they cried unto the Lord and the priests sounded the trumpets. Then the men of Judah gave a shout. And as the men of Judah shouted, it came to pass that God smote Jeroboam and all Israel before Abijah and Judah. And the children of Israel fled before Judah, and God delivered them into their hand. And Abijah and his people slew them with a great slaughter, so there fell down slain of Israel five hundred thousand chosen men. Thus, the children of Israel were brought under at that time, and the children of Judah prevailed because they relied upon the Lord God of their fathers.

6 And Abijah pursued after Jeroboam and took cities from him: Beth-el with the towns thereof, and Jeshanah with the towns thereof, and Ephron with the towns thereof. Neither did Jeroboam recover strength again in the days of Abijah. And the Lord struck him, and he died. But Abijah waxed mighty, and married fourteen wives, and

begot twenty-two sons and sixteen daughters. And the rest of the acts of Abijah, and his ways, and his sayings, are written in the history of the prophet Iddo.

7 So Abijah slept with his fathers, and they buried him in the city of David. And Asa his son reigned in his stead. In his days, the land was quiet ten years.

6 And Asa did that which was good and right in the eyes of the Lord his God, for he took away the altars of the strange gods and the high places, and broke down the images and cut down the groves, and commanded Judah to seek the Lord God of their fathers and to do the law and the commandment. Also, he took away out of all the cities of Judah the high places and the images. And the kingdom was quiet before him.

2 And he built fortified cities in Judah, for the land had rest, and he had no war in those years because the Lord had given him rest. Therefore, he said unto Judah, Let us build these cities, and make about them walls and towers, gates and bars, while the land is yet before us because we have sought the Lord our God; we have sought him, and he has given us rest on every side. So they built and prospered.

3 And Asa had an army of men that bore shields and spears out of Judah, three hundred thousand, and out of Benjamin that bore shields and drew bows, two hundred eighty thousand. All these were mighty men of valor.

4 And there came out against them Zerah the Ethiopian, with a host of a thousand thousand, and three hundred chariots, and came unto Mareshah. Then Asa went out against him, and they set the battle in array in the valley of Zephathah at Mareshah. And Asa cried unto the Lord his God and said, Lord, it is nothing with you to help, whether with many or with them that have no power. Help us, O Lord our God, for we rest on you, and in your name we go against this multitude. O Lord, you are our God, let not man prevail against you.

5 So the Lord smote the Ethiopians before Asa and before Judah, and the Ethiopians fled. And Asa and the people that were with him pursued them unto Gerar. And the Ethiopians were overthrown, that they could not recover themselves, for they were destroyed before the Lord and before his host. And they carried away very much spoil. And

they smote all the cities round about Gerar, for the fear of the Lord came upon them. And they spoiled all the cities, for there was exceedingly much spoil in them. They smote also the tents of cattle, and carried away sheep and camels in abundance, and returned to Jerusalem.

6 And the spirit of God came upon Azariah the son of Oded. And he went out to meet Asa and said unto him, Hear me, Asa, and all Judah and Benjamin. The Lord is with you, while you are with him; and if you seek him, he will be found of you. But if you forsake him, he will forsake you. Now for a long season Israel has been without the true God, and without a teaching priest, and without law. But when they in their trouble did turn unto the Lord God of Israel and sought him, he was found of them. And in those times, there was no peace to him that went out, nor to him that came in, but great vexations were upon all the inhabitants of the countries. And nation was destroyed of nation, and city of city, for God did vex them with all adversity. Be strong therefore and let not your hands be weak, for your work shall be rewarded.

7 And when Asa heard these words and the prophecy of Oded the prophet, he took courage and put away the abominable idols out of all the land of Judah and Benjamin, and out of the cities which he had taken from Mount Ephraim, and renewed the altar of the Lord that was before the porch of the Lord. And he gathered all Judah and Benjamin, and the strangers with them out of Ephraim and Manasseh, and out of Simeon — for they fell to him out of Israel in abundance when they saw that the Lord his God was with him — so they gathered themselves together at Jerusalem in the third month in the fifteenth year of the reign of Asa.

8 And they offered unto the Lord, the same time, of the spoil which they had brought — seven hundred oxen and seven thousand sheep. And they entered into a covenant to seek the Lord God of their fathers with all their heart and with all their soul, that whoever would not seek the Lord God of Israel should be put to death, whether small or great, whether man or woman. And they swore unto the Lord with a loud voice, and with shouting, and with trumpets, and with horns. And all Judah rejoiced at the oath, for they had sworn with all their heart and sought him with their whole desire, and he was found of them. And the Lord gave them rest round about.

9 And also concerning Maacah, the mother of Asa the king, he removed her from being queen because she had made an idol in a grove. And Asa cut down her idol, and stamped it, and burned it at the brook Kidron. But the high places were not taken away out of Israel.

10 Nevertheless, the heart of Asa was perfect all his days. And he brought into the house of God the things that his father had dedicated, and that he himself had dedicated — silver, and gold, and vessels. And there was no more war unto the thirty-fifth year of the reign of Asa.

11 In the thirty-sixth year of the reign of Asa, Baasha king of Israel came up against Judah and built Ramah, to the intent that he might let none go out or come in to Asa king of Judah. Then Asa brought out silver and gold, out of the treasures of the house of the Lord and of the king's house, and sent to Benhadad king of Syria that dwelled at Damascus, saying, There is a league between me and you, as there was between my father and your father. Behold, I have sent you silver and gold. Go break your league with Baasha king of Israel, that he may depart from me.

12 And Benhadad listened unto king Asa, and sent the captains of his armies against the cities of Israel. And they smote Ijon, and Dan, and Abel-Maim, and all the store cities of Naphtali. And it came to pass, when Baasha heard it, that he left off building of Ramah and let his work cease. Then Asa the king took all Judah. And they carried away the stones of Ramah and the timber thereof with which Baasha was building. And he built with them Geba and Mizpah.

13 And at that time, Hanani the seer came to Asa king of Judah, and said unto him, Because you have relied on the king of Syria and not relied on the Lord your God, therefore is the host of the king of Syria escaped out of your hand. Were not the Ethiopians and the Lubim a huge host with very many chariots and horsemen? Yet, because you did rely on the Lord, he delivered them into your hand. For the eyes of the Lord run to and fro throughout the whole earth, to show himself strong in the behalf of them whose heart is perfect toward him. Herein you have done foolishly. Therefore from henceforth you shall have wars. Then Asa was angry with the seer and put him in a prison house, for he was in a rage with him because of this thing. And Asa oppressed some of the people the same time.

¹⁴ And behold, the acts of Asa, first and last, they are written in the book of the kings of Judah and Israel. And Asa in the thirty-ninth year of his reign was diseased in his feet, until his disease was exceedingly great. Yet in his disease he sought not to the Lord, but to the physicians. And Asa slept with his fathers, and died in the forty-first year of his reign. And they buried him in his own sepulchers which he had made for himself in the city of David, and laid him in the bed which was filled with sweet odors and diverse kinds of spices prepared by the apothecaries' art. And they made a very great burning for him.

7 And Jehoshaphat his son reigned in his stead, and strengthened himself against Israel. And he placed forces in all the fortified cities of Judah, and set garrisons in the land of Judah and in the cities of Ephraim which Asa his father had taken.

² And the Lord was with Jehoshaphat because he walked in the first ways of his father David, and sought not unto Baalim but sought to the Lord God of his father, and walked in his commandments and not after the doings of Israel. Therefore, the Lord established the kingdom in his hand. And all Judah brought to Jehoshaphat presents, and he had riches and honor in abundance. And his heart was lifted up in the ways of the Lord. Moreover, he took away the high places and groves out of Judah.

³ Also in the third year of his reign, he sent to his princes — even to Benhail, and to Obadiah, and to Zechariah, and to Nethanel, and to Micaiah — to teach in the cities of Judah. And with them he sent Levites, even Shemaiah, and Nethaniah, and Zebadiah, and Asahel, and Shemiramoth, and Jehonathan, and Adonijah, and Tobijah, and Tobadonijah — Levites, and with them, Elishama and Jehoram — priests. And they taught in Judah, and had the book of the law of the Lord with them, and went about throughout all the cities of Judah, and taught the people.

⁴ And the fear of the Lord fell upon all the kingdoms of the lands that were round about Judah, so that they made no war against Jehoshaphat. Also, some of the Philistines brought Jehoshaphat presents and tribute silver; and the Arabians brought him flocks, seven thousand seven hundred rams and seven thousand seven hundred he-goats.

5 And Jehoshaphat waxed great exceedingly, and he built in Judah castles and cities of store, and he had much business in the cities of Judah. And the men of war, mighty men of valor, were in Jerusalem. And these are the numbers of them according to the house of their fathers: of Judah, the captains of thousands: Adnah the chief, and with him mighty men of valor, three hundred thousand; and next to him was Jehohanan the captain, and with him two hundred eighty thousand; and next to him was Amasiah the son of Zichri, who willingly offered himself unto the Lord, and with him two hundred thousand mighty men of valor. And of Benjamin: Eliada, a mighty man of valor, and with him armed men with bow and shield, two hundred thousand; and next to him was Jehozabad, and with him a hundred eighty thousand ready, prepared for the war. These waited on the king besides those whom the king put in the fortified cities throughout all Judah.

6 Now Jehoshaphat had riches and honor in abundance, and joined alliance with Ahab. And after certain years, he went down to Ahab, to Samaria. And Ahab killed sheep and oxen for him in abundance, and for the people that he had with him, and persuaded him to go up with him to Ramoth-Gilead. And Ahab king of Israel said unto Jehoshaphat king of Judah, Will you go with me to Ramoth-Gilead? And he answered him, I am as you are, and my people as your people, and we will be with you in the war.

7 And Jehoshaphat said unto the king of Israel, Inquire, I pray you, at the word of the Lord today. Therefore, the king of Israel gathered together of prophets four hundred men, and said unto them, Shall we go to Ramoth-Gilead to battle? Or shall I refrain? And they said, Go up, for God will deliver it into the king's hand.

8 But Jehoshaphat said, Is there not here a prophet of the Lord besides, that we might inquire of him? And the king of Israel said unto Jehoshaphat, There is yet one man by whom we may inquire of the Lord, but I hate him, for he never prophesied good unto me, but always evil. The same is Micaiah the son of Imlah. And Jehoshaphat said, Let not the king say so. And the king of Israel called for one of his officers and said, Fetch quickly Micaiah the son of Imlah.

9 And the king of Israel and Jehoshaphat king of Judah sat either of them on his throne, clothed in their robes, and they sat in a void

place at the entering in of the gate of Samaria. And all the prophets prophesied before them. And Zedekiah the son of Chenaanah had made him horns of iron, and said, Thus says the Lord: With these you shall push Syria until they are consumed. And all the prophets prophesied so, saying, Go up to Ramoth-Gilead and prosper, for the Lord shall deliver it into the hand of the king.

10 And the messenger that went to call Micaiah spoke to him, saying, Behold, the words of the prophets declare good to the king with one assent. Let your word therefore, I pray you, be like one of theirs, and speak good. And Micaiah said, As the Lord lives, even what my God says, that will I speak.

11 And when he had come to the king, the king said unto him, Micaiah, shall we go to Ramoth-Gilead to battle? Or shall I refrain? And he said, Go up and prosper, and they shall be delivered into your hand. And the king said to him, How many times shall I adjure you that you say nothing but the truth to me in the name of the Lord?

12 Then he said, I did see all Israel scattered upon the mountains, as sheep that have no shepherd. And the Lord said, These have no master; let them return, therefore, every man to his house in peace. And the king of Israel said to Jehoshaphat, Did I not tell you that he would not prophesy good unto me, but evil?

13 Again he said, Therefore hear the word of the Lord: I saw the Lord sitting upon his throne, and all the host of heaven standing on his right hand and on his left. And the Lord said, Who shall entice Ahab king of Israel, that he may go up and fall at Ramoth-Gilead? And one spoke, saying after this manner, and another saying after that manner. Then there came out of them a lying spirit, and stood before the Lord and said, I will entice him. And the Lord said unto him, With what? And he said, I will go out and be a lying spirit in the mouth of all his prophets. And the Lord said, You shall entice him, and you shall also prevail. Go out and do so, for all these have sinned against me. Now therefore behold, the Lord has found a lying spirit in the mouth of these your prophets, and the Lord has spoken evil against you.

14 Then Zedekiah the son of Chenaanah came near and smote Micaiah upon the cheek, and said, Which way went the spirit of the Lord from me to speak unto you? And Micaiah said, Behold, you

shall see on that day when you shall go into an inner chamber to hide
yourself.

¹⁵ Then the king of Israel said, Take Micaiah and carry him back to
Amon the governor of the city, and to Joash the king's son, and say,
Thus says the king: Put this man in the prison, and feed him with
bread of affliction and with water of affliction until I return in peace.
And Micaiah said, If you certainly return in peace, then has the Lord
not spoken by me. And he said, Listen, all you people.

¹⁶ So the king of Israel and Jehoshaphat the king of Judah went up
to Ramoth-Gilead. And the king of Israel said unto Jehoshaphat, I will
disguise myself and will go to the battle, but you put on your robes.
So the king of Israel disguised himself, and they went to the battle.

¹⁷ Now the king of Syria had commanded the captains of the chariots
that were with him, saying, Fight not with small or great, save only
with the king of Israel. And it came to pass, when the captains of
the chariots saw Jehoshaphat, that they said, It is the king of Israel.
Therefore, they encompassed about him to fight. But Jehoshaphat cried
out, and the Lord helped him and God moved them from him; for it
came to pass that, when the captains of the chariots perceived that it
was not the king of Israel, they turned back again from pursuing him.

¹⁸ And a certain man drew a bow at a venture, and smote the king
of Israel between the joints of the harness. Therefore he said to his
chariot man, Turn your hand, that you may carry me out of the host,
for I am wounded. And the battle increased that day. Nevertheless, the
king of Israel propped himself up in his chariot against the Syrians
until the evening. And about the time of the sun going down, he died.

¹⁹ And Jehoshaphat the king of Judah returned to his house in peace,
to Jerusalem. And Jehu the son of Hanani, the seer, went out to meet
him, and said to king Jehoshaphat, Should you help the ungodly
and love them that hate the Lord? Therefore is wrath upon you from
before the Lord. Nevertheless, there are good things found in you, in
that you have taken away the groves out of the land and have prepared
your heart to seek God.

²⁰ And Jehoshaphat dwelled at Jerusalem. And he went out again
through the people, from Beersheba to Mount Ephraim, and brought
them back unto the Lord God of their fathers. And he set judges in the
land throughout all the fortified cities of Judah, city by city. And said to

the judges, Take heed what you do, for you judge not for man but for the Lord, who is with you in the judgment. Wherefore, now let the fear of the Lord be upon you. Take heed and do it, for there is no iniquity with the Lord our God, nor respect of persons, nor taking of bribes.

21 Moreover, in Jerusalem did Jehoshaphat set of the Levites, and the priests, and of the chief of the fathers of Israel, for the judgment of the Lord and for controversies, when they returned to Jerusalem. And he charged them, saying, Thus shall you do in the fear of the Lord, faithfully, and with a perfect heart. And whatever cause shall come to you of your brethren that dwell in their cities, between blood and blood, between law and commandment, statutes and judgments, you shall even warn them that they trespass not against the Lord, and so wrath come upon you and upon your brethren. This do, and you shall not trespass.

22 And behold, Amariah the chief priest is over you in all matters of the Lord, and Zebadiah the son of Ishmael, the ruler of the house of Judah, for all the king's matters. Also, the Levites shall be officers before you. Deal courageously and the Lord shall be with the good.

23 It came to pass after this also, the children of Moab and the children of Ammon (and with them, others besides the Ammonites) came against Jehoshaphat to battle. Then there came some that told Jehoshaphat, saying, There comes a great multitude against you from beyond the sea on this side of Syria. And behold, they are in Hazazon-Tamar, which was called Engedi. And Jehoshaphat feared, and set himself to seek the Lord, and proclaimed a fast throughout all Judah. And Judah gathered themselves together to ask of the Lord; even out of all the cities of Judah they came to seek the Lord.

24 And Jehoshaphat stood in the congregation of Judah and Jerusalem, in the house of the Lord, before the new court, and said, O Lord God of our fathers — you, God, who are in Heaven, and rule over all the kingdoms of the heathen, and in your hand you have power and might so that none is able to withstand you — you, our God, did drive out the inhabitants of this land before your people Israel, and gave it to the seed of Abraham your friend for ever. And they dwelled therein, and have built you a sanctuary therein for your name, saying, If evil comes upon us — the sword, judgment, or pestilence, or famine — we

stand before this house and in your presence, for your name is in this house, and cry unto you in our affliction; then you will hear and help.

25 And now behold, the children of Ammon and Moab and Mount Seir—whom you would not let Israel invade when they came out of the land of Egypt, but they turned from them and destroyed them not—behold, they reward us not, but have come to cast us out of your possession which you have given us to inherit. O our God, will you not judge them? For we have no might against this great company that comes against us, neither know we what to do. But our eyes are upon you.

26 And all Judah stood before the Lord with their little ones, their wives, and their children.

27 Then upon Jahaziel the son of Zechariah, the son of Benaiah, the son of Jeiel, the son of Mattaniah, a Levite of the sons of Asaph, came the spirit of the Lord in the midst of the congregation. And he said, Listen, all Judah, and you inhabitants of Jerusalem, and you, king Jehoshaphat. Thus says the Lord unto you: Be not afraid nor dismayed by reason of this great multitude; for the battle is not yours, but God's. Tomorrow go down against them. Behold, they come up by the cliff of Ziz, and you shall find them at the end of the brook, before the wilderness of Jeruel. You shall not go to fight in this day. Set yourselves, stand still, and see the salvation of the Lord with you. O Judah and Jerusalem, fear not, nor be dismayed. Tomorrow go out against them, for the Lord will be with you.

28 And Jehoshaphat bowed his head with his face to the ground, and all Judah and the inhabitants of Jerusalem fell before the Lord, worshipping the Lord. And the Levites of the children of the Kohathites and of the children of the Korahites stood up to praise the Lord God of Israel with a loud voice on high.

29 And they rose early in the morning and went forth into the wilderness of Tekoa. And as they went forth, Jehoshaphat stood and said, Hear me, O Judah, and you inhabitants of Jerusalem. Believe in the Lord your God; so shall you be established. Believe his prophets; so shall you prosper. And when he had consulted with the people, he appointed singers unto the Lord, and that should praise the beauty of holiness as they went out before the army, and to say, Praise the Lord, for his mercy endures for ever.

³⁰ And when they began to sing and to praise, the Lord set ambushes against the children of Ammon, Moab, and Mount Seir who had come against Judah, and they were smitten; for the children of Ammon and Moab stood up against the inhabitants of Mount Seir utterly to slay and destroy them. And when they had made an end of the inhabitants of Seir, every one helped to destroy another.

³¹ And when Judah came toward the watchtower in the wilderness, they looked unto the multitude, and behold, they were dead bodies fallen to the earth, and none escaped. And when Jehoshaphat and his people came to take away the spoil of them, they found among them in abundance both riches (with the dead bodies) and precious jewels, which they stripped off for themselves, more than they could carry away. And they were three days in gathering of the spoil, it was so much. And on the fourth day, they assembled themselves in the valley of Berachah — for there they blessed the Lord, therefore the name of the same place was called the valley of Berachah unto this day.

³² Then they returned, every man of Judah and Jerusalem, and Jehoshaphat in the forefront of them, to go again to Jerusalem with joy; for the Lord had made them to rejoice over their enemies. And they came to Jerusalem with psalteries and harps and trumpets, unto the house of the Lord. And the fear of God was on all the kingdoms of those countries when they had heard that the Lord fought against the enemies of Israel. So the realm of Jehoshaphat was quiet, for his God gave him rest round about.

³³ And Jehoshaphat reigned over Judah. He was thirty-five years old when he began to reign, and he reigned twenty-five years in Jerusalem. And his mother's name was Azubah, the daughter of Shilhi. And he walked in the way of Asa his father and departed not from it, doing right in the sight of the Lord. Nevertheless, the high places were not taken away, for as yet the people had not prepared their hearts unto the God of their fathers.

³⁴ Now the rest of the acts of Jehoshaphat, first and last, behold, they are written in the book of Jehu the son of Hanani, who is mentioned in the book of the kings of Israel.

³⁵ And after this did Jehoshaphat king of Judah join himself with Ahaziah king of Israel, who did very wickedly. And he joined himself with him to make ships to go to Tarshish, and they made the ships

in Ezion-Geber. Then Eliezer, the son of Dodavahu of Mareshah, prophesied against Jehoshaphat, saying, Because you have joined yourself with Ahaziah, the Lord has broken your works. And the ships were broken, that they were not able to go to Tarshish.

8 Now Jehoshaphat slept with his fathers, and was buried with his fathers in the city of David; and Jehoram his son reigned in his stead. And he had brethren, the sons of Jehoshaphat: Azariah, and Jehiel, and Zechariah, and Azariah, and Michael, and Shephatiah — all these were the sons of Jehoshaphat king of Israel. And their father gave them great gifts of silver, and of gold, and of precious things, with fortified cities in Judah; but the kingdom gave he to Jehoram because he was the firstborn.

2 Now when Jehoram was risen up to the kingdom of his father, he strengthened himself and slew all his brethren with the sword, and diverse also of the princes of Israel. Jehoram was thirty-two years old when he began to reign, and he reigned eight years in Jerusalem. And he walked in the way of the kings of Israel, like did the house of Ahab; for he had the daughter of Ahab to wife and he wrought evil in the eyes of the Lord. Nevertheless, the Lord would not destroy the house of David because of the covenant that he had made with David, and as he promised to give a light to him and to his sons for ever.

3 In his days, the Edomites revolted from under the dominion of Judah and made themselves a king. Then Jehoram went forth with his princes and all his chariots with him, and he rose up by night and smote the Edomites who encompassed him in, and the captains of the chariots. So the Edomites revolted from under the hand of Judah unto this day.

4 The same time did Libnah revolt from under his hand because he had forsaken the Lord God of his fathers. Moreover, he made high places in the mountains of Judah, and caused the inhabitants of Jerusalem to commit fornication, and compelled Judah to it.

5 And there came a writing to him from Elijah the prophet, saying, Thus says the Lord God of David your father: Because you have not walked in the ways of Jehoshaphat your father, nor in the ways of Asa king of Judah, but have walked in the way of the kings of Israel, and have made Judah and the inhabitants of Jerusalem to go whoring like

unto the whoredoms of the house of Ahab, and also have slain your brethren of your father's house, who were better than yourself. Behold, with a great plague will the Lord smite your people, and your children, and your wives, and all your goods; and you shall have great sickness by disease of your bowels, until your bowels fall out by reason of the sickness, day by day.

6 Moreover, the Lord stirred up against Jehoram the spirit of the Philistines and of the Arabians that were near the Ethiopians, and they came up into Judah, and broke into it, and carried away all the substance that was found in the king's house, and his sons also, and his wives, so that there was not a son left him save Jehoahaz, the youngest of his sons.

7 And after all this, the Lord smote him in his bowels with an incurable disease. And it came to pass that in process of time, after the end of two years, his bowels fell out by reason of his sickness. So he died of awful diseases. And his people made no burning for him like the burning of his fathers.

8 Thirty-two years old was he when he began to reign, and he reigned in Jerusalem eight years, and departed without being desired. Nevertheless, they buried him in the city of David, but not in the sepulchers of the kings. And the inhabitants of Jerusalem made Ahaziah, his youngest son, king in his stead; for the band of men that came with the Arabians to the camp had slain all the eldest.

9 So Ahaziah the son of Jehoram king of Judah reigned; twenty-two years old was Ahaziah when he began to reign, and he reigned one year in Jerusalem. His mother's name also was Athaliah, the daughter of Omri.

2 He also walked in the ways of the house of Ahab, for his mother was his counselor to do wickedly. Wherefore, he did evil in the sight of the Lord like the house of Ahab, for they were his counselors after the death of his father, to his destruction. He walked also after their counsel, and went with Joram the son of Ahab, king of Israel, to war against Hazael king of Syria at Ramoth-Gilead, and the Syrians smote Joram. And he returned to be healed in Jezreel because of the wounds which were given him at Ramah when he fought with Hazael king of Syria.

3 And Azariah the son of Jehoram, king of Judah, went down to see Joram the son of Ahab at Jezreel, because he was sick. And the destruction of Ahaziah was of God, by coming to Joram; for when he had come, he went out with Joram against Jehu the son of Nimshi, whom the Lord had anointed to cut off the house of Ahab.

4 And it came to pass that when Jehu was executing judgment upon the house of Ahab, and found the princes of Judah and the sons of the brethren of Ahaziah that ministered to Ahaziah, he slew them. And he sought Ahaziah, and they caught him—for he was hidden in Samaria—and brought him to Jehu. And when they had slain him, they buried him—Because, said they, he is the son of Jehoshaphat, who sought the Lord with all his heart. So the house of Ahaziah had no power to keep still the kingdom.

5 But when Athaliah the mother of Ahaziah saw that her son was dead, she arose and destroyed all the royal seed of the house of Judah. But Jehoshabeath, the daughter of the king, took Joash the son of Ahaziah, and stole him from among the king's sons that were slain, and put him and his nurse in a bedchamber. So Jehoshabeath, the daughter of king Jehoram, the wife of Jehoiada the priest—for she was the sister of Ahaziah—hid him from Athaliah, so that she slew him not. And he was with them hidden in the house of God six years. And Athaliah reigned over the land.

10 And in the seventh year, Jehoiada strengthened himself and took the captains of hundreds—Azariah the son of Jeroham, and Ishmael the son of Jehohanan, and Azariah the son of Obed, and Maaseiah the son of Adaiah, and Elishaphat the son of Zichri—into covenant with him. And they went about in Judah and gathered the Levites out of all the cities of Judah, and the chief of the fathers of Israel; and they came to Jerusalem. And all the congregation made a covenant with the king in the house of God.

2 And he said unto them, Behold, the king's son shall reign, as the Lord has said of the sons of David. This is the thing that you shall do: a third part of you entering on the Sabbath, of the priests and of the Levites, shall be porters of the doors. And a third part shall be at the king's house, and a third part at the gate of the foundation. And all the people shall be in the courts of the house of the Lord. But let none come

into the house of the Lord, save the priests and they that minister of the Levites. They shall go in, for they are holy. But all the people shall keep the watch of the Lord. And the Levites shall encompass the king round about, every man with his weapons in his hand, and whoever else comes into the house, he shall be put to death. But be with the king when he comes in and when he goes out.

3 So the Levites and all Judah did according to all things that Jehoiada the priest had commanded, and took every man his men that were to come in on the Sabbath, with them that were to go out on the Sabbath (for Jehoiada the priest dismissed not the courses). Moreover, Jehoiada the priest delivered to the captains of hundreds spears, and bucklers, and shields, that had been king David's, which were in the house of God. And he set all the people, every man having his weapon in his hand, from the right side of the temple to the left side of the temple, along by the altar and the temple, by the king round about.

4 Then they brought out the king's son, and put upon him the crown, and gave him the testimony, and made him king. And Jehoiada and his sons anointed him and said, God save the king.

5 Now when Athaliah heard the noise of the people running and praising the king, she came to the people, into the house of the Lord. And she looked, and behold, the king stood at his pillar at the entering in, and the princes and the trumpets by the king. And all the people of the land rejoiced and sounded with trumpets, also the singers with instruments of music, and such as taught to sing praise. Then Athaliah rent her clothes, and said, Treason, treason.

6 Then Jehoiada the priest brought out the captains of hundreds that were set over the host, and said unto them, Have her out of the ranks, and whoever follows her, let him be slain with the sword— for the priest said, Slay her not in the house of the Lord. So they laid hands on her, and when she had come to the entrance of the horse gate by the king's house, they slew her there.

7 And Jehoiada made a covenant—between him, and between all the people, and between the king—that they should be the Lord's people. Then all the people went to the house of Baal and broke it down, and broke his altars and his images in pieces, and slew Mattan the priest of Baal before the altars.

8 Also, Jehoiada appointed the offices of the house of the Lord by the hand of the priests, the Levites whom David had distributed in the house of the Lord, to offer the burnt offerings of the Lord as it is written in the law of Moses, with rejoicing and with singing as it was ordained by David. And he set the porters at the gates of the house of the Lord, that none who was unclean in anything should enter in.

9 And he took the captains of hundreds, and the nobles, and the governors of the people, and all the people of the land, and brought down the king from the house of the Lord. And they came through the high gate into the king's house and set the king upon the throne of the kingdom. And all the people of the land rejoiced. And the city was quiet after they had slain Athaliah with the sword.

11 Joash was seven years old when he began to reign, and he reigned forty years in Jerusalem. His mother's name also was Zibiah of Beersheba. And Joash did right in the sight of the Lord all the days of Jehoiada the priest. And Jehoiada took for him two wives, and he begot sons and daughters.

2 And it came to pass, after this, Joash was determined to repair the house of the Lord. And he gathered together the priests and the Levites, and said to them, Go out unto the cities of Judah, and gather of all Israel money to repair the house of your God from year to year, and see that you hasten the matter. Nevertheless, the Levites hastened not.

3 And the king called for Jehoiada the chief, and said unto him, Why have you not required of the Levites to bring in out of Judah and out of Jerusalem the collection of Moses the servant of the Lord and of the congregation of Israel for the tabernacle of witness? For the sons of Athaliah, that wicked woman, had broken up the house of God, and also all the dedicated things of the house of the Lord did they bestow upon the Baalim.

4 And at the king's commandment, they made a chest and set it outside at the gate of the house of the Lord. And they made a proclamation through Judah and Jerusalem to bring in to the Lord the collection of Moses the servant of God upon Israel in the wilderness. And all the princes and all the people rejoiced, and brought in, and cast into the chest until they had made an end.

5 Now it came to pass that when the chest was brought unto the king's office by the hand of the Levites, and when they saw that there was much money, the king's scribe and the high priest's officer came and emptied the chest, and took it, and carried it to his place again. Thus they did day by day, and gathered money in abundance. And the king and Jehoiada gave it to such as did the work of the service of the house of the Lord, and hired masons and carpenters to repair the house of the Lord, and also such as wrought iron and brass to mend the house of the Lord.

6 So the workmen worked, and the work was perfected by them, and they set the house of God in his state and strengthened it. And when they had finished it, they brought the rest of the money before the king and Jehoiada, whereof were made vessels for the house of the Lord, even vessels to minister and to offer with, and spoons, and vessels of gold and silver. And they offered burnt offerings in the house of the Lord continually, all the days of Jehoiada.

7 But Jehoiada waxed old, and was full of days when he died; a hundred thirty years old was he when he died. And they buried him in the city of David among the kings because he had done good in Israel, both toward God and toward his house.

8 Now after the death of Jehoiada, the princes of Judah came and did reverence to the king. Then the king listened unto them. And they left the house of the Lord God of their fathers and served groves and idols. And wrath came upon Judah and Jerusalem for this their trespass. Yet he sent prophets to them, to bring them again unto the Lord, and they testified against them; but they would not give ear.

9 And the spirit of God came upon Zechariah the son of Jehoiada the priest, who stood above the people and said unto them, Thus says God: Why do you transgress the commandments of the Lord, that you cannot prosper? Because you have forsaken the Lord, he has also forsaken you.

10 And they conspired against him and stoned him with stones at the commandment of the king, in the court of the house of the Lord. Thus, Joash the king remembered not the kindness which Jehoiada his father had done to him, but slew his son. And when he died, he said, The Lord look upon me and require me.

11 And it came to pass, at the end of the year, that the host of Syria came up against him. And they came to Judah and Jerusalem, and

destroyed all the princes of the people from among the people, and sent all the spoil of them unto the king of Damascus; for the army of the Syrians came with a small company of men, and the Lord delivered a very great host into their hand, because they had forsaken the Lord God of their fathers. So they executed judgment against Joash.

12 And when they were departed from him — for they left him in great diseases — his own servants conspired against him for the blood of the sons of Jehoiada the priest and slew him on his bed; and he died. And they buried him in the city of David, but they buried him not in the sepulchers of the kings. And these are they that conspired against him: Zabad the son of Shimeath an Ammonitess, and Jehozabad the son of Shimrith a Moabitess.

13 Now his sons, and the greatness of the burdens upon him, and the repairing of the house of God, behold, they are written in the history of the book of the kings. And Amaziah his son reigned in his stead.

12 Amaziah was twenty-five years old when he began to reign, and he reigned twenty-nine years in Jerusalem. And his mother's name was Jehoaddan, of Jerusalem. And he did right in the sight of the Lord, but not with a perfect heart. Now it came to pass, when the kingdom was established to him, that he slew his servants that had killed the king, his father. But he slew not their children, but did as it is written in the law in the book of Moses, where the Lord commanded, saying, The fathers shall not die for the children, neither shall the children die for the fathers, but every man shall die for his own sin.

2 Moreover, Amaziah gathered Judah together and made them captains over thousands and captains over hundreds, according to the houses of their fathers, throughout all Judah and Benjamin. And he numbered them from twenty years old and above, and found them three hundred thousand choice men able to go forth to war that could handle spear and shield. He hired also a hundred thousand mighty men of valor out of Israel for a hundred talents of silver.

3 But there came a man of God to him, saying, O king, let not the army of Israel go with you, for the Lord is not with Israel — namely, with all the children of Ephraim; but if you will go do it, be strong for the battle; God shall make you fall before the enemy, for God has power to help and to cast down. And Amaziah said to the man of God,

But what shall we do for the hundred talents which I have given to the army of Israel? And the man of God answered, The Lord is able to give you much more than this.

4 Then Amaziah separated them, the army that had come to him out of Ephraim, to go home again. Wherefore, their anger was greatly kindled against Judah and they returned home in great anger.

5 And Amaziah strengthened himself and led forth his people, and went to the valley of salt and smote, of the children of Seir, ten thousand. And ten thousand alive did the children of Judah carry away captive, and brought them unto the top of the rock, and cast them down from the top of the rock, that they all were broken in pieces.

6 But the soldiers of the army whom Amaziah sent back, that they should not go with him to battle, fell upon the cities of Judah, from Samaria even unto Bethhoron, and smote three thousand of them, and took much spoil.

7 Now it came to pass, after Amaziah had come from the slaughter of the Edomites, that he brought the gods of the children of Seir and set them up to be his gods, and bowed down himself before them and burned incense unto them. Wherefore, the anger of the Lord was kindled against Amaziah and he sent unto him a prophet, who said unto him, Why have you sought after the gods of the people, which could not deliver their own people out of your hand?

8 And it came to pass as he talked with him that the king said unto him, Are you made of the king's counsel? Cease; why should you be smitten? Then the prophet ceased, and said, I know that God has determined to destroy you because you have done this and have not listened unto my counsel.

9 Then Amaziah king of Judah took advice, and sent to Joash the son of Jehoahaz, the son of Jehu, king of Israel, saying, Come, let us see one another in the face. And Joash king of Israel sent to Amaziah king of Judah, saying, The thistle that grew in Lebanon sent to the cedar that grew in Lebanon, saying, Give your daughter to my son to wife. And there passed by a wild beast that was in Lebanon and trod down the thistle. You say, Behold, you have smitten the Edomites; and your heart lifts you up to boast. Abide now at home. Why should you meddle to your hurt, that you should fall? Even you and Judah with you?

10 But Amaziah would not hear, for it came of God, that he might deliver them into the hand of their enemies because they sought after the gods of Edom. So Joash the king of Israel went up, and they saw one another in the face, both he and Amaziah king of Judah, at Bethshemesh which belongs to Judah. And Judah was put to the worse before Israel, and they fled every man to his tent. And Joash the king of Israel took Amaziah king of Judah, the son of Joash, the son of Jehoahaz, at Bethshemesh, and brought him to Jerusalem, and broke down the wall of Jerusalem from the gate of Ephraim to the corner gate — four hundred cubits. And he took all the gold and the silver, and all the vessels that were found in the house of God with Obededom, and the treasures of the king's house, the hostages also, and returned to Samaria.

11 And Amaziah the son of Joash, king of Judah, lived after the death of Joash son of Jehoahaz, king of Israel, fifteen years. Now the rest of the acts of Amaziah, first and last, behold, are they not written in the book of the kings of Judah and Israel?

12 Now after the time that Amaziah did turn away from following the Lord, they made a conspiracy against him in Jerusalem. And he fled to Lachish, but they sent to Lachish after him and slew him there. And they brought him upon horses and buried him with his fathers in the city of Judah.

13 Then all the people of Judah took Uzziah, who was sixteen years old, and made him king in the place of his father Amaziah. He built Eloth and restored it to Judah after the king slept with his fathers.

2 Sixteen years old was Uzziah when he began to reign, and he reigned fifty-two years in Jerusalem. His mother's name also was Jecoliah, of Jerusalem. And he did right in the sight of the Lord, according to all that his father Amaziah did. And he sought God in the days of Zechariah, who had understanding in the visions of God. And as long as he sought the Lord, God made him to prosper.

3 And he went forth and warred against the Philistines, and broke down the wall of Gath, and the wall of Jabneh, and the wall of Ashdod, and built cities about Ashdod and among the Philistines. And God helped him against the Philistines, and against the Arabians that

dwelled in Gur-Baal, and the Meunites. And the Ammonites gave gifts to Uzziah, and his name spread abroad even to the entering in of Egypt, for he strengthened himself exceedingly.

4 Moreover, Uzziah built towers in Jerusalem at the corner gate, and at the valley gate, and at the turning of the wall, and fortified them. Also, he built towers in the desert and dug many wells, for he had many cattle (both in the low country and in the plains), husbandmen also, and vine dressers in the mountains and in Carmel, for he loved husbandry.

5 Moreover, Uzziah had a host of fighting men that went out to war by bands, according to the number of their account by the hand of Jeiel the scribe and Maaseiah the ruler, under the hand of Hananiah, one of the king's captains. The whole number of the chief of the fathers of the mighty men of valor were two thousand six hundred. And under their hand was an army, three hundred seven thousand five hundred, that made war with mighty power to help the king against the enemy. And Uzziah prepared for them throughout all the host shields, and spears, and helmets, and habergeons, and bows, and slings to cast stones. And he made in Jerusalem engines, invented by skillful men, to be on the towers and upon the bulwarks to shoot arrows and great stones. And his name spread far abroad, for he was marvelously helped until he was strong.

6 But when he was strong, his heart was lifted up to his destruction; for he transgressed against the Lord his God, and went into the temple of the Lord to burn incense upon the altar of incense. And Azariah the priest went in after him, and with him eighty priests of the Lord that were valiant men. And they withstood Uzziah the king and said unto him, It appertains not unto you, Uzziah, to burn incense unto the Lord, but to the priests, the sons of Aaron that are consecrated to burn incense. Go out of the sanctuary, for you have trespassed, neither shall it be for your honor from the Lord God.

7 Then Uzziah was angry, and had a censer in his hand to burn incense; and while he was angry with the priests, the leprosy even rose up in his forehead before the priests in the house of the Lord, from beside the incense altar. And Azariah the chief priest, and all the priests, looked upon him; and behold, he was leprous in his forehead. And they thrust him out from there, yea, he himself hastened also to go out because the Lord had smitten him.

8 And Uzziah the king was a leper unto the day of his death, and dwelled in a separate house, being a leper; for he was cut off from the house of the Lord. And Jotham his son was over the king's house, judging the people of the land.

9 Now the rest of the acts of Uzziah, first and last, did Isaiah the prophet, the son of Amoz, write. So Uzziah slept with his fathers, and they buried him with his fathers in the field of the burial which belonged to the kings; for they said, He is a leper. And Jotham his son reigned in his stead.

14 Jotham was twenty-five years old when he began to reign, and he reigned sixteen years in Jerusalem. His mother's name also was Jerushah, the daughter of Zadok. And he did right in the sight of the Lord, according to all that his father Uzziah did. Nevertheless, he entered not into the temple of the Lord. And the people did yet corruptly.

2 He built the high gate of the house of the Lord, and on the wall of Ophel he built much. Moreover, he built cities in the mountains of Judah, and in the forests he built castles and towers.

3 He fought also with the king of the Ammonites and prevailed against them. And the children of Ammon gave him the same year a hundred talents of silver, and ten thousand measures of wheat, and ten thousand of barley. So much did the children of Ammon pay unto him, both the second year and the third. So Jotham became mighty because he prepared his ways before the Lord his God.

4 Now the rest of the acts of Jotham, and all his wars and his ways, they are written in the book of the kings of Israel and Judah. He was twenty-five years old when he began to reign, and reigned sixteen years in Jerusalem. And Jotham slept with his fathers, and they buried him in the city of David. And Ahaz his son reigned in his stead.

15 Ahaz was twenty years old when he began to reign, and he reigned sixteen years in Jerusalem. But he did not right in the sight of the Lord like David his father, for he walked in the ways of the kings of Israel, and made also molten images for the Baalim. Moreover, he burned incense in the valley of the son of Hinnom, and burned his children in the fire, after the abominations of the

heathen whom the Lord had cast out before the children of Israel. He sacrificed also and burned incense in the high places, and on the hills, and under every green tree.

2 Wherefore, the Lord his God delivered him into the hand of the king of Syria. And they smote him, and carried away a great multitude of them captives, and brought them to Damascus.

3 And he was also delivered into the hand of the king of Israel, who smote him with a great slaughter; for Pekah the son of Remaliah slew in Judah a hundred twenty thousand in one day, all valiant men, because they had forsaken the Lord God of their fathers. And Zichri, a mighty man of Ephraim, slew Maaseiah the king's son, and Azrikam the governor of the house, and Elkanah next to the king. And the children of Israel carried away captive of their brethren two hundred thousand women, sons, and daughters, and took also away much spoil from them, and brought the spoil to Samaria.

4 But a prophet of the Lord was there, whose name was Oded. And he went out before the host that came to Samaria, and said unto them, Behold, because the Lord God of your fathers was angry with Judah, he has delivered them into your hand, and you have slain them in a rage that reaches up unto Heaven. And now you purpose to keep under the children of Judah and Jerusalem for bondmen and bondwomen unto you. But are there not with you, even with you, sins against the Lord your God? Now hear me therefore and deliver the captives again whom you have taken captive of your brethren, for the fierce wrath of the Lord is upon you.

5 Then certain of the heads of the children of Ephraim — Azariah the son of Johanan, Berechiah the son of Meshillemoth, and Jehizkiah the son of Shallum, and Amasa the son of Hadlai — stood up against them that came from the war, and said unto them, You shall not bring in the captives here; for whereas we have offended against the Lord, you intend to add to our sins and to our trespass. For our trespass is great, and there is fierce wrath against Israel.

6 So the armed men left the captives and the spoil before the princes and all the congregation. And the men who were expressed by name rose up and took the captives, and with the spoil clothed all that were naked among them, and arrayed them, and shod them, and gave them to eat and to drink, and anointed them, and carried all the feeble of

them upon asses, and brought them to Jericho, the city of palm trees, to their brethren. Then they returned to Samaria.

⁷At that time did king Ahaz send unto the kings of Assyria to help him, for again the Edomites had come and smitten Judah and carried away captives. The Philistines also had invaded the cities of the low country and of the south of Judah, and had taken Bethshemesh, and Aijalon, and Gederoth, and Soco with the villages thereof, and Timnah with the villages thereof, Gimzo also and the villages thereof, and they dwelled there (for the Lord brought Judah low because of Ahaz king of Israel, for he made Judah naked, and transgressed seriously against the Lord). And Tiglath-Pileser king of Assyria came unto him and distressed him, but strengthened him not; for Ahaz took away a portion out of the house of the Lord, and out of the house of the king, and of the princes, and gave it unto the king of Assyria; but he helped him not.

⁸And in the time of his distress did he trespass yet more against the Lord — this is that king Ahaz — for he sacrificed unto the gods of Damascus which smote him, and he said, Because the gods of the kings of Syria help them, therefore will I sacrifice to them, that they may help me. But they were the ruin of him and of all Israel.

⁹And Ahaz gathered together the vessels of the house of God, and cut in pieces the vessels of the house of God, and shut up the doors of the house of the Lord, and he made himself altars in every corner of Jerusalem. And in every single city of Judah he made high places to burn incense unto other gods, and provoked to anger the Lord God of his fathers.

¹⁰Now the rest of his acts and of all his ways, first and last, behold, they are written in the book of the kings of Judah and Israel. And Ahaz slept with his fathers, and they buried him in the city, even in Jerusalem. But they brought him not into the sepulchers of the kings of Israel. And Hezekiah his son reigned in his stead.

16 Hezekiah began to reign when he was twenty-five years old, and he reigned twenty-nine years in Jerusalem. And his mother's name was Abijah, the daughter of Zechariah. And he did that which was right in the sight of the Lord, according to all that David his father had done.

2 He, in the first year of his reign, in the first month, opened the doors of the house of the Lord and repaired them. And he brought in the priests and the Levites, and gathered them together into the east street, and said unto them, Hear me, you Levites; sanctify now yourselves, and sanctify the house of the Lord God of your fathers, and carry forth the filthiness out of the holy place. For our fathers have trespassed and done evil in the eyes of the Lord our God, and have forsaken him, and have turned away their faces from the habitation of the Lord, and turned their backs. Also, they have shut up the doors of the porch and put out the lamps, and have not burned incense nor offered burnt offerings in the holy place unto the God of Israel. Wherefore, the wrath of the Lord was upon Judah and Jerusalem, and he has delivered them to trouble, to astonishment, and to hissing, as you see with your eyes; for behold, our fathers have fallen by the sword, and our sons and our daughters and our wives are in captivity for this.

3 Now it is in my heart to make a covenant with the Lord God of Israel, that his fierce wrath may turn away from us. My sons, be not now negligent, for the Lord has chosen you to stand before him, to serve him, and that you should minister unto him and burn incense.

4 Then the Levites arose: Mahath the son of Amasai and Joel the son of Azariah, of the sons of the Kohathites; and of the sons of Merari: Kish the son of Abdi and Azariah the son of Jehallelel; and of the Gershonites: Joah the son of Zimmah and Eden the son of Joah; and of the sons of Elizaphan: Shimri and Jeiel; and of the sons of Asaph: Zechariah and Mattaniah; and of the sons of Heman: Jehiel and Shimei; and of the sons of Jeduthun: Shemaiah and Uzziel.

5 And they gathered their brethren and sanctified themselves, and came according to the commandment of the king, by the words of the Lord, to cleanse the house of the Lord. And the priests went into the inner part of the house of the Lord to cleanse it, and brought out all the uncleanness that they found in the temple of the Lord, into the court of the house of the Lord. And the Levites took it, to carry it out abroad into the brook Kidron. Now they began on the first day of the first month to sanctify, and on the eighth day of the month came they to the porch of the Lord. So they sanctified the house of the Lord in eight days, and in the sixteenth day of the first month, they made an end.

⁶ Then they went in to Hezekiah the king and said, We have cleansed all the house of the Lord, and the altar of burnt offering with all the vessels thereof, and the showbread table with all the vessels thereof. Moreover, all the vessels which king Ahaz in his reign did cast away in his transgression have we prepared and sanctified, and behold, they are before the altar of the Lord.

⁷ Then Hezekiah the king rose early, and gathered the rulers of the city and went up to the house of the Lord. And they brought seven bullocks, and seven rams, and seven lambs, and seven he-goats for a sin offering for the kingdom, and for the sanctuary, and for Judah. And he commanded the priests, the sons of Aaron, to offer them on the altar of the Lord. So they killed the bullocks, and the priests received the blood and sprinkled it on the altar. Likewise, when they had killed the rams, they sprinkled the blood upon the altar. They killed also the lambs and they sprinkled the blood upon the altar. And they brought forth the he-goats for the sin offering before the king and the congregation, and they laid their hands upon them, and the priests killed them, and they made reconciliation with their blood upon the altar to make an atonement for all Israel; for the king commanded the burnt offering and the sin offering for all Israel.

⁸ And he set the Levites in the house of the Lord with cymbals, with psalteries, and with harps, according to the commandment of David, and of Gad the king's seer, and Nathan the prophet; for so was the commandment of the Lord by his prophets. And the Levites stood with the instruments of David, and the priests with the trumpets.

⁹ And Hezekiah commanded to offer the burnt offering upon the altar. And when the burnt offering began, the song of the Lord began with the trumpets and with the instruments ordained by David king of Israel. And all the congregation worshipped, and the singers sang, and the trumpeters sounded until the burnt offering was finished.

¹⁰ And when they had made an end of offering, the king and all that were present with him bowed themselves and worshipped. Moreover, Hezekiah the king and the princes commanded the Levites to sing praise unto the Lord, with the words of David and of Asaph the seer. And they sang praises with gladness, and they bowed their heads and worshipped.

11 Then Hezekiah answered and said, Now you have consecrated yourselves unto the Lord. Come near and bring sacrifices and thank offerings into the house of the Lord. And the congregation brought in sacrifices and thank offerings, and as many as were of a free heart, burnt offerings. And the number of the burnt offerings which the congregation brought was seventy bullocks, a hundred rams, two hundred lambs — all these were for a burnt offering to the Lord. And the consecrated things were six hundred oxen and three thousand sheep. But the priests were too few, so that they could not flay all the burnt offerings. Wherefore, their brethren the Levites did help them until the work was ended, and until the priests had sanctified themselves (for the Levites were more upright in heart to sanctify themselves than the priests). And also the burnt offerings were in abundance, with the fat of the peace offerings and the drink offerings for every burnt offering.

12 So the service of the house of the Lord was set in order. And Hezekiah rejoiced, and all the people, that God had prepared the people; for the thing was done suddenly.

13 And Hezekiah sent to all Israel and Judah, and wrote letters also to Ephraim and Manasseh, that they should come to the house of the Lord at Jerusalem to keep the Passover unto the Lord God of Israel; for the king had taken counsel, and his princes, and all the congregation in Jerusalem, to keep the Passover in the second month, for they could not keep it at that time because the priests had not sanctified themselves sufficiently, neither had the people gathered themselves together to Jerusalem. And the thing pleased the king and all the congregation. So they established a decree to make proclamation throughout all Israel, from Beersheba even to Dan, that they should come to keep the Passover unto the Lord God of Israel at Jerusalem, for they had not done it of a long time as it was written.

14 So the messengers went with the letters from the king and his princes throughout all Israel and Judah, and according to the commandment of the king, saying, You children of Israel, return unto the Lord God of Abraham, Isaac, and Israel, and he will return to the remnant of you that are escaped out of the hand of the kings of Assyria. And be not you like your fathers and like your brethren who trespassed against the Lord God of their fathers, who therefore gave them up to desolation, as you see. Now be not stiff-necked as your fathers; yield

yourselves unto the Lord and enter into his sanctuary which he has sanctified for ever, and serve the Lord your God, that the fierceness of his wrath may turn away from you. For if you return unto the Lord, your brethren and your children shall find compassion before them that lead them captive, so that they shall come again into this land; for the Lord your God is gracious and merciful, and will not turn away his face from you if you return unto him.

15 So the messengers passed from city to city through the country of Ephraim and Manasseh, even unto Zebulun; but they laughed them to scorn and mocked them. Nevertheless, diverse of Asher, and Manasseh, and of Zebulun humbled themselves and came to Jerusalem. Also in Judah, the hand of God was to give them one heart to do the commandment of the king and of the princes by the word of the Lord.

16 And there assembled at Jerusalem many people to keep the Feast of Unleavened Bread in the second month, a very great congregation. And they arose and took away the altars that were in Jerusalem, and all the altars for incense took they away and cast them into the brook Kidron.

17 Then they killed the passover on the fourteenth day of the second month. And the priests and the Levites were ashamed, and sanctified themselves, and brought in the burnt offerings into the house of the Lord. And they stood in their place after their manner, according to the law of Moses the man of God. The priests sprinkled the blood which they received of the hand of the Levites, for there were many in the congregation that were not sanctified. Therefore, the Levites had the charge of the killing of the passovers for everyone that was not clean, to sanctify them unto the Lord. For a multitude of the people, even many of Ephraim, and Manasseh, Issachar, and Zebulun had not cleansed themselves; yet did they eat the passover otherwise than it was written. But Hezekiah prayed for them, saying, The good Lord pardon everyone that prepares his heart to seek God, the Lord God of his fathers, though not according to the purification of the sanctuary. And the Lord listened to Hezekiah and healed the people.

18 And the children of Israel that were present at Jerusalem kept the Feast of Unleavened Bread seven days with great gladness. And the Levites and the priests praised the Lord day by day, singing with loud instruments unto the Lord. And Hezekiah spoke encouragingly unto all the Levites that taught the good knowledge of the Lord. And they

did eat throughout the feast seven days, offering peace offerings and making confession to the Lord God of their fathers.

¹⁹ And the whole assembly took counsel to keep another seven days. And they kept another seven days with gladness. For Hezekiah king of Judah did give to the congregation a thousand bullocks and seven thousand sheep. And the princes gave to the congregation a thousand bullocks and ten thousand sheep, and a great number of priests sanctified themselves. And all the congregation of Judah, with the priests and the Levites, and all the congregation that came out of Israel, and the strangers that came out of the land of Israel and that dwelled in Judah, rejoiced. So there was great joy in Jerusalem; for since the time of Solomon the son of David, king of Israel, there was not the like in Jerusalem. Then the priests the Levites arose and blessed the people. And their voice was heard, and their prayer came up to his holy dwelling place, even unto Heaven.

²⁰ Now when all this was finished, all Israel that were present went out to the cities of Judah, and broke the images in pieces, and cut down the groves, and threw down the high places and the altars out of all Judah and Benjamin, in Ephraim also, and Manasseh, until they had utterly destroyed them all. Then all the children of Israel returned, every man to his possession, into their own cities.

²¹ And Hezekiah appointed the courses of the priests and the Levites after their courses, every man according to his service, the priests and Levites for burnt offerings and for peace offerings, to minister, and to give thanks, and to praise in the gates of the tents of the Lord.

²² He appointed also the king's portion of his substance for the burnt offerings, namely for the morning and evening burnt offerings, and the burnt offerings for the Sabbaths, and for the new moons, and for the set feasts, as it is written in the law of the Lord. Moreover, he commanded the people that dwelled in Jerusalem to give the portion of the priests and the Levites, that they might be encouraged in the law of the Lord.

²³ And as soon as the commandment came abroad, the children of Israel brought in abundance the firstfruits of grain, wine, and oil, and honey, and of all the increase of the field; and the tithe of all things brought they in abundantly. And concerning the children of Israel and Judah that dwelled in the cities of Judah, they also brought in the tithe

of oxen and sheep, and the tithe of holy things which were consecrated unto the Lord their God, and laid them by heaps. In the third month, they began to lay the foundation of the heaps, and finished them in the seventh month.

24 And when Hezekiah and the princes came and saw the heaps, they blessed the Lord and his people Israel. Then Hezekiah questioned with the priests and the Levites concerning the heaps, and Azariah the chief priest of the house of Zadok answered him and said, Since the people began to bring the offerings into the house of the Lord, we have had enough to eat, and have left plenty; for the Lord has blessed his people, and that which is left is this great store.

25 Then Hezekiah commanded to prepare chambers in the house of the Lord. And they prepared them, and brought in the offerings, and the tithes, and the dedicated things faithfully, over which Conaniah the Levite was ruler, and Shimei his brother was the next.

26 And Jehiel, and Azaziah, and Nahath, and Asahel, and Jerimoth, and Jozabad, and Eliel, and Ismachiah, and Mahath, and Benaiah were overseers under the hand of Conaniah and Shimei his brother, at the commandment of Hezekiah the king and Azariah the ruler of the house of God.

27 And Kore the son of Imnah the Levite, the porter toward the east, was over the freewill offerings of God, to distribute the offerings of the Lord and the most holy things. And next to him were Eden, and Miniamin, and Jeshua, and Shemaiah, Amariah, and Shecaniah in the cities of the priests, in their set office, to give to their brethren by courses, as well to the great as to the small: besides their genealogy of males, from three years old and upward, even unto everyone that enters into the house of the Lord, his daily portion for their service in their charges according to their courses; both to the genealogy of the priests by the house of their fathers and the Levites from twenty years old and upward in their charges by their courses, and to the genealogy of all their little ones, their wives, and their sons, and their daughters, through all the congregation (for in their set office they sanctified themselves in holiness); also of the sons of Aaron, the priests who were in the fields of the suburbs of their cities, in every single city, the men that were expressed by name, to give portions to all the

males among the priests, and to all that were reckoned by genealogies among the Levites.

28 And thus did Hezekiah throughout all Judah, and wrought good and right and truth before the Lord his God. And in every work that he began in the service of the house of God, and in the law, and in the commandments, to seek his God, he did with all his heart and prospered.

29 After these things and the establishment thereof, Sennacherib king of Assyria came and entered into Judah, and encamped against the fortified cities, and thought to win them for himself.

30 And when Hezekiah saw that Sennacherib had come, and that he was purposed to fight against Jerusalem, he took counsel with his princes and his mighty men to stop the waters of the fountains which were outside the city, and they did help him. So there were gathered many people together who stopped all the fountains and the brook that ran through the midst of the land, saying, Why should the kings of Assyria come and find much water? Also, he strengthened himself, and built up all the wall that was broken, and raised it up to the towers, and another wall outside, and repaired Millo in the city of David, and made darts and shields in abundance.

31 And he set captains of war over the people, and gathered them together to him in the street of the gate of the city, and spoke encouragingly to them, saying, Be strong and courageous. Be not afraid nor dismayed for the king of Assyria, nor for all the multitude that is with him, for there is more with us than with him. With him is an arm of flesh, but with us is the Lord our God, to help us and to fight our battles. And the people rested themselves upon the words of Hezekiah king of Judah.

32 After this did Sennacherib king of Assyria send his servants to Jerusalem — but he himself laid siege against Lachish, and all his power with him — unto Hezekiah king of Judah, and unto all Judah that were at Jerusalem, saying, Thus says Sennacherib king of Assyria: On what do you trust, that you abide in the siege in Jerusalem? Does not Hezekiah persuade you to give over yourselves to die by famine and by thirst? Saying, The Lord our God shall deliver us out of the hand of the king of Assyria? Has not the same Hezekiah taken away

his high places and his altars, and commanded Judah and Jerusalem, saying, You shall worship before one altar and burn incense upon it?

33 Do you not know what I and my fathers have done unto all the people of other lands? Were the gods of the nations of those lands in any way able to deliver their lands out of my hand? Who was there among all the gods of those nations that my fathers utterly destroyed that could deliver his people out of my hand, that your god should be able to deliver you out of my hand? Now therefore let not Hezekiah deceive you nor persuade you on this manner, neither yet believe him. For no god of any nation or kingdom was able to deliver his people out of my hand, and out of the hand of my fathers. How much less shall your god deliver you out of my hand?

34 And his servants spoke yet against the Lord God and against his servant Hezekiah. He wrote also letters to rail on the Lord God of Israel and to speak against him, saying, As the gods of the nations of other lands have not delivered their people out of my hand, so shall not the god of Hezekiah deliver his people out of my hand. Then they cried with a loud voice in the Jews' speech unto the people of Jerusalem that were on the wall, to frighten them and to trouble them, that they might take the city. And they spoke against the God of Jerusalem, as against the gods of the people of the earth which were the work of the hands of man.

35 And for this cause, Hezekiah the king and the prophet Isaiah, the son of Amoz, prayed and cried to Heaven. And the Lord sent an angel who cut off all the mighty men of valor, and the leaders and captains in the camp of the king of Assyria. So he returned with shame of face to his own land. And when he had come into the house of his god, they that came forth of his own body slew him there with the sword.

36 Thus, the Lord saved Hezekiah and the inhabitants of Jerusalem from the hand of Sennacherib the king of Assyria, and from the hand of all other, and guided them on every side. And many brought gifts unto the Lord to Jerusalem, and presents to Hezekiah king of Judah, so that he was magnified in the sight of all nations from that point forward.

37 In those days, Hezekiah was sick to the death and prayed unto the Lord. And he spoke unto him and he gave him a sign. But Hezekiah rendered not again according to the benefit done unto him, for his heart was lifted up. Therefore, there was wrath upon him and upon

Judah and Jerusalem. Notwithstanding, Hezekiah humbled himself for the pride of his heart, both he and the inhabitants of Jerusalem, so that the wrath of the Lord came not upon them in the days of Hezekiah.

38 And Hezekiah had exceedingly many riches and honor. And he made himself treasuries for silver, and for gold, and for precious stones, and for spices, and for shields, and for all manner of pleasant jewels; storehouses also for the increase of grain, and wine, and oil; and stalls for all manner of beasts, and enclosures for flocks. Moreover, he provided himself cities, and possessions of flocks and herds in abundance; for God had given him substance, very much.

39 This same Hezekiah also stopped the upper watercourse of Gihon, and brought it straight down to the west side of the city of David. And Hezekiah prospered in all his works. Nevertheless, in the business of the ambassadors of the princes of Babylon who sent unto him to inquire of the wonder that was done in the land, God left him, to try him, that he might know all that was in his heart.

40 Now the rest of the acts of Hezekiah and his goodness, behold, they are written in the vision of Isaiah the prophet, the son of Amoz, and in the book of the kings of Judah and Israel. And Hezekiah slept with his fathers, and they buried him in the chiefest of the sepulchers of the sons of David. And all Judah and the inhabitants of Jerusalem did him honor at his death. And Manasseh his son reigned in his stead.

17 Manasseh was twelve years old when he began to reign, and he reigned fifty-five years in Jerusalem, but did evil in the sight of the Lord like unto the abominations of the heathen whom the Lord had cast out before the children of Israel. For he built again the high places which Hezekiah his father had broken down, and he reared up altars for the Baalim, and made groves, and worshipped all the host of heaven and served them. Also, he built altars in the house of the Lord whereof the Lord had said, In Jerusalem shall my name be for ever. And he built altars for all the host of heaven in the two courts of the house of the Lord. And he caused his children to pass through the fire in the valley of the son of Hinnom. Also, he observed times, and used enchantments, and used witchcraft, and dealt with a familiar spirit and with wizards. He wrought much evil in the sight of the Lord to provoke him to anger.

2 And he set a carved image, the idol which he had made, in the house of God, of which God had said to David and to Solomon his son, In this house and in Jerusalem, which I have chosen before all the tribes of Israel, will I put my name for ever. Neither will I anymore remove the foot of Israel from out of the land which I have appointed for your fathers, so that they will take heed to do all that I have commanded them, according to the whole law and the statutes and the ordinances by the hand of Moses. So Manasseh made Judah and the inhabitants of Jerusalem to err, and to do worse than the heathen whom the Lord had destroyed before the children of Israel.

3 And the Lord spoke to Manasseh and to his people, but they would not listen. Wherefore, the Lord brought upon them the captains of the host of the king of Assyria, who took Manasseh among the thorns, and bound him with fetters, and carried him to Babylon. And when he was in affliction, he implored the Lord his God, and humbled himself greatly before the God of his fathers, and prayed unto him; and he was entreated of him, and heard his supplication, and brought him again to Jerusalem, into his kingdom. Then Manasseh knew that the Lord, he was God.

4 Now after this, he built a wall outside the city of David on the west side of Gihon, in the valley, even to the entrance at the fish gate, and encompassed about Ophel, and raised it up a very great height, and put captains of war in all the fortified cities of Judah.

5 And he took away the strange gods, and the idol out of the house of the Lord, and all the altars that he had built in the mount of the house of the Lord and in Jerusalem, and cast them out of the city. And he repaired the altar of the Lord and sacrificed thereon peace offerings and thank offerings, and commanded Judah to serve the Lord God of Israel. Nevertheless, the people did sacrifice still in the high places, yet unto the Lord their God only.

6 Now the rest of the acts of Manasseh, and his prayer unto his God, and the words of the seers that spoke to him in the name of the Lord God of Israel, behold, they are written in the book of the kings of Israel. His prayer also, and how God was entreated of him, and all his sin and his trespass, and the places wherein he built high places and set up groves and engraved images before he was humbled, behold, they are written among the sayings of the seers. So Manasseh slept

with his fathers, and they buried him in his own house. And Amon his son reigned in his stead.

7 Amon was twenty-two years old when he began to reign, and reigned two years in Jerusalem. But he did evil in the sight of the Lord, as did Manasseh his father; for Amon sacrificed unto all the carved images which Manasseh his father had made, and served them, and humbled not himself before the Lord, as Manasseh his father had humbled himself. But Amon trespassed more and more.

8 And his servants conspired against him and slew him in his own house. But the people of the land slew all them that had conspired against king Amon. And the people of the land made Josiah his son king in his stead.

18 Josiah was eight years old when he began to reign, and he reigned in Jerusalem thirty-one years. And he did right in the sight of the Lord, and walked in the ways of David his father, and declined neither to the right hand nor to the left. For in the eighth year of his reign, while he was yet young, he began to seek after the God of David his father.

2 And in the twelfth year, he began to purge Judah and Jerusalem from the high places, and the groves, and the carved images, and the molten images. And they broke down the altars of the Baalim in his presence. And the images that were on high above them he cut down. And the groves, and the carved images, and the molten images he broke in pieces, and made dust of them, and strewed it upon the graves of them that had sacrificed unto them. And he burned the bones of the priests upon their altars, and cleansed Judah and Jerusalem. And so did he in the cities of Manasseh, and Ephraim, and Simeon, even unto Naphtali, with their mattocks round about. And when he had broken down the altars and the groves, and had beaten the engraved images into powder, and cut down all the idols throughout all the land of Israel, he returned to Jerusalem.

3 Now in the eighteenth year of his reign, when he had purged the land and the house, he sent Shaphan the son of Azaliah, and Maaseiah the governor of the city, and Joah the son of Joahaz, the recorder, to repair the house of the Lord his God.

4 And when they came to Hilkiah the high priest, they delivered the money that was brought into the house of God, which the Levites that kept the doors had gathered of the hand of Manasseh and Ephraim, and of all the remnant of Israel, and of all Judah and Benjamin, and they returned to Jerusalem. And they put it in the hand of the workmen that had the oversight of the house of the Lord, and they gave it to the workmen that worked in the house of the Lord to repair and amend the house. Even to the craftsmen and builders they gave it, to buy hewn stone and timber for couplings, and to floor the houses which the kings of Judah had destroyed.

5 And the men did the work faithfully. And the overseers of them were Jahath and Obadiah, the Levites of the sons of Merari, and Zechariah and Meshullam, of the sons of the Kohathites, to set it forward. And other of the Levites — all that were skilled with instruments of music — also, they were over the bearers of burdens, and were overseers of all that wrought the work in any manner of service. And of the Levites there were scribes, and officers, and porters.

6 And when they brought out the money that was brought into the house of the Lord, Hilkiah the priest found a book of the law of the Lord given by Moses. And Hilkiah answered and said to Shaphan the scribe, I have found the book of the law in the house of the Lord. And Hilkiah delivered the book to Shaphan.

7 And Shaphan carried the book to the king and brought the word of the king back again, saying, All that was committed to your servants, they do. And they have gathered together the money that was found in the house of the Lord and have delivered it into the hand of the overseers and to the hand of the workmen. Then Shaphan the scribe told the king, saying, Hilkiah the priest has given me a book. And Shaphan read it before the king.

8 And it came to pass, when the king had heard the words of the law, that he rent his clothes. And the king commanded Hilkiah, and Ahikam the son of Shaphan, and Abdon the son of Micah, and Shaphan the scribe, and Asaiah (a servant of the king's), saying, Go inquire of the Lord for me, and for them that are left in Israel and in Judah, concerning the words of the book that is found. For great is the wrath of the Lord that is poured out upon us because our fathers have not kept the word of the Lord, to do after all that is written in this book.

⁹ And Hilkiah, and they that the king had appointed, went to Huldah the prophetess, the wife of Shallum the son of Tikvath, the son of Hasrah, keeper of the wardrobe—now she dwelled in Jerusalem in the college—and they spoke to her to that effect.

¹⁰ And she answered them, Thus says the Lord God of Israel: Tell the man that sent you to me, Thus says the Lord: Behold, I will bring evil upon this place and upon the inhabitants thereof, even all the curses that are written in the book which they have read before the king of Judah, because they have forsaken me and have burned incense unto other gods, that they might provoke me to anger with all the works of their hands. Therefore, my wrath shall be poured out upon this place and shall not be quenched.

¹¹ And as for the king of Judah who sent you to inquire of the Lord, so shall you say unto him, Thus says the Lord God of Israel: Concerning the words which you have heard, because your heart was tender, and you did humble yourself before God when you heard his words against this place and against the inhabitants thereof, and humbled yourself before me, and did rend your clothes and weep before me, I have even heard you also, says the Lord. Behold, I will gather you to your fathers, and you shall be gathered to your grave in peace, neither shall your eyes see all the evil that I will bring upon this place and upon the inhabitants of the same. So they brought the king word again.

¹² Then the king sent and gathered together all the elders of Judah and Jerusalem. And the king went up into the house of the Lord, and all the men of Judah, and the inhabitants of Jerusalem, and the priests, and the Levites, and all the people, great and small. And he read in their ears all the words of the book of the covenant that was found in the house of the Lord.

¹³ And the king stood in his place and made a covenant before the Lord, to walk after the Lord and to keep his commandments, and his testimonies, and his statutes, with all his heart and with all his soul, to perform the words of the covenant which are written in this book. And he caused all that were present in Jerusalem and Benjamin to stand. And the inhabitants of Jerusalem did according to the covenant of God, the God of their fathers.

¹⁴ And Josiah took away all the abominations out of all the countries that pertained to the children of Israel, and made all that were present

in Israel to serve, even to serve the Lord their God. And all his days they departed not from following the Lord, the God of their fathers.

15 Moreover, Josiah kept a Passover unto the Lord in Jerusalem. And they killed the passover on the fourteenth of the first month. And he set the priests in their charges and encouraged them to the service of the house of the Lord, and said unto the Levites that taught all Israel, who were holy unto the Lord, Put the holy ark in the house which Solomon the son of David, king of Israel, did build. It shall not be a burden upon your shoulders.

16 Serve now the Lord your God and his people Israel, and prepare yourselves by the houses of your fathers after your courses, according to the writing of David king of Israel and according to the writing of Solomon his son. And stand in the holy place according to the divisions of the families of the fathers of your brethren the people, and after the division of the families of the Levites. So kill the passover and sanctify yourselves, and prepare your brethren that they may do according to the word of the Lord by the hand of Moses.

17 And Josiah gave to the people of the flock, lambs and kids, all for the passover offerings for all that were present, to the number of thirty thousand, and three thousand bullocks. These were of the king's substance.

18 And his princes gave willingly unto the people, to the priests, and to the Levites. Hilkiah and Zechariah and Jehiel, rulers of the house of God, gave unto the priests for the passover offerings two thousand six hundred small cattle, and three hundred oxen. Conaniah also, and Shemaiah and Nethanel, his brethren, and Hashabiah, and Jeiel, and Jozabad, chief of the Levites, gave unto the Levites for passover offerings five thousand small cattle and five hundred oxen.

19 So the service was prepared, and the priests stood in their place and the Levites in their courses, according to the king's commandment. And they killed the passover, and the priests sprinkled the blood from their hands, and the Levites flayed them. And they removed the burnt offerings, that they might give according to the divisions of the families of the people, to offer unto the Lord as it is written in the book of Moses. And so did they with the oxen. And they roasted the passover with fire, according to the ordinance. But the other holy offerings

boiled they in pots, and in cauldrons, and in pans, and divided them speedily among all the people.

20 And afterward they made ready for themselves and for the priests, because the priests, the sons of Aaron, were busied in offering of burnt offerings and the fat until night. Therefore, the Levites prepared for themselves and for the priests, the sons of Aaron.

21 And the singers, the sons of Asaph, were in their place, according to the commandment of David, and Asaph, and Heman, and Jeduthun the king's seer. And the porters waited at every gate. They did not need to depart from their service, for their brethren the Levites prepared for them.

22 So all the service of the Lord was prepared the same day, to keep the Passover and to offer burnt offerings upon the altar of the Lord, according to the commandment of king Josiah. And the children of Israel that were present kept the Passover at that time, and the Feast of Unleavened Bread seven days. And there was no Passover like that kept in Israel from the days of Samuel the prophet. Neither did all the kings of Israel keep such a Passover as Josiah kept, and the priests, and the Levites, and all Judah and Israel that were present, and the inhabitants of Jerusalem. In the eighteenth year of the reign of Josiah was this Passover kept.

23 After all this, when Josiah had prepared the temple, Necho king of Egypt came up to fight at Carchemish by Euphrates, and Josiah went out against him. But he sent ambassadors to him, saying, What have I to do with you, you king of Judah? I come not against you this day, but against the house with which I have war. For God commanded me to make haste. Cease from meddling with God, who is with me, that he destroy you not.

24 Nevertheless, Josiah would not turn his face from him, but disguised himself that he might fight with him, and listened not unto the words of Necho from the mouth of God, and came to fight in the valley of Megiddo. And the archers shot at king Josiah. And the king said to his servants, Take me away, for I am severely wounded. His servants therefore took him out of that chariot and put him in the second chariot that he had. And they brought him to Jerusalem, and he died, and was buried in one of the sepulchers of his fathers. And all Judah and Jerusalem mourned for Josiah.

²⁵ And Jeremiah lamented for Josiah. And all the singing men and the singing women spoke of Josiah in their lamentations to this day, and made them an ordinance in Israel. And behold, they are written in the lamentations.

²⁶ Now the rest of the acts of Josiah, and his goodness, according to that which was written in the law of the Lord, and his deeds, first and last, behold, they are written in the book of the kings of Israel and Judah.

19

Then the people of the land took Jehoahaz the son of Josiah and made him king in his father's stead in Jerusalem. Jehoahaz was twenty-three years old when he began to reign, and he reigned three months in Jerusalem. And the king of Egypt deposed him at Jerusalem, and condemned the land in a hundred talents of silver and a talent of gold. And the king of Egypt made Eliakim his brother king over Judah and Jerusalem, and turned his name to Jehoiakim. And Necho took Jehoahaz his brother and carried him to Egypt.

² Jehoiakim was twenty-five years old when he began to reign, and he reigned eleven years in Jerusalem. And he did evil in the sight of the Lord his God. Against him came up Nebuchadnezzar king of Babylon, and bound him in fetters to carry him to Babylon. Nebuchadnezzar also carried of the vessels of the house of the Lord to Babylon, and put them in his temple at Babylon.

³ Now the rest of the acts of Jehoiakim, and his abominations which he did, and that which was found in him, behold, they are written in the book of the kings of Israel and Judah. And Jehoiachin his son reigned in his stead.

⁴ Jehoiachin was eight years old when he began to reign, and reigned three months and ten days in Jerusalem. And he did evil in the sight of the Lord. And when the year was expired, king Nebuchadnezzar sent and brought him to Babylon with the goodly vessels of the house of the Lord, and made Zedekiah his brother king over Judah and Jerusalem.

⁵ Zedekiah was twenty-one years old when he began to reign, and reigned eleven years in Jerusalem. And he did evil in the sight of the Lord his God, and humbled not himself before Jeremiah the prophet speaking from the mouth of the Lord. And he also rebelled against king

Nebuchadnezzar, who had made him swear by God. But he stiffened his neck and hardened his heart from turning unto the Lord God of Israel. Moreover, all the chief of the priests and the people transgressed very much, after all the abominations of the heathen, and polluted the house of the Lord which he had hallowed in Jerusalem.

⁶ And the Lord God of their fathers sent to them by his messengers, rising up early and sending because he had compassion on his people and on his dwelling place. But they mocked the messengers of God, and despised his words, and misused his prophets, until the wrath of the Lord arose against his people, until there was no remedy.

⁷ Therefore, he brought upon them the king of the Chaldees, who slew their young men with the sword in the house of their sanctuary, and had no compassion upon young man or virgin, old man or him that stooped for age. He gave them all into his hand. And all the vessels of the house of God, great and small, and the treasures of the house of the Lord, and the treasures of the king, and of his princes — all these he brought to Babylon. And they burned the house of God, and broke down the wall of Jerusalem, and burned all the palaces thereof with fire, and destroyed all the goodly vessels thereof.

⁸ And them that had escaped from the sword he carried away to Babylon, where they were servants to him and his sons until the reign of the kingdom of Persia, to fulfill the word of the Lord by the mouth of Jeremiah until the land had enjoyed her Sabbaths. For as long as she lay desolate, she kept Sabbath, to fulfill seventy years.

⁹ Now in the first year of Cyrus king of Persia, that the word of the Lord spoken by the mouth of Jeremiah might be accomplished, the Lord stirred up the spirit of Cyrus king of Persia, that he made a proclamation throughout all his kingdom, and put it also in writing, saying, Thus says Cyrus king of Persia: All the kingdoms of the earth has the Lord God of Heaven given me. And he has charged me to build him a house in Jerusalem, which is in Judah. Who is there among you of all his people? The Lord his God be with him, and let him go up.

EZRA

Now in the first year of Cyrus king of Persia, that the word of the Lord by the mouth of Jeremiah might be fulfilled, the Lord stirred up the spirit of Cyrus king of Persia, that he made a proclamation throughout all his kingdom and put it also in writing, saying, Thus says Cyrus king of Persia: The Lord God of Heaven has given me all the kingdoms of the earth and he has charged me to build him a house at Jerusalem, which is in Judah. Who is there among you of all his people? His God be with him, and let him go up to Jerusalem, which is in Judah, and build the house of the Lord God of Israel — he is the God which is in Jerusalem. And whoever remains in any place where he sojourns, let the men of his place help him with silver, and with gold, and with goods, and with beasts, besides the freewill offering for the house of God that is in Jerusalem.

2 Then rose up the chief of the fathers of Judah and Benjamin, and the priests and the Levites, with all them whose spirit God had raised, to go up to build the house of the Lord which is in Jerusalem. And all they that were about them strengthened their hands with vessels of silver, with gold, with goods, and with beasts, and with precious things, besides all that was willingly offered. Also, Cyrus the king brought forth the vessels of the house of the Lord, which Nebuchadnezzar had brought forth out of Jerusalem and had put them in the house of his gods, even those did Cyrus king of Persia bring forth by the hand of Mithredath the treasurer, and numbered them unto Sheshbazzar, the prince of Judah. And this is the number of them: thirty dishes of gold; a thousand dishes of silver; twenty-nine knives; thirty basins of gold; silver basins of a second sort, four hundred ten; and other vessels, a thousand. All the vessels of gold and of silver were five thousand four hundred. All these did Sheshbazzar bring up with them of the captivity that were brought up from Babylon unto Jerusalem.

3 Now these are the children of the province that went up out of captivity, of those who had been carried away (whom Nebuchadnezzar the king of Babylon had carried away unto Babylon) and came again unto Jerusalem and Judah, everyone unto his city who came with Zerubbabel: Joshua, Nehemiah, Seraiah, Reelaiah, Mordecai, Bilshan, Mispar, Bigvai, Rehum, Baanah.

4 The number of the men of the people of Israel: The children of Parosh — two thousand one hundred seventy-two; the children of Shephatiah — three hundred seventy-two; the children of Arah — seven hundred seventy-five; the children of Pahathmoab, of the children

of Jeshua and Joab — two thousand eight hundred twelve; the children of Elam — a thousand two hundred fifty-four; the children of Zattu — nine hundred forty-five; the children of Zaccai — seven hundred sixty; the children of Bani — six hundred forty-two; the children of Bebai — six hundred twenty-three; the children of Azgad — a thousand two hundred twenty-two; the children of Adonikam — six hundred sixty-six. The children of Bigvai — two thousand fifty-six. The children of Adin — four hundred fifty-four; the children of Ater (of Hezekiah) — ninety-eight; the children of Bezai — three hundred twenty-three; the children of Jorah — a hundred twelve; the children of Hashum — two hundred twenty-three; the children of Gibbar — ninety-five; the children of Bethlehem — a hundred twenty-three; the men of Netophah — fifty-six; the men of Anathoth — a hundred twenty-eight; the children of Azmaveth — forty-two; the children of Kiriath-Jearim, Chephirah, and Beeroth — seven hundred forty-three; the children of Ramah and Gaba — six hundred twenty-one; the men of Michmash — a hundred twenty-two; the men of Beth-el and Ai — two hundred twenty-three; the children of Nebo — fifty-two; the children of Magbish — a hundred fifty-six; the children of the other Elam — a thousand two hundred fifty-four; the children of Harim — three hundred twenty; the children of Lod, Hadid, and Ono — seven hundred twenty-five; the children of Jericho — three hundred forty-five; the children of Senaah — three thousand six hundred thirty.

5 The priests: the children of Jedaiah, of the house of Jeshua — nine hundred seventy-three; the children of Immer — a thousand fifty-two; the children of Pashur — one thousand two hundred forty-seven; the children of Harim — one thousand seventeen.

6 The Levites: the children of Jeshua and Kadmiel, of the children of Hodaviah — seventy-four.

7 The singers: the children of Asaph — a hundred twenty-eight.

8 The children of the porters: the children of Shallum, the children of Ater, the children of Talmon, the children of Akkub, the children of Hatita, the children of Shobai, in all — a hundred thirty-nine.

9 The temple servants: the children of Ziha, the children of Hasupha, the children of Tabbaoth, the children of Keros, the children of Siaha, the children of Padon, the children of Lebanah, the children of Hagabah, the children of Akkub, the children of Hagab, the children

of Shalmai, the children of Hanan, the children of Giddel, the children of Gahar, the children of Reaiah, the children of Rezin, the children of Nekoda, the children of Gazzam, the children of Uzza, the children of Paseah, the children of Besai, the children of Asnah, the children of Meunim, the children of Nephusim, the children of Bakbuk, the children of Hakupha, the children of Harhur, the children of Bazluth, the children of Mehida, the children of Harsha, the children of Barkos, the children of Sisera, the children of Thamah, the children of Neziah, the children of Hatipha.

10 The children of Solomon's servants: the children of Sotai, the children of Hassophereth, the children of Peruda, the children of Jaalah, the children of Darkon, the children of Giddel, the children of Shephatiah, the children of Hattil, the children of Pochereth of Zebaim, the children of Ami.

11 All the temple servants and the children of Solomon's servants were three hundred ninety-two.

12 And these were they who went up from Telmelah, Telharsa, Cherub, Addan, and Immer, but they could not show their father's house and their seed whether they were of Israel: the children of Delaiah, the children of Tobiah, the children of Nekoda — six hundred fifty-two. And of the children of the priests: the children of Habaiah, the children of Hakkoz, the children of Barzillai, who took a wife of the daughters of Barzillai the Gileadite and were called after their name. These sought their register among those that were reckoned by genealogy, but they were not found. Therefore were they as polluted, put from the priesthood. And the Tirshatha said unto them that they should not eat of the most holy things until there stood up a priest with Urim and with Thummim.

13 The whole congregation together was forty-two thousand three hundred sixty, besides their servants and their maids, of whom there were seven thousand three hundred thirty-seven. And there were among them two hundred singing men and singing women. Their horses were seven hundred thirty-six; their mules — two hundred forty-five; their camels — four hundred thirty-five; their asses — six thousand seven hundred twenty.

14 And some of the chief of the fathers, when they came to the house of the Lord which is at Jerusalem, offered freely for the house of God,

to set it up in his place. They gave after their ability unto the treasure of the work sixty-one thousand drams of gold, and five thousand pounds of silver, and one hundred priests' garments. So the priests, and the Levites, and some of the people, and the singers, and the porters, and the temple servants dwelled in their cities, and all Israel in their cities.

15 And when the seventh month had come and the children of Israel were in the cities, the people gathered themselves together as one man to Jerusalem. Then stood up Joshua the son of Jozadak, and his brethren the priests, and Zerubbabel the son of Shealtiel, and his brethren, and built the altar of the God of Israel, to offer burnt offerings thereon, as it is written in the law of Moses the man of God. And they set the altar upon his bases, for fear was upon them because of the people of those countries. And they offered burnt offerings thereon unto the Lord, even burnt offerings morning and evening. They kept also the Feast of Tabernacles as it is written, and offered the daily burnt offerings by number according to the custom, as the duty of every day required, and afterward offered the continual burnt offering, both of the new moons, and of all the set feasts of the Lord that were consecrated, and of everyone that willingly offered a freewill offering unto the Lord. From the first day of the seventh month began they to offer burnt offerings unto the Lord. But the foundation of the temple of the Lord was not yet laid. They gave money also unto the masons, and to the carpenters, and food, and drink, and oil unto them of Sidon, and to them of Tyre, to bring cedar trees from Lebanon to the sea of Joppa, according to the grant that they had of Cyrus king of Persia.

16 Now in the second year of their coming unto the house of God at Jerusalem, in the second month began Zerubbabel the son of Shealtiel, and Joshua the son of Jozadak, and the remnant of their brethren the priests and the Levites, and all they that had come out of the captivity unto Jerusalem, and appointed the Levites, from twenty years old and upward, to set forward the work of the house of the Lord. Then stood Joshua with his sons and his brethren, Kadmiel and his sons, the sons of Judah, together, to set forward the workmen in the house of God: the sons of Henadad, with their sons and their brethren the Levites.

17 And when the builders laid the foundation of the temple of the Lord, they set the priests in their apparel with trumpets, and the Levites the sons of Asaph with cymbals, to praise the Lord after the

ordinance of David king of Israel. And they sang together by course in praising and giving thanks unto the Lord because he is good, for his mercy endures for ever toward Israel. And all the people shouted with a great shout when they praised the Lord, because the foundation of the house of the Lord was laid. But many of the priests and Levites, and chief of the fathers who were old men that had seen the first house, when the foundation of this house was laid before their eyes, wept with a loud voice. And many shouted aloud for joy, so that the people could not discern the noise of the shout of joy from the noise of the weeping of the people; for the people shouted with a loud shout, and the noise was heard afar off.

18 Now when the adversaries of Judah and Benjamin heard that the children of the captivity built the temple unto the Lord God of Israel, then they came to Zerubbabel, and to the chief of the fathers, and said unto them, Let us build with you, for we seek your God as you do, and we do sacrifice unto him since the days of Esarhaddon king of Assyria, who brought us up here. But Zerubbabel, and Joshua, and the rest of the chief of the fathers of Israel said unto them, You have nothing to do with us to build a house unto our God, but we ourselves together will build unto the Lord God of Israel, as king Cyrus the king of Persia has commanded us. Then the people of the land weakened the hands of the people of Judah, and troubled them in building, and hired counselors against them to frustrate their purpose all the days of Cyrus king of Persia, even until the reign of Darius king of Persia. And in the reign of Ahasuerus, in the beginning of his reign, wrote they unto him an accusation against the inhabitants of Judah and Jerusalem. And in the days of Artaxerxes wrote Bishlam, Mithredath, Tabeel, and the rest of their companions, unto Artaxerxes king of Persia, and the writing of the letter was written in the Syrian tongue and interpreted in the Syrian tongue.

19 Rehum the chancellor and Shimshai the scribe wrote a letter against Jerusalem to Artaxerxes the king in this sort. Then wrote Rehum the chancellor, and Shimshai the scribe, and the rest of their companions — the Dinaites, the Apharsathchites, the Tarpelites, the Apharsites, the Archevites, the Babylonians, the Susanchites, the Dehavites, and the Elamites — and the rest of the nations whom the great and noble Osnappar brought over and set in the cities of Samaria,

and the rest that are on this side of the river, and at such a time. This is the copy of the letter that they sent unto him, even unto Artaxerxes the king:

20 Your servants, the men on this side of the river: And at such a time, be it known unto the king that the Jews who came up from you to us have come unto Jerusalem, building the rebellious and the bad city, and have set up the walls thereof and joined the foundations. Be it known now unto the king that if this city is built and the walls set up again, then will they not pay toll, tribute, and custom, and so you shall damage the revenue of the kings. Now because we have maintenance from the king's palace, and it was not meet for us to see the king's dishonor, therefore have we sent and certified to the king that search may be made in the book of the records of your fathers; so shall you find in the book of the records and know that this city is a rebellious city, and hurtful unto kings and provinces, and that they have moved sedition within the same of old time, for which cause was this city destroyed. We certify to the king that if this city is built again and the walls thereof set up, by this means you shall have no portion on this side of the river.

21 Then sent the king an answer: Unto Rehum the chancellor, and to Shimshai the scribe, and to the rest of their companions that dwell in Samaria, and unto the rest beyond the river: Peace. And at such a time, the letter which you sent unto us has been plainly read before me. And I commanded, and search has been made, and it is found that this city of old time has made insurrection against kings, and that rebellion and sedition have been made therein. There have been mighty kings also over Jerusalem, who have ruled over all countries beyond the river, and toll, tribute, and custom was paid unto them. Give now commandment to cause these men to cease, and that this city be not built until another commandment shall be given from me. Take heed now that you fail not to do this. Why should damage grow to the hurt of the kings?

22 Now when the copy of king Artaxerxes' letter was read before Rehum, and Shimshai the scribe, and their companions, they went up in haste to Jerusalem, unto the Jews, and made them to cease by force and power. Then ceased the work of the house of God which is

at Jerusalem. So it ceased unto the second year of the reign of Darius king of Persia.

23 Then the prophets — Haggai the prophet and Zechariah the son of Iddo — prophesied unto the Jews that were in Judah and Jerusalem in the name of the God of Israel, even unto them. Then Zerubbabel the son of Shealtiel and Joshua the son of Jozadak rose up and began to build the house of God which is at Jerusalem. And with them were the prophets of God helping them.

24 At the same time came to them Tattenai, governor on this side of the river, and Shetharboznai, and their companions, and said thus unto them: Who has commanded you to build this house and to make up this wall? Then said we unto them after this manner: What are the names of the men that make this building? But the eye of their God was upon the elders of the Jews, that they could not cause them to cease until the matter came to Darius. And then they returned an answer by letter concerning this matter. The copy of the letter that Tattenai, governor on this side of the river, and Shetharboznai, and his companions the Apharsachites who were on this side of the river sent unto Darius the king. They sent a letter unto him wherein was written thus:

25 Unto Darius the king: All peace. Be it known unto the king that we went into the province of Judah, to the house of the great God which is built with great stones, and timber is laid in the walls, and this work goes fast on and prospers in their hands. Then asked we those elders, and said unto them thus: Who commanded you to build this house and to make up these walls? We asked their names also, to certify to you that we might write the names of the men that were the chief of them. And thus they returned us an answer, saying, We are the servants of the God of Heaven and earth, and build the house that was built these many years ago which a great king of Israel built and set up. But after our fathers had provoked the God of Heaven unto wrath, he gave them into the hand of Nebuchadnezzar the king of Babylon, the Chaldean who destroyed this house and carried the people away into Babylon. But in the first year of Cyrus the king of Babylon, the same king Cyrus made a decree to build this house of God. And the vessels also of gold and silver of the house of God, which Nebuchadnezzar took out of the temple that was in Jerusalem and

brought them into the temple of Babylon, those did Cyrus the king take out of the temple of Babylon, and they were delivered unto one whose name was Sheshbazzar, whom he had made governor, and said unto him, Take these vessels, go. Carry them into the temple that is in Jerusalem, and let the house of God be built in his place. Then came the same Sheshbazzar and laid the foundation of the house of God which is in Jerusalem. And since that time even until now has it been in building, and yet it is not finished. Now therefore if it seem good to the king, let there be search made in the king's treasure house which is there at Babylon, whether it be so that a decree was made of Cyrus the king to build this house of God at Jerusalem, and let the king send his pleasure to us concerning this matter.

26 Then Darius the king made a decree, and search was made in the house of the scrolls where the treasures were laid up in Babylon. And there was found at Ecbatana, in the palace that is in the province of the Medes, a scroll, and therein was a record thus written:

27 In the first year of Cyrus the king, the same Cyrus the king made a decree concerning the house of God at Jerusalem: Let the house be built, the place where they offered sacrifices, and let the foundations thereof be strongly laid: the height thereof sixty cubits, and the breadth thereof sixty cubits, with three rows of great stones and a row of new timber. And let the expenses be given out of the king's house. And also let the golden and silver vessels of the house of God, which Nebuchadnezzar took forth out of the temple which is at Jerusalem and brought unto Babylon, be restored and brought again unto the temple which is at Jerusalem, every one to his place, and place them in the house of God.

28 Now therefore Tattennai, governor beyond the river, Shetharboznai, and your companions the Apharsachites who are beyond the river, are far from there. Let the work of this house of God alone. Let the governor of the Jews and the elders of the Jews build this house of God in his place. Moreover, I make a decree what you shall do to the elders of these Jews for the building of this house of God: that of the king's goods, even of the tribute beyond the river, forthwith expenses be given unto these men, that they be not hindered. And that which they have need of, both young bullocks, and rams, and lambs, for the burnt offerings of the God of Heaven, wheat, salt, wine, and oil, according to the appointment of the priests who are at Jerusalem, let

it be given them day by day without fail, that they may offer sacrifices of sweet savors unto the God of Heaven, and pray for the life of the king and of his sons. Also, I have made a decree that whoever shall alter this word, let timber be pulled down from his house, and being set up, let him be hung thereon, and let his house be made a dunghill for this. And the God that has caused his name to dwell there destroy all kings and people that shall apply their hand to alter and to destroy this house of God which is at Jerusalem. I, Darius, have made a decree; let it be done with speed.

²⁹ Then Tattennai, governor on this side of the river, Shetharboznai, and their companions, according to that which Darius the king had sent, so they did speedily. And the elders of the Jews built, and they prospered through the prophesying of Haggai the prophet and Zechariah the son of Iddo. And they built and finished it according to the commandment of the God of Israel, and according to the commandment of Cyrus, and Darius, and Artaxerxes king of Persia. And this house was finished on the third day of the month Adar, which was in the sixth year of the reign of Darius the king. And the children of Israel, the priests, and the Levites, and the rest of the children of the captivity kept the dedication of this house of God with joy, and offered at the dedication of this house of God a hundred bullocks, two hundred rams, four hundred lambs; and for a sin offering for all Israel, twelve he-goats, according to the number of the tribes of Israel. And they set the priests in their divisions and the Levites in their courses for the service of God which is at Jerusalem, as it is written in the book of Moses.

³⁰ And the children of the captivity kept the Passover upon the fourteenth day of the first month; for the priests and the Levites were purified together, all of them were pure, and killed the passover for all the children of the captivity, and for their brethren the priests, and for themselves. And the children of Israel who had come again out of captivity, and all such as had separated themselves unto them from the filthiness of the heathen of the land to seek the Lord God of Israel, did eat, and kept the Feast of Unleavened Bread seven days with joy. For the Lord had made them joyful, and turned the heart of the king of Assyria unto them, to strengthen their hands in the work of the house of God, the God of Israel.

2 Now after these things, in the reign of Artaxerxes king of Persia, Ezra the son of Seraiah, the son of Azariah, the son of Hilkiah, the son of Shallum, the son of Zadok, the son of Ahitub, the son of Amariah, the son of Azariah, the son of Meraioth, the son of Zerahiah, the son of Uzzi, the son of Bukki, the son of Abishua, the son of Phinehas, the son of Eleazar, the son of Aaron the chief priest — this Ezra went up from Babylon. And he was a ready scribe in the law of Moses which the Lord God of Israel had given. And the king granted him all his request, according to the hand of the Lord his God upon him. And there went up some of the children of Israel, and of the priests, and the Levites, and the singers, and the porters, and the temple servants unto Jerusalem in the seventh year of Artaxerxes the king. And he came to Jerusalem in the fifth month which was in the seventh year of the king, for upon the first day of the first month began he to go up from Babylon, and on the first day of the fifth month came he to Jerusalem, according to the good hand of his God upon him; for Ezra had prepared his heart to seek the law of the Lord and to do it, and to teach in Israel statutes and judgments. Now this is the copy of the letter that the king Artaxerxes gave unto Ezra the priest, the scribe, even a scribe of the words of the commandments of the Lord and of his statutes to Israel:

2 Artaxerxes, king of kings, unto Ezra the priest, a scribe of the law of the God of Heaven: Perfect peace. And at such a time, I make a decree that all they of the people of Israel and of his priests and Levites in my realm, who are determined of their own free will to go up to Jerusalem, go with you, forasmuch as you are sent of the king and of his seven counselors to inquire concerning Judah and Jerusalem according to the law of your God which is in your hand, and to carry the silver and gold which the king and his counselors have freely offered unto the God of Israel whose habitation is in Jerusalem, and all the silver and gold that you can find in all the province of Babylon with the freewill offering of the people and of the priests, offering willingly for the house of their God which is in Jerusalem, that you may buy speedily with this money bullocks, rams, lambs, with their meal offerings and their drink offerings, and offer them upon the altar of the house of your God which is in Jerusalem. And whatever shall seem good to you and to your brethren to do with the rest of the silver and the gold, that

do after the will of your God. The vessels also that are given you for
the service of the house of your God, those deliver before the God of
Jerusalem. And whatever more shall be needful for the house of your
God which you shall have occasion to bestow, bestow it out of the
king's treasure house.

3 And I, even I, Artaxerxes the king, do make a decree to all the
treasurers who are beyond the river, that whatever Ezra the priest, the
scribe of the law of the God of Heaven, shall require of you, it be done
speedily; unto a hundred talents of silver, and to a hundred measures
of wheat, and to a hundred baths of wine, and to a hundred baths of
oil, and salt without prescribing how much. Whatever is commanded
by the God of Heaven, let it be diligently done for the house of the
God of Heaven. For why should there be wrath against the realm of
the king and his sons? Also, we certify to you that, touching any of
the priests and Levites, singers, porters, temple servants, or ministers
of this house of God, it shall not be lawful to impose toll, tribute, or
custom upon them.

4 And you, Ezra, after the wisdom of your God that is in your hand,
set magistrates and judges who may judge all the people that are
beyond the river, all such as know the laws of your God, and teach
them that know them not. And whoever will not do the law of your
God and the law of the king, let judgment be executed speedily upon
him, whether it be unto death, or to banishment, or to confiscation of
goods, or to imprisonment.

5 Blessed be the Lord God of our fathers, who has put such a thing
as this in the king's heart, to beautify the house of the Lord which is
in Jerusalem, and has extended mercy unto me before the king and
his counselors, and before all the king's mighty princes. And I was
strengthened as the hand of the Lord my God was upon me, and I
gathered together out of Israel chief men to go up with me.

6 These are now the chief of their fathers, and this is the genealogy
of them that went up with me from Babylon in the reign of Artaxerxes
the king: of the sons of Phinehas: Gershom; of the sons of Ithamar:
Daniel; of the sons of David: Hattush of the sons of Shecaniah; of the
sons of Parosh: Zechariah, and with him were reckoned by genealogy
of the males a hundred fifty; of the sons of Pahathmoab: Eliehoenai
the son of Zerahiah, and with him two hundred males; of the sons of

Shecaniah: the son of Jahaziel, and with him three hundred males; of the sons also of Adin: Ebed the son of Jonathan, and with him fifty males; and of the sons of Elam: Jeshaiah the son of Athaliah, and with him seventy males; and of the sons of Shephatiah: Zebadiah the son of Michael, and with him eighty males; of the sons of Joab: Obadiah the son of Jehiel, and with him two hundred eighteen males; and of the sons of Shelomith: the son of Josiphiah, and with him a hundred sixty males; and of the sons of Bebai: Zechariah the son of Bebai, and with him twenty-eight males; and of the sons of Azgad: Johanan the son of Hakkatan, and with him a hundred ten males; and of the last sons of Adonikam, whose names are these: Eliphelet, Jeuel, and Shemaiah, and with them sixty males; of the sons also of Bigvai: Uthai and Zabbud, and with them seventy males.

7 And I gathered them together to the river that runs to Ahava and there stayed we in tents three days. And I viewed the people and the priests, and found there none of the sons of Levi. Then sent I for Eliezer, for Ariel, for Shemaiah, and for Elnathan, and for Jarib, and for Elnathan, and for Nathan, and for Zechariah, and for Meshullam — chief men; also for Joiarib and for Elnathan — men of understanding. And I sent them with commandment unto Iddo the chief at the place Casiphia, and I told them what they should say unto Iddo and to his brethren the temple servants at the place Casiphia, that they should bring unto us ministers for the house of our God. And by the good hand of our God upon us they brought us a man of understanding of the sons of Mahli, the son of Levi, the son of Israel; and Sherebiah, with his sons and his brethren, eighteen; and Hashabiah, and with him Jeshaiah of the sons of Merari, his brethren and their sons, twenty; also of the temple servants whom David and the princes had appointed for the service of the Levites, two hundred twenty temple servants. All of them were expressed by name.

8 Then I proclaimed a fast there, at the river of Ahava, that we might afflict ourselves before our God to seek of him a right way for us, and for our little ones, and for all our substance. For I was ashamed to ask of the king a band of soldiers and horsemen to help us against the enemy in the way, because we had spoken unto the king, saying, The hand of our God is upon all them for good that seek him, but his power

and his wrath is against all them that forsake him. So we fasted and implored our God for this, and he was entreated of us.

⁹ Then I separated twelve of the chief of the priests — Sherebiah, Hashabiah, and ten of their brethren with them — and weighed unto them the silver, and the gold, and the vessels, even the offering of the house of our God which the king, and his counselors, and his lords, and all Israel there present had offered. I even weighed unto their hand six hundred fifty talents of silver, and silver vessels a hundred talents, and of gold a hundred talents, also twenty basins of gold of a thousand drams, and two vessels of fine copper, precious as gold. And I said unto them, You are holy unto the Lord, the vessels are holy also, and the silver and the gold are a freewill offering unto the Lord God of your fathers. Watch and keep them until you weigh them before the chief of the priests and the Levites and chief of the fathers of Israel at Jerusalem in the chambers of the house of the Lord. So took the priests and the Levites the weight of the silver, and the gold, and the vessels, to bring them to Jerusalem unto the house of our God.

¹⁰ Then we departed from the river of Ahava on the twelfth day of the first month to go unto Jerusalem. And the hand of our God was upon us, and he delivered us from the hand of the enemy and of such as lay in wait by the way. And we came to Jerusalem and stayed there three days.

¹¹ Now on the fourth day was the silver and the gold and the vessels weighed in the house of our God (by the hand of Meremoth, the son of Uriah the priest, and with him was Eleazar the son of Phinehas, and with them was Jozabad the son of Jeshua, and Noadiah the son of Binnui — Levites) by number and by weight of every one. And all the weight was written at that time.

¹² Also, the children of those that had been carried away, who had come out of the captivity, offered burnt offerings unto the God of Israel: twelve bullocks for all Israel, ninety-six rams, seventy-seven lambs, twelve he-goats for a sin offering — all this was a burnt offering unto the Lord. And they delivered the king's commissions unto the king's lieutenants, and to the governors on this side of the river, and they furthered the people and the house of God.

¹³ Now when these things were done, the princes came to me, saying, The people of Israel and the priests and the Levites have not separated

themselves from the people of the lands, doing according to their abominations — even of the Canaanites, the Hittites, the Perizzites, the Jebusites, the Ammonites, the Moabites, the Egyptians, and the Amorites; for they have taken of their daughters for themselves and for their sons, so that the holy seed have mingled themselves with the people of those lands — yea, the hand of the princes and rulers has been chief in this trespass. And when I heard this thing, I rent my garment and my mantle, and plucked off the hair of my head and of my beard, and sat down astonished. Then were assembled unto me everyone that trembled at the words of the God of Israel because of the transgression of those that had been carried away. And I sat astonished until the evening sacrifice.

14 And at the evening sacrifice I arose up from my self-abasement, and having rent my garment and my mantle, I fell upon my knees and spread out my hands unto the Lord my God, and said, O my God, I am ashamed and blush to lift up my face to you, my God, for our iniquities are increased over our head, and our trespass is grown up unto the heavens. Since the days of our fathers have we been in a great trespass unto this day. And for our iniquities have we, our kings, and our priests been delivered into the hand of the kings of the lands, to the sword, to captivity, and to a spoil, and to confusion of face, as it is this day. And now for a little space, grace has been shown from the Lord our God, to leave us a remnant to escape, and to give us a nail in his holy place, that our God may lighten our eyes and give us a little reviving in our bondage. For we were bondmen, yet our God has not forsaken us in our bondage, but has extended mercy unto us in the sight of the kings of Persia, to give us a reviving, to set up the house of our God and to repair the desolations thereof, and to give us a wall in Judah and in Jerusalem.

15 And now, O our God, what shall we say after this? For we have forsaken your commandments which you have commanded by your servants the prophets, saying, The land unto which you go to possess is an unclean land with the filthiness of the people of the lands, with their abominations which have filled it from one end to another with their uncleanness. Now therefore give not your daughters unto their sons, neither take their daughters unto your sons, nor seek their peace or their wealth for ever, that you may be strong, and eat the good of the

land, and leave it for an inheritance to your children for ever. And after all that has come upon us for our evil deeds and for our great trespass, seeing that you, our God, have punished us less than our iniquities deserve, and have given us such deliverance as this, should we again break your commandments and join in alliance with the people of these abominations? Would you not be angry with us until you had consumed us, so that there should be no remnant nor escaping? O Lord God of Israel, you are righteous, for we remain yet escaped, as it is this day. Behold, we are before you in our trespasses, for we cannot stand before you because of this.

16 Now when Ezra had prayed, and when he had confessed, weeping and casting himself down before the house of God, there assembled unto him out of Israel a very great congregation of men and women and children, for the people wept very bitterly. And Shecaniah the son of Jehiel, one of the sons of Elam, answered and said unto Ezra, We have trespassed against our God and have taken strange wives of the people of the land. Yet now there is hope in Israel concerning this thing. Now therefore let us make a covenant with our God to put away all the wives and such as are born of them, according to the counsel of my lord and of those that tremble at the commandment of our God, and let it be done according to the law. Arise, for this matter belongs unto you. We also will be with you. Be of good courage, and do it. Then Ezra arose and made the chief priests, the Levites, and all Israel to swear that they should do according to this word. And they swore.

17 Then Ezra rose up from before the house of God and went into the chamber of Johanan the son of Eliashib. And when he came there, he did eat no bread, nor drink water, for he mourned because of the transgression of them that had been carried away. And they made proclamation throughout Judah and Jerusalem unto all the children of the captivity that they should gather themselves together unto Jerusalem, and that whoever would not come within three days, according to the counsel of the princes and the elders, all his substance should be forfeited, and himself separated from the congregation of those that had been carried away.

18 Then all the men of Judah and Benjamin gathered themselves together unto Jerusalem within three days. It was the ninth month, on the twentieth day of the month, and all the people sat in the street

of the house of God, trembling because of this matter and for the great rain. And Ezra the priest stood up and said unto them, You have transgressed and have taken strange wives to increase the trespass of Israel. Now therefore make confession unto the Lord God of your fathers, and do his pleasure, and separate yourselves from the people of the land and from the strange wives. Then all the congregation answered and said with a loud voice, As you have said, so must we do. But the people are many, and it is a time of much rain, and we are not able to stand outside; neither is this a work of one day or two, for we are many that have transgressed in this thing. Let now our rulers of all the congregation stand, and let all them who have taken strange wives in our cities come at appointed times, and with them the elders of every city, and the judges thereof, until the fierce wrath of our God for this matter be turned from us. Only Jonathan the son of Asahel and Jahzeiah the son of Tikvah were employed about this matter, and Meshullam and Shabbethai the Levite helped them.

¹⁹ And the children of the captivity did so. And Ezra the priest, with certain chief of the fathers after the house of their fathers, and all of them by their names, were separated, and sat down in the first day of the tenth month to examine the matter. And they made an end with all the men that had taken strange wives by the first day of the first month.

²⁰ And among the sons of the priests there were found that had taken strange wives, namely, of the sons of Joshua the son of Jozadak, and his brethren: Maaseiah, and Eliezer, and Jarib, and Gedaliah (and they gave their hands that they would put away their wives, and being guilty, they offered a ram of the flock for their trespass); and of the sons of Immer: Hanani and Zebadiah; and of the sons of Harim: Maaseiah, and Elijah, and Shemaiah, and Jehiel, and Uzziah; and of the sons of Pashur: Elioenai, Maaseiah, Ishmael, Nethanel, Jozabad, and Elasah; also of the Levites: Jozabad, and Shimei, and Kelaiah (the same is Kelita), Pethahiah, Judah, and Eliezer; of the singers also: Eliashib; and of the porters: Shallum, and Telem, and Uri. Moreover, of Israel, of the sons of Parosh: Ramiah, and Izziah, and Malchiah, and Miamin, and Eleazar, and Malchijah, and Benaiah; and of the sons of Elam: Mattaniah, Zechariah, and Jehiel, and Abdi, and Jeremoth, and Elijah; and of the sons of Zattu: Elioenai, Eliashib, Mattaniah, and Jeremoth, and Zabad, and Aziza; of the sons also of Bebai: Jehohanan, Hananiah,

Zabbai, and Athlai; and of the sons of Bani: Meshullam, Malluch, and Adaiah, Jashub, and Sheal, and Ramoth; and of the sons of Pahathmoab: Adna, and Chelal, Benaiah, Maaseiah, Mattaniah, Bezalel, and Binnui, and Manasseh; and of the sons of Harim: Eliezer, Ishijah, Malchiah, Shemaiah, Shimeon, Benjamin, Malluch, and Shemariah; of the sons of Hashum: Mattenai, Mattattah, Zabad, Eliphelet, Jeremai, Manasseh, and Shimei; of the sons of Bani: Maadai, Amram, and Uel, Benaiah, Bedeiah, Cheluhi, Vaniah, Meremoth, Eliashib, Mattaniah, Mattenai, and Jaasu, and Bani, and Binnui, Shimei, and Shelemiah, and Nathan, and Adaiah, Machnadebai, Shashai, Sharai, Azarel, and Shelemiah, Shemariah, Shallum, Amariah, and Joseph; of the sons of Nebo: Jeiel, Mattithiah, Zabad, Zebina, Jaddai, and Joel, Benaiah.

21 All these had taken strange wives, and some of them had wives by whom they had children.

THE BOOK OF NEHEMIAH

The words of Nehemiah the son of Hacaliah.

AND it came to pass in the month Chislev, in the twentieth year, as I was in Shushan the palace, that Hanani, one of my brethren, came, he and certain men of Judah. And I asked them concerning the Jews that had escaped who were left of the captivity, and concerning Jerusalem. And they said unto me, The remnant that are left of the captivity there in the province are in great affliction and reproach; the wall of Jerusalem also is broken down, and the gates thereof are burned with fire.

2 And it came to pass, when I heard these words, that I sat down and wept, and mourned certain days, and fasted and prayed before the God of Heaven, and said, I implore you, O Lord God of Heaven, the great and terrible God that keeps covenant and mercy for them that love him and observe his commandments, let your ear now be attentive and your eyes open, that you may hear the prayer of your servant which I pray before you now day and night for the children of Israel your servants, and confess the sins of the children of Israel which we have sinned against you. Both I and my father's house have sinned. We have dealt very corruptly against you and have not kept the commandments, nor the statutes, nor the judgments which you

commanded your servant Moses. Remember, I implore you, the word that you commanded your servant Moses, saying, If you transgress, I will scatter you abroad among the nations; but if you turn unto me, and keep my commandments and do them, though there were of you cast out unto the utmost part of the heaven, yet will I gather you from there and will bring them unto the place that I have chosen to set my name there. Now these are your servants and your people whom you have redeemed by your great power and by your strong hand. O Lord, I implore you, let now your ear be attentive to the prayer of your servant and to the prayer of your servants who desire to fear your name, and prosper, I pray you, your servant this day, and grant him mercy in the sight of this man.

3 For I was the king's cupbearer, and it came to pass in the month Nisan, in the twentieth year of Artaxerxes the king, that wine was before him, and I took up the wine and gave it unto the king. Now I had not been previously sad in his presence, wherefore the king said unto me, Why is your countenance sad, seeing you are not sick? This is nothing else but sorrow of heart. Then I was very much afraid and said unto the king, Let the king live for ever. Why should not my countenance be sad when the city, the place of my fathers' sepulchers, lies waste, and the gates thereof are consumed with fire? Then the king said unto me, For what do you make request? So I prayed to the God of Heaven. And I said unto the king, If it please the king, and if your servant have found favor in your sight, that you would send me unto Judah, unto the city of my fathers' sepulchers, that I may build it. And the king said unto me — the queen also sitting by him — For how long shall your journey be? And when will you return? So it pleased the king to send me, and I set him a time. Moreover, I said unto the king, If it please the king, let letters be given to me, to the governors beyond the river, that they may convey me over until I come into Judah, and a letter unto Asaph the keeper of the king's forest, that he may give me timber to make beams for the gates of the palace which appertained to the house, and for the wall of the city, and for the house that I shall enter into. And the king granted me according to the good hand of my God upon me.

2 Then I came to the governors beyond the river and gave them the king's letters. Now the king had sent captains of the army and horsemen with me. When Sanballat the Horonite, and Tobiah the servant, the Ammonite, heard of it, it grieved them exceedingly that there had come a man to seek the welfare of the children of Israel. So I came to Jerusalem and was there three days. And I arose in the night, I and some few men with me, neither told I any man what my God had put in my heart to do at Jerusalem, neither was there any beast with me save the beast that I rode upon. And I went out by night by the gate of the valley, even before the dragon well and to the dung port, and viewed the walls of Jerusalem which were broken down and the gates thereof were consumed with fire. Then I went on to the gate of the fountain and to the king's pool, but there was no place for the beast that was under me to pass. Then went I up in the night by the brook and viewed the wall, and turned back and entered by the gate of the valley, and so returned. And the rulers knew not where I went or what I did, neither had I as yet told it to the Jews, nor to the priests, nor to the nobles, nor to the rulers, nor to the rest that did the work.

2 Then I said unto them, You see the distress that we are in, how Jerusalem lies waste and the gates thereof are burned with fire. Come and let us build up the wall of Jerusalem, that we be no more a reproach. Then I told them of the hand of my God which was good upon me, as also the king's words that he had spoken unto me. And they said, Let us rise up and build. So they strengthened their hands for this good work. But when Sanballat the Horonite, and Tobiah the servant, the Ammonite, and Geshem the Arabian heard it, they laughed us to scorn, and despised us, and said, What is this thing that you do? Will you rebel against the king? Then I answered them and said unto them, The God of Heaven, he will prosper us, therefore we his servants will arise and build; but you have no portion, nor right, nor memorial in Jerusalem.

3 Then Eliashib the high priest rose up with his brethren the priests, and they built the sheep gate; they sanctified it and set up the doors of it—even unto the tower of Meah they sanctified it, unto the tower of Hananel. And next unto him built the men of Jericho. And next to them built Zaccur the son of Imri. But the fish gate did the sons of Hassenaah build, who also laid the beams thereof and set up the doors thereof, the locks thereof, and the bars thereof. And next unto

them repaired Meremoth the son of Uriah, the son of Hakkoz. And next unto them repaired Meshullam the son of Berechiah, the son of Meshezabeel. And next unto them repaired Zadok the son of Baana. And next unto them the Tekoites repaired, but their nobles put not their necks to the work of their Lord.

4 Moreover, the old gate was repaired by Jehoiada the son of Paseah, and Meshullam the son of Besodeiah; they laid the beams thereof and set up the doors thereof, and the locks thereof, and the bars thereof. And next unto them repaired Melatiah the Gibeonite and Jadon the Meronothite, the men of Gibeon and of Mizpah, unto the throne of the governor on this side of the river. Next unto him repaired Uzziel the son of Harhaiah, of the goldsmiths. Next unto him also repaired Hananiah the son of the apothecaries. And they fortified Jerusalem unto the broad wall. And next unto them repaired Rephaiah the son of Hur, the ruler of the half part of Jerusalem. And next unto them repaired Jedaiah the son of Harumaph, even opposite his house. And next unto him repaired Hattush the son of Hashabneiah. Malchijah the son of Harim and Hasshub the son of Pahathmoab repaired the other piece and the tower of the furnaces. And next unto him repaired Shallum the son of Hallohesh, the ruler of the half part of Jerusalem, he and his daughters.

5 The valley gate was repaired by Hanun and the inhabitants of Zanoah; they built it and set up the doors thereof, the locks thereof, and the bars thereof, and a thousand cubits on the wall unto the dung gate. But the dung gate was repaired by Malchijah the son of Rechab, the ruler of part of Bethhaccerem; he built it and set up the doors thereof, the locks thereof, and the bars thereof. But the gate of the fountain was repaired by Shallun the son of Colhozeh, the ruler of part of Mizpah; he built it, and covered it, and set up the doors thereof, the locks thereof, and the bars thereof, and the wall of the pool of Siloah by the king's garden, and unto the stairs that go down from the city of David. After him repaired Nehemiah the son of Azbuk, the ruler of the half part of Bethzur, unto the place opposite the sepulchers of David, and to the pool that was made, and unto the house of the mighty. After him repaired the Levites — Rehum the son of Bani. Next unto him repaired Hashabiah, the ruler of the half part of Keilah, in his part. After him repaired their brethren — Bavvai the

son of Henadad, the ruler of the half part of Keilah. And next to him repaired Ezer the son of Jeshua, the ruler of Mizpah, another piece in front of the ascent to the armory at the turning. After him, Baruch the son of Zabbai earnestly repaired the other piece, from the turning unto the door of the house of Eliashib the high priest. After him repaired Meremoth the son of Uriah, the son of Hakkoz, another piece from the door of the house of Eliashib even to the end of the house of Eliashib. And after him repaired the priests — the men of the plain. After him repaired Benjamin and Hasshub in front of their house. After him repaired Azariah the son of Maaseiah, the son of Ananiah, by his house. After him repaired Binnui the son of Henadad another piece from the house of Azariah unto the turning, even unto the corner, Palal the son of Uzai in front of the turning and the tower which projects out from the king's high house that was by the court of the prison. After him Pedaiah the son of Parosh (moreover, the temple servants dwelled in Ophel), unto the place in front of the water gate toward the east and the tower that projects out. After them the Tekoites repaired another piece in front of the great tower that projects out, even unto the wall of Ophel.

6 From above the horse gate repaired the priests, every one in front of his house. After them repaired Zadok the son of Immer in front of his house. After him repaired also Shemaiah the son of Shecaniah, the keeper of the east gate. After him repaired Hananiah the son of Shelemiah and Hanun the sixth son of Zalaph, another piece. After him repaired Meshullam the son of Berechiah in front of his chamber. After him repaired Malchijah the goldsmith's son unto the place of the temple servants and of the merchants, in front of the gate Miphkad, and to the ascent of the corner. And between the ascent of the corner unto the sheep gate repaired the goldsmiths and the merchants.

7 But it came to pass that when Sanballat heard that we built the wall, he was angry and took great indignation, and mocked the Jews. And he spoke before his brethren and the army of Samaria and said, What are these feeble Jews doing? Will they fortify themselves? Will they sacrifice? Will they make an end in a day? Will they revive the stones out of the heaps of the rubbish which are burned? Now Tobiah the Ammonite was by him, and he said, Even that which they build, if a fox go up, he shall even break down their stone wall.

8 Hear, O our God, for we are despised, and turn their reproach upon their own head, and give them for a prey in the land of captivity, and cover not their iniquity, and let not their sin be blotted out from before you; for they have provoked you to anger before the builders. So built we the wall, and all the wall was joined together unto the half thereof, for the people had a mind to work.

9 But it came to pass that when Sanballat, and Tobiah, and the Arabians, and the Ammonites, and the Ashdodites heard that the walls of Jerusalem were made up, and that the breaches began to be stopped, then they were very angry and conspired all of them together to come and to fight against Jerusalem and to hinder it. Nevertheless, we made our prayer unto our God and set a watch against them day and night because of them. And Judah said, The strength of the bearers of burdens is decayed, and there is much rubbish, so that we are not able to build the wall. And our adversaries said, They shall not know, neither see, until we come in the midst among them and slay them, and cause the work to cease. And it came to pass that when the Jews who dwelled by them came, they said unto us ten times, From all places where you shall return unto us, they will be upon you. Therefore set I in the lower places behind the wall, and on the higher places, I even set the people after their families with their swords, their spears, and their bows. And I looked and rose up, and said unto the nobles, and to the rulers, and to the rest of the people, Be not afraid of them. Remember the Lord, who is great and terrible, and fight for your brethren, your sons and your daughters, your wives and your houses.

10 And it came to pass, when our enemies heard that it was known unto us and God had brought their counsel to naught, that we returned all of us to the wall, every one unto his work. And it came to pass from that time forth that the half of my servants labored in the work, and the other half of them held both the spears, the shields, and the bows, and the habergeons. And the rulers were behind all the house of Judah. They who built on the wall and they that bore burdens with those that loaded, everyone with one of his hands labored in the work, and with the other hand held a weapon. For the builders, everyone had his sword girded by his side and so built. And he that sounded the trumpet was by me. And I said unto the nobles, and to the rulers, and to the rest of the people, The work is great and large, and we are separated upon the

wall, one far from another. In what place therefore you hear the sound of the trumpet, assemble there unto us. Our God shall fight for us.

11 So we labored in the work. And half of them held the spears from the rising of the morning until the stars appeared. Likewise, at the same time said I unto the people, Let everyone with his servant lodge within Jerusalem, that in the night they may be a guard to us, and labor on the day. So neither I, nor my brethren, nor my servants, nor the men of the guard who followed me, none of us put off our clothes, saving that everyone put them off for washing.

12 And there was a great cry of the people and of their wives against their brethren the Jews; for there were that said, We, our sons, and our daughters are many, therefore we take up grain for them, that we may eat and live. Some also there were that said, We have mortgaged our lands, vineyards, and houses, that we might buy grain because of the dearth. There were also that said, We have borrowed money for the king's tribute upon our lands and vineyards. Yet now our flesh is as the flesh of our brethren, our children as their children, and behold, we bring into bondage our sons and our daughters to be servants, and some of our daughters are brought unto bondage already; neither is it in our power to redeem them, for other men have our lands and vineyards.

13 And I was very angry when I heard their cry and these words. Then I consulted with myself, and I rebuked the nobles and the rulers and said unto them, You exact usury, every one of his brother. And I set a great assembly against them. And I said unto them, We after our ability have redeemed our brethren the Jews who were sold unto the heathen, and will you even sell your brethren? Or shall they be sold unto us? Then held they their peace, and found nothing to answer. Also, I said, It is not good that you do. Ought you not to walk in the fear of our God because of the reproach of the heathen our enemies? I likewise, and my brethren, and my servants might exact of them money and grain. I pray you, let us leave off this usury. Restore, I pray you, to them, even this day, their lands, their vineyards, their oliveyards, and their houses; also the hundredth part of the money, and of the grain, the wine, and the oil that you exact of them. Then said they, We will restore unto them, and will require nothing of them, so will we do as you say. Then I called the priests and took an oath of them that they

should do according to this promise. Also, I shook my lap and said, So God shake out every man from his house and from his labor that performs not this promise, even thus be he shaken out and emptied. And all the congregation said, Amen — and praised the Lord. And the people did according to this promise.

¹⁴ Moreover, from the time that I was appointed to be their governor in the land of Judah, from the twentieth year even unto the thirty-second year of Artaxerxes the king — that is, twelve years — I and my brethren have not eaten the bread of the governor. But the former governors that had been before me were burdensome unto the people, and had taken of them bread and wine, besides forty shekels of silver. Yea, even their servants bore rule over the people, but so did not I because of the fear of God. Yea, also I continued in the work of this wall, neither bought we any land. And all my servants were gathered there unto the work. Moreover, there were at my table a hundred fifty of the Jews and rulers besides those that came unto us from among the heathen that are about us. Now that which was prepared for me daily was one ox and six choice sheep, also fowls were prepared for me, and once in ten days, store of all sorts of wine. Yet for all this I required not the bread of the governor because the bondage was heavy upon this people. Think upon me, my God, for good, according to all that I have done for this people.

¹⁵ Now it came to pass, when Sanballat, and Tobiah, and Geshem the Arabian, and the rest of our enemies heard that I had built the wall and there was no breach left therein — though at that time I had not set up the doors upon the gates — that Sanballat and Geshem sent unto me, saying, Come, let us meet together in the villages in the plain of Ono. But they thought to do me mischief. And I sent messengers unto them, saying, I am doing a great work, so that I cannot come down. Why should the work cease while I leave it and come down to you? Yet they sent unto me four times after this sort, and I answered them after the same manner. Then sent Sanballat his servant unto me in like manner the fifth time, with an open letter in his hand, wherein was written: It is reported among the heathen, and Geshem says you and the Jews think to rebel, for which cause you build the wall, that you may be their king according to these words. And you have also appointed prophets to preach of you at Jerusalem, saying, There is

a king in Judah. And now shall it be reported to the king according to these words. Come now therefore and let us take counsel together. Then I sent unto him, saying, There are no such things done as you say, but you feign them out of your own heart. For they all made us afraid, saying, Their hands shall be weakened from the work, that it be not done. Now therefore, O God, strengthen my hands.

16 Afterward I came unto the house of Shemaiah the son of Delaiah, the son of Mehetabel who was shut up, and he said, Let us meet together in the house of God, within the temple, and let us shut the doors of the temple, for they will come to slay you, yea, in the night will they come to slay you. And I said, Should such a man as I flee? And who is my enemy that such a man as I would go into the temple to save his life? I will not go in. And behold, I perceived that God had not sent him, but that he pronounced this prophecy against me for Tobiah and Sanballat had hired him. Therefore, should I be afraid of him he hired, and do so as he said and sin, and that they might have me for an evil report, that they might reproach me? My God, think upon Tobiah and Sanballat according to these their works, and on the prophetess Noadiah and the rest of the prophets that would have put me in fear.

17 So the wall was finished in the twenty-fifth of Elul, in fifty-two days. And it came to pass that when all our enemies heard, and all the heathen that were about us saw, they were much cast down in their own eyes, for they perceived that this work was wrought of our God. Moreover, in those days, the nobles of Judah sent many letters unto Tobiah, and the letters of Tobiah came unto them; for there were many in Judah sworn unto him, because he was the son-in-law of Shecaniah the son of Arah, and his son Jehohanan had taken the daughter of Meshullam the son of Berechiah. Also, they reported his good deeds before me, and uttered my words to him. Tobiah sent letters to put me in fear.

18 Now it came to pass, when the wall was built, and I had set up the doors, and the porters and the singers and the Levites were appointed, that I gave my brother Hanani, and Hananiah the ruler of the palace, charge over Jerusalem, for he was a faithful man, and feared God above many. And I said unto them, Let not the gates of Jerusalem be opened until the sun is hot; and while they stand by, let them shut the doors and bar them, and appoint watches of the inhabitants of Jerusalem,

everyone in his watch and everyone in front of his house. Now the city was large and great, but the people few therein and the houses not built.

¹⁹ And my God put into my heart to gather together the nobles, and the rulers, and the people, that they might be reckoned by genealogy. And I found a register of the genealogy of them who came up at the first, and found written therein:

²⁰ These are the children of the province that went up out of the captivity, of those that had been carried away, whom Nebuchadnezzar the king of Babylon had carried away, and came again to Jerusalem and to Judah, every one unto his city, who came with Zerubbabel, Joshua, Nehemiah, Azariah, Raamiah, Nahamani, Mordecai, Bilshan, Mispereth, Bigvai, Rehum, Baanah.

²¹ The number of the men of the people of Israel: the children of Parosh — two thousand one hundred seventy-two; the children of Shephatiah — three hundred seventy-two; the children of Arah — seven hundred seventy-five; the children of Pahathmoab (of the children of Jeshua and Joab) — two thousand eight hundred twelve; the children of Elam — a thousand two hundred fifty-four; the children of Zattu — nine hundred forty-five; the children of Zaccai — seven hundred sixty; the children of Bani — six hundred forty-two; the children of Bebai — six hundred twenty-three; the children of Azgad — a thousand two hundred twenty-two; the children of Adonikam — six hundred sixty-six; the children of Bigvai — two thousand fifty-six; the children of Adin — four hundred fifty-four; the children of Ater of Hezekiah) — ninety-eight; the children of Hashum — two hundred twenty-three; the children of Bezai — three hundred twenty-three; the children of Jorah — a hundred twelve; the children of Gibeon — ninety-five; the men of Bethlehem and Netophah — a hundred eighty-eight; the men of Anathoth — a hundred twenty-eight; the men of Bethazmaveth — forty-two; the men of Kiriath-Jearim, Chephirah, and Beeroth — seven hundred forty-three; the men of Ramah and Geba — six hundred twenty-one; the men of Michmash — a hundred twenty-two; the men of Beth-el and Ai — two hundred twenty-three; the men of the other Nebo — fifty-two; the children of the other Elam — a thousand two hundred fifty-four; the children of Harim — three hundred twenty; the children of Jericho — three hundred forty-five; the children of

Lod, Hadid, and Ono — seven hundred twenty-five; the children of Senaah — three thousand six hundred thirty.

22 The priests: the children of Jedaiah (of the house of Jeshua) — nine hundred seventy-three; the children of Immer — a thousand fifty-two; the children of Pashur — a thousand two hundred forty-seven; the children of Harim — a thousand seventeen.

23 The Levites: the children of Jeshua (of Kadmiel, of the children of Hodevah) — seventy-four.

24 The singers of the children of Asaph — one hundred twenty-eight.

25 The porters: the children of Shallum, the children of Ater, the children of Talmon, the children of Akkub, the children of Hatita, the children of Shobai — a hundred thirty-nine.

26 The temple servants: the children of Ziha, the children of Hasupha, the children of Tabbaoth, the children of Keros, the children of Sia, the children of Padon, the children of Lebanah, the children of Hagabah, the children of Shalmai, the children of Hanan, the children of Giddel, the children of Gahar, the children of Reaiah, the children of Rezin, the children of Nekoda, the children of Gazzam, the children of Uzza, the children of Paseah, the children of Besai, the children of Meunim, the children of Nephishesim, the children of Bakbuk, the children of Hakupha, the children of Harhur, the children of Bazluth, the children of Mehida, the children of Harsha, the children of Barkos, the children of Sisera, the children of Thamah, the children of Neziah, the children of Hatipha.

27 The children of Solomon's servants: the children of Sotai, the children of Sophereth, the children of Perida, the children of Jaala, the children of Darkon, the children of Giddel, the children of Shephatiah, the children of Hattil, the children of Pochereth of Zebaim, the children of Amon. All the temple servants and the children of Solomon's servants were three hundred ninety-two.

28 And these were they who went up also from Telmelah, Telharesha, Cherub, Addan, and Immer, but they could not show their father's house, nor their seed, whether they were of Israel: the children of Delaiah, the children of Tobiah, the children of Nekoda — six hundred fifty-two. And of the priests: the children of Habaiah, the children of Hakkoz, the children of Barzillai (who took one of the daughters of Barzillai the Gileadite to wife and was called after their name). These

sought their register among those that were reckoned by genealogy, but it was not found. Therefore were they, as polluted, put from the priesthood. And the governor said unto them that they should not eat of the most holy things until there stood up a priest with Urim and Thummim.

29 The whole congregation together was forty-two thousand three hundred sixty, besides their manservants and their maidservants, of whom there were seven thousand three hundred thirty-seven. And they had two hundred forty-five singing men and singing women; their horses — seven hundred thirty-six; their mules — two hundred forty-five; their camels — four hundred thirty-five; six thousand seven hundred twenty asses.

30 And some of the chief of the fathers gave unto the work. The governor gave to the treasure a thousand drams of gold, fifty basins, five hundred thirty priests' garments. And some of the chief of the fathers gave to the treasure of the work twenty thousand drams of gold, and two thousand two hundred pounds of silver. And that which the rest of the people gave was twenty thousand drams of gold, and two thousand pounds of silver, and sixty-seven priests' garments. So the priests, and the Levites, and the porters, and the singers, and some of the people, and the temple servants, and all Israel dwelled in their cities; and when the seventh month came, the children of Israel were in their cities.

31 And all the people gathered themselves together as one man into the street that was before the water gate, and they spoke unto Ezra the scribe to bring the book of the law of Moses which the Lord had commanded to Israel. And Ezra the priest brought the law before the congregation, both of men and women and all that could hear with understanding, upon the first day of the seventh month. And he read therein before the street that was before the water gate from the morning until midday, before the men and the women and those that could understand; and the ears of all the people were attentive unto the book of the law. And Ezra the scribe stood upon a pulpit of wood which they had made for the purpose. And beside him stood Mattithiah, and Shema, and Anaiah, and Uriah, and Hilkiah, and Maaseiah, on his right hand, and on his left hand, Pedaiah, and Mishael, and Malchijah, and Hashum, and Hashbaddanah, Zechariah, and Meshullam. And

Ezra opened the book in the sight of all the people, for he was above all the people. And when he opened it, all the people stood up. And Ezra blessed the Lord, the great God. And all the people answered, Amen, amen — with lifting up their hands, and they bowed their heads and worshipped the Lord with their faces to the ground. Also, Jeshua, and Bani, and Sherebiah, Jamin, Akkub, Shabbethai, Hodiah, Maaseiah, Kelita, Azariah, Jozabad, Hanan, Pelaiah, and the Levites caused the people to understand the law, and the people stood in their place. So they read in the book, in the law of God distinctly, and gave the sense, and caused them to understand the reading.

32 And Nehemiah, who is the governor, and Ezra the priest, the scribe, and the Levites that taught the people, said unto all the people, This day is holy unto the Lord your God. Mourn not, nor weep (for all the people wept when they heard the words of the law). Then he said unto them, Go your way, eat the fat and drink the sweet, and send portions unto them for whom nothing is prepared, for this day is holy unto our Lord. Neither be sorry, for the joy of the Lord is your strength. So the Levites stilled all the people, saying, Hold your peace, for the day is holy, neither be grieved. And all the people went their way to eat and to drink, and to send portions, and to make great mirth because they had understood the words that were declared unto them.

33 And on the second day were gathered together the chief of the fathers of all the people, the priests, and the Levites, unto Ezra the scribe, even to understand the words of the law. And they found written in the law which the Lord had commanded by Moses that the children of Israel should dwell in booths in the feast of the seventh month, and that they should publish and proclaim in all their cities and in Jerusalem, saying, Go forth unto the mount and fetch olive branches, and pine branches, and myrtle branches, and palm branches, and branches of thick trees, to make booths as it is written. So the people went forth, and brought them, and made themselves booths, everyone upon the roof of his house, and in their courts, and in the courts of the house of God, and in the street of the water gate, and in the street of the gate of Ephraim. And all the congregation of them that had come again out of the captivity made booths and sat under the booths, for since the days of Joshua the son of Nun unto that day had not the children of Israel done so. And there was very great gladness. Also day

by day, from the first day unto the last day, he read in the book of the law of God. And they kept the feast seven days, and on the eighth day was a solemn assembly according unto the manner.

34 Now in the twenty-fourth day of this month, the children of Israel were assembled with fasting and with sackcloth and earth upon them. And the seed of Israel separated themselves from all strangers, and stood and confessed their sins and the iniquities of their fathers. And they stood up in their place and read in the book of the law of the Lord their God one fourth part of the day, and another fourth part they confessed and worshipped the Lord their God. Then stood up (upon the stairs of the Levites) Jeshua, and Bani, Kadmiel, Shebaniah, Bunni, Sherebiah, Bani, and Chenani, and cried with a loud voice unto the Lord their God.

35 Then the Levites — Jeshua, and Kadmiel, Bani, Hashabneiah, Sherebiah, Hodiah, Shebaniah, and Pethahiah — said, Stand up and bless the Lord your God for ever and ever, and blessed be your glorious name, which is exalted above all blessing and praise. You, you Lord alone, you have made heaven, the Heaven of heavens, with all their host; the earth and all things that are therein; the seas and all that is therein; and you preserve them all. And the host of heaven worships you. You are the Lord the God who did choose Abram, and brought him forth out of Ur of the Chaldees, and gave him the name of Abraham, and found his heart faithful before you, and made a covenant with him to give the land of the Canaanites, the Hittites, the Amorites, and the Perizzites, and the Jebusites, and the Girgashites — to give it, I say, to his seed, and have performed your words (for you are righteous), and did see the affliction of our fathers in Egypt, and heard their cry by the Red Sea. And you showed signs and wonders upon Pharaoh, and on all his servants, and on all the people of his land, for you knew that they dealt proudly against them. So did you get yourself a name, as it is this day. And you did divide the sea before them, so that they went through the midst of the sea on the dry land. And their persecutors you threw into the depths as a stone into the mighty waters. Moreover, you led them in the day by a cloudy pillar and in the night by a pillar of fire, to give them light in the way wherein they should go. You came down also upon Mount Sinai, and spoke with them from Heaven, and gave them right judgments and true laws, good statutes and commandments,

and made known unto them your holy Sabbath, and commanded
them precepts, statutes, and laws by the hand of Moses your servant,
and gave them bread from heaven for their hunger, and brought
forth water for them out of the rock for their thirst, and promised
them that they should go in to possess the land which you had sworn
to give them. But they and our fathers dealt proudly, and hardened
their necks, and listened not to your commandments, and refused to
obey, neither were mindful of your wonders that you did among them,
but hardened their necks, and in their rebellion appointed a captain
to return to their bondage.

36 But you are a God ready to pardon, gracious and merciful, slow
to anger, and of great kindness, and forsook them not. Yea, when they
had made themselves a molten calf and said, This is your God that
brought you up out of Egypt—and had wrought great provocations,
yet you in your abundant mercies forsook them not in the wilderness;
the pillar of the cloud departed not from them by day, to lead them
in the way, neither the pillar of fire by night, to show them light and
the way wherein they should go. You gave also your good spirit to
instruct them, and withheld not your manna from their mouth, and
gave them water for their thirst. Yea, forty years did you sustain them
in the wilderness; they lacked nothing, their clothes waxed not old,
and their feet swelled not. Moreover, you gave them kingdoms and
nations, and did divide them into every corner. So they possessed the
land of Sihon, and the land of the king of Heshbon, and the land of
Og king of Bashan. Their children also you multiplied as the stars of
heaven and brought them into the land concerning which you had
promised to their fathers that they should go in to possess it. So the
children went in and possessed the land, and you subdued before
them the inhabitants of the land, the Canaanites, and gave them into
their hands, with their kings and the people of the land, that they
might do with them as they would. And they took strong cities and a
fat land, and possessed houses full of all goods, wells dug, vineyards,
and oliveyards, and fruit trees in abundance. So they did eat and
were filled, and became fat and delighted themselves in your great
goodness. Nevertheless, they were disobedient and rebelled against
you, and cast your law behind their backs, and slew your prophets who
testified against them to turn them to you, and they wrought great

provocations. Therefore, you delivered them into the hand of their enemies, who vexed them. And in the time of their trouble, when they cried unto you, you heard them from Heaven, and according to your abundant mercies you gave them saviors who saved them out of the hand of their enemies. But after they had rest, they did evil again before you, therefore you left them in the hand of their enemies, so that they had the dominion over them. Yet when they returned and cried unto you, you heard them from Heaven, and many times did you deliver them according to your mercies, and testified against them, that you might bring them again unto your law. Yet they dealt proudly and listened not unto your commandments, but sinned against your judgments — which if a man do, he shall live in them — and withdrew the shoulder, and hardened their neck, and would not hear. Yet many years did you bear them, and testified against them by your spirit in your prophets; yet would they not give ear. Therefore, you gave them into the hand of the people of the lands. Nevertheless, for your great mercies' sake you did not utterly consume them nor forsake them, for you are a gracious and merciful God.

37 Now therefore, our God, the great, the mighty, and the terrible God, who keeps covenant and mercy, let not all the trouble seem little before you that has come upon us, on our kings, on our princes, and on our priests, and on our prophets, and on our fathers, and on all your people, since the time of the kings of Assyria unto this day. Nevertheless, you are just in all that is brought upon us, for you have done right, but we have done wickedly. Neither have our kings, our princes, our priests, nor our fathers kept your law, nor listened unto your commandments and your testimonies with which you did testify against them. For they have not served you in their kingdom, and in your great goodness that you gave them, and in the large and fat land which you gave before them, neither turned they from their wicked works. Behold, we are servants this day, and for the land that you gave unto our fathers to eat the fruit thereof and the good thereof, behold, we are servants in it. And it yields much increase unto the kings whom you have set over us because of our sins. Also, they have dominion over our bodies and over our cattle at their pleasure, and we are in great distress. And because of all this, we make a sure covenant and write it, and our princes, Levites, and priests seal unto it.

38 Now those that sealed: Nehemiah the governor (the son of Hacaliah), and Zedekiah, Seraiah, Azariah, Jeremiah, Pashur, Amariah, Malchijah, Hattush, Shebaniah, Malluch, Harim, Meremoth, Obadiah, Daniel, Ginnethon, Baruch, Meshullam, Abijah, Mijamin, Maaziah, Bilgai, Shemaiah — these were the priests. And the Levites: both Jeshua the son of Azaniah, Binnui of the sons of Henadad, Kadmiel, and their brethren (Shebaniah, Hodiah, Kelita, Pelaiah, Hanan, Mica, Rehob, Hashabiah, Zaccur, Sherebiah, Shebaniah, Hodiah, Bani, Beninu). The chief of the people: Parosh, Pahathmoab, Elam, Zattu, Bani, Bunni, Azgad, Bebai, Adonijah, Bigvai, Adin, Ater, Hizkijah, Azzur, Hodiah, Hashum, Bezai, Hariph, Anathoth, Nebai, Magpiash, Meshullam, Hezir, Meshezabeel, Zadok, Jaddua, Pelatiah, Hanan, Anaiah, Hoshea, Hananiah, Hasshub, Hallohesh, Pilha, Shobek, Rehum, Hashabnah, Maaseiah, and Ahijah, Hanan, Anan, Malluch, Harim, Baanah.

39 And the rest of the people — the priests, the Levites, the porters, the singers, the temple servants, and all they that had separated themselves from the people of the lands unto the law of God, their wives, their sons and their daughters, everyone having knowledge and having understanding — they cleaved to their brethren, their nobles, and entered into an oath that a curse should come upon them if they did not walk in God's law which was given by Moses the servant of God; and to observe and do all the commandments of the Lord their God, and his judgment and statutes; and that they would not give their daughters unto the people of the land, nor take the daughters of the people for their sons. And if the people of the land bring merchandise or any provisions on the Sabbath day to sell, we would not buy it of them on the Sabbath, or on the holy day, and we would leave the seventh year and the exaction of every debt.

40 Also, we made ordinances for us to charge ourselves yearly with the third part of a shekel for the service of the house of our God, for the showbread, and for the continual meal offering, and for the continual burnt offering of the Sabbaths, of the new moons, for the set feasts, and for the holy things, and for the sin offerings to make an atonement for Israel, and for all the work of the house of our God.

41 And we cast the lots among the priests, the Levites, and the people, for the wood offering, to bring it into the house of our God after the houses of our fathers, at times appointed year by year, to burn upon the altar of the Lord our God as it is written in the law; and to bring the firstfruits of our ground, and the firstfruits of all fruit of all trees year by year unto the house of the Lord; also, the firstborn of our sons and of our cattle, as it is written in the law, and the firstlings of our herds and of our flocks, to bring to the house of our God, unto the priests that minister in the house of our God; and that we should bring the firstfruits of our dough, and our offerings, and the fruit of all manner of trees, of wine, and of oil, unto the priests, to the chambers of the house of our God; and the tithes of our ground unto the Levites, that the same Levites might have the tithes in all the cities of our tillage. And the priest (the son of Aaron) shall be with the Levites when the Levites take tithes, and the Levites shall bring up the tithe of the tithes unto the house of our God, to the chambers, into the treasure house. For the children of Israel and the children of Levi shall bring the offering of the grain, of the new wine, and the oil, unto the chambers where are the vessels of the sanctuary, and the priests that minister, and the porters, and the singers. And we will not forsake the house of our God.

42 And the rulers of the people dwelled at Jerusalem. The rest of the people also cast lots, to bring one of ten to dwell in Jerusalem the holy city, and nine parts in other cities. And the people blessed all the men that willingly offered themselves to dwell at Jerusalem.

43 Now these are the chief of the province that dwelled in Jerusalem (but in the cities of Judah dwelled everyone in his possession in their cities — Israel, the priests, and the Levites, and the temple servants, and the children of Solomon's servants — and at Jerusalem dwelled of the children of Judah and of the children of Benjamin): of the children of Judah: Athaiah the son of Uzziah, the son of Zechariah, the son of Amariah, the son of Shephatiah, the son of Mahalalel, of the children of Perez; and Maaseiah the son of Baruch, the son of Colhozeh, the son of Hazaiah, the son of Adaiah, the son of Joiarib, the son of Zechariah, the son of Shiloni. All the sons of Perez that dwelled at Jerusalem were four hundred sixty-eight valiant men.

44 And these are the sons of Benjamin: Sallu the son of Meshullam, the son of Joed, the son of Pedaiah, the son of Kolaiah, the son of Maaseiah, the son of Ithiel, the son of Jesaiah; and after him Gabbai, Sallai — nine hundred twenty-eight; and Joel the son of Zichri was their overseer, and Judah the son of Senuah, second over the city.

⁴⁵ Of the priests: Jedaiah, the son of Joiarib; Jachin; Seraiah the son of Hilkiah, the son of Meshullam, the son of Zadok, the son of Meraioth, the son of Ahitub, the ruler of the house of God. And their brethren that did the work of the house were eight hundred twenty-two. And Adaiah the son of Jeroham, the son of Pelaliah, the son of Amzi, the son of Zechariah, the son of Pashur, the son of Malchiah, and his brethren, chief of the fathers — two hundred forty-two; and Amashsai the son of Azarel, the son of Ahzai, the son of Meshillemoth, the son of Immer, and their brethren, mighty men of valor — one hundred twenty-eight. And their overseer was Zabdiel, the son of one of the great men.

⁴⁶ Also of the Levites: Shemaiah the son of Hasshub, the son of Azrikam, the son of Hashabiah, the son of Bunni; and Shabbethai and Jozabad of the chief of the Levites had the oversight of the outward business of the house of God. And Mattaniah the son of Mica, the son of Zabdi, the son of Asaph, was the principal to begin the thanksgiving in prayer; and Bakbukiah, the second among his brethren, and Abda the son of Shammua, the son of Galal, the son of Jeduthun. All the Levites in the holy city were two hundred eighty-four.

⁴⁷ Moreover, the porters: Akkub, Talmon, and their brethren that kept the gates were a hundred seventy-two. And the residue of Israel, of the priests the Levites, were in all the cities of Judah, everyone in his inheritance. But the temple servants dwelled in Ophel, and Ziha and Gishpa over the temple servants.

⁴⁸ The overseer also of the Levites at Jerusalem: Uzzi the son of Bani, the son of Hashabiah, the son of Mattaniah, the son of Mica, of the sons of Asaph, the singers over the business of the house of God; for it was the king's commandment concerning them that a certain portion should be for the singers due for every day. And Pethahiah, the son of Meshezabeel, of the children of Zerah, the son of Judah, was at the king's hand in all matters concerning the people.

⁴⁹ And for the villages with their fields, some of the children of Judah dwelled at Kiriath-Arba and in the villages thereof; and at Dibon and in the villages thereof; and at Jekabzeel and in the villages thereof; and at Jeshua, and at Moladah, and at Bethpelet, and at Hazar-Shual, and at Beersheba and in the villages thereof; and at Ziklag, and at Meconah and in the villages thereof; and at Enrimmon, and at Zorah, and at Jarmuth, Zanoah, Adullam, and in their villages; at Lachish

and the fields thereof; at Azekah and in the villages thereof. And they dwelled from Beersheba unto the valley of Hinnom.

⁵⁰ The children also of Benjamin from Geba dwelled at Michmash, and Aija, and Beth-el, and in their villages, and at Anathoth, Nob, Ananiah, Hazor, Ramah, Gittaim, Hadid, Zeboim, Neballat, Lod, and Ono, the valley of craftsmen. And of the Levites were divisions in Judah and in Benjamin.

⁵¹ Now these are the priests and the Levites that went up with Zerubbabel the son of Shealtiel and Jeshua: Seraiah, Jeremiah, Ezra, Amariah, Malluch, Hattush, Shecaniah, Rehum, Meremoth, Iddo, Ginnetho, Abijah, Miamin, Maadiah, Bilgah, Shemaiah, and Joiarib, Jedaiah, Sallu, Amok, Hilkiah, Jedaiah — these were the chief of the priests and of their brethren in the days of Jeshua. Moreover, the Levites: Jeshua, Binnui, Kadmiel, Sherebiah, Judah, and Mattaniah, who was over the thanksgiving, he and his brethren. Also, Bakbukiah and Unni, their brethren, were opposite them in the watches.

⁵² And Jeshua begot Joiakim, Joiakim also begot Eliashib, and Eliashib begot Joiada, and Joiada begot Jonathan, and Jonathan begot Jaddua. And in the days of Joiakim were priests, the chief of the fathers: of Seraiah, Meraiah; of Jeremiah, Hananiah; of Ezra, Meshullam; of Amariah, Jehohanan; of Malluchi, Jonathan; of Shebaniah, Joseph; of Harim, Adna; of Meraioth, Helkai; of Iddo, Zechariah; of Ginnethon, Meshullam; of Abijah, Zichri; of Miniamin, of Moadiah: Piltai; of Bilgah, Shammua; of Shemaiah, Jehonathan; and of Joiarib, Mattenai; of Jedaiah, Uzzi; of Sallai, Kallai; of Amok, Eber; of Hilkiah, Hashabiah; of Jedaiah, Nethanel.

⁵³ The Levites in the days of Eliashib, Joiada, and Johanan, and Jaddua, were recorded — chief of the fathers, also the priests — to the reign of Darius the Persian. The sons of Levi, the chief of the fathers, were written in the book of the chronicles, even until the days of Johanan the son of Eliashib. And the chief of the Levites: Hashabiah, Sherebiah, and Jeshua the son of Kadmiel, with their brethren opposite them, to praise and to give thanks, according to the commandment of David the man of God, watch corresponding with watch. Mattaniah, and Bakbukiah, Obadiah, Meshullam, Talmon, Akkub were porters keeping the watch at the thresholds of the gates. These were in the

days of Joiakim the son of Jeshua, the son of Jozadak, and in the days of Nehemiah the governor, and of Ezra the priest, the scribe.

54 And at the dedication of the wall of Jerusalem they sought the Levites out of all their places, to bring them to Jerusalem, to keep the dedication with gladness, both with thanksgivings and with singing, with cymbals, psalteries, and with harps. And the sons of the singers gathered themselves together, both out of the plain country round about Jerusalem, and from the villages of the Netophathites, also from the house of Gilgal, and out of the fields of Geba and Azmaveth, for the singers had built themselves villages round about Jerusalem. And the priests and the Levites purified themselves, and purified the people, and the gates, and the wall.

55 Then I brought up the princes of Judah upon the wall and appointed two great companies of them that gave thanks, whereof one went on the right hand upon the wall toward the dung gate. And after them went Hoshaiah, and half of the princes of Judah, and Azariah, Ezra, and Meshullam, Judah, and Benjamin, and Shemaiah, and Jeremiah, and certain of the priests' sons with trumpets, namely Zechariah the son of Jonathan, the son of Shemaiah, the son of Mattaniah, the son of Micaiah, the son of Zaccur, the son of Asaph, and his brethren Shemaiah, and Azarel, Milalai, Gilalai, Maai, Nethanel, and Judah, Hanani, with the musical instruments of David the man of God, and Ezra the scribe before them. And at the fountain gate which was opposite them, they went up by the stairs of the city of David at the ascent of the wall above the house of David, even unto the water gate eastward.

56 And the other company of them that gave thanks went opposite them, and I after them, and the half of the people upon the wall—from beyond the tower of the furnaces even unto the broad wall, and from above the gate of Ephraim, and above the old gate, and above the fish gate, and the tower of Hananel, and the tower of Meah, even unto the sheep gate. And they stood still in the prison gate. So stood the two companies of them that gave thanks in the house of God, and I, and the half of the rulers with me, and the priests—Eliakim, Maaseiah, Miniamin, Micaiah, Elioenai, Zechariah, and Hananiah with trumpets—and Maaseiah, and Shemaiah, and Eleazar, and Uzzi, and Jehohanan, and Malchijah, and Elam, and Ezer. And the singers sang

loud, with Jezrahiah their overseer. Also that day they offered great sacrifices and rejoiced, for God had made them rejoice with great joy. The wives also and the children rejoiced, so that the joy of Jerusalem was heard even afar off.

57 And at that time were some appointed over the chambers for the treasures, for the offerings, for the firstfruits, and for the tithes, to gather into them out of the fields of the cities the portions of the law for the priests and Levites, for Judah rejoiced for the priests and for the Levites that waited. And both the singers and the porters kept the charge of their God and the charge of the purification, according to the commandment of David and of Solomon his son. For in the days of David and Asaph of old, there were chief of the singers, and songs of praise and thanksgiving unto God. And all Israel, in the days of Zerubbabel and in the days of Nehemiah, gave the portions of the singers and the porters, every day his portion, and they sanctified holy things unto the Levites, and the Levites sanctified them unto the children of Aaron.

58 On that day, they read in the book of Moses in the audience of the people, and therein was found written that the Ammonite and the Moabite should not come into the congregation of God for ever, because they met not the children of Israel with bread and with water but hired Balaam against them, that he should curse them. Nevertheless, our God turned the curse into a blessing. Now it came to pass, when they had heard the law, that they separated from Israel all the mixed multitude.

59 And before this, Eliashib the priest, having the oversight of the chamber of the house of our God, was related to Tobiah. And he had prepared for him a great chamber where previously they laid the meal offerings, the frankincense, and the vessels, and the tithes of the grain, the new wine, and the oil, which was commanded to be given to the Levites, and the singers, and the porters, and the offerings of the priests. But in all this time, I was not at Jerusalem; for in the thirty-second year of Artaxerxes king of Babylon came I unto the king, and after certain days I obtained leave of the king. And I came to Jerusalem, and understood of the evil that Eliashib did for Tobiah in preparing him a chamber in the courts of the house of God, and it grieved me severely. Therefore, I cast forth all the household stuff of Tobiah out

of the chamber. Then I commanded, and they cleansed the chambers, and there brought I again the vessels of the house of God, with the meal offering and the frankincense.

⁶⁰ And I perceived that the portions of the Levites had not been given them, for the Levites and the singers that did the work were fled, every one to his field. Then I contended with the rulers and said, Why is the house of God forsaken? And I gathered them together and set them in their place. Then brought all Judah the tithe of the grain, and the new wine, and the oil unto the treasuries. And I made treasurers over the treasuries: Shelemiah the priest, and Zadok the scribe, and of the Levites: Pedaiah; and next to them was Hanan the son of Zaccur, the son of Mattaniah; for they were counted faithful, and their office was to distribute unto their brethren. Remember me, O my God, concerning this, and wipe not out my good deeds that I have done for the house of my God and for the offices thereof.

⁶¹ In those days saw I in Judah some treading wine presses on the Sabbath, and bringing in sheaves of wheat and loading asses, as also wine, grapes, and figs, and all manner of burdens, which they brought into Jerusalem on the Sabbath day. And I testified against them in the day wherein they sold provisions. There dwelled men of Tyre also therein, who brought fish and all manner of merchandise, and sold on the Sabbath unto the children of Judah and in Jerusalem. Then I contended with the nobles of Judah and said unto them, What evil thing is this that you do, and profane the Sabbath day? Did not your fathers thus, and did not our God bring all this evil upon us and upon this city? Yet you bring more wrath upon Israel by profaning the Sabbath.

⁶² And it came to pass that when the gates of Jerusalem began to be dark before the Sabbath, I commanded that the gates should be shut, and charged that they should not be opened until after the Sabbath. And some of my servants set I at the gates, that there should no burden be brought in on the Sabbath day. So the merchants and sellers of all kind of merchandise lodged outside Jerusalem once or twice, then I testified against them and said unto them, Why do you lodge about the wall? If you do so again, I will lay hands on you. From that time forth came they no more on the Sabbath. And I commanded the Levites that they should cleanse themselves and that they should come and

keep the gates, to sanctify the Sabbath day. Remember me, O my God, concerning this also, and spare me according to the greatness of your mercy.

⁶³ In those days also I saw Jews that had married wives of Ashdod, of Ammon, and of Moab, and their children spoke half in the speech of Ashdod, and could not speak in the Jews' language, but according to the language of each people. And I contended with them, and cursed them, and smote certain of them, and plucked off their hair, and made them swear by God, saying, You shall not give your daughters unto their sons, nor take their daughters unto your sons, or for yourselves. Did not Solomon king of Israel sin by these things? Yet among many nations was there no king like him, who was beloved of his God, and God made him king over all Israel. Nevertheless, even him did foreign women cause to sin. Shall we then listen unto you to do all this great evil, to transgress against our God in marrying strange wives? And one of the sons of Joiada, the son of Eliashib the high priest, was son-in-law to Sanballat the Horonite, therefore I chased him from me. Remember them, O my God, because they have defiled the priesthood, and the covenant of the priesthood and of the Levites.

⁶⁴ Thus I cleansed them from all strangers, and appointed the watches of the priests and the Levites, every one in his business, and for the wood offering at times appointed, and for the firstfruits. Remember me, O my God, for good.

THE BOOK OF ESTHER

Now it came to pass in the days of Ahasuerus — this is Ahasuerus who reigned from India even unto Ethiopia over a hundred twenty-seven provinces — in those days when the king Ahasuerus sat on the throne of his kingdom, which was in Shushan the palace, in the third year of his reign, he made a feast unto all his princes and his servants, the power of Persia and Media, the nobles and princes of the provinces before him, when he showed the riches of his glorious kingdom and the honor of his excellent majesty many days, even a hundred eighty days. And when these days were expired, the king made a feast unto all the people that were present in Shushan the palace, both unto great and small, seven days in the court of the garden of the king's palace, where were white, green, and blue hangings fastened with cords of fine linen and purple to silver rings and pillars of marble. The beds were of gold and silver upon a pavement of red, and blue, and white, and black marble. And they gave them drink in vessels of gold — the vessels being diverse one from another — and royal wine in abundance, according to the state of the king. And the drinking was according to the law, none did compel, for so the king had appointed to all the officers of his house that they should do according to every man's pleasure. Also, Vashti the queen made a feast for the women in the royal house which belonged to king Ahasuerus.

2 On the seventh day, when the heart of the king was merry with wine, he commanded Mehuman, Biztha, Harbona, Bigtha, and Abagtha, Zethar, and Carcas — the seven chamberlains that served in the presence of Ahasuerus the king — to bring Vashti the queen before the king with the royal crown, to show the people and the princes her beauty, for she was fair to look on. But the queen Vashti refused to come at the king's commandment by chamberlains. Therefore was the king very angry, and his anger burned in him.

3 Then the king said to the wise men who knew the times (for so was the king's manner toward all that knew law and judgment, and the next unto him was Carshena, Shethar, Admatha, Tarshish, Meres, Marsena, and Memucan — the seven princes of Persia and Media who saw the king's face, who sat the first in the kingdom), What shall we do unto the queen Vashti according to law, because she has not performed the commandment of the king Ahasuerus by the chamberlains? And Memucan answered before the king and the princes, Vashti the queen has not done wrong to the king only, but also to all the princes, and to all the people that are in all the provinces of the king Ahasuerus; for this deed of the queen shall come abroad unto all women, so that they shall despise their husbands in their eyes when it shall be reported the king Ahasuerus commanded Vashti the queen to be brought in before him, but she came not. Likewise shall the ladies of Persia and Media say this day unto all the king's princes who have heard of the deed of the queen. Thus shall there arise too much contempt and wrath. If it please the king, let there go a royal commandment from him, and let it be written among the laws of the Persians and the Medes that it be not altered, that Vashti come no more before king Ahasuerus, and

let the king give her royal estate unto another that is better than she. And when the king's decree which he shall make shall be published throughout all his empire — for it is great — all the wives shall give to their husbands honor, both to great and small.

4 And the saying pleased the king and the princes. And the king did according to the word of Memucan, for he sent letters into all the king's provinces, into every province according to the writing thereof and to every people after their language, that every man should bear rule in his own house and that it should be published according to the language of every people.

5 After these things, when the wrath of king Ahasuerus was appeased, he remembered Vashti and what she had done, and what was decreed against her. Then said the king's servants that ministered unto him, Let there be fair young virgins sought for the king. And let the king appoint officers in all the provinces of his kingdom, that they may gather together all the fair young virgins unto Shushan the palace, to the house of the women, unto the custody of Hegai the king's chamberlain, keeper of the women, and let their things for purification be given them. And let the maiden who pleases the king be queen instead of Vashti. And the thing pleased the king, and he did so.

6 Now in Shushan the palace there was a certain Jew whose name was Mordecai, the son of Jair, the son of Shimei, the son of Kish, a Benjamite who had been carried away from Jerusalem with the captivity, who had been carried away with Jeconiah king of Judah, whom Nebuchadnezzar the king of Babylon had carried away. And he brought up Hadassah — that is, Esther, his uncle's daughter — for she had neither father nor mother; and the maid was fair and beautiful, whom Mordecai, when her father and mother were dead, took for his own daughter.

7 So it came to pass, when the king's commandment and his decree was heard and when many maidens were gathered together unto Shushan the palace to the custody of Hegai, that Esther was brought also unto the king's house to the custody of Hegai, keeper of the women. And the maiden pleased him, and she obtained kindness of him, and he speedily gave her her things for purification, with such things as belonged to her and seven maidens meet to be given her out of the king's house. And he preferred her and her maids unto the best

place of the house of the women. Esther had not shown her people nor her kindred, for Mordecai had charged her that she should not show it. And Mordecai walked every day before the court of the women's house, to know how Esther did and what should become of her.

8 Now when every maid's turn had come to go in to king Ahasuerus, after she had been twelve months according to the manner of the women (for so were the days of their purifications accomplished — that is, six months with oil of myrrh, and six months with sweet odors and with other things for the purifying of the women), then, thus came every maiden unto the king: whatever she desired was given her to go with her out of the house of the women unto the king's house. In the evening she went, and on the next day she returned into the second house of the women, to the custody of Shaashgaz the king's chamberlain who kept the concubines; she came in unto the king no more except the king delighted in her and that she was called by name.

9 Now when the turn of Esther, the daughter of Abihail the uncle of Mordecai, who had taken her for his daughter, had come to go in unto the king, she asked for nothing but what Hegai the king's chamberlain, the keeper of the women, appointed. And Esther obtained favor in the sight of all them that looked upon her. So Esther was taken unto king Ahasuerus, into his royal house in the tenth month, which is the month Tebeth, in the seventh year of his reign.

10 And the king loved Esther above all the women, and she obtained grace and favor in his sight more than all the virgins, so that he set the royal crown upon her head and made her queen instead of Vashti. Then the king made a great feast unto all his princes and his servants, even Esther's feast. And he made a release to the provinces and gave gifts according to the state of the king.

11 And when the virgins were gathered together the second time, then Mordecai sat in the king's gate. Esther had not yet shown her kindred nor her people, as Mordecai had charged her; for Esther did the commandment of Mordecai like when she was brought up with him. In those days, while Mordecai sat in the king's gate, two of the king's chamberlains, Bigthana and Teresh of those who kept the door, were angry and sought to lay hand on the king Ahasuerus. And the thing was known to Mordecai, who told it unto Esther the queen, and Esther attested to the king in Mordecai's name. And when inquisition

was made of the matter, it was found out; therefore, they were both hanged on a tree. And it was written in the book of the chronicles before the king.

12 After these things did king Ahasuerus promote Haman, the son of Hammedatha the Agagite, and advanced him, and set his seat above all the princes that were with him. And all the king's servants that were in the king's gate bowed and reverenced Haman, for the king had so commanded concerning him. But Mordecai bowed not, nor did him reverence. Then the king's servants who were in the king's gate said unto Mordecai, Why do you transgress the king's commandment? Now it came to pass, when they spoke daily unto him and he listened not unto them, that they told Haman, to see whether Mordecai's matters would stand; for he had told them that he was a Jew. And when Haman saw that Mordecai bowed not, nor did him reverence, then was Haman full of wrath. And he disdained to lay hands on Mordecai alone; for they had shown him the people of Mordecai, wherefore Haman sought to destroy all the Jews that were throughout the whole kingdom of Ahasuerus, even the people of Mordecai.

13 In the first month — that is, the month Nisan — in the twelfth year of king Ahasuerus, they cast Pur — that is, the lot — before Haman from day to day, and from month to month, to the twelfth month — that is, the month Adar. And Haman said unto king Ahasuerus, There is a certain people scattered abroad and dispersed among the people in all the provinces of your kingdom, and their laws are different from all people, neither keep they the king's laws; therefore, it is not for the king's profit to suffer them. If it please the king, let it be written that they may be destroyed, and I will pay ten thousand talents of silver to the hands of those that have the charge of the business, to bring it into the king's treasuries. And the king took his ring from his hand, and gave it unto Haman the son of Hammedatha the Agagite, the Jews' enemy. And the king said unto Haman, The silver is given to you, the people also, to do with them as it seems good to you.

14 Then were the king's scribes called on the thirteenth day of the first month, and there was written according to all that Haman had commanded unto the king's lieutenants, and to the governors that were over every province, and to the rulers of every people of every province according to the writing thereof, and to every people after

their language; in the name of king Ahasuerus was it written, and sealed with the king's ring. And the letters were sent by messengers into all the king's provinces to destroy, to kill, and to cause to perish all Jews, both young and old, little children and women, in one day, even upon the thirteenth day of the twelfth month, which is the month Adar, and to take the spoil of them for a prey. The copy of the writing for a commandment to be given in every province was published unto all people, that they should be ready against that day. The messengers went out, being hastened by the king's commandment, and the decree was given in Shushan the palace. And the king and Haman sat down to drink, but the city Shushan was perplexed.

¹⁵ When Mordecai perceived all that was done, Mordecai rent his clothes, and put on sackcloth with ashes, and went out into the midst of the city, and cried with a loud and a bitter cry, and came even before the king's gate; for none might enter into the king's gate clothed with sackcloth. And in every province, wherever the king's commandment and his decree came, there was great mourning among the Jews, and fasting, and weeping, and wailing; and many lay in sackcloth and ashes.

¹⁶ So Esther's maids and her chamberlains came and told it to her. Then was the queen exceedingly grieved. And she sent raiment to clothe Mordecai, and to take away his sackcloth from him, but he received it not. Then called Esther for Hathach, one of the king's chamberlains whom he had appointed to attend upon her, and gave him a commandment to Mordecai, to know what it was and why it was. So Hathach went forth to Mordecai, unto the street of the city which was before the king's gate. And Mordecai told him of all that had happened unto him, and of the sum of the money that Haman had promised to pay to the king's treasuries for the Jews, to destroy them. Also, he gave him the copy of the writing of the decree that was given at Shushan to destroy them, to show it unto Esther, and to declare it unto her, and to charge her that she should go in unto the king, to make supplication unto him and to make request before him for her people.

¹⁷ And Hathach came and told Esther the words of Mordecai. Again Esther spoke unto Hathach and gave him commandment unto Mordecai: All the king's servants and the people of the king's provinces do know that whoever, whether man or woman, shall come unto the king into the inner court, who is not called, there is one law of his: to

put him to death, except such to whom the king shall hold out the golden scepter, that he may live. But I have not been called to come in unto the king these thirty days. And they told to Mordecai Esther's words.

¹⁸ Then Mordecai commanded to answer Esther, Think not with yourself that you shall escape in the king's house more than all the Jews, for if you altogether hold your peace at this time, then shall there enlargement and deliverance arise to the Jews from another place, but you and your father's house shall be destroyed. And who knows whether you have come to the kingdom for such a time as this?

¹⁹ Then Esther bid them return Mordecai this answer: Go gather together all the Jews that are present in Shushan, and fast for me, and neither eat nor drink three days, night or day. I also and my maidens will fast likewise, and so will I go in unto the king, which is not according to the law; and if I perish, I perish. So Mordecai went his way and did according to all that Esther had commanded him.

²⁰ Now it came to pass, on the third day, that Esther put on her royal apparel, and stood in the inner court of the king's house, across from the king's house; and the king sat upon his royal throne in the royal house, across from the gate of the house. And it was so, when the king saw Esther the queen standing in the court, she obtained favor in his sight, and the king held out to Esther the golden scepter that was in his hand. So Esther drew near and touched the top of the scepter. Then said the king unto her, What do you desire, queen Esther, and what is your request? It shall be even given you to the half of the kingdom. And Esther answered, If it seem good unto the king, let the king and Haman come this day unto the banquet that I have prepared for him. Then the king said, Cause Haman to make haste, that he may do as Esther has said.

²¹ So the king and Haman came to the banquet that Esther had prepared. And the king said unto Esther at the banquet of wine, What is your petition? — and it shall be granted you. And what is your request? — even to the half of the kingdom it shall be performed. Then answered Esther and said, My petition and my request is: if I have found favor in the sight of the king, and if it please the king to grant my petition and to perform my request, let the king and Haman come

to the banquet that I shall prepare for them, and I will do tomorrow as the king has said.

22 Then went Haman forth that day joyful and with a glad heart; but when Haman saw Mordecai in the king's gate, that he stood not up nor moved for him, he was full of indignation against Mordecai; nevertheless, Haman restrained himself. And when he came home, he sent and called for his friends and Zeresh his wife, and Haman told them of the glory of his riches, and the multitude of his children, and all the things wherein the king had promoted him, and how he had advanced him above the princes and servants of the king. Haman said moreover, Yea, Esther the queen did let no man come in with the king unto the banquet that she had prepared but myself, and tomorrow am I invited unto her also with the king. Yet all this avails me nothing, so long as I see Mordecai the Jew sitting at the king's gate. Then said Zeresh his wife and all his friends unto him, Let a gallows be made of fifty cubits high, and tomorrow speak unto the king that Mordecai may be hung thereon; then go in merrily with the king unto the banquet. And the thing pleased Haman, and he caused the gallows to be made.

23 On that night could not the king sleep, and he commanded to bring the book of records of the chronicles, and they were read before the king. And it was found written that Mordecai had told of Bigthana and Teresh, two of the king's chamberlains, the keepers of the door, who sought to lay hand on the king Ahasuerus. And the king said, What honor and dignity has been done to Mordecai for this? Then said the king's servants that ministered unto him, There is nothing done for him. And the king said, Who is in the court? Now Haman had come into the outward court of the king's house, to speak unto the king to hang Mordecai on the gallows that he had prepared for him. And the king's servants said unto him, Behold, Haman stands in the court. And the king said, Let him come in. So Haman came in. And the king said unto him, What shall be done unto the man whom the king delights to honor? Now Haman thought in his heart, To whom would the king delight to do honor more than to myself? And Haman answered the king, For the man whom the king delights to honor, Let the royal apparel be brought which the king uses to wear, and the horse that the king rides upon, and the royal crown which is set upon his head, and let this apparel and horse be delivered to the

hand of one of the king's most noble princes, that they may array the man whom the king delights to honor, and bring him on horseback through the street of the city, and proclaim before him, Thus shall it be done to the man whom the king delights to honor. Then the king said to Haman, Make haste, and take the apparel and the horse as you have said, and do even so to Mordecai the Jew that sits at the king's gate. Let nothing fail of all that you have spoken. Then took Haman the apparel and the horse, and arrayed Mordecai, and brought him on horseback through the street of the city, and proclaimed before him, Thus shall it be done unto the man whom the king delights to honor.

24 And Mordecai came again to the king's gate, but Haman hastened to his house mourning and having his head covered. And Haman told Zeresh his wife and all his friends everything that had befallen him. Then said his wise men and Zeresh his wife unto him, If Mordecai is of the seed of the Jews, before whom you have begun to fall, you shall not prevail against him but shall surely fall before him. And while they were yet talking with him, the king's chamberlains came and hastened to bring Haman unto the banquet that Esther had prepared.

25 So the king and Haman came to banquet with Esther the queen. And the king said again unto Esther, on the second day at the banquet of wine, What is your petition, queen Esther? — and it shall be granted you. And what is your request? — and it shall be performed, even to the half of the kingdom. Then Esther the queen answered and said, If I have found favor in your sight, O king, and if it please the king, let my life be given me at my petition, and my people at my request; for we are sold, I and my people, to be destroyed, to be slain, and to perish. But if we had been sold for bondmen and bondwomen, I would have held my tongue, although the enemy could not offset the king's damage. Then the king Ahasuerus answered and said unto Esther the queen, Who is he, and where is he, that dared presume in his heart to do so? And Esther said, The adversary and enemy is this wicked Haman. Then Haman was afraid before the king and the queen.

26 And the king, arising from the banquet of wine in his wrath, went into the palace garden. And Haman stood up to make request for his life to Esther the queen, for he saw that there was evil determined against him by the king. Then the king returned out of the palace garden into the place of the banquet of wine, and Haman was fallen

upon the bed on which Esther was. Then said the king, Will he force
the queen also before me in the house? As the word went out of the
king's mouth, they covered Haman's face. And Harbona, one of the
chamberlains, said before the king, Behold also, the gallows fifty
cubits high which Haman had made for Mordecai, who had spoken
good for the king, stands in the house of Haman. Then the king said,
Hang him thereon. So they hung Haman on the gallows that he had
prepared for Mordecai; then was the king's wrath pacified.

27 On that day did the king Ahasuerus give the house of Haman, the
Jews' enemy, unto Esther the queen. And Mordecai came before the
king, for Esther had told what he was unto her. And the king took off
his ring, which he had taken from Haman, and gave it unto Mordecai.
And Esther set Mordecai over the house of Haman.

28 And Esther spoke yet again before the king, and fell down at his
feet, and implored him with tears to put away the mischief of Haman
the Agagite and his device that he had devised against the Jews. Then
the king held out the golden scepter toward Esther. So Esther arose
and stood before the king, and said, If it please the king, and if I have
found favor in his sight, and the thing seem right before the king, and
I am pleasing in his eyes, let it be written to reverse the letters devised
by Haman the son of Hammedatha the Agagite which he wrote to
destroy the Jews who are in all the king's provinces. For how can I
endure to see the evil that shall come unto my people, or how can I
endure to see the destruction of my kindred?

29 Then the king Ahasuerus said unto Esther the queen and to
Mordecai the Jew, Behold, I have given Esther the house of Haman,
and him they have hung upon the gallows because he laid his hand
upon the Jews. Write also for the Jews as it pleases you, in the king's
name, and seal it with the king's ring; for the writing which is written
in the king's name and sealed with the king's ring may no man reverse.

30 Then were the king's scribes called at that time in the third
month — that is, the month Sivan — on the twenty-third day thereof;
and it was written according to all that Mordecai commanded unto
the Jews, and to the lieutenants, and the deputies and rulers of the
provinces which are from India unto Ethiopia, a hundred twenty-seven
provinces, unto every province according to the writing thereof and
unto every people after their language, and to the Jews according to

their writing and according to their language. And he wrote in the king Ahasuerus' name and sealed it with the king's ring, and sent letters by messengers on horseback, and riders on mules, camels, and young dromedaries, wherein the king granted the Jews who were in every city to gather themselves together, and to stand for their life, to destroy, to slay, and to cause to perish all the power of the people and province that would assault them, both little ones and women, and to take the spoil of them for a prey, upon one day in all the provinces of king Ahasuerus, namely upon the thirteenth day of the twelfth month, which is the month Adar. The copy of the writing for a commandment to be given in every province was published unto all people, and that the Jews should be ready against that day to avenge themselves on their enemies. So the messengers that rode upon mules and camels went out, being hastened and pressed on by the king's commandment. And the decree was given at Shushan the palace.

31 And Mordecai went out from the presence of the king in royal apparel of blue and white, and with a great crown of gold, and with a garment of fine linen and purple; and the city of Shushan rejoiced and was glad. The Jews had light, and gladness, and joy, and honor. And in every province and in every city wherever the king's commandment and his decree came, the Jews had joy and gladness, a feast and a good day. And many of the people of the land became Jews, for the fear of the Jews fell upon them.

32 Now in the twelfth month — that is, the month Adar — on the thirteenth day of the same, when the king's commandment and his decree drew near to be put in execution, in the day that the enemies of the Jews hoped to have power over them — though it was turned to the contrary, that the Jews had rule over them that hated them — the Jews gathered themselves together in their cities throughout all the provinces of the king Ahasuerus, to lay hand on such as sought their hurt. And no man could withstand them, for the fear of them fell upon all people. And all the rulers of the provinces, and the lieutenants, and the deputies, and officers of the king helped the Jews, because the fear of Mordecai fell upon them; for Mordecai was great in the king's house and his fame went out throughout all the provinces, for this man Mordecai waxed greater and greater. Thus the Jews smote all their enemies with the stroke of the sword, and slaughter, and

destruction, and did what they desired unto those that hated them. And in Shushan the palace, the Jews slew and destroyed five hundred men, and Parshandatha, and Dalphon, and Aspatha, and Poratha, and Adalia, and Aridatha, and Parmashta, and Arisai, and Aridai, and Vaizatha—the ten sons of Haman the son of Hammedatha, the enemy of the Jews—slew they, but on the spoil laid they not their hand. On that day, the number of those that were slain in Shushan the palace was brought before the king.

33 And the king said unto Esther the queen, The Jews have slain and destroyed five hundred men in Shushan the palace, and the ten sons of Haman. What have they done in the rest of the king's provinces? Now what is your petition?—and it shall be granted you. Or what is your request further?—and it shall be done. Then said Esther, If it please the king, let it be granted to the Jews who are in Shushan to do tomorrow also according unto this day's decree, and let Haman's ten sons be hung upon the gallows. And the king commanded it so to be done. And the decree was given at Shushan, and they hung Haman's ten sons. For the Jews that were in Shushan gathered themselves together on the fourteenth day also of the month Adar, and slew three hundred men at Shushan, but on the prey they laid not their hand.

34 But the other Jews that were in the king's provinces gathered themselves together, and stood for their lives, and had rest from their enemies, and slew of their foes seventy-five thousand; but they laid not their hands on the prey. On the thirteenth day of the month Adar, and on the fourteenth day of the same, they rested and made it a day of feasting and gladness.

35 But the Jews that were at Shushan assembled together on the thirteenth day thereof and on the fourteenth thereof. And on the fifteenth day of the same, they rested and made it a day of feasting and gladness. Therefore, the Jews of the villages that dwelled in the unwalled towns made the fourteenth day of the month Adar a day of gladness and feasting, and a good day, and of sending portions one to another.

36 And Mordecai wrote these things, and sent letters unto all the Jews that were in all the provinces of the king Ahasuerus, both near and far, to establish this among them: that they should keep the fourteenth day of the month Adar, and the fifteenth day of the same, yearly, as

the days wherein the Jews rested from their enemies, and the month which was turned unto them from sorrow to joy, and from mourning into a good day, that they should make them days of feasting and joy, and of sending portions one to another, and gifts to the poor.

37 And the Jews undertook to do as they had begun, and as Mordecai had written unto them, because Haman the son of Hammedatha the Agagite, the enemy of all the Jews, had devised against the Jews to destroy them, and had cast Pur (that is, the lot) to consume them and to destroy them. But when Esther came before the king, he commanded by letters that his wicked device which he devised against the Jews should return upon his own head, and that he and his sons should be hung on the gallows. Wherefore, they called these days Purim, after the name of Pur. Therefore, for all the words of this letter, and of that which they had seen concerning this matter and which had come unto them, the Jews ordained and took upon them — and upon their seed, and upon all such as joined themselves unto them, so as it should not fail — that they would keep these two days according to their writing, and according to their appointed time every year; and that these days should be remembered and kept throughout every generation, every family, every province, and every city; and that these days of Purim should not fail from among the Jews, nor the memorial of them perish from their seed.

38 Then Esther the queen, the daughter of Abihail, and Mordecai the Jew, wrote with all authority to confirm this second letter of Purim. And he sent the letters unto all the Jews, to the hundred twenty-seven provinces of the kingdom of Ahasuerus, with words of peace and truth, to confirm these days of Purim in their times appointed, according as Mordecai the Jew and Esther the queen had enjoined them, and as they had decreed for themselves and for their seed — the matters of the fastings and their cry. And the decree of Esther confirmed these matters of Purim, and it was written in the book.

39 And the king Ahasuerus laid a tribute upon the land and upon the isles of the sea. And all the acts of his power and of his might, and the declaration of the greatness of Mordecai unto which the king advanced him, are they not written in the book of the chronicles of the kings of Media and Persia? For Mordecai the Jew was next unto king Ahasuerus, and great among the Jews, and accepted of the multitude

of his brethren, seeking the wealth of his people and speaking peace to all his seed.

THE BOOK OF JOB

THERE was a man in the land of Uz whose name was Job, and that man was perfect and upright, and one that feared God and eschewed evil. And there were born unto him seven sons and three daughters. His substance also was seven thousand sheep, and three thousand camels, and five hundred yoke of oxen, and five hundred she-asses, and a very great household, so that this man was the greatest of all the men of the east. And his sons went and feasted in their houses, every one his day, and sent and called for their three sisters to eat and to drink with them. And it was so, when the days of their feasting were gone about, that Job sent and sanctified them, and rose up early in the morning, and offered burnt offerings according to the number of them all. For Job said, It may be that my sons have sinned and cursed God in their hearts. Thus did Job continually.

2 Now there was a day when the children of God came to present themselves before the Lord, and Satan came also among them. And the Lord said unto Satan, From where do you come? Then Satan answered the Lord and said, From going to and fro in the earth, and from walking up and down in it.

3 And the Lord said unto Satan, Have you considered my servant Job, that there is none like him in the earth? A perfect and an upright man, one that fears God and eschews evil. Then Satan answered the Lord and said, Does Job fear God for naught? Have you not made a hedge about him, and about his house, and about all that he has on every side? You have blessed the work of his hands and his substance is increased in the land. But put forth your hand now and touch all that he has, and he will curse you to your face. And the Lord said unto Satan, Behold, all that he has is in your power, only upon himself put not forth your hand. So Satan went forth from the presence of the Lord.

4 And there was a day when his sons and his daughters were eating and drinking wine in their eldest brother's house. And there came a messenger unto Job and said, The oxen were plowing and the asses feeding beside them, and the Sabeans fell upon them and took them

away; yea, they have slain the servants with the edge of the sword; and I only am escaped alone to tell you.

5 While he was yet speaking, there came also another and said, The fire of God is fallen from heaven, and has burned up the sheep and the servants and consumed them; and I only am escaped alone to tell you.

6 While he was yet speaking, there came also another and said, The Chaldeans made out three bands and fell upon the camels, and have carried them away, yea, and slain the servants with the edge of the sword; and I only am escaped alone to tell you.

7 While he was yet speaking, there came also another and said, Your sons and your daughters were eating and drinking wine in their eldest brother's house, and behold, there came a great wind from the wilderness and smote the four corners of the house, and it fell upon the young men and they are dead; and I only am escaped alone to tell you.

8 Then Job arose and rent his mantle, and shaved his head, and fell down upon the ground and worshipped, and said, Naked came I out of my mother's womb, and naked shall I return there. The Lord gave and the Lord has taken away. Blessed be the name of the Lord.

9 In all this Job sinned not, nor charged God foolishly.

2 Again, there was a day when the children of God came to present themselves before the Lord, and Satan came also among them, to present himself before the Lord. And the Lord said unto Satan, From where do you come? And Satan answered the Lord and said, From going to and fro in the earth, and from walking up and down in it.

2 And the Lord said unto Satan, Have you considered my servant Job, that there is none like him in the earth? A perfect and an upright man, one that fears God and eschews evil. And still he holds fast his integrity, although you moved against him to destroy him without cause. And Satan answered the Lord and said, Skin for skin, yea, all that a man has will he give for his life. But put forth your hand now and touch his bone and his flesh, and he will curse you to your face. And the Lord said unto Satan, Behold, he is in your hand, but save his life.

3 So Satan went forth from the presence of the Lord and smote Job with terrible boils from the sole of his foot unto his crown. And he took himself a potsherd to scrape himself with and he sat down among the ashes. Then said his wife unto him, Do you still retain your integrity?

Curse God and die. But he said unto her, You speak as one of the foolish women speak. What? Shall we receive good at the hand of God, and shall we not receive evil? In all this, Job did not sin with his lips.

⁴ Now when Job's three friends heard of all this evil that had come upon him, they came every one from his own place — Eliphaz the Temanite, and Bildad the Shuhite, and Zophar the Naamathite — for they had made an appointment together to come to mourn with him and to comfort him. And when they lifted up their eyes afar off and knew him not, they lifted up their voice and wept. And they rent every one his mantle and sprinkled dust upon their heads toward heaven. So they sat down with him upon the ground seven days and seven nights, and none spoke a word unto him, for they saw that his grief was very great.

⁵ After this, Job opened his mouth and cursed his day. And Job spoke and said, Let the day perish wherein I was born, and the night in which it was said, There is a boy conceived. Let that day be darkness. Let not God regard it from above, neither let the light shine upon it. Let darkness and the shadow of death stain it. Let a cloud dwell upon it. Let the blackness of the day terrify it. As for that night, let darkness seize upon it. Let it not be joined unto the days of the year. Let it not come into the number of the months. Behold, let that night be solitary. Let no joyful voice come therein. Let them curse it that curse the day, who are ready to raise up their mourning. Let the stars of the twilight thereof be dark. Let it look for light, but have none. Neither let it see the dawning of the day, because it shut not up the doors of my mother's womb, nor hid sorrow from my eyes.

⁶ Why died I not from the womb? Why did I not give up the ghost when I came out of the belly? Why did the knees receive me? Or why the breasts, that I should suck? For now should I have lain still and been quiet. I should have slept. Then I would have been at rest with kings and counselors of the earth who built desolate places for themselves, or with princes that had gold, who filled their houses with silver, or as a hidden untimely birth, I would not have been, as infants who never saw light. There the wicked cease from troubling, and there the weary be at rest. There the prisoners rest together; they hear not the voice of the oppressor. The small and great are there, and the servant is free from his master.

7 Why is light given to him that is in misery and life unto the bitter in soul, who long for death but it comes not? And dig for it more than for hidden treasures? Who rejoice exceedingly and are glad when they can find the grave? Why is light given to a man whose way is hidden and whom God has hedged in? For my sighing comes before I eat, and my roarings are poured out like the waters; for the thing which I greatly feared has come upon me, and that which I was afraid of has come unto me. I was not in safety, neither had I rest, neither was I quiet; yet trouble came.

3 Then Eliphaz the Temanite answered and said, If we attempt to speak with you, will you be grieved? But who can withhold himself from speaking? Behold, you have instructed many, and you have strengthened the weak hands. Your words have upheld him that was falling, and you have strengthened the feeble knees. But now it has come upon you, and you faint. It touches you, and you are troubled. Is not this your fear, your confidence, your hope, and the uprightness of your ways?

2 Remember, I pray you: who perished, being innocent? Or where were the righteous cut off? Even as I have seen, they that plow iniquity and sow wickedness reap the same. By the blast of God they perish, and by the breath of his nostrils are they consumed. The roaring of the lion, and the voice of the fierce lion, and the teeth of the young lions are broken. The old lion perishes for lack of prey, and the stout lion's whelps are scattered abroad.

3 Now a thing was secretly brought to me and my ear received a little thereof. In thoughts from the visions of the night, when deep sleep falls on men, fear came upon me, and trembling which made all my bones to shake. Then a spirit passed before my face; the hair of my flesh stood up. It stood still, but I could not discern the form thereof. An image was before my eyes. There was silence, and I heard a voice saying, Shall mortal man be more just than God? Shall a man be more pure than his Maker? Behold, he put no trust in his servants, and his angels he charged with folly. How much less them that dwell in houses of clay, whose foundation is in the dust, who are crushed before the moth! They are destroyed from morning to evening. They

perish for ever without any regarding it. Does not their excellence in them go away? They die even without wisdom.

4 Call now, if there be any that will answer you; and to which of the saints will you turn? For wrath kills the foolish man, and envy slays the silly one. I have seen the foolish taking root, but suddenly I cursed his habitation. His children are far from safety, and they are crushed in the gate. Neither is there any to deliver them whose harvest the hungry eats up and takes it even out of the thorns; and the robber swallows up their substance. Although affliction comes not forth of the dust, neither does trouble spring out of the ground. Yet man is born unto trouble as the sparks fly upward.

5 I would seek unto God, and unto God would I commit my cause, who does great things, and unsearchable, marvelous things without number; who gives rain upon the earth and sends waters upon the fields; to set up on high those that be low, that those who mourn may be exalted to safety. He disappoints the devices of the crafty so that their hands cannot perform their enterprise. He takes the wise in their own craftiness, and the counsel of the froward is carried headlong. They meet with darkness in the daytime, and grope in the noonday as in the night. But he saves the poor from the sword, from their mouth, and from the hand of the mighty. So the poor has hope, and iniquity stops her mouth.

6 Behold, happy is the man whom God corrects; therefore, despise not the chastening of the Almighty. For he makes sore, and binds up; he wounds, and his hands make whole. He shall deliver you in six troubles, yea, in seven there shall no evil touch you. In famine he shall redeem you from death, and in war from the power of the sword. You shall be hidden from the scourge of the tongue, neither shall you be afraid of destruction when it comes. At destruction and famine you shall laugh, neither shall you be afraid of the beasts of the earth; for you shall be in league with the stones of the field, and the beasts of the field shall be at peace with you. And you shall know that your tabernacle shall be in peace, and you shall visit your habitation and shall not sin. You shall know also that your seed shall be great, and your offspring as the grass of the earth. You shall come to your grave in a full age, like a shock of grain comes in in his season.

⁷ Behold this, we have examined it, so it is. Hear it and know it for your good.

⁸ But Job answered and said, Oh that my grief were thoroughly weighed, and my calamity laid in the balances together, for now it would be heavier than the sand of the sea. Therefore, my words are swallowed up. For the arrows of the Almighty are within me, the poison whereof drinks up my spirit. The terrors of God do set themselves in array against me. Does the wild ass bray when he has grass? Or lows the ox over his fodder? Can that which is unsavory be eaten without salt? Or is there any taste in the white of an egg? The things that my soul refused to touch are as my sorrowful food.

⁹ Oh that I might have my request, and that God would grant me the thing that I long for, even that it would please God to destroy me, that he would let loose his hand and cut me off. Then should I yet have comfort, yea, I would harden myself in sorrow. Let him not spare, for I have not concealed the words of the Holy One.

¹⁰ What is my strength, that I should hope? And what is my end, that I should prolong my life? Is my strength the strength of stones? Or is my flesh of brass? Is not my help in me? And is wisdom driven quite from me?

¹¹ To him that is afflicted, pity should be shown from his friend, but he forsakes the fear of the Almighty. My brethren have dealt deceitfully as a brook, and as the stream of brooks they pass away, which are darkened by reason of the ice, and wherein the snow is hidden. When they wax warm, they vanish. When it is hot, they are consumed out of their place. The paths of their way are turned aside; they go to nothing and perish. The troops of Tema looked, the companies of Sheba waited for them. They were confounded because they had hoped; they came there and were ashamed. For now you are nothing; you see my casting down and are afraid. Did I say, Bring unto me? Or, Give a reward for me of your substance? Or, Deliver me from the enemy's hand? Or, Redeem me from the hand of the mighty?

¹² Teach me, and I will hold my tongue; and cause me to understand wherein I have erred. How forcible are right words! But what does your arguing prove? Do you imagine to reprove words, and the speeches of one that is desperate, as wind? Yea, you overwhelm the fatherless, and you dig a pit for your friend.

¹³ Now therefore be content; look upon me, for it is evident unto you if I lie. Return, I pray you, let it not be iniquity; yea, return again, my righteousness is in me. Is there iniquity in my tongue? Cannot my taste discern perverse things?

¹⁴ Is there not an appointed time to man upon earth? Are not his days also like the days of a hired hand? As a servant earnestly desires the shadow, and as a hired hand looks for the reward of his work, so am I made to possess months of vanity, and wearisome nights are appointed to me. When I lie down, I say, When shall I arise and the night be gone? And I am full of tossings to and fro unto the dawning of the day.

¹⁵ My flesh is clothed with worms and clods of dust. My skin has broken and become loathsome. My days are swifter than a weaver's shuttle and are spent without hope. O remember that my life is wind. My eye shall no more see good. The eye of him that has seen me shall see me no more; your eyes are upon me, and I am not. As the cloud is consumed and vanishes away, so he that goes down to the grave shall come up no more. He shall return no more to his house, neither shall his place know him anymore.

¹⁶ Therefore, I will not restrain my mouth, I will speak in the anguish of my spirit, I will complain in the bitterness of my soul. Am I a sea, or a whale, that you set a watch over me? When I say, My bed shall comfort me, my couch shall ease my complaint — then you scare me with dreams and terrify me through visions, so that my soul chooses strangling and death rather than my life. I loathe it. I would not live always. Let me alone, for my days are vanity.

¹⁷ What is man that you should magnify him? And that you should set your heart upon him? And that you should visit him every morning and try him every moment? How long will you not depart from me, nor let me alone until I swallow down my spittle? I have sinned. What shall I do unto you, O you preserver of men? Why have you set me as a mark against you so that I am a burden to myself? And why do you not pardon my transgression and take away my iniquity? For now shall I sleep in the dust, and you shall seek me in the morning, but I shall not be.

4 Then answered Bildad the Shuhite and said, How long will you speak these things? And how long shall the words of your

mouth be like a strong wind? Does God pervert judgment? Or does the Almighty pervert justice? If your children have sinned against him and he has cast them away for their transgression, if you would seek unto God early and make your supplication to the Almighty, if you were pure and upright, surely now he would awake for you and make the habitation of your righteousness prosperous. Though your beginning was small, yet your latter end should greatly increase.

2 For inquire, I pray you, of the former age, and prepare yourself to the search of their fathers; for we are but of yesterday, and know nothing because our days upon earth are a shadow. Shall not they teach you, and tell you, and utter words out of their heart? Can the rush grow up without mire? Can the reeds grow without water? While it is yet in his greenness and not cut down, it withers before any other herb; so are the paths of all that forget God. And the hypocrite's hope shall perish, whose hope shall be cut off and whose trust shall be a spider's web. He shall lean upon his house, but it shall not stand. He shall hold it fast, but it shall not endure. He is green before the sun and his branch shoots forth in his garden. His roots are wrapped about the heap and see the place of stones. If he destroy him from his place, then it shall deny him, saying, I have not seen you. Behold, this is the joy of his way, and out of the earth shall others grow.

3 Behold, God will not cast away a perfect man, neither will he help the evildoers, until he fill your mouth with laughing and your lips with rejoicing. They that hate you shall be clothed with shame and the dwelling place of the wicked shall come to naught.

4 Then Job answered and said, I know it is so, truly. But how should man be just with God? If he will contend with him, he cannot answer him one of a thousand. He is wise in heart and mighty in strength (who has hardened himself against him and has prospered?), who removes the mountains, and they know not, who overturns them in his anger; who shakes the earth out of her place, and the pillars thereof tremble; who commands the sun and it rises not, and seals up the stars; who alone spreads out the heavens, and treads upon the waves of the sea; who makes Arcturus, Orion, and Pleiades, and the chambers of the south; who does great things past finding out, yea, and wonders without number. He goes by me, and I see him not; he passes on also, but I perceive him not. Behold, he takes away. Who can hinder him?

Who will say unto him, What are you doing? If God will not withdraw his anger, the proud helpers do stoop under him.

5 How much less shall I answer him and choose out my words to reason with him? — whom, though I were righteous, yet would I not answer; but I would make supplication to my judge. If I had called and he had answered me, yet would I not believe that he had listened unto my voice; for he breaks me with a tempest and multiplies my wounds without cause. He will not suffer me to take my breath, but fills me with bitterness. If I speak of strength, behold, he is strong; and if of judgment, who shall set me a time to plead? If I justify myself, my own mouth shall condemn me. If I say, I am perfect, it shall also prove me perverse.

6 Though I were perfect, yet would I not know my soul. I would despise my life. This is one thing, therefore I said it: He destroys the perfect and the wicked. If the scourge slay suddenly, he will laugh at the trial of the innocent. The earth is given into the hand of the wicked, he covers the faces of the judges thereof. If not, where and who is he?

7 Now my days are swifter than a messenger; they flee away, they see no good. They are passed away as the swift ships, as the eagle that hastens to the prey. If I say, I will forget my complaint, I will leave off my sadness and comfort myself — I am afraid of all my sorrows, I know that you will not hold me innocent. If I am wicked, why then labor I in vain? If I wash myself with snow water and make my hands never so clean, yet shall you plunge me in the ditch and my own clothes shall abhor me.

8 For he is not a man, as I am, that I should answer him, and we should come together in judgment. Neither is there any arbiter between us that might lay his hand upon us both. Let him take his rod away from me, and let not his fear terrify me. Then would I speak and not fear him; but it is not so with me.

9 My soul is weary of my life. I will leave my complaint upon myself. I will speak in the bitterness of my soul. I will say unto God, Do not condemn me, show me why you contend with me. Is it good unto you that you should oppress? That you should despise the work of your hands and shine upon the counsel of the wicked? Do you have eyes of flesh? Or do you see as a man sees? Are your days as the days of man? Are your years as man's days, that you inquire after my iniquity and

search after my sin? You know that I am not wicked, and there is none that can deliver out of your hand.

10 Your hands have made me and fashioned me together round about, yet you do destroy me. Remember, I implore you, that you have made me as the clay. And will you bring me into dust again? Have you not poured me out as milk, and curdled me like cheese? You have clothed me with skin and flesh, and have knit me together with bones and sinews. You have granted me life and favor, and your visitation has preserved my spirit.

11 And these things have you hidden in your heart, I know that this is with you: If I sin, then you mark me, and you will not acquit me from my iniquity. If I am wicked, woe unto me. And if I am righteous, yet will I not lift up my head. I am full of confusion, therefore see my affliction, for it increases. You hunt me as a fierce lion, and again you show yourself marvelous upon me. You renew your witnesses against me and increase your indignation upon me. Changes and war are against me.

12 Why then have you brought me forth out of the womb? Oh that I had given up the ghost, and no eye had seen me. I should have been as though I had not been. I should have been carried from the womb to the grave. Are not my days few? Cease then, and let me alone, that I may take comfort a little before I go where I shall not return, even to the land of darkness and the shadow of death; a land of darkness as darkness itself, and of the shadow of death, without any order and where the light is as darkness.

5 Then answered Zophar the Naamathite and said, Should not the multitude of words be answered? And should a man full of talk be justified? Should your lies make men hold their peace? And when you mock, shall no man make you ashamed? For you have said, My doctrine is pure, and I am clean in your eyes. But oh that God would speak and open his lips against you, and that he would show you the secrets of wisdom, that they are double to that which is. Know therefore that God exacts of you less than your iniquity deserves.

2 Can you by searching find out God? Can you find out the Almighty unto perfection? It is as high as heaven; what can you do? Deeper than hell, what can you know? The measure thereof is longer than the earth

and broader than the sea. If he cut off and shut up or gather together, then who can hinder him? For he knows vain men. He sees wickedness also. Will he not then consider it? For vain man would be wise, though man be born like a wild ass's colt.

3 If you prepare your heart and stretch out your hands toward him, if iniquity is in your hand, put it far away and let not wickedness dwell in your tabernacles; for then shall you lift up your face without spot. Yea, you shall be steadfast and shall not fear, because you shall forget your misery and remember it as waters that pass away. And your age shall be clearer than the noonday. You shall shine forth, you shall be as the morning. And you shall be secure, because there is hope. Yea, you shall dig about you, and you shall take your rest in safety. Also, you shall lie down and none shall make you afraid. Yea, many shall make suit unto you, but the eyes of the wicked shall fail and they shall not escape, and their hope shall be as the giving up of the ghost.

4 And Job answered and said, No doubt but you are the people, and wisdom shall die with you. But I have understanding as well as you. I am not inferior to you. Yea, who knows not such things as these?

5 I am as one mocked of his neighbor, who calls upon God and he answers him. The just upright man is laughed to scorn. He that is ready to slip with his feet is as a lamp despised in the thought of him that is at ease. The tabernacles of robbers prosper, and they that provoke God are secure, into whose hand God brings abundantly.

6 But ask now the beasts and they shall teach you, and the fowls of the air and they shall tell you. Or speak to the earth and it shall teach you, and the fishes of the sea shall declare unto you. Who knows not in all these that the hand of the Lord has wrought this? In whose hand is the soul of every living thing, and the breath of all mankind. Does not the ear try words, and the mouth taste his food? With the elder is wisdom, and in length of days understanding.

7 With him is wisdom and strength. He has counsel and understanding. Behold, he breaks down and it cannot be built again. He shuts up a man and there can be no opening. Behold, he withholds the waters and they dry up; also, he sends them out and they overturn the earth. With him is strength and wisdom. The deceived and the deceiver are his. He leads counselors away spoiled, and makes the judges fools. He loosens the bond of kings, and girds their loins with a girdle. He

leads princes away spoiled, and overthrows the mighty. He removes away the speech of the trusty, and takes away the understanding of the aged. He pours contempt upon princes, and weakens the strength of the mighty. He reveals deep things out of darkness, and brings out to light the shadow of death. He increases the nations and destroys them. He enlarges the nations and overthrows them again. He takes away the heart of the chief of the people of the earth, and causes them to wander in a wilderness where there is no way. They grope in the dark without light, and he makes them to stagger like a drunken man.

8 Behold, my eye has seen all this, my ear has heard and understood it. What you know do I know also. I am not inferior unto you. Surely I would speak to the Almighty, and I desire to reason with God. But you are forgers of lies, you are all physicians of no value. Oh that you would altogether hold your peace, and it should be your wisdom. Hear now my reasoning and listen to the pleadings of my lips.

9 Will you speak wickedly for God, and talk deceitfully for him? Will you respect his person? Will you contend for God? Is it good that he should search you out? Or as one man mocks another, do you so mock him? He will surely reprove you if you do secretly respect persons. Shall not his excellence make you afraid and his dread fall upon you? Your remembrances are like unto ashes, your bodies to bodies of clay.

10 Hold your peace, let me alone that I may speak, and let come on me what will. Why do I take my flesh in my teeth and put my life in my hand? Though he slay me, yet will I trust in him; but I will maintain my own ways before him. He also shall be my salvation, for a hypocrite shall not come before him. Hear diligently my speech and my declaration with your ears. Behold, now I have prepared my case, I know that I shall be justified. Who is he that will plead with me? For now if I hold my tongue, I shall give up the ghost.

11 Only do not two things unto me, then will I not hide myself from you: withdraw your hand far from me, and let not your dread make me afraid. Then call, and I will answer. Or let me speak, and you answer me. How many are my iniquities and sins? Make me to know my transgression and my sin. Why do you hide your face, and hold me for your enemy? Will you break a leaf driven to and fro? And will you pursue the dry stubble? For you write bitter things against me, and make me to possess the iniquities of my youth. You put my

feet also in the stocks and look narrowly unto all my paths. You set a print upon the heels of my feet.

12 And he, as a rotten thing, consumes, as a garment that is moth-eaten. Man that is born of a woman is of few days and full of trouble. He comes forth like a flower and is cut down. He flees also as a shadow and continues not. And do you open your eyes upon such a one, and bring me into judgment with you? Who can bring a clean thing out of an unclean? Not one. Seeing his days are determined, the number of his months are with you, you have appointed his bounds that he cannot pass. Turn from him that he may rest until he shall accomplish, as a hired hand, his day.

13 For there is hope of a tree, if it is cut down, that it will sprout again, and that the tender branch thereof will not cease. Though the root thereof wax old in the earth, and the stock thereof die in the ground, yet through the scent of water it will bud and bring forth boughs like a plant. But man dies and wastes away. Yea, man gives up the ghost, and where is he? As the waters fail from the sea and the flood decays and dries up, so man lies down and rises not until the heavens are no more. They shall not awake, nor be roused out of their sleep.

14 Oh that you would hide me in the grave, that you would keep me secret until your wrath is past, that you would appoint me a set time and remember me. If a man die, shall he live again? All the days of my appointed time will I wait until my change come. You shall call, and I will answer you. You will have a desire to the work of your hands; for now you number my steps. Do you not watch over my sin? My transgression is sealed up in a bag, and you sew up my iniquity.

15 And surely the mountain falling comes to naught, and the rock is removed out of his place. The waters wear the stones. You wash away the things which grow out of the dust of the earth, and you destroy the hope of man. You prevail for ever against him, and he passes. You change his countenance and send him away. His sons come to honor and he knows it not, and they are brought low, but he perceives it not of them. But his flesh upon him shall have pain, and his soul within him shall mourn.

6 Then answered Eliphaz the Temanite, and said, Should a wise man utter vain knowledge and fill his belly with the east wind?

Should he reason with unprofitable talk or with speeches by which he can do no good? Yea, you cast off fear and restrain prayer before God. For your mouth utters your iniquity, and you choose the tongue of the crafty. Your own mouth condemns you and not I. Yea, your own lips testify against you.

2 Are you the first man that was born? Or were you made before the hills? Have you heard the secret of God? And do you restrain wisdom to yourself? What do you know that we know not? What do you understand which is not in us? With us are both the gray-headed and very aged men, much older than your father. Are the consolations of God small with you? Is there any secret thing with you? Why does your heart carry you away? And what do your eyes wink at, that you turn your spirit against God and let such words go out of your mouth?

3 What is man, that he should be clean? And he who is born of a woman, that he should be righteous? Behold, he puts no trust in his saints; yea, the heavens are not clean in his sight. How much more abominable and filthy is man who drinks iniquity like water! I will show you; hear me. And that which I have seen, I will declare, which wise men have told from their fathers and have not hid it, unto whom alone the earth was given and no stranger passed among them.

4 The wicked man travails with pain all his days, and the number of years is hidden to the oppressor. A dreadful sound is in his ears. In prosperity the destroyer shall come upon him. He believes not that he shall return out of darkness, and he is waited for of the sword. He wanders abroad for bread, saying, Where is it? He knows that the day of darkness is ready at his hand. Trouble and anguish shall make him afraid. They shall prevail against him as a king ready to the battle.

5 For he stretches out his hand against God and strengthens himself against the Almighty. He runs upon him, even on his neck, upon the thick bosses of his bucklers, because he covers his face with his fatness and makes layers of fat on his flanks. And he dwells in desolate cities and in houses which no man inhabits, which are ready to become heaps. He shall not be rich, neither shall his substance continue, neither shall he prolong the perfection thereof upon the earth. He shall not depart out of darkness. The flame shall dry up his branches, and by the breath of his mouth shall he go away.

⁶ Let not him that is deceived trust in vanity, for vanity shall be his recompense. It shall be accomplished before his time, and his branch shall not be green. He shall shake off his unripe grape as the vine and shall cast off his flower as the olive. For the congregation of hypocrites shall be desolate, and fire shall consume the tabernacles of bribery. They conceive mischief and bring forth vanity, and their belly prepares deceit.

⁷ Then Job answered and said, I have heard many such things. Miserable comforters are you all. Shall vain words have an end? Or what emboldens you that you answer? I also could speak as you do. If your soul were in my soul's stead, I could heap up words against you and shake my head at you. But I would strengthen you with my mouth, and the moving of my lips should lessen your grief.

⁸ Though I speak, my grief is not lessened. And though I refrain, what am I eased? But now he has made me weary. You have made desolate all my company. And you have filled me with wrinkles, which is a witness against me. And my leanness rising up in me bears witness to my face. He tears me in his wrath who hates me, he gnashes upon me with his teeth. My enemy sharpens his eyes upon me. They have gaped upon me with their mouth. They have smitten me upon the cheek reproachfully. They have gathered themselves together against me.

⁹ God has delivered me to the ungodly, and turned me over into the hands of the wicked. I was at ease, but he has broken me asunder. He has also taken me by my neck and shaken me to pieces, and set me up for his mark. His archers encompass me round about, he cleaves my kidneys asunder and does not spare. He pours out my bile upon the ground. He breaks me with breach upon breach. He runs upon me like a giant.

¹⁰ I have sewed sackcloth upon my skin and defiled my horn in the dust. My face is foul with weeping and on my eyelids is the shadow of death, not for any injustice in my hands. Also, my prayer is pure.

¹¹ O earth, cover not my blood, and let my cry have no place. Also, now behold, my witness is in Heaven and my record is on high. My friends scorn me, but my eye pours out tears unto God. Oh that one might plead for a man with God, as a man pleads for his neighbor.

¹² When a few years have come, then I shall go the way where I shall not return. My breath is corrupt. My days are extinct. The graves are

ready for me. Are there not mockers with me? And does not my eye continue in their provocation?

13 Lay down now, put me in a surety with you; who is he that will strike hands with me? For you have hidden their heart from understanding; therefore shall you not exalt them. He that speaks flattery to his friends, even the eyes of his children shall fail.

14 He has made me also a byword of the people, and previously I was as a tabor. My eye also is dim by reason of sorrow, and all my members are as a shadow. Upright men shall be astonished at this, and the innocent shall stir up himself against the hypocrite. The righteous also shall hold on his way, and he that has clean hands shall be stronger and stronger.

15 But as for you all, do return and come now, for I cannot find one wise man among you. My days are past, my purposes are broken off, even the thoughts of my heart. They change the night into day, the light is short because of darkness. If I wait, the grave is my house. I have made my bed in the darkness. I have said to corruption, You are my father; to the worm, You are my mother and my sister. And where is now my hope? As for my hope, who shall see it? They shall go down to the bars of the pit when our rest together is in the dust.

7 Then answered Bildad the Shuhite and said, How long will it be before you make an end of words? Mark and afterward we will speak. Why are we counted as beasts and reputed vile in your sight? He tears himself in his anger. Shall the earth be forsaken for you? And shall the rock be removed out of his place?

2 Yea, the light of the wicked shall be put out, and the spark of his fire shall not shine. The light shall be dark in his tabernacle, and his candle shall be put out with him. The steps of his strength shall be distressed, and his own counsel shall cast him down. For he is cast into a net by his own feet and he walks upon a snare. The trap shall take him by the heel, and the robber shall prevail against him. The snare is laid for him in the ground, and a trap for him in the way.

3 Terrors shall make him afraid on every side and shall drive him to his feet. His strength shall be famished, and destruction ready at his side. It shall devour the strength of his skin, even the firstborn of death shall devour his strength. His confidence shall be rooted out

of his tabernacle, and it shall bring him to the king of terrors. It shall dwell in his tabernacle because it is none of his. Brimstone shall be scattered upon his habitation. His roots shall be dried up beneath, and above shall his branch be cut off.

4 His remembrance shall perish from the earth, and he shall have no name in the street. He shall be driven from light into darkness, and chased out of the world. He shall neither have son nor grandson among his people, nor any remaining in his dwellings. They that come after him shall be astonished at his day, as they that went before were frightened. Surely such are the dwellings of the wicked, and this is the place of him that knows not God.

5 Then Job answered and said, How long will you vex my soul and break me in pieces with words? These ten times have you reproached me. You are not ashamed that you make yourselves strangers to me. And be it indeed that I have erred, my error remains with myself. If indeed you will magnify yourselves against me and plead against me my reproach, know now that God has overthrown me and has encompassed me with his net.

6 Behold, I cry out of wrong, but I am not heard. I cry aloud, but there is no judgment. He has walled up my way that I cannot pass, and he has set darkness in my paths. He has stripped me of my glory and taken the crown from my head. He has destroyed me on every side and I am gone, and my hope has he removed like a tree. He has also kindled his wrath against me and he counts me unto him as one of his enemies. His troops come together and raise up their way against me, and encamp round about my tabernacle.

7 He has put my brethren far from me, and my acquaintances are truly estranged from me. My kinsfolk have failed and my familiar friends have forgotten me. They that dwell in my house and my maids count me for a stranger. I am a foreigner in their sight. I called my servant and he gave me no answer. I entreated him with my mouth. My breath is strange to my wife, though I entreated for the children's sake of my own body. Yea, young children despised me. I arose and they spoke against me. All my intimate friends abhorred me, and they whom I loved are turned against me. My bone cleaves to my skin and to my flesh, and I am escaped by the skin of my teeth.

8 Have pity upon me, have pity upon me, O you my friends, for the hand of God has touched me. Why do you persecute me as God and are not satisfied with my flesh?

9 Oh that my words were now written. Oh that they were printed in a book, that they were engraved with an iron pen and lead in the rock for ever. For I know my redeemer lives and he shall stand at the latter day upon the earth. And after my skin worms destroy this body, yet in my flesh shall I see God, whom I shall see for myself, and my eyes shall behold, and not another, though my reins be consumed within me.

10 But you should say, Why do we persecute him, seeing the root of the matter is found in me? Be afraid of the sword, for wrath brings the punishments of the sword, that you may know there is a judgment.

8 Then answered Zophar the Naamathite, and said, Therefore do my thoughts cause me to answer, and for this I make haste. I have heard the rebuke of my reproach, and the spirit of my understanding causes me to answer.

2 Do you not know this of old, since man was placed upon earth, that the triumphing of the wicked is short and the joy of the hypocrite but for a moment? Though his excellence mount up to the heavens and his head reach unto the clouds, yet he shall perish for ever like his own dung. They who have seen him shall say, Where is he? He shall fly away as a dream and shall not be found. Yea, he shall be chased away as a vision of the night. The eye also which saw him shall see him no more, neither shall his place anymore behold him. His children shall seek to please the poor and his hands shall restore their goods. His bones are full of the sin of his youth which shall lie down with him in the dust.

3 Though wickedness be sweet in his mouth, though he hide it under his tongue, though he spare it and forsake it not but keep it still within his mouth, yet his food in his bowels is turned, it is the venom of asps within him. He has swallowed down riches and he shall vomit them up again; God shall cast them out of his belly. He shall suck the poison of asps, the viper's tongue shall slay him. He shall not see the rivers, the floods, the brooks of honey and butter. That which he labored for shall he restore and shall not swallow it down. According to his substance shall the restitution be, and he shall not rejoice therein, because he has

oppressed and has forsaken the poor, because he has violently taken away a house which he built not.

4 Surely he shall not feel quietness in his belly. He shall not save of that which he desired. There shall none of his food be left, therefore shall no man look for his goods. In the fullness of his sufficiency he shall be in distress. Every hand of the wicked shall come upon him. When he is about to fill his belly, God shall cast the fury of his wrath upon him and shall rain it upon him while he is eating. He shall flee from the iron weapon and the bow of steel shall strike him through; it is drawn and comes out of the body, yea, the glittering sword comes out of his bile.

5 Terrors are upon him. All darkness shall be hidden in his secret places. A fire not blown shall consume him, it shall go ill with him that is left in his tabernacle. The Heaven shall reveal his iniquity and the earth shall rise up against him. The increase of his house shall depart and his goods shall flow away in the day of his wrath. This is the portion of a wicked man from God and the heritage appointed unto him by God.

6 But Job answered and said, Hear diligently my speech, and let this be your consolations. Suffer me that I may speak; and after I have spoken, mock on. As for me, is my complaint to man? And if it were so, why should not my spirit be troubled? Mark me, and be astonished, and lay your hand upon your mouth. Even when I remember, I am afraid, and trembling takes hold on my flesh.

7 Why do the wicked live, become old, yea, are mighty in power? Their seed is established in their sight with them, and their offspring before their eyes. Their houses are safe from fear, neither is the rod of God upon them. Their bull breeds and fails not. Their cow calves and casts not her calf. They send forth their little ones like a flock and their children dance. They take the tambourine and harp and rejoice at the sound of the organ. They spend their days in wealth and in a moment go down to the grave. Therefore, they say unto God, Depart from us, for we desire not the knowledge of your ways. What is the Almighty, that we should serve him? And what profit should we have if we pray unto him? Behold, their good is not in their hand. The counsel of the wicked is far from me.

8 How oft is the candle of the wicked put out! And how oft comes their destruction upon them! God distributes sorrows in his anger. They are as stubble before the wind and as chaff that the storm carries away. God lays up his iniquity for his children. He rewards him, and he shall know it. His eyes shall see his destruction, and he shall drink of the wrath of the Almighty. For what pleasure has he in his house after him when the number of his months is cut off in the middle?

9 Shall any teach God knowledge, seeing he judges those that are high? One dies in his full strength, being wholly at ease and quiet. His breasts are full of milk and his bones are moistened with marrow. And another dies in the bitterness of his soul and never eats with pleasure. They shall lie down alike in the dust, and the worms shall cover them.

10 Behold, I know your thoughts and the devices which you wrongfully imagine against me. For you say, Where is the house of the prince? And where are the dwelling places of the wicked? Have you not asked them that go by the way? And do you not know their tokens, that the wicked is reserved to the day of destruction? They shall be brought forth to the day of wrath. Who shall declare his way to his face? And who shall repay him what he has done? Yet shall he be brought to the grave and shall remain in the tomb. The clods of the valley shall be sweet unto him, and every man shall draw after him, as there are innumerable before him. How then do you comfort me in vain, seeing in your answers there remains falsehood?

9 Then Eliphaz the Temanite answered and said, Can a man be profitable unto God as he that is wise may be profitable unto himself? Is it any pleasure to the Almighty that you are righteous? Or is it gain to him that you make your ways perfect? Will he reprove you for fear of you? Will he enter with you into judgment?

2 Is not your wickedness great and your iniquities infinite? For you have taken a pledge from your brother for naught, and stripped the naked of their clothing. You have not given water to the weary to drink, and you have withheld bread from the hungry. But the mighty man, he had the earth, and the honorable man dwelled in it. You have sent widows away empty and the arms of the fatherless have been broken. Therefore, snares are round about you and sudden fear troubles you, or darkness you cannot see and abundance of waters cover you.

3 Is not God in the height of Heaven? And behold the height of the stars, how high they are. And you say, How does God know? Can he judge through the dark cloud? Thick clouds are a covering to him that he sees not, and he walks in the circuit of heaven. Have you marked the old way which wicked men have trodden, who were cut down out of time? Whose foundation was overflowed with a flood, who said unto God, Depart from us? And what can the Almighty do for them? Yet he filled their houses with good things. But the counsel of the wicked is far from me. The righteous see and are glad, and the innocent laugh them to scorn. Whereas our substance is not cut down, but the remnant of them the fire consumes.

4 Acquaint now yourself with him, and be at peace; thereby good shall come unto you. Receive, I pray you, the law from his mouth, and lay up his words in your heart. If you return to the Almighty, you shall be built up. You shall put away iniquity far from your tabernacles. Then shall you lay up gold as dust, and the gold of Ophir as the stones of the brooks. Yea, the Almighty shall be your defense, and you shall have plenty of silver. For then shall you have your delight in the Almighty, and shall lift up your face unto God. You shall make your prayer unto him and he shall hear you, and you shall pay your vows. You shall also decree a thing and it shall be established unto you, and the light shall shine upon your ways. When men are cast down, then you shall say, There is lifting up; and he shall save the humble person. He shall deliver the island of the innocent, and it is delivered by the pureness of your hands.

5 Then Job answered and said, Even today is my complaint bitter. My stroke is heavier than my groaning. Oh that I knew where I might find him, that I might come even to his seat. I would order my case before him, and fill my mouth with arguments. I would know the words which he would answer me, and understand what he would say unto me. Will he plead against me with his great power? No, but he would put strength in me. There the righteous might dispute with him; so should I be delivered for ever from my judge.

6 Behold, I go forward, but he is not there; and backward, but I cannot perceive him. On the left hand, where he does work, but I cannot behold him. He hides himself on the right hand that I cannot see him, but he knows the way that I take. When he has tried me, I

shall come forth as gold. My foot has held his steps, his way have I kept and not declined, neither have I gone back from the commandment of his lips. I have esteemed the words of his mouth more than my necessary food.

7 But he is in one, and who can turn him? And what his soul desires, even that he does; for he performs the thing that is appointed for me, and many such things are with him. Therefore am I troubled at his presence; when I consider, I am afraid of him. For God makes my heart soft and the Almighty troubles me, because I was not cut off before the darkness, neither has he covered the darkness from my face.

8 Why, seeing times are not hidden from the Almighty, do they that know him not see his days? Some remove the landmarks; they violently take away flocks and feed thereof. They drive away the ass of the fatherless, they take the widow's ox for a pledge. They turn the needy out of the way. The poor of the earth hide themselves together. Behold, as wild asses in the desert go they forth to their work; rising early for a prey, the wilderness yields food for them and for their children. They reap everyone his fodder in the field, and they gather the vintage of the wicked. They cause the naked to lodge without clothing, that they have no covering in the cold. They are wet with the showers of the mountains, and embrace the rock for lack of a shelter. They pluck the fatherless from the breast, and take a pledge of the poor. They cause him to go naked without clothing, and they take away the sheaf from the hungry who make oil within their walls, and tread their winepresses, and suffer thirst. Men groan from out of the city, and the soul of the wounded cries out. Yet God lays not folly to them.

9 They are of those that rebel against the light. They know not the ways thereof, nor abide in the paths thereof. The murderer rising with the light kills the poor and needy, and in the night is as a thief. The eye also of the adulterer waits for the twilight, saying, No eye shall see me, and disguises his face. In the dark they dig through houses which they had marked for themselves in the daytime. They know not the light, for the morning is to them even as the shadow of death. If one know them, they are in the terrors of the shadow of death.

10 He is swift as the waters. Their portion is cursed in the earth. He beholds not the way of the vineyards. Drought and heat consume the snow waters, so does the grave those who have sinned. The womb

shall forget him. The worm shall feed sweetly on him. He shall be no more remembered, and wickedness shall be broken as a tree. He treats with evil the barren that bears not, and does not good to the widow. He draws also the mighty with his power. He rises up, and no man is sure of life. Though it is given him to be in safety, on which he rests, yet his eyes are upon their ways. They are exalted for a little while, but have gone and brought low. They are taken out of the way as all other, and cut off as the tops of the ears of grain. And if it be not so now, who will make me a liar and make my speech worth nothing?

10 Then Bildad the Shuhite answered and said, Dominion and fear are with him, he makes peace in his high places. Is there any number of his armies? And upon whom does not his light arise? How then can man be justified with God? Or how can he be clean that is born of a woman? Behold even to the moon, and it shines not, yea, the stars are not pure in his sight. How much less man that is a worm, and the son of man which is a worm!

2 But Job answered and said, How have you helped him that is without power, saved the arm that has no strength? How have you counseled him that has no wisdom? And how have you plentifully declared the thing as it is? To whom have you uttered words, and whose spirit came from you?

3 Dead things are formed from under the waters, and the inhabitants thereof; hell is naked before him, and destruction has no covering. He stretches out the north over the empty place, and hangs the earth upon nothing. He binds up the waters in his thick clouds, and the cloud is not rent under them. He holds back the face of his throne and spreads his cloud upon it. He has encompassed the waters with bounds until the day and night come to an end. The pillars of heaven tremble and are astonished at his reproof. He divides the sea with his power, and by his understanding he smites through the proud. By his spirit he has garnished the heavens; his hand has formed the crooked serpent.

4 Behold, these are parts of his ways, but how little a portion is heard of him? But the thunder of his power, who can understand?

5 Moreover, Job continued his parable and said, As God liveth, who has taken away my judgment, and the Almighty who has vexed my soul, all the while my breath is in me and the spirit of God is in my

nostrils, my lips shall not speak wickedness nor my tongue utter deceit. God forbid that I should justify you. Until I die, I will not remove my integrity from me. My righteousness I hold fast and will not let it go. My heart shall not reproach me so long as I live.

6 Let my enemy be as the wicked, and he that rises up against me as the unrighteous. For what is the hope of the hypocrite, though he has gained, when God takes away his soul? Will God hear his cry when trouble comes upon him? Will he delight himself in the Almighty? Will he always call upon God? I will teach you by the hand of God; that which is with the Almighty will I not conceal. Behold, all you yourselves have seen it. Why then are you thus altogether vain?

7 This is the portion of a wicked man with God, and the heritage of oppressors which they shall receive of the Almighty: if his children be multiplied, it is for the sword, and his offspring shall not be satisfied with bread. Those that remain of him shall be buried in death, and his widows shall not weep. Though he heap up silver as the dust and prepare raiment as the clay, he may prepare it, but the just shall put it on, and the innocent shall divide the silver. He builds his house as a moth, and as a booth that the keeper makes. The rich man shall lie down, but he shall not be gathered. He opens his eyes, and he is not. Terrors take hold on him as waters, a tempest steals him away in the night. The east wind carries him away and he departs, and as a storm hurls him out of his place. For God shall cast upon him and not spare; he would gladly flee out of his hand. Men shall clap their hands at him and shall hiss him out of his place.

8 Surely there is a vein for the silver, and a place for gold where they refine it. Iron is taken out of the earth, and brass is molten out of the stone. He sets an end to darkness and searches out all perfection, the stones of darkness, and the shadow of death. The flood breaks out from the inhabitant, even the waters forgotten of the foot; they are dried up, they have gone away from men. As for the earth, out of it comes bread, and underneath it is turned up as by fire. The stones of it are the place of sapphires, and it has dust of gold. There is a path which no fowl knows, and which the vulture's eye has not seen. The lion's whelps have not trodden it, nor the fierce lion passed by it. He puts forth his hand upon the rock, he overturns the mountains by the roots. He cuts out rivers among the rocks and his eye sees every

precious thing. He binds the floods from overflowing, and the thing that is hidden brings he forth to light.

9 But where shall wisdom be found? And where is the place of understanding? Man knows not the price thereof, neither is it found in the land of the living. The depth says, It is not in me; and the sea says, It is not with me. It cannot be gotten for gold, neither shall silver be weighed for the price thereof. It cannot be valued with the gold of Ophir, with the precious onyx, or the sapphire. The gold and the crystal cannot equal it, and the exchange of it shall not be for jewels of fine gold. No mention shall be made of coral or of pearls, for the price of wisdom is above rubies. The topaz of Ethiopia shall not equal it, neither shall it be valued with pure gold.

10 Where then comes wisdom? And where is the place of understanding? Seeing it is hidden from the eyes of all living and kept close from the fowls of the air. Destruction and death say, We have heard the fame thereof with our ears. God understands the way thereof, and he knows the place thereof; for he looks to the ends of the earth and sees under the whole heaven, to make the weight for the winds, and he weighs the waters by measure. When he made a decree for the rain and a way for the lightning of the thunder, then did he see it and declare it. He prepared it, yea, and searched it out. And unto man he said, Behold, the fear of the Lord, that is wisdom, and to depart from evil is understanding.

11 Moreover, Job continued his parable and said, Oh that I were as in months past, as in the days when God preserved me, when his candle shone upon my head and when by his light I walked through darkness; as I was in the days of my youth, when the secret of God was upon my tabernacle, when the Almighty was yet with me, when my children were about me, when I washed my steps with butter and the rock poured me out rivers of oil.

12 When I went out to the gate through the city, when I prepared my seat in the street, the young men saw me and hid themselves, and the aged arose and stood up. The princes refrained from talking and laid their hand on their mouth. The nobles held their peace and their tongue cleaved to the roof of their mouth. When the ear heard me, then it blessed me; and when the eye saw me, it gave witness to me, because I delivered the poor that cried, and the fatherless, and him that

had none to help him. The blessing of him that was ready to perish came upon me, and I caused the widow's heart to sing for joy. I put on righteousness and it clothed me, my judgment was as a robe and a diadem. I was eyes to the blind, and feet was I to the lame. I was a father to the poor, and the cause which I knew not, I searched out. And I broke the jaws of the wicked and plucked the spoil out of his teeth.

13 Then I said, I shall die in my nest, and I shall multiply my days as the sand. My root was spread out by the waters, and the dew lay all night upon my branch. My glory was fresh in me and my bow was renewed in my hand.

14 Unto me men gave ear and waited, and kept silence at my counsel. After my words they spoke not again, and my speech dropped upon them; and they waited for me as for the rain, and they opened their mouth wide as for the spring rain. If I laughed on them, they believed it not, and the light of my countenance they cast not down. I chose out their way, and sat chief and dwelled as a king in the army, as one that comforts the mourners.

15 But now they that are younger than I have me in derision, whose fathers I would have disdained to have set with the dogs of my flock. Yea, to what might the strength of their hands profit me, in whom old age was perished? For lack and famine, they were solitary, fleeing into the wilderness in former time, desolate and waste, who cut up mallows by the bushes and juniper roots for their food. They were driven forth from among men. They cried after them as after a thief, to dwell in the cliffs of the valleys, in caves of the earth, and in the rocks. Among the bushes they brayed, under the nettles they were gathered together. They were children of fools, yea, children of base men. They were viler than the earth.

16 And now am I their song, yea, I am their byword. They abhor me, they flee far from me and refrain not to spit in my face. Because he has loosened my cord and afflicted me, they have also let loose the bridle before me. Upon my right hand rise the youth. They push away my feet, and they raise up against me the ways of their destruction. They mar my path, they set forward my calamity, they have no helper. They came upon me as a wide breaking in of waters. In the desolation they rolled themselves upon me. Terrors are turned upon me. They pursue my soul as the wind, and my welfare passes away as a cloud.

17 And now my soul is poured out upon me, the days of affliction have taken hold upon me. My bones are pierced in me in the night season, and my sinews take no rest. By the great force of my disease is my garment changed, it binds me about as the collar of my coat. He has cast me into the mire, and I have become like dust and ashes.

18 I cry unto you and you do not hear me, I stand up and you regard me not. You are become cruel to me; with your strong hand you oppose yourself against me. You lift me up to the wind, you cause me to ride upon it, and dissolve my substance. For I know that you will bring me to death and to the house appointed for all living. Nevertheless, he will not stretch out his hand to the grave, though they cry in his destruction.

19 Did not I weep for him that was in trouble? Was not my soul grieved for the poor? When I looked for good, then evil came unto me; and when I waited for light, there came darkness. My inward parts boiled, and rested not. The days of affliction confronted me. I went mourning without the sun. I stood up and I cried in the congregation. I am a brother to dragons and a companion to owls. My skin is black upon me and my bones are burned with heat. My harp also is turned to mourning, and my organ into the voice of them that weep.

20 I made a covenant with my eyes. Why then should I think upon a virgin? For what portion of God is there from above? And what inheritance of the Almighty from on high? Is not destruction to the wicked, and a strange punishment to the workers of iniquity? Does not he see my ways and count all my steps?

21 If I have walked with vanity or if my foot has hastened to deceit, let me be weighed in an even balance, that God may know my integrity. If my step has turned out of the way, and my heart walked after my eyes, and if any blot has cleaved to my hands, then let me sow and let another eat; yea, let my offspring be rooted out.

22 If my heart has been deceived by a woman, or if I have laid wait at my neighbor's door, then let my wife grind unto another and let others bow down upon her. For this is a heinous crime, yea, it is an iniquity to be punished by the judges; for it is a fire that consumes to destruction, and would root out all my increase.

23 If I did despise the cause of my manservant or of my maidservant when they contended with me, what then shall I do when God rises

up? And when he visits, what shall I answer him? Did not he that made me in the womb make him? And did not one fashion us in the womb?

24 If I have withheld the poor from their desire, or have caused the eyes of the widow to fail, or have eaten my morsel myself, alone, and the fatherless has not eaten thereof — for from my youth he was brought up with me as with a father, and I have guided her from my mother's womb — if I have seen any perish for lack of clothing or any poor without covering, if his loins have not blessed me and if he were not warmed with the fleece of my sheep, if I have lifted up my hand against the fatherless when I saw my help in the gate, then let my arm fall from my shoulder blade and my arm be broken from the bone. For destruction from God was a terror to me, and by reason of his highness I could not endure.

25 If I have made gold my hope, or have said to the fine gold, You are my confidence — if I rejoiced because my wealth was great and because my hand had gotten much, if I beheld the sun when it shone or the moon walking in brightness, and my heart has been secretly enticed or my mouth has kissed my hand, this also was an iniquity to be punished by the judge, for I should have denied the God that is above.

26 If I rejoiced at the destruction of him that hated me, or lifted up myself when evil found him — neither have I suffered my mouth to sin by wishing a curse to his soul; if the men of my tabernacle said not, Oh that we had of his flesh, we cannot be satisfied — the stranger did not lodge in the street, but I opened my doors to the traveler; if I covered my transgressions as Adam, by hiding my iniquity in my bosom, did I fear a great multitude, or did the contempt of families terrify me, that I kept silence and went not out of the door?

27 Oh that one would hear me. Behold, my desire is that the Almighty would answer me, and that my adversary had written a book. Surely I would take it upon my shoulder and bind it as a crown to me. I would declare unto him the number of my steps. As a prince would I go near unto him.

28 If my land cry against me, or that the furrows likewise thereof complain, if I have eaten the fruits thereof without money, or have caused the owners thereof to lose their life, let thistles grow instead of wheat, and cockle instead of barley.

29 The words of Job are ended.

11 So these three men ceased to answer Job because he was righteous in his own eyes. Then was kindled the wrath of Elihu, the son of Barachel the Buzite, of the kindred of Ram. Against Job was his wrath kindled, because he justified himself rather than God. Also against his three friends was his wrath kindled, because they had found no answer, and yet had condemned Job. Now Elihu had waited until Job had spoken because they were older than he. When Elihu saw that there was no answer in the mouth of these three men, then his wrath was kindled.

2 And Elihu, the son of Barachel the Buzite, answered and said, I am young and you are very old; wherefore, I was afraid and dared not show you my opinion. I said, Days should speak, and multitude of years should teach wisdom. But there is a spirit in man, and the inspiration of the Almighty gives them understanding. Great men are not always wise, neither do the aged understand judgment.

3 Therefore, I said, Listen to me, I also will show my opinion. Behold, I waited for your words, I gave ear to your reasons while you searched out what to say. Yea, I paid attention to you, and behold, there was none of you that refuted Job or that answered his words, lest you should say, We have found out wisdom, God thrusts him down, not man. Now he has not directed his words against me, neither will I answer him with your speeches.

4 They were dismayed, they answered no more, they left off speaking. When I had waited — for they spoke not, but stood still, and answered no more — I said, I will answer also my part. I also will show my opinion. For I am full of matter, the spirit within me constrains me. Behold, my belly is as wine which has no vent, it is ready to burst like new bottles. I will speak, that I may be refreshed. I will open my lips and answer. Let me not, I pray you, respect any man's person, neither let me give flattering titles unto man. For I know not to give flattering titles; in so doing, my Maker would soon take me away.

5 Wherefore, Job, I pray you, hear my speeches and listen to all my words. Behold, now I have opened my mouth, my tongue has spoken in my mouth. My words shall be of the uprightness of my heart, and my lips shall utter knowledge clearly. The spirit of God has made me, and the breath of the Almighty has given me life. If you can answer me, set your words in order before me, stand up. Behold, I am according

to your wish in God's stead. I also am formed out of the clay. Behold, my terror shall not make you afraid, neither shall my hand be heavy upon you.

6 Surely you have spoken in my hearing, and I have heard the voice of your words, saying, I am clean, without transgression; I am innocent, neither is there iniquity in me. Behold, he finds accusations against me, he counts me for his enemy, he puts my feet in the stocks, he marks all my paths. Behold, in this you are not just.

7 I will answer you that God is greater than man. Why do you quarrel against him? For he gives not account of all of his matters. For God speaks once — yea, twice — yet man perceives it not. In a dream, in a vision of the night, when deep sleep falls upon men in slumberings upon the bed, then he opens the ears of men and seals their instruction, that he may withdraw man from his purpose and hide pride from man. He keeps back his soul from the pit, and his life from perishing by the sword.

8 He is chastened also with pain upon his bed, and the multitude of his bones with strong pain, so that his life abhors bread and his soul dainty food. His flesh is consumed away, that it cannot be seen, and his bones that were not seen stick out. Yea, his soul draws near unto the grave and his life to the destroyers.

9 If there be a messenger with him, an interpreter, one among a thousand to show unto man his uprightness, then he is gracious unto him and says, Deliver him from going down to the pit, I have found a ransom, his flesh shall be fresher than a child's, he shall return to the days of his youth — he shall pray unto God, and he will be favorable unto him, and he shall see his face with joy; for he will render unto man his righteousness.

10 He looks upon men, and if any say, I have sinned and perverted that which was right, and it profited me not — he will deliver his soul from going into the pit, and his life shall see the light. Behold all these things God oftentimes works with man, to bring back his soul from the pit, to be enlightened with the light of the living.

11 Mark well, O Job, listen unto me. Hold your peace and I will speak. If you have anything to say, answer me. Speak, for I desire to justify you. If not, listen unto me. Hold your peace and I shall teach you wisdom.

12 Furthermore, Elihu answered and said, Hear my words, O you wise men, and give ear unto me, you that have knowledge; for the ear tries words as the mouth tastes food. Let us choose to us judgment. Let us know among ourselves what is good. For Job has said, I am righteous, and God has taken away my judgment. Should I lie against my right? My wound is incurable without transgression. What man is like Job, who drinks up scorning like water, who goes in company with the workers of iniquity and walks with wicked men? For he has said, It profits a man nothing that he should delight himself with God.

13 Therefore, listen unto me you men of understanding. Far be it from God that he should do wickedness, and from the Almighty that he should commit iniquity; for the work of a man shall he render unto him, and cause every man to find according to his ways. Yea, surely God will not do wickedly, neither will the Almighty pervert judgment. Who has given him a charge over the earth? Or who has disposed the whole world? If he set his heart upon man, if he gather unto himself his spirit and his breath, all flesh shall perish together and man shall return unto dust.

14 If now you have understanding, hear this. Listen to the voice of my words. Shall even he that hates right govern? And will you condemn him that is most just? Is it fit to say to a king, You are wicked, and to princes, You are ungodly? How much less to him that accepts not the persons of princes, nor regards the rich more than the poor? For they all are the work of his hands. In a moment shall they die, and the people shall be troubled at midnight and pass away, and the mighty shall be taken away without hand.

15 For his eyes are upon the ways of man and he sees all his goings. There is no darkness, nor shadow of death, where the workers of iniquity may hide themselves. For he will not lay upon man more than right, that he should enter into judgment with God. He shall break in pieces mighty men without number, and set others in their stead. Therefore, he knows their works, and he overturns them in the night so that they are destroyed. He strikes them as wicked men in the open sight of others because they turned back from him and would not consider any of his ways, so that they cause the cry of the poor to come unto him; and he hears the cry of the afflicted.

16 When he gives quietness, who then can make trouble? And when he hides his face, who then can behold him? Whether it be done against a nation, or against a man only, that the hypocrite reign not, lest the people be ensnared.

17 Surely it is meet to be said unto God, I have borne chastisement, I will not offend anymore. That which I see not, teach me; if I have done iniquity, I will do no more. Should it be according to your mind? He will recompense it, whether you refuse or whether you choose, and not I. Therefore, speak what you know.

18 Let men of understanding tell me, and let a wise man listen unto me. Job has spoken without knowledge and his words were without wisdom. My desire is that Job may be tried unto the end because of his answers for wicked men, for he adds rebellion unto his sin. He claps his hands among us and multiplies his words against God.

19 Elihu spoke moreover and said, Do you think this to be right that you said: My righteousness is more than God's? For you said, What advantage will it be unto you? — and, What profit shall I have if I be cleansed from my sin? I will answer you, and your companions with you.

20 Look unto the heavens and see, and behold the clouds which are higher than you. If you sin, what do you do against him? Or if your transgressions be multiplied, what do you do unto him? If you are righteous, what do you give him? Or what does he receive of your hand? Your wickedness may hurt a man as you are, and your righteousness may profit the son of man.

21 By reason of the multitude of oppressions, they make the oppressed to cry; they cry out by reason of the arm of the mighty. But none says, Where is God my Maker, who gives songs in the night, who teaches us more than the beasts of the earth and makes us wiser than the fowls of heaven? There they cry, but none gives answer because of the pride of evil men. Surely God will not hear vanity, neither will the Almighty regard it. Although you say you shall not see him, yet judgment is before him. Therefore, trust in him. But now, because it is not so, he has visited in his anger. Yet he knows it not in great extremity; therefore does Job open his mouth in vain, he multiplies words without knowledge.

22 Elihu also proceeded and said, Suffer me a little and I will show you that I have yet to speak on God's behalf. I will fetch my knowledge from afar and will ascribe righteousness to my Maker; for truly my words shall not be false. He that is perfect in knowledge is with you.

23 Behold, God is mighty and despises not any. He is mighty in strength and wisdom. He preserves not the life of the wicked, but gives right to the poor. He withdraws not his eyes from the righteous, but with kings on the throne, yea, he does establish them for ever and they are exalted. And if they be bound in fetters and be held in cords of affliction, then he shows them their work and their transgressions, that they have exceeded. He opens also their ear to discipline and commands that they return from iniquity. If they obey and serve him, they shall spend their days in prosperity and their years in pleasures. But if they obey not, they shall perish by the sword and they shall die without knowledge.

24 But the hypocrites in heart heap up wrath, they cry not when he binds them. They die in youth and their life is among the unclean. He delivers the poor in his affliction and opens their ears in oppression.

25 Even so would he have removed you out of the tight place into a broad place where there is no confinement, and that which should be set on your table should be full of fatness. But you have fulfilled the judgment of the wicked; judgment and justice take hold on you. Because there is wrath, beware lest he take you away with his stroke; then a great ransom cannot deliver you. Will he esteem your riches? No, not gold, nor all the forces of strength. Desire not the night when people are cut off in their place. Take heed, regard not iniquity, for this you have chosen rather than affliction.

26 Behold, God exalts by his power. Who teaches like him? Who has enjoined him his way? Or who can say, You have wrought iniquity? Remember that you magnify his work, which men behold. Every man may see it, man may behold it afar off. Behold, God is great and we know him not, neither can the number of his years be searched out.

27 For he makes small the drops of water, they pour down rain according to the vapor thereof, which the clouds do drop and distill upon man abundantly. Also, can any understand the spreadings of the clouds or the noise of his tabernacle? Behold, he spreads his light upon it and covers the bottom of the sea. For by them he judges the

people. He gives food in abundance. With clouds he covers the light, and commands it not to shine by the cloud that comes between. The noise thereof shows concerning it; the cattle also, concerning the vapor.

28 At this also my heart trembles and is moved out of his place. Hear attentively the noise of his voice and the sound that goes out of his mouth. He directs it under the whole heaven, and his lightning unto the ends of the earth. After it a voice roars, he thunders with the voice of his excellence, and he will not restrain them when his voice is heard. God thunders marvelously with his voice.

29 Great things does he which we cannot comprehend. For he says to the snow, Be on the earth; likewise to the small rain and to the great rain of his strength. He seals up the hand of every man, that all men may know his work. Then the beasts go into dens and remain in their places. Out of the south comes the whirlwind, and cold out of the north. By the breath of God, frost is given and the breadth of the waters is narrowed. Also by watering, he wearies the thick cloud. He scatters his bright cloud and it is turned round about by his counsels, that they may do whatever he commands them upon the face of the world in the earth. He causes it to come — whether for correction, or for his land, or for mercy.

30 Listen unto this, O Job. Stand still and consider the wondrous works of God. Do you know when God disposed them and caused the light of his cloud to shine? Do you know the balancings of the clouds, the wondrous works of him who is perfect in knowledge? How your garments are warm when he quiets the earth by the south wind? Have you, with him, spread out the sky, which is strong and as a molten mirror?

31 Teach us what we shall say unto him, for we cannot order our speech by reason of darkness. Shall it be told him that I speak? If a man speak, surely he shall be swallowed up. And now men see not the bright light which is in the clouds, but the wind passes and cleanses them. Fair weather comes out of the north; with God is terrible majesty. Touching the Almighty, we cannot find him out. He is excellent in power, and in judgment, and in plenty of justice. He will not afflict. Men do therefore fear him. He respects not any that are wise of heart.

12 Then the Lord answered Job out of the whirlwind and said, Who is this that darkens counsel by words without knowledge? Gird up now your loins like a man, for I will demand of you, and you answer me.

2 Where were you when I laid the foundations of the earth? Declare, if you have understanding. Who has laid the measures thereof, if you know? Or who has stretched the line upon it? Upon what are the foundations thereof fastened? Or who laid the cornerstone thereof, when the morning stars sang together and all the sons of God shouted for joy? Or who shut up the sea with doors when it broke forth, as if it had issued out of the womb? When I made the cloud the garment thereof, and thick darkness a swaddling band for it, and broke up for it my decreed place, and set bars and doors, and said, Hitherto shall you come, but no further, and here shall your proud waves be stopped?

3 Have you commanded the morning since your days, and caused the daybreak to know his place? That it might take hold of the ends of the earth, that the wicked might be shaken out of it? It is turned as clay to the seal and they stand as a garment. And from the wicked their light is withheld, and the high arm shall be broken.

4 Have you entered into the springs of the sea? Or have you walked in the search of the depth? Have the gates of death been opened unto you? Or have you seen the doors of the shadow of death? Have you perceived the breadth of the earth? Declare, if you know it all.

5 Where is the way where light dwells? And as for darkness, where is the place thereof, that you should take it to the bound thereof, and that you should know the paths to the house thereof? Do you know it because you were then born? Or because the number of your days is great?

6 Have you entered into the treasuries of the snow? Or have you seen the treasuries of the hail which I have reserved against the time of trouble, against the day of battle and war? By what way is the light parted which scatters the east wind upon the earth? Who has divided a watercourse for the overflowing of waters, or a way for the lightning of thunder? To cause it to rain on the earth where no man is, on the wilderness wherein there is no man, to satisfy the desolate and waste ground and to cause the bud of the tender herb to spring forth? Has the rain a father? Or who has begotten the drops of dew? Out of whose

womb came the ice? And the hoary frost of heaven, who has begotten it? The waters are hidden as with a stone, and the face of the deep is frozen.

7 Can you bind the sweet influences of Pleiades, or loosen the bands of Orion? Can you bring forth Mazzaroth in his season, or can you guide Arcturus with his sons? Do you know the ordinances of heaven? Can you set the dominion thereof in the earth?

8 Can you lift up your voice to the clouds, that abundance of waters may cover you? Can you send lightnings, that they may go and say unto you, Here we are? Who has put wisdom in the inward parts? Or who has given understanding to the heart? Who can number the clouds in wisdom? Or who can stop the bottles of heaven when the dust grows into hardness and the clods cleave fast together?

9 Will you hunt the prey for the lion? Or fill the appetite of the young lions when they crouch in their dens and abide in the cover to lie in wait? Who provides for the raven his food, when his young ones cry unto God, they wander for lack of food?

10 Do you know the time when the wild goats of the rock bring forth? Can you mark when the hinds do calve? Can you number the months they fulfill? Or do you know the time when they bring forth? They bow themselves, they bring forth their young ones, they cast out their sorrows. Their young ones are in good condition, they grow up with grain. They go forth and return not unto them.

11 Who has sent out the wild ass free? Or who has loosened the bands of the wild ass, whose house I have made the wilderness and the barren land his dwellings? He scorns the multitude of the city, neither regards he the crying of the driver. The range of the mountains is his pasture and he searches after every green thing.

12 Will the re'em be willing to serve you or abide by your crib? Can you bind the re'em with his band in the furrow? Or will he harrow the valleys after you? Will you trust him because his strength is great? Or will you leave your labor to him? Will you believe him that he will bring home your seed and gather it into your barn?

13 Did you give the beautiful wings unto the peacocks, or wings and feathers unto the ostrich? Which leaves her eggs in the earth and warms them in dust, and forgets that the foot may crush them or that the wild beast may break them? She is hardened against her young ones as though they were not hers. Her labor is in vain without fear

because God has deprived her of wisdom, neither has he imparted to her understanding. When she lifts up herself on high, she scorns the horse and his rider.

¹⁴ Have you given the horse strength? Have you clothed his neck with thunder? Can you make him afraid as a grasshopper? The glory of his nostrils is terrible. He paws in the valley and rejoices in his strength. He goes on to meet the armed men. He mocks at fear and is not frightened, neither turns he back from the sword. The quiver rattles against him, the glittering spear and the shield. He swallows the ground with fierceness and rage, neither believes he that it is the sound of the trumpet. He says among the trumpets, Ha, ha — and he smells the battle afar off, the thunder of the captains and the shouting.

¹⁵ Does the hawk fly by your wisdom and stretch her wings toward the south? Does the eagle mount up at your command and make her nest on high? She dwells and abides on the rock, upon the crag of the rock and the strong place. From there she seeks the prey and her eyes behold afar off. Her young ones also suck up blood, and where the slain are, there is she.

¹⁶ Moreover, the Lord answered Job and said, Shall he that contends with the Almighty instruct? He that reproves God, let him answer it.

¹⁷ Then Job answered the Lord and said, Behold, I am vile, what shall I answer you? I will lay my hand upon my mouth. Once have I spoken, but I will not answer. Yea, twice, but I will proceed no further.

¹⁸ Then answered the Lord unto Job out of the whirlwind, and said, Gird up your loins now like a man. I will demand of you, and declare unto me, will you also disannul my judgment? Will you condemn me, that you may be righteous? Do you have an arm like God, or can you thunder with a voice like him?

¹⁹ Adorn yourself now with majesty and excellence, and array yourself with glory and beauty. Cast abroad the rage of your wrath, and behold everyone that is proud and abase him. Look on everyone that is proud and bring him low, and tread down the wicked in their place. Hide them in the dust together and bind their faces in secret. Then will I also confess unto you that your own right hand can save you.

²⁰ Behold now behemoth, which I made with you. He eats grass as an ox. Behold now, his strength is in his loins and his force is in the navel of his belly. He moves his tail like a cedar. The sinews of his

stones are wrapped together. His bones are as strong pieces of brass, his bones are like bars of iron. He is the chief of the ways of God. He that made him can make his sword to approach unto him. Surely the mountains bring him forth food where all the beasts of the field play. He lies under the shady trees in the cover of the reed and fens. The shady trees cover him with their shadow, the willows of the brook encompass him about. Behold, he drinks up a river and hastens not, he trusts that he can draw up Jordan into his mouth. He takes it with his eyes, his nose pierces through snares.

21 Can you draw out leviathan with a hook, or his tongue with a cord which you let down? Can you put a hook into his nose, or bore his jaw through with a thorn? Will he make many supplications unto you? Will he speak soft words unto you? Will he make a covenant with you? Will you take him for a servant for ever? Will you play with him as with a bird? Or will you bind him for your maidens? Shall the companions make a banquet of him? Shall they part him among the merchants? Can you fill his skin with barbed irons, or his head with fish spears? Lay your hand upon him, remember the battle, do no more. Behold, the hope of him is in vain. Shall not one be cast down even at the sight of him? None is so fierce that dare stir him up.

22 Who then is able to stand before me? Who has preempted me, that I should repay him? Whatever is under the whole heaven is mine.

23 I will not conceal his parts, nor his power, nor his comely proportion. Who can uncover the face of his garment? Or who can come to him with his double bridle? Who can open the doors of his face? His teeth are terrible round about. His scales are his pride, shut up together as with a close seal. One is so near to another that no air can come between them. They are joined one to another, they stick together, that they cannot be divided. By his sneezings a light does shine, and his eyes are like the eyelids of the morning. Out of his mouth go burning lamps, and sparks of fire leap out. Out of his nostrils goes smoke, as out of a boiling pot or cauldron. His breath kindles coals and a flame goes out of his mouth. In his neck remains strength, and sorrow is turned into joy before him. The flakes of his flesh are joined together, they are firm in themselves, they cannot be moved. His heart is as firm as a stone, yea, as hard as a piece of the lower millstone.

²⁴When he raises up himself, the mighty are afraid; by reason of breakings, they purify themselves. The sword of him that lays at him cannot hold—the spear, the dart, nor the habergeon. He esteems iron as straw and brass as rotten wood. The arrow cannot make him flee. Sling stones are turned with him into stubble. Darts are counted as stubble. He laughs at the shaking of a spear. Sharp stones are under him. He spreads sharp pointed things upon the mire. He makes the deep to boil like a pot, he makes the sea like a pot of ointment. He makes a path to shine after him, one would think the deep to be greying. Upon earth there is not his like, who is made without fear. He beholds all high things. He is a king over all the children of pride.

²⁵ Then Job answered the Lord and said, I know that you can do everything and that no thought can be withheld from you. Who is he that hides counsel without knowledge? Therefore have I uttered that I understood not things too wonderful for me, which I knew not. Hear, I implore you, and I will speak. I will demand of you and you declare unto me. I have heard of you by the hearing of the ear, but now my eye sees you. Wherefore, I abhor myself and repent in dust and ashes.

13 And it was so, that after the Lord had spoken these words unto Job, the Lord said to Eliphaz the Temanite, My wrath is kindled against you and against your two friends, for you have not spoken of me right, as my servant Job has. Therefore, take unto you now seven bullocks and seven rams, and go to my servant Job, and offer up for yourselves a burnt offering, and my servant Job shall pray for you, for him will I accept, lest I deal with you after your folly, in that you have not spoken of me right—like my servant Job. So Eliphaz the Temanite, and Bildad the Shuhite, and Zophar the Naamathite went and did according as the Lord commanded them.

² The Lord also accepted Job. And the Lord turned the captivity of Job when he prayed for his friends; also, the Lord gave Job twice as much as he had before. Then came there unto him all his brethren, and all his sisters, and all they that had been of his acquaintance before, and did eat bread with him in his house. And they bemoaned him and comforted him over all the evil that the Lord had brought upon him. Every man also gave him a piece of money, and everyone an earring of gold.

³ So the Lord blessed the latter end of Job more than his beginning; for he had fourteen thousand sheep, and six thousand camels, and a thousand yoke of oxen, and a thousand she-asses. He had also seven sons, and three daughters — and he called the name of the first Jemimah, and the name of the second Keziah, and the name of the third Kerenhappuch. And in all the land were no women found so fair as the daughters of Job. And their father gave them inheritance among their brethren.

⁴ After this Job lived a hundred forty years, and saw his sons, and his sons' sons, even four generations. So Job died, being old and full of days.

THE BOOK OF PSALMS

PSALM 1

BLESSED is the man that walks not in the counsel of the ungodly, nor stands in the way of sinners, nor sits in the seat of the scornful, but his delight is in the law of the Lord, and in his law does he meditate day and night. And he shall be like a tree planted by the rivers of water, that brings forth his fruit in his season. His leaf also shall not wither, and whatever he does shall prosper.

² The ungodly are not so, but are like the chaff, which the wind drives away. Therefore, the ungodly shall not stand in the judgment, nor sinners in the congregation of the righteous. For the Lord knows the way of the righteous, but the way of the ungodly shall perish.

PSALM 2

WHY do the heathen rage and the people imagine a vain thing? The kings of the earth set themselves and the rulers take counsel together, against the Lord and against his anointed, saying, Let us break their bands asunder and cast away their cords from us.

² He that sits in the Heavens shall laugh; the Lord shall have them in derision. Then shall he speak unto them in his wrath, and vex them in his severe displeasure, Yet have I set my king upon my holy hill of Zion. I will declare the decree: the Lord has said unto me, You are my son; this day have I begotten you. Ask of me and I shall give you the heathen for your inheritance, and the farthest parts of the earth for

your possession. You shall break them with a rod of iron. You shall dash them in pieces like a potter's vessel.

3 Be wise now therefore, O you kings. Be instructed, you judges of the earth. Serve the Lord with fear and rejoice with trembling. Kiss the Son lest he be angry and you perish from the way when his wrath is kindled but a little. Blessed are all they that put their trust in him.

PSALM 3

A psalm of David, when he fled from Absalom his son.

LORD, how they are increased that trouble me! Many are they that rise up against me. Many there are who say of my soul, There is no help for him in God. Selah.

2 But you, O Lord, are a shield for me, my glory, and the lifter up of my head. I cried unto the Lord with my voice and he heard me out of his holy hill. Selah. I laid me down and slept. I awoke, for the Lord sustained me. I will not be afraid of ten thousands of people that have set themselves against me round about.

3 Arise, O Lord. Save me, O my God, for you have smitten all my enemies upon the cheekbone. You have broken the teeth of the ungodly. Salvation belongs unto the Lord; your blessing is upon your people. Selah.

PSALM 4

To the chief musician on stringed instruments, a psalm of David.

HEAR me when I call, O God of my righteousness. You have enlarged me when I was in distress. Have mercy upon me and hear my prayer.

2 O you sons of men, how long will you turn my glory into shame? How long will you love vanity and seek after lies? Selah. But know that the Lord has set apart him that is godly for himself. The Lord will hear when I call unto him. Stand in awe and sin not. Commune with your own heart upon your bed and be still. Selah. Offer the sacrifices of righteousness and put your trust in the Lord.

3 There are many that say, Who will show us any good? Lord, lift up the light of your countenance upon us. You have put gladness in my heart, more than in the time that their grain and their wine increased.

I will both lay me down in peace and sleep, for you Lord, only, make me dwell in safety.

PSALM 5

To the chief musician, upon wind instruments, a psalm of David.

GIVE ear to my words, O Lord. Consider my meditation. Listen unto the voice of my cry, my King and my God, for unto you will I pray. My voice shall you hear in the morning, O Lord. In the morning will I direct my prayer unto you and will look up.

2 For you are not a God who has pleasure in wickedness, neither shall evil dwell with you. The foolish shall not stand in your sight. You hate all workers of iniquity. You shall destroy them that speak lies. The Lord will abhor the bloody and deceitful man. But as for me, I will come into your house in the multitude of your mercy, and in your fear will I worship toward your holy temple. Lead me, O Lord, in your righteousness because of my enemies. Make your way straight before my face.

3 For there is no faithfulness in their mouth. Their inward part is wickedness. Their throat is an open sepulcher. They flatter with their tongue. Destroy them, O God. Let them fall by their own counsels. Cast them out in the multitude of their transgressions, for they have rebelled against you. But let all those that put their trust in you rejoice. Let them ever shout for joy because you defend them. Let them also that love your name be joyful in you; for you, Lord, will bless the righteous. With favor will you encompass him as with a shield.

PSALM 6

To the chief musician, on stringed instruments upon Sheminith,
a psalm of David.

O Lord, rebuke me not in your anger, neither chasten me in your hot displeasure. Have mercy upon me, O Lord, for I am weak. O Lord, heal me, for my bones are vexed. My soul is also seriously vexed, but you, O Lord — how long? Return, O Lord. Deliver my soul. Oh save me for your mercies' sake. For in death there is no remembrance of you; in the grave, who shall give you thanks? I am weary with my groaning. All night I make my bed to swim. I water my couch with my tears. My eye is consumed because of grief. It waxes old because of all my enemies.

2 Depart from me, all you workers of iniquity, for the Lord has heard the voice of my weeping. The Lord has heard my supplication. The Lord will receive my prayer. Let all my enemies be ashamed and severely vexed. Let them return and be ashamed suddenly.

PSALM 7
Shiggaion of David, which he sang unto the Lord
concerning the words of Cush the Benjamite.

O Lord my God, in you do I put my trust. Save me from all them that persecute me, and deliver me, lest he tear my soul like a lion, rending it in pieces while there is none to deliver. O Lord my God, if I have done this, if there is iniquity in my hands, if I have rewarded evil unto him that was at peace with me — yea, I have delivered him that without cause is my enemy — let the enemy persecute my soul and take it. Yea, let him tread down my life upon the earth and lay my honor in the dust. Selah.

2 Arise, O Lord, in your anger. Lift up yourself because of the rage of my enemies and awake for me to the judgment that you have commanded. So shall the congregation of the people encompass you about. For their sakes therefore return on high. The Lord shall judge the people. Judge me, O Lord, according to my righteousness and according to my integrity that is in me. Oh let the wickedness of the wicked come to an end, but establish the just; for the righteous God tries the hearts and reins. My defense is of God, who saves the upright in heart. God judges the righteous, and God is angry with the wicked every day.

3 If he turn not, he will sharpen his sword. He has bent his bow and made it ready. He has also prepared for him the instruments of death. He ordains his arrows against the persecutors. Behold, he travails with iniquity, and has conceived mischief and brought forth falsehood. He made a pit, and dug it, and is fallen into the ditch which he made. His mischief shall return upon his own head and his violent dealing shall come down upon his own crown. I will praise the Lord according to his righteousness and will sing praise to the name of the Lord Most High.

PSALM 8

To the chief Musician upon Gittith, a psalm of David.

O Lord our Lord, how excellent is your name in all the earth, who has set your glory above the heavens. Out of the mouth of babes and sucklings have you ordained strength because of your enemies, that you might still the enemy and the avenger.

2 When I consider your heavens, the work of your fingers, the moon and the stars which you have ordained, what is man that you are mindful of him? And the son of man that you visit him? For you have made him a little lower than the angels and have crowned him with glory and honor. You made him to have dominion over the works of your hands. You have put all things under his feet, all sheep and oxen, yea, and the beasts of the field, the fowl of the air, and the fish of the sea, and whatever passes through the paths of the seas. O Lord our Lord, how excellent is your name in all the earth.

PSALM 9

To the chief musician upon Muthlabben, a psalm of David.

I WILL praise you, O Lord, with my whole heart. I will show forth all your marvelous works. I will be glad and rejoice in you. I will sing praise to your name, O you Most High. When my enemies are turned back, they shall fall and perish at your presence. For you have maintained my right and my cause. You sat in the throne judging right. You have rebuked the heathen; you have destroyed the wicked; you have put out their name for ever and ever.

2 O you enemy, destructions have come to a perpetual end and you have destroyed cities. Their memorial is perished with them, but the Lord shall endure for ever. He has prepared his throne for judgment and he shall judge the world in righteousness. He shall minister judgment to the people in uprightness. The Lord also will be a refuge for the oppressed, a refuge in times of trouble. And they that know your name will put their trust in you, for you, Lord, have not forsaken them that seek you. Sing praises to the Lord who dwells in Zion. Declare among the people his doings. When he makes inquisition for blood, he remembers them. He forgets not the cry of the humble.

³ Have mercy upon me, O Lord. Consider my trouble which I suffer of them that hate me — you that lift me up from the gates of death — that I may show forth all your praise in the gates of the daughter of Zion. I will rejoice in your salvation.

⁴ The heathen are sunk down in the pit that they made. In the net which they hid is their own foot taken. The Lord is known by the judgment which he executes, the wicked is snared in the work of his own hands. Higgaion. Selah. The wicked shall be turned into hell, and all the nations that forget God. For the needy shall not always be forgotten, the expectation of the poor shall not perish for ever. Arise, O Lord. Let not man prevail. Let the heathen be judged in your sight. Put them in fear, O Lord, that the nations may know themselves to be but men. Selah.

PSALM 10

WHY do you stand afar off, O Lord? Why do you hide yourself in times of trouble? The wicked, in his pride, does persecute the poor. Let them be taken in the devices that they have imagined. For the wicked boasts of his heart's desire, and blesses the covetous whom the Lord abhors. The wicked, through the pride of his countenance, will not seek after God. God is not in all his thoughts. His ways are always grievous. Your judgments are far above, out of his sight. As for all his enemies — he sneers at them. For he has said in his heart, I shall not be moved; never in adversity. His mouth is full of cursing and deceit; and his heart is full of fraud, and under his tongue, mischief and vanity.

² He sits in the lurking places of the villages. In the secret places does he murder the innocent. His eyes are secretly set against the poor. He lies in wait secretly as a lion in his den. He lies in wait to catch the poor. He does catch the poor when he draws him into his net. He crouches to the strong ones; and humbles himself, that the poor may fall by his devices. He has said in his heart, God has forgotten. He hides his face; he will never see it.

³ Arise, O Lord. O God, lift up your hand. Forget not the humble. The wicked despise God; wherefore, he does say in his heart, You will not require iniquity at my hand. O Lord, you have seen all this, for you behold mischief and spite, to repay with your hand. The poor commits himself unto you; you are the helper of the fatherless. O Lord,

you will break the arm of the wicked, and of the evil; and seek out his wickedness until you find none that remain. And the Lord shall be King for ever and ever over his people; for the wicked shall perish out of his land. Lord, you have heard the desire of the humble. You will prepare their heart. You will cause your ear to hear, to judge the fatherless and the oppressed, that the man of the earth may no more oppress.

PSALM 11

To the chief musician, a psalm of David.

IN that day, you shall come, O Lord, and I will put my trust in you. You shall say unto your people, For my ear has heard your voice. You shall say unto every soul, Flee unto my mountain — and the righteous shall flee like a bird that is let go from the snare of the fowler. For the wicked bend their bow, they make ready their arrow upon the string, that they may secretly shoot at the upright in heart to destroy their foundation. But the foundations of the wicked shall be destroyed, and what can they do?

2 For the Lord, when he shall come into his holy temple, sitting upon God's throne in Heaven, his eyes shall pierce the wicked. Behold, his eyelids shall try the children of men, and he shall redeem the righteous, and they shall be tried. The Lord loves the righteous; but the wicked and him that loves violence, his soul hates. Upon the wicked he shall rain snares, fire, and brimstone, and a horrible tempest — the portion of their cup. For the righteous Lord loves righteousness. His countenance does behold the upright.

PSALM 12

To the chief musician upon Sheminith, a psalm of David.

IN that day, you shall help, O Lord, the poor and the meek of the earth; for the godly man shall cease to be found and the faithful fail from among the children of men. They shall speak vanity, everyone with his neighbor. With flattering lips and with a double heart do they speak. But the Lord shall cut off all flattering lips, the tongue that speaks proud things, who have said, With our tongue will we prevail. Our lips are our own. Who shall be Lord over us? Therefore, thus says the Lord: I will arise in that day. I will stand upon the earth and I will judge the earth for the oppression of the poor, for the sighing of the needy. And their cry has entered into my ear.

2 Therefore, the Lord shall sit in judgment upon all those who say in their hearts, We all sit in safety — and sneer at him. These are the words of the Lord, yea, pure words, like silver tried in a furnace of earth, purified seven times. You shall save your people, O Lord. You shall keep them. You shall preserve them from the wickedness of these generations for ever. The wicked walk on every side and the vilest men are exalted, but in the day of their pride, you shall visit them.

PSALM 13
To the chief musician, a psalm of David.

How long, O Lord, will you withdraw yourself from me? How long will you hide your face from me, that I may not see you? Will you forget me and cast me off from your presence for ever? How long shall I take counsel in my soul, sorrowing in my heart daily? How long shall my enemy be exalted over me? Consider me, O Lord, and hear my cry, O my God, and lighten my eyes lest I sleep the death of the ungodly, lest my enemy say, I have prevailed against him. Those that trouble me rejoice when I am moved. But I have trusted in your mercy. My heart shall rejoice in your salvation. I will sing unto the Lord because he has dealt bountifully with me.

PSALM 14
To the chief musician, a psalm of David.

THE fool has said in his heart, There is no man that has seen God because he shows himself not unto us, therefore there is no God. Behold, they are corrupt. They have done abominable works and none of them does good.

2 For the Lord looked down from Heaven upon the children of men, and by his voice said unto his servant, Seek among the children of men to see if there are any that do understand God. And he opened his mouth unto the Lord and said, Behold all these who say they are yours. The Lord answered and said, They are all gone aside. They are together become filthy. You can behold none of these that are doing good — no, not one. All they have for their teachers are workers of iniquity, and there is no knowledge in them. They are they who eat

up my people. They eat bread and call not upon the Lord. They are in great fear, for God dwells in the generation of the righteous. He is the counsel of the poor because they are ashamed of the wicked and flee unto the Lord for their refuge. They are ashamed of the counsel of the poor because the Lord is his refuge. Oh that Zion were established out of Heaven, the salvation of Israel. O Lord, when will you establish Zion? When the Lord brings back the captives of his people, Jacob shall rejoice, Israel shall be glad.

PSALM 15

A psalm of David.

LORD, who shall abide in your tabernacle? Who shall dwell in your holy hill of Zion? He that walks uprightly, and works righteousness, and speaks the truth in his heart. He that backbites not with his tongue, nor does evil to his neighbor, nor takes up a reproach against his neighbor, in whose eyes a vile person is despised; but he honors them that fear the Lord, swears not falsely to hurt any man, and changes not. He that puts not out his money to usury, nor takes reward against the innocent. He that does these things shall never be moved.

PSALM 16

Michtam of David.

PRESERVE me, O God, for in you do I put my trust. You have said unto me, you are the Lord my God. My goodness is extended unto you, and to all the saints that dwell in the earth, and the excellent, in whom is all my delight. And the wicked, there is no delight in them; Their sorrows shall be multiplied upon all those who hasten to seek another god: Their drink offerings of blood will I not accept, nor take up their names into my lips.

2 Therefore, you, Lord, are the portion of my inheritance, and of my cup; You maintain my lot. The lines are fallen unto me in pleasant places, Yea, I have a goodly heritage. I will bless the Lord, who has given me counsel. My reins also instruct me in the night seasons. I have set the Lord always before me. Because he is at my right hand, I shall not be moved. Therefore, my heart is glad and my glory rejoices. My flesh also shall rest in hope; for you will not leave my soul in hell, neither will you suffer your Holy One to see corruption. You will show

me the path of life. In your presence is fullness of joy. At your right hand there are pleasures for ever.

PSALM 17

A Prayer of David.

Give me right word, O Lord. Speak and your servant shall hear you. Attend unto my cry and give ear unto my prayer. I come not unto you out of feigned lips. Let my sentence come forth from your presence. Let your eyes behold the things that are equal. You have proved my heart. You have visited me in the night. You have tried me. You shall find nothing evil in me, for I am purposed. My mouth shall not transgress concerning the works of men. By the word of your lips I have kept out of the paths of the destroyer. Hold up my goings in your paths, that my footsteps slip not.

2 I have called upon you for you will hear me, O God, my speech, and incline your ear unto me. Show your marvelous, loving kindness, O you that save them who put their trust in you. By your right hand, from those that rise up, keep me as the apple of the eye. Hide me under the shadow of your wings from the wicked that oppress me. My deadly enemies encompass me about. They are enclosed in their own fat. With their mouth they speak proudly. They have now encompassed us in our steps. They have set their eyes, bowing down to the earth as a lion is greedy of his prey, and as a young lion lurking in secret places.

3 Arise, O Lord, disappoint him; cast him down. Deliver my soul from the wicked by your sword, from men by your strong hand, yea, O Lord, from men of the world, for their portion is in their life, and whose belly you fill with your good things. They are full of children, and they die and leave the rest of their inheritance to their babes. As for me, I will behold your face in righteousness. I shall be satisfied when I awake with your likeness.

PSALM 18

To the chief musician, a psalm of David, the servant of the Lord who spoke unto the Lord the words of this song in the day that the Lord delivered him from the hand of all his enemies and from the hand of Saul. And he said:

I will love you, O Lord, my strength. The Lord is my rock, and my fortress, and my deliverer, my God, my strength in whom I will trust, my buckler, and the horn of my salvation, and my high tower. I will call upon the Lord for he is to be praised. So shall I be saved from my enemies.

2 The sorrows of death encompassed me and the floods of ungodly men made me afraid. The sorrows of hell encompassed me about. The snares of death confronted me. In my distress I called upon the Lord and cried unto my God. He heard my voice out of his temple, and my cry came before him, even into his ears.

3 Then the earth shook and trembled. The foundations also of the hills moved and were shaken because he was angry. There went up a smoke out of his nostrils, and fire out of his mouth devoured; coals were kindled by it. He bowed the heavens also and came down, and darkness was under his feet. And he rode upon a cherub and did fly, yea, he did fly upon the wings of the wind. He made darkness his secret place, his pavilion round about him were dark waters and thick clouds of the skies. At the brightness that was before him his thick clouds passed, hailstones and coals of fire. The Lord also thundered in the heavens, and the Highest gave his voice: hailstones and coals of fire. Yea, he sent out his arrows and scattered them, and he shot out lightnings and routed them. Then the channels of waters were seen and the foundations of the world were uncovered at your rebuke, O Lord, at the blast of the breath of your nostrils. He sent from above. He took me. He drew me out of many waters. He delivered me from my strong enemy and from them who hated me, for they were too strong for me. They confronted me in the day of my calamity, but the Lord was my support. He brought me forth also into a large place. He delivered me because he delighted in me.

4 The Lord rewarded me according to my righteousness. According to the cleanness of my hands has he recompensed me. For I have kept the ways of the Lord and have not wickedly departed from my God. For all his judgments were before me, and I did not put away his statutes from me. I was also upright before him and I kept myself from my iniquity. Therefore has the Lord recompensed me according to my righteousness, according to the cleanness of my hands in his eyesight. With the merciful you will show yourself merciful. With an upright man you will show yourself upright. With the pure you will show yourself pure. And with the froward you will show yourself froward.

For you will save the afflicted people, but will bring down high looks. For you will light my candle.

⁵ The Lord my God will enlighten my darkness. For by you I have run through a troop and by my God have I leaped over a wall. O God, your ways are perfect. The word of the Lord is tried, is a buckler to all those who trust in him.

⁶ For who is God save the Lord? Or who is a rock save our God? Our God that girds me with strength and makes my way perfect, he makes my feet like hinds' feet and sets me upon my high places. He teaches my hands to war so that a bow of steel is broken by my arms. You have also given me the shield of your salvation, and your right hand has held me up, and your gentleness has made me great. You have enlarged my steps under me that my feet did not slip. I have pursued my enemies and overtaken them. Neither did I return until they were consumed. I have wounded them, that they were not able to rise. They are fallen under my feet. For you have girded me with strength unto the battle. You have subdued under me those that rose up against me. You have also given me the necks of my enemies, that I might destroy them that hate me. They cried but found none to save unto the Lord, but he answered them not. Then did I beat them small as the dust before the wind. I did cast them out as the dirt in the streets.

⁷ You have delivered me from the strivings of the people, and you have made me the head of the heathen. A people whom I have not known shall serve me. As soon as they hear of me, they shall obey me. The strangers shall submit themselves unto me. The strangers shall fade away and be frightened out of their strongholds. The Lord lives, and blessed be my rock and let the God of my salvation be exalted. It is God that avenges me and subdues the people under me, he delivers me from my enemies. Yea, you lift me up above those that rise up against me. You have delivered me from the violent man. Therefore will I give thanks unto you, O Lord, among the heathen, and sing praises unto your name. Great deliverance gives he to his king, and shows mercy to his anointed, to David, and to his seed for ever.

PSALM 19
To the chief musician, a psalm of David.

THE heavens declare the glory of God and the firmament shows his handiwork. Day unto day utters speech, and night unto night shows knowledge. No speech nor language can be if their voice is not heard. Their line is gone out through all the earth, and their words to the end of the world. In them has he set a tabernacle for the sun, which is as a bridegroom coming out of his chamber, and rejoices as a strong man to run a race: his going forth is from the end of the heaven, and his circuit unto the ends of it. And there is nothing hidden from the heat thereof.

2 The law of the Lord is perfect, converting the soul. The testimony of the Lord is sure, making wise the simple. The statutes of the Lord are right, rejoicing the heart. The commandment of the Lord is pure, enlightening the eyes. The fear of the Lord is clean, enduring for ever; the judgments of the Lord are true and righteous altogether, more to be desired are they than gold — yea, than much fine gold; sweeter also than honey and the honeycomb. Moreover, by them is your servant warned, and in keeping of them there is great reward.

3 Who can understand his errors? Cleanse me from secret faults. Keep back your servant also from presumptuous acts. Let them not have dominion over me. Then shall I be upright, and I shall be innocent from the great transgression. Let the words of my mouth and the meditation of my heart be acceptable in your sight, O Lord, my strength and my redeemer.

PSALM 20
To the chief musician, a psalm of David.

THE Lord hear you in the day of trouble. The name of the God of Jacob defend you, send you help from the sanctuary, and strengthen you out of Zion. Remember all your offerings and accept your burnt sacrifice. Selah. Grant according to your own heart and fulfill all your counsel. We will rejoice in your salvation, and in the name of our God we will set up our banners. The Lord fulfill all your petitions.

2 Now I know that the Lord saves his anointed. He will hear him from his holy Heaven with the saving strength of his right hand. Some trust in chariots and some in horses, but we will remember the name of the Lord our God. They are brought down and fallen, but we are risen and stand upright. Save, Lord. Let the king hear us when we call.

PSALM 21

To the chief musician, a psalm of David.

THE king shall rejoice in your strength, O Lord, and in your salvation. How greatly shall he rejoice. You have given him his heart's desire and have not withheld the request of his lips. Selah. For you meet him with the blessings of goodness. You set a crown of pure gold on his head. He asked life of you, and you gave it to him, even length of days for ever and ever, his glory is great in your salvation. Honor and majesty have you laid upon him, for you have made him most blessed for ever. You have made him exceedingly glad with your countenance, for the king trusts in the Lord, and through the mercy of the Most High he shall not be moved.

2 Your hand shall find out all your enemies, your right hand shall find out those that hate you. You shall make them as a fiery oven in the time of your anger. The Lord shall swallow them up in his wrath and the fire shall devour them. Their fruit shall you destroy from the earth, and their seed from among the children of men. For they intended evil against you, they imagined a mischievous device which they are not able to perform. Therefore shall you make them turn their back when you shall make ready your arrows upon your strings against the face of them.

3 Be exalted, Lord, in your own strength; so will we sing and praise your power.

PSALM 22

To the chief musician upon Aijeleth Shahar, a psalm of David.

MY God, why have you forsaken me? My God, hear the words of my roaring. You are far from helping me. O my God, I cry in the daytime, but you answer not, and in the night season, and am not silent. But you are holy that inhabit the Heavens. You are worthy of the praises of Israel. Our fathers trusted in you. They trusted and you did deliver them. They cried unto you and were delivered. They trusted in you and were not confounded.

2 But I am a worm, and loved of no man, a reproach of man and despised of the people. All they that see me laugh me to scorn. They shoot out the lip, they shake the head, saying, He trusted on the Lord, that he would deliver him; let him deliver him, seeing he delighted in him.

3 But you are he that took me out of the womb. You did make me hope when I was upon my mother's breasts. I was cast upon you from the womb. You were my God from my mother's breasts.

4 Be not far from me — for trouble is near — for there is none to help. Many armies have encompassed me; strong armies of Bashan have beset me around. They gaped upon me with their mouths like a ravening and roaring lion. I am poured out like water and all my bones are out of joint. My heart is like wax, it is melted in the midst of my inward parts. My strength is dried up like a potsherd, and my tongue cleaves to my jaws, and you have brought me into the dust of death. For dogs have encompassed me, the assembly of the wicked have enclosed me. They pierced my hands and my feet. I may tally all my bones. They look and stare upon me. They part my garments among them and cast lots upon my vesture. But be not far from me, O Lord. O my strength, hasten to help me. Deliver my soul from the sword, my darling from the power of the dog. Save me from the lion's mouth, for you have heard me speak from the secret places of the wilderness through the horns of the re'em.

5 I will declare your name unto my brethren. In the midst of the congregation will I praise you. You that fear the Lord, praise him; all you, the seed of Jacob, glorify him; and fear him, all you, the seed of Israel. For he has not despised nor abhorred the affliction of the afflicted. Neither has he hidden his face from him, but when he cried unto him, he heard. My praise shall be of you in the great congregation. I will pay my vows before them that fear him. The meek shall eat and be satisfied. They shall praise the Lord that seek him. Your heart shall live for ever. All the ends of the world shall remember and turn unto the Lord, and all the kindreds of the nations shall worship before you. For the kingdom is the Lord's and he is the governor among the nations. All they that are fat upon earth shall eat and worship. All they that go

down to the dust shall bow before him, and none can keep alive his own soul. A seed shall serve him; it shall be accounted to the Lord for a generation. They shall come and shall declare his righteousness unto a people that shall be born — what he has done.

PSALM 23
A psalm of David.

THE Lord is my shepherd. I shall not lack. He makes me to lie down in green pastures. He leads me beside the still waters. He restores my soul. He leads me in the paths of righteousness for his name's sake. Yea, though I walk through the valley of the shadow of death, I will fear no evil, for you are with me. Your rod and your staff — they comfort me.

2 You prepare a table before me in the presence of my enemies. You anoint my head with oil. My cup runs over. Surely goodness and mercy shall follow me all the days of my life, and I will dwell in the house of the Lord for ever.

PSALM 24
A psalm of David.

THE earth is the Lord's, and the fullness thereof — the world and they that dwell therein. For he has founded it upon the seas and established it upon the waters. Who shall ascend into the hill of the Lord? Or who shall stand in his holy place? He that has clean hands and a pure heart, who has not lifted up his soul unto vanity nor sworn deceitfully. He shall receive the blessing from the Lord and righteousness from the God of his salvation. This is the generation of them that seek him, that seek your face, O Jacob. Selah.

2 Lift up your heads, O you generations of Jacob, and be lifted up. And the Lord, strong and mighty — the Lord, mighty in battle, who is the King of glory — shall establish you for ever. And he will roll away the heavens and will come down to redeem his people, to make you an everlasting name, to establish you upon his everlasting rock. Lift up your heads, O you generations of Jacob. Lift up your heads, you everlasting generations. And the Lord of Hosts, the King of kings, even the King of glory shall come unto you, and shall redeem his people, and shall establish them in righteousness. Selah.

PSALM 25
A psalm of David.

UNTO you, O Lord, do I lift up my soul. O my God, I trust in you. Let me not be ashamed. Let not my enemies triumph over me. Yea, let none that wait on you be ashamed. Let them be ashamed who transgress without cause. Show me your ways, O Lord. Teach me your paths. Lead me in your truth and teach me, for you are the God of my salvation. On you do I wait all day. Remember, O Lord, your tender mercies and your loving kindnesses, for they have been ever of old. Remember not the sins of my youth nor my transgressions. According to your mercy remember me, for your goodness' sake, O Lord.

2 Good and upright is the Lord, therefore will he teach sinners in the way. The meek will he guide in judgment and the meek will he teach his way. All the paths of the Lord are mercy and truth unto such as keep his covenant and his testimonies.

3 For your name's sake, O Lord, pardon my iniquity, for it is great. What man is he that fears the Lord? Him shall he teach in the way that he shall choose. His soul shall dwell at ease and his seed shall inherit the earth. The secret of the Lord is with them that fear him, and he will show them his covenant. My eyes are ever toward the Lord, for he shall pluck my feet out of the net.

4 Turn unto me and have mercy upon me, for I am desolate and afflicted. The troubles of my heart are enlarged. O bring me out of my distresses. Look upon my affliction and my pain and forgive all my sins. Consider my enemies, for they are many and they hate me with cruel hatred. O keep my soul and deliver me. Let me not be ashamed, for I put my trust in you. Let integrity and uprightness preserve me, for I wait on you. Redeem Israel, O God, out of all his troubles.

PSALM 26
A psalm of David.

JUDGE me, O Lord, for I have walked in my integrity. I have trusted also in the Lord. Therefore, I shall not slide. Examine me, O Lord, and prove me. Try my reins and my heart, for your loving kindness is before my eyes and I have walked in your truth. I have not sat with vain people, neither will I go in with deceivers. I have hated the congregation of evildoers and will not sit with the wicked. I will wash my hands in innocence; so will I go about your altar, O Lord, that I may publish with the voice of thanksgiving and tell of all your wondrous works. Lord, I have loved the habitation of your house and the place where your honor dwells.

2 Gather not my soul with sinners, nor my life with bloody men in whose hands is mischief — and their right hand is full of bribes. But as for me, I will walk in my integrity. Redeem me and be merciful unto me. My foot stands in an even place. In the congregations will I bless the Lord.

PSALM 27
A psalm of David.

THE Lord is my light and my salvation. Whom shall I fear? The Lord is the strength of my life. Of whom shall I be afraid? When the wicked, even my enemies and my foes, came upon me to eat up my flesh, they stumbled and fell. Though a host should encamp against me, my heart shall not fear. Though war should rise against me, in this I am confident. One thing have I desired of the Lord that I will seek after: that I may dwell in the house of the Lord all the days of my life, to behold the beauty of the Lord and to inquire in his temple. For in the time of trouble, he shall hide me in his pavilion. In the secret of his tabernacle shall he hide me. He shall set me up upon a rock. And now shall my head be lifted up above my enemies round about me. Therefore will I offer in his tabernacle sacrifices of joy. I will sing, yea, I will sing praises unto the Lord.

2 Hear, O Lord, when I cry with my voice. Have mercy also upon me and answer me. When you said, Seek my face — my heart said unto you, Your face, Lord, will I seek. Hide not your face far from me. Put not your servant away in anger. You have been my help. Leave me not, neither forsake me, O God of my salvation. When my father and my mother forsake me, then the Lord will take me up. Teach me your way, O Lord, and lead me in a plain path because of my enemies. Deliver me not over unto the will of my enemies, for false witnesses are risen up against me, and such as breathe out cruelty. Unless I had believed to see the goodness of the Lord in the land of the living, you would deliver

my soul into hell. You did say unto me, Wait on the Lord, be of good courage, and he shall strengthen your heart. Wait, I say, on the Lord.

PSALM 28
A psalm of David.

UNTO you will I cry, O Lord, my rock. Be not silent to me, lest if you be silent to me, I become like them that go down into the pit. Hear the voice of my supplications when I cry unto you, when I lift up my hands toward your Holy of Holies. Draw me not away with the wicked and with the workers of iniquity who speak peace to their neighbors, but mischief is in their hearts. Give them according to their deeds and according to the wickedness of their endeavors. Give them after the work of their hands. Render to them their desert. Because they regard not the works of the Lord nor the operation of his hands, he shall destroy them and not build them up.

2 Blessed be the Lord because he has heard the voice of my supplications. The Lord is my strength and my shield. My heart trusted in him and I am helped. Therefore, my heart greatly rejoices and with my song will I praise him. The Lord is their strength, and he is the saving strength of his anointed. Save your people and bless your inheritance. Feed them also, and lift them up for ever.

PSALM 29
A psalm of David.

GIVE unto the Lord, O you mighty. Give unto the Lord glory and strength. Give unto the Lord the glory due unto his name. Worship the Lord in the beauty of holiness. The voice of the Lord is upon the waters. The God of glory thunders. The Lord is upon many waters. The voice of the Lord is powerful. The voice of the Lord is full of majesty. The voice of the Lord breaks the cedars; yea, the Lord breaks the cedars of Lebanon. He makes them also to skip like a calf — Lebanon and Sirion like a young re'em. The voice of the Lord divides the flames of fire. The voice of the Lord shakes the wilderness; the Lord shakes the wilderness of Kadesh. The voice of the Lord makes the hinds to calve and strips bare the forests. And in his temple does everyone speak of his glory. The Lord sits upon the flood. Yea, the Lord sits King for ever. The Lord will give strength unto his people. The Lord will bless his people with peace.

PSALM 30

A psalm and song at the dedication of the house of David.

I WILL extol you, O Lord, for you have lifted me up and have not made my foes to rejoice over me. O Lord my God, I cried unto you and you have healed me. O Lord, you have brought up my soul from the grave. You have kept me alive that I should not go down to the pit. Sing unto the Lord, O saints of his, and give thanks at the remembrance of his holiness. For his anger kindles against the wicked. They repent, and in a moment it is turned away and they are in his favor and he gives them life. Therefore weeping may endure for a night, but joy comes in the morning.

2 And in my prosperity I said, I shall never be moved. Lord, by your favor you have made my mountain to stand strong. You did hide your face and I was troubled. I cried to you, O Lord, and unto the Lord I made supplication. When I go down to the pit, my blood shall return to the dust. I will praise you. My soul shall declare your truth, for what profit am I if I do it not? Hear, O Lord, and have mercy upon me. Lord, be my helper. You have turned for me my mourning into dancing. You have put off my sackcloth and girded me with gladness. To the end that my soul may give glory to your name and sing praise to you and not be silent — O Lord my God, I will give thanks unto you for ever.

PSALM 31

To the chief musician, a psalm of David.

IN you, O Lord, do I put my trust. Let me never be ashamed. Deliver me in your righteousness. Bow down your ear to me. Deliver me speedily. Be my strong rock for a house of defense to save me, for you are my rock and my fortress. Therefore, for your name's sake, lead me and guide me. Pull me out of the net that they have laid secretly for me, for you are my strength. Into your hand I commit my spirit. You have redeemed me, O Lord God of truth. I have hated them that regard lying vanities, but I trust in the Lord. I will be glad and rejoice in your mercy, for you have considered my trouble. You have known my soul in adversities and have not shut me up into the hand of the enemy. You have set my feet in a large room.

2 Have mercy upon me, O Lord, for I am in trouble. My eye is consumed with grief, yea, my soul and my belly. For my life is spent with grief and my years with sighing. My strength fails because of my iniquity and my bones are consumed. I was a reproach among all my enemies — but especially among my neighbors — and a fear to my acquaintance. They that did see me outside fled from me. I am forgotten as a dead man, out of mind. I am like a broken vessel, for I have heard the slander of many. Fear was on every side. While they took counsel together against me, they devised to take away my life.

3 But I trusted in you, O Lord. I said, You are my God. My times are in your hand. Deliver me from the hand of my enemies and from them that persecute me. Make your face to shine upon your servant. Save me for your mercies' sake. Let me not be ashamed, O Lord, for I have called upon you. Let the wicked be ashamed and let them be silent in the grave. Let the lying lips be put to silence which speak grievous things proudly and contemptuously against the righteous.

4 Oh how great is your goodness which you have laid up for them that fear you, which you have wrought for them that trust in you before the sons of men. You shall hide them in the secret of your presence from the pride of man. You shall keep them secretly in a pavilion from the strife of tongues. Blessed be the Lord, for he has shown me his marvelous kindness in a strong city. For I said in my haste, I am cut off from before your eyes. Nevertheless, you heard the voice of my supplications when I cried unto you. O love the Lord, all you his saints, for the Lord preserves the faithful and plentifully rewards the proud doer. Be of good courage and he shall strengthen your heart, all you that hope in the Lord.

PSALM 32

A psalm of David, Maskil.

BLESSED are they whose transgressions are forgiven and who have no sins to be covered. Blessed is the man unto whom the Lord imputes not iniquity and in whose spirit there is no guile.

2 When I kept silence, my spirit failed within me. When I opened my mouth, my bones waxed old through my speaking all the day

long. For day and night, your spirit was heavy upon me. My moisture is turned into the drought of summer. Selah. I acknowledged my sin unto you, and my iniquity have I not hidden. I said, I will confess my transgressions unto the Lord — and you forgave the iniquity of my sin. Selah. For this shall everyone that is godly pray unto you in a time when you may be found. Surely in the floods of great waters they shall not come near unto him. You are my hiding place. You shall preserve me from trouble. You shall encompass me about with songs of deliverance. Selah.

3 You have said, I will instruct you and teach you in the way which you shall go. I will guide you with my eye. Be not as the horse or as the mule which have no understanding, whose mouth must be held in with bit and bridle lest they come near unto you. Many sorrows shall be to the wicked, but he that trusts in the Lord — mercy shall encompass him about. Be glad in the Lord and rejoice, you righteous, and shout for joy, all you that are upright in heart.

PSALM 33

REJOICE in the Lord, O you righteous. To praise the Lord is comely for the upright in heart. Praise the Lord with your voice. Sing unto him with the psaltery and harp, an instrument with ten strings. Sing unto him a new song. Play skillfully with a loud noise.

2 For the word of the Lord is given to the upright and all his works are done in truth. He loves righteousness and judgment. The earth is full of the goodness of the Lord. By the word of the Lord were the heavens made, and all the host of them by the breath of his mouth. He gathers the waters of the sea together as a heap. He lays up the deep in storehouses. Let all the earth fear the Lord. Let all the inhabitants of the world stand in awe of him. For he spoke, and it was finished. He commanded, and it stood fast. The Lord brings the counsel of the heathen to naught. He makes the devices of the people of no effect. The counsel of the Lord stands for ever and the thoughts of his heart are to all generations. Blessed are the nations and the people whom the Lord God has chosen for his own inheritance.

3 The Lord looks from Heaven, he beholds all the sons of men. From the place of his habitation, he looks upon all the inhabitants of the earth. He fashions their hearts alike. He considers all their works.

There is no king saved by the multitude of a host. A mighty man is not delivered by much strength. A horse is a vain thing for safety, neither shall he deliver any by his great strength. Behold, the eye of the Lord is upon them that fear him, upon them that hope in his mercy to deliver their soul from death and to keep them alive in a time of famine. Our soul waits for the Lord. He is our help and our shield. For our heart shall rejoice in him because we have trusted in his holy name. Let your mercy, O Lord, be upon us according as we hope in you.

PSALM 34

*A psalm of David when he changed his behavior before Abimelech,
who drove him away and he departed.*

I WILL bless the Lord at all times. His praise shall continually be in my mouth. My soul shall make her boast in the Lord. The humble shall hear thereof and be glad. O magnify the Lord with me and let us exalt his name together.

2 I sought the Lord, and he heard me and delivered me from all my fears. They looked unto him and were lightened, and their faces were not ashamed. This poor man cried, and the Lord heard him and saved him out of all his troubles. The angel of the Lord encamps round about them that fear him and delivers them. O taste and see that the Lord is good. Blessed is the man that trusts in him. O fear the Lord, you his saints, for there is no lack to them that fear him. The young lions do lack, and suffer hunger; but they that seek the Lord shall not lack any good thing.

3 Come, you children, listen unto me. I will teach you the fear of the Lord. What man is he who desires life and loves many days that he may see good? Keep your tongue from evil and your lips from speaking guile. Depart from evil and do good. Seek peace and pursue it.

4 The eyes of the Lord are upon the righteous and his ears are open unto their cry. The face of the Lord is against them that do evil, to cut off the remembrance of them from the earth. The righteous cry and the Lord hears and delivers them out of all their troubles. The Lord is near unto them that are of a broken heart and saves such as be of a contrite spirit. Many are the afflictions of the righteous, but the Lord delivers him out of them all. He keeps all his bones; not one of them is broken. Evil shall slay the wicked and they that hate the righteous

shall be desolate. The Lord redeems the soul of his servants and none of them that trust in him shall be desolate.

PSALM 35
A psalm of David.

PLEAD my cause, O Lord, with them that quarrel with me. Fight against them that fight against me. Take hold of shield and buckler and stand up for my help. Draw out also the spear and stop the way against them that persecute me. Say unto my soul, I am your salvation. Let them be confounded and put to shame that seek after my soul. Let them be turned back and brought to confusion that devise my hurt. Let them be as chaff before the wind and let the angel of the Lord chase them. Let their way be dark and slippery and let the angel of the Lord persecute them. For without cause have they hidden for me their net in a pit which, without cause, they have dug for my soul. Let destruction come upon him unawares, and let his net that he has hidden catch himself; into that very destruction let him fall. And my soul shall be joyful in the Lord, it shall rejoice in his salvation. All my bones shall say, Lord, who is like unto you who delivers the poor from him that is too strong for him? Yea, the poor and the needy from him that spoils him?

2 False witnesses did rise up. They laid to my charge things that I knew not. They rewarded me evil for good, for the purpose of the spoiling of my soul. But as for me, when they were sick, my clothing was sackcloth. I humbled my soul with fasting, and my prayer returned into my own bosom. I behaved myself as though he had been my friend or brother. I bowed down heavily, as one that mourns for his mother. But in my adversity they rejoiced and gathered themselves together. Yea, the abusers gathered themselves together against me and I knew it not. They did tear me, and ceased not. With hypocritical mockers in feasts, they gnashed upon me with their teeth. Lord, how long will you look on? Rescue my soul from their destructions, my darling from the lions. I will give you thanks in the great congregation. I will praise you among many people.

3 Let not them that are my enemies wrongfully rejoice over me. Neither let them wink with the eye that hate me without a cause. For they speak not peace, but they devise deceitful matters against them

that are quiet in the land. Yea, they opened their mouth wide against me and said, Aha, aha, our eye has seen it. This you have seen, O Lord. Keep not silence. O Lord, be not far from me. Stir up yourself and awake to my judgment, even unto my cause, my God and my Lord. Judge me, O Lord my God, according to your righteousness, and let them not rejoice over me. Let them not say in their hearts, Ah, so would we have it. Let them not say, We have swallowed him up. Let them be ashamed and brought to confusion together that rejoice in my hurt. Let them be clothed with shame and dishonor that magnify themselves against me. Let them shout for joy and be glad that favor my righteous cause. Yea, let them say continually, Let the Lord be magnified, who has pleasure in the prosperity of his servant. And my tongue shall speak of your righteousness and of your praise all day long.

PSALM 36
To the chief musician, a psalm of David the servant of the Lord.

THE wicked who live in transgression say in their hearts, There is no condemnation—for there is no fear of God before their eyes. For they flatter themselves in their own eyes until their iniquities are found to be hateful. The words of their mouth are full of iniquity and deceit. The wicked man has left off to be wise and to do good. He devises mischief upon his bed. He sets himself in a way that is not good.

2 O Lord, you are in the heavens; they are full of your mercy. And the thoughts of a righteous man ascend up unto you, whose throne is far above the clouds. He is filled with your righteousness, like the great mountains, and with your judgment, like a great deep. O Lord, you preserve man and beast. How excellent is your loving kindness, O God. Therefore, the children of men put their trust under the shadow of your wings. They shall be abundantly satisfied with the fatness of your house, and you shall make them drink of the river of your pleasures. For with you is the fountain of life. In your light shall we see light.

3 O continue your loving kindness unto them that know you and your righteousness to the upright in heart. Let not the foot of pride come against me, and let not the hand of the wicked remove me. They are the workers of iniquity and shall fall. They shall be cast down and shall not be able to rise.

PSALM 37
A psalm of David.

FRET not yourself because of evildoers, neither be envious against the workers of iniquity. For they shall soon be cut down like the grass and wither as the green herb. Trust in the Lord and do good; so shall you dwell in the land, and truly you shall be fed. Delight yourself also in the Lord and he shall give you the desires of your heart. Commit your way unto the Lord. Trust also in him and he shall bring it to pass. And he shall bring forth your righteousness as the light and your judgment as the noonday. Rest in the Lord and wait patiently for him. Fret not yourself because of him who prospers in his way, because of the man who brings wicked devices to pass. Cease from anger and forsake wrath. Fret not yourself in any way to do evil. For evildoers shall be cut off, but those that wait upon the Lord — they shall inherit the earth; for yet a little while, and the wicked shall not be. Yea, you shall diligently consider his place, and it shall not be. But the meek shall inherit the earth and shall delight themselves in the abundance of peace. The wicked plots against the just and gnashes upon him with his teeth. The Lord shall laugh at him, for he sees that his day is coming. The wicked have drawn out the sword and have bent their bow to cast down the poor and needy and to slay such as be of upright conduct. Their sword shall enter into their own heart and their bows shall be broken. A little that a righteous man has is better than the riches of many wicked; for the arms of the wicked shall be broken, but the Lord upholds the righteous. The Lord knows the days of the upright and their inheritance shall be for ever. They shall not be ashamed in the evil time, and in the days of famine, they shall be satisfied. But the wicked shall perish and the enemies of the Lord shall be as the fat of lambs. They shall consume; into smoke shall they consume away. The wicked borrows and pays not again, but the righteous shows mercy and gives. For such as are blessed of him shall inherit the earth and they that are cursed of him shall be cut off.

2 The steps of a good man are ordered by the Lord and he delights in his way. Though he fall, he shall not be utterly cast down, for the Lord upholds him with his hand. I have been young, and now am old; yet have I not seen the righteous forsaken nor his seed begging bread.

He is ever merciful and lends, and his seed is blessed. Depart from evil, and do good, and dwell for ever. For the Lord loves judgment and forsakes not his saints, they are preserved for ever; but the seed of the wicked shall be cut off. The righteous shall inherit the land and dwell therein for ever. The mouth of the righteous speaks wisdom and his tongue talks of judgment. The law of his God is in his heart. None of his steps shall slide. The wicked watches the righteous and seeks to slay him. The Lord will not leave him in his hand nor condemn him when he is judged.

³ Wait on the Lord and keep his way and he shall exalt you to inherit the land. When the wicked are cut off, you shall see it. I have seen the wicked in great power, spreading himself like a green bay tree. Yet he passed away, and behold, he was not. Yea, I sought him, but he could not be found. Mark the perfect man and behold the upright, for the end of that man is peace. But the transgressors shall be destroyed together. The end of the wicked shall come and they shall be cut off, but the salvation of the righteous is of the Lord. He is their strength in the time of trouble. And the Lord shall help them and deliver them; he shall deliver them from the wicked and save them because they trust in him.

PSALM 38

A psalm of David, to bring to remembrance.

O Lord, rebuke me not in your wrath, neither chasten me in your hot displeasure, for your arrows stick fast in me and your hand presses me heavily. There is no soundness in my flesh because of your anger, neither is there any rest in my bones because of my sin. For my iniquities have gone over my head; as a heavy burden, they are too heavy for me. My wounds stink and are corrupt because of my foolishness. I am troubled. I am bowed down greatly. I go mourning all the day long, for my loins are filled with a loathsome distress and no soundness is found in my flesh. I am feeble, and broken, and very sore. I have wept by reason of the groaning of my heart. Lord, all my desire is before you and my groaning is not hidden from you. My heart pants; my strength fails me. As for the light of my eyes, it also is gone from me.

2 My loved ones and my friends stand aloof because of my sore, and my kinsmen stand afar off. They also that seek after my life lay snares for me, and they that seek my hurt speak mischievous things and imagine deceits all the day long. But I, as a deaf man, heard not, and I was as a dumb man that opens not his mouth. Thus, I was as a man that hears not and in whose mouth are no reproofs. For in you, O Lord, do I hope. You will hear, O Lord my God, for I said, Hear me lest otherwise they should rejoice over me. When my foot slips, they magnify themselves against me; for I am ready to stumble and my sorrow is continually before me. For I will declare my iniquity; I will be sorry for my sin. But my enemies are lively, and they are strong, and they that hate me wrongfully are multiplied. They also that render evil for good are my adversaries because I follow the thing that good is. Forsake me not, O Lord. O my God, be not far from me. Make haste to help me, O Lord, my salvation.

PSALM 39
To the chief musician, even to Jeduthun, a psalm of David.

I SAID, I will take heed to my ways that I sin not with my tongue. I will keep my mouth with a bridle while the wicked is before me. I was dumb with silence. I held my peace, even from good, and my sorrow was stirred. My heart was hot within me. While I was musing, the fire burned.

2 Then spoke I with my tongue, Lord, make me to know my end and the measure of my days, what it is, that I may know how frail I am. Behold, you have made my days as a handbreadth and my age is as nothing before you. Truly every man at his best state is altogether vanity. Selah. Surely every man walks in a vain show. Surely they are disquieted in vain. He heaps up riches and knows not who shall gather them. And now, Lord, what do I wait for? My hope is in you. Deliver me from all my transgressions. Make me not the reproach of the foolish. I was dumb and opened not my mouth because you did chasten me. Remove your stroke away from me or I shall be consumed by the blow of your hand. When you, with rebukes, do correct man for iniquity, you make his beauty to consume away like a moth. Surely every man is vanity. Selah. Hear my prayer, O Lord, and give ear unto my cry. Hold not your peace at my tears, for I am a stranger with you

and a sojourner, as all my fathers were. O spare me that I may recover strength before I go from here and be no more.

PSALM 40

To the chief musician, a psalm of David.

I WAITED patiently for the Lord, and he inclined unto me and heard my cry. He brought me up also out of a horrible pit, out of the miry clay, and set my feet upon a rock and established my goings. And he has put a new song in my mouth, even praise unto our God. Many shall see, and fear, and shall trust in the Lord. Blessed is that man that makes the Lord his trust and respects not the proud, nor such as turn aside to lies. Many, O Lord my God, are your wonderful works which you have done, and your thoughts which are toward us. They cannot be reckoned up in order unto you; if I would declare and speak of them, they are more than can be numbered.

2 Sacrifice and offering you did not desire. My ears have you opened. Burnt offering and sin offering have you not required. Then said I, Behold, I come. In the volume of the book it is written of me. I delight to do your will, O my God, yea, your law is within my heart. I have preached righteousness in the great congregation. Behold, I have not restrained my lips, O Lord, you know. I have not hidden your righteousness within my heart. I have declared your faithfulness and your salvation. I have not concealed your loving kindness and your truth from the great congregation. Withhold not your tender mercies from me, O Lord. Let your loving kindness and your truth continually preserve me.

3 For innumerable evils have encompassed me about. My iniquities have taken hold upon me so that I am not able to look up. They are more than the hairs of my head. Therefore, my heart fails me. Be pleased, O Lord, to deliver me. O Lord, make haste to help me. Let them be ashamed and confounded together that seek after my soul to destroy it. Let them be driven backward and put to shame that wish me evil. Let them be desolate, for a reward of their shame, that say unto me, Aha, aha.

4 Let all those that seek you rejoice and be glad in you. Let such as love your salvation say continually, The Lord be magnified. But I am

poor and needy, yet the Lord thinks upon me. You are my help and my deliverer. Make no delay, O my God.

PSALM 41

To the chief musician, a psalm of David.

BLESSED is he that considers the poor. The Lord will deliver him in time of trouble. The Lord will preserve him and keep him alive, and he shall be blessed upon the earth. And you will not deliver him unto the will of his enemies. The Lord will strengthen him upon the bed of languishing. You will make all his pains to cease when he is laid in his bed of sickness.

2 I said, Lord, be merciful unto me. Heal my soul for I have sinned against you. My enemies speak evil of me: When shall he die and his name perish? And if he come to see me, he speaks vanity. His heart gathers iniquity to itself. When he goes abroad, he tells it. All that hate me whisper together against me, against me do they devise my hurt: An evil disease, say they, cleaves fast unto him, and now that he lies, he shall rise up no more. Yea, my own familiar friend, in whom I trusted, who did eat of my bread, has lifted up his heel against me. But you, O Lord, be merciful unto me and raise me up that I may repay them. By this I know that you favor me: because my enemy does not triumph over me. And as for me, you uphold me in my integrity and set me before your face for ever. Blessed be the Lord God of Israel from everlasting and to everlasting. Amen and Amen.

PSALM 42

To the chief musician, Maskil, for the sons of Korah.

As the hart pants after the water brooks, so pants my soul after you, O God. My soul thirsts to see God, to see the living God. When shall I come and appear before you, O God? My tears have been poured out unto you day and night while my enemies continually say unto me, Where is your God? When I remember these my enemies, I pour out my soul unto you, for I had gone with the multitude. I also went with them to the house of God with the voice of joy and praise, with the multitude that kept holy day. Why are you cast down, O my soul? And why are you disquieted in me? Hope in God, for I shall yet praise him for the help of his countenance.

2 O my God, my soul is cast down within me. Therefore will I remember you from the land of Jordan and of the Hermonites, from the hill Mizar. Deep calls unto deep at the noise of your waterspouts. All your waves and your billows have gone over me.

3 Yet the Lord will command his loving kindness in the daytime, and in the night his song shall be with me and my prayer unto the God of my life. I will say unto God, my rock, Why have you forgotten me? Why do I go mourning because of the oppression of the enemy? As with a sword in my bones, my enemies reproach me while they say daily unto me, Where is your God? Why are you cast down, O my soul? And why are you disquieted within me? Hope in God, for I shall yet praise him who is the health of my countenance and my God.

PSALM 43

JUDGE me, O God, and plead my cause against an ungodly nation. O deliver me from the deceitful and unjust man. For you are the God of my strength. Why do you cast me off? Why do I go mourning because of the oppression of the enemy? O send out your light and your truth. Let them lead me. Let them bring me unto your holy hill and to your tabernacles. Then will I go unto the altar of God, unto God, my exceeding joy. Yea, upon the harp will I praise you, O God my God.

2 Why are you cast down, O my soul? And why are you disquieted within me? Hope in God, for I shall yet praise him who is the health of my countenance and my God.

PSALM 44

To the chief musician, for the sons of Korah, Maskil.

WE have heard with our ears, O God. Our fathers have told us what work you did in their days, in the times of old — how you did drive out the heathen with your hand and planted them, how you did afflict the people and cast them out. For they got not the land in possession by their own sword, neither did their own arm save them, but your right hand, and your arm, and the light of your countenance, because you had a favor unto them. You are my King, O God. Command deliverances for Jacob. Through you will we push down our enemies. Through your name will we tread them under that rise up against us. For I will not trust in my bow, neither shall my sword save me;

but you have saved us from our enemies and have put them to shame that hated us. In God we boast all the day long and praise your name for ever. Selah.

2 But you have cast off and put us to shame, and go not forth with our armies. You make us to turn back from the enemy, and they who hate us spoil for themselves. You have given us like sheep appointed for food and have scattered us among the heathen. You sell your people for naught and do not increase your wealth by their price. You make us a reproach to our neighbors, a scorn and a derision to them that are round about us. You make us a byword among the heathen, a shaking of the head among the people. My confusion is continually before me, and the shame of my face has covered me for the voice of him that reproaches and blasphemes by reason of the enemy and avenger.

3 All this has come upon us, yet have we not forgotten you, neither have we dealt falsely in your covenant. Our heart is not turned back, neither have our steps declined from your way, though you have badly broken us in the place of dragons and covered us with the shadow of death. If we have forgotten the name of our God or stretched out our hands to a strange god, shall not God search this out? For he knows the secrets of the heart. Yea, for your sake are we killed all day long. We are counted as sheep for the slaughter.

4 Awake; why do you sleep, O Lord? Arise; cast us not off for ever. Why do you hide your face and forget our affliction and our oppression? For our soul is bowed down to the dust. Our belly cleaves unto the earth. Arise for our help and redeem us for your mercies' sake.

PSALM 45

To the chief musician upon Shoshannim, for the sons of Korah, Maskil,
a song of loves.

My heart is overflowing with a good matter. I speak of the things which I have made touching the king. My tongue is the pen of a ready writer.

2 You are fairer than the children of men. Grace is poured into your lips. Therefore, God has blessed you for ever. Gird your sword upon your thigh, O Most Mighty, with your glory and your majesty. And in your majesty, ride prosperously because of truth, and meekness, and righteousness. And your right hand shall teach you terrible things.

Your arrows are sharp in the heart of the king's enemies whereby the people fall under you. Your throne, O God, is for ever and ever. The scepter of your kingdom is a right scepter. You love righteousness and hate wickedness. Therefore, God, your God, has anointed you with the oil of gladness above your fellows. All your garments smell of myrrh, and aloes, and cassia, out of the ivory palaces whereby they have made you glad. Kings' daughters were among your honorable women. Upon your right hand did stand the queen in gold of Ophir.

3 Listen, O daughter, and consider, and incline your ear: Forget also your own people and your father's house. So shall the king greatly desire your beauty; for he is your Lord, and worship him. And the daughter of Tyre shall be there with a gift, even the rich among the people shall entreat your favor. The king's daughter is all glorious within; her clothing is of crafted gold. She shall be brought unto the king in raiment of needlework. The virgins, her companions that follow her, shall be brought unto you. With gladness and rejoicing shall they be brought. They shall enter into the king's palace.

4 Instead of your fathers shall be your children, whom you may make princes in all the earth. I will make your name to be remembered in all generations. Therefore shall the people praise you for ever and ever.

PSALM 46
To the chief musician for the sons of Korah, a song upon Alamoth.

GOD is our refuge and strength, a present help in trouble. Therefore, we will not fear though the earth shall be removed, and though the mountains shall be carried into the midst of the sea, and the waters thereof roar, being troubled, and the mountains shake with the swelling thereof.

2 Yet there shall be a river, the streams whereof shall make glad the city of God, the holy of the tabernacle of the Most High. For Zion shall come and God shall be in her midst; she shall not be moved. God shall help her right early. The heathen shall be enraged and their kingdoms shall be moved, and the Lord shall utter his voice, and the earth shall be melted. The Lord of Hosts, who shall be with us, the God of Jacob, our refuge. Selah.

3 Come, behold the works of the Lord, what desolations he shall make in the earth in the latter days. He makes wars to cease unto the

end of the earth. He breaks the bow and cuts the spear asunder. He burns the chariot in the fire and says unto the nations, Be still and know that I am God. I will be exalted among the heathen. I will be exalted in the earth. The Lord of Hosts shall be with us, the God of Jacob, our refuge.

PSALM 47

To the chief musician, a psalm for the sons of Korah.

O CLAP YOUR HANDS, all you people. Shout unto God with the voice of triumph. For the Lord Most High is terrible, he is a great king over all the earth. He shall subdue the people under us and the nations under our feet. He shall choose our inheritance for us, the excellence of Jacob, whom he loved. Selah. God is gone up with a shout, the Lord with the sound of a trumpet. Sing praises to God, sing praises. Sing praises unto our King, sing praises. For God is the King of all the earth, sing praises with understanding. God reigns over the heathen. God sits upon the throne of his holiness. The princes of the people are gathered together, even the people of the God of Abraham, for the shields of the earth belong unto God. He is greatly exalted.

PSALM 48

A song and psalm for the sons of Korah.

G REAT is the Lord and greatly to be praised in the city of our God, in the mountain of his holiness — beautiful for situation, the joy of the whole earth is Mount Zion on the sides of the north, the city of the great King. God is known in her palaces for a refuge, for behold, the kings were assembled, they passed by together. They saw it and so they marveled; they were troubled, and hastened away. Fear took hold upon them there, and pain as of a woman in travail. You break the ships of Tarshish with an east wind. As we have heard, so have we seen in the city of the Lord of Hosts, in the city of our God. God will establish it for ever. Selah.

2 We have thought of your loving kindness, O God, in the midst of your temple. According to your name, O God, so is your praise unto the ends of the earth. Your right hand is full of righteousness. Let Mount Zion rejoice. Let the daughters of Judah be glad because of your judgments. Walk about Zion and go round about her. Tally the

towers thereof. Mark well her bulwarks, consider her palaces, that you may tell it to the generation following. For this God is our God for ever and ever. He will be our guide even unto death.

PSALM 49

To the chief musician, a psalm for the sons of Korah.

HEAR this, all you people. Give ear, all you inhabitants of the world, both low and high, rich and poor together. My mouth shall speak of wisdom and the meditation of my heart shall be of understanding. I will incline my ear to a parable. I will open my dark saying upon the harp.

2 Why should I fear in the days of evil, when the iniquity of my foes shall encompass me about. They that trust in their wealth and boast themselves in the multitude of their riches — none can, by any means, redeem his brother, nor give to God a ransom for him that he should still live for ever, that it ceases not for ever to see corruption. For the redemption of their souls are through God, and precious. For he sees wise men die; likewise, the fool and the brutish person perish, and leave their wealth to others, their inward thought of their houses for ever, their dwelling places, to all generations. Lands they called after their own names, and they are honorable. Nevertheless, man in honor abides not. He is also like the beasts that perish. This I speak of them who walk in their way and forsake the Almighty in their folly, yet their posterity approve their sayings. Selah.

3 Like sheep they are laid in the grave. Death shall feed on them, and the upright shall have dominion over them in the morning, and their beauty shall consume in the grave from their dwelling. But God will redeem my soul from the power of the grave, for he shall receive me. Selah.

4 Be not afraid when one is made rich, when the glory of his house is increased. For when he dies, he shall carry nothing away. His glory shall not descend after him. Though while he lived, he blessed his soul, and men will praise you when you do well to yourself, he shall go to the generation of his fathers; they shall never see light. Man that is in honor, and understands not, is like the beasts that perish.

PSALM 50
A psalm of Asaph.

THE mighty God, even the Lord, has spoken and called the earth from the rising of the sun unto the going down thereof. Out of Zion, the perfection of beauty, God has shined. Our God shall come and shall not keep silence. A fire shall devour before him, and it shall be very tempestuous round about him. He shall call to the heavens from above, and to the earth, that he may judge his people: Gather my saints together unto me, those that have made a covenant with me by sacrifice. And the heavens shall declare his righteousness, for God is judge himself. Selah.

2 Hear, O my people, and I will speak, O Israel, and I will testify against you—I am God, even your God. I will not reprove you for your sacrifices or your burnt offerings continually before me. I will take no bullock out of your house nor he-goats out of your folds. For every beast of the forest is mine, and the cattle upon a thousand hills. I know all the fowls of the mountains, and the wild beasts of the field are mine. If I were hungry, I would not tell you, for the world is mine and the fullness thereof. Will I eat the flesh of bulls or drink the blood of goats? Offer unto God thanksgiving, and pay your vows unto the Most High; and call upon me in the day of trouble. I will deliver you and you shall glorify me.

3 But unto the wicked, God says, What do you have to do with declaring my statutes, or that you should take my covenant in your mouth, seeing you hate instruction and cast my words behind you? When you saw a thief, then you consented with him, and have been partaker with adulterers. You give your mouth to evil and your tongue frames deceit. You sit and speak against your brother, you slander your own mother's son. These things have you done, and I kept silence. You thought that I was altogether such a one as yourself. But I will reprove you and set covenants in order before your eyes. Now consider this, you that forget God, lest I tear you in pieces and none can deliver: whoever offers praise glorifies me, and to him that orders his conduct aright will I show the salvation of God.

PSALM 51

To the chief musician, a psalm of David when Nathan the prophet
came unto him after he had gone in to Bathsheba.

HAVE mercy upon me, O God, according to your loving kindness. According unto the multitude of your tender mercies, blot out my transgressions. Wash me thoroughly from my iniquity and cleanse me from my sin. For I acknowledge my transgressions and my sin is ever before me. Against you, you only, have I sinned and done evil in your sight, that you might be justified when you speak and be clear when you judge. Behold, I was shaped in iniquity, and in sin did my mother conceive me. Behold, you desire truth in the inward parts, and in the hidden part you shall make me to know wisdom.

2 Purge me with hyssop and I shall be clean. Wash me and I shall be whiter than snow. Make me to hear joy and gladness, that the bones which you have broken may rejoice. Hide your face from my sins and blot out all my iniquities. Create in me a clean heart, O God, and renew a right spirit within me. Cast me not away from your presence and take not your holy spirit from me. Restore unto me the joy of your salvation and uphold me with your free spirit. Then will I teach transgressors your ways and sinners shall be converted unto you. Deliver me from bloodguiltiness, O God — you, God of my salvation — and my tongue shall sing aloud of your righteousness. O Lord, open my lips and my mouth shall show forth your praise.

3 For you desire not sacrifice, else would I give it. You delight not in burnt offering. The sacrifices of God are a broken spirit, a broken and a contrite heart. O God, you will not despise.

4 Do good in your good pleasure unto Zion. Build the walls of Jerusalem. Then shall you be pleased with the sacrifices of righteousness, with burnt offering, and whole burnt offering. Then shall they offer bullocks upon your altar.

PSALM 52

To the chief musician, Maskil, a psalm of David when Doeg the Edomite came and told Saul and said unto him, David has come to the house of Ahimelech.

WHY do you boast yourself in mischief, O mighty man? The goodness of God endures continually. Your tongue devises mischiefs, like a sharp razor working deceitfully. You love evil more than good, and lying rather than to speak righteousness. Selah.

2 You love all devouring words, O you deceitful tongue. God shall likewise destroy you for ever. He shall take you away, and pluck you out of your dwelling place, and root you out of the land of the living. Selah. The righteous also shall see, and fear, and shall laugh at him. Behold the man who made not God his strength, but trusted in the abundance of his riches and strengthened himself in his wickedness.

3 But I am like a green olive tree in the House of God. I trust in the mercy of God for ever and ever. I will praise you for ever because you have done wonderful work. I will wait on your name, for you are good before your saints.

PSALM 53

To the chief musician upon Mahalath, Maskil, a psalm of David.

THE fool has said in his heart, There is no God. Such are corrupt and they have done abominable iniquity. There are none that do good. God looked down from Heaven upon the children of men to see if there were any that did understand, that did seek God. Every one of them is gone back. They are altogether become filthy. The workers of iniquity have no knowledge. They eat up my people as they eat bread. They have not called upon God. There is none that does good, no, not one. They were in great fear, for God has scattered the bones of him that encamps against him.

2 O Lord, you have put to shame those who have said in their hearts, There was no fear — because you have despised them. Oh that Zion had come, the salvation of Israel, for out of Zion shall they be judged when God brings back the captives of his people. And Jacob shall rejoice; Israel shall be glad.

PSALM 54

To the chief musician on stringed instruments, Maskil, a psalm of David,
when the Ziphim came and said to Saul,
Doth not David hide himself with us?

SAVE me, O God, by your name, and judge me by your strength. Hear my prayer, O God. Give ear to the words of my mouth. For strangers are risen up against me and oppressors seek after my soul. They have not set God before them. Selah.

2 Behold, God is my helper. The Lord is with them that uphold my soul. He shall reward evil unto my enemies. Cut them off in your truth. I will freely sacrifice unto you. I will praise your name, O Lord, for it is good. For he has delivered me out of all trouble and my eye has seen his desire upon my enemies.

PSALM 55

To the chief musician on stringed instruments, Maskil, a psalm of David.

GIVE ear to my prayer, O God, and hide not yourself from my supplication. Attend unto me and hear me. I mourn in my complaint and make a noise because of the voice of the enemy, because of the oppression of the wicked; for they cast iniquity upon me, and in wrath they hate me. My heart is bitterly pained within me, and the terrors of death are fallen upon me. Fearfulness and trembling have come upon me, and horror has overwhelmed me. And I said, Oh that I had wings like a dove, for then I would fly away and be at rest. Behold, then would I wander far off and remain in the wilderness. Selah. I would hasten my escape from the windy storm and tempest. Destroy, O Lord, and divide their tongues, for I have seen violence and strife in the city. Day and night they go about it, upon the walls thereof. Mischief also and sorrow are in the midst of it. Wickedness is in the midst thereof. Deceit and guile depart not from her streets.

2 For it was not an enemy that reproached me, neither he that hated me that did magnify himself against me. If so, then I could have borne it. I would have hidden myself from him. But it was a man of my equal, my guide and my acquaintance. We took sweet counsel together and walked unto the house of God in company.

³ Let death seize upon them and let them go down quick into hell, for wickedness is in their dwellings and among them. As for me, I will call upon God, and the Lord shall save me. Evening, and morning, and at noon will I pray and cry aloud, and he shall hear my voice. He has delivered my soul in peace from the battle that was against me, for there were many with me. God shall hear and afflict them, even he that abides of old. Selah.

⁴ Because they have no changes, therefore they fear not God. They have put forth their hand against such as be at peace with them. They have broken the Lord's covenant. The words of their mouth were smoother than butter, but war was in their heart. Their words were softer than oil, yet they have drawn swords.

⁵ Cast your burden upon the Lord and he shall sustain you. He shall never suffer the righteous to be moved. But you, O God, shall bring them down into the pit of destruction. Bloody and deceitful men shall not live out half their days, but I will trust in you.

PSALM 56

To the chief musician upon Jonath-elem-rechokim, Michtam of David, when the Philistines took him in Gath.

BE merciful unto me, O God, for man would swallow me up. He, fighting daily, oppresses me. My enemies would daily swallow me up, for they are many that fight against me, O you Most High. What? Am I afraid? I will trust in you. In God I will praise his word. In God I have put my trust. I will not fear what flesh can do unto me. Every day they wrest my words. All their thoughts are against me for evil. They gather themselves together. They hide themselves. They mark my steps when they wait for my soul. Shall they escape by iniquity? In your anger, cast down the people, O God. You tell my wanderings. Put my tears into your bottle. Are they not in your book? When I cry unto you, then shall my enemies turn back. This I know, for God is for me. In God will I praise his word. In the Lord will I praise his word. In God have I put my trust. I will not be afraid what man can do unto me. Your vows are upon me, O God. I will render praises unto you, for you have delivered my soul from death. Will you not deliver my feet from falling, that I may walk before God in the light of the living?

PSALM 57

To the chief musician, Al-taschith, Michtam of David,
when he fled from Saul in the cave.

BE merciful unto me, O God, be merciful unto me, for my soul trusts in you. Yea, in the shadow of your wings will I make my refuge until these calamities are passed over. I will cry unto God Most High, unto God that performs all things for me. He shall send from Heaven and save me from the reproach of him that would swallow me up. Selah. God shall send forth his mercy and his truth. My soul is among lions and I lie even among them that are set on fire, even the sons of men whose teeth are spears and arrows, and their tongue a sharp sword. Be exalted, O God, above the heavens. Let your glory be above all the earth. They have prepared a net for my steps. My soul is bowed down. They have dug a pit before me, into the midst whereof they are fallen themselves. Selah.

2 My heart is fixed, O God, my heart is fixed. I will sing and give praise. Wake up, my glory. Awake, psaltery and harp. I myself will awake early. I will praise you, O Lord, among the people. I will sing unto you among the nations. For your mercy is great unto the heavens and your truth unto the clouds. Be exalted, O God, above the heavens. Let your glory be above all the earth.

PSALM 58

To the chief musician, Al-taschith, Michtam of David.

DO you indeed speak righteousness, O congregation? Do you judge uprightly, O you sons of men? Yea, in heart you work wickedness. You weigh the violence of your hands in the earth. The wicked are estranged from the womb, they go astray as soon as they are born, speaking lies. Their poison is like the poison of a serpent. They are like the deaf adder that stops her ear, which will not listen to the voice of charmers, charming never so wisely. Break their teeth, O God, in their mouth. Break out the great teeth of the young lions, O Lord. Let them melt away as waters which run continually. When he bends his bow to shoot his arrows, let them be as cut in pieces. As a snail which melts, let every one of them pass away, like the untimely birth of a woman, that they may not see the sun. Before your pots can

feel the thorns, he shall take them away as with a whirlwind, both
living and in his wrath. The righteous shall rejoice when he sees the
vengeance. He shall wash his feet in the blood of the wicked, so that
a man shall say, Truly there is a reward for the righteous. Truly he is
a God that judges in the earth.

PSALM 59

To the chief musician, Al-taschith, Michtam of David
when Saul sent and they watched the house to kill him.

DELIVER me from my enemies, O my God. Defend me from them
that rise up against me. Deliver me from the workers of iniquity
and save me from bloody men. For behold, they lie in wait for my soul.
The mighty are gathered against me, not for my transgression nor for
my sin, O Lord. They run and prepare themselves without my fault.
Awake to help me and behold. You, therefore, O Lord God of hosts,
the God of Israel, awake to visit all the heathen. Be not merciful to
any wicked transgressors. Selah. They return at evening. They make
a noise like a dog and go round about the city. Behold, they belch out
with their mouth, swords are in their lips. For who, say they, does hear?

2 But you, O Lord, shall laugh at them. You shall have all the heathen
in derision. Because of his strength will I wait upon you, for God is
my defense. The God of my mercy shall go before me. God shall let me
see my desire upon my enemies. Slay them not lest my people forget.
Scatter them by your power and bring them down, O Lord our shield.
For the sin of their mouth and the words of their lips, let them even
be taken in their pride, and for cursing and lying which they speak.
Consume them in wrath; consume them that they may not be, and let
them know that God rules in Jacob unto the ends of the earth. Selah.
And at evening, let them return and let them make a noise like a dog
and go round about the city. Let them wander up and down for food,
and grudge if they are not satisfied.

3 But I will sing of your power, yea, I will sing aloud of your mercy
in the morning. For you have been my defense and refuge in the day
of my trouble. Unto you, O my strength, will I sing, for God is my
defense and the God of my mercy.

PSALM 60

To the chief musician upon Sushaneduth, Michtam of David,
to teach; when he strove with Aram-naharaim and with Aram-zobah
when Joab returned and smote of Edom in the valley of salt twelve thousand.

O GOD, you have cast us off. You have scattered us. You have been displeased. O turn yourself to us again. You have made the earth to tremble. You have broken it. Heal the breaches thereof, for it shakes. You have shown your people hard things. You have made us to drink the wine of astonishment. You have given a banner to them that fear you, that it may be displayed because of the truth. Selah. That your beloved may be delivered, save with your right hand and hear me.

2 God has spoken in his holiness; I will rejoice. I will divide Shechem and mete out the valley of Succoth. Gilead is mine and Manasseh is mine. Ephraim also is the strength of my head. Judah is my lawgiver. Moab is my washpot. Over Edom will I cast out my shoe. Philistia, triumph because of me. Who will bring me into the strong city? Who will lead me into Edom? Will not you, O God, who had cast us off? And you, O God, who did not go out with our armies? Give us help from trouble, for vain is the help of man. Through God we shall do valiantly, for he it is that shall tread down our enemies.

PSALM 61

To the chief musician upon a stringed instrument, a psalm of David.

HEAR my cry, O God. Attend unto my prayer. From the end of the earth will I cry unto you when my heart is overwhelmed. Lead me to the rock that is higher than I. For you have been a shelter for me and a strong tower from the enemy. I will abide in your tabernacle for ever. I will trust in the cover of your wings. Selah. For you, O God, have heard my vows. You have given me the heritage of those that fear your name.

2 You will prolong the king's life and his years as many generations. He shall abide before God for ever. O prepare mercy and truth which may preserve him. So will I sing praise unto your name for ever, that I may daily perform my vows.

PSALM 62

To the chief musician, to Jeduthun, a psalm of David.

TRULY my soul waits upon God. From him comes my salvation. He only is my rock and my salvation. He is my defense. I shall not be greatly moved. How long will you imagine mischief against a man? You shall be slain, all of you. As a bowing wall shall you be, and as a tottering fence. They only consult to cast him down from his excellence. They delight in lies. They bless with their mouth, but they curse inwardly. Selah.

2 My soul, wait only upon God, for my expectation is from him. He only is my rock and my salvation. He is my defense. I shall not be moved. In God is my salvation and my glory. The rock of my strength and my refuge is in God. Trust in him at all times, you people. Pour out your heart before him. God is a refuge for us. Selah.

3 Surely men of low degree are vanity and men of high degree are a lie. To be laid in the balance, they are altogether lighter than vanity. Trust not in oppression and become not vain in robbery. If riches increase, set not your heart upon them. God has spoken once; twice have I heard this: that power belongs unto God. Also unto you, O Lord, belongs mercy, for you render to every man according to his work.

PSALM 63

A psalm of David, when he was in the wilderness of Judah.

O GOD, you are my God. Early will I seek you. My soul thirsts for you, my flesh longs for you in a dry and thirsty land where no water is. To see your power and your glory, so as I have seen you in the sanctuary. Because your loving kindness is better than life, my lips shall praise you. Thus will I bless you while I live. I will lift up my hands in your name. My soul shall be satisfied as with marrow and fatness, and my mouth shall praise you with joyful lips when I remember you upon my bed and meditate on you in the night watches. Because you have been my help, therefore in the shadow of your wings will I rejoice. My soul follows hard after you. Your right hand upholds me.

2 But those that seek my soul to destroy it shall go into the lower parts of the earth. They shall fall by the sword. They shall be a portion

for foxes. But the king shall rejoice in God. Everyone that swears by him shall glory, but the mouth of them that speak lies shall be stopped.

PSALM 64

To the chief musician, a psalm of David.

HEAR my voice, O God, in my prayer. Preserve my life from fear of the enemy. Hide me from the secret counsel of the wicked, from the insurrection of the workers of iniquity who sharpen their tongue like a sword and bend their bows to shoot their arrows, even bitter words that they may shoot in secret at the perfect. Suddenly do they shoot at him and fear not. They encourage themselves in an evil matter. They speak of laying snares secretly. They say, Who shall see them? They search out iniquities. They accomplish a diligent search. Both the inward thought of every one of them and the heart, is deep.

2 But God shall shoot at them with an arrow; suddenly shall they be wounded. So they shall make their own tongue to fall upon themselves. All that see them shall flee away. And all men shall fear and shall declare the work of God, for they shall wisely consider of his doing. The righteous shall be glad in the Lord and shall trust in him, and all the upright in heart shall glory.

PSALM 65

To the chief musician, a psalm and song of David.

PRAISE waits for you, O God, in Zion, and unto you shall the vow be performed. O you that hear prayer, unto you shall all flesh come. Iniquities prevail against me. As for our transgressions, you shall purge them away. Blessed is the man whom you choose and cause to approach unto you that he may dwell in your courts. We shall be satisfied with the goodness of your house, even of your holy temple.

2 By terrible things in righteousness will you answer us, O God of our salvation, who are the confidence of all the ends of the earth and of them that are afar off upon the sea; who, by his strength, sets fast the mountains, being girded with power; who stills the noise of the seas, the noise of their waves, and the tumult of the people. They also that dwell in the outermost parts are afraid at your tokens. You make the outgoings of the morning and evening to rejoice.

3 You visit the earth and water it. You greatly enrich it with the river of God, which is full of water. You prepare them grain when you have so provided for it. You water the ridges thereof abundantly. You settle the furrows thereof. You make it soft with showers. You bless the springing thereof. You crown the year with your goodness and your paths drop fatness. They drop upon the pastures of the wilderness, and the little hills rejoice on every side. The pastures are clothed with flocks. The valleys also are covered over with grain. They shout for joy, they also sing.

PSALM 66
To the chief musician, a song or psalm.

MAKE a joyful noise unto God, all you lands. Sing forth the honor of his name. Make his praise glorious. Say unto God, How terrible are you in your works. Through the greatness of your power shall your enemies submit themselves unto you. All the earth shall worship you and shall sing unto you. They shall sing to your name. Selah.

2 Come and see the works of God. He is terrible in his doing toward the children of men. He turned the sea into dry land. They went through the waters on foot. There did we rejoice in him. He rules by his power for ever. His eyes behold the nations. Let not the rebellious exalt themselves. Selah. O bless our God, you people, and make the voice of his praise to be heard, which holds our soul in life and suffers not our feet to be moved. For you, O God, have proved us. You have tried us as silver is tried. You brought us into the net. You laid affliction upon our loins. You have caused men to ride over our heads. We went through fire and through water, but you brought us out into a wealthy place.

3 I will go into your house with burnt offerings. I will pay you my vows which my lips have uttered and my mouth has spoken when I was in trouble. I will offer unto you burnt sacrifices of fatlings with the incense of rams. I will offer bullocks with goats. Selah.

4 Come and hear, all you that fear God, and I will declare what he has done for my soul. I cried unto him with my mouth, and he was extolled with my tongue. If I regard iniquity in my heart, the Lord will not hear me. But truly God has heard me. He has attended to

the voice of my prayer. Blessed be God, who has not turned away my prayer, nor his mercy from me.

PSALM 67

To the chief musician on stringed instruments, a psalm or song.

GOD be merciful unto us, and bless us, and cause his face to shine upon us. Selah. That your way may be known upon earth, your salvation among all nations, let the people praise you, O God. Let all the people praise you. O let the nations be glad and sing for joy, for you shall judge the people righteously and govern the nations upon earth. Selah. Let the people praise you, O God; let all the people praise you. Then shall the earth yield her increase, and God, even our own God, shall bless us. God shall bless us, and all the ends of the earth shall fear him.

PSALM 68

To the chief musician, a psalm or song of David.

LET God arise. Let his enemies be scattered. Let them also that hate him flee before him. As smoke is driven away, so drive them away. As wax melts before the fire, so let the wicked perish at the presence of God. But let the righteous be glad. Let them rejoice before God. Yea, let them exceedingly rejoice. Sing unto God. Sing praises to his name. Extol him that rides upon the heavens by his name, Jah, and rejoice before him. A father of the fatherless and a judge of the widows is God in his holy habitation. God sets the solitary in families. He brings out those who are bound with chains, but the rebellious dwell in a dry land.

2 O God, when you went forth before your people, when you did march through the wilderness, Selah, the earth shook, the heavens also dropped at the presence of God; even Sinai itself was moved at the presence of God, the God of Israel. You, O God, did send a plentiful rain whereby you did confirm your inheritance when it was weary. Your congregation has dwelled therein. You, O God, have prepared of your goodness for the poor. The Lord gave the word; great was the company of those that published it. Kings of armies did flee in haste and she that tarried at home divided the spoil. Though you have lain among the pots, yet shall you be as the wings of a dove covered with silver, and her feathers with yellow gold. When the Almighty scattered

kings in it, it was white as snow in Salmon. The hill of God is as the hill of Bashan, a high hill as the hill of Bashan. Why do you leap, you high hills? This is the hill which God desires to dwell in. Yea, the Lord will dwell in it for ever. The chariots of God are twenty thousand, even thousands of angels. The Lord is among them, as in Sinai, in the holy place. You have ascended on high. You have taken captive the captor. You have received gifts for men, yea, for the rebellious also, that the Lord God might dwell among them. Blessed be the Lord who daily loads us with benefits, even the God of our salvation. Selah.

3 He that is our God is the God of salvation, and unto God the Lord belong the escapes from death. But God shall wound the head of his enemies and the hairy scalp of such a one as goes on still in his trespasses. The Lord said, I will bring again from Bashan. I will bring my people again from the depths of the sea, that your foot may be dipped in the blood of your enemies and the tongue of your dogs in the same.

4 They have seen your goings, O God, even the goings of my God, my King, in the sanctuary. The singers went before, the players on instruments followed after. Among them were the damsels playing with tambourines. Bless you, God, in the congregations, even the Lord, from the fountain of Israel. There is little Benjamin with their ruler, the princes of Judah and their council, the princes of Zebulun, and the princes of Naphtali.

5 Your God has commanded your strength. Strengthen, O God, that which you have wrought for us. Because of your temple at Jerusalem shall kings bring presents unto you. Rebuke the company of spearmen, the multitude of the bulls with the calves of the people until everyone submit himself with pieces of silver. Scatter the people that delight in war. Princes shall come out of Egypt. Ethiopia shall soon stretch out her hands unto God.

6 Sing unto God, you kingdoms of the earth. O sing praises unto the Lord. Selah. To him that rides upon the heavens of heavens which were of old, behold, he does send out his voice, and that a mighty voice. Ascribe strength unto God. His excellence is over Israel and his strength is in the clouds. O God, you are terrible out of your holy places. The God of Israel is he that gives strength and power unto his people. Blessed be God.

PSALM 69

To the chief musician upon Shoshannim, a psalm of David.

SAVE me, O God, for the waters have come in unto my soul. I sink in deep mire where there is no standing. I have come into deep waters where the floods overflow me. I am weary of my crying. My throat is dried. My eyes fail while I wait for my God. They that hate me without a cause are more than the hairs of my head. They that would destroy me, being my enemies wrongfully, are mighty. Then I restored that which I took not away. O God, you know my foolishness, and my sins are not hidden from you.

2 Let not them that wait on you, O Lord God of Hosts, be ashamed for my sake. Let not those that seek you be confounded for my sake, O God of Israel, because for your sake I have borne reproach. Shame has covered my face. I am become a stranger unto my brethren and a foreigner unto my mother's children. For the zeal of your house has eaten me up, and the reproaches of them that reproached you are fallen upon me. When I wept and chastened my soul with fasting, that was to my reproach. I made sackcloth also my garment, and I became a proverb to them. They that sit in the gate speak against me, and I was the song of the drunkards.

3 But as for me, my prayer is unto you, O Lord, in an acceptable time. O God, in the multitude of your mercy, hear me in the truth of your salvation. Deliver me out of the mire and let me not sink. Let me be delivered from them that hate me and out of the deep waters. Let not the flood overflow me, neither let the deep swallow me up, and let not the pit shut her mouth upon me. Hear me, O Lord, for your loving kindness is good. Turn unto me according to the multitude of your tender mercies, and hide not your face from your servant, for I am in trouble. Hear me speedily. Draw near unto my soul and redeem it. Deliver me because of my enemies. You have known my reproach, and my shame, and my dishonor. My adversaries are all before you. Reproach has broken my heart, and I am full of heaviness; and I looked for some to take pity, but there was none, and for comforters, but I found none. They gave me also gall for my food, and in my thirst they gave me vinegar to drink.

⁴ Let their table become a snare before them. And that which should have been for their welfare, let it become a trap. Let their eyes be darkened that they see not and make their loins continually to shake. Pour out your indignation upon them and let your wrathful anger take hold of them. Let their habitation be desolate and let none dwell in their tents. For they persecute him whom you have smitten, and they talk to the grief of those whom you have wounded. Add iniquity unto their iniquity and let them not come into your righteousness. Let them be blotted out of the book of the living and not be written with the righteous.

⁵ But I am poor and sorrowful. Let your salvation, O God, set me up on high. I will praise the name of God with a song and will magnify him with thanksgiving. This also shall please the Lord better than an ox or bullock that has horns and hooves.

⁶ The humble shall see this and be glad, and your heart shall live that seek God. For the Lord hears the poor and despises not his prisoners.

⁷ Let the heaven and earth praise him, the seas, and everything that moves therein. For God will save Zion and will build the cities of Judah that they may dwell there and have it in possession. The seed also of his servants shall inherit it, and they that love his name shall dwell therein.

PSALM 70

To the chief musician, a psalm of David, to bring to remembrance.

MAKE haste, O God, to deliver me. Make haste to help me, O Lord. Let them be ashamed and confounded that seek after my soul. Let them be turned backward and put to confusion that desire my hurt. Let them be turned back for a reward of their shame that say, Aha, aha. Let all those that seek you rejoice and be glad in you, and let such as love your salvation say continually, Let God be magnified. But I am poor and needy. Make haste unto me, O God. You are my help and my deliverer. O Lord, make no delay.

PSALM 71

IN you, O Lord, do I put my trust. Let me never be put to confusion. Deliver me in your righteousness and cause me to escape. Incline your ear unto me and save me. Be my strong habitation unto which I may continually come. You have given commandment to save me, for you are my rock and my fortress. Deliver me, O my God, out of the hand of the wicked, out of the hand of the unrighteous and cruel man. For you are my hope, O Lord God. You are my trust from my youth. By you I have been held up from the womb. You are he that took me out of my mother's inward parts. My praise shall be continually of you. I am as a wonder unto many, but you are my strong refuge. Let my mouth be filled with your praise and with your honor all the day.

2 Cast me not off in the time of old age. Forsake me not when my strength fails. For my enemies speak against me and they that lay wait for my soul take counsel together, saying, God has forsaken him, persecute and take him, for there is none to deliver him. O God, do not be far from me. O my God, make haste for my help. Let them be confounded and consumed that are adversaries to my soul. Let them be covered with reproach and dishonor that seek my hurt.

3 But I will hope continually and will yet praise you more and more. My mouth shall show forth your righteousness and your salvation all the day, for I do not know the numbers thereof. I will go in the strength of the Lord God. I will make mention of your righteousness, even of yours only. O God, you have taught me from my youth, and hitherto have I declared your wondrous works; now also, when I am old and gray-headed. O God, forsake me not until I have shown your strength unto this generation and your power to everyone that is to come. Your righteousness also, O God, is very high, who have done great things. O God, who is like unto you? You, who have shown me great and severe troubles, shall quicken me again and shall bring me up again from the depths of the earth. You shall increase my greatness and comfort me on every side. I will also praise you with the psaltery, even your truth, O my God. Unto you will I sing with the harp, O you Holy One of Israel. My lips shall greatly rejoice when I sing unto you, and my soul which you have redeemed. My tongue also shall talk of your righteousness all the day long. For they are confounded, for they are brought unto shame that seek my hurt.

PSALM 72
A psalm for Solomon.

GIVE the king your judgments, O God, and your righteousness unto the king's son. He shall judge your people with righteousness and your poor with judgment. The mountains shall bring peace to the people and the little hills by righteousness. He shall judge the poor of the people. He shall save the children of the needy and shall break in pieces the oppressor. They shall fear you as long as the sun and moon endure, throughout all generations. He shall come down like rain upon the mown grass, as showers that water the earth. In his days shall the righteous flourish, and abundance of peace, so long as the moon endures. He shall have dominion also from sea to sea, and from the river unto the ends of the earth. They that dwell in the wilderness shall bow before him, and his enemies shall lick the dust. The kings of Tarshish and of the isles shall bring presents. The kings of Sheba and Seba shall offer gifts. Yea, all kings shall fall down before him. All nations shall serve him.

2 For he shall deliver the needy when he cries, the poor also, and him that has no helper. He shall spare the poor and needy and shall save the souls of the needy. He shall redeem their soul from deceit and violence, and precious shall their blood be in his sight. And he shall live, and to him shall be given of the gold of Sheba. Prayer also shall be made for him continually, and daily shall he be praised. There shall be a handful of grain in the earth upon the top of the mountains. The fruit thereof shall shake like Lebanon. And they of the city shall flourish like grass of the earth. His name shall endure for ever. His name shall be continued as long as the sun, and men shall be blessed in him. All nations shall call him blessed.

3 Blessed be the Lord God, the God of Israel, who only does wondrous things. And blessed be his glorious name for ever. And let the whole earth be filled with his glory. Amen and amen.

4 The prayers of David, the son of Jesse, are ended.

PSALM 73
A psalm of Asaph.

Truly God is good to Israel, even to such as are of a clean heart. But as for me, my feet were almost gone. My steps had well near slipped. For I was envious at the foolish when I saw the prosperity of the wicked. For there are no bands in their death, but their strength is firm. They are not in trouble as other men, neither are they plagued like other men. Therefore, pride encompasses them about as a chain. Violence covers them as a garment. Their eyes stand out with fatness. They have more than heart could wish. They are corrupt and speak wickedly concerning oppression. They speak loftily. They set their mouth against the heavens, and their tongue walks through the earth. Therefore, his people return here, and waters of a full cup are wrung out to them. And they say, How does God know? And is there knowledge in the Most High? Behold, these are the ungodly who prosper in the world. They increase in riches. Truly I have cleansed my heart in vain and washed my hands in innocence. For all the day long I have been plagued, and chastened every morning.

2 If I say I will speak thus, behold, I should offend against the generation of your children. When I thought to know this, it was too painful for me until I went into the sanctuary of God. Then I understood their end. Surely you did set them in slippery places. You cast them down into destruction. How they are brought into desolation as in a moment. They are utterly consumed with terrors, as a dream when one awakes. So, O Lord, when you awake, you shall despise their image. Thus my heart was grieved, and I was pricked in my reins. So foolish was I, and ignorant. I was as a beast before you.

3 Nevertheless, I am continually with you. You have held me by my right hand. You shall guide me with your counsel and afterward receive me to glory. Whom do I have in Heaven but you? And there is none upon earth that I desire besides you. My flesh and my heart fails, but God is the strength of my heart and my portion for ever. For behold, they that are far from you shall perish. You have destroyed all them that go whoring from you. But it is good for me to draw near to God. I have put my trust in the Lord God, that I may declare all your works.

PSALM 74
Maskil of Asaph.

O GOD, why have you cast us off for ever? Why does your anger smoke against the sheep of your pasture? Remember your congregation, which you have purchased of old; the rod of your inheritance, which you have redeemed; this Mount Zion, wherein you have dwelled. Lift up your feet unto the perpetual desolations, even all that the enemy has done wickedly in the sanctuary. Your enemies roar in the midst of your congregations. They set up their ensigns for signs. A man was famous according as he had lifted up axes upon the thick trees. But now they break down the carved work thereof at once with axes and hammers. They have cast fire into your sanctuary. They have defiled by casting down the dwelling place of your name to the ground. They said in their hearts, Let us destroy them together. They have burned up all the synagogues of God in the land. We see not our signs. There is no more any prophet, neither is there among us any that knows how long. O God, how long shall the adversary reproach? Shall the enemy blaspheme your name for ever? Why do you withdraw your hand, even your right hand? Pluck it out of your bosom.

2 For God is my King of old, working salvation in the midst of the earth. You did divide the sea by your strength. You broke the heads of the dragons in the waters. You broke the heads of leviathan in pieces and gave him to be food to the people inhabiting the wilderness. You did cleave the fountain and the waters. You dried up mighty rivers. The day is yours. The night also is yours. You have established the light and the sun. You have set all the borders of the earth. You have made summer and winter.

3 Remember this: that the enemy has reproached, O Lord, and that the foolish people have blasphemed your name. O deliver not the soul of your turtledove unto the multitude of the wicked. Forget not the congregation of your poor for ever. Have respect unto the covenant. For the dark places of the earth are full of the habitations of cruelty. O let not the oppressed return ashamed. Let the poor and needy praise your name. Arise, O God, plead your own cause. Remember how the foolish man reproaches you daily. Forget not the voice of your enemies. The tumult of those that rise up against you increases continually.

PSALM 75

To the chief musician, Al-taschith, a psalm or song of Asaph.

UNTO you, O God, do we give thanks. Unto you do we give thanks; for your name is near, your wondrous works declare. When I shall receive the congregation, I will judge uprightly. The earth and all the inhabitants thereof are dissolved. I bear up the pillars of it. Selah.

2 I said unto the fools, Deal not foolishly, and to the wicked, Lift not up the horn. Lift not up your horn on high. Speak not with a stiff neck. For promotion comes neither from the east, nor from the west, nor from the south.

3 But God is the judge. He puts down one and sets up another. For in the hand of the Lord there is a cup, and the wine is red. It is full of mixture, and he pours out of the same. But the dregs thereof, all the wicked of the earth shall wring them out and drink them. But I will declare for ever. I will sing praises to the God of Jacob. All the horns of the wicked also will I cut off, but the horns of the righteous shall be exalted.

PSALM 76

To the chief musician on stringed instruments, a psalm or song of Asaph.

IN Judah is God known, his name is great in Israel. In Salem also is his tabernacle, and his dwelling place in Zion. There he broke the arrows of the bow, the shield, and the sword, and the battle. Selah. You are more glorious and excellent than the mountains of prey. The stouthearted are spoiled. They have slept their sleep, and none of the men of might have found their hands. At your rebuke, O God of Jacob, both the chariot and horse are cast into a dead sleep.

2 You, even you, are to be feared. And who may stand in your sight when once you are angry? You did cause judgment to be heard from Heaven. The earth feared and was still when God arose to judgment, to save all the meek of the earth. Selah. Surely the wrath of man shall praise you; the remainder of wrath shall you restrain. Vow and pay unto the Lord your God. Let all that are round about him bring presents unto him that ought to be feared. He shall cut off the spirit of princes. He is terrible to the kings of the earth.

PSALM 77

To the chief musician, to Jeduthun, a psalm of Asaph.

I CRIED unto God with my voice, even unto God with my voice, and he gave ear unto me. In the day of my trouble I sought the Lord. My sore ran in the night and ceased not. My soul refused to be comforted. I remembered God and was troubled. I complained, and my spirit was overwhelmed. Selah. You hold my eyes waking. I am so troubled that I cannot speak. I have considered the days of old, the years of ancient times. I call to remembrance my song in the night. I commune with my own heart, and my spirit made diligent search.

2 Will the Lord cast off for ever? And will he be favorable no more? Is his mercy completely gone for ever? Does his promise fail for ever? Has God forgotten to be gracious? Has he in anger shut up his tender mercies? Selah.

3 And I said, This is my infirmity, but I will remember the years of the right hand of the Most High. I will remember the works of the Lord. Surely, I will remember your wonders of old. I will meditate also of all your work and talk of your doings. Your way, O God, is in the sanctuary. Who is so great a God as our God? You are the God that does wonders. You have declared your strength among the people. You have with your arm redeemed your people, the sons of Jacob and Joseph. Selah.

4 The waters saw you, O God. The waters saw you. They were afraid. The depths also were troubled. The clouds poured out water. The skies sent out a sound. Your arrows also went abroad. The voice of your thunder was in the heaven, the lightnings lightened the world. The earth trembled and shook. Your way is in the sea, and your path in the great waters, and your footsteps are not known. You led your people like a flock by the hand of Moses and Aaron.

PSALM 78

Maskil of Asaph.

G IVE ear, O my people, to my law. Incline your ears to the words of my mouth. I will open my mouth in a parable. I will utter dark sayings of old, which we have heard and known and our fathers have told us. We will not hide them from their children, showing to the generation to come the praises of the Lord, and his strength, and his wonderful works that he has done. For he established a testimony in Jacob and appointed a law in Israel, which he commanded our fathers that they should make them known to their children, that the generation to come might know them, even the children who should be born, who should arise and declare them to their children, that they might set their hope in God and not forget the works of God, but keep his commandments, and might not be as their fathers, a stubborn and rebellious generation — a generation that set not their heart aright and whose spirit was not steadfast with God. The children of Ephraim, being armed and carrying bows, turned back in the day of battle. They kept not the covenant of God, and refused to walk in his law, and forgot his works and his wonders that he had shown them.

2 Marvelous things did he in the sight of their fathers in the land of Egypt, in the field of Zoan. He divided the sea and caused them to pass through, and he made the waters to stand as a heap. In the daytime also he led them with a cloud, and all the night with a light of fire. He cleaved the rocks in the wilderness and gave them drink as out of the great depths. He brought streams also out of the rock and caused waters to run down like rivers.

3 And they sinned yet more against him by provoking the Most High in the wilderness. And they tested God in their heart by asking food for their lust. Yea, they spoke against God. They said, Can God furnish a table in the wilderness? Behold, he smote the rock that the waters gushed out and the streams overflowed. Can he give bread also? Can he provide flesh for his people? Therefore, the Lord heard this and was angry. So a fire was kindled against Jacob, and anger also came up against Israel because they believed not in God and trusted not in his salvation, though he had commanded the clouds from above, and opened the doors of heaven, and had rained down manna upon them to eat, and had given them of the grain of heaven. Man did eat angels' food. He sent them food in abundance. He caused an east wind to blow in the heaven, and by his power he brought in the south wind. He rained flesh also upon them as dust, and feathered fowls like the sand of the sea. And he let it fall in the midst of their camp, round about their habitations. So they did eat and were well filled. For he gave them their own desire. They were not estranged from their lust. But while their food was yet in their mouths, the wrath of God came

upon them and slew the fattest of them and smote down the chosen men of Israel.

4 For all this, they sinned still and believed not for his wondrous works. Therefore, their days did he consume in vanity and their years in trouble. When he slew them, then they sought him, and they returned and inquired early after God, and they remembered that God was their rock and the high God their redeemer. Nevertheless, they did flatter him with their mouth, and they lied unto him with their tongues. For their heart was not right with him, neither were they steadfast in his covenant. But he, being full of compassion, forgave their iniquity and destroyed them not. Yea, many a time he turned his anger away and did not stir up all his wrath; for he remembered that they were but flesh, a wind that passes away and comes not again.

5 How oft did they provoke him in the wilderness and grieve him in the desert! Yea, they turned back and tested God and limited the Holy One of Israel. They remembered not his hand nor the day when he delivered them from the enemy, how he had wrought his signs in Egypt and his wonders in the field of Zoan, and had turned their rivers into blood and their waters, that they could not drink. He sent diverse sorts of flies among them which devoured them, and frogs which destroyed them. He gave also their increase unto the caterpillar and their labor unto the locust. He destroyed their vines with hail and their sycamore trees with frost. He gave up their cattle also to the hail, and their flocks to hot thunderbolts. He cast upon them the fierceness of his anger, wrath, and indignation, and trouble by sending evil angels among them. He made a way to his anger. He spared not their soul from death, but gave their life over to the pestilence and smote all the first born in Egypt, the chief of their strength in the tabernacles of Ham, but made his own people to go forth like sheep, and guided them in the wilderness like a flock. And he led them on safely so that they feared not, but the sea overwhelmed their enemies. And he brought them to the border of his sanctuary, even to this mountain, which his right hand had purchased. He cast out the heathen also before them, and divided them an inheritance by line, and made the tribes of Israel to dwell in their tents.

6 Yet they tested and provoked the Most High God and kept not his testimonies, but turned back and dealt unfaithfully like their fathers.

They were turned aside like a deceitful bow. For they provoked him to anger with their high places and moved him to jealousy with their engraved images. When God heard this, he was angry, and greatly abhorred Israel, so that he forsook the tabernacle of Shiloh, the tent which he placed among men, and delivered his strength into captivity and his glory into the enemy's hand. He gave his people over also unto the sword and was angry with his inheritance. The fire consumed their young men and their maidens were not given to marriage. Their priests fell by the sword and their widows made no lamentation.

7 Then the Lord awoke as one out of sleep, and like a mighty man that shouts by reason of wine, and he smote his enemies in the rear, he put them to a perpetual reproach. Moreover, he refused the tabernacle of Joseph and chose not the tribe of Ephraim, but chose the tribe of Judah, the mount Zion, which he loved. And he built his sanctuary like high palaces, like the earth which he has established for ever. He chose David also, his servant, and took him from the sheepfolds. From following the ewes great with young, he brought him to feed Jacob his people and Israel his inheritance. So he fed them according to the integrity of his heart and guided them by the skillfulness of his hands.

PSALM 79
A psalm of Asaph.

O GOD, the heathen have come into your inheritance, your holy temple they have defiled. They have laid Jerusalem on heaps. The dead bodies of your servants they have given to be food unto the fowls of the heaven, the flesh of your saints unto the beasts of the earth. Their blood they have shed like water round about Jerusalem, and there was none to bury them. We are become a reproach to our neighbors, a scorn and derision to them that are round about us.

2 How long, Lord? Will you be angry for ever? Shall your jealousy burn like fire? Pour out your wrath upon the heathen that have not known you and upon the kingdoms that have not called upon your name, for they have devoured Jacob and laid waste his dwelling place.

3 O remember not against us former iniquities. Let your tender mercies speedily meet us, for we are brought very low. Help us, O God of our salvation, for the glory of your name, and deliver us and purge away our sins for your name's sake. Why should the heathen say,

Where is their God? Let him be known among the heathen in our sight by the revenging of the blood of your servants which is shed. Let the sighing of the prisoner come before you. According to the greatness of your power, preserve those that are appointed to die, and render unto our neighbors sevenfold into their bosom their reproach with which they have reproached you, O Lord, so we your people and sheep of your pasture will give you thanks for ever. We will show forth your praise to all generations.

PSALM 80
To the chief musician upon Shoshannim-Eduth, a psalm of Asaph.

GIVE ear, O Shepherd of Israel, you that lead Joseph like a flock. You that dwell between the cherubim, shine forth. Before Ephraim and Benjamin and Manasseh, stir up your strength, and come and save us. Turn us again, O God, and cause your face to shine, and we shall be saved.

2 O Lord God of Hosts, how long will you be angry against the prayer of your people? You feed them with the bread of tears and give them tears to drink in great measure. You make us a strife unto our neighbors, and our enemies laugh among themselves. Turn us again, O God of Hosts, and cause your face to shine, and we shall be saved.

3 You have brought a vine out of Egypt, you have cast out the heathen and planted it. You prepared room before it and did cause it to take deep root, and it filled the land. The hills were covered with the shadow of it, and the boughs thereof were like the goodly cedars. She sent out her boughs unto the sea and her branches unto the river. Why have you then broken down her hedges so that all they who pass by the way do pluck her? The boar out of the wood does waste it, and the wild beast of the field does devour it. Return, we implore you, O God of Hosts. Look down from Heaven, and behold, and visit this vine and the vineyard which your right hand has planted, and the branch that you made strong for yourself. It is burned with fire. It is cut down. They perish at the rebuke of your countenance. Let your hand be upon the man of your right hand, upon the son of man whom you made strong for yourself, so will not we go back from you. Quicken us, and we will call upon your name. Turn us again, O Lord God of Hosts, cause your face to shine, and we shall be saved.

PSALM 81
To the chief musician upon Gittith, a psalm of Asaph.

SING aloud unto God our strength. Make a joyful noise unto the God of Jacob. Take a psalm and bring here the tambourine, the pleasant harp with the psaltery. Sound the trumpet in the new moon, in the time appointed, on our solemn feast day; for this was a statute for Israel and a law of the God of Jacob. This he ordained in Joseph for a testimony when he went out through the land of Egypt, where I heard a language that I understood not:

2 I removed his shoulder from the burden, his hands were delivered from the pots. You called in trouble, and I delivered you. I answered you in the secret place of thunder. I proved you at the waters of Meribah. Selah. Hear, O my people, and I will testify unto you, O Israel, if you will listen unto me. There shall no strange god be in you, neither shall you worship any strange god. I am the Lord your God who brought you out of the land of Egypt. Open your mouth wide and I will fill it. But my people would not listen to my voice, and Israel would have none of me. So I gave them up unto their own hearts' lust, and they walked in their own counsels. Oh that my people had listened unto me and Israel had walked in my ways. I should soon have subdued their enemies and turned my hand against their adversaries. The haters of the Lord should have submitted themselves unto him, but their time should have endured for ever. He should have fed them also with the finest of the wheat, and with honey out of the rock I should have satisfied you.

PSALM 82
A psalm of Asaph.

GOD stands in the congregation of the mighty, he judges among the gods. How long will you suffer them to judge unjustly, and respect the persons of the wicked? Selah. Defend the poor and fatherless. Do justice to the afflicted and needy. Deliver the poor and needy. Rid them out of the hand of the wicked. They know not, neither will they understand. They walk on in darkness. All the foundations of the earth are out of course.

2 I have said, You are gods, and all of you are children of the Most High. But you shall die like men and fall like one of the princes. Arise, O God, judge the earth, for you shall inherit all nations.

PSALM 83
A song or psalm of Asaph.

KEEP not silence, O God. Hold not your peace, and be not still, O God. For behold, your enemies make a tumult, and they that hate you have lifted up the head. They have taken crafty counsel against your people and consulted against your hidden ones. They have said, Come and let us cut them off from being a nation, that the name of Israel may be no more in remembrance. For they have consulted together with one consent, they are confederate against you: the tabernacles of Edom and the Ishmaelites, of Moab and the Hagrites, Gebal, and Ammon, and Amalek, the Philistines with the inhabitants of Tyre; Assyria also is joined with them. They have helped the children of Lot. Selah.

2 Do unto them as unto the Midianites, as to Sisera, as to Jabin at the brook of Kishon, who perished at Endor. They became as dung for the earth. Make their nobles like Oreb and like Zeeb, yea, all their princes as Zebah and as Zalmunna, who said, Let us take to ourselves the houses of God in possession. O my God, make them like a wheel, as the stubble before the wind, as the fire burns a wood, and as the flame sets the mountains on fire. So persecute them with your tempest and make them afraid with your storm. Fill their faces with shame, that they may seek your name, O Lord. Let them be confounded and troubled for ever. Yea, let them be put to shame and perish, that men may know that you — whose name alone is Jehovah — are the Most High over all the earth.

PSALM 84
To the chief musician upon Gittith, a psalm for the sons of Korah.

How amiable are your tabernacles, O Lord of Hosts. My soul longs, yea, even faints for the courts of the Lord. My heart and my flesh cry out for the living God. Yea, the sparrow has found a house and the swallow a nest for herself where she may lay her young — even your altars, O Lord of Hosts, my King and my God. Blessed are they that dwell in your house. They will be still praising you. Selah. Blessed is the man whose strength is in you, in whose heart are the ways of them who, passing through the valley of Baca, make it a well. The rain also fills the pools. They go from strength to strength. Every one of them in Zion appears before God. O Lord God of Hosts, hear my prayer. Give ear, O God of Jacob. Selah. Behold, O God our shield, and look upon the face of your anointed; for a day in your courts is better than a thousand. I would rather be a doorkeeper in the house of my God than to dwell in the tents of wickedness. For the Lord God is a sun and shield. The Lord will give grace and glory. No good thing will he withhold from them that walk uprightly. O Lord of Hosts, blessed is the man that trusts in you.

PSALM 85
To the chief musician, a psalm for the sons of Korah.

Lord, you have been favorable unto your land. You have brought back the captives of Jacob, you have forgiven the iniquity of your people, you have covered all their sin. Selah. You have taken away all your wrath. You have turned yourself from the fierceness of your anger. Turn us, O God of our salvation, and cause your anger toward us to cease. Will you be angry with us for ever? Will you draw out your anger to all generations? Will you not revive us again, that your people may rejoice in you? Show us your mercy, O Lord, and grant us your salvation.

2 I will hear what God the Lord will speak, for he will speak peace unto his people and to his saints. But let them not return to folly. Surely his salvation is near them that fear him, that glory may dwell in our land. Mercy and truth are met together. Righteousness and peace have kissed each other. Truth shall spring out of the earth, and righteousness shall look down from Heaven. Yea, the Lord shall give that which is good, and our land shall yield her increase. Righteousness shall go before him and shall set us in the way of his steps.

PSALM 86
A Prayer of David.

Bow down your ear, O Lord, hear me, for I am poor and needy. Preserve my soul, for I am holy. O my God, save your servant that trusts in you. Be merciful unto me, O Lord, for I cry unto you daily. Rejoice the soul of your servant, for unto you, O Lord, do I lift up my soul. For you, Lord, are good, and ready to forgive, and plenteous in mercy unto all them that call upon you. Give ear, O Lord, unto my prayer, and attend to the voice of my supplications. In the day of my trouble I will call upon you, for you will answer me. Among the gods there is none like unto you, O Lord, neither are there any works like unto your works. All nations whom you have made shall come and worship before you, O Lord, and shall glorify your name; for you are great and do wondrous things. You are God alone. Teach me your way, O Lord. I will walk in your truth. Unite my heart to fear your name. I will praise you, O Lord my God, with all my heart, and I will glorify your name for ever; for great is your mercy toward me, and you have delivered my soul from the lowest hell. O God, the proud are risen against me, and the assemblies of violent men have sought after my soul and have not set you before them. But you, O Lord, are a God full of compassion, and gracious, long-suffering, and plenteous in mercy and truth. O turn unto me and have mercy upon me. Give your strength unto your servant, and save the son of your handmaid. Show me a token for good, that they who hate me may see it and be ashamed, because you, Lord, have helped me and comforted me.

PSALM 87
A psalm or song for the sons of Korah.

HIS foundation is in the holy mountains. The Lord loves the gates of Zion more than all the dwellings of Jacob. Glorious things are spoken of you, O city of God. Selah. I will make mention of Rahab and Babylon to them that know me. Behold Philistia and Tyre with Ethiopia. This man was born there. And of Zion it shall be said, This and that man were born in her, and the highest himself shall establish her. The Lord shall count when he writes up the people that this man was born there. Selah. As well the singers as the players on instruments shall be there. All my springs are in you.

PSALM 88
A song or psalm for the sons of Korah, to the chief musician
upon Mahalath Leannoth, Maskil of Heman the Ezrahite.

O LORD God of my salvation, I have cried day and night before you. Let my prayer come before you. Incline your ear unto my cry, for my soul is full of troubles and my life draws near unto the grave. I am counted with them that go down into the pit. I am as a man that has no strength, free among the dead, like the slain that lie in the grave whom you remember no more and they are cut off from your hand. You have laid me in the lowest pit, in darkness, in the depths. Your wrath lies hard upon me and you have afflicted me with all your waves. Selah. You have put away my acquaintance far from me. You have made me an abomination unto them. I am shut up and I cannot come forth. My eye mourns by reason of affliction. Lord, I have called daily upon you, I have stretched out my hands unto you.

2 Will you show wonders to the dead? Shall the dead arise and praise you? Selah. Shall your loving kindness be declared in the grave? Or your faithfulness in destruction? Shall your wonders be known in the dark? And your righteousness in the land of forgetfulness?

3 But unto you I have cried, O Lord, and in the morning shall my prayer go before you. Lord, why do you cast off my soul? Why do you hide your face from me? I am afflicted and ready to die from my youth up. While I suffer your terrors, I am distracted. Your fierce wrath goes over me. Your terrors have cut me off. They came round about me daily like water. They encompassed me about together. Loved one and friend you have put far from me, and my acquaintance into darkness.

PSALM 89
Maskil of Ethan the Ezrahite.

I WILL sing of the mercies of the Lord for ever. With my mouth will I make known your faithfulness to all generations. For I have said, Mercy shall be built up for ever. Your faithfulness shall you establish in the very heavens.

2 I have made a covenant with my chosen. I have sworn unto David my servant, Your seed will I establish for ever and build up your throne to all generations. Selah.

3 And the heavens shall praise your wonders, O Lord, your faithfulness also in the congregation of the saints. For who in the heaven can be compared unto the Lord? Who among the sons of the mighty can be likened unto the Lord? God is greatly to be feared in the assembly of the saints and to be had in reverence of all them that are about him. O Lord God of Hosts, who is a strong Lord like unto

you? Or to your faithfulness round about you? You rule the raging of
the sea. When the waves thereof arise, you still them. You have broken
Rahab in pieces as one that is slain. You have scattered your enemies
with your strong arm. The heavens are yours. The earth also is yours.
As for the world and the fullness thereof, you have founded them. The
north and the south, you have created them. Tabor and Hermon shall
rejoice in your name. You have a mighty arm. Strong is your hand, and
high is your right hand. Justice and judgment are the habitation of
your throne. Mercy and truth shall go before your face. Blessed is the
people that know the joyful sound. They shall walk, O Lord, in the
light of your countenance. In your name they shall rejoice all the day,
and in your righteousness shall they be exalted. For you are the glory
of their strength, and in your favor our horn shall be exalted. For the
Lord is our defense and the Holy One of Israel is our king.

4 Then you spoke in vision to your holy one and said, I have laid help
upon one that is mighty, I have exalted one chosen out of the people. I
have found David, my servant. With my holy oil have I anointed him
with whom my hand shall be established. My arm also shall strengthen
him. The enemy shall not exact upon him, nor the son of wickedness
afflict him. And I will beat down his foes before his face and plague
them that hate him. But my faithfulness and my mercy shall be with
him, and in my name his horn shall be exalted. I will set his hand also
in the sea and his right hand in the rivers. He shall cry unto me, You
are my father, my God, and the rock of my salvation. Also, I will make
him my firstborn, higher than the kings of the earth. My mercy I will
keep for him for ever, and my covenant shall stand fast with him. His
seed also will I make to endure for ever, and his throne as the days of
Heaven. If his children forsake my law and walk not in my judgments,
if they break my statutes and keep not my commandments, then will
I visit their transgression with the rod and their iniquity with stripes.
Nevertheless, my loving kindness will I not utterly take from him,
nor suffer my faithfulness to fail. My covenant will I not break, nor
alter the thing that is gone out of my lips; once have I sworn by my
holiness that I will not lie unto David. His seed shall endure for ever,
and his throne as the sun before me. It shall be established for ever as
the moon and as a faithful witness in heaven. Selah.

⁵ But you have cast off and abhorred, you have been angry with your anointed. You have made void the covenant of your servant. You have profaned his crown by casting it to the ground. You have broken down all his hedges. You have brought his strongholds to ruin. All that pass by the way spoil him. He is a reproach to his neighbors. You have set up the right hand of his adversaries. You have made all his enemies to rejoice. You have also turned the edge of his sword and have not made him to stand in the battle. You have made his glory to cease and cast his throne down to the ground. The days of his youth have you shortened. You have covered him with shame. Selah. How long, Lord? Will you hide yourself for ever? Shall your wrath burn like fire? Remember how short my time is. Why have you made all men in vain? What man is he that lives and shall not see death? Shall he deliver his soul from the hand of the grave? Selah. Lord, where are your former loving kindnesses which you swore unto David in your truth? Remember, Lord, the reproach of your servants, how I do bear in my bosom the reproach of all the mighty people with which your enemies have reproached, O Lord, with which they have reproached the footsteps of your anointed. Blessed be the Lord for ever. Amen and amen.

PSALM 90
A Prayer of Moses, the man of God.

LORD, you have been our dwelling place in all generations. Before the mountains were brought forth or ever you had formed the earth and the world, even from everlasting to everlasting, you are God. You turn man to destruction and say, Return, you children of men. For a thousand years in your sight are but as yesterday when it is past and as a watch in the night. You carry them away as with a flood. They are as a sleep. In the morning they are like grass which grows up. In the morning it flourishes and grows up. In the evening it is cut down and withers.

² For we are consumed by your anger, and by your wrath are we troubled. You have set our iniquities before you, our secret sins in the light of your countenance. For all our days are passed away in your wrath. We spend our years as a tale that is told. The days of our years are seventy years. And if by reason of strength they are eighty years,

yet is their strength labor and sorrow, for it is soon cut off and we fly away. Who knows the power of your anger? Even according to your fear, so is your wrath. So teach us to number our days, that we may apply our hearts unto wisdom. Return us, O Lord.

3 How long will you hide your face from your servants, and let them repent of all their hard speeches they have spoken concerning you? O satisfy us early with your mercy, that we may rejoice and be glad all our days. Make us glad according to the days wherein you have afflicted us and the years wherein we have seen evil. Let your work appear unto your servants and your glory unto their children. And let the beauty of the Lord our God be upon us, and establish the work of our hands upon us. Yea, the work of our hands, establish it.

PSALM 91

HE that dwells in the secret place of the Most High shall abide under the shadow of the Almighty. I will say of the Lord, He is my refuge and my fortress. My God, in him will I trust. Surely he shall deliver you from the snare of the fowler and from the noxious pestilence. He shall cover you with his feathers, and under his wings shall you trust. His truth shall be your shield and buckler. You shall not be afraid for the terror by night, nor for the arrow that flies by day, nor for the pestilence that walks in darkness, nor for the destruction that wastes at noonday. A thousand shall fall at your side and ten thousand at your right hand, but it shall not come near to you. Only with your eyes shall you behold and see the reward of the wicked. Because you have made the Lord — who is my refuge, even the Most High — your habitation, there shall no evil befall you, neither shall any plague come near your dwelling. For he shall give his angels charge over you, to keep you in all your ways. They shall bear you up in their hands lest you dash your foot against a stone. You shall tread upon the lion and adder. The young lion and the dragon shall you trample under feet.

2 Because he has set his love upon me, therefore will I deliver him. I will set him on high because he has known my name. He shall call upon me, and I will answer him. I will be with him in trouble. I will deliver him and honor him. With long life will I satisfy him and show him my salvation.

PSALM 92

A psalm or song for the Sabbath day.

IT is a good thing to give thanks unto the Lord and to sing praises unto your name, O Most High, to show forth your loving kindness in the morning and your faithfulness every night, upon an instrument of ten strings, and upon the psaltery, upon the harp with a solemn sound.

2 For you, Lord, have made me glad through your work. I will triumph in the works of your hands. O Lord, how great are your works. And your thoughts are very deep. A brutish man knows not, neither does a fool understand this. When the wicked spring as the grass and when all the workers of iniquity do flourish, it is that they shall be destroyed for ever. But you, Lord, are most high for ever. For behold your enemies, O Lord, for behold, your enemies shall perish. All the workers of iniquity shall be scattered, but my horn shall you exalt like the horn of a re'em. I shall be anointed with fresh oil. My eye also shall see my desire on my enemies, and my ears shall hear my desire of the wicked that rise up against me.

3 The righteous shall flourish like the palm tree, he shall grow like a cedar in Lebanon. Those that are planted in the house of the Lord shall flourish in the courts of our God. They shall still bring forth fruit in old age. They shall be fat and flourishing to show that the Lord is upright. He is my rock, and there is no unrighteousness in him.

PSALM 93

THE Lord reigns. He is clothed with majesty. The Lord is clothed with strength with which he has girded himself. The world also is established that it cannot be moved. Your throne is established of old. You are from everlasting. The floods have lifted up, O Lord, the floods have lifted up their voice. The floods lift up their waves. The Lord on high is mightier than the noise of many waters, yea, than the mighty waves of the sea. Your testimonies are very sure. Holiness becomes your house, O Lord, for ever.

PSALM 94

O LORD God to whom vengeance belongs, O God to whom vengeance belongs, show yourself. Lift yourself up, you judge of the earth. Render a reward to the proud. Lord, how long shall the wicked, how long shall the wicked triumph? How long shall they utter and speak hard things, and all the workers of iniquity boast themselves? They break in pieces your people, O Lord, and afflict your heritage. They slay the widow and the stranger, and murder the fatherless. Yet they say, The Lord shall not see, neither shall the God of Jacob regard it.

2 Understand, you brutish among the people; and you fools, when will you be wise? He that planted the ear, shall he not hear? He that formed the eye, shall he not see? He that chastises the heathen, shall he not correct? He that teaches man knowledge, shall he not know? The Lord knows the thoughts of man, that they are vanity.

3 Blessed is the man whom you chasten, O Lord, and teach him out of your law, that you may give him rest from the days of adversity until the pit be dug for the wicked. For the Lord will not cast off his people, neither will he forsake his inheritance. But judgment shall return unto righteousness, and all the upright in heart shall follow it.

4 Who will rise up for me against the evildoers? Or who will stand up for me against the workers of iniquity? Unless the Lord had been my help, my soul would have almost dwelled in silence. When I said, My foot slips—your mercy, O Lord, held me up. In the multitude of my thoughts within me, your comforts delight my soul.

5 Shall the throne of iniquity have fellowship with you, which frames mischief by a law? They gather themselves together against the soul of the righteous and condemn the innocent blood. But the Lord is my defense, and my God is the rock of my refuge. And he shall bring upon them their own iniquity and shall cut them off in their own wickedness. Yea, the Lord our God shall cut them off.

PSALM 95

O COME let us sing unto the Lord, let us make a joyful noise to the rock of our salvation. Let us come before his presence with thanksgiving and make a joyful noise unto him with psalms. For the Lord is a great God and a great King above all gods. In his hand are the deep places of the earth. The strength of the hills is his also. The sea is his, and he made it, and his hands formed the dry land. O come let us worship and bow down. Let us kneel before the Lord our maker.

² For he is our God, and we are the people of his pasture and the sheep of his hand. Today if you will hear his voice, harden not your heart as in the provocation, and as in the day of temptation in the wilderness, when your fathers tested me, proved me, and saw my work. Forty years long was I grieved with this generation, and said, It is a people that do err in their heart, and they have not known my ways, unto whom I swore in my wrath that they should not enter into my rest.

PSALM 96

O SING unto the Lord a new song. Sing unto the Lord, all the earth. Sing unto the Lord. Bless his name. Show forth his salvation from day to day. Declare his glory among the heathen, his wonders among all people. For the Lord is great, and greatly to be praised. He is to be feared above all gods, for all the gods of the nations are idols. But the Lord made the heavens. Honor and majesty are before him. Strength and beauty are in his sanctuary. Give unto the Lord, O you kindreds of the people, give unto the Lord glory and strength. Give unto the Lord the glory due unto his name. Bring an offering and come into his courts. O worship the Lord in the beauty of holiness. Fear before him, all the earth. Say among the heathen that the Lord reigns. The world also shall be established that it shall not be moved. He shall judge the people righteously. Let the heavens rejoice and let the earth be glad. Let the sea roar and the fullness thereof. Let the field be joyful and all that is therein. Then shall all the trees of the wood rejoice before the Lord, for he comes, for he comes to judge the earth. He shall judge the world with righteousness and the people with his truth.

PSALM 97

THE Lord reigns. Let the earth rejoice. Let the multitude of isles be glad. Clouds and darkness are round about him. Righteousness and judgment are the habitation of his throne. A fire goes before him and burns up his enemies round about. His lightnings enlightened the world; the earth saw and trembled. The hills melted like wax at the presence of the Lord, at the presence of the Lord of the whole earth. The heavens declare his righteousness, and all the people see his glory. Confounded be all they that serve engraved images, that boast themselves of idols. Worship him, all you gods. Zion heard and was glad, and the daughters of Judah rejoiced because of your judgments, O Lord. For you, Lord, are high above all the earth. You are exalted far above all gods. You that love the Lord hate evil. He preserves the souls of his saints, he delivers them out of the hand of the wicked. Light is sown for the righteous and gladness for the upright in heart. Rejoice in the Lord, you righteous, and give thanks at the remembrance of his holiness.

PSALM 98
A psalm.

O SING unto the Lord a new song, for he has done marvelous things. His right hand and his holy arm has gotten him the victory. The Lord has made known his salvation. His righteousness has he openly shown in the sight of the heathen. He has remembered his mercy and his truth toward the house of Israel. All the ends of the earth have seen the salvation of our God. Make a joyful noise unto the Lord, all the earth. Make a loud noise and rejoice and sing praise. Sing unto the Lord with the harp—with the harp and the voice of a psalm. With trumpets and sound of horn, make a joyful noise before the Lord, the King. Let the sea roar and the fullness thereof, the world and they that dwell therein. Let the waters clap their hands. Let the hills be joyful together before the Lord, for he comes to judge the earth. With righteousness shall he judge the world, and the people with equity.

PSALM 99

T HE Lord reigns. Let the people tremble. He sits between the cherubim. Let the earth be moved. The Lord is great in Zion and he is high above all the people. Let them praise your great and terrible name, for it is holy. The king's strength also loves judgment. You do establish equity. You execute judgment and righteousness in Jacob. Exalt the Lord our God and worship at his footstool, for he is holy.

2 Moses and Aaron among his priests, and Samuel among them that call upon his name, they called upon the Lord and he answered them. He spoke unto them in the cloudy pillar. They kept his testimonies and the ordinance that he gave them. You answered them, O Lord our God. You were a God that forgave them, though you took vengeance of their inventions.

³ Exalt the Lord our God and worship at his holy hill, for the Lord our God is holy.

PSALM 100

A psalm of praise.

MAKE a joyful noise unto the Lord, all you lands. Serve the Lord with gladness. Come before his presence with singing. Know that the Lord, he is God. It is he that has made us, and not we ourselves. We are his people and the sheep of his pasture. Enter into his gates with thanksgiving and into his courts with praise. Be thankful unto him and bless his name, for the Lord is good. His mercy is everlasting, and his truth endures to all generations.

PSALM 101

A psalm of David.

I WILL sing of mercy and judgment. Unto you, O Lord, will I sing. I will behave myself wisely in a perfect way. O when will you come unto me? I will walk within my house with a perfect heart. I will set no wicked thing before my eyes. I hate the work of them that turn aside, it shall not cleave to me. A froward heart shall depart from me. I will not know a wicked person. Whoever secretly slanders his neighbor, him will I cut off. Him that has a high look and a proud heart, I will not suffer. My eyes shall be upon the faithful of the land that they may dwell with me. He that walks in a perfect way, he shall serve me. He that works deceit shall not dwell within my house. He that tells lies shall not remain in my sight. I will early destroy all the wicked of the land, that I may cut off all wicked doers from the city of the Lord.

PSALM 102

A prayer of the afflicted, when he is overwhelmed,
and pours out his complaint before the Lord.

HEAR my prayer, O Lord, and let my cry come unto you. Hide not your face from me in the day when I am in trouble. Incline your ear unto me. In the day when I call, answer me speedily. For my days are consumed like smoke, and my bones are burned as a hearth. My heart is smitten and withered like grass, so that I forget to eat my bread. By reason of the voice of my groaning, my bones cleave to my skin. I am

like a pelican of the wilderness. I am like an owl of the desert. I watch
and am as a sparrow alone upon the housetop. My enemies reproach
me all the day, and they that are mad against me are sworn against me.
For I have eaten ashes like bread and mingled my drink with weeping
because of your indignation and your wrath. For you have lifted me
up and cast me down. My days are like a shadow that declines, and I
am withered like grass.

2 But you, O Lord, shall endure for ever, and your remembrance
unto all generations. You shall arise and have mercy upon Zion, for
the time to favor her, yea, the set time has come. For your servants
take pleasure in her stones, and favor the dust thereof. So the heathen
shall fear the name of the Lord, and all the kings of the earth your
glory. When the Lord shall build up Zion, he shall appear in his glory.
He will regard the prayer of the destitute and not despise their prayer.
This shall be written for the generation to come. And the people who
shall be gathered shall praise the Lord, for he has looked down from
the height of his sanctuary. From Heaven did the Lord behold the
earth, to hear the groaning of the prisoner, to release those that are
appointed to death, to declare the name of the Lord in Zion and his
praise in Jerusalem, when the people are gathered together, and the
kingdoms, to serve the Lord.

3 He weakened my strength in the way; he shortened my days. I said,
O my God, take me not away in the middle of my days. Your years are
throughout all generations. Of old you have laid the foundation of the
earth, and the heavens are the work of your hands. They shall perish,
but you shall endure. Yea, all of them shall wax old like a garment. As
a vesture shall you change them, and they shall be changed. But you
are the same, and your years shall have no end. The children of your
servants shall continue, and their seed shall be established before you.

PSALM 103
A psalm of David.

BLESS the Lord, O my soul, and all that is within me, bless his
holy name. Bless the Lord, O my soul, and forget not all his
benefits — who forgives all your iniquities, who heals all your diseases,
who redeems your life from destruction, who crowns you with loving
kindness and tender mercies, who satisfies your mouth with good

things, so that your youth is renewed like the eagle's. The Lord executes righteousness and judgment for all that are oppressed. He made known his ways unto Moses, his acts unto the children of Israel. The Lord is merciful and gracious, slow to anger and plenteous in mercy. He will not always chide, neither will he keep his anger for ever. He has not dealt with us after our sins nor rewarded us according to our iniquities. For as the heaven is high above the earth, so great is his mercy toward them that fear him. As far as the east is from the west, so far has he removed our transgressions from us. Like a father pities his children, so the Lord pities them that fear him; for he knows our frame, he remembers that we are dust.

2 As for man, his days are as grass. As a flower of the field, so he flourishes. For the wind passes over it, and it is gone, and the place thereof shall know it no more. But the mercy of the Lord is from everlasting to everlasting upon them that fear him, and his righteousness unto children's children — to such as keep his covenant and to those that remember his commandments to do them. The Lord has prepared his throne in the Heavens, and his kingdom rules over all. Bless the Lord, you his angels that excel in strength, that do his commandments, listening unto the voice of his word. Bless the Lord, all you his hosts, you ministers of his that do his pleasure. Bless the Lord, all his works in all places of his dominion. Bless the Lord, O my soul.

PSALM 104

Bless the Lord, O my soul. O Lord my God, you are very great. You are clothed with honor and majesty — who covers yourself with light as with a garment; who stretches out the heavens like a curtain; who lays the beams of his chambers in the waters; who makes the clouds his chariot; who walks upon the wings of the wind; who makes his angels spirits, his ministers a flaming fire; who laid the foundations of the earth, that it should not be removed for ever.

2 You covered it with the deep as with a garment. The waters stood above the mountains. At your rebuke, they fled; at the voice of your thunder, they hastened away. They go up by the mountains, they go down by the valleys, unto the place which you have founded for them. You have set a bound that they may not pass over, that they turn not again to cover the earth. He sends the springs into the valleys which

run among the hills. They give drink to every beast of the field. The wild asses quench their thirst. By them shall the fowls of the heaven have their habitation, which sing among the branches. He waters the hills from his chambers.

3 The earth is satisfied with the fruit of your works. He causes the grass to grow for the cattle, and herb for the service of man, that he may bring forth food out of the earth, and wine that makes glad the heart of man, and oil to make his face to shine, and bread which strengthens man's heart. The trees of the Lord are full of sap, the cedars of Lebanon which he has planted, where the birds make their nests. As for the stork, the fir trees are her house; the high hills are a refuge for the wild goats and the rocks for the conies.

4 He appointed the moon for seasons. The sun knows his going down. You make darkness and it is night, wherein all the beasts of the forest do creep forth. The young lions roar after their prey and seek their food from God. The sun rises, they gather themselves together, and lay themselves down in their dens. Man goes forth unto his work and to his labor until the evening. O Lord, how abundant are your works. In wisdom you have made them all.

5 The earth is full of your riches; so is this great and wide sea in which are innumerable creeping things, both small and great beasts. There go the ships, and you have made leviathan to play therein. These wait all upon you, that you may give them their food in due season. That you give them, they gather. You open your hand, they are filled with good. You hide your face, they are troubled. You take away their breath, they die and return to their dust. You send forth your spirit, they are created and you renew the face of the earth. The glory of the Lord shall endure for ever. The Lord shall rejoice in his works. He looks on the earth and it trembles. He touches the hills and they smoke.

6 I will sing unto the Lord as long as I live. I will sing praise to my God while I have my being. My meditation of him shall be sweet. I will be glad in the Lord. Let the sinners be consumed out of the earth, and let the wicked be no more. Bless the Lord, O my soul. Praise the Lord.

PSALM 105

O GIVE thanks unto the Lord. Call upon his name. Make known his deeds among the people. Sing unto him, sing psalms unto him. Talk of all his wondrous works. Glory in his holy name. Let the heart of them rejoice that seek the Lord. Seek the Lord and his strength, seek his face ever.

2 Remember his marvelous works that he has done, his wonders, and the judgments of his mouth, O you seed of Abraham his servant, you children of Jacob his chosen. He is the Lord our God. His judgments are in all the earth. He has remembered his covenant for ever — the word which he commanded to a thousand generations — which covenant he made with Abraham, and his oath unto Isaac, and confirmed the same unto Jacob for a law, and to Israel for an everlasting covenant, saying, Unto you will I give the land of Canaan, the lot of your inheritance, when they were but a few men in number, yea, very few and strangers in it. When they went from one nation to another, from one kingdom to another people, he suffered no man to do them wrong. Yea, he reproved kings for their sakes, saying, Touch not my anointed and do my prophets no harm.

3 Moreover, he called for a famine upon the land. He broke the whole support of bread. He sent a man before them, even Joseph, who was sold for a servant, whose feet they hurt with fetters. He was laid in iron until the time that his word came. The word of the Lord tried him. The king sent and released him, even the ruler of the people, and let him go free. He made him lord of his house and ruler of all his substance, to bind his princes at his pleasure and teach his elders wisdom. Israel also came into Egypt, and Jacob sojourned in the land of Ham. And he increased his people greatly and made them stronger than their enemies. He turned their heart to hate his people, to deal subtly with his servants.

4 He sent Moses his servant and Aaron whom he had chosen. They showed his signs among them, and wonders in the land of Ham. He sent darkness and made it dark, and they rebelled not against his word. He turned their waters into blood and slew their fish. Their land brought forth frogs in abundance in the chambers of their kings. He spoke and there came diverse sorts of flies and lice in all their borders.

He gave them hail for rain and flaming fire in their land. He smote their vines also, and their fig trees, and broke the trees of their borders. He spoke and the locusts came, and caterpillars, and that without number, and did eat up all the herbs in their land and devoured the fruit of their ground. He smote also all the first born in their land, the chief of all their strength. He brought them forth also with silver and gold, and there was not one feeble person among their tribes. Egypt was glad when they departed, for the fear of them fell upon them. He spread a cloud for a covering, and fire to give light in the night. The people asked and he brought quails, and satisfied them with the bread of Heaven. He opened the rock and the waters gushed out; they ran in the dry places like a river. For he remembered his holy promise unto Abraham his servant. And he brought forth his people with joy, and his chosen with gladness, and gave them the lands of the heathen; and they inherited the labor of the people, that they might observe his statutes and keep his laws. Praise the Lord.

PSALM 106

PRAISE the Lord. O give thanks unto the Lord, for he is good, for his mercy endures for ever. Who can utter the mighty acts of the Lord? Who can show forth all his praise? Blessed are they that keep judgment, and he that does righteousness at all times. Remember me, O Lord, with the favor of your people. O visit me with your salvation, that I may see the good of your chosen, that I may rejoice in the gladness of your nation, that I may glory with your inheritance.

2 We have sinned with our fathers. We have committed iniquity. We have done wickedly. Our fathers understood not your wonders in Egypt. They remembered not the multitude of your mercies, but provoked you at the sea, at the Red Sea. Nevertheless, he saved them for his name's sake, that he might make his mighty power to be known. He rebuked the Red Sea also, and it was dried up, so he led them through the depths as through the wilderness. And he saved them from the hand of him that hated them, and redeemed them from the hand of the enemy. And the waters covered their enemies; there was not one of them left. Then they believed his words, they sang his praise.

3 They soon forgot his works. They waited not for his counsel, but lusted exceedingly in the wilderness and tested God in the desert. And

he gave them their request, but sent leanness into their soul. They envied Moses also in the camp, and Aaron, the saint of the Lord. The earth opened and swallowed up Dathan, and covered the company of Abiram, and a fire was kindled in their company. The flame burned up the wicked. They made a calf in Horeb and worshipped the molten image. Thus, they changed their glory into the similitude of an ox that eats grass. They forgot God their savior, who had done great things in Egypt—wondrous works in the land of Ham, and terrible things by the Red Sea. Therefore, he said that he would destroy them, had not Moses his chosen stood before him in the breach to turn away his wrath lest he should destroy them. Yea, they despised the pleasant land. They believed not his word, but murmured in their tents and listened not unto the voice of the Lord. Therefore, he lifted up his hand against them to overthrow them in the wilderness, to overthrow their seed also among the nations, and to scatter them in the lands. They joined themselves also unto Baal-Peor, and ate the sacrifices of the dead. Thus, they provoked him to anger with their inventions, and the plague broke in upon them. Then Phineas stood up and executed judgment, and so the plague was stopped. And that was counted unto him for righteousness, unto all generations for ever.

4 They angered him also at the waters of strife, so that it went ill with Moses for their sakes, because they provoked his spirit so that he spoke rashly with his lips. They did not destroy the nations concerning whom the Lord commanded them, but were mingled among the heathen and learned their works. And they served their idols, which were a snare unto them. Yea, they sacrificed their sons and their daughters unto devils, and shed innocent blood, even the blood of their sons and of their daughters whom they sacrificed unto the idols of Canaan; and the land was polluted with blood. Thus were they defiled with their own works, and went whoring with their own inventions. Therefore was the wrath of the Lord kindled against his people, insomuch that he abhorred his own inheritance. And he gave them into the hand of the heathen, and they that hated them ruled over them. Their enemies also oppressed them, and they were brought into subjection under their hand. Many times did he deliver them, but they provoked him with their counsel and were brought low for their iniquity.

⁵ Nevertheless, he regarded their affliction when he heard their cry. And he remembered for them his covenant, and spared his people according to the multitude of his mercies. He made them also to be pitied of all those that carried them captives.

⁶ Save us, O Lord our God, and gather us from among the heathen, to give thanks unto your holy name and to triumph in your praise. Blessed be the Lord God of Israel, from everlasting to everlasting. And let all the people say, Amen. Praise the Lord.

PSALM 107

O GIVE thanks unto the Lord, for he is good, for his mercy endures for ever. Let the redeemed of the Lord say so, whom he has redeemed from the hand of the enemy and gathered them out of the lands from the east and from the west, from the north and from the south.

² They wandered in the wilderness in a solitary way. They found no city to dwell in. Hungry and thirsty, their soul fainted in them. Then they cried unto the Lord in their trouble, and he delivered them out of their distresses. And he led them forth by the right way, that they might go to a city of habitation. Oh that men would praise the Lord for his goodness and for his wonderful works to the children of men. For he satisfies the longing soul and fills the hungry soul with goodness.

³ Such as sit in darkness and in the shadow of death, being bound in affliction and iron because they rebelled against the words of God and spurned the counsel of the Most High, therefore he brought down their heart with labor. They fell down and there was none to help. Then they cried unto the Lord in their trouble, and he saved them out of their distresses. He brought them out of darkness and the shadow of death, and broke their bands asunder. Oh that men would praise the Lord for his goodness and for his wonderful works to the children of men; for he has broken the gates of brass and cut the bars of iron asunder.

⁴ Fools, because of their transgression and because of their iniquities, are afflicted. Their soul abhors all manner of food, and they draw near unto the gates of death. Then they cry unto the Lord in their trouble, and he saves them out of their distresses. He sent his word, and healed them, and delivered them from their destructions. Oh that men would praise the Lord for his goodness and for his wonderful works to the

children of men. And let them sacrifice the sacrifices of thanksgiving and declare his works with rejoicing.

⁵ They that go down to the sea in ships, that do business in great waters, these see the works of the Lord and his wonders in the deep. For he commands and raises the stormy wind which lifts up the waves thereof. They mount up to the heaven, they go down again to the depths. Their soul is melted because of trouble. They reel to and fro, and stagger like a drunk man, and are at their wits' end. Then they cry unto the Lord in their trouble and he brings them out of their distresses. He makes the storm a calm, so that the waves thereof are still. Then they are glad because they are quiet, so he brings them unto their desired haven. Oh that men would praise the Lord for his goodness and for his wonderful works to the children of men. Let them exalt him also in the congregation of the people and praise him in the assembly of the elders.

⁶ He turns rivers into a wilderness and the watersprings into dry ground, a fruitful land into barrenness, for the wickedness of them that dwell therein. He turns the wilderness into a standing water and dry ground into watersprings. And there he makes the hungry to dwell, that they may prepare a city for habitation, and sow the fields, and plant vineyards which may yield fruits of increase. He blesses them also, so that they are multiplied greatly, and suffers not their cattle to decrease. Again they are diminished and brought low through oppression, affliction, and sorrow. He pours contempt upon princes and causes them to wander in the wilderness where there is no way. Yet he sets the poor on high from affliction and makes him families like a flock. The righteous shall see it and rejoice, and all iniquity shall stop her mouth. Whoever is wise and will observe these things, even they shall understand the loving kindness of the Lord.

PSALM 108

A song or psalm of David.

O GOD, my heart is fixed. I will sing and give praise even with my glory. Awake, psaltery and harp. I myself will awake early. I will praise you, O Lord, among the people, and I will sing praises unto you among the nations. For your mercy is great above the heavens, and your truth reaches unto the clouds. Be exalted, O God, above the heavens, and your glory above all the earth.

2 That your beloved may be delivered, save with your right hand and answer me. God has spoken in his holiness, I will rejoice. I will divide Shechem and mete out the valley of Succoth. Gilead is mine, Manasseh is mine. Ephraim is also the strength of my head; Judah is my lawgiver; Moab is my washpot. Over Edom will I cast out my shoe. Over Philistia will I triumph.

3 Who will bring me into the strong city? Who will lead me into Edom? Will not you, O God, who have cast us off? And will not you, O God, go forth with our hosts? Give us help from trouble, for vain is the help of man. Through God we shall do valiantly, for he it is that shall tread down our enemies.

PSALM 109
To the chief musician, a psalm of David.

HOLD not your peace, O God of my praise, for the mouth of the wicked and the mouth of the deceitful are opened against me. They have spoken against me with a lying tongue. They encompassed me about. They spoke against me also with words of hatred, and fought against me without a cause. And notwithstanding my love, they are my adversaries, yet I will continue in prayer for them. And they have rewarded me evil for good, and hatred for my love.

2 Set a wicked man over them, and let Satan stand at his right hand. When they shall be judged, let them be condemned, and let their prayer become sin. Let their days be few. Let another take their office. Let their children be fatherless and their wives widows. Let their children be continually vagabonds and beg. Let them seek also out of their desolate places. Let the extortioner catch all that they have, and let the stranger spoil their labor. Let there be none to extend mercy unto them, neither let there be any to favor their fatherless children. Let their posterity be cut off. In the generation following, let their names be blotted out. Let the iniquity of their fathers be remembered before the Lord, and let not the sin of their mothers be blotted out. Let them be before the Lord continually, that he may cut off the memory of them from the earth, because they remembered not to show mercy, but persecuted the poor and needy man, that they might even slay

the broken in heart. As they loved cursing, so let it come upon them. As they did not delight in blessing, so let it be far from them. As they clothed themselves with cursing as with their garments, so let it come into their inward parts like water, and like oil into their bones. Let it be unto them as a garment covers them, and for a belt with which they are girded continually. This shall be the reward of my adversaries from the Lord and of them who speak evil against my soul.

3 But do deliver me, O Lord my God, for your name's sake, because your mercy is good; therefore, deliver me. For I am poor and needy, and my heart is wounded within me. I am gone like the shadow when it declines. I am tossed up and down as the locust. My knees are weak through fasting, and my flesh fails of fatness. I became also a reproach unto them. When they looked upon me, they shook their heads. Help me, O Lord my God. O save me according to your mercy, that they may know that this is your hand, that you, Lord, have done it. Let them curse, but you bless. When they arise, let them be ashamed, but let your servant rejoice. Let my adversaries be clothed with shame, and let them cover themselves with their own confusion as with a mantle. I will greatly praise the Lord with my mouth, yea, I will praise him among the multitude. For he shall stand at the right hand of the poor to save him from those that condemn his soul.

PSALM 110

A psalm of David.

THE Lord said unto my lord, Sit at my right hand until I make your enemies your footstool. The Lord shall send the rod of your strength out of Zion. Rule in the midst of your enemies. Your people shall be willing in the day of your power, in the beauties of holiness from the womb of the morning. You have the dew of your youth. The Lord has sworn and will not repent, You are a priest for ever after the Order of Melchizedek. The Lord at your right hand shall strike through kings in the day of his wrath. He shall judge among the heathen. He shall fill these streets with their dead bodies. He shall wound the heads over many countries. He shall drink of the brook in the way. Therefore shall he lift up the head.

PSALM 111

P RAISE the Lord. I will praise the Lord with my whole heart in the
assembly of the upright and in the congregation. The works of
the Lord are great, sought out of all them that have pleasure therein.
His work is honorable and glorious, and his righteousness endures for
ever. He has made his wonderful works to be remembered. The Lord
is gracious and full of compassion. He has given food unto them that
fear him. He will ever be mindful of his covenant. He has shown his
people the power of his works, that he may give them the heritage of
the heathen. The works of his hands are verity and judgment. All his
commandments are sure. They stand fast for ever and ever, and are
done in truth and uprightness. He sent redemption unto his people. He
has commanded his covenant for ever. Holy and reverend is his name.
The fear of the Lord is the beginning of wisdom. A good understanding
have all they that do his commandments. His praise endures for ever.

PSALM 112

P RAISE the Lord. Blessed is the man who fears the Lord and delights
greatly in his commandments. His seed shall be mighty upon
earth. The generation of the upright shall be blessed, wealth and riches
shall be in his house, and his righteousness endures for ever. Unto the
upright there arises light in the darkness — he is gracious, and full of
compassion, and righteous. A good man shows favor and lends. He will
guide his affairs with discretion. Surely he shall not be moved for ever.
The righteous shall be in everlasting remembrance. He shall not be
afraid of evil tidings. His heart is fixed, trusting in the Lord. His heart
is established. He shall not be afraid until he see judgment executed
upon his enemies. He has dispersed; he has given to the poor. His
righteousness endures for ever. His horn shall be exalted with honor.
The wicked shall see it and be grieved. He shall gnash with his teeth
and melt away. The desire of the wicked shall perish.

PSALM 113

P RAISE the Lord. Praise, O you servants of the Lord, praise the
name of the Lord. Blessed be the name of the Lord from this time
forth and for ever. From the rising of the sun unto the going down of

the same, the Lord's name is to be praised. The Lord is high above all nations and his glory above the heavens. Who is like unto the Lord our God who dwells on high, who humbles himself to behold the things that are in Heaven and in the earth? He raises up the poor out of the dust and lifts the needy out of the dunghill, that he may set him with princes, even with the princes of his people. He makes the barren woman to keep house, to be a joyful mother of children. Praise the Lord.

PSALM 114

WHEN Israel went out of Egypt, the house of Jacob from a people of strange language, Judah was his sanctuary and Israel his dominion. The sea saw it and fled. Jordan was driven back. The mountains skipped like rams and the little hills like lambs. What ailed you, O you sea, that you fled? You Jordan, that you were driven back? You mountains, that you skipped like rams, and you little hills like lambs? Tremble, you earth, at the presence of the Lord, at the presence of the God of Jacob, who turned the rock into a standing water, the flint into a fountain of waters.

PSALM 115

NOT unto us, O Lord, not unto us, but unto your name be glory, for your mercy and for your truth's sake. Why should the heathen say, Where is now their God? But our God is in the Heavens. He has done whatever he has pleased. Their idols are silver and gold, the work of men's hands. They have mouths, but they speak not. Eyes have they, but they see not. They have ears, but they hear not. Noses have they, but they smell not. They have hands, but they handle not. Feet have they, but they walk not, neither speak they through their throat. They that make them are like unto them; so is everyone that trusts in them.

2 O Israel, trust in the Lord. He is your help and your shield. O house of Aaron, trust in the Lord. He is your help and your shield. You that fear the Lord, trust in the Lord. He is your help and your shield. The Lord has been mindful of us. He will bless us. He will bless the house of Israel. He will bless the house of Aaron. He will bless them that fear the Lord, both small and great. The Lord shall increase you more and more, you and your children. You are blessed of the Lord who made Heaven and earth. The heaven, even the heavens, are the Lord's, but

the earth he has given to the children of men. The dead praise not the Lord, neither any that go down into silence. But we will bless the Lord from this time forth and for ever. Praise the Lord.

PSALM 116

I LOVE the Lord because he has heard my voice and my supplications, because he has inclined his ear unto me; therefore will I call upon him as long as I live. The sorrows of death encompassed me, and the pains of hell got hold upon me. I found trouble and sorrow. Then I called upon the name of the Lord: O Lord, I implore you, deliver my soul. Gracious is the Lord, and righteous. Yea, our God is merciful. The Lord preserves the simple. I was brought low, and he helped me. Return unto your rest, O my soul, for the Lord has dealt bountifully with you. For you have delivered my soul from death, my eyes from tears, and my feet from falling. I will walk before the Lord in the land of the living. I believed, therefore have I spoken. I was greatly afflicted. I said in my haste, All men are liars.

2 What shall I render unto the Lord for all his benefits toward me? I will take the cup of salvation and call upon the name of the Lord. I will pay my vows unto the Lord now in the presence of all his people. Precious in the sight of the Lord is the death of his saints. O Lord, truly I am your servant. I am your servant and the son of your handmaid. You have loosened my bonds. I will offer to you the sacrifice of thanksgiving and will call upon the name of the Lord. I will pay my vows unto the Lord now in the presence of all his people, in the courts of the Lord's house — in your midst, O Jerusalem. Praise the Lord.

PSALM 117

O PRAISE the Lord, all you nations. Praise him, all you people. For his merciful kindness is great toward us and the truth of the Lord endures for ever. Praise the Lord.

PSALM 118

O GIVE thanks unto the Lord, for he is good, because his mercy endures for ever. Let Israel now say that his mercy endures for ever. Let the house of Aaron now say that his mercy endures for ever. Let them now that fear the Lord say that his mercy endures for ever.

² I called upon the Lord in distress. The Lord answered me and set me in a large place. The Lord is on my side. I will not fear. What can man do unto me? The Lord takes my part with them that help me; therefore, I shall see my desire upon them that hate me. It is better to trust in the Lord than to put confidence in man. It is better to trust in the Lord than to put confidence in princes. All nations encompassed me about, but in the name of the Lord will I destroy them. They encompassed me about, yea, they encompassed me about, but in the name of the Lord I will destroy them. They encompassed me about like bees. They are quenched as the fire of thorns, for in the name of the Lord I will destroy them. You have thrust heavily at me, that I might fall, but the Lord helped me. The Lord is my strength and song, and is become my salvation. The voice of rejoicing and salvation is in the tabernacles of the righteous. The right hand of the Lord does valiantly. The right hand of the Lord is exalted. The right hand of the Lord does valiantly. I shall not die, but live and declare the works of the Lord. The Lord has chastened me severely, but he has not given me over unto death.

³ Open to me the gates of righteousness — I will go into them, and I will praise the Lord — this gate of the Lord into which the righteous shall enter. I will praise you, for you have heard me and have become my salvation. The stone which the builders refused has become the head stone of the corner. This is the Lord's doing. It is marvelous in our eyes. This is the day which the Lord has made. We will rejoice and be glad in it. Save now, I implore you, O Lord. O Lord I implore you, send now prosperity. Blessed be he that comes in the name of the Lord. We have blessed you out of the house of the Lord. God is the Lord who has shown us light. Bind the sacrifice with cords, even unto the horns of the altar. You are my God and I will praise you. You are my God, I will exalt you. O give thanks unto the Lord, for he is good, for his mercy endures for ever.

PSALM 119
ALEPH

BLESSED are the undefiled in the way, who walk in the law of the Lord. Blessed are they that keep his testimonies and that seek him with the whole heart. They also do no iniquity. They walk in his ways. You have commanded us to keep your precepts diligently. Oh that my ways were directed to keep your statutes. Then I shall not be ashamed, when I have respect unto all your commandments. I will praise you with uprightness of heart when I shall have learned your righteous judgments. I will keep your statutes. O forsake me not utterly.

BETH

2 How shall a young man cleanse his way? By taking heed to it according to your word. With my whole heart have I sought you; Oh let me not wander from your commandments. Your word I have hidden in my heart, that I might not sin against you. Blessed are you, O Lord. Teach me your statutes. With my lips have I declared all the judgments of your mouth. I have rejoiced in the way of your testimonies as much as in all riches. I will meditate upon your precepts and have respect unto your ways. I will delight myself in your statutes. I will not forget your word.

GIMEL

3 Deal bountifully with your servant, that I may live and keep your word. Open your eyes, that I may behold wondrous things out of your law. I am a stranger in the earth. Hide not your commandments from me. My heart breaks, for my soul longs after your judgments at all times. You have rebuked the proud. They are cursed who do err from your commandments. Remove from me reproach and contempt, for I have kept your testimonies. Princes also did sit and speak against me, but your servant did meditate in your statutes. Your testimonies also are my delight and my counselors.

DALETH

4 My soul cleaves unto the dust. Quicken me according to your word. I have declared my ways and you heard me. Teach me your statutes, make me to understand the way of your precepts; so shall I talk of your wondrous works. My soul melts for heaviness. Strengthen me according to your word. Remove from me the way of lying and grant me your law graciously. I have chosen the way of truth. Your judgments have I laid before me. I have stuck unto your testimonies. O Lord, put me not to shame. I will run the way of your commandments when you shall enlarge my heart.

HE

5 Teach me, O Lord, the way of your statutes, and I shall keep it to the end. Give me understanding and I shall keep your law, yea, I shall observe it with my whole heart. Make me to go in the path of your commandments, for therein do I delight. Incline my heart unto your testimonies and not to covetousness. Turn away my eyes from beholding vanity and quicken me in your way. Establish your word unto your servant who is devoted to your fear. Turn away my reproach, which I fear, for your judgments are good. Behold, I have longed after your precepts. Quicken me in your righteousness.

VAU

6 Let your mercies come also unto me, O Lord, even your salvation according to your word. So shall I have that with which to answer him who reproaches me, for I trust in your word. And take not the word of truth utterly out of my mouth, for I have hoped in your judgments. So shall I keep your law continually for ever and ever. And I will walk at liberty, for I seek your precepts. I will speak of your testimonies also before kings and will not be ashamed. And I will delight myself in your commandments, which I have loved. My hands also will I lift up unto your commandments, which I have loved, and I will meditate upon your statutes.

ZAIN

7 Remember the word unto your servant, upon which you have caused me to hope. This is my comfort in my affliction, for your word has quickened me. The proud have had me greatly in derision, yet have I not declined from your law. I remembered your judgments of old, O Lord, and have comforted myself. Horror has taken hold upon me because of the wicked that forsake your law. Your statutes have been my songs in the house of my pilgrimage. I have remembered your name, O Lord, in the night, and have kept your law. This I had because I kept your precepts.

CHETH

⁸You are my portion, O Lord. I have said that I would keep your words. I entreated your favor with my whole heart. Be merciful unto me according to your word. I thought on my ways and turned my feet unto your testimonies. I made haste and delayed not to keep your commandments. The bands of the wicked have robbed me, but I have not forgotten your law. At midnight I will rise to give thanks unto you because of your righteous judgments. I am a companion of all them that fear you and of them that keep your precepts. The earth, O Lord, is full of your mercy. Teach me your statutes.

TETH

⁹You have dealt well with your servant, O Lord, according unto your word. Teach me good judgment and knowledge, for I have believed your commandments. Before I was afflicted, I went astray, but now have I kept your word. You are good and do good. Teach me your statutes. The proud have forged a lie against me, but I will keep your precepts with my whole heart. Their heart is as fat as grease, but I delight in your law. It is good for me that I have been afflicted, that I might learn your statutes. The law of your mouth is better unto me than thousands of gold and silver.

JOD

¹⁰Your hands have made me and fashioned me. Give me understanding, that I may learn your commandments. They that fear you will be glad when they see me because I have hoped in your word. I know, O Lord, that your judgments are right and that you in faithfulness have afflicted me. Let, I pray you, your merciful kindness be for my comfort, according to your word unto your servant. Let your tender mercies come unto me, that I may live, for your law is my delight. Let the proud be ashamed, for they dealt perversely with me without a cause; but I will meditate upon your precepts. Let those that fear you turn unto me, and those that have known your testimonies. Let my heart be sound in your statutes, that I be not ashamed.

CAPH

11 My soul faints for your salvation, but I hope in your word. My eyes fail for your word, saying, When will you comfort me? For I have become like a bottle in the smoke, yet do I not forget your statutes. How many are the days of your servant? When will you execute judgment on them that persecute me? The proud have dug pits for me which are not after your law. All your commandments are faithful. They persecute me wrongfully. Help me. They had almost consumed me upon earth, but I forsook not your precepts. Quicken me after your loving kindness; so I shall keep the testimony of your mouth.

LAMED

12 For ever, O Lord, your word is settled in Heaven. Your faithfulness is unto all generations. You have established the earth, and it stands. They continue this day according to your ordinances, for all are your servants. Unless your law had been my delights, I should then have perished in my affliction. I will never forget your precepts, for with them you have quickened me. I am yours. Save me, for I have sought your precepts. The wicked have waited for me, to destroy me, but I will consider your testimonies. I have seen an end of all perfection, but your commandment is exceedingly broad.

MEM

13 Oh how I love your law. It is my meditation all the day. You through your commandments have made me wiser than my enemies, for they are ever with me. I have more understanding than all my teachers, for your testimonies are my meditation. I understand more than the elders because I keep your precepts. I have restrained my feet from every evil way, that I might keep your word. I have not departed from your judgments, for you have taught me. How sweet are your words unto my taste, yea, sweeter than honey to my mouth. Through your precepts I get understanding, therefore I hate every false way.

NUN

14 Your word is a lamp unto my feet and a light unto my path. I have sworn and I will perform it, that I will keep your righteous judgments.

I am afflicted very much. Quicken me, O Lord, according unto your word. Accept, I implore you, the freewill offerings of my mouth, O Lord, and teach me your judgments. My soul is continually in your hand, and I do not forget your law. The wicked have laid a snare for me, yet I erred not from your precepts. Your testimonies have I taken as a heritage for ever, for they are the rejoicing of my heart. I have inclined my heart to perform your statutes always, even unto the end.

SAMECH

¹⁵ I hate vain thoughts, but your law do I love. You are my hiding place and my shield. I hope in your word. Depart from me, you evildoers, for I will keep the commandments of my God. Uphold me according unto your word, that I may live, and let me not be ashamed of my hope. Hold me up and I shall be safe, and I will have respect unto your statutes continually. You have trodden down all them that err from your statutes, for their deceit is falsehood. You put away all the wicked of the earth like dross, therefore I love your testimonies. My flesh trembles for fear of you and I am afraid of your judgments.

AIN

¹⁶ I have done judgment and justice. Leave me not to my oppressors. Be surety for your servant for good. Let not the proud oppress me. My eyes fail for your salvation and for the word of your righteousness. Deal with your servant according to your mercy, and teach me your statutes. I am your servant. Give me understanding, that I may know your testimonies and the time, O Lord, for me to work; for they have made void your law. Therefore, I love your commandments above gold, yea, above fine gold. Therefore, I esteem all your precepts concerning all things to be right, and I hate every false way.

PE

¹⁷ Your testimonies are wonderful, therefore does my soul keep them. The entrance of your words gives light; they give understanding unto the simple. I opened my mouth and panted, for I longed for your commandments. Look upon me and be merciful unto me, as you used to do unto those that love your name. Order my steps in your word, and let not any iniquity have dominion over me. Deliver me from the

oppression of man; so will I keep your precepts. Make your face to shine upon your servant, and teach me your statutes. Rivers of waters run down my eyes because they keep not your law.

TZADDI

[18] Righteous are you, O Lord, and upright are your judgments. Your testimonies that you have commanded are righteous and very faithful. My zeal has consumed me because my enemies have forgotten your words. Your word is very pure, therefore your servant loves it. I am small and despised; yet I do not forget your precepts. Your righteousness is an everlasting righteousness and your law is the truth. Trouble and anguish have taken hold on me, yet your commandments are my delights. The righteousness of your testimonies is everlasting. Give me understanding and I shall live.

KOPH

[19] I cried with my whole heart, Hear me, O Lord, I will keep your statutes. I cried unto you, Save me, and I shall keep your testimonies. I rose before the dawning of the morning and cried; I hoped in your word. My eyes anticipate the night watches, that I might meditate in your word. Hear my voice according unto your loving kindness. O Lord, quicken me according to your judgment. They draw near that follow after mischief. They are far from your law. You are near, O Lord, and all your commandments are truth. Concerning your testimonies, I have known of old that you have founded them for ever.

RESH

[20] Consider my affliction and deliver me, for I do not forget your law. Plead my cause and deliver me. Quicken me according to your word. Salvation is far from the wicked, for they seek not your statutes. Great are your tender mercies, O Lord. Quicken me according to your judgments. Many are my persecutors and my enemies, yet I do not decline from your testimonies. I beheld the transgressors and was grieved because they kept not your word. Consider how I love your precepts. Quicken me, O Lord, according to your loving kindness. Your word is true from the beginning, and every one of your righteous judgments endures for ever.

SCHIN

21 Princes have persecuted me without a cause, but my heart stands
in awe of your word. I rejoice at your word as one that finds great spoil.
I hate and abhor lying; but your law do I love. Seven times a day do
I praise you because of your righteous judgments. Great peace have
they who love your law, and nothing shall offend them. Lord, I have
hoped for your salvation and done your commandments. My soul has
kept your testimonies and I love them exceedingly. I have kept your
precepts and your testimonies, for all my ways are before you.

TAU

22 Let my cry come near before you, O Lord. Give me understanding
according to your word. Let my supplication come before you. Deliver
me according to your word. My lips shall utter praise when you have
taught me your statutes. My tongue shall speak of your word, for all
your commandments are righteousness. Let your hand help me, for
I have chosen your precepts. I have longed for your salvation, O Lord,
and your law is my delight. Let my soul live, and it shall praise you.
And let your judgments help me. I have gone astray like a lost sheep.
Seek your servant, for I do not forget your commandments.

PSALM 120
A song of degrees.

IN my distress I cried unto the Lord, and he heard me. Deliver my
soul, O Lord, from lying lips and from a deceitful tongue. What
shall be given unto you? Or what shall be done unto you, you false
tongue? Sharp arrows of the mighty with coals of juniper. Woe is me,
that I sojourn in Meshech, that I dwell in the tents of Kedar. My soul
has long dwelled with him that hates peace. I am for peace, but when
I speak, they are for war.

PSALM 121
A song of degrees.

I WILL lift up my eyes unto the hills from where my help comes — my
help comes from the Lord who made heaven and earth. Behold, he
that keeps Israel shall neither slumber nor sleep. He will not suffer your

foot to be moved. He that keeps you will not slumber. The Lord is your keeper. The Lord is your shade upon your right hand. The sun shall not smite you by day, nor the moon by night. The Lord shall preserve you from all evil. He shall preserve your soul. The Lord shall preserve your going out and your coming in from this time forth, and even for ever.

PSALM 122

A song of degrees of David.

I WAS glad when they said unto me, Let us go into the house of the Lord. Our feet shall stand within your gates, O Jerusalem. Jerusalem is built as a city that is compacted together, where the tribes go up — the tribes of the Lord — unto the testimony of Israel, to give thanks unto the name of the Lord. For there are set thrones of judgment, the thrones of the house of David. Pray for the peace of Jerusalem. They shall prosper that love you. Peace be within your walls and prosperity within your palaces. For my brethren and companions' sakes, I will now say, Peace be within you. Because of the house of the Lord our God, I will seek your good.

PSALM 123

A song of degrees.

U NTO you I lift up my eyes, O you that dwell in the Heavens. Behold, as the eyes of servants look unto the hand of their masters, and as the eyes of a maiden unto the hand of her mistress, so our eyes wait upon the Lord our God until he has mercy upon us. Have mercy upon us, O Lord, have mercy upon us, for we are exceedingly filled with contempt. Our soul is exceedingly filled with the scorning of those that are at ease and with the contempt of the proud.

PSALM 124

A song of degrees of David.

N OW may Israel say, If the Lord was not on our side when men rose up against us, then they would have swallowed us up quick when their wrath was kindled against us. Then the waters would have overwhelmed us, the stream would have gone over our soul. Then the proud waters would have gone over our soul. Blessed be the Lord, who has not given us as a prey to their teeth. Our soul is escaped as a bird out of the snare of the fowlers. The snare is broken and we are escaped. Our help is in the name of the Lord who made heaven and earth.

PSALM 125
A song of degrees.

THEY that trust in the Lord in Mount Zion cannot be removed, but abides for ever. As the mountains are round about Jerusalem, so the Lord is round about his people from henceforth, even for ever. For the rod of the wicked shall not rest upon the lot of the righteous lest the righteous put forth their hands unto iniquity. Do good, O Lord, unto the good and unto the upright in their hearts. As for such as turn aside unto their crooked ways, the Lord shall lead them forth with the workers of iniquity. But peace shall be upon Israel.

PSALM 126
A song of degrees.

WHEN the Lord turned again the captivity of Zion, we were like them that dream. Then our mouth was filled with laughter and our tongue with singing. Then said they among the heathen, The Lord has done great things for them. The Lord has done great things for us, of which we are glad. Return our prosperity, O Lord, as the streams in the south. They that sow in tears shall reap in joy. He that goes forth and weeps, bearing precious seed, shall doubtless come again with rejoicing, bringing his sheaves with him.

PSALM 127
A song of degrees for Solomon.

EXCEPT the Lord build the house, they labor in vain that build it. Except the Lord keep the city, the watchman wakes but in vain. It is vain for you to rise up early, to sit up late, to eat the bread of sorrows, for so he gives his beloved sleep. Behold, children are a heritage of the Lord, and the fruit of the womb is his reward. As arrows are in the hand of a mighty man, so are children of the youth. Happy is the man that has his quiver full of them. They shall not be ashamed, but they shall speak with the enemies in the gate.

PSALM 128

A song of degrees.

Blessed is everyone that fears the Lord, that walks in his ways, for you shall eat the labor of your hands. Happy shall you be, and it shall be well with you. Your wife shall be as a fruitful vine by the sides of your house, your children like olive plants round about your table. Behold that thus shall the man be blessed that fears the Lord. The Lord shall bless you out of Zion, and you shall see the good of Jerusalem all the days of your life. Yea, you shall see your children's children and peace upon Israel.

PSALM 129

A song of degrees.

Many a time have they afflicted me from my youth. May Israel now say, Many a time have they afflicted me from my youth, yet they have not prevailed against me. The plowers plowed upon my back, they made long their furrows. The Lord is righteous, he has cut asunder the cords of the wicked. Let them all be confounded and turned back that hate Zion. Let them be as the grass upon the housetops, which withers before it grows up, with which the reaper fills not his hand, nor he that binds sheaves his bosom. Neither do they who go by say, The blessing of the Lord be upon you, we bless you in the name of the Lord.

PSALM 130

A song of degrees.

Out of the depths have I cried unto you, O Lord. Lord, hear my voice. Let your ears be attentive to the voice of my supplications. If you, Lord, should mark iniquities, O Lord, who shall stand? But there is forgiveness with you, that you may be feared. I wait for the Lord. My soul does wait, and in his word do I hope. My soul waits for the Lord more than they that watch for the morning—I say, more than they that watch for the morning. Let Israel hope in the Lord, for with the Lord there is mercy, and with him is plenteous redemption. And he shall redeem Israel from all his iniquities.

PSALM 131
A song of degrees of David.

LORD, my heart is not haughty, nor my eyes lofty, neither do I exercise myself in great matters or in things too high for me. Surely I have behaved and quieted myself as a child that is weaned of his mother. My soul is even as a weaned child. Let Israel hope in the Lord from henceforth and for ever.

PSALM 132
A song of degrees.

LORD, remember David and all his afflictions, how he swore unto the Lord and vowed unto the Mighty God of Jacob, Surely I will not come into the tabernacle of my house nor go up into my bed. I will not give sleep to my eyes or slumber to my eyelids until I find a place for the Lord, a habitation for the Mighty God of Jacob. Behold, we heard of it at Ephrathah; we found it in the fields of the wood. We will go into his tabernacles, we will worship at his footstool. Arise, O Lord, into your rest, you and the ark of your strength. Let your priests be clothed with righteousness, and let your saints shout for joy. For your servant David's sake, turn not away the face of your anointed.

2 The Lord has sworn in truth unto David (he will not turn from it), Of the fruit of your body will I set upon your throne; if your children will keep my covenant and my testimony that I shall teach them, their children shall also sit upon your throne for ever. For the Lord has chosen Zion, he has desired it for his habitation: this is my rest for ever. Here will I dwell, for I have desired it. I will abundantly bless her provision. I will satisfy her poor with bread. I will also clothe her priests with salvation, and her saints shall shout aloud for joy. There will I make the horn of David to bud. I have ordained a lamp for my anointed. His enemies will I clothe with shame, but upon himself shall his crown flourish.

PSALM 133
A song of degrees of David.

BEHOLD, how good and how pleasant it is for brethren to dwell together in unity, it is like the precious ointment upon the head that ran down upon the beard, even Aaron's beard, that went down to the skirts of his garments as the dew of Hermon that descended upon the mountains of Zion, for there the Lord commanded the blessing, even life for ever.

PSALM 134

A song of degrees.

BEHOLD, bless the Lord, all you servants of the Lord, who by night stand in the house of the Lord. Lift up your hands in the sanctuary and bless the Lord. The Lord, who has made heaven and earth, bless you out of Zion.

PSALM 135

PRAISE the Lord. Praise the name of the Lord. Praise him, O you servants of the Lord. You that stand in the house of the Lord, in the courts of the house of our God, praise the Lord, for the Lord is good. Sing praises unto his name, for it is pleasant. For the Lord has chosen Jacob unto himself, and Israel for his peculiar treasure. For I know that the Lord is great and that our Lord is above all gods.

2 Whatever the Lord pleased, that did he in heaven, and in earth, in the seas, and all deep places. He causes the vapors to ascend from the ends of the earth. He makes lightnings for the rain. He brings the wind out of his treasuries; who smote the first born of Egypt, both of man and beast; who sent tokens and wonders into your midst, O Egypt, upon Pharaoh and upon all his servants; who smote great nations and slew mighty kings — Sihon king of the Amorites, and Og king of Bashan, and all the kingdoms of Canaan — and gave their land for a heritage, a heritage unto Israel his people. Your name, O Lord, endures for ever, and your memorial, O Lord, throughout all generations. For the Lord will judge his people, and he will not repent himself concerning his servants.

3 The idols of the heathen are silver and gold, the work of men's hands. They have mouths, but they speak not. Eyes have they, but they see not. They have ears, but they hear not, neither is there any breath in their mouths. They that make them are like unto them; so is everyone that trusts in them. Bless the Lord, O house of Israel. Bless the Lord, O house of Aaron. Bless the Lord, O house of Levi. You that

fear the Lord, bless the Lord. Blessed be the Lord out of Zion. Blessed be the Lord out of Jerusalem. Praise the Lord.

PSALM 136

O GIVE thanks unto the Lord, for he is good, for his mercy endures for ever. O give thanks unto the God of gods, for his mercy endures for ever. O give thanks to the Lord of lords, for his mercy endures for ever; to him who alone does great wonders, for his mercy endures for ever; to him that by wisdom made the heavens, for his mercy endures for ever; to him that stretched out the earth above the waters, for his mercy endures for ever; to him that made great lights, for his mercy endures for ever: the sun to rule by day, for his mercy endures for ever, the moon and stars to rule by night, for his mercy endures for ever; to him that smote Egypt in their first born, for his mercy endures for ever, and brought out Israel from among them, for his mercy endures for ever, with a strong hand and with a stretched out arm, for his mercy endures for ever; to him who divided the Red Sea into parts, for his mercy endures for ever, and made Israel to pass through the midst of it, for his mercy endures for ever, but overthrew Pharaoh and his host in the Red Sea, for his mercy endures for ever; to him who led his people through the wilderness, for his mercy endures for ever; to him who smote great kings, for his mercy endures for ever, and slew famous kings, for his mercy endures for ever: Sihon, king of the Amorites, for his mercy endures for ever, and Og the king of Bashan, for his mercy endures for ever, and gave their land for a heritage, for his mercy endures for ever, even a heritage unto Israel his servant, for his mercy endures for ever; who remembered us in our low estate, for his mercy endures for ever, and has redeemed us from our enemies, for his mercy endures for ever; who gives food to all flesh, for his mercy endures for ever.

2 O give thanks unto the God of Heaven, for his mercy endures for ever.

PSALM 137

B Y the rivers of Babylon, there we sat down. Yea, we wept when we remembered Zion. We hung our harps upon the willows in the midst thereof, for there they that carried us away captive required of us a song, and they that wasted us required of us mirth, saying, Sing us one of the songs of Zion. How shall we sing the Lord's song in a strange land? If I forget you, O Jerusalem, let my right hand forget its skill. If I do not remember you, let my tongue cleave to the roof of my mouth, if I prefer not Jerusalem above my chief joy. Remember, O Lord, the children of Edom in the day of Jerusalem, who said, Raze it, raze it, even to the foundation thereof. O daughter of Babylon, who are to be destroyed, happy shall he be that rewards you as you have served us. Happy shall he be that takes and dashes your little ones against the stones.

PSALM 138
A psalm of David.

I WILL praise you with my whole heart. Before the gods I will sing praise unto you. I will worship toward your holy temple, and praise your name for your loving kindness and for your truth; for you have magnified your word above all your name. In the day when I cried, you answered me and strengthened me with strength in my soul. All the kings of the earth shall praise you, O Lord, when they hear the words of your mouth. Yea, they shall sing in the ways of the Lord, for great is the glory of the Lord. Though the Lord be high, yet he has respect unto the lowly; but the proud he knows afar off. Though I walk in the midst of trouble, you will revive me. You shall stretch forth your hand against the wrath of my enemies, and your right hand shall save me. The Lord will perfect me in knowledge concerning his kingdom. I will praise you, O Lord, for ever, for you are merciful and will not forsake the works of your own hands.

PSALM 139
To the chief musician, a psalm of David.

O Lord, you have searched me and known me. You know my sitting down and my rising up. You understand my thought afar off. You encompass my path and my lying down, and are acquainted with all my ways. For there is not a word in my tongue, but behold, O Lord, you know it altogether. You have beset me behind and before, and laid your hand upon me. Such knowledge is too wonderful for me. It is high. I cannot attain unto it. Where shall I go from your spirit? Or where shall I flee from your presence? If I ascend up into Heaven, you are there. If I make my bed in hell, behold, you are there. If I take the wings of the morning and dwell in the farthest parts of the sea, even there shall your hand lead me, and your right hand shall hold me.

2 If I say, Surely the darkness shall cover me, even the night shall be light about me, yea, the darkness hides not from you, but the night shines as the day. The darkness and the light are both alike to you.

3 For you have possessed my reins. You have covered me in my mother's womb. I will praise you, for I am fearfully and wonderfully made. Marvelous are your works, and that my soul knows right well. My substance was not hidden from you when I was made in secret and curiously worked in the lowest parts of the earth. Your eyes did see my substance, yet being imperfect. And in your book all my members were written, which in continuance were fashioned when as yet I knew none of them. How precious also are your thoughts unto me, O God, how great is the sum of them. If I should count them, they are more in number than the sand. When I awake, I am still with you.

4 Surely you will slay the wicked, O God. Depart from me therefore you bloody men; for they speak against you wickedly, and your enemies take your name in vain. Do not I hate them, O Lord, that hate you? And am I not grieved with those that rise up against you? I hate them with perfect hatred. I count them my enemies. Search me, O God, and know my heart. Try me and know my thoughts. And see if there is any wicked way in me, and lead me in the way everlasting.

PSALM 140
To the chief musician, a psalm of David.

DELIVER me, O Lord, from the evil man, preserve me from the violent man, who imagine mischiefs in their heart; continually are they gathered together for war. They have sharpened their tongues like a serpent. Adders' poison is under their lips. Selah. Keep me, O Lord, from the hands of the wicked. Preserve me from the violent man who has purposed to overthrow my goings. The proud have hidden a snare for me, and cords. They have spread a net by the wayside. They have set traps for me. Selah.

2 I said unto the Lord, You are my God, hear the voice of my supplications, O Lord. O God the Lord, the strength of my salvation,

you have covered my head in the day of battle. Grant not, O Lord, the desires of the wicked. Further not his wicked device lest they exalt themselves. Selah. As for the head of those that encompass me about, let the mischief of their own lips cover them. Let burning coals fall upon them. Let them be cast into the fire, into deep pits, that they rise not up again. Let not an evil speaker be established in the earth. Evil shall hunt the violent man to overthrow him.

³ I know that the Lord will maintain the cause of the afflicted and the right of the poor. Surely the righteous shall give thanks unto your name. The upright shall dwell in your presence.

PSALM 141
A psalm of David.

LORD, I cry unto you. Make haste unto me. Give ear unto my voice when I cry unto you. Let my prayer be set forth before you as incense, and the lifting up of my hands as the evening sacrifice. Set a watch, O Lord, before my mouth; keep the door of my lips. Incline not my heart to any evil thing, to practice wicked works with men that work iniquity, and let me not eat of their dainties. When the righteous smite me with the word of the Lord, it is a kindness, and when they reprove me, it shall be an excellent oil and shall not destroy my faith; for yet my prayer also shall be for them. I do not delight in their calamities. When their judges are overthrown in stony places, they shall hear my words, for they are sweet. Our bones are scattered at the grave's mouth as when one cuts and chops wood upon the earth. But my eyes are unto you, O God the Lord. In you is my trust. Leave not my soul destitute. Keep me from the snares which they have laid for me and the traps of the workers of iniquity. Let the wicked fall into their own nets while I thus escape.

PSALM 142
Maskil of David: A prayer when he was in the cave.

I CRIED unto the Lord with my voice. With my voice unto the Lord did I make my supplication. I poured out my complaint before him. I showed before him my trouble. When my spirit was overwhelmed within me, then you knew my path. In the way wherein I walked have they secretly laid a snare for me. I looked on my right hand and beheld, but there was no man that would know me. Refuge failed me. No man cared for my soul. I cried unto you, O Lord. I said, You are my refuge and my portion in the land of the living. Attend unto my cry, for I am brought very low. Deliver me from my persecutors, for they are stronger than I. Bring my soul out of prison, that I may praise your name. The righteous shall encompass me about, for you shall deal bountifully with me.

PSALM 143
A psalm of David.

HEAR my prayer, O Lord. Give ear to my supplications. In your faithfulness answer me, and in your righteousness. And enter not into judgment with your servant, for in your sight shall no man living be justified. For the enemy has persecuted my soul. He has smitten my life down to the ground, he has made me to dwell in darkness as those that have been long dead. Therefore is my spirit overwhelmed within me; my heart within me is desolate.

2 I remember the days of old. I meditate on all your works. I muse on the work of your hands. I stretch forth my hands unto you. My soul thirsts after you as a thirsty land. Selah. Hear me speedily, O Lord. My spirit fails. Hide not your face from me lest I be like unto them that go down into the pit. Cause me to hear your loving kindness in the morning, for in you do I trust. Cause me to know the way wherein I should walk, for I lift up my soul unto you. Deliver me, O Lord, from my enemies. I flee unto you to hide me. Teach me to do your will, for you are my God. Your spirit is good. Lead me into the land of uprightness. Quicken me, O Lord, for your name's sake. For your righteousness' sake bring my soul out of trouble, and of your mercy cut off my enemies and destroy all them that afflict my soul, for I am your servant.

PSALM 144
A psalm of David.

BLESSED be the Lord, my strength, who teaches my hands to war and my fingers to fight — my goodness and my fortress, my high tower and my deliverer, my shield and he in whom I trust, who subdues my people under me. Lord, what is man that you take knowledge of him?

Or the son of man that you make account of him? Man is like vanity, his days are as a shadow that passes away. Bow your heavens, O Lord, and come down. Touch the mountains and they shall smoke. Cast forth lightning and scatter them. Shoot out your arrows and destroy them. Send your hand from above. Rid me and deliver me out of great waters, from the hand of strange children whose mouths speak vanity and their right hand is a right hand of falsehood.

2 I will sing a new song unto you, O God. Upon a psaltery and an instrument of ten strings will I sing praises unto you. It is he that gives salvation unto kings, who delivers David his servant from the hurtful sword. Rid me and deliver me from the hand of strange children, whose mouths speak vanity and their right hand is a right hand of falsehood, that our sons may be as plants grown up in their youth; that our daughters may be as cornerstones, polished after the similitude of a palace; that our granaries may be full, affording all manner of store; that our sheep may bring forth thousands and ten thousands in our streets; that our oxen may be strong to labor; that there be no breaking in nor going out; that there be no complaining in our streets. Happy is that people that is in such a case; yea, happy is that people whose God is the Lord.

PSALM 145
David's psalm of praise.

I WILL extol you, my God, O king, and I will bless your name for ever and ever. Every day will I bless you, and I will praise your name for ever and ever. Great is the Lord, and greatly to be praised. And his greatness is unsearchable. One generation shall praise your works to another and shall declare your mighty acts. I will speak of the glorious honor of your majesty and of your wondrous works, and men shall speak of the might of your terrible acts. And I will declare your greatness. They shall abundantly utter the memory of your great goodness and shall sing of your righteousness. The Lord is gracious, and full of compassion, slow to anger, and of great mercy. The Lord is good to all, and his tender mercies are over all his works. All your works shall praise you, O Lord, and your saints shall bless you. They shall speak of the glory of your kingdom and talk of your power, to make known to the sons of men his mighty acts and the glorious majesty

of his kingdom. Your kingdom is an everlasting kingdom, and your
dominion endures throughout all generations. The Lord upholds
all that fall and raises up all those that are bowed down. The eyes of
all wait upon you, and you give them their food in due season. You
open your hand and satisfy the desire of every living thing. The Lord
is righteous in all his ways and holy in all his works. The Lord is near
unto all them that call upon him, to all that call upon him in truth.
He will fulfill the desire of them that fear him. He also will hear their
cry and will save them. The Lord preserves all them that love him, but
all the wicked will he destroy. My mouth shall speak the praise of the
Lord. And let all flesh bless his holy name for ever and ever.

PSALM 146

PRAISE the Lord. Praise the Lord, O my soul. While I live will I
praise the Lord. I will sing praises unto my God while I have any
being. Put not your trust in princes, nor in the son of man in whom
there is no help. His breath goes forth, he returns to his earth; in that
very day his thoughts perish. Happy is he that has the God of Jacob
for his help, whose hope is in the Lord his God who made heaven, and
earth, the sea, and all that therein is; who keeps truth for ever; who
executes judgment for the oppressed; who gives food to the hungry.
The Lord releases the prisoners. The Lord opens the eyes of the blind.
The Lord raises the bowed down. The Lord loves the righteous. The
Lord preserves the strangers. He relieves the fatherless and widow,
but the way of the wicked he turns upside down. The Lord shall reign
for ever, even your God, O Zion, unto all generations. Praise the Lord.

PSALM 147

PRAISE the Lord, for it is good to sing praises unto our God; for it is
pleasant and praise is comely. The Lord does build up Jerusalem;
he gathers together the outcasts of Israel. He heals the broken in
heart and binds up their wounds. He tallies the number of the stars;
he calls them all by their names. Great is our Lord, and of great power.
His understanding is infinite. The Lord lifts up the meek; he casts the
wicked down to the ground. Sing unto the Lord with thanksgiving.
Sing praise upon the harp unto our God, who covers the heaven with
clouds; who prepares rain for the earth; who makes grass to grow upon

the mountains. He gives to the beast his food, and to the young ravens which cry. He delights not in the strength of the horse. He takes not pleasure in the legs of a man. The Lord takes pleasure in them that fear him, in those that hope in his mercy.

2 Praise the Lord, O Jerusalem. Praise your God, O Zion, for he has strengthened the bars of your gates. He has blessed your children within you. He makes peace in your borders and fills you with the finest of the wheat. He sends forth his commandment upon earth. His word runs very swiftly. He gives snow like wool. He scatters the hoarfrost like ashes. He casts forth his ice like morsels. Who can stand before his cold? He sends out his word and melts them. He causes his wind to blow and the waters flow. He shows his word unto Jacob, his statutes and his judgments unto Israel. He has not dealt so with any nation, and as for his judgments, they have not known them. Praise the Lord.

PSALM 148

P RAISE the Lord. Praise the Lord from the heavens. Praise him in the heights. Praise him, all his angels. Praise him, all his hosts. Praise him, sun and moon. Praise him, all you stars of light. Praise him, you Heavens of heavens and you waters that are above the heavens. Let them praise the name of the Lord, for he commanded and they were created. He has also established them for ever and ever. He has made a decree which shall not pass. Praise the Lord from the earth, you dragons and all depths, fire and hail, snow and vapor, stormy wind fulfilling his word, mountains and all hills, fruitful trees and all cedars, beast and all cattle, creeping things and flying fowl, kings of the earth and all people, princes and all judges of the earth, both young men and virgins, old men and children. Let them praise the name of the Lord, for his name alone is excellent. His glory is above the earth and heaven. He also exalts the horn of his people, the praise of all his saints, even of the children of Israel — a people near unto him. Praise the Lord.

PSALM 149

P RAISE the Lord. Sing unto the Lord a new song, and his praise in the congregation of saints. Let Israel rejoice in him that made him. Let the children of Zion be joyful in their King. Let them praise his name in the dance. Let them sing praises unto him with the tambourine and harp. For the Lord takes pleasure in his people, he will beautify the meek with salvation. Let the saints be joyful in glory. Let them sing aloud upon their beds. Let the high praises of God be in their mouth, and a two-edged sword in their hand — to execute vengeance upon the heathen and punishments upon the people, to bind their kings with chains and their nobles with fetters of iron, to execute upon them the judgment written. This honor, all his saints have. Praise the Lord.

PSALM 150

Praise the Lord. Praise God in his sanctuary. Praise him in the firmament of his power. Praise him for his mighty acts. Praise him according to his excellent greatness. Praise him with the sound of the trumpet. Praise him with the psaltery and harp. Praise him with the tambourine and dance. Praise him with stringed instruments and organs. Praise him upon the loud cymbals. Praise him upon the high sounding cymbals. Let everything that has breath praise the Lord. Praise the Lord.

THE PROVERBS

The proverbs of Solomon the son of David, king of Israel: to know wisdom and instruction; to perceive the words of understanding; to receive the instruction of wisdom, justice, and judgment, and equity; to give subtlety to the simple, to the young man knowledge and discretion. A wise man will hear and will increase learning, and a man of understanding shall attain unto wise counsels; to understand a proverb, and the interpretation — the words of the wise, and their dark sayings. The fear of the Lord is the beginning of knowledge, but fools despise wisdom and instruction.

My son, hear the instruction of your father, and forsake not the law of your mother; for they shall be an ornament of grace unto your head, and chains about your neck. My son, if sinners entice you, consent not. If they say, Come with us, let us lay wait for blood, let us lurk secretly for the innocent without cause, let us swallow them up alive as the grave, and whole, as those that go down into the pit; we shall find all precious substance, we shall fill our houses with spoil, cast in your lot among us, let us all have one purse — my son, walk not in the way with them. Restrain your foot from their path, for their feet run to evil and make haste to shed blood — surely in vain the net is spread in the sight of any bird — and they lay wait for their own blood, they lurk secretly for their own lives. So are the ways of everyone that is greedy of gain which take away the life of the owners thereof.

2 Wisdom cries outside; she utters her voice in the streets, she cries in the chief place of concourse, in the openings of the gates. In the city she utters her words, saying, How long, you simple ones, will you love simplicity? And the scorners delight in their scorning? And fools hate knowledge? Turn at my reproof. Behold, I will pour out my spirit unto you, I will make known my words unto you.

3 Because I have called and you refused, I have stretched out my hand and no man regarded, but you have despised all my counsel and would have none of my reproof, I also will laugh at your calamity; I will mock when your fear comes. When your fear comes as desolation and your destruction comes as a whirlwind, when distress and anguish comes upon you — then shall they call upon me; but I will not answer. They shall seek me early, but they shall not find me, for they hated knowledge and did not choose the fear of the Lord. They would have none of my counsel, they despised all my reproof. Therefore shall they eat of the fruit of their own way, and be filled with their own devices; for the turning away of the simple shall slay them, and the prosperity of fools shall destroy them.

4 But whoever listens unto me shall dwell safely, and shall be quiet from fear of evil.

5 My son, if you will receive my words and hide my commandments with you, so that you incline your ear unto wisdom and apply your heart to understanding, yea, if you cry after knowledge and lift up your voice for understanding, if you seek her as silver and search for her as for hidden treasures, then shall you understand the fear of the Lord and find the knowledge of God; for the Lord gives wisdom, out of his mouth comes knowledge and understanding. He lays up sound wisdom for the righteous, he is a buckler to them that walk uprightly. He keeps the paths of judgment and preserves the way of his saints. Then shall you understand righteousness, and judgment, and equity, yea, every good path.

6 When wisdom enters into your heart and knowledge is pleasant unto your soul, discretion shall preserve you, understanding shall keep you, to deliver you from the way of the evil man, from the man that speaks froward things, who leave the paths of uprightness to walk in the ways of darkness, who rejoice to do evil and delight in the frowardness of the wicked, whose ways are crooked, and they froward in their paths; to deliver you from the strange woman, even from the stranger who flatters with her words, who forsakes the guide of her youth and forgets the covenant of her God — for her house inclines unto death and her paths unto the dead, none that go unto her return again, neither take they hold of the paths of life — that you may walk in the way of good men, and keep the paths of the righteous. For the upright shall dwell in the land and the perfect shall remain in it, but the wicked shall be cut off from the earth and the transgressors shall be rooted out of it.

7 My son, forget not my law, but let your heart keep my commandments; for length of days, and long life, and peace shall they add to you. Let not mercy and truth forsake you; bind them about your neck, write them upon the tablet of your heart. So shall you find favor and good understanding in the sight of God and man.

8 Trust in the Lord with all your heart, and lean not unto your own understanding. In all your ways acknowledge him, and he shall direct your paths. Be not wise in your own eyes. Fear the Lord, and depart from evil; it shall be health to your navel and marrow to your bones.

9 Honor the Lord with your substance, and with the firstfruits of all your increase. So shall your barns be filled with plenty, and your presses shall burst out with new wine.

10 My son, despise not the chastening of the Lord, neither be weary of his correction; for whom the Lord loves, he corrects, even as a father the son in whom he delights.

11 Happy is the man that finds wisdom, and the man that gets understanding; for the merchandise of it is better than the merchandise of silver, and the gain thereof than fine gold. She is more precious than rubies, and all the things you can desire are not to be compared unto her. Length of days is in her right hand; and in her left hand, riches and honor. Her ways are ways of pleasantness, and all her paths are peace. She is a tree of life to them that lay hold upon her, and happy is

everyone that retains her. The Lord, by wisdom, has founded the earth; by understanding has he established the heavens; by his knowledge, the depths are broken up and the clouds drop down the dew. My son, do not let them depart from your eyes.

12 Keep sound wisdom and discretion; so shall they be life unto your soul and grace to your neck. Then shall you walk in your way safely, and your foot shall not stumble. When you lie down, you shall not be afraid; yea, you shall lie down and your sleep shall be sweet.

13 Be not afraid of sudden fear, neither of the desolation of the wicked when it comes; for the Lord shall be your confidence, and shall keep your foot from being taken.

14 Withhold not good from them to whom it is due, when it is in the power of your hand to do it. Say not unto your neighbor, Go, and come again, and tomorrow I will give—when you have it by you. Devise not evil against your neighbor, seeing he dwells securely by you. Quarrel not with a man without cause, if he has done you no harm.

15 Envy not the oppressor, and choose none of his ways; for the froward is abomination to the Lord, but his secret is with the righteous. The curse of the Lord is in the house of the wicked, but he blesses the habitation of the just. Surely he scorns the scorners, but he gives grace unto the lowly. The wise shall inherit glory, but shame shall be the promotion of fools.

16 Hear, you children, the instruction of a father, and attend to know understanding; for I give you good teachings. Forsake not my law; for I was my father's son, tender and only-beloved in the sight of my mother. He taught me also, and said unto me, Let your heart retain my words; keep my commandments, and live. Get wisdom, get understanding; forget it not, neither decline from the words of my mouth. Forsake her not, and she shall preserve you; love her, and she shall keep you. Wisdom is the principal thing; therefore, get wisdom; and with all your getting, get understanding. Exalt her, and she shall promote you. She shall bring you to honor when you do embrace her. She shall give to your head an ornament of grace: a crown of glory shall she deliver to you.

17 Hear, O my son, and receive my sayings, and the years of your life shall be many. I have taught you in the way of wisdom, I have led you in right paths. When you go, your steps shall not be distressed; and

when you run, you shall not stumble. Take fast hold of instruction, let her not go; keep her, for she is your life.

¹⁸ Enter not into the path of the wicked, and go not in the way of evil men. Avoid it, pass not by it, turn from it and pass away; for they sleep not except they have done mischief, and their sleep is taken away unless they cause some to fall. For they eat the bread of wickedness, and drink the wine of violence. But the path of the just is as the shining light, that shines more and more unto the perfect day; the way of the wicked is as darkness, they know not at what they stumble.

¹⁹ My son, attend to my words, incline your ear unto my sayings. Let them not depart from your eyes, keep them in the midst of your heart; for they are life unto those that find them, and health to all their flesh. Keep your heart with all diligence, for out of it are the issues of life. Put away from you a froward mouth, and perverse lips put far from you. Let your eyes look right on, and let your eyelids look straight before you. Ponder the path of your feet, and let all your ways be established. Turn not to the right hand nor to the left; remove your foot from evil.

²⁰ My son, attend unto my wisdom and bow your ear to my understanding, that you may regard discretion and that your lips may keep knowledge. For the lips of a strange woman drop as a honeycomb, and her mouth is smoother than oil; but her end is bitter as wormwood, sharp as a two-edged sword. Her feet go down to death, her steps take hold on hell. Lest you should ponder the path of life, her ways are moveable, that you cannot know them. Hear me now therefore, O you children, and depart not from the words of my mouth. Remove your way far from her, and come not near the door of her house, lest you give your honor unto others and your years unto the cruel; lest strangers be filled with your wealth and your labors be in the house of a stranger, and you mourn at the last, when your flesh and your body are consumed, and say, How I have hated instruction, and my heart despised reproof, and have not obeyed the voice of my teachers, nor inclined my ear to them that instructed me! I was almost in all evil in the midst of the congregation and assembly.

²¹ Drink waters out of your own cistern, and running waters out of your own well. Let your fountains be dispersed abroad, and rivers of waters in the streets. Let them be only your own, and not strangers' with you. Let your fountain be blessed, and rejoice with the wife of

your youth. Let her be as the loving hind and pleasant roe; let her breasts satisfy you at all times, and you be ravished always with her love. And why will you, my son, be ravished with a strange woman, and embrace the bosom of a stranger?

22 For the ways of man are before the eyes of the Lord, and he ponders all his goings. His own iniquities shall take the wicked himself, and he shall be held with the cords of his sins. He shall die without instruction, and in the greatness of his folly he shall go astray.

23 My son, if you be surety for your friend, if you have stricken your hand with a stranger, you are snared with the words of your mouth, you are caught with the words of your mouth. Do this now, my son, and deliver yourself: when you have come into the hand of your friend, go humble yourself, and make sure your friend. Give not sleep to your eyes, nor slumber to your eyelids. Deliver yourself as a roe from the hand of the hunter, and as a bird from the hand of the fowler.

24 Go to the ant, you sluggard. Consider her ways and be wise—which having no guide, overseer, or ruler, provides her food in the summer and gathers her food in the harvest. How long will you sleep, O sluggard? When will you arise out of your sleep? Yet a little sleep, a little slumber, a little folding of the hands to sleep; so shall your poverty come as one that travels, and your lack as an armed man.

25 A naughty person, a wicked man, walks with a froward mouth. He winks with his eyes, he speaks with his feet, he teaches with his fingers. Frowardness is in his heart, he devises mischief continually; he sows discord. Therefore shall his calamity come suddenly; suddenly shall he be broken without remedy.

26 These six things does the Lord hate, yea, seven are an abomination unto him: a proud look, a lying tongue, and hands that shed innocent blood, a heart that devises wicked imaginations, feet that be swift in running to mischief, a false witness that speaks lies, and he that sows discord among brethren.

27 My son, keep your father's commandment, and forsake not the law of your mother. Bind them continually upon your heart, and tie them about your neck. When you go, it shall lead you; when you sleep, it shall keep you; and when you awake, it shall talk with you. For the commandment is a lamp, and the law is light; and reproofs of instruction are the way of life.

²⁸ To keep you from the evil woman, from the flattery of the tongue of a strange woman, lust not after her beauty in your heart, neither let her catch you with her eyelids; for by means of a whorish woman, a man is brought to a piece of bread, and the adulteress will hunt for the precious life. Can a man take fire in his bosom and his clothes not be burned? Can one go upon hot coals and his feet not be burned? So he that goes in to his neighbor's wife, whoever touches her shall not be innocent.

²⁹ Men do not despise a thief if he steal to satisfy his soul when he is hungry; but if he be found, he shall restore sevenfold, he shall give all the substance of his house.

³⁰ But whoever commits adultery with a woman lacks understanding; he that does it destroys his own soul. A wound and dishonor shall he get, and his reproach shall not be wiped away. For jealousy is the rage of a man, therefore he will not spare in the day of vengeance. He will not regard any ransom, neither will he rest content, though you give many gifts.

³¹ My son, keep my words, and lay up my commandments with you. Keep my commandments and live, and my law as the apple of your eye. Bind them upon your fingers, write them upon the tablet of your heart. Say unto wisdom, You are my sister — and call understanding your kinswoman, that they may keep you from the strange woman, from the stranger who flatters with her words.

³² For at the window of my house I looked through my lattice, and beheld among the simple ones; I discerned among the youths a young man, void of understanding, passing through the street near her corner; and he went the way to her house in the twilight, in the evening, in the black and dark night. And behold, there met him a woman, with the attire of a harlot and subtle of heart. (She is loud and stubborn; her feet remain not in her house — now is she outside, now in the streets, and lies in wait at every corner.) So she caught him, and kissed him, and with an impudent face said unto him, I have peace offerings with me, this day have I paid my vows. Therefore came I forth to meet you, diligently to seek your face, and I have found you. I have adorned my bed with coverings of tapestry, with carved works, with fine linen of Egypt. I have perfumed my bed with myrrh, aloes, and cinnamon. Come, let us take our fill of love until the morning, let us

solace ourselves with loves; for the master of the house is not at home, he is gone, a long journey; he has taken a bag of money with him and will come home at the day appointed. With her much fair speech she caused him to yield, with the flattering of her lips she forced him. He goes after her immediately, as an ox goes to the slaughter, or as a fool to the correction of the stocks, until a dart strike through his liver; as a bird hastens to the snare, and knows not that it is for his life.

33 Listen unto me now therefore, O you children, and attend to the words of my mouth. Let not your heart decline to her ways, go not astray in her paths; for she has cast down many wounded, yea, many strong men have been slain by her. Her house is the way to hell, going down to the chambers of death.

34 Does not Wisdom cry, and understanding put forth her voice? She stands in the top of high places, by the way in the places of the paths. She cries at the gates, at the entry of the city, at the coming in at the doors. Unto you, O men, I call, and my voice is to the sons of man. O you simple, understand Wisdom; and you fools, be of an understanding heart.

35 Hear, for I will speak of excellent things, and the opening of my lips shall be right things; for my mouth shall speak truth, and wickedness is an abomination to my lips. All the words of my mouth are in righteousness, there is nothing froward or perverse in them. They are all plain to him that understands, and right to them that find knowledge. Receive my instruction, and not silver, and knowledge rather than choice gold. For wisdom is better than rubies, and all the things that may be desired are not to be compared to it.

36 I, Wisdom, dwell with prudence, and find out knowledge of clever inventions. The fear of the Lord is to hate evil. Pride, and arrogance, and the evil way, and the froward mouth, do I hate. Counsel is mine, and sound wisdom. I am understanding, I have strength. By me kings reign and princes decree justice. By me princes rule, and nobles — even all the judges of the earth. I love them that love me, and those that seek me early shall find me. Riches and honor are with me — yea, durable riches and righteousness. My fruit is better than gold, yea, than fine gold, and my revenue than choice silver. I lead in the way of righteousness, in the midst of the paths of judgment, that I may cause those that love me to inherit substance; and I will fill their treasuries.

37 The Lord possessed me in the beginning of his way, before his works of old. I was set up from everlasting, from the beginning, or ever the earth was. When there were no depths, I was brought forth, when there were no fountains abounding with water. Before the mountains were settled, before the hills was I brought forth, while as yet he had not made the earth, nor the fields, nor the highest part of the dust of the world. When he prepared the heavens, I was there. When he set a compass upon the face of the depth, when he established the clouds above, when he strengthened the fountains of the deep, when he gave to the sea his decree that the waters should not pass his commandment, when he appointed the foundations of the earth — then I was by him, as one brought up with him, and I was daily his delight, rejoicing always before him, rejoicing in the habitable part of his earth; and my delights were with the sons of men.

38 Now therefore listen unto me, O you children, for blessed are they that keep my ways. Hear instruction, and be wise, and refuse it not. Blessed is the man that hears me, watching daily at my gates, waiting at the posts of my doors; for whoever finds me finds life and shall obtain favor of the Lord; but he that sins against me wrongs his own soul. All they that hate me love death.

39 Wisdom has built her house, she has hewn out her seven pillars. She has killed her beasts, she has mingled her wine, she has also furnished her table.

40 She has sent forth her maidens. She cries upon the highest places of the city, Whoever is simple, let him turn in here. As for him that lacks understanding, she says to him, Come, eat of my bread and drink of the wine which I have mingled.

41 Forsake the foolish and live, and go in the way of understanding. He that reproves a scorner gets to himself shame, and he that rebukes a wicked man gets himself a blot. Reprove not a scorner, lest he hate you; rebuke a wise man, and he will love you. Give instruction to a wise man and he will be yet wiser, teach a just man and he will increase in learning. The fear of the Lord is the beginning of wisdom, and the knowledge of the holy is understanding; for by me your days shall be multiplied and the years of your life shall be increased. If you are wise, you shall be wise for yourself; but if you scorn, you alone shall bear it.

⁴²A foolish woman is clamorous, she is simple and knows nothing; for she sits at the door of her house, on a seat in the high places of the city, to call passengers who go right on their ways, Whoever is simple, let him turn in here. And as for him that lacks understanding, she says to him, Stolen waters are sweet, and bread eaten in secret is pleasant. But he knows not that the dead are there, and that her guests are in the depths of hell.

2 *The Proverbs of Solomon.*
A wise son makes a glad father, but a foolish son is the heaviness of his mother.

2 Treasures of wickedness profit nothing, but righteousness delivers from death.

3 The Lord will not suffer the soul of the righteous to famish, but he casts away the substance of the wicked.

4 He becomes poor that deals with a slack hand, but the hand of the diligent makes rich.

5 He that gathers in summer is a wise son, but he that sleeps in harvest is a son that causes shame.

6 Blessings are upon the head of the just, but violence covers the mouth of the wicked.

7 The memory of the just is blessed, but the name of the wicked shall rot.

8 The wise in heart will receive commandments, but a prattling fool shall fall.

9 He that walks uprightly walks surely, but he that perverts his ways shall be known.

10 He that winks with the eye causes sorrow, but a prattling fool shall fall.

11 The mouth of a righteous man is a well of life, but violence covers the mouth of the wicked.

12 Hatred stirs up strife, but love covers all sins.

13 In the lips of him that has understanding, wisdom is found; but a rod is for the back of him that is void of understanding.

14 Wise men lay up knowledge, but the mouth of the foolish is near destruction.

¹⁵ The rich man's wealth is his strong city, the destruction of the poor is their poverty.

¹⁶ The labor of the righteous tends to life, the fruit of the wicked to sin.

¹⁷ He is in the way of life that keeps instruction, but he that refuses reproof errs.

¹⁸ He that hides hatred with lying lips, and he that utters a slander, is a fool.

¹⁹ In the multitude of words there lacks not sin, but he that restrains his lips is wise.

²⁰ The tongue of the just is as choice silver, the heart of the wicked is worth little.

²¹ The lips of the righteous feed many, but fools die for lack of wisdom.

²² The blessing of the Lord, it makes rich, and he adds no sorrow with it.

²³ It is as sport to a fool to do mischief, but a man of understanding has wisdom.

²⁴ The fear of the wicked, it shall come upon him; but the desire of the righteous shall be granted.

²⁵ As the whirlwind passes, so is the wicked no more; but the righteous is an everlasting foundation.

²⁶ As vinegar to the teeth, and as smoke to the eyes, so is the sluggard to them that send him.

²⁷ The fear of the Lord prolongs days, but the years of the wicked shall be shortened.

²⁸ The hope of the righteous shall be gladness, but the expectation of the wicked shall perish.

²⁹ The way of the Lord is strength to the upright, but destruction shall be to the workers of iniquity.

³⁰ The righteous shall never be removed, but the wicked shall not inhabit the earth.

³¹ The mouth of the just brings forth wisdom, but the froward tongue shall be cut out.

³² The lips of the righteous know what is acceptable, but the mouth of the wicked speaks frowardness.

³³ A false balance is abomination to the Lord; but a just weight is his delight.

³⁴ When pride comes, then comes shame; but with the lowly is wisdom.

³⁵ The integrity of the upright shall guide them, but the perverseness of transgressors shall destroy them.

³⁶ Riches profit not in the day of wrath, but righteousness delivers from death.

³⁷ The righteousness of the perfect shall direct his way, but the wicked shall fall by his own wickedness.

³⁸ The righteousness of the upright shall deliver them, but transgressors shall be taken in their own wickedness.

³⁹ When a wicked man dies, his expectation shall perish, and the hope of unjust men perishes.

⁴⁰ The righteous is delivered out of trouble, and the wicked comes in his stead.

⁴¹ A hypocrite with his mouth destroys his neighbor, but through knowledge shall the just be delivered.

⁴² When it goes well with the righteous, the city rejoices; and when the wicked perish, there is shouting.

⁴³ By the blessing of the upright, the city is exalted; but it is overthrown by the mouth of the wicked.

⁴⁴ He that is void of wisdom despises his neighbor, but a man of understanding holds his peace.

⁴⁵ A talebearer reveals secrets, but he that is of a faithful spirit conceals the matter.

⁴⁶ Where no counsel is, the people fall; but in the multitude of counselors there is safety.

⁴⁷ He that is surety for a stranger shall smart for it, and he that hates being surety is sure.

⁴⁸ A gracious woman retains honor, and strong men retain riches.

⁴⁹ The merciful man does good to his own soul, but he that is cruel troubles his own flesh.

⁵⁰ The wicked works a deceitful work; but to him that sows righteousness shall be a sure reward.

⁵¹ As righteousness tends to life, so he that pursues evil pursues it to his own death.

⁵² They that are of a froward heart are abomination to the Lord; but such as are upright in their way are his delight.

53 Though hand join in hand, the wicked shall not be unpunished, but the seed of the righteous shall be delivered.

54 As a jewel of gold in a swine's snout, so is a fair woman who is without discretion.

55 The desire of the righteous is only good, but the expectation of the wicked is wrath.

56 There is that scatters, and yet increases; and there is that withholds more than is meet, but it tends to poverty.

57 The liberal soul shall be made fat, and he that waters shall be watered also himself.

58 He that withholds grain, the people shall curse him; but blessing shall be upon the head of him that sells it.

59 He that diligently seeks good procures favor; but he that seeks mischief, it shall come unto him.

60 He that trusts in his riches shall fall, but the righteous shall flourish as a branch.

61 He that troubles his own house shall inherit the wind, and the fool shall be servant to the wise of heart.

62 The fruit of the righteous is a tree of life, and he that wins souls is wise.

63 Behold, the righteous shall be recompensed in the earth, much more the wicked and the sinner.

64 Whoever loves instruction loves knowledge, but he that hates reproof is brutish.

65 A good man obtains favor of the Lord, but a man of wicked devices will he condemn.

66 A man shall not be established by wickedness, but the root of the righteous shall not be moved.

67 A virtuous woman is a crown to her husband; but she that makes ashamed is as rottenness in his bones.

68 The thoughts of the righteous are right, but the counsels of the wicked are deceit.

69 The words of the wicked are to lie in wait for blood, but the mouth of the upright shall deliver them.

70 The wicked are overthrown, and are not; but the house of the righteous shall stand.

⁷¹ A man shall be commended according to his wisdom, but he that is of a perverse heart shall be despised.

⁷² He that is despised and has a servant is better than he that honors himself and lacks bread.

⁷³ A righteous man regards the life of his beast; but the tender mercies of the wicked are cruel.

⁷⁴ He that tills his land shall be satisfied with bread, but he that follows vain people is void of understanding.

⁷⁵ The wicked desires the net of evil men, but the root of the righteous yields fruit.

⁷⁶ The wicked is snared by the transgression of his lips, but the just shall come out of trouble.

⁷⁷ A man shall be satisfied with good by the fruit of his mouth, and the recompense of a man's hands shall be rendered unto him.

⁷⁸ The way of a fool is right in his own eyes, but he that listens unto counsel is wise.

⁷⁹ A fool's wrath is quickly known, but a prudent man covers shame.

⁸⁰ He that speaks truth shows forth righteousness; but a false witness, deceit.

⁸¹ There is that speaks like the piercings of a sword, but the tongue of the wise is health.

⁸² The lip of truth shall be established for ever, but a lying tongue is but for a moment.

⁸³ Deceit is in the heart of them that imagine evil, but to the counselors of peace is joy.

⁸⁴ There shall no evil happen to the just, but the wicked shall be filled with mischief.

⁸⁵ Lying lips are abomination to the Lord, but they that deal truly are his delight.

⁸⁶ A prudent man conceals knowledge, but the heart of fools proclaims foolishness.

⁸⁷ The hand of the diligent shall bear rule, but the slothful shall be under tribute.

⁸⁸ Heaviness in the heart of man makes it stoop, but a good word makes it glad.

⁸⁹ The righteous is more excellent than his neighbor, but the way of the wicked seduces them.

⁹⁰ The slothful man roasts not that which he took in hunting, but the substance of a diligent man is precious.

⁹¹ In the way of righteousness is life, and in the pathway thereof, there is no death.

⁹² A wise son hears his father's instruction, but a scorner hears not rebuke.

⁹³ A man shall eat good by the fruit of his mouth, but the soul of the transgressors shall eat violence.

⁹⁴ He that keeps his mouth keeps his life, but he that opens wide his lips shall have destruction.

⁹⁵ The soul of the sluggard desires, and has nothing; but the soul of the diligent shall be made fat.

⁹⁶ A righteous man hates lying, but a wicked man is loathsome and comes to shame.

⁹⁷ Righteousness keeps him that is upright in the way, but wickedness overthrows the sinner.

⁹⁸ There is that makes himself rich, yet has nothing; there is that makes himself poor, yet has great riches.

⁹⁹ The ransom of a man's life are his riches, but the poor hears not rebuke.

¹⁰⁰ The light of the righteous rejoices, but the lamp of the wicked shall be put out.

¹⁰¹ Only by pride comes contention, but with the well-advised is wisdom.

¹⁰² Wealth gotten by vanity shall be diminished, but he that gathers by labor shall increase.

¹⁰³ Hope deferred makes the heart sick; but when the desire comes, it is a tree of life.

¹⁰⁴ Whoever despises the word shall be destroyed, but he that fears the commandment shall be rewarded.

¹⁰⁵ The law of the wise is a fountain of life, to depart from the snares of death.

¹⁰⁶ Good understanding gives favor, but the way of transgressors is hard.

¹⁰⁷ Every prudent man deals with knowledge, but a fool lays open his folly.

108 A wicked messenger falls into mischief, but a faithful ambassador is health.

109 Poverty and shame shall be to him that refuses instruction, but he that regards reproof shall be honored.

110 The desire accomplished is sweet to the soul, but it is abomination to fools to depart from evil.

111 He that walks with wise men shall be wise, but a companion of fools shall be destroyed.

112 Evil pursues sinners; but to the righteous, good shall be repaid.

113 A good man leaves an inheritance to his children's children, and the wealth of the sinner is laid up for the just.

114 Much food is in the tillage of the poor, but there is that which is destroyed for lack of judgment.

115 He that spares his rod hates his son, but he that loves him chastens him early.

116 The righteous eats to the satisfying of his soul, but the belly of the wicked shall lack.

117 Every wise woman builds her house, but the foolish plucks it down with her hands.

118 He that walks in his uprightness fears the Lord, but he that is perverse in his ways despises him.

119 In the mouth of the foolish is a rod of pride, but the lips of the wise shall preserve them.

120 Where no oxen are, the crib is clean; but much increase is by the strength of the ox.

121 A faithful witness will not lie, but a false witness will utter lies.

122 A scorner seeks wisdom and finds it not, but knowledge is easy unto him that understands.

123 Go from the presence of a foolish man when you perceive not in him the lips of knowledge.

124 The wisdom of the prudent is to understand his way, but the folly of fools is deceit.

125 Fools make a mock at sin, but among the righteous there is favor.

126 The heart knows his own bitterness, and a stranger does not meddle with his joy.

127 The house of the wicked shall be overthrown, but the tabernacle of the upright shall flourish.

128 There is a way which seems right unto a man, but the end thereof are the ways of death.

129 Even in laughter the heart is sorrowful, and the end of that mirth is heaviness.

130 The backslider in heart shall be filled with his own ways, and a good man shall be satisfied from himself.

131 The simple believes every word, but the prudent man looks well to his going.

132 A wise man fears and departs from evil, but the fool rages and is confident.

133 He that is soon angry deals foolishly, and a man of wicked devices is hated.

134 The simple inherit folly, but the prudent are crowned with knowledge.

135 The evil bow before the good, and the wicked at the gates of the righteous.

136 The poor is hated even of his own neighbor, but the rich has many friends.

137 He that despises his neighbor sins, but he that has mercy on the poor, happy is he.

138 Do they not err that devise evil? But mercy and truth shall be to them that devise good.

139 In all labor there is profit, but the talk of the lips tends only to poverty.

140 The crown of the wise is their riches, but the foolishness of fools is folly.

141 A true witness delivers souls, but a deceitful witness speaks lies.

142 In the fear of the Lord is strong confidence, and his children shall have a place of refuge.

143 The fear of the Lord is a fountain of life, to depart from the snares of death.

144 In the multitude of people is the king's honor, but in the lack of people is the destruction of the prince.

145 He that is slow to wrath is of great understanding, but he that is hasty of spirit exalts folly.

146 A sound heart is the life of the flesh, but envy, the rottenness of the bones.

¹⁴⁷ He that oppresses the poor reproaches his Maker, but he that honors him has mercy on the poor.

¹⁴⁸ The wicked is driven away in his wickedness, but the righteous has hope in his death.

¹⁴⁹ Wisdom rests in the heart of him that has understanding, but that which is in the midst of fools is made known.

¹⁵⁰ Righteousness exalts a nation, but sin is a reproach to any people.

¹⁵¹ The king's favor is toward a wise servant, but his wrath is against him that causes shame.

¹⁵² A soft answer turns away wrath, but grievous words stir up anger.

¹⁵³ The tongue of the wise uses knowledge aright, but the mouth of fools pours out foolishness.

¹⁵⁴ The eyes of the Lord are in every place, beholding the evil and the good.

¹⁵⁵ A wholesome tongue is a tree of life, but perverseness therein is a breach in the spirit.

¹⁵⁶ A fool despises his father's instruction, but he that regards reproof is prudent.

¹⁵⁷ In the house of the righteous is much treasure, but in the revenues of the wicked is trouble.

¹⁵⁸ The lips of the wise disperse knowledge, but the heart of the foolish does not so.

¹⁵⁹ The sacrifice of the wicked is an abomination to the Lord, but the prayer of the upright is his delight.

¹⁶⁰ The way of the wicked is an abomination unto the Lord, but he loves him that follows after righteousness.

¹⁶¹ Correction is grievous unto him that forsakes the way, and he that hates reproof shall die.

¹⁶² Hell and destruction are before the Lord, how much more then the hearts of the children of men!

¹⁶³ A scorner loves not one that reproves him, neither will he go unto the wise.

¹⁶⁴ A merry heart makes a cheerful countenance, but by sorrow of the heart the spirit is broken.

¹⁶⁵ The heart of him that has understanding seeks knowledge, but the mouth of fools feeds on foolishness.

166 All the days of the afflicted are evil, but he that is of a merry heart has a continual feast.

167 Better is little with the fear of the Lord, than great treasure and trouble with it.

168 Better is a dinner of herbs where love is, than a fattened ox and hatred with it.

169 A wrathful man stirs up strife, but he that is slow to anger appeases strife.

170 The way of the slothful man is as a hedge of thorns, but the way of the righteous is made plain.

171 A wise son makes a glad father, but a foolish man despises his mother.

172 Folly is joy to him that is destitute of wisdom, but a man of understanding walks uprightly.

173 Without counsel, purposes are disappointed, but in the multitude of counselors they are established.

174 A man has joy by the answer of his mouth; and a word spoken in due season, how good is it!

175 The way of life is above to the wise, that he may depart from hell beneath.

176 The Lord will destroy the house of the proud, but he will establish the border of the widow.

177 The thoughts of the wicked are an abomination to the Lord, but the words of the pure are pleasant words.

178 He that is greedy of gain troubles his own house, but he that hates bribes shall live.

179 The heart of the righteous studies to answer, but the mouth of the wicked pours out evil things.

180 The Lord is far from the wicked, but he hears the prayer of the righteous.

181 The light of the eyes rejoices the heart, and a good report makes the bones fat.

182 The ear that hears the reproof of life abides among the wise.

183 He that refuses instruction despises his own soul, but he that hears reproof gets understanding.

184 The fear of the Lord is the instruction of wisdom, and before honor is humility.

185 The preparations of the heart in man, and the answer of the tongue, is from the Lord.

186 All the ways of a man are clean in his own eyes, but the Lord weighs the spirits.

187 Commit your works unto the Lord, and your thoughts shall be established.

188 The Lord has made all things for himself, yea, even the wicked for the day of evil.

189 Everyone that is proud in heart is an abomination to the Lord; though hand join in hand, he shall not be unpunished.

190 By mercy and truth, iniquity is purged; and by the fear of the Lord, men depart from evil.

191 When a man's ways please the Lord, he makes even his enemies to be at peace with him.

192 Better is a little with righteousness, than great revenues without right.

193 A man's heart devises his way, but the Lord directs his steps.

194 A divine sentence is in the lips of the king, his mouth transgresses not in judgment.

195 A just weight and balance are the Lord's; all the weights of the bag are his work.

196 It is an abomination to kings to commit wickedness, for the throne is established by righteousness.

197 Righteous lips are the delight of kings, and they love him that speaks right.

198 The wrath of a king is as messengers of death, but a wise man will pacify it.

199 In the light of the king's countenance is life, and his favor is as a cloud of the spring rain.

200 How much better is it to get wisdom than gold, and to get understanding rather to be chosen than silver!

201 The highway of the upright is to depart from evil; he that keeps his way preserves his soul.

202 Pride goes before destruction, and a haughty spirit before a fall.

203 Better it is to be of a humble spirit with the lowly, than to divide the spoil with the proud.

204 He that handles a matter wisely shall find good; and whoever trusts in the Lord, happy is he.

205 The wise in heart shall be called prudent, and the sweetness of the lips increases learning.

206 Understanding is a wellspring of life unto him that has it; but the instruction of fools is folly.

207 The heart of the wise teaches his mouth and adds learning to his lips.

208 Pleasant words are as a honeycomb—sweet to the soul, and health to the bones.

209 There is a way that seems right unto a man, but the end thereof are the ways of death.

210 He that labors, labors for himself, for his mouth craves it of him.

211 An ungodly man digs up evil, and in his lips there is as a burning fire.

212 A froward man sows strife, and a whisperer separates chief friends.

213 A violent man entices his neighbor and leads him into a way that is not good.

214 He shuts his eyes to devise froward things; moving his lips, he brings evil to pass.

215 The graying head is a crown of glory, if it is found in the way of righteousness.

216 He that is slow to anger is better than the mighty, and he that rules his spirit than he that takes a city.

217 The lot is cast into the lap, but the whole disposing thereof is of the Lord.

218 Better is a dry morsel, and quietness with it, than a house full of sacrifices with strife.

219 A wise servant shall have rule over a son that causes shame, and shall have part of the inheritance among the brethren.

220 The refining pot is for silver, and the furnace for gold, but the Lord tries the hearts.

221 A wicked doer gives heed to false lips, and a liar gives ear to a naughty tongue.

222 Whoever mocks the poor reproaches his Maker, and he that is glad at calamities shall not be unpunished.

223 Children's children are the crown of old men, and the glory of children are their fathers.

224 Excellent speech becomes not a fool, much less do lying lips a prince.

225 A bribe is as a precious stone in the eyes of him that has it; wherever it turns, it prospers.

226 He that covers a transgression seeks love, but he that repeats a matter separates close friends.

227 A reproof enters more into a wise man than a hundred stripes into a fool.

228 An evil man seeks only rebellion; therefore, a cruel messenger shall be sent against him.

229 Let a bear robbed of her whelps meet a man, rather than a fool in his folly.

230 Whoever rewards evil for good, evil shall not depart from his house.

231 The beginning of strife is as when one lets out water; therefore, leave off contention before it is meddled with.

232 He that justifies the wicked, and he that condemns the just, even they both are abomination to the Lord.

233 Why is there a price in the hand of a fool to get wisdom, seeing he has no heart to it?

234 A friend loves at all times, and a brother is born for adversity.

235 A man void of understanding strikes hands and becomes surety in the presence of his friend.

236 He loves transgression that loves strife, and he that exalts his gate seeks destruction.

237 He that has a froward heart finds no good, and he that has a perverse tongue falls into mischief.

238 He that begets a fool does it to his sorrow, and the father of a fool has no joy.

239 A merry heart does good like a medicine, but a broken spirit dries the bones.

240 A wicked man takes a bribe out of the bosom to pervert the ways of judgment.

241 Wisdom is before him that has understanding, but the eyes of a fool are in the ends of the earth.

242 A foolish son is a grief to his father, and bitterness to her that bore him.

243 Also, to punish the just is not good, nor to strike princes for equity.

244 He that has knowledge spares his words, and a man of understanding is of an excellent spirit.

245 Even a fool, when he holds his peace, is counted wise, and he that shuts his lips is esteemed a man of understanding.

246 Through desire, a man having separated himself seeks and meddles with all wisdom.

247 A fool has no delight in understanding, but that his heart may reveal itself.

248 When the wicked comes then contempt also comes, and with ignominy, reproach.

249 The words of a man's mouth are as deep waters, and the wellspring of wisdom as a flowing brook.

250 It is not good to respect the person of the wicked to overthrow the righteous in judgment.

251 A fool's lips enter into contention, and his mouth calls for strokes.

252 A fool's mouth is his destruction, and his lips are the snare of his soul.

253 The words of a talebearer are as wounds, and they go down into the innermost parts of the belly.

254 He also that is slothful in his work is brother to him that is a great waster.

255 The name of the Lord is a strong tower, the righteous runs into it and is safe.

256 The rich man's wealth is his strong city, and as a high wall, in his own imagination.

257 Before destruction, the heart of man is haughty, and before honor is humility.

258 He that answers a matter before he hears it, it is folly and shame unto him.

259 The spirit of a man will sustain his infirmity; but a wounded spirit, who can bear?

260 The heart of the prudent gets knowledge, and the ear of the wise seeks knowledge.

261 A man's gift makes room for him, and brings him before great men.

262 He that is first in his own cause seems just, but his neighbor comes and examines him.

263 The lot causes contentions to cease, and parts between the mighty.

264 A brother offended is harder to be won than a strong city, and their contentions are like the bars of a castle.

265 A man's belly shall be satisfied with the fruit of his mouth, and with the increase of his lips shall he be filled.

266 Death and life are in the power of the tongue, and they that love it shall eat the fruit thereof.

267 Whoever finds a good wife has obtained favor of the Lord.

268 The poor uses entreaties, but the rich answers roughly.

269 A man that has friends must show himself friendly, and there is a friend that sticks closer than a brother.

270 Better is the poor that walks in his integrity, than he that is perverse in his lips and is a fool.

271 Also, that the soul be without knowledge — it is not good; and he that hastens with his feet sins.

272 The foolishness of man perverts his way, and his heart frets against the Lord.

273 Wealth makes many friends, but the poor is separated from his neighbor.

274 A false witness shall not be unpunished, and he that speaks lies shall not escape.

275 Many will entreat the favor of the prince, and every man is a friend to him that gives gifts.

276 All the brethren of the poor do hate him; how much more do his friends go far from him? He pursues them with words, yet they are absent to him.

277 He that gets wisdom loves his own soul, he that keeps understanding shall find good.

278 A false witness shall not be unpunished, and he that speaks lies shall perish.

279 Delight is not fitting for a fool, much less for a servant to have rule over princes.

280 The discretion of a man defers his anger, and it is his glory to pass over a transgression.

281 The king's wrath is as the roaring of a lion, but his favor is as dew upon the grass.

282 A foolish son is the calamity of his father, and the contentions of a wife are a continual dripping.

283 House and riches are the inheritance of fathers, and a prudent wife is from the Lord.

284 Slothfulness casts into a deep sleep, and an idle soul shall suffer hunger.

285 He that keeps the commandment keeps his own soul, but he that despises his ways shall die.

286 He that has pity upon the poor lends unto the Lord, and that which he has given will he pay him again.

287 Chasten your son while there is hope, and let not your soul spare for his crying.

288 A man of great wrath shall suffer punishment; for if you deliver him, yet you must do it again.

289 Hear counsel and receive instruction, that you may be wise in your latter end.

290 There are many devices in a man's heart; nevertheless, the counsel of the Lord—that shall stand.

291 The desire of a man is his kindness, and a poor man is better than a liar.

292 The fear of the Lord tends to life, and he that has it shall abide satisfied; he shall not be visited with evil.

293 A slothful man hides his hand in his bosom, and will not so much as bring it to his mouth again.

294 Smite a scorner, and the simple will beware; and reprove one that has understanding, and he will understand knowledge.

295 He that wastes his father, and chases away his mother, is a son that causes shame and brings reproach.

296 Cease, my son, to hear the instruction that causes to err from the words of knowledge.

297 An ungodly witness scorns judgment, and the mouth of the wicked devours iniquity.

298 Judgments are prepared for scorners, and stripes for the back of fools.

299 Wine is a mocker, strong drink is raging, and whoever is deceived thereby is not wise.

300 The fear of a king is as the roaring of a lion; whoever provokes him to anger sins against his own soul.

301 It is an honor for a man to cease from strife, but every fool will be meddling.

302 The sluggard will not plow by reason of the cold, therefore shall he beg in harvest and have nothing.

303 Counsel in the heart of man is like deep water, but a man of understanding will draw it out.

304 Most men will proclaim every one his own goodness; but a faithful man, who can find?

305 The just man walks in his integrity, his children are blessed after him.

306 A king that sits in the throne of judgment scatters away all evil with his eyes.

307 Who can say, I have made my heart clean, I am pure from my sin?

308 Diverse weights and diverse measures, both of them are alike: abomination to the Lord.

309 Even a child is known by his doings, whether his work is pure and whether it is right.

310 The hearing ear and the seeing eye, the Lord has made even both of them.

311 Love not sleep, lest you come to poverty; open your eyes and you shall be satisfied with bread.

312 It is naught, it is naught, says the buyer; but when he is gone his way, then he boasts.

313 There is gold, and a multitude of rubies, but the lips of knowledge are a precious jewel.

314 Take his garment that is surety for a stranger, and take a pledge of him for a strange woman.

315 Bread of deceit is sweet to a man, but afterward his mouth shall be filled with gravel.

316 Every purpose is established by counsel, and with good advice make war.

317 He that goes about as a talebearer reveals secrets; therefore, meddle not with him that flatters with his lips.

318 Whoever curses his father or his mother, his lamp shall be put out in obscure darkness.

319 An inheritance may be gotten hastily at the beginning, but the end thereof shall not be blessed.

320 Say not, I will recompense evil — but wait on the Lord, and he shall save you.

321 Diverse weights are an abomination unto the Lord, and a false balance is not good.

322 Man's goings are of the Lord; how can a man then understand his own way?

323 It is a snare to the man who devours that which is holy, and after, vows to make inquiry.

324 A wise king scatters the wicked, and brings the wheel over them.

325 The spirit of man is the candle of the Lord, searching all the inward parts of the belly.

326 Mercy and truth preserve the king, and his throne is upheld by mercy.

327 The glory of young men is their strength, and the beauty of old men is the gray head.

328 The blueness of a wound cleanses away evil, so do stripes the inward parts of the belly.

329 The king's heart is in the hand of the Lord as the rivers of water: he turns it wherever he will.

330 Every way of a man is right in his own eyes, but the Lord ponders the hearts.

331 To do justice and judgment is more acceptable to the Lord than sacrifice.

332 A haughty look, and a proud heart, and the plowing of the wicked is sin.

333 The thoughts of the diligent tend only to plenteousness; but of everyone that is hasty, only to lack.

334 The getting of treasures by a lying tongue is a vanity tossed to and fro of them that seek death.

335 The robbery of the wicked shall destroy them, because they refuse to do judgment.

336 The way of man is froward and strange; but as for the pure, his work is right.

337 It is better to dwell in a corner of the housetop than with a brawling woman in a wide house.

338 The soul of the wicked desires evil, his neighbor finds no favor in his eyes.

339 When the scorner is punished, the simple is made wise; and when the wise is instructed, he receives knowledge.

340 The righteous man wisely considers the house of the wicked, but God overthrows the wicked for their wickedness.

341 Whoever stops his ears at the cry of the poor, he also shall cry himself, but shall not be heard.

342 A gift in secret pacifies anger, and a reward in the bosom, strong wrath.

343 It is joy to the just to do judgment, but destruction shall be to the workers of iniquity.

344 The man that wanders out of the way of understanding shall remain in the congregation of the dead.

345 He that loves pleasure shall be a poor man; he that loves wine and oil shall not be rich.

346 The wicked shall be a ransom for the righteous, and the transgressor for the upright.

347 It is better to dwell in the wilderness than with a contentious and an angry woman.

348 There is treasure to be desired, and oil, in the dwelling of the wise; but a foolish man spends it up.

349 He that follows after righteousness and mercy finds life, righteousness, and honor.

350 A wise man scales the city of the mighty, and casts down the strength of the confidence thereof.

351 Whoever keeps his mouth and his tongue keeps his soul from troubles.

352 Proud and haughty scorner is his name, who deals in proud wrath.

353 The desire of the slothful kills him, for his hands refuse to labor. He covets greedily all the day long, but the righteous gives and spares not.

354 The sacrifice of the wicked is abomination; how much more when he brings it with a wicked mind!

355 A false witness shall perish, but the man that hears speaks constantly.

356 A wicked man hardens his face, but as for the upright, he directs his way.

357 There is no wisdom, nor understanding, nor counsel against the Lord.

358 The horse is prepared against the day of battle, but safety is of the Lord.

359 A good name is rather to be chosen than great riches, and loving favor rather than silver and gold.

360 The rich and poor meet together, the Lord is the maker of them all.

361 A prudent man foresees the evil and hides himself, but the simple pass on and are punished.

362 By humility and the fear of the Lord are riches, and honor, and life.

363 Thorns and snares are in the way of the froward; he that does keep his soul shall be far from them.

364 Train up a child in the way he should go, and when he is old, he will not depart from it.

365 The rich rules over the poor, and the borrower is servant to the lender.

366 He that sows iniquity shall reap vanity, and the rod of his anger shall fail.

367 He that has a bountiful eye shall be blessed, for he gives of his bread to the poor.

368 Cast out the scorner, and contention shall go out; yea, strife and reproach shall cease.

369 He that loves pureness of heart, for the grace of his lips, the king shall be his friend; for the eyes of the Lord preserve knowledge, but he overthrows the words of the transgressor.

370 The slothful man says, There is a lion outside, I shall be slain in the streets.

371 The mouth of strange women is a deep pit; he that is abhorred of the Lord shall fall therein.

372 Foolishness is bound in the heart of a child, but the rod of correction shall drive it far from him.

373 He that oppresses the poor to increase his riches, and he that gives to the rich, shall surely come to lack.

3 Bow down your ear, and hear the words of the wise, and apply your heart unto my knowledge, for it is a pleasant thing if you keep them within you; they shall likewise be fitted in your lips. That your trust may be in the Lord, I have made known to you this day, even to you. Have not I written to you excellent things in counsels and knowledge? That I might make you know the certainty of the words of truth? That you might answer the words of truth to them that send unto you?

2 Rob not the poor, because he is poor, neither oppress the afflicted in the gate; for the Lord will plead their cause, and spoil the soul of those that spoiled them.

3 Make no friendship with an angry man, and with a furious man you shall not go, lest you learn his ways and get a snare to your soul.

4 Be not one of them that strike hands, or of them that are sureties for debts.

5 If you have nothing to pay, why should he take away your bed from under you?

6 Remove not the ancient landmark, which your fathers have set.

7 Do you see a man diligent in his business? He shall stand before kings, he shall not stand before mean men.

8 When you sit to eat with a ruler, consider diligently what is before you, and put a knife to your throat if you are a man given to appetite. Be not desirous of his dainties, for they are deceitful food.

9 Labor not to be rich, cease from your own wisdom.

10 Will you set your eyes upon that which is not? For riches certainly make themselves wings; they fly away as an eagle toward heaven.

11 Eat not the bread of him that has an evil eye, neither desire his dainty foods; for as he thinks in his heart, so is he. Eat and drink, says he to you, but his heart is not with you. The morsel which you have eaten shall you vomit up, and lose your sweet words. Speak not in the ears of a fool, for he will despise the wisdom of your words. Remove not the old landmark, and enter not into the fields of the fatherless; for their redeemer is mighty, he shall plead their cause with you.

12 Apply your heart unto instruction, and your ears to the words of knowledge.

¹³ Withhold not correction from the child, for if you beat him with the rod, he shall not die. You shall beat him with the rod, and shall deliver his soul from hell.

¹⁴ My son, if your heart is wise, my heart shall rejoice, even mine. Yea, my reins shall rejoice when your lips speak right things. Let not your heart envy sinners, but be in the fear of the Lord all the day long; for surely there is an end, and your expectation shall not be cut off. Hear, my son, and be wise, and guide your heart in the way. Be not among winebibbers, among riotous eaters of flesh; for the drunkard and the glutton shall come to poverty, and drowsiness shall clothe a man with rags.

¹⁵ Listen unto your father that begot you, and despise not your mother when she is old. Buy the truth, and sell it not; also wisdom, and instruction, and understanding. The father of the righteous shall greatly rejoice, and he that begets a wise child shall have joy of him. Your father and your mother shall be glad, and she that bore you shall rejoice. My son, give me your heart, and let your eyes observe my ways. For a whore is a deep ditch, and a strange woman is a narrow pit; she also lies in wait as for a prey, and increases the transgressors among men.

¹⁶ Who has woe? Who has sorrow? Who has contentions? Who has babbling? Who has wounds without cause? Who has redness of eyes? They that linger long at the wine; they that go to seek mixed wine. Look not upon the wine when it is red, when it gives his color in the cup, when it moves itself aright. At the last it bites like a serpent and stings like an adder. Your eyes shall behold strange women, and your heart shall utter perverse things. Yea, you shall be as he that lies down in the midst of the sea, or as he that lies upon the top of a mast. They have stricken me, shall you say, and I was not sick; they have beaten me, and I felt it not. When shall I awake? I will seek it yet again.

¹⁷ Be not envious against evil men, neither desire to be with them; for their heart studies destruction, and their lips talk of mischief.

¹⁸ Through wisdom is a house built, and by understanding it is established, and by knowledge shall the chambers be filled with all precious and pleasant riches.

¹⁹ A wise man is strong, yea, a man of knowledge increases strength. For by wise counsel you shall make your war, and in multitude of counselors there is safety.

²⁰ Wisdom is too high for a fool; he opens not his mouth in the gate.

²¹ He that devises to do evil shall be called a mischievous person.

²² The thought of foolishness is sin, and the scorner is an abomination to men.

²³ If you faint in the day of adversity, your strength is small.

²⁴ If you refuse to deliver them that are drawn unto death, and those that are ready to be slain — if you say, Behold, we knew it not — does not he that ponders the heart consider it? And he that keeps your soul, does not he know it? And shall not he render to every man according to his works?

²⁵ My son, eat honey because it is good, and the honeycomb which is sweet to your taste; so shall the knowledge of wisdom be unto your soul; when you have found it, then there shall be a reward and your expectation shall not be cut off.

²⁶ Lay not wait, O wicked man, against the dwelling of the righteous; spoil not his resting place. For a just man falls seven times and rises up again, but the wicked shall fall into mischief.

²⁷ Rejoice not when your enemy falls, and do not let your heart be glad when he stumbles, lest the Lord see it and it displease him, and he turn away his wrath from him. Fret not yourself because of evil men, neither be envious at the wicked, for there shall be no reward to the evil man; the candle of the wicked shall be put out.

²⁸ My son, fear the Lord and the king, and meddle not with them that are given to change; for their calamity shall rise suddenly, and who knows the ruin of them both?

These things also belong to the wise.

²⁹ It is not good to have respect of persons in judgment. He that says unto the wicked, You are righteous — him shall the people curse; nations shall abhor him. But to them that rebuke him shall be delight, and a good blessing shall come upon them. Every man shall kiss his lips that give a right answer.

³⁰ Prepare your work outside, and make it fit for yourself in the field; and afterward build your house.

³¹ Be not a witness against your neighbor without cause, and deceive not with your lips. Say not, I will do so to him as he has done to me, I will render to the man according to his work.

³² I went by the field of the slothful, and by the vineyard of the man void of understanding; and behold, it was all grown over with thorns, and nettles had covered the face thereof, and the stone wall thereof was broken down. Then I saw, and considered it well; I looked upon it, and received instruction. Yet a little sleep, a little slumber, a little folding of the hands to sleep—so shall your poverty come as one that travels, and your lack as an armed man.

These are also proverbs of Solomon, which the men of Hezekiah king of Judah copied out.

4 It is the glory of God to conceal a thing, but the honor of kings to search out a matter.

² The heaven for height, and the earth for depth, and the heart of kings is unsearchable.

³ Take away the dross from the silver, and there shall come forth a vessel for the metalsmith.

⁴ Take away the wicked from before the king, and his throne shall be established in righteousness.

⁵ Put not forth yourself in the presence of the king, and stand not in the place of great men; for better it is that it be said unto you, Come up here—than that you should be put lower in the presence of the prince whom your eyes have seen.

⁶ Go not forth hastily to quarrel, lest you know not what to do in the end thereof, when your neighbor has put you to shame. Debate your cause with your neighbor himself, and reveal not a secret to another, lest he that hears it put you to shame, and your infamy turns not away.

⁷ A word fitly spoken is like apples of gold in pictures of silver.

⁸ As an earring of gold, and an ornament of fine gold, so is a wise reprover upon an obedient ear.

⁹ As the cold of snow in the time of harvest, so is a faithful messenger to them that send him; for he refreshes the soul of his masters.

¹⁰ Whoever boasts himself of a false gift is like clouds and wind without rain.

11 By long enduring is a prince persuaded, and a soft tongue breaks the bone.

12 Have you found honey? Eat so much as is sufficient for you, lest you be filled with it and vomit it.

13 Withdraw your foot from your neighbor's house, lest he be weary of you and so hate you.

14 A man that bears false witness against his neighbor is a club, and a sword, and a sharp arrow.

15 Confidence in an unfaithful man in time of trouble is like a broken tooth, and a foot out of joint.

16 As he that takes away a garment in cold weather, and as vinegar upon natron, so is he that sings songs to a heavy heart.

17 If your enemy is hungry, give him bread to eat, and if he is thirsty, give him water to drink; for you shall heap coals of fire upon his head, and the Lord shall reward you.

18 The north wind drives away rain; so does an angry countenance a backbiting tongue.

19 It is better to dwell in the corner of the housetop than with a brawling woman and in a wide house.

20 As cold waters to a thirsty soul, so is good news from a far country.

21 A righteous man falling down before the wicked is as a troubled fountain and a corrupt spring.

22 It is not good to eat much honey; so for men to search their own glory is not glory.

23 He that has no rule over his own spirit is like a city that is broken down and without walls.

24 As snow in summer, and as rain in harvest, so honor is not fitting for a fool.

25 As the bird by wandering, as the swallow by flying, so the causeless curse shall not come.

26 A whip for the horse, a bridle for the ass, and a rod for the fool's back.

27 Answer not a fool according to his folly, lest you also be like unto him.

28 Answer a fool according to his folly, lest he be wise in his own eyes.

29 He that sends a message by the hand of a fool cuts off the feet and drinks damage.

30 The legs of the lame are not equal; so is a parable in the mouth of fools.

31 As he that binds a stone in a sling, so is he that gives honor to a fool.

32 As a thorn goes up into the hand of a drunkard, so is a parable in the mouth of fools.

33 The great God that formed all things both rewards the fool and rewards transgressors.

34 As a dog returns to his vomit, so a fool returns to his folly.

35 Do you see a man wise in his own eyes? There is more hope for a fool than of him.

36 The slothful man says, There is a lion in the way, a lion is in the streets.

37 As the door turns upon his hinges, so does the slothful upon his bed.

38 The slothful hides his hand in his bosom, it grieves him to bring it again to his mouth.

39 The sluggard is wiser in his own eyes than seven men that can render a reason.

40 He that passes by, and meddles with strife belonging not to him, is like one that takes a dog by the ears.

41 As a madman who casts fiery darts, arrows, and death, so is the man that deceives his neighbor and says, Am I not in sport?

42 Where no wood is, there the fire goes out; so where there is no talebearer, the strife ceases.

43 As coals are to burning coals, and wood to fire, so is a contentious man to kindle strife.

44 The words of a talebearer are as wounds, and they go down into the innermost parts of the belly.

45 Burning lips and a wicked heart are like a potsherd covered with silver dross. He that hates disguises it with his lips, and lays up deceit within him. When he speaks fair, believe him not, for there are seven abominations in his heart whose hatred is covered by deceit; his wickedness shall be shown before the whole congregation.

46 Whoever digs a pit shall fall therein; and he that rolls a stone, it will return upon him.

47 A lying tongue hates those that are afflicted by it, and a flattering mouth works ruin.

⁴⁸ Boast not yourself of tomorrow, for you know not what a day may bring forth.

⁴⁹ Let another man praise you, and not your own mouth; a stranger, and not your own lips.

⁵⁰ A stone is heavy, and the sand weighty; but a fool's wrath is heavier than them both.

⁵¹ Wrath is cruel, and anger is overwhelming; but who is able to stand before envy?

⁵² Open rebuke is better than secret love.

⁵³ Faithful are the wounds of a friend, but the kisses of an enemy are deceitful.

⁵⁴ The full soul loathes a honeycomb; but to the hungry soul, every bitter thing is sweet.

⁵⁵ As a bird that wanders from her nest, so is a man that wanders from his place.

⁵⁶ Ointment and perfume rejoice the heart; so does the sweetness of a man's friend by hearty counsel.

⁵⁷ Your own friend, and your father's friend, forsake not, neither go into your brother's house in the day of your calamity; for better is a neighbor that is near than a brother far off.

⁵⁸ My son, be wise and make my heart glad, that I may answer him who reproaches me.

⁵⁹ A prudent man foresees the evil and hides himself, but the simple pass on and are punished.

⁶⁰ Take his garment that is surety for a stranger, and take a pledge of him for a strange woman.

⁶¹ He that blesses his friend with a loud voice, rising early in the morning, it shall be counted a curse to him.

⁶² A continual dripping in a very rainy day and a contentious woman are alike. Whoever hides her hides the wind, and the ointment of his right hand, which betrays itself.

⁶³ Iron sharpens iron; so a man sharpens the countenance of his friend.

⁶⁴ Whoever keeps the fig tree shall eat the fruit thereof; so he that waits on his master shall be honored.

⁶⁵ As in water face answers to face, so the heart of man to man.

⁶⁶ Hell and destruction are never full; so the eyes of man are never satisfied.

67 As the refining pot for silver and the furnace for gold, so is a man to his praise.

68 Though you should grind a fool in a mortar among wheat with a pestle, yet his foolishness will not depart from him.

69 Be diligent to know the state of your flocks, and look well to your herds; for riches are not for ever, and does the crown endure to every generation? The hay appears, and the tender grass shows itself, and herbs of the mountains are gathered. The lambs are for your clothing, and the goats are the price of the field. And you shall have goats' milk enough for your food, for the food of your household, and for the maintenance of your maidens.

70 The wicked flee when no man pursues, but the righteous are bold as a lion.

71 For the transgression of a land, many are the princes thereof; but by a man of understanding and knowledge, the state thereof shall be prolonged.

72 A poor man that oppresses the poor is like a sweeping rain which leaves no food.

73 They that forsake the law praise the wicked, but such as keep the law contend with them.

74 Evil men understand not judgment, but they that seek the Lord understand all things.

75 Better is the poor that walks in his uprightness than he that is perverse in his ways, though he be rich.

76 Whoever keeps the law is a wise son, but he that is a companion of riotous men shames his father.

77 He that by usury and unjust gain increases his substance, he shall gather it for him that will pity the poor.

78 He that turns away his ear from hearing the law, even his prayer shall be abomination.

79 Whoever causes the righteous to go astray in an evil way, he shall fall himself into his own pit; but the upright shall have good things in possession.

80 The rich man is wise in his own eyes, but the poor that has understanding searches him out.

81 When righteous men do rejoice, there is great glory; but when the wicked rise, a man is hidden.

82 He that covers his sins shall not prosper, but whoever confesses and forsakes them shall have mercy.

83 Happy is the man that fears always, but he that hardens his heart shall fall into mischief.

84 As a roaring lion and a roaming bear, so is a wicked ruler over the poor people.

85 The prince that lacks understanding is also a great oppressor, but he that hates covetousness shall prolong his days.

86 A man that does violence to the blood of any person shall flee to the pit; let no man stop him.

87 Whoever walks uprightly shall be saved, but he that is perverse in his ways shall fall at once.

88 He that tills his land shall have plenty of bread, but he that follows after vain people shall have poverty enough.

89 A faithful man shall abound with blessings, but he that makes haste to be rich shall not be innocent.

90 To have respect of persons is not good; for, for a piece of bread, that man will transgress.

91 He that hastens to be rich has an evil eye, and considers not that poverty shall come upon him.

92 He that rebukes a man afterward shall find more favor than he that flatters with the tongue.

93 Whoever robs his father or his mother and says, It is no transgression — the same is the companion of a destroyer.

94 He that is of a proud heart stirs up strife, but he that puts his trust in the Lord shall be made fat.

95 He that trusts in his own heart is a fool; but whoever walks wisely, he shall be delivered.

96 He that gives unto the poor shall not lack, but he that hides his eyes shall have many a curse.

97 When the wicked rise, men hide themselves; but when they perish, the righteous increase.

98 He that being often reproved hardens his neck shall suddenly be destroyed, and that without remedy.

99 When the righteous are in authority, the people rejoice; but when the wicked bears rule, the people mourn.

100 Whoever loves wisdom rejoices his father, but he that keeps company with harlots spends his substance.

101 The king by judgment establishes the land, but he that receives bribes overthrows it.

102 A man that flatters his neighbor spreads a net for his feet.

103 In the transgression of an evil man there is a snare, but the righteous does sing and rejoice.

104 The righteous considers the cause of the poor, but the wicked regards not to know it.

105 Scornful men bring a city into a snare, but wise men turn away wrath.

106 If a wise man contends with a foolish man, whether he rage or laugh, there is no rest.

107 The bloodthirsty hate the upright, but the just seek his soul.

108 A fool utters all his mind, but a wise man keeps it in until afterward.

109 If a ruler listen to lies, all his servants are wicked.

110 The poor and the deceitful man meet together; the Lord lightens both their eyes.

111 The king that faithfully judges the poor, his throne shall be established for ever.

112 The rod and reproof give wisdom, but a child left to himself brings his mother to shame.

113 When the wicked are multiplied, transgression increases; but the righteous shall see their fall.

114 Correct your son and he shall give you rest, yea, he shall give delight unto your soul.

115 Where there is no vision, the people perish; but he that keeps the law, happy is he.

116 A servant will not be corrected by words; for though he understand, he will not answer.

117 Do you see a man that is hasty in his words? There is more hope for a fool than for him.

118 He that delicately brings up his servant from a child shall have him become his son at the length.

119 An angry man stirs up strife, and a furious man abounds in transgression.

120 A man's pride shall bring him low, but honor shall uphold the humble in spirit.

121 Whoever is partner with a thief hates his own soul; he hears cursing, and betrays it not.

122 The fear of man brings a snare, but whoever puts his trust in the Lord shall be safe.

123 Many seek the ruler's favor, but every man's judgment comes from the Lord.

124 An unjust man is an abomination to the just, and he that is upright in the way is abomination to the wicked.

The words of Agur the son of Jakeh, the prophecy the man spoke unto Ithiel, even unto Ithiel and Ucal.

5 Surely I am more brutish than any man, and have not the understanding of a man. I neither learned wisdom nor have the knowledge of the holy. Who has ascended up into Heaven, or descended? Who has gathered the wind in his fists? Who has bound the waters in a garment? Who has established all the ends of the earth? What is his name, and what is his son's name, if you can tell?

2 Every word of God is pure. He is a shield unto them that put their trust in him. Add not unto his words, lest he reprove you and you be found a liar.

3 Two things have I required of you, do not deny me them before I die: remove far from me vanity and lies, give me neither poverty nor riches; feed me with food suitable for me, lest I be full and deny you, and say, Who is the Lord? Or lest I be poor and steal, and take the name of my God in vain.

4 Accuse not a servant unto his master, lest he curse you and you be found guilty.

5 There is a generation that curses their father and does not bless their mother; there is a generation that are pure in their own eyes, and yet is not washed from their filthiness; there is a generation, oh how lofty are their eyes, and their eyelids are lifted up; there is a generation whose swords are as teeth, and their knives as molars, to devour the poor from off the earth and the needy from among men!

6 The horse leech has two daughters, crying, Give, give!

7 There are three things that are never satisfied, yea, four things say not, It is enough: the grave, and the barren womb, the earth that is not filled with water, and the fire say not, It is enough.

8 The eye that mocks at his father and despises to obey his mother, the ravens of the valley shall pick it out, and the young eagles shall eat it.

9 There are three things which are too wonderful for me, yea, four which I know not: the way of an eagle in the air, the way of a serpent upon a rock, the way of a ship in the midst of the sea, and the way of a man with a maid.

10 Such is the way of an adulterous woman: she eats, and wipes her mouth, and says, I have done no wickedness.

11 For three things the earth is disquieted, and for four which it cannot bear: for a servant when he reigns, and a fool when he is filled with food, for an odious woman when she is married, and a handmaid that is heir to her mistress.

12 There are four things which are little upon the earth but they are exceedingly wise: the ants are a people not strong, yet they prepare their food in the summer; the conies are but a feeble folk, yet they make their houses in the rocks; the locusts have no king, yet they go forth all of them by bands; the spider takes hold with her hands, and is in kings' palaces.

13 There are three things which go well, yea, four are comely in going: a lion, which is strongest among beasts and turns not away for any; a greyhound; a he-goat also; and a king against whom there is no rising up.

14 If you have done foolishly in lifting up yourself, or if you have thought evil, lay your hand upon your mouth. Surely the churning of milk brings forth butter, and the wringing of the nose brings forth blood; so the forcing of wrath brings forth strife.

The words of king Lemuel — the prophecy that his mother taught him.

6 What, my son? And what, the son of my womb? And what, the son of my vows? Give not your strength unto women, nor your ways to that which destroys kings. It is not for kings, O Lemuel, it is not for kings to drink wine, nor for princes strong drink, lest they drink and forget the law, and pervert the judgment of any of the afflicted. Give

strong drink unto him that is ready to perish, and wine unto those that be of heavy hearts. Let him drink and forget his poverty, and remember his misery no more.

2 Open your mouth for the dumb, in the cause of all such as are appointed to destruction. Open your mouth, judge righteously, and plead the cause of the poor and needy.

3 Who can find a virtuous woman? For her price is far above rubies. The heart of her husband does safely trust in her, so that he shall have no need of spoil. She will do him good and not evil all the days of her life. She seeks wool and flax, and works willingly with her hands. She is like the merchants' ships, she brings her food from afar. She rises also while it is yet night, and gives food to her household and a portion to her maidens. She considers a field and buys it; with the fruit of her hands she plants a vineyard. She girds her loins with strength, and strengthens her arms. She perceives that her merchandise is good, her candle goes not out by night. She lays her hands to the spindle, and her hands hold the rod. She stretches out her hand to the poor, yea, she reaches forth her hands to the needy. She is not afraid of the snow for her household, for all her household are clothed with scarlet. She makes herself coverings of tapestry, her clothing is silk and purple. Her husband is known in the gates, when he sits among the elders of the land. She makes fine linen and sells it, and delivers girdles unto the merchant. Strength and honor are her clothing, and she shall rejoice in time to come. She opens her mouth with wisdom and in her tongue is the law of kindness. She looks well to the ways of her household and eats not the bread of idleness. Her children arise up and call her blessed; her husband also, and he praises her. Many daughters have done virtuously, but you excel them all. Favor is deceitful and beauty is vain; but a woman that fears the Lord, she shall be praised. Give her of the fruit of her hands, and let her own works praise her in the gates.

ECCLESIASTES OR THE PREACHER

The words of the Preacher, the son of David, king in Jerusalem.

VANITY of vanities, says the Preacher, vanity of vanities — all is vanity. What profit has a man of all his labor which he takes under the sun? One generation passes away and another generation comes, but the earth stands for ever. The sun also rises, and the sun goes down, and hastens to his place where he arose. The wind goes toward the south, and turns about unto the north; it whirls about continually, and the wind returns again according to his circuits. All the rivers run into the sea, yet the sea is not full; unto the place from which the rivers come, there they return again. All things are full of labor, man cannot utter it; the eye is not satisfied with seeing, nor the ear filled with hearing. The thing that has been, it is that which shall be; and that which is done is that which shall be done, and there is no new thing under the sun. Is there anything whereof it may be said, See, this is new? It has been already of old time, which was before us. There is no remembrance of former things, neither shall there be any remembrance of things that are to come, with those that shall come after.

2 I, the Preacher, was king over Israel in Jerusalem, and I gave my heart to seek and search out by wisdom concerning all things that are done under heaven. This severe travail has God given to the sons of man to be exercised with. I have seen all the works that are done under the sun, and behold, all is vanity and vexation of spirit. That which is crooked cannot be made straight, and that which is lacking cannot be numbered.

3 I communed with my own heart, saying, Behold, I have come to great estate, and have gotten more wisdom than all they that have been before me in Jerusalem; yea, my heart had great experience of wisdom and knowledge, and I gave my heart to know wisdom and to know madness and folly. I perceived that this also is vexation of spirit, for in much wisdom is much grief; and he that increases knowledge increases sorrow.

4 I said in my heart, Go to now, I will prove you with mirth; therefore, enjoy pleasure. And behold, this also is vanity. I said of laughter, It is mad — and of mirth, What does it do? I sought in my heart to give myself unto wine (yet acquainting my heart with wisdom) and to lay hold on folly, until I might see what was that good for the sons of men, which they should do under the heaven all the days of their life.

5 I made myself great works, I built myself houses, I planted myself vineyards, I made myself gardens and orchards, and I planted trees in them of all kind of fruits. I made myself pools of water, to water the wood that brings forth trees. I got myself servants and maidens, and

had servants born in my house. Also, I had great possessions of great and small cattle, above all that were in Jerusalem before me. I gathered myself also silver and gold, and the peculiar treasure of kings and of the provinces. I got myself men singers and women singers, and the delights of the sons of men as musical instruments, and that of all sorts. So I was great, and increased more than all that were before me in Jerusalem. Also my wisdom remained with me, and whatever my eyes desired, I kept not from them. I withheld not my heart from any joy, for my heart rejoiced in all my labor, and this was my portion of all my labor.

6 Then I looked on all the works that my hands had wrought, and on the labor that I had labored to do, and behold — all was vanity and vexation of spirit, and there was no profit under the sun.

7 And I turned myself to behold wisdom, and madness, and folly; for what can the man do that comes after the king? Even that which has been already done. Then I saw that wisdom excels folly, as far as light excels darkness. The wise man's eyes are in his head, but the fool walks in darkness. And I myself perceived also that one event happens to them all. Then I said in my heart, As it happens to the fool, so it happens even to me; and why was I then more wise? Then I said in my heart that this also is vanity; for there is no remembrance of the wise more than of the fool, for ever, seeing that which now is in the days to come, shall all be forgotten. And how does the wise man die? As the fool.

8 Therefore I hated life because the work that is wrought under the sun is grievous unto me, for all is vanity and vexation of spirit. Yea, I hated all my labor which I had taken under the sun, because I should leave it unto the man that shall be after me, and who knows whether he shall be a wise man or a fool? Yet shall he have rule over all my labor wherein I have labored, and wherein I have shown myself wise under the sun. This is also vanity. Therefore, I went about to cause my heart to despair of all the labor which I took under the sun. For there is a man whose labor is in wisdom, and in knowledge, and in equity; yet to a man that has not labored therein shall he leave it for his portion; this also is vanity and a great evil. For what has man of all his labor, and of the vexation of his heart, wherein he has labored under the sun? For all his days are sorrows, and his travail — grief. Yea, his heart takes not rest in the night. This is also vanity.

9 There is nothing better for a man than that he should eat and drink, and that he should make his soul enjoy good in his labor. This also I saw, that it was from the hand of God; for who can eat, or who else can hasten unto this, more than I? For God gives to a man that is good in his sight wisdom, and knowledge, and joy; but to the sinner he gives travail, to gather and to heap up, that he may give to him that is good before God. This also is vanity and vexation of spirit.

10 To everything there is a season, and a time to every purpose under the heaven: a time to be born, and a time to die; a time to plant, and a time to pluck up that which is planted; a time to kill, and a time to heal; a time to break down, and a time to build up; a time to weep, and a time to laugh; a time to mourn, and a time to dance; a time to cast away stones, and a time to gather stones together; a time to embrace, and a time to refrain from embracing; a time to get, and a time to lose; a time to keep, and a time to cast away; a time to rend, and a time to sew; a time to keep silence, and a time to speak; a time to love, and a time to hate; a time of war, and a time of peace.

11 What profit has he that works in that wherein he labors? I have seen the travail which God has given to the sons of men, to be exercised in it. He has made everything beautiful in his time. Also he has set the world in their heart, so that no man can find out the work that God makes, from the beginning to the end. I know that there is no good in them but for a man to rejoice, and to do good in his life; and also that every man should eat and drink and enjoy the good of all his labor, it is the gift of God.

12 I know that whatever God does, it shall be for ever; nothing can be put to it, nor anything taken from it. And God does it that men should fear before him. That which has been is now, and that which is to be has already been, and God requires that which is past.

13 And moreover, I saw under the sun the place of judgment, that wickedness was there; and the place of righteousness, that iniquity was there. I said in my heart, God shall judge the righteous and the wicked, for there is a time there for every purpose and for every work.

14 I said in my heart, concerning the estate of the sons of men, that God might manifest them and that they might see that they themselves are beasts; for that which befalls the sons of men befalls beasts. Even one thing befalls them — as the one dies, so dies the other. Yea, they

have all one breath, so that a man has no preeminence above a beast, for all is vanity. All go unto one place, all are of the dust and all turn to dust again. Who knows the spirit of man that goes upward and the spirit of the beast that goes downward to the earth? Wherefore, I perceive that there is nothing better than that a man should rejoice in his own works, for that is his portion. For who shall bring him to see what shall be after him?

15 So I returned, and considered all the oppressions that are done under the sun, and behold the tears of such as were oppressed, and they had no comforter; and on the side of their oppressors there was power, but they had no comforter. Wherefore, I praised the dead who are already dead, more than the living who are yet alive. Yea, better is he than both they, who has not yet been, who has not seen the evil work that is done under the sun.

16 Again I considered all travail and every right work, that for this a man is envied of his neighbor. This is also vanity and vexation of spirit. The fool folds his hands together and eats his own flesh. Better is a handful with quietness than both the hands full with travail and vexation of spirit.

17 Then I returned, and I saw vanity under the sun: there is one alone, and there is not a second; yea, he has neither child nor brother, yet is there no end of all his labor, neither is his eye satisfied with riches. Neither says he, For whom do I labor and bereave my soul of good? This is also vanity, yea, it is a severe travail. Two are better than one because they have a good reward for their labor; for if they fall, the one will lift up his fellow. But woe to him that is alone when he falls, for he has not another to help him up. Again if two lie together, then they have heat; but how can one be warm alone? And if one prevail against him, two shall withstand him, and a threefold cord is not quickly broken.

18 Better is a poor and a wise child than an old and foolish king who will no more be admonished; for out of prison he comes to reign, whereas also he that is born in his kingdom becomes poor. I considered all the living who walk under the sun, with the second child that shall stand up in his stead. There is no end of all the people, even of all that have been before them; they also that come after shall not rejoice in him. Surely this also is vanity and vexation of spirit.

¹⁹ Keep your foot when you go to the house of God, and be more ready to hear than to give the sacrifice of fools; for they consider not that they do evil. Be not rash with your mouth, and let not your heart be hasty to utter anything before God, for God is in Heaven and you upon earth; therefore, let your words be few. For a dream comes through the multitude of business, and a fool's voice is known by multitude of words.

²⁰ When you vow a vow unto God, defer not to pay it, for he has no pleasure in fools. Pay that which you have vowed. Better is it that you should not vow than that you should vow and not pay. Suffer not your mouth to cause your flesh to sin, neither say you before the angel that it was an error. Why should God be angry at your voice and destroy the work of your hands? For in the multitude of dreams and many words, there are also diverse vanities; but fear God.

²¹ If you see the oppression of the poor, and violent perverting of judgment and justice in a province, marvel not at the matter; for he that is higher than the highest regards, and there is higher than they. Moreover, the profit of the earth is for all; the king himself is served by the field. He that loves silver shall not be satisfied with silver, nor he that loves abundance with increase; this also is vanity. When goods increase, they are increased that eat them; and what good is there to the owners thereof, saving the beholding of them with their eyes? The sleep of a laboring man is sweet, whether he eat little or much; but the abundance of the rich will not suffer him to sleep.

²² There is a grievous evil which I have seen under the sun, namely riches kept for the owners thereof, to their hurt. But those riches perish by evil travail, and he begets a son, and there is nothing in his hand. As he came forth of his mother's womb, naked shall he return to go as he came, and shall take nothing of his labor which he may carry away in his hand. And this also is a grievous evil: that in all points as he came, so shall he go. And what profit has he that has labored for the wind? All his days also he eats in darkness, and he has much sorrow and wrath with his sickness.

²³ Behold that which I have seen: it is good and comely for one to eat and to drink, and to enjoy the good of all his labor that he takes under the sun all the days of his life which God gives him, for it is his portion. Every man also to whom God has given riches, and wealth, and has

given him power to eat thereof, and to take his portion, and to rejoice in his labor — this is the gift of God; for he shall not much remember the days of his life, because God answers him in the joy of his heart.

24 There is an evil which I have seen under the sun, and it is common among men: a man to whom God has given riches, wealth, and honor, so that he lacks nothing for his soul of all that he desires, yet God gives him not power to eat thereof, but a stranger eats it. This is vanity, and it is an evil disease.

25 If a man beget a hundred children and live many years, so that the days of his years are many, and his soul is not filled with good, and also that he has no burial, I say that an untimely birth is better than he; for he comes in with vanity and departs in darkness, and his name shall be covered with darkness. Moreover, he has not seen the sun, nor known anything; this has more rest than the other. Yea, though he live a thousand years twice over, yet has he seen no good. Do not all go to one place?

26 All the labor of man is for his mouth, and yet the appetite is not filled. For what has the wise more than the fool? What has the poor, that knows to walk before the living? Better is the sight of the eyes than the wandering of the desire; this is also vanity and vexation of spirit. That which has been is named already, and it is known that it is man; neither may he contend with him that is mightier than he. Seeing there are many things that increase vanity, what is man the better? For who knows what is good for man in this life, all the days of his vain life which he spends as a shadow? For who can tell a man what shall be after him under the sun?

27 A good name is better than precious ointment, and the day of death than the day of one's birth. It is better to go to the house of mourning than to go to the house of feasting, for that is the end of all men, and the living will lay it to his heart. Sorrow is better than laughter, for by the sadness of the countenance the heart is made better. The heart of the wise is in the house of mourning; but the heart of fools is in the house of mirth. It is better to hear the rebuke of the wise than for a man to hear the song of fools; for as the crackling of thorns under a pot, so is the laughter of the fool. This also is vanity.

28 Surely oppression makes a wise man mad, and a bribe destroys the heart. Better is the end of a thing than the beginning thereof; and

the patient in spirit is better than the proud in spirit. Be not hasty in your spirit to be angry, for anger rests in the bosom of fools. Say not, What is the cause that the former days were better than these? — for you do not inquire wisely concerning this. Wisdom is good with an inheritance, and by it there is profit to them that see the sun; for wisdom is a defense, and money is a defense, but the excellence of knowledge is that wisdom gives life to them that have it.

29 Consider the work of God: for who can make that straight which he has made crooked? In the day of prosperity, be joyful; but in the day of adversity, consider: God also has set the one alongside the other, to the end that man should find nothing after him.

30 All things have I seen in the days of my vanity: there is a just man that perishes in his righteousness, and there is a wicked man that prolongs his life in his wickedness. Be not overly righteous, neither make yourself overly wise; why should you destroy yourself? Be not overly wicked, neither be foolish; why should you die before your time? It is good that you should take hold of this, yea, also from this withdraw not your hand; for he that fears God shall come forth of them all.

31 Wisdom strengthens the wise more than ten mighty men who are in the city. For there is not a just man upon earth that does good and sins not. Also, take no heed unto all words that are spoken, lest you hear your servant curse you; for oftentimes also your own heart knows that you yourself likewise have cursed others. All this have I proved by wisdom. I said, I will be wise — but it was far from me. That which is far off, and exceedingly deep, who can find it out? I applied my heart to know, and to search, and to seek out wisdom, and the reason of things, and to know the wickedness of folly, even of foolishness and madness. And I find more bitter than death the woman whose heart is snares and nets, and her hands as bands. Whoever pleases God shall escape from her, but the sinner shall be taken by her.

32 Behold, this have I found, says the Preacher, counting one by one to find out the account, which yet my soul seeks but I find not: one man among a thousand have I found, but a woman among all those have I not found. Behold, this only have I found: that God has made man upright, but they have sought out many inventions. Who is as the wise man? And who knows the interpretation of a thing? A man's wisdom makes his face to shine, and the boldness of his face shall be changed.

³³ I counsel you to keep the king's commandment, and that in regard of the oath of God. Be not hasty to go out of his sight. Stand not in an evil thing, for he does whatever pleases him. Where the word of a king is, there is power; and who may say unto him, What are you doing? Whoever keeps the commandment shall feel no evil thing, and a wise man's heart discerns both time and judgment; because to every purpose there is time and judgment, therefore the misery of man is great upon him. For he knows not that which shall be, for who can tell him when it shall be? There is no man that has power over the spirit to retain the spirit, neither has he power in the day of death; and there is no discharge in that war, neither shall wickedness deliver those that are given to it.

³⁴ All this have I seen, and applied my heart unto every work that is done under the sun. There is a time wherein one man rules over another to his own hurt. And so I saw the wicked buried who had come and gone from the place of the holy, and they were forgotten in the city where they had so done; this also is vanity. Because sentence against an evil work is not executed speedily, therefore the heart of the sons of men is fully set in them to do evil. Though a sinner do evil a hundred times and his days be prolonged, yet surely I know that it shall be well with them that fear God, who fear before him. But it shall not be well with the wicked, neither shall he prolong his days, which are as a shadow, because he fears not before God.

³⁵ There is a vanity which is done upon the earth: that there are just men unto whom it happens according to the work of the wicked; again, there are wicked men to whom it happens according to the work of the righteous. I said that this also is vanity. Then I commended mirth, because a man has no better thing under the sun than to eat, and to drink, and to be merry; for that shall abide with him of his labor the days of his life which God gives him under the sun.

³⁶ When I applied my heart to know wisdom, and to see the business that is done upon the earth — for also there is that neither day nor night sees sleep with his eyes — then I beheld all the work of God, that a man cannot find out the work that is done under the sun; because though a man labor to seek it out, yet he shall not find it. Yea further, though a wise man think to know it, yet shall he not be able to find it.

37 For all this I considered in my heart, even to declare all this: that the righteous, and the wise, and their works are in the hand of God; no man knows either love or hatred by all that is before them. All things come alike to all, there is one event to the righteous and to the wicked; to the good and to the clean, and to the unclean; to him that sacrifices, and to him that sacrifices not; as is the good, so is the sinner; and he that swears, as he that fears an oath. This is an evil among all things that are done under the sun: that there is one event unto all.

38 Yea, also the heart of the sons of men is full of evil, and madness is in their heart while they live; and after that, they go to the dead. For to him that is joined to all the living there is hope, for a living dog is better than a dead lion. For the living know that they shall die, but the dead know not anything, neither have they anymore a reward, for the memory of them is forgotten. Also, their love, and their hatred, and their envy, is now perished; neither have they anymore a portion for ever in anything that is done under the sun.

39 Go your way, eat your bread with joy, and drink your wine with a merry heart; for God now accepts your works. Let your garments be always white, and let your head lack no ointment. Live joyfully with the wife whom you love, all the days of the life of your vanity which he has given you under the sun, all the days of your vanity; for that is your portion in this life and in your labor which you take under the sun. Whatever your hand finds to do, do it with your might; for there is no work, nor device, nor knowledge, nor wisdom in the grave where you go.

40 I returned and saw under the sun that the race is not to the swift, nor the battle to the strong, neither yet bread to the wise, nor yet riches to men of understanding, nor yet favor to men of skill; but time and chance happens to them all, for man also knows not his time. As the fishes that are taken in an evil net, and as the birds that are caught in the snare, so are the sons of men snared in an evil time when it falls suddenly upon them.

41 This wisdom have I seen also under the sun, and it seemed great unto me: There was a little city, and few men within it. And there came a great king against it, and besieged it, and built great bulwarks against it. Now there was found in it a poor wise man, and he by his wisdom delivered the city; yet no man remembered that same poor

man. Then I said, Wisdom is better than strength; nevertheless, the poor man's wisdom is despised and his words are not heard. The words of wise men are heard in quiet more than the cry of him that rules among fools. Wisdom is better than weapons of war, but one sinner destroys much good.

⁴² Dead flies cause the ointment of the apothecary to send forth a stinking savor; so does a little folly him that is in reputation for wisdom and honor. A wise man's heart is at his right hand, but a fool's heart at his left. Yea also, when he that is a fool walks by the way, his wisdom fails him, and he says to everyone that he is a fool. If the spirit of the ruler rise up against you, leave not your place, for yielding pacifies great offenses.

⁴³ There is an evil which I have seen under the sun, as an error which proceeds from the ruler: Folly is set in great dignity, and the rich sit in low place; I have seen servants upon horses, and princes walking as servants upon the earth.

⁴⁴ He that digs a pit shall fall into it, and whoever breaks a hedge, a serpent shall bite him. Whoever removes stones shall be hurt by them, and he that chops wood shall be endangered thereby. If the iron is blunt and he does not whet the edge, then he must apply more strength; but wisdom is profitable to direct.

⁴⁵ Surely the serpent will bite without enchantment, and a babbler is no better.

⁴⁶ The words of a wise man's mouth are gracious, but the lips of a fool will swallow up himself. The beginning of the words of his mouth is foolishness, and the end of his talk is mischievous madness. A fool also is full of words.

⁴⁷ A man cannot tell what shall be; and what shall be after him, who can tell him?

⁴⁸ The labor of the foolish wearies every one of them, because he knows not how to go to the city.

⁴⁹ Woe to you, O land, when your king is a child and your princes eat in the morning. Blessed are you, O land, when your king is the son of nobles and your princes eat in due season, for strength and not for drunkenness.

⁵⁰ By much slothfulness, the building decays; and through idleness of the hands, the house drops through.

51 A feast is made for laughter and wine makes merry, but money answers all things.

52 Curse not the king, no not in your thought, and curse not the rich in your bedchamber; for a bird of the air shall carry the voice, and that which has wings shall tell the matter.

53 Cast your bread upon the waters, for you shall find it after many days. Give a portion to seven and also to eight, for you know not what evil shall be upon the earth.

54 If the clouds are full of rain, they empty themselves upon the earth; and if the tree fall toward the south or toward the north, in the place where the tree falls, there it shall be. He that observes the wind shall not sow, and he that regards the clouds shall not reap.

55 As you know not what is the way of the spirit, nor how the bones do grow in the womb of her that is with child, even so you know not the works of God, who makes all. In the morning sow your seed, and in the evening withhold not your hand, for you know not which shall prosper, either this or that, or whether they both alike shall be good.

56 Truly the light is sweet, and a pleasant thing it is for the eyes to behold the sun; but if a man live many years and rejoice in them all, yet let him remember the days of darkness, for they shall be many. All that comes is vanity.

57 Rejoice, O young man, in your youth, and let your heart cheer you in the days of your youth, and walk in the ways of your heart, and in the sight of your eyes. But know that for all these things, God will bring you into judgment. Therefore, remove sorrow from your heart and put away evil from your flesh, for childhood and youth are vanity.

58 Remember now your Creator in the days of your youth, while the evil days come not, nor the years draw near when you shall say, I have no pleasure in them; while the sun, or the light, or the moon, or the stars be not darkened, nor the clouds return after the rain; in the day when the keepers of the house shall tremble, and the strong men shall bow themselves, and the grinders cease because they are few, and those that look out of the windows be darkened; and the doors shall be shut in the streets when the sound of the grinding is low; and he shall rise up at the voice of the bird, and all the daughters of music shall be brought low; also when they shall be afraid of that which is high, and fears shall be in the way; and the almond tree shall flourish, and the

grasshopper shall be a burden, and desire shall fail; because man goes to his long home, and the mourners go about the streets; or ever the silver cord be removed, or the golden bowl be broken, or the pitcher be broken at the fountain, or the wheel broken at the cistern — then shall the dust return to the earth as it was, and the spirit shall return unto God who gave it. Vanity of vanities, says the Preacher, all is vanity.

59 And moreover, because the Preacher was wise, he still taught the people knowledge; yea, he gave good heed, and sought out, and set in order many proverbs. The Preacher sought to find out acceptable words, and that which was written was upright, even words of truth. The words of the wise are as goads, and as nails fastened by the masters of assemblies, which are given from one shepherd; and further by these, my son, be admonished. Of making many books there is no end, and much study is a weariness of the flesh.

60 Let us hear the conclusion of the whole matter: fear God and keep his commandments, for this is the whole duty of man; for God shall bring every work into judgment with every secret thing, whether it be good or whether it be evil.

THE BOOK OF THE PROPHET ISAIAH

The vision of Isaiah the son of Amoz which he saw concerning Judah and Jerusalem in the days of Uzziah, Jotham, Ahaz, and Hezekiah, kings of Judah.

HEAR, O heavens, and give ear, O earth, for the Lord has spoken: I have nourished and brought up children, and they have rebelled against me. The ox knows his owner and the ass his master's crib, but Israel does not know, my people does not consider. Ah sinful nation, a people loaded with iniquity, a seed of evildoers, children that are corrupters. They have forsaken the Lord, they have provoked the Holy One of Israel unto anger, they have gone away backward. Why should you be stricken anymore? You will revolt more and more. The whole head is sick and the whole heart faint. From the sole of the foot even unto the head there is no soundness in it, but wounds, and bruises, and putrifying sores — they have not been closed, neither bound up, neither mollified with ointment. Your country is desolate, your cities are burned with fire. Your land, strangers devour it in your presence; and it is desolate, as overthrown by strangers. And the daughter of Zion is left as a cottage in a vineyard, as a lodge in a garden of cucumbers, as a besieged city. Except the Lord of Hosts had left unto us a very small remnant, we should have been as Sodom and we should have been like unto Gomorrah.

2 Hear the word of the Lord, you rulers of Sodom; give ear unto the law of our God, you people of Gomorrah. To what purpose is the multitude of your sacrifices unto me? — says the Lord. I am full of the burnt offerings of rams and the fat of fed beasts, and I delight not in the blood of bullocks, or of lambs, or of he-goats. When you come to appear before me, who has required this at your hand, to tread my courts? Bring no more vain offerings. Incense is an abomination unto me. The new moons, and Sabbaths, the calling of assemblies I cannot bear — it is iniquity, even the solemn meeting. Your new moons and your appointed feasts my soul hates; they are a trouble unto me, I am weary to bear them. And when you spread forth your hands, I will hide my eyes from you; yea, when you make many prayers, I will not hear.

3 Your hands are full of blood. Wash yourself, make yourself clean; put away the evil of your doings from before my eyes. Cease to do evil, learn to do well. Seek judgment, relieve the oppressed, judge the fatherless, plead for the widow. Come now and let us reason together, says the Lord. Though your sins be as scarlet, they shall be as white as snow; though they be red like crimson, they shall be as wool. If you are willing and obedient, you shall eat the good of the land, but if you refuse and rebel, you shall be devoured with the sword; for the mouth of the Lord has spoken it.

4 How the faithful city has become a harlot! It was full of judgment; righteousness lodged in it, but now — murderers. Your silver has become dross, your wine mixed with water, your princes are rebellious and are companions of thieves. Everyone loves bribes and follows after rewards; they judge not the fatherless, neither does the cause of the widow come unto them. Therefore says the Lord, the Lord of Hosts, the Mighty One of Israel, Ah, I will ease myself of my adversaries and avenge myself of my enemies, and I will turn my hand upon you, and purely purge away your dross, and take away all your tin. And I will restore your judges as at the first, and your counselors as at the beginning. Afterward, you shall be called the city of righteousness, the faithful city. Zion shall be redeemed with judgment and her converts

with righteousness. And the destruction of the transgressors and of the sinners shall be together, and they that forsake the Lord shall be consumed. For they shall be ashamed of the oaks which you have desired, and you shall be confounded for the gardens that you have chosen. For you shall be as an oak whose leaf fades, and as a garden that has no water. And the strong shall be as tinder, and the maker of it as a spark; and they shall both burn together, and none shall quench them.

5 The word that Isaiah, the son of Amoz, saw concerning Judah and Jerusalem; and it shall come to pass in the last days, when the mountain of the Lord's house shall be established in the top of the mountains, and shall be exalted above the hills, and all nations shall flow unto it. And many people shall go and say, Come and let us go up to the mountain of the Lord, to the house of the God of Jacob, and he will teach us of his ways and we will walk in his paths. For out of Zion shall go forth the law, and the word of the Lord from Jerusalem. And he shall judge among the nations and shall rebuke many people. And they shall beat their swords into plowshares and their spears into pruning hooks; nation shall not lift up sword against nation, neither shall they learn war anymore.

6 O house of Jacob, come and let us walk in the light of the Lord, yea, come, for you have all gone astray, everyone to his wicked ways. Therefore, O Lord, you have forsaken your people, the house of Jacob, because they are replenished from the east, and listen unto fortune-tellers like the Philistines, and they please themselves in the children of strangers. Their land also is full of silver and gold, neither is there any end of their treasures. Their land is also full of horses, neither is there any end of their chariots. Their land also is full of idols; they worship the work of their own hands, that which their own fingers have made. And the mean man bows not down and the great man humbles himself not; therefore, forgive him not.

7 O you wicked ones, enter into the rock and hide yourselves in the dust, for the fear of the Lord and his majesty shall smite you. And it shall come to pass that the lofty looks of man shall be humbled, and the haughtiness of men shall be bowed down, and the Lord alone shall be exalted in that day. For the day of the Lord of Hosts soon comes upon all nations, yea, upon everyone; yea, upon the proud and lofty, and upon everyone who is lifted up; and he shall be brought low. Yea, and

the day of the Lord shall come upon all the cedars of Lebanon, for they are high and lifted up, and upon all the oaks of Bashan, and upon all the high mountains, and upon all the hills, and upon all the nations which are lifted up, and upon every people, and upon every high tower, and upon every fortified wall, and upon all the ships of the sea, and upon all the ships of Tarshish, and upon all pleasant pictures. And the loftiness of man shall be bowed down, and the haughtiness of men shall be made low, and the Lord alone shall be exalted in that day. And the idols he shall utterly abolish. And they shall go into the holes of the rocks and into the caves of the earth, for the fear of the Lord shall come upon them and the glory of his majesty shall smite them when he arises to shake terribly the earth. In that day, a man shall cast his idols of silver and his idols of gold, which he has made for himself to worship, to the moles and to the bats, to go into the clefts of the rocks and into the tops of the rugged rocks; for the fear of the Lord shall come upon them and the majesty of the Lord shall smite them when he arises to shake terribly the earth. Cease from man, whose breath is in his nostrils, for wherein is he to be accounted of?

8 For behold, the Lord, the Lord of Hosts does take away from Jerusalem and from Judah the supply and the support, the whole support of bread and the whole supply of water, the mighty man, and the man of war, the judge, and the prophet, and the prudent, and the elder, the captain of fifty, and the honorable man, and the counselor, and the expert craftsman, and the eloquent orator. And I will give children unto them to be their princes, and babes shall rule over them. And the people shall be oppressed, everyone by another and everyone by his neighbor. The child shall behave himself proudly against the elder, and the base against the honorable. When a man shall take hold of his brother of the house of his father, and shall say, You have clothing, be our ruler and let not this ruin come under your hand — in that day shall he swear, saying, I will not be a healer, for in my house there is neither bread nor clothing; make me not a ruler of the people. For Jerusalem is ruined and Judah is fallen because their tongues and their doings have been against the Lord, to provoke the eyes of his glory. The show of their countenance does witness against them, and does declare their sin to be even as Sodom; they cannot hide it. Woe unto their souls, for they have rewarded evil unto themselves.

Say unto the righteous that it is well with them, for they shall eat the fruit of their doings. Woe unto the wicked, for they shall perish, for the reward of their hands shall be upon them.

9 And my people, children are their oppressors and women rule over them. O my people, they who lead you cause you to err and destroy the way of your paths. The Lord stands up to plead, and stands to judge the people. The Lord will enter into judgment with the elders of his people and the princes thereof; for you have eaten up the vineyard and the spoil of the poor in your houses. What do you mean? You beat my people to pieces and grind the faces of the poor, says the Lord God of Hosts.

10 Moreover, the Lord says, Because the daughters of Zion are haughty, and walk with stretched forth necks and wanton eyes, walking and mincing as they go, and making a tinkling with their feet, therefore the Lord will smite with a scab the crown of the head of the daughters of Zion, and the Lord will expose their secret parts. In that day, the Lord will take away the finery of tinkling ornaments, and cauls, and round ornaments like the moon, the chains, and the bracelets, and the mufflers, the bonnets, and the ornaments of the legs, and the headbands, and the perfume vessels, and the earrings, the rings, and nose jewels, the changeable suits of apparel, and the mantles, and the wimples, and the crisping pins, the mirrors, and the fine linen, and the hoods, and the veils. And it shall all come to pass, instead of sweet smell there shall be stink; and instead of a belt, a rope; and instead of well-set hair, baldness; and instead of a stomacher, a girding of sackcloth; burning instead of beauty. Your men shall fall by the sword, and your mighty in the war. And her gates shall lament and mourn, and she shall be desolate, shall sit upon the ground.

11 And in that day, seven women shall take hold of one man, saying, We will eat our own bread and wear our own apparel, only let us be called by your name to take away our reproach.

12 In that day shall the branch of the Lord be beautiful and glorious, the fruit of the earth excellent and comely to them that are escaped of Israel. And it shall come to pass, they that are left in Zion and remain in Jerusalem shall be called holy, everyone that is written among the living in Jerusalem when the Lord shall have washed away the filth of the daughters of Zion, and shall have purged the blood of Jerusalem

from the midst thereof by the spirit of judgment and by the spirit of burning. And the Lord will create upon every dwelling place of Mount Zion, and upon her assemblies, a cloud and smoke by day, and the shining of a flaming fire by night; for upon all, the glory of Zion shall be a defense. And there shall be a tabernacle for a shadow in the daytime from the heat, and for a place of refuge, and a cover from storm and from rain.

13 And then will I sing to my well-beloved a song of my beloved, touching his vineyard: My well-beloved has a vineyard in a very fruitful hill. And he fenced it, and gathered out the stones thereof, and planted it with the choicest vine, and built a tower in the midst of it, and also made a winepress therein. And he expected that it should bring forth grapes, and it brought forth wild grapes. And now O inhabitants of Jerusalem and men of Judah, judge, I pray you, between me and my vineyard. What could have been done more to my vineyard that I have not done in it? Therefore, when I looked that it should bring forth grapes, it brought forth wild grapes. And now come, I will tell you what I will do to my vineyard: I will take away the hedge thereof, and it shall be eaten up; and I will break down the wall thereof, and it shall be trodden down; and I will lay it waste. It shall not be pruned nor dug, but there shall come up briers and thorns. I will also command the clouds that they rain no rain upon it. For the vineyard of the Lord of Hosts is the house of Israel, and the men of Judah his pleasant plant. And he looked for judgment, and behold, oppression; for righteousness, but behold, a cry.

14 Woe unto them that join house to house until there can be no place that they may be placed alone in the midst of the earth. In my ears says the Lord of Hosts, Truly many houses shall be desolate, and great and fair cities without inhabitant. Yea, ten acres of vineyard shall yield one bath, and the seed of a homer shall yield an ephah.

15 Woe unto them that rise up early in the morning that they may follow strong drink, that continue until night, and wine inflame them. And the harp and the viol, the tambourine and pipe, and wine are in their feasts, but they regard not the work of the Lord, neither consider the operation of his hands. Therefore, my people have gone into captivity because they have no knowledge, and their honorable men are famished, and their multitude dried up with thirst. Therefore,

hell has enlarged herself, and opened her mouth without measure; and their glory, and their multitude, and their pomp, and he that rejoices shall descend into it. And the mean man shall be brought down, and the mighty man shall be humbled, and the eyes of the lofty shall be humbled; but the Lord of Hosts shall be exalted in judgment, and God that is holy shall be sanctified in righteousness. Then shall the lambs feed after their manner, and the waste places of the fat ones shall strangers eat.

16 Woe unto them that draw iniquity with cords of vanity and sin as with a cart rope, that say, Let him make speed; hasten his work, that we may see it; and let the counsel of the Holy One of Israel draw near and come, that we may know it.

17 Woe unto them that call evil good and good evil, that put darkness for light and light for darkness, that put bitter for sweet and sweet for bitter.

18 Woe unto the wise in their own eyes and prudent in their own sight.

19 Woe unto the mighty to drink wine, and men of strength to mingle strong drink, who justify the wicked for reward, and take away the righteousness of the righteous from him. Therefore, as the fire devours the stubble and the flame consumes the chaff, their root shall be as rottenness and their blossom shall go up as dust, because they have cast away the law of the Lord of Hosts, and despised the word of the Holy One of Israel. Therefore is the anger of the Lord kindled against his people, and he has stretched forth his hand against them and has smitten them. And the hills did tremble, and their carcasses were torn in the middle of the streets. For all this his anger is not turned away, but his hand stretched out still.

20 And he will lift up an ensign to the nations from far, and will hiss unto them from the end of the earth. And behold, they shall come with speed, swiftly; none shall be weary nor stumble among them; none shall slumber nor sleep; neither shall the girdle of their loins be loosened, nor the latchet of their shoes be broken; whose arrows shall be sharp, and all their bows bent, and their horses' hooves shall be counted like flint, and their wheels like a whirlwind, their roaring like a lion. They shall roar like young lions; yea, they shall roar, and lay hold of the prey, and shall carry away safe, and none shall deliver.

And in that day, they shall roar against them like the roaring of the sea; and if they look unto the land, behold, darkness and sorrow, and the light is darkened in the heavens thereof.

2 In the year that king Uzziah died, I saw also the Lord sitting upon a throne, high and lifted up, and his train filled the temple. Above it stood the seraphim. Each one had six wings: with two he covered his face, and with two he covered his feet, and with two he did fly. And one cried unto another, and said, Holy, holy, holy is the Lord of Hosts! The whole earth is full of his glory! And the posts of the door moved at the voice of him that cried, and the house was filled with smoke.

2 Then said I, Woe is me, for I am undone because I am a man of unclean lips, and I dwell in the midst of a people of unclean lips; for my eyes have seen the King, the Lord of Hosts. Then flew one of the seraphim unto me, having a live coal in his hand, which he had taken with the tongs from off the altar. And he laid it upon my mouth and said, Behold, this has touched your lips, and your iniquity is taken away, and your sin purged. Also, I heard the voice of the Lord, saying, Whom shall I send? And who will go for us? Then said I, Here am I; send me. And he said, Go and tell this people, Hear indeed — but they understand not; and, See indeed — but they perceived not. Make the heart of this people fat, and make their ears heavy, and shut their eyes, lest they see with their eyes, and hear with their ears, and understand with their hearts, and convert and be healed. Then said I, Lord, how long? And he said, Until the cities are wasted without inhabitant, and the houses without man, and the land is utterly desolate, and the Lord have removed men far away; for there shall be a great forsaking in the midst of the land. But yet in it there shall be a tenth, and they shall return and shall be eaten as a teil tree and as an oak, whose substance is in them when they cast their leaves, so the holy seed shall be the substance thereof.

3 It came to pass in the days of Ahaz the son of Jotham, the son of Uzziah king of Judah, that Rezin the king of Syria, and Pekah the son of Remaliah king of Israel, went up toward Jerusalem to war against it, but could not prevail against it. And it was told to the house of David, saying, Syria is confederate with Ephraim. And his heart

was moved, and the heart of his people, as the trees of the wood are moved with the wind.

2 Then said the Lord unto Isaiah, Go forth now to meet Ahaz — you, and Shear-jashub [A remnant shall repent/return] your son — at the end of the conduit of the upper pool in the highway of the fuller's field. And say unto him, Take heed and be quiet; fear not, neither be faint-hearted for the two tails of these smoking firebrands, for the fierce anger of Rezin with Syria, and of the son of Remaliah, because Syria, Ephraim, and the son of Remaliah have taken evil counsel against you, saying, Let us go up against Judah and vex it, and let us make a breach therein for us, and set a king in the midst of it, yea, the son of Tabeal. Thus says the Lord: It shall not stand, neither shall it come to pass. For the head of Syria is Damascus, and the head of Damascus, Rezin. And within sixty-five years shall Ephraim be broken, that it be not a people. And the head of Ephraim is Samaria, and the head of Samaria is Remaliah's son. If you will not believe, surely you shall not be established.

3 Moreover, the Lord spoke again unto Ahaz, saying, Ask a sign of the Lord your God; ask it either in the depth or in the height above. But Ahaz said, I will not ask, neither will I test the Lord. And he said, Hear now, O house of David: Is it a small thing for you to weary men, but will you weary my God also? Therefore, the Lord himself shall give you a sign: behold, a virgin shall conceive, and shall bear a son, and shall call his name Immanuel. Butter and honey shall he eat, that he may know to refuse the evil and to choose the good. For before the child shall know to refuse the evil and choose the good, the land that you abhor shall be forsaken of both her kings. The Lord shall bring upon you, and upon your people, and upon your father's house days that have not come from the day that Ephraim departed from Judah — the king of Assyria. And it shall come to pass in that day that the Lord shall hiss for the fly that is in the outermost part of Egypt, and for the bee that is in the land of Assyria. And they shall come and shall rest all of them in the desolate valleys, and in the holes of the rocks, and upon all thorns, and upon all bushes. In the same day shall the Lord shave with a razor that is hired — by them beyond the river, by the king of Assyria — the head, and the hair of the feet; and it shall also consume the beard. And it shall come to pass, in that day, a man shall nourish a

young cow and two sheep. And it shall come to pass, for the abundance of milk they shall give, he shall eat butter; for butter and honey shall everyone eat that is left in the land. And it shall come to pass, in that day, every place shall be, where there were a thousand vines at a thousand pieces of silver, which shall be for briers and thorns. With arrows and with bows shall men come there because all the land shall become briers and thorns. And all hills that shall be dug with the mattock, there shall not come there the fear of briers and thorns, but it shall be for the sending forth of oxen, and the treading of lesser cattle.

4 Moreover, the word of the Lord said unto me, Take a great scroll, and write on it in common script: Maher-shalal-hash-baz [Hasten the plunder, hurry the spoil]. And I took unto me faithful witnesses to record — Uriah the priest and Zechariah the son of Jeberechiah. And I went unto the prophetess, and she conceived and bore a son. Then said the Lord to me, Call his name Maher-shalal-hash-baz. For behold, the child shall not have knowledge to cry, My father and my mother — before the riches of Damascus and the spoil of Samaria shall be taken away before the king of Assyria.

5 The Lord spoke also unto me again, saying, Forasmuch as this people refuse the waters of Shiloah that go softly, and rejoice in Rezin and Remaliah's son, now therefore behold, the Lord brings up upon them the waters of the river, strong and many, even the king of Assyria and all his glory. And he shall come up over all his channels, and go over all his banks, and he shall pass through Judah. He shall overflow and go over, he shall reach even to the neck. And the stretching out of his wings shall fill the breadth of your land, O Immanuel. Associate yourselves, O you people, and you shall be broken in pieces. And give ear, all you of far countries: Gird yourselves, and you shall be broken in pieces; gird yourselves, and you shall be broken in pieces. Take counsel together, and it shall come to naught; speak the word, and it shall not stand; for God is with us.

6 For the Lord spoke thus to me with a strong hand, and instructed me that I should not walk in the way of this people, saying, Say not, A conspiracy — to all to whom this people shall say, A conspiracy; neither fear their fear nor be afraid. Sanctify the Lord of Hosts himself, and let him be your fear, and let him be your dread, and he shall be for a sanctuary; but for a stone of stumbling and for a rock of offense to

both the houses of Israel, for a trap and a snare to the inhabitants of Jerusalem. And many among them shall stumble and fall, and be broken, and be snared, and be taken.

7 Bind up the testimony, seal the law among my disciples. And I will wait upon the Lord that hides his face from the house of Jacob, and I will look for him. Behold, I and the children whom the Lord has given me are for signs and for wonders in Israel from the Lord of Hosts who dwells in Mount Zion. And when they shall say unto you, Seek unto them that have familiar spirits, and unto wizards that peep and mutter — should not a people seek unto their God? For the living to hear from the dead — to the law and to the testimony? And if they speak not according to this word, it is because there is no light in them. And they shall pass through it hard-pressed and hungry; and it shall come to pass that when they shall be hungry, they shall fret themselves, and curse their king and their God, and look upward. And they shall look unto the earth and behold trouble and darkness, dimness of anguish, and shall be driven to darkness.

4 Nevertheless, the dimness shall not be such as was in her vexation, when at the first he lightly afflicted the land of Zebulun, and the land of Naphtali, and afterward did more grievously afflict by the way of the Red Sea beyond Jordan, in Galilee of the nations. The people that walked in darkness have seen a great light; they that dwell in the land of the shadow of death, upon them has the light shone. You have multiplied the nation and increased the joy; they joy before you according to the joy in harvest, and as men rejoice when they divide the spoil. For you have broken the yoke of his burden, and the staff of his shoulder, the rod of his oppressor, as in the day of Midian, for every battle of the warrior with confused noise and garments rolled in blood; but this shall be with burning and fuel of fire. For unto us a child is born, unto us a son is given, and the government shall be upon his shoulder. And his name shall be called Wonderful Counselor, the Mighty God, the Everlasting Father, the Prince of Peace. Of the increase of government and peace there is no end, upon the throne of David and upon his kingdom, to order it and to establish it with judgment and with justice from henceforth even for ever. The zeal of the Lord of Hosts will perform this.

2 The Lord sent his word unto Jacob, and it has lighted upon Israel. And all the people shall know, even Ephraim and the inhabitants of Samaria, that say in the pride and in the stoutness of heart, The bricks are fallen down, but we will build with hewn stones; the sycamores are cut down, but we will change them into cedars. Therefore, the Lord shall set up the adversaries of Rezin against him and join his enemies together — the Syrians before and the Philistines behind — and they shall devour Israel with open mouth. For all this his anger is not turned away, but his hand is stretched out still.

3 For the people turns not unto him that smites them, neither do they seek the Lord of Hosts. Therefore, the Lord will cut off from Israel head and tail, branch and rush, in one day. The elder and honorable, he is the head; and the prophet that teaches lies, he is the tail. For the leaders of this people cause them to err, and they that are led of them are destroyed. Therefore, the Lord shall have no joy in their young men, neither shall have mercy on their fatherless and widows; for every one of them is a hypocrite and an evildoer, and every mouth speaks folly. For all this his anger is not turned away, but his hand is stretched out still.

4 For wickedness burns as the fire; it shall devour the briers and thorns, and shall kindle in the thickets of the forest, and they shall mount up like the lifting up of smoke. Through the wrath of the Lord of Hosts is the land darkened, and the people shall be as the fuel of the fire; no man shall spare his brother. And he shall snatch on the right hand and be hungry, and he shall eat on the left hand and they shall not be satisfied. They shall eat, every man, the flesh of his own arm: Manasseh, Ephraim; and Ephraim, Manasseh; they together shall be against Judah. For all this his anger is not turned away, but his hand stretched out still.

5 Woe unto them that decree unrighteous decrees and that write grievousness which they have prescribed, to turn aside the needy from judgment and to take away the right from the poor of my people, that widows may be their prey and that they may rob the fatherless. And what will you do in the day of visitation, and in the desolation which shall come from far? To whom will you flee for help? And where will you leave your glory? Without me they shall bow down under the

prisoners, and they shall fall under the slain. For all this his anger is not turned away, but his hand is stretched out still.

6 O Assyrian, the rod of my anger, and the staff in their hand is my indignation. I will send him against a hypocritical nation, and against the people of my wrath will I give him a charge to take the spoil, and to take the prey, and to tread them down like the mire of the streets. Nevertheless, he means not so, neither does his heart think so, but in his heart it is to destroy and cut off nations not a few. For he says, Are not my princes altogether kings? Is not Calno as Carchemish? Is not Hamath as Arpad? Is not Samaria as Damascus? As my hand has founded the kingdoms of the idols, and whose engraved images did excel them of Jerusalem and of Samaria, shall I not, as I have done unto Samaria and her idols, so do to Jerusalem and to her idols?

7 Wherefore, it shall come to pass that when the Lord has performed his whole work upon Mount Zion and upon Jerusalem, I will punish the fruit of the stout heart of the king of Assyria, and the glory of his haughty looks. For he says, By the strength of my hand and by my wisdom I have done these things, for I am prudent. And I have moved the borders of the people, and have robbed their treasures, and I have put down the inhabitants like a valiant man. And my hand has found as a nest the riches of the people, and as one gathers eggs that are left have I gathered all the earth; and there was none that moved the wing, or opened the mouth, or peeped.

8 Shall the ax boast itself against him that hews with it? Shall the saw magnify itself against him that shakes it? As if the rod should shake itself against them that lift it up, or as if the staff should lift up itself as if it were no wood. Therefore shall the Lord, the Lord of Hosts, send among his fat ones leanness; and under his glory he shall kindle a burning like the burning of a fire. And the Light of Israel shall be for a fire, and his Holy One for a flame, and shall burn and devour his thorns and his briers in one day, and shall consume the glory of his forest and of his fruitful field, both soul and body. And they shall be as when a standard-bearer faints. And the rest of the trees of his forest shall be few, that a child may write them.

5 And it shall come to pass in that day that the remnant of Israel, and such as are escaped of the house of Jacob, shall no more again rely

upon him that smote them, but shall rely upon the Lord, the Holy One of Israel, in truth. The remnant shall return, yea, even the remnant of Jacob, unto the mighty God. For though your people Israel be as the sand of the sea, yet a remnant of them shall return. The consumption decreed shall overflow with righteousness; for the Lord God of Hosts shall make a consumption, even determined, in all the land.

2 Therefore, thus says the Lord God of Hosts: O my people that dwell in Zion, be not afraid of the Assyrian (he shall smite you with a rod, and shall lift up his staff against you, after the manner of Egypt), for yet a very little while and the indignation shall cease, and my anger, in their destruction. And the Lord of Hosts shall stir up a scourge for him, according to the slaughter of Midian at the rock of Oreb; and as his rod was upon the sea, so shall he lift it up after the manner of Egypt. And it shall come to pass in that day, that his burden shall be taken away from off your shoulder, and his yoke from off your neck, and the yoke shall be destroyed because of the anointing.

3 He has come to Aiath, he has passed to Migron; at Michmash, he has laid up his things. They have gone over the passage, they have taken up their lodging at Geba. Ramath is afraid, Gibeah of Saul is fled. Lift up your voice, O daughter of Gallim; cause it to be heard unto Laish, O poor Anathoth. Madmenah is removed, the inhabitants of Gebim gather themselves to flee. As yet shall he remain at Nob that day; he shall shake his hand against the mount of the daughter of Zion, the hill of Jerusalem. Behold, the Lord, the Lord of Hosts shall lop the bough with terror, and the high ones of stature shall be hewn down, and the haughty shall be humbled. And he shall cut down the thickets of the forest with iron, and Lebanon shall fall by a mighty one.

4 And there shall come forth a rod out of the stem of Jesse, and a branch shall grow out of his roots. And the spirit of the Lord shall rest upon him — the spirit of wisdom and understanding, the spirit of counsel and might, the spirit of knowledge and of the fear of the Lord — and shall make him of quick understanding in the fear of the Lord. And he shall not judge after the sight of his eyes, neither reprove after the hearing of his ears, but with righteousness shall he judge the poor, and reprove with equity for the meek of the earth. And he shall smite the earth with the rod of his mouth, and with the breath of his lips shall he slay the wicked. And righteousness shall be the girdle of

his loins, and faithfulness the girdle of his reins. The wolf also shall dwell with the lamb, and the leopard shall lie down with the kid; and the calf, and the young lion, and the fatling together, and a little child shall lead them. And the cow and the bear shall feed, their young ones shall lie down together, and the lion shall eat straw like the ox. And the sucking child shall play on the hole of the asp, and the weaned child shall put his hand on the cockatrice's den. They shall not hurt nor destroy in all my holy mountain, for the earth shall be full of the knowledge of the Lord as the waters cover the sea. And in that day, there shall be a root of Jesse who shall stand for an ensign of the people; to it shall the gentiles seek, and his rest shall be glorious.

5 And it shall come to pass in that day that the Lord shall set his hand again the second time to recover the remnant of his people which shall be left from Assyria, and from Egypt, and from Pathros, and from Cush, and from Elam, and from Shinar, and from Hamath, and from the islands of the sea. And he shall set up an ensign for the nations, and shall assemble the outcasts of Israel, and gather together the dispersed of Judah, from the four corners of the earth. The envy also of Ephraim shall depart, and the adversaries of Judah shall be cut off. Ephraim shall not envy Judah and Judah shall not vex Ephraim. But they shall fly upon the shoulders of the Philistines toward the west, they shall spoil them of the east together, they shall lay their hand upon Edom and Moab, and the children of Ammon shall obey them. And the Lord shall utterly destroy the tongue of the Egyptian sea, and with his mighty wind he shall shake his hand over the river, and shall smite it in the seven streams, and make men go over with dry feet. And there shall be a highway for the remnant of his people which shall be left from Assyria, like it was to Israel in the day that he came up out of the land of Egypt.

6 And in that day, you shall say, O Lord, I will praise you; though you were angry with me, your anger is turned away and you comforted me. Behold, God is my salvation. I will trust and not be afraid, for the Lord Jehovah is my strength and my song; he also has become my salvation. Therefore, with joy shall you draw water out of the wells of salvation. And in that day shall you say, Praise the Lord, call upon his name, declare his doings among the people, make mention that his name is exalted. Sing unto the Lord, for he has done excellent things;

this is known in all the earth. Cry out and shout, you inhabitant of Zion, for great is the Holy One of Israel in your midst.

The burden of Babylon, which Isaiah the son of Amoz did see.

6 Lift up a banner upon the high mountain, exalt the voice unto them, shake the hand, that they may go into the gates of the nobles. I have commanded my sanctified ones, I have also called my mighty ones, for my anger is not upon them that rejoice in my highness. The noise of the multitude in the mountains, as of a great people, a tumultuous noise of the kingdoms of nations gathered together; the Lord of Hosts musters the host of the battle. They come from a far country, from the end of heaven — yea, the Lord and the weapons of his indignation — to destroy the whole land.

2 Howl, for the day of the Lord is at hand; it shall come as a destruction from the Almighty. Therefore shall all hands be faint, every man's heart shall melt, and they shall be afraid. Pangs and sorrows shall take hold of them, they shall be in pain as a woman that travails; they shall be amazed one at another, their faces shall be as flames. Behold, the day of the Lord comes, cruel both with wrath and fierce anger, to lay the land desolate; and he shall destroy the sinners thereof out of it. For the stars of heaven and the constellations thereof shall not give their light; the sun shall be darkened in his going forth, and the moon shall not cause her light to shine. And I will punish the world for evil, and the wicked for their iniquity. And I will cause the arrogance of the proud to cease, and will lay low the haughtiness of the terrible. I will make a man more precious than fine gold, even a man than the golden wedge of Ophir. Therefore, I will shake the heavens, and the earth shall remove out of her place, in the wrath of the Lord of Hosts and in the day of his fierce anger. And it shall be as the chased roe, and as a sheep that no man takes up; they shall every man turn to his own people and flee everyone into his own land. Everyone that is proud shall be thrust through, and everyone that is joined to the wicked shall fall by the sword. Their children also shall be dashed to pieces before their eyes, their houses shall be spoiled, and their wives violated. Behold, I will stir up the Medes against them, who shall not regard silver and gold, they shall not delight in it. Their bows also shall dash the young men

to pieces, and they shall have no pity on the fruit of the womb; their eye shall not spare children.

3 And Babylon, the glory of kingdoms, the beauty of the Chaldees' excellence, shall be as when God overthrew Sodom and Gomorrah. It shall never be inhabited, neither shall it be dwelled in from generation to generation, neither shall the Arabian pitch tent there, neither shall the shepherds make their fold there. But wild beasts of the desert shall lie there, and their houses shall be full of howling creatures, and owls shall dwell there, and satyrs shall dance there. And the wild beasts of the islands shall cry in their desolate houses, and dragons in their pleasant palaces. And her time is near to come, and her days shall not be prolonged, for I will destroy her speedily; yea, for I will be merciful unto my people, but the wicked shall perish.

4 For the Lord will have mercy on Jacob, and will yet choose Israel, and set them in their own land, and the strangers shall be joined with them, and they shall cleave to the house of Jacob. And the people shall take them and bring them to their place, yea, from far unto the ends of the earth, and they shall return to their lands of promise. And the house of Israel shall possess them in the land of the Lord for servants and handmaids; and they shall take them captives, whose captives they were, and they shall rule over their oppressors.

5 And it shall come to pass in that day that the Lord shall give you rest from your sorrow, and from your fear, and from the hard bondage wherein you were made to serve. And it shall come to pass in that day, that you shall take up this proverb against the king of Babylon, and say, How has the oppressor ceased, the golden city ceased. The Lord has broken the staff of the wicked, the scepters of the rulers. He who smote the people in wrath with a continual stroke, he that ruled the nations in anger, is persecuted, and none hinders. The whole earth is at rest and is quiet; they break forth into singing. Yea, the fir trees rejoice at you, and also the cedars of Lebanon, saying, Since you are laid down, no feller has come up against us. Hell from beneath is moved for you to meet you at your coming. It stirs up the dead for you, even all the chief ones of the earth; it has raised up from their thrones all the kings of the nations. All they shall speak and say unto you, Have you also become weak as us? Have you become like unto us? Your pomp

is brought down to the grave, and the noise of your viols; the worm is spread under you, and the worms cover you.

6 How are you fallen from Heaven, O Lucifer, son of the morning! Are you cut down to the ground, which did weaken the nations? For you have said in your heart, I will ascend into Heaven; I will exalt my throne above the stars of God; I will sit also upon the mount of the congregation, in the sides of the north; I will ascend above the heights of the clouds; I will be like the Most High. Yet you shall be brought down to hell, to the sides of the pit. They that see you shall narrowly look upon you, and shall consider you, and shall say, Is this the man that made the earth to tremble, that did shake kingdoms, and made the world as a wilderness, and destroyed the cities thereof, and opened not the house of his prisoners? All the kings of the nations, yea, all of them lie in glory, every one of them in his own house. But you are cast out of your grave like an abominable branch, and the remnant of those that are slain, thrust through with a sword, that go down to the stones of the pit, as a carcass trodden under feet. You shall not be joined with them in burial because you have destroyed your land and slain your people; the seed of evildoers shall never be renowned.

7 Prepare slaughter for his children for the iniquities of their fathers, that they do not rise, nor possess the land, nor fill the face of the world with cities. For I will rise up against them, says the Lord of Hosts, and cut off from Babylon the name, and remnant, and son, and grandson, says the Lord. I will also make it a possession for the bittern and pools of water; and I will sweep it with the broom of destruction, says the Lord of Hosts. The Lord of Hosts has sworn, saying, Surely as I have thought, so shall it come to pass; and as I have purposed, so shall it stand, that I will break the Assyrian in my land, and upon my mountains tread him underfoot. Then shall his yoke depart from off them, and his burden depart from off their shoulders. This is the purpose that is purposed upon the whole earth, and this is the hand that is stretched out upon all the nations. For the Lord of Hosts has purposed, and who shall disannul? And his hand stretched out, and who shall turn it back?

In the year that king Ahaz died was this burden.

8 Rejoice not, whole Palestina, because the rod of him that smote you is broken; for out of the serpent's root shall come forth a cockatrice,

and his fruit shall be a fiery flying serpent. And the first born of the poor shall feed, and the needy shall lie down in safety. And I will kill your root with famine, and he shall slay your remnant. Howl, O gate; cry, O city; you, whole Palestina, are dissolved, for there shall come from the north a smoke, and none shall be alone in his appointed times. What shall then answer the messengers of the nation? That the Lord has founded Zion, and the poor of his people shall trust in it.

The burden of Moab.

9 Because in the night Ar of Moab is laid waste and brought to silence, because in the night Kir of Moab is laid waste, and brought to silence, he is gone up to Bajith and to Dibon, the high places, to weep. Moab shall howl over Nebo and over Medeba; on all their heads shall be baldness, and every beard cut off. In their streets they shall gird themselves with sackcloth; on the tops of their houses and in their streets everyone shall howl, weeping abundantly. And Heshbon shall cry, and Elealeh; their voice shall be heard even unto Jahaz. Therefore, the armed soldiers of Moab shall cry out, his life shall be grievous unto him. My heart shall cry out for Moab; his fugitives shall flee unto Zoar, a heifer of three years old. For by the mounting up of Luhith with weeping shall they go up in it; for in the way of Horonaim they shall raise up a cry of destruction. For the waters of Nimrim shall be desolate, for the hay is withered away, the grass fails, there is no green thing. Therefore, the abundance they have gotten, and that which they have laid up, shall they carry away to the brook of the willows. For the cry is gone round about the borders of Moab, the howling thereof unto Eglaim, and the howling thereof unto Beerelim. For the waters of Dimon shall be full of blood, for I will bring more upon Dimon — lions upon him that escapes of Moab and upon the remnant of the land.

10 Send the lamb to the ruler of the land, from Sela to the wilderness, unto the mount of the daughter of Zion. For it shall be that as a wandering bird cast out of the nest, so the daughters of Moab shall be at the fords of Arnon. Take counsel, execute judgment. Make your shadow as the night in the middle of the noonday. Hide the outcasts, betray not him that wanders. Let my outcasts dwell with you, Moab; be a cover to them from the face of the spoiler. For the extortioner is at an end, the spoiler ceases, the oppressors are consumed out of

the land. And in mercy shall the throne be established; and he shall sit upon it in truth, in the tabernacle of David, judging, and seeking judgment, and hasting righteousness. We have heard of the pride of Moab — of his haughtiness and his pride, for he is very proud — and his wrath, his lies, and all his evil works. Therefore shall Moab howl for Moab, everyone shall howl. For the foundations of Kirhareseth shall you mourn — surely they are stricken. For the fields of Heshbon languish, and the vine of Sibmah; the lords of the heathen have broken down the principal plants thereof. They have come even unto Jazer, they wandered through the wilderness; her branches are stretched out, they have gone over the sea. Therefore, I will bewail with the weeping of Jazer the vine of Sibmah. I will water you with my tears, O Heshbon and Elealeh, for the shouting for your summer fruits and for your harvest is fallen. And gladness is taken away, and joy out of the plentiful field. And in the vineyards there shall be no singing, neither shall there be shouting. The treaders shall tread out no wine in their presses; I have made their vintage shouting to cease. Wherefore my heart shall sound like a harp for Moab, and my inward parts for Kirhareseth. And it shall come to pass, when it is seen that Moab is weary on the high place, that he shall come to his sanctuary to pray, but he shall not prevail.

11 This is the word that the Lord has spoken concerning Moab since that time. But now the Lord has spoken, saying, Within three years, as the years of a hired hand, and the glory of Moab shall be despised, with all that great multitude, and the remnant shall be very small and feeble.

The burden of Damascus.

12 Behold, Damascus is taken away from being a city, and it shall be a ruinous heap; the cities of Aroer are forsaken, they shall be for flocks which shall lie down, and none shall make them afraid. The fortress shall also cease from Ephraim, and the kingdom from Damascus; and the remnant of Syria, they shall be as the glory of the children of Israel, says the Lord of Hosts. And in that day it shall come to pass that the glory of Jacob shall be made thin, and the fatness of his flesh shall wax lean. And it shall be as when the harvestman gathers the grain, and reaps the ears with his arm; and it shall be as he that gathers ears in the valley of Rephaim. Yet gleaning grapes shall be left in it, as the shaking

of an olive tree, two or three berries in the top of the uppermost bough, four or five in the outermost fruitful branches thereof, says the Lord God of Israel. At that day shall a man look to his Maker, and his eyes shall have respect to the Holy One of Israel. And he shall not look to the altars, the work of his hands, neither shall respect that which his fingers have made, either the groves or the images. In that day shall his strong cities be as a forsaken bough and an uppermost branch, which they left because of the children of Israel; and there shall be desolation. Because you have forgotten the God of your salvation and have not been mindful of the Rock of your strength, therefore shall you plant pleasant plants and shall set it with strange slips. In the day shall you make your plant to grow, and in the morning shall you make your seed to flourish; but the harvest shall be a heap in the day of grief and of desperate sorrow.

13 Woe to the multitude of many people, who make a noise like the noise of the seas, and to the rushing of nations, that make a rushing like the rushing of mighty waters. The nations shall rush like the rushing of many waters, but God shall rebuke them, and they shall flee far off, and shall be chased as the chaff of the mountains before the wind, and like a rolling thing before the whirlwind. And behold, at evening—trouble; and before the morning, he is not. This is the portion of them that spoil us, and the lot of them that rob us.

14 Woe to the land shadowing with wings, which is beyond the rivers of Ethiopia, that sends ambassadors by the sea, even in vessels of papyrus upon the waters, saying, Go, you swift messengers, to a nation now lost yet defiant, to a people terrible from their beginning until now, a nation meted out and trodden down, whose land the rivers have spoiled. All you inhabitants of the world and dwellers on the earth, see, when he lifts up an ensign on the mountains; and when he blows a trumpet, hear. For so the Lord said unto me: I will take my rest and I will consider in my dwelling place, like a clear heat upon herbs and like a cloud of dew in the heat of harvest. For before the harvest, when the bud is perfect and the sour grape is ripening in the flower, he shall both cut off the sprigs with pruning hooks and take away and cut down the branches. They shall be left together unto the fowls of the mountains and to the beasts of the earth; and the fowls shall summer upon them, and all the beasts of the earth shall winter

upon them. In that time shall the present be brought unto the Lord of Hosts, of a people who were lost yet defiant, and from a people terrible from their beginning until now, a nation meted out and trodden underfoot, whose land the rivers have spoiled, to the place of the name of the Lord of Hosts: the mount Zion.

The burden of Egypt.

15 Behold, the Lord rides upon a swift cloud and shall come into Egypt; and the idols of Egypt shall be moved at his presence, and the heart of Egypt shall melt in the midst of it. And I will set the Egyptians against the Egyptians and they shall fight, every one against his brother and every one against his neighbor, city against city and kingdom against kingdom. And the spirit of Egypt shall fail in the midst thereof, and I will destroy the counsel thereof; and they shall seek to the idols, and to the charmers, and to them that have familiar spirits, and to the wizards. And the Egyptians will I give over into the hand of a cruel lord, and a fierce king shall rule over them, says the Lord, the Lord of Hosts. And the waters shall fail from the sea, and the river shall be wasted and dried up. And they shall turn the rivers far away, and the brooks of defense shall be emptied and dried up; the reeds and rushes shall wither. The papyrus by the brooks, by the mouth of the brooks, and everything sowed by the brooks shall wither, be driven away, and be no more. The fishers also shall mourn, and all they that cast fishhooks into the brooks shall lament, and they that spread nets upon the waters shall languish. Moreover, they that work in fine flax and they that weave networks shall be confounded. And they shall be broken in the purposes thereof, all that make sluices and ponds for fish.

16 Surely the princes of Zoan are fools, the counsel of the wise counselors of Pharaoh has become brutish. How do you say unto Pharaoh, I am the son of the wise, the son of ancient kings? Where are they? Where are your wise men? And let them tell you now, and let them know what the Lord of Hosts has purposed upon Egypt. The princes of Zoan have become fools, the princes of Noph are deceived; they have also seduced Egypt, even they that are the cornerstone of the tribes thereof. The Lord has mingled a perverse spirit in the midst thereof, and they have caused Egypt to err in every work thereof, as a drunk man staggers in his vomit. Neither shall there be any work for

Egypt, which the head or tail, branch or rush may do. In that day shall Egypt be like unto women, and it shall be afraid and fear because of the shaking of the hand of the Lord of Hosts which he shakes over it. And the land of Judah shall be a terror unto Egypt; everyone that makes mention thereof shall be afraid in himself because of the counsel of the Lord of Hosts which he has determined against it.

17 In that day shall five cities in the land of Egypt speak the language of Canaan, and swear to the Lord of Hosts; one shall be called the city of destruction. In that day shall there be an altar to the Lord in the center of the land of Egypt, and a pillar at the border thereof to the Lord. And it shall be for a sign and for a witness unto the Lord of Hosts in the land of Egypt, for they shall cry unto the Lord because of the oppressors; and he shall send them a savior, and a great one, and he shall deliver them. And the Lord shall be known to Egypt, and the Egyptians shall know the Lord in that day and shall do sacrifice and offering; yea, they shall vow a vow unto the Lord and perform it. And the Lord shall smite Egypt, he shall smite and heal it, and they shall return even to the Lord, and he shall be entreated of them and shall heal them. In that day shall there be a highway out of Egypt to Assyria, and the Assyrian shall come into Egypt, and the Egyptian into Assyria, and the Egyptians shall serve with the Assyrians. In that day shall Israel be the third with Egypt and with Assyria, even a blessing in the midst of the land whom the Lord of Hosts shall bless, saying, Blessed be Egypt my people, and Assyria the work of my hands, and Israel my inheritance.

18 In the year that Tartan came unto Ashdod (when Sargon the king of Assyria sent him), and fought against Ashdod and took it, at the same time spoke the Lord by Isaiah the son of Amoz, saying, Go and remove the sackcloth from off your loins and put off your shoes from your feet. And he did so, walking naked and barefoot.

19 And the Lord said, Like my servant Isaiah has walked naked and barefoot three years for a sign and wonder upon Egypt and upon Ethiopia, so shall the king of Assyria lead away the Egyptians prisoners, and the Ethiopians captives, young and old, naked and barefoot, even with their buttocks uncovered, to the shame of Egypt. And they shall be afraid and ashamed of Ethiopia, their expectation, and of Egypt, their glory; and the inhabitant of this isle shall say in that day, Behold,

such is our expectation, where we flee for help to be delivered from the king of Assyria. And how shall we escape?

The burden of the Desert of the Sea.

20 As whirlwinds in the south pass through, so it comes from the desert, from a terrible land. A grievous vision is declared unto me: the treacherous dealer deals treacherously, and the spoiler spoils. Go up, O Elam; besiege, O Media; all the sighing thereof have I made to cease. Therefore are my loins filled with pain, pangs have taken hold upon me, as the pangs of a woman that travails. I was bowed down at the hearing of it, I was dismayed at the seeing of it. My heart panted, fearfulness frightened me, the night of my pleasure has he turned into fear unto me. Prepare the table, watch in the watchtower, eat, drink; arise, you princes, and anoint the shield. For thus has the Lord said unto me: Go, set a watchman, let him declare what he sees. And he saw a chariot with a couple of horsemen, a chariot of asses, and a chariot of camels, and he listened diligently with much heed. And he cried, A lion! My lord, I stand continually upon the watchtower in the daytime, and I am set in my watch whole nights; and behold, here comes a chariot of men with a couple of horsemen. And he answered and said, Babylon is fallen, is fallen; and all the engraved images of her gods he has broken unto the ground. O my threshing and the grain of my floor, that which I have heard of the Lord of Hosts, the God of Israel, have I declared unto you.

The burden of Dumah.

21 He calls to me out of Seir, Watchman, what of the night? Watchman, what of the night? The watchman said, The morning comes, and also the night. If you will inquire, inquire; return, come.

The burden upon Arabia.

22 In the forest in Arabia shall you lodge, O traveling companies of Dedanim. The inhabitants of the land of Tema brought water to him that was thirsty, they met with their bread him that fled. For they fled from the swords, from the drawn sword, and from the bent bow, and from the grievousness of war. For thus has the Lord said unto me: Within a year, according to the years of a hired hand, and all the

glory of Kedar shall fail. And the residue of the number of archers, the mighty men of the children of Kedar, shall be diminished, for the Lord God of Israel has spoken it.

The burden of the Valley of Vision.

23 What ails you now, that you are wholly gone up to the housetops, you that are full of stirs, a tumultuous city, a joyous city? Your slain men are not slain with the sword, nor dead in battle. All your rulers are fled together, they are bound by the archers; all that are found in you are bound together, who have fled from far. Therefore said I, Look away from me; I will weep bitterly. Labor not to comfort me because of the spoiling of the daughter of my people. For it is a day of trouble, and of treading down, and of perplexity by the Lord God of hosts in the valley of vision, breaking down the walls, and of crying to the mountains. And Elam bore the quiver with chariots of men and horsemen, and Kir uncovered the shield. And it shall come to pass that your choicest valleys shall be full of chariots, and the horsemen shall set themselves in array at the gate. And he uncovered the covering of Judah, and you did look in that day to the armor of the house of the forest. You have seen also the breaches of the city of David, that they are many, and you gathered together the waters of the lower pool. And you have numbered the houses of Jerusalem, and the houses have you broken down to fortify the wall. You made also a ditch between the two walls for the water of the old pool, but you have not looked unto the maker thereof, neither had respect unto him that fashioned it long ago. And in that day did the Lord God of Hosts call to weeping, and to mourning, and to baldness, and to girding with sackcloth; and behold, joy and gladness, slaying oxen and killing sheep, eating flesh and drinking wine: Let us eat and drink, for tomorrow we shall die. And it was revealed in my ears by the Lord of Hosts, Surely this iniquity shall not be purged from you until you die, says the Lord God of Hosts.

24 Thus says the Lord God of Hosts: Go, get yourself unto this treasurer, even unto Shebna, who is over the house, and say, What do you have here? And whom do you have here, that you have hewn yourself out a sepulcher here as he that hews himself out a sepulcher on high, and that carves a habitation for himself in a rock? Behold, the Lord will carry you away with a mighty captivity and will surely

cover you. He will surely violently turn and toss you like a ball into a
large country. There shall you die, and there the chariots of your glory
shall be the shame of your lord's house. And I will drive you from
your station, and from your state shall he pull you down. And it shall
come to pass in that day that I will call my servant, Eliakim the son
of Hilkiah, and I will clothe him with your robe, and strengthen him
with your sash, and I will commit your government into his hand. And
he shall be a father to the inhabitants of Jerusalem and to the house of
Judah. And the key of the house of David will I lay upon his shoulder;
so he shall open and none shall shut, and he shall shut and none shall
open. And I will fasten him as a nail in a sure place, and he shall be
for a glorious throne to his father's house. And they shall hang upon
him all the glory of his father's house: the offspring and the offshoots,
all vessels of small quantity, from the vessels of cups even to all the
vessels of flagons. In that day, says the Lord of Hosts, shall the nail that
is fastened in the sure place be removed, and be cut down, and fall; and
the burden that was upon it shall be cut off, for the Lord has spoken it.

The burden of Tyre.

25 Howl, ships of Tarshish, for it is laid waste, so that there is no
house, no entering in; from the land of Kittim it is revealed to them.
Be still, you inhabitants of the isle, you whom the merchants of Sidon
that pass over the sea have replenished. And by great waters, the seed
of Shihor, the harvest of the river is her revenue, and she is a mart
of nations. Be ashamed, O Sidon, for the sea has spoken, even the
strength of the sea, saying, I travail not, nor bring forth children,
neither do I nourish up young men, nor bring up virgins. As at the
report concerning Egypt, so shall they be greatly pained at the report
of Tyre. Pass over to Tarshish; howl, you inhabitants of the isle. Is this
your joyous city, whose antiquity is of ancient days? Her own feet shall
carry her afar off to sojourn. Who has taken this counsel against Tyre,
the crowning city, whose merchants are princes, whose traffickers are
the honorable of the earth? The Lord of Hosts has purposed it, to stain
the pride of all glory and to bring into contempt all the honorable of
the earth. Pass through your land as a river, O daughter of Tarshish,
there is no more strength in you. He stretched out his hand over the sea,

he shook the kingdoms. The Lord has given a commandment against the merchant city, to destroy the strongholds thereof.

26 And he said, You shall no more rejoice, O you oppressed virgin, daughter of Sidon. Arise, pass over to Kittim; there also shall you have no rest. Behold the land of the Chaldeans. This people was not until the Assyrian founded it for them that dwell in the wilderness. They set up the towers thereof, they raised up the palaces thereof. And he brought it to ruin.

27 Howl, you ships of Tarshish, for your strength is laid waste. And it shall come to pass in that day that Tyre shall be forgotten seventy years, according to the days of one king; and after the end of seventy years shall Tyre sing as a harlot: Take a harp, go about the city, you harlot that has been forgotten; make sweet melody, sing many songs, that you may be remembered. And it shall come to pass after the end of seventy years that the Lord will visit Tyre, and she shall turn to her hire, and shall commit fornication with all the kingdoms of the world upon the face of the earth. And her merchandise and her hire shall be holiness to the Lord. It shall not be treasured nor laid up, for her merchandise shall be for them that dwell before the Lord, to eat sufficiently and for durable clothing.

7 Behold, the Lord makes the earth empty, and makes it waste, and turns it upside down, and scatters abroad the inhabitants thereof. And it shall be, as with the people, so with the priest; as with the servant, so with his master; as with the maid, so with her mistress; as with the buyer, so with the seller; as with the lender, so with the borrower; as with the taker of usury, so with the giver of usury to him. The land shall be utterly emptied and utterly spoiled, for the Lord has spoken this word. The earth mourns and fades away; the world languishes and fades away; the haughty people of the earth do languish. The earth also is defiled under the inhabitants thereof, because they have transgressed the laws, changed the ordinance, broken the everlasting covenant. Therefore has the curse devoured the earth, and they that dwell therein are desolate; therefore, the inhabitants of the earth are burned, and few men left. The new wine mourns, the vine languishes, all the merry-hearted do sigh. The mirth of tambourines ceases, the noise of them that rejoice ends, the joy of the harp ceases. They shall

not drink wine with a song; strong drink shall be bitter to them that drink it. The city of confusion is broken down; every house is shut up, that no man may come in. There is a crying for wine in the streets, all joy is darkened, the mirth of the land is gone. In the city is left desolation, and the gate is smitten with destruction. When thus it shall be in the midst of the land among the people, there shall be as the shaking of an olive tree, and as the gleaning-grapes when the vintage is done. They shall lift up their voice, they shall sing for the majesty of the Lord, they shall cry aloud from the sea. Wherefore, glorify the Lord in the fires, even the name of the Lord God of Israel in the isles of the sea.

2 From the farthest part of the earth have we heard songs, even glory to the righteous. But I said, My leanness, my leanness, woe unto me. The treacherous dealers have dealt treacherously; yea, the treacherous dealers have dealt very treacherously. Fear, and the pit, and the snare are upon you, O inhabitant of the earth. And it shall come to pass that he who flees from the noise of the fear shall fall into the pit; and he that comes up out of the midst of the pit shall be taken in the snare. For the windows from on high are open, and the foundations of the earth do shake. The earth is utterly broken down, the earth is clean dissolved, the earth is moved exceedingly. The earth shall reel to and fro like a drunkard, and shall be removed like a cottage; and the transgression thereof shall be heavy upon it, and it shall fall and not rise again. And it shall come to pass in that day that the Lord shall punish the host of the high ones that are on high, and the kings of the earth upon the earth. And they shall be gathered together as prisoners are gathered in the pit, and shall be shut up in the prison; and after many days shall they be visited. Then the moon shall be confounded and the sun ashamed, when the Lord of Hosts shall reign in Mount Zion, and in Jerusalem, and before his elders gloriously.

3 O Lord, you are my God; I will exalt you. I will praise your name, for you have done wonderful things, your counsels of old are faithfulness and truth. For you have made of a city a heap, of a fortified city a ruin, a palace of strangers to be no city; it shall never be built. Therefore shall the strong people glorify you, the city of the terrible nations shall fear you. For you have been a strength to the poor, a strength to the needy in his distress, a refuge from the storm, a shadow from the heat, when the blast of the terrible ones is as a storm against the

wall. You shall bring down the noise of strangers as the heat in a dry place, even the heat with the shadow of a cloud; the branch of the terrible ones shall be brought low. And in this mountain shall the Lord of Hosts make unto all people a feast of fat things, a feast of aged wines — of fat things full of marrow, of aged wines well refined. And he will destroy in this mountain the face of the covering cast over all people and the veil that is spread over all nations. He will swallow up death in victory. And the Lord God will wipe away tears from off all faces, and the rebuke of his people shall he take away from off all the earth; for the Lord has spoken it. And it shall be said in that day, Behold, this is our God; we have waited for him and he will save us; this is the Lord, we have waited for him; we will be glad and rejoice in his salvation. For in this mountain shall the hand of the Lord rest, and Moab shall be trodden down under him even as straw is trodden down for the dunghill. And he shall spread forth his hands in the midst of them, as he that swims spreads forth his hands to swim; and he shall bring down their pride together with the spoils of their hands. And the fortress of the high fort of your walls shall he bring down, lay low, and bring to the ground, even to the dust.

4 In that day shall this song be sung in the land of Judah: We have a strong city; salvation will God appoint for walls and bulwarks. Open the gates, that the righteous nation which keeps the truth may enter in. You will keep him in perfect peace whose mind is fixed on you because he trusts in you. Trust in the Lord for ever, for in the Lord JEHOVAH is everlasting strength. For he brings down them that dwell on high, the lofty city he lays it low; he lays it low, even to the ground; he brings it even to the dust. The foot shall tread it down, even the feet of the poor and the steps of the needy. The way of the just is uprightness; you, Most Upright, do weigh the path of the just. Yea, in the way of your judgments, O Lord, have we waited for you; the desire of our soul is to your name and to the remembrance of you. With my soul have I desired you in the night, yea, with my spirit within me will I seek you early; for when your judgments are in the earth, the inhabitants of the world will learn righteousness. Let favor be shown to the wicked, yet will he not learn righteousness. In the land of uprightness will he deal unjustly, and will not behold the majesty of the Lord. Lord, when your hand is lifted up, they will not see; but they shall see and be ashamed

for their envy at the people, yea, the fire of your enemies shall devour them. Lord, you will ordain peace for us, for you also have wrought all our works in us. O Lord our God, other lords besides you have had dominion over us, but by you only will we make mention of your name. They are dead, they shall not live; they are deceased, they shall not rise. Therefore have you visited and destroyed them, and made all their memory to perish. You have increased the nation, O Lord, you have increased the nation. You are glorified, you had removed it far, unto all the ends of the earth.

5 Lord, in trouble have they visited you, they poured out a prayer when your chastening was upon them. Like a woman with child that draws near the time of her delivery is in pain, and cries out in her pangs, so have we been in your sight, O Lord. We have been with child, we have been in pain, we have, as it were, brought forth wind. We have not wrought any deliverance in the earth, neither have the inhabitants of the world fallen. Your dead men shall live, together with my dead body shall they arise. Awake and sing, you that dwell in dust, for your dew is as the dew of herbs, and the earth shall cast out the dead. Come, my people, enter into your chambers and shut your doors about you. Hide yourself as for a little moment, until the indignation be passed over. For behold, the Lord comes out of his place to punish the inhabitants of the earth for their iniquity. The earth also shall disclose her blood and shall no more cover her slain.

6 In that day, the Lord, with his severe and great and strong sword, shall punish leviathan the piercing serpent, even leviathan that crooked serpent; and he shall slay the dragon that is in the sea.

7 In that day, sing unto her, A vineyard of red wine, I the Lord do keep it. I will water it every moment, lest any hurt it. I will keep it night and day. Fury is not in me. Who would set the briers and thorns against me in battle? I would go through them, I would burn them together. Or let him take hold of my strength, that he may make peace with me, and he shall make peace with me. He shall cause them that come of Jacob to take root; Israel shall blossom, and bud, and fill the face of the world with fruit. Has he smitten him as he smote those that smote him? Or is he slain according to the slaughter of them that are slain by him? In measure, when it shoots forth, you will debate with it; he holds back his rough wind in the day of the east wind. By this therefore

shall the iniquity of Jacob be purged, and this is all the fruit to take away his sin: when he makes all the stones of the altar as chalkstones that are beaten asunder, the groves and images shall not stand up. Yet the fortified city shall be desolate, and the habitation forsaken and left like a wilderness. There shall the calf feed, and there shall he lie down and consume the branches thereof. When the boughs thereof are withered, they shall be broken off; the women come and set them on fire For it is a people of no understanding, therefore he that made them will not have mercy on them, and he that formed them will show them no favor. And it shall come to pass in that day that the Lord shall beat off from the channel of the river unto the stream of Egypt, and you shall be gathered one by one, O you children of Israel. And it shall come to pass in that day that the great trumpet shall be blown, and they shall come who were ready to perish in the land of Assyria, and the outcasts in the land of Egypt, and shall worship the Lord in the holy mount at Jerusalem.

8 Woe to the crown of pride, to the drunkards of Ephraim whose glorious beauty is a fading flower, which are on the head of the fat valleys of them that are overcome with wine. Behold, the Lord has a mighty and strong one, which, as a tempest of hail and a destroying storm, as a flood of mighty waters overflowing, shall cast down to the earth with the hand. The crown of pride, the drunkards of Ephraim, shall be trodden under feet, and the glorious beauty which is on the head of the fat valley shall be a fading flower, and as the hasty fruit before the summer, which, when he that looks upon it sees, while it is yet in his hand, he eats it up.

2 In that day shall the Lord of Hosts be for a crown of glory and for a diadem of beauty unto the residue of his people, and for a spirit of judgment to him that sits in judgment, and for strength to them that turn the battle to the gate. But they also have erred through wine, and through strong drink are out of the way. The priest and the prophet have erred through strong drink, they are swallowed up of wine, they are out of the way through strong drink; they err in vision, they stumble in judgment. For all tables are full of vomit and filthiness, so that there is no place clean.

3 Whom shall he teach knowledge? And whom shall he make to understand doctrine? Those who are weaned from the milk and drawn from the breasts, for precept must be upon precept — precept upon precept, line upon line, line upon line, here a little, and there a little. For with stammering lips and another tongue will he speak to this people, to whom he said, This is the rest with which you may cause the weary to rest, and this is the refreshing — yet they would not hear. But the word of the Lord was unto them precept upon precept, precept upon precept, line upon line, line upon line, here a little and there a little, that they might go, and fall backward, and be broken, and snared, and taken.

4 Wherefore, hear the word of the Lord, you scornful men that rule this people which is in Jerusalem. Because you have said, We have made a covenant with death, and with hell are we at agreement; when the overflowing scourge shall pass through, it shall not come unto us, for we have made lies our refuge and under falsehood have we hidden ourselves — therefore, thus says the Lord God: Behold, I lay in Zion for a foundation a stone, a tried stone, a precious cornerstone, a sure foundation. He that believes shall not make haste. Judgment also will I lay to the line, and righteousness to the plummet; and the hail shall sweep away the refuge of lies, and the waters shall overflow the hiding place. And your covenant with death shall be disannulled, and your agreement with hell shall not stand; when the overflowing scourge shall pass through, then you shall be trodden down by it. From the time that it goes forth, it shall take you; for morning by morning shall it pass over, by day and by night. And it shall be a vexation only to understand the report. For the bed is shorter than that a man can stretch himself on it, and the covering narrower than that he can wrap himself in it. For the Lord shall rise up as in Mount Perazim, he shall be angry as in the valley of Gibeon, that he may do his work, his strange work, and bring to pass his act, his strange act. Now therefore, be not mockers, lest your bands be made strong; for I have heard from the Lord God of hosts a consumption, even determined upon the whole earth.

5 Give ear, and hear my voice; listen, and hear my speech. Does the plowman plow all day to sow? Does he open and break the clods of his ground? When he has made plain the face thereof, does he not cast abroad the caraway, and scatter the cumin, and cast in the principal

wheat, and the appointed barley and the rye in their place? For his God does instruct him to discretion, and does teach him. For the caraway are not threshed with a threshing instrument, neither is a cart wheel turned about upon the cumin; but the caraway are beaten out with a staff, and the cumin with a rod. Bread grain is ground because he will not ever be threshing it, nor break it with the wheel of his cart, nor bruise it with his horsemen. This also comes forth from the Lord of Hosts, who is wonderful in counsel and excellent in working.

6 Woe to Ariel, to Ariel, the city where David dwelled. Add year to year; let them kill sacrifices. Yet I will distress Ariel, and there shall be heaviness and sorrow; for thus has the Lord said unto me: It shall be unto Ariel that I the Lord will camp against her round about, and will lay siege against her with a mount, and I will raise forts against her. And she shall be brought down and shall speak out of the ground, and her speech shall be low, out of the dust; and her voice shall be as of one that has a familiar spirit, out of the ground, and her speech shall whisper out of the dust. Moreover, the multitude of her strangers shall be like small dust, and the multitude of the terrible ones shall be as chaff that passes away; yea, it shall be at an instant, suddenly. For they shall be visited of the Lord of Hosts with thunder, and with earthquake, and great noise, with storm, and tempest, and the flame of devouring fire. And the multitude of all the nations that fight against Ariel, even all that fight against her and her stronghold, and that distress her, shall be as a dream of a night vision. Yea, it shall be unto them even as unto a hungry man who dreams, and behold, he eats, but he awakes and his soul is empty; or like unto a thirsty man who dreams, and behold, he drinks, but he awakes and behold, he is faint and his soul has appetite. Yea, even so shall the multitude of all the nations be that fight against Mount Zion.

7 For behold, all you that do iniquity, pause yourselves and wonder, for you shall cry out and cry. Yea, you shall be drunk, but not with wine; you shall stagger, but not with strong drink. For behold, the Lord has poured out upon you the spirit of deep sleep, for behold, you have closed your eyes, and you have rejected the prophets, and your rulers and the seers has he covered because of your iniquities.

9 And it shall come to pass that the Lord God shall bring forth unto you the words of a book, and they shall be the words of them who have slumbered. And behold, the book shall be sealed, and in the book shall be a revelation from God, from the beginning of the world to the ending thereof. Wherefore because of the things which are sealed up, the things which are sealed shall not be delivered in the day of the wickedness and abominations of the people; wherefore, the book shall be kept from them. But the book shall be delivered unto a man, and he shall deliver the words of the book, which are the words of those who have slumbered in the dust, and he shall deliver these words unto another. But the words which are sealed he shall not deliver, neither shall he deliver the book, for the book shall be sealed by the power of God, and the revelation which was sealed shall be kept in the book until the own due time of the Lord, that they may come forth; for behold, they reveal all things from the foundation of the world unto the end thereof.

2 And the day comes that the words of the book which were sealed shall be read upon the housetops, and they shall be read by the power of Christ. And all things shall be revealed unto the children of men which ever have been among the children of men, and which ever will be, even unto the end of the earth. Wherefore at that day when the book shall be delivered unto the man of whom I have spoken, the book shall be hidden from the eyes of the world, that the eyes of none shall behold it, save it be that three witnesses shall behold it by the power of God, besides him to whom the book shall be delivered; and they shall testify to the truth of the book and the things therein. And there is no other who shall view it, save it be a few according to the will of God, to bear testimony of his word unto the children of men. For the Lord God has said that the words of the faithful should speak as if it were from the dead.

3 Wherefore the Lord God will proceed to bring forth the words of the book; and in the mouth of as many witnesses as seems him good will he establish his word; and woe be unto him that rejects the word of God. But behold, it shall come to pass that the Lord God shall say unto him to whom he shall deliver the book, Take these words which are not sealed and deliver them to another, that he may show them unto the learned, saying, Read this, I pray you. And the learned shall

say, Bring here the book and I will read them. And now because of the glory of the world and to get gain will they say this, and not for the glory of God. And the man shall say, I cannot bring the book, for it is sealed. Then shall the learned say, I cannot read it. Wherefore, it shall come to pass that the Lord God will deliver again the book and the words thereof to him that is not learned; and the man that is not learned shall say, I am not learned.

4 Then shall the Lord God say unto him, The learned shall not read them, for they have rejected them, and I am able to do my own work; wherefore, you shall read the words which I shall give unto you. Touch not the things which are sealed, for I will bring them forth in my own due time, for I will show unto the children of men that I am able to do my own work. Wherefore, when you have read the words which I have commanded you, and obtained the witnesses whom I have promised unto you, then shall you seal up the book again and hide it up unto me, that I may preserve the words which you have not read, until I shall see fit in my own wisdom to reveal all things unto the children of men. For behold, I am God, and I am a God of miracles, and I will show unto the world that I am the same yesterday, today, and for ever, and I work not among the children of men save it be according to their faith.

5 And again it shall come to pass that the Lord shall say unto him that shall read the words that shall be delivered him, Forasmuch as this people draw near unto me with their mouth, and with their lips do honor me, but have removed their hearts far from me, and their fear towards me is taught by the precepts of men; therefore, I will proceed to do a marvelous work among this people, yea, a marvelous work and a wonder, for the wisdom of their wise and learned shall perish, and the understanding of their prudent shall be hidden.

6 And woe unto them that seek deep to hide their counsel from the Lord, and their works are in the dark, and they say, Who sees us? And who knows us? And they also say, Surely your turning of things upside down shall be esteemed as the potter's clay. But behold, I will show unto them, says the Lord of Hosts, that I know all their works. For shall the work say of him that made it, He made me not? Or shall the thing framed say of him that framed it, He had no understanding? But behold, says the Lord of Hosts, I will show unto the children of men that it is not yet a very little while and Lebanon shall be turned into a

fruitful field, and the fruitful field shall be esteemed as a forest. And in that day shall the deaf hear the words of the book, and the eyes of the blind shall see out of obscurity and out of darkness. And the meek also shall increase, and their joy shall be in the Lord, and the poor among men shall rejoice in the Holy One of Israel. For assuredly as the Lord lives, they shall see that the terrible one is brought to naught, and the scorner is consumed; and all that watch for iniquity are cut off, and they that make a man an offender for a word, and lay a snare for him that reproves in the gate, and turn aside the just for a thing of naught. Therefore thus says the Lord, who redeemed Abraham, concerning the house of Jacob: Jacob shall not now be ashamed, neither shall his face now wax pale. But when he sees his children, the work of my hands, in his midst, they shall sanctify my name, and sanctify the Holy One of Jacob, and shall fear the God of Israel. They also that erred in spirit shall come to understanding, and they that murmured shall learn doctrine.

⁷ Woe to the rebellious children, says the Lord, that take counsel, but not of me; and that cover with a covering, but not of my spirit, that they may add sin to sin; that walk to go down into Egypt, and have not asked at my mouth, to strengthen themselves in the strength of Pharaoh and to trust in the shadow of Egypt. Therefore shall the strength of Pharaoh be your shame, and the trust in the shadow of Egypt your confusion. For his princes were at Zoan, and his ambassadors came to Hanes; they were all ashamed of a people that could not profit them, nor be a help nor profit, but a shame and also a reproach.

The burden of the beasts of the south.

⁸ Into the land of trouble and anguish from which come the young and old lion, the viper and fiery flying serpent, they will carry their riches upon the shoulders of young asses and their treasures upon the humps of camels, to a people that shall not profit them. For the Egyptians shall help in vain and to no purpose, therefore have I cried concerning this, Their strength is to sit still.

⁹ Now go, write it before them upon plates and note it in a book, that it may be for the time to come, for ever and ever — that this is a rebellious people, lying children, children that will not hear the law of the Lord, who say to the seers, See not — and to the prophets, Prophesy not unto us right things, speak unto us smooth things, prophesy

deceits, get out of the way, turn aside out of the path, cause the Holy One of Israel to cease from before us. Wherefore, thus says the Holy One of Israel: Because you despise this word, and trust in oppression and perverseness, and rely thereon, therefore this iniquity shall be to you as a breach ready to fall, swelling out in a high wall, whose breaking comes suddenly, at an instant. And he shall break it as the breaking of the potter's vessel that is broken in pieces, he shall not spare, so that there shall not be found in the bursting of it a shard to take fire from the hearth, or to take water out of the pit. For thus says the Lord God, the Holy One of Israel: In returning and rest shall you be saved, in quietness and in confidence shall be your strength, and you would not. But you said, No, for we will flee upon horses — therefore shall you flee. And, We will ride upon the swift — therefore shall they that pursue you be swift. One thousand shall flee at the rebuke of one; at the rebuke of five shall you flee, until you are left as a beacon upon the top of a mountain, and as an ensign on a hill.

10 And therefore will the Lord wait, that he may be gracious unto you, and therefore will he be exalted, that he may have mercy upon you; for the Lord is a God of judgment. Blessed are all they that wait for him. For the people shall dwell in Zion at Jerusalem, you shall weep no more. He will be very gracious unto you at the voice of your cry; when he shall hear it, he will answer you. And though the Lord give you the bread of adversity and the water of affliction, yet shall not your teachers be removed into a corner anymore, but your eyes shall see your teachers, and your ears shall hear a word behind you, saying, This is the way, walk in it. When you turn to the right hand and when you turn to the left, you shall defile also the covering of your engraved images of silver, and the ornament of your molten images of gold; you shall cast them away as a menstruous cloth, you shall say unto it, Depart from here. Then shall he give the rain of your seed that you shall sow the ground with, and bread of the increase of the earth, and it shall be fat and plenteous. In that day shall your cattle feed in large pastures. The oxen likewise, and the young asses that plow the ground, shall eat clean feed which has been winnowed with the winnowing fork and with the winnowing shovel. And there shall be upon every high mountain, and upon every high hill, rivers and streams of waters in the day of the great slaughter, when the towers

fall. Moreover, the light of the moon shall be as the light of the sun, and the light of the sun shall be sevenfold, as the light of seven days, in the day that the Lord binds up the breach of his people and heals the stroke of their wound.

10 Behold, the name of the Lord comes from far, burning with his anger, and the burden thereof is heavy. His lips are full of indignation and his tongue as a devouring fire, and his breath as an overflowing stream shall reach to the middle of the neck, to sift the nations with the sieve of vanity. And there shall be a bridle in the jaws of the people causing them to err. You shall have a song as in the night when a holy solemnity is kept, and gladness of heart as when one goes with a pipe, to come into the mountain of the Lord, to the Mighty One of Israel. And the Lord shall cause his glorious voice to be heard, and shall show the lighting down of his arm with the indignation of his anger and with the flame of a devouring fire, with scattering, and tempest, and hailstones. For through the voice of the Lord shall the Assyrian be beaten down which smote with a rod. And in every place where the grounded staff shall pass which the Lord shall lay upon him, it shall be with tambourines and harps; and in battles of shaking will he fight with it. For Topheth is ordained of old, yea, for the king it is prepared; he has made it deep and large, the pile thereof is fire and much wood; the breath of the Lord, like a stream of brimstone, does kindle it.

2 Woe to them that go down to Egypt for help, and rely on horses and trust in chariots because they are many, and in horsemen because they are very strong, but they look not unto the Holy One of Israel, neither seek the Lord. Yet he also is wise, and will bring evil, and will not call back his words, but will arise against the house of the evildoers and against the help of them that work iniquity. Now the Egyptians are men, and not God, and their horses flesh, and not spirit.

3 When the Lord shall stretch out his hand, both he that helps shall fall and he that is helped shall fall down, and they all shall fail together. For thus has the Lord spoken unto me: Like the lion and the young lion roaring on his prey when a multitude of shepherds is called forth against him, he will not be afraid of their voice nor abase himself for the noise of them; so shall the Lord of Hosts come down to fight for

Mount Zion and for the hill thereof. As birds flying, so will the Lord of Hosts defend Jerusalem; defending also he will deliver it, and passing over he will preserve it.

⁴ Turn unto him from whom the children of Israel have deeply revolted. For in that day, every man shall cast away his idols of silver and his idols of gold which your own hands have made unto you for a sin. Then shall the Assyrian fall with the sword, not of a mighty man; and the sword (not of a mean man) shall devour him, but he shall flee from the sword, and his young men shall be defeated. And he shall pass over to his stronghold for fear, and his princes shall be afraid of the ensign, says the Lord, whose fire is in Zion and his furnace in Jerusalem.

11 Behold, a king shall reign in righteousness and princes shall rule in judgment. And a man shall be as a hiding place from the wind and a cover from the tempest, as rivers of water in a dry place, as the shadow of a great rock in a weary land. And the eyes of them that see shall not be dim, and the ears of them that hear shall listen. The heart also of the rash shall understand knowledge, and the tongue of the stammerers shall be ready to speak plainly. The vile person shall be no more called liberal, nor the scoundrel said to be bountiful. For the vile person will speak villany and his heart will work iniquity, to practice hypocrisy and to utter error against the Lord, to make empty the soul of the hungry, and he will cause the drink of the thirsty to fail. The instruments also of the scoundrel are evil; he devises wicked devices to destroy the poor with lying words, even when the needy speak right. But the liberal devises liberal things, and by liberal things shall he stand.

² Rise up, you women that are at ease, hear my voice, you careless daughters; give ear unto my speech. Many days and years shall you be troubled, you careless women, for the vintage shall fail, the gathering shall not come. Tremble, you women that are at ease, be troubled, you careless ones. Strip yourselves and make yourselves bare, and gird sackcloth upon your loins. They shall lament for the teats, for the pleasant fields, for the fruitful vine. Upon the land of my people shall come up thorns and briers, yea, upon all the houses of joy in the joyous city, because the palaces shall be forsaken, the multitude of the houses shall be left desolate, the forts and towers shall be for

dens for ever — a joy of wild asses, a pasture of flocks, until the spirit is poured upon us from on high, and the wilderness is a fruitful field, and the fruitful field is counted for a forest. Then judgment shall dwell in the wilderness and righteousness remain in the fruitful field. And the work of righteousness shall be peace, and the effect of righteousness: quietness and assurance for ever. And my people shall dwell in a peaceable habitation, and in sure dwellings, and in quiet resting places when it shall hail, coming down on the forest, and the city shall be low in a low place. Blessed are you that sow beside all waters, that send forth there the feet of the ox and the ass.

3 Woe to you who spoil and you were not spoiled, and deal treacherously and they dealt not treacherously with you. When you shall cease to spoil, you shall be spoiled, and when you shall make an end to dealing treacherously, they shall deal treacherously with you.

4 O Lord, be gracious unto us; we have waited for you. Be their arm every morning, their salvation also in the time of trouble. At the noise of the tumult the people fled, at the lifting up of yourself the nations were scattered. And your spoil shall be gathered like the gathering of the caterpillar, as the running to and fro of locusts shall he run upon them. The Lord is exalted, for he dwells on high, he has filled Zion with judgment and righteousness. And wisdom and knowledge shall be the stability of your times and strength of salvation; the fear of the Lord is his treasure. Behold, their valiant ones shall cry outside, the ambassadors of peace shall weep bitterly. The highways lie waste, the wayfaring man ceases — he has broken the covenant, he has despised the cities, he regards no man. The earth mourns and languishes, Lebanon is ashamed and hewn down, Sharon is like a wilderness, and Bashan and Carmel shake off their fruits.

5 Now will I rise, says the Lord, now will I be exalted, now will I lift up myself. You shall conceive chaff, you shall bring forth stubble; your breath, as fire, shall devour you. And the people shall be as the burnings of lime, as thorns cut up shall they be burned in the fire. Hear, you that are far off, what I have done; and you that are near, acknowledge my might. The sinners in Zion are afraid; fearfulness has surprised the hypocrites. Who among us shall dwell with the devouring fire? Who among us shall dwell with everlasting burnings? He that walks righteously and speaks uprightly, he that despises the gain of

oppressions, that shakes his hands from holding of bribes, that stops his ears from hearing of blood, and shuts his eyes from seeing evil — he shall dwell on high. His place of defense shall be the strongholds of rocks; bread shall be given him, his waters shall be sure. Your eyes shall see the king in his beauty, they shall behold the land that is very far off. Your heart shall meditate in terror. Where is the scribe? Where is the receiver? Where is he that counted the towers? You shall not see a fierce people, a people of a deeper speech than you can perceive, of a stammering tongue that you cannot understand. Look upon Zion, the city of our solemnities. Your eyes shall see Jerusalem, a quiet habitation, a tabernacle that shall not be taken down — not one of the stakes thereof shall ever be removed, neither shall any of the cords thereof be broken. But there the glorious Lord will be unto us a place of broad rivers and streams, wherein shall go no galley with oars, neither shall gallant ship pass thereby. For the Lord is our judge, the Lord is our lawgiver, the Lord is our king — he will save us. Your tacklings are slack; they could not well strengthen their mast, they could not spread the sail. Then is the prey of a great spoil divided; the lame take the prey. And the inhabitant shall not say, I am sick. The people that dwell therein shall be forgiven their iniquity.

12 Come near, you nations, to hear; and listen, you people. Let the earth hear, and all that is therein, the world and all things that come forth of it. For the indignation of the Lord is upon all nations and his fury upon all their armies. He has utterly destroyed them, he has delivered them to the slaughter. Their slain also shall be cast out, and their stink shall come up out of their carcasses, and the mountains shall be melted with their blood. And all the host of heaven shall be dissolved, and the heavens shall be rolled together as a scroll, and all their host shall fall down as the leaf falls off from the vine and as a falling fig from the fig tree. For my sword shall be bathed in Heaven; behold, it shall come down upon Idumea and upon the people of my curse, to judgment. The sword of the Lord is filled with blood, it is made fat with fatness, and with the blood of lambs and goats, with the fat of the kidneys of rams; for the Lord has a sacrifice in Bozrah and a great slaughter in the land of Idumea.

2 And the re'ems shall come down with them, and the bullocks with the bulls; and their land shall be soaked with blood, and their dust made fat with fatness. For it is the day of the Lord's vengeance and the year of recompenses for the controversy of Zion. And the streams thereof shall be turned into pitch, and the dust thereof into brimstone, and the land thereof shall become burning pitch. It shall not be quenched night nor day. The smoke thereof shall go up for ever, from generation to generation it shall lie waste; none shall pass through it for ever and ever. But the cormorant and the bittern shall possess it, the owl also, and the raven shall dwell in it; and he shall stretch out upon it the line of confusion and the stones of emptiness. They shall call the nobles thereof to the kingdom, but none shall be there, and all her princes shall be nothing. And thorns shall come up in her palaces, nettles and brambles in the fortresses thereof; and it shall be a habitation of dragons and a court for owls. The wild beasts of the desert shall also meet with the wild beasts of the island, and the satyr shall cry to his fellow; the screech owl also shall rest there, and find for herself a place of rest. There shall the great owl make her nest, and lay, and hatch, and gather under her shadow. There shall the vultures also be gathered, every one with her mate.

3 Seek out of the book of the Lord and read the names written therein; no one of these shall fail. None shall lack their mate; for my mouth, it has commanded, and my spirit, it has gathered them. And I have cast the lot for them, and I have divided it unto them by line; they shall possess it for ever, from generation to generation they shall dwell therein.

4 The wilderness and the solitary place shall be glad for them, and the desert shall rejoice and blossom as the rose. It shall blossom abundantly and rejoice, even with joy and singing. The glory of Lebanon shall be given unto it, the excellence of Carmel and Sharon. They shall see the glory of the Lord and the excellence of our God.

5 Strengthen the weak hands and confirm the feeble knees. Say to them that are of a fearful heart, Be strong, fear not; behold, your God will come with vengeance, even God with a recompense; he will come and save you. Then the eyes of the blind shall be opened and the ears of the deaf shall be unstopped. Then shall the lame man leap as a hart, and the tongue of the dumb sing. For in the wilderness shall waters

break out, and streams in the desert; and the parched ground shall become a pool, and the thirsty land springs of water. In the habitation of dragons, where each lay, shall be grass with reeds and rushes. And a highway shall be there, for a way shall be cast up, and it shall be called the way of holiness. The unclean shall not pass over upon it, but it shall be cast up for those who are clean; and the wayfaring men, though they are accounted fools, shall not err therein. No lion shall be there, nor any ravenous beast shall go up thereon; it shall not be found there, but the redeemed shall walk there. And the ransomed of the Lord shall return and come to Zion with songs and everlasting joy upon their heads. They shall obtain joy and gladness, and sorrow and sighing shall flee away.

13 Now it came to pass in the fourteenth year of king Hezekiah that Sennacherib king of Assyria came up against all the fortified cities of Judah and took them. And the king of Assyria sent Rabshakeh from Lachish to Jerusalem, unto king Hezekiah, with a great army. And he stood by the conduit of the upper pool in the highway of the fuller's field. Then came forth unto him Eliakim (Hilkiah's son) who was over the house, and Shebna the scribe, and Joah (Asaph's son) the recorder.

2 And Rabshakeh said unto them, Say now to Hezekiah, Thus says the great king, the king of Assyria: What confidence is this wherein you trust? I say your words are but vain when you say, I have counsel and strength for war. Now, on whom do you trust, that you rebel against me? Behold, you trust in the staff of this broken reed — on Egypt — on which, if a man lean, it will go into his hand and pierce it. So is Pharaoh king of Egypt to all that trust in him. But if you say to me, We trust in the Lord our God — is it not he whose high places and whose altars Hezekiah has taken away, and said to Judah and to Jerusalem, You shall worship before this altar? Now therefore give pledges, I pray you, to my master the king of Assyria, and I will give you two thousand horses, if you are able on your part to set riders upon them. How then will you turn away the face of one captain of the least of my master's servants, and put your trust on Egypt for chariots and for horsemen? And have I now come up without the Lord against this land to destroy it? The Lord said unto me, Go up against this land and destroy it.

³ Then said Eliakim, and Shebna, and Joah unto Rabshakeh, Speak, I pray you, unto your servants in the Syrian language, for we understand it; and speak not to us in the Jews' language, in the ears of the people that are on the wall. But Rabshakeh said, Has my master sent me to your master and to you to speak these words? Has he not sent me to the men that sit upon the wall, that they may eat their own dung and drink their own piss with you?

⁴ Then Rabshakeh stood and cried with a loud voice in the Jews' language, and said, Hear the words of the great king, the king of Assyria! Thus says the king: Let not Hezekiah deceive you, for he shall not be able to deliver you. Neither let Hezekiah make you trust in the Lord, saying, The Lord will surely deliver us, this city shall not be delivered into the hand of the king of Assyria. Listen not to Hezekiah, for thus says the king of Assyria: Make an agreement with me by a present, and come out to me, and eat everyone of his vine and everyone of his fig tree, and drink everyone the waters of his own cistern, until I come and take you away to a land like your own land — a land of grain and wine, a land of bread and vineyards. Beware lest Hezekiah persuade you, saying, The Lord will deliver us. Have any of the gods of the nations delivered his land out of the hand of the king of Assyria? Where are the gods of Hamath and Arphad? Where are the gods of Sepharvaim? And have they delivered Samaria out of my hand? Who are they among all the gods of these lands that have delivered their land out of my hand, that the Lord should deliver Jerusalem out of my hand?

⁵ But they held their peace and answered him not a word, for the king's commandment was, saying, Answer him not. Then came Eliakim (the son of Hilkiah) that was over the household, and Shebna the scribe, and Joah (the son of Asaph) the recorder, to Hezekiah with their clothes rent, and told him the words of Rabshakeh.

⁶ And it came to pass when king Hezekiah heard it that he rent his clothes, and covered himself with sackcloth, and went into the house of the Lord. And he sent Eliakim who was over the household, and Shebna the scribe, and the elders of the priests covered with sackcloth, unto Isaiah the prophet, the son of Amoz. And they said unto him, Thus says Hezekiah: This day is a day of trouble, and of rebuke, and of blasphemy, for the children have come to the birth and there is not

strength to bring forth. It may be the Lord your God will hear the words of Rabshakeh, whom the king of Assyria his master has sent to reproach the living God, and will reprove the words which the Lord your God has heard; wherefore, lift up your prayer for the remnant that is left.

7 So the servants of king Hezekiah came to Isaiah, and Isaiah said unto them, Thus shall you say unto your master: Thus says the Lord: Be not afraid of the words that you have heard, with which the servants of the king of Assyria have blasphemed me. Behold, I will send a blast upon him, and he shall hear a rumor and return to his own land; and I will cause him to fall by the sword in his own land.

8 So Rabshakeh returned and found the king of Assyria warring against Libnah (for he had heard that he was departed from Lachish). And he heard say concerning Tirhakah king of Ethiopia: He has come forth to make war with you. And when he heard it, he sent messengers to Hezekiah, saying, Thus shall you speak to Hezekiah king of Judah, saying, Let not your God in whom you trust deceive you, saying Jerusalem shall not be given into the hand of the king of Assyria. Behold, you have heard what the kings of Assyria have done to all lands by destroying them utterly, and shall you be delivered? Have the gods of the nations delivered them whom my fathers have destroyed—as Gozan, and Haran, and Rezeph, and the children of Eden who were in Telassar? Where is the king of Hamath, and the king of Arphad, and the king of the city of Sepharvaim, Hena, and Ivvah?

9 And Hezekiah received the letter from the hand of the messengers and read it; and Hezekiah went up unto the house of the Lord and spread it before the Lord. And Hezekiah prayed unto the Lord, saying, O Lord of Hosts, God of Israel who dwells between the cherubim, you are the God, even you alone, of all the kingdoms of the earth; you have made Heaven and earth. Incline your ear, O Lord, and hear; open your eyes, O Lord, and see; and hear all the words of Sennacherib which he has sent to reproach the living God. Truly, Lord, the kings of Assyria have laid waste all the nations and their countries, and have cast their gods into the fire—for they were no gods, but the work of men's hands, wood and stone; therefore, they have destroyed them. Now therefore, O Lord our God, save us from his hand, that all the kingdoms of the earth may know that you are the Lord, even you only.

¹⁰ Then Isaiah the son of Amoz sent unto Hezekiah, saying, Thus says the Lord God of Israel: Whereas you have prayed to me against Sennacherib king of Assyria, this is the word which the Lord has spoken concerning him: The virgin, the daughter of Zion, has despised you and laughed you to scorn; the daughter of Jerusalem has shaken her head at you. Whom have you reproached and blasphemed? And against whom have you exalted your voice and lifted up your eyes on high? Even against the Holy One of Israel. By your servants have you reproached the Lord, and have said, By the multitude of my chariots have I come up to the height of the mountains, to the sides of Lebanon, and I will cut down the tall cedars thereof and the choice fir trees thereof; and I will enter into the height of his border, and the forest of his Carmel. I have dug and drunk water, and with the soles of my feet have I dried up all the rivers of the besieged places. Have you not heard long ago how I have done it? And of ancient times that I have formed it? Now have I brought it to pass, that you should be, to lay waste fortified cities into ruinous heaps. Therefore, their inhabitants were of small power, they were dismayed and confounded. They were as the grass of the field, and as the green herb, as the grass on the housetops, and as grain blasted before it is grown up. But I know your abode, and your going out, and your coming in, and your rage against me. Because your rage against me and your tumult has come up into my ears, therefore will I put my hook in your nose and my bridle in your lips, and I will turn you back by the way by which you came.

¹¹ And this shall be a sign unto you: you shall eat this year such as grows of itself; and the second year, that which springs of the same; and in the third year, you sow, and reap, and plant vineyards, and eat the fruit thereof. And the remnant that is escaped of the house of Judah shall again take root downward, and bear fruit upward. For out of Jerusalem shall go forth a remnant, and they that escape out of Jerusalem shall come up upon Mount Zion; the zeal of the Lord of Hosts shall do this.

¹² Therefore, thus says the Lord concerning the king of Assyria: He shall not come into this city, nor shoot an arrow there, nor come before it with shields, nor cast a bank against it. By the way that he came, by the same shall he return and shall not come into this city, says the Lord. For I will defend this city to save it for my own sake, and for my

servant David's sake. Then the angel of the Lord went forth and smote in the camp of the Assyrians a hundred and eighty-five thousand; and when they who were left arose early in the morning, behold, they were all dead corpses. So Sennacherib king of Assyria departed, and went and returned, and dwelled at Nineveh. And it came to pass, as he was worshipping in the house of Nisroch his god, that Adrammelech and Sharezer — his sons — smote him with the sword; and they escaped into the land of Armenia, and Esarhaddon his son reigned in his stead.

¹³ In those days was Hezekiah sick unto death. And Isaiah the prophet, the son of Amoz, came unto him and said unto him, Thus says the Lord: Set your house in order, for you shall die and not live. Then Hezekiah turned his face toward the wall and prayed unto the Lord, and said, Remember now, O Lord, I implore you, how I have walked before you in truth and with a perfect heart, and have done that which is good in your sight. And Hezekiah wept severely. Then came the word of the Lord to Isaiah, saying, Go and say to Hezekiah, Thus says the Lord, the God of David your father: I have heard your prayer, I have seen your tears; behold, I will add unto your days fifteen years. And I will deliver you and this city out of the hand of the king of Assyria, and I will defend this city. And this shall be a sign unto you from the Lord, that the Lord will do this thing that he has spoken: behold, I will bring again the shadow of the degrees, which is gone down in the sun dial of Ahaz, ten degrees backward. So the sun returned ten degrees, by which degrees it was gone down.

¹⁴ The writing of Hezekiah king of Judah, when he had been sick and was recovered of his sickness: I said in the cutting off of my days I shall go to the gates of the grave, I am deprived of the residue of my years. I said I shall not see the Lord, even the Lord, in the land of the living; I shall behold man no more with the inhabitants of the world. My age is departed and is removed from me as a shepherd's tent. I have cut off like a weaver my life; he will cut me off with withering sickness. From day even to night will you make an end of me. I reckoned until morning that as a lion, so will he break all my bones; from day even to night will you make an end of me. Like a crane or a swallow, so did I chatter; I did mourn as a dove. My eyes fail with looking upward. O Lord, I am oppressed, undertake for me. What shall I say? He has both spoken unto me and himself has healed me. I shall go softly all my years,

that I may not walk in the bitterness of my soul. O Lord, you who are the life of my spirit, in whom I live, so will you recover me and make me to live; and in all these things I will praise you. Behold, I had great bitterness instead of peace; but you have, in love to my soul, saved me from the pit of corruption, for you have cast all my sins behind your back. For the grave cannot praise you, death cannot celebrate you, they that go down into the pit cannot hope for your truth. The living, the living, he shall praise you, as I do this day; the father to the children shall make known your truth. The Lord was ready to save me; therefore, we will sing my songs to the stringed instruments all the days of our life in the house of the Lord.

¹⁵ For Isaiah had said, Let them take a lump of figs and lay it for a plaster upon the boil, and he shall recover. Hezekiah also had said, What is the sign that I shall go up to the house of the Lord?

¹⁶ At that time, Merodach-baladan, the son of Baladan king of Babylon, sent letters and a present to Hezekiah, for he had heard that he had been sick and was recovered. And Hezekiah was glad of them, and showed them the house of his precious things — the silver, and the gold, and the spices, and the precious ointment, and all the house of his armor, and all that was found in his treasures. There was nothing in his house, nor in all his dominion, that Hezekiah showed them not. Then came Isaiah the prophet unto king Hezekiah, and said unto him, What did these men say? And from where did they come unto you? And Hezekiah said, They have come from a far country unto me, even from Babylon. Then said he, What have they seen in your house? And Hezekiah answered, All that is in my house have they seen; there is nothing among my treasures that I have not shown them. Then said Isaiah to Hezekiah, Hear the word of the Lord of Hosts: Behold, the days come that all that is in your house, and that which your fathers have laid up in store until this day, shall be carried to Babylon. Nothing shall be left, says the Lord. And of your sons that shall issue from you, whom you shall beget, shall they take away; and they shall be eunuchs in the palace of the king of Babylon. Then said Hezekiah to Isaiah, Good is the word of the Lord which you have spoken. He said moreover, For there shall be peace and truth in my days.

¹⁷ Comfort, comfort my people, says your God. Speak comfortingly to Jerusalem, and cry unto her that her warfare is accomplished, that

her iniquity is pardoned; for she has received of the Lord's hand double for all her sins.

14 The voice of him that cries in the wilderness: Prepare the way of the Lord, make straight in the desert a highway for our God. Every valley shall be exalted, and every mountain and hill shall be made low, and the crooked shall be made straight, and the rough places plain. And the glory of the Lord shall be revealed and all flesh shall see it together, for the mouth of the Lord has spoken it. The voice said, Cry. And he said, What shall I cry? All flesh is grass, and all the goodliness thereof is as the flower of the field. The grass withers, the flower fades, because the spirit of the Lord blows upon it; surely the people is grass. The grass withers, the flower fades, but the word of our God shall stand for ever.

2 O Zion, that brings good tidings, go up into the high mountain. O Jerusalem, that brings good tidings, lift up your voice with strength; lift it up, be not afraid. Say unto the cities of Judah, Behold your God. Behold, the Lord God will come with strong hand, and his arm shall rule for him. Behold, his reward is with him and his work before him. He shall feed his flock like a shepherd, he shall gather the lambs with his arm and carry them in his bosom, and shall gently lead those that are with young.

3 Who has measured the waters in the hollow of his hand, and meted out heaven with the span, and comprehended the dust of the earth in a measure, and weighed the mountains in scales and the hills in a balance? Who has directed the spirit of the Lord, or being his counselor has taught him? With whom took he counsel, and who instructed him and taught him in the path of judgment, and taught him knowledge, and showed to him the way of understanding? Behold, the nations are as a drop of a bucket and are counted as the small dust of the balance; behold, he takes up the isles as a very little thing. And Lebanon is not sufficient to burn, nor the beasts thereof sufficient for a burnt offering. All nations before him are as nothing, and they are counted to him less than nothing, and vanity.

4 To whom then will you liken God? Or what likeness will you compare unto him? The workman melts an engraved image, and the goldsmith spreads it over with gold and casts silver chains. He that is

so impoverished that he has no offering chooses a tree that will not rot; he seeks unto him an expert workman to prepare an engraved image that shall not be moved.

5 Have you not known? Have you not heard? Has it not been told to you from the beginning? Have you not understood from the foundations of the earth? It is he that sits upon the circle of the earth, and the inhabitants thereof are as grasshoppers; who stretches out the heavens as a curtain, and spreads them out as a tent to dwell in; that brings the princes to nothing. He makes the judges of the earth as vanity. Yea, they shall not be planted; yea, they shall not be sowed; yea, their stock shall not take root in the earth; and he shall also blow upon them and they shall wither, and the whirlwind shall take them away as stubble. To whom then will you liken me, or shall I be equal? — says the Holy One. Lift up your eyes on high and behold who has created these things, that brings out their host by number. He calls them all by names by the greatness of his might, for he is strong in power; not one fails. Why do you say, O Jacob, and speak, O Israel, My way is hidden from the Lord and my judgment is passed over from my God? Have you not known, have you not heard, that the everlasting God, the Lord, the Creator of the ends of the earth faints not, neither is weary? There is no searching of his understanding. He gives power to the fatigued, and to them that have no might he increases strength. Even the youths shall faint and be weary, and the young men shall utterly fall; but they that wait upon the Lord shall renew their strength, they shall mount up with wings as eagles, they shall run and not be weary, and they shall walk and not faint.

15 Keep silence before me, O islands, and let the people renew their strength. Let them come near, then let them speak; let us come near together to judgment. Who raised up the righteous man from the east, called him to his foot, gave the nations before him, and made him rule over kings? He gave them as the dust to his sword, and as driven stubble to his bow. He pursued them and passed safely, even by the way that he had not gone with his feet.

2 Who has wrought and done it, calling the generations from the beginning? I, the Lord, the first and with the last — I am he. The isles saw it and feared; the ends of the earth were afraid, drew near, and came.

They helped everyone his neighbor, and everyone said to his brother, Be of good courage. So the carpenter encouraged the goldsmith, and he that smooths with the hammer him that smote the anvil, saying, It is ready for the soldering. And he fastened it with nails, that it should not be moved.

3 But you, Israel, are my servant, Jacob whom I have chosen, the seed of Abraham my friend, you whom I have taken from the ends of the earth, and called you from the chief men thereof, and said unto you, You are my servant; I have chosen you and not cast you away. Fear not, for I am with you; be not dismayed, for I am your God. I will strengthen you, yea, I will help you, yea, I will uphold you with the right hand of my righteousness. Behold, all they that were incensed against you shall be ashamed and confounded; they shall be as nothing, and they that quarrel with you shall perish. You shall seek them and shall not find them, even them that contended with you. They that war against you shall be as nothing and as a thing of naught. For I the Lord your God will hold your right hand, saying unto you, Fear not; I will help you. Fear not, you worm Jacob and you men of Israel; I will help you, says the Lord, and your redeemer, the Holy One of Israel. Behold, I will make you a new sharp threshing instrument having teeth. You shall thresh the mountains and beat them small, and shall make the hills as chaff. You shall winnow them, and the wind shall carry them away, and the whirlwind shall scatter them; and you shall rejoice in the Lord and shall glory in the Holy One of Israel.

4 When the poor and needy seek water and there is none, and their tongue fails for thirst, I the Lord will hear them, I the God of Israel will not forsake them. I will open rivers in high places and fountains in the midst of the valleys; I will make the wilderness a pool of water and the dry land springs of water. I will plant in the wilderness the cedar, the shittah tree, and the myrtle, and the oil tree. I will set in the desert the fir tree, and the pine, and the box tree together, that they may see, and know, and consider, and understand together that the hand of the Lord has done this, and the Holy One of Israel has created it.

5 Produce your cause, says the Lord; bring forth your strong reasons, says the King of Jacob. Let them bring them forth and show us what shall happen. Let them show the former things, what they are, that we may consider them and know the latter end of them; or declare

to us things to come, show the things that are to come hereafter, that we may know that you are gods. Yea, do good or do evil, that we may be dismayed and behold it together. Behold, you are of nothing, and your work of naught; an abomination is he that chooses you. I have raised up one from the north, and he shall come. From the rising of the sun shall he call upon my name, and he shall come upon princes as upon mortar and as the potter treads clay.

6 Who has declared from the beginning, that we may know? And previously, that we may say, He is righteous? Yea, there is none that shows, yea, there is none that declares, yea, there is none that hears your words. The first shall say to Zion, Behold, behold them; and I will give to Jerusalem one that brings good tidings. For I beheld, and there was no man even among them and there was no counselor that, when I asked of them, could answer a word. Behold, they are all vanity; their works are nothing, their molten images are wind and confusion.

7 Behold my servant, whom I uphold, my elect in whom my soul delights; I have put my spirit upon him, he shall bring forth judgment to the gentiles. He shall not cry, nor lift up, nor cause his voice to be heard in the street. A bruised reed shall he not break and the smoking flax shall he not quench; he shall bring forth judgment unto truth. He shall not fail nor be discouraged until he has set judgment in the earth, and the isles shall wait for his law.

8 Thus says God the Lord, he that created the heavens and stretched them out, he that spread forth the earth and that which comes out of it, he that gives breath unto the people upon it and spirit to them that walk therein: I, the Lord, have called you in righteousness, and will hold your hand, and will keep you, and give you for a covenant of the people, for a light of the gentiles — to open the blind eyes, to bring out the prisoners from the prison, and them that sit in darkness out of the prison house. I am the Lord — that is my name; and my glory will I not give to another, neither my praise to engraved images. Behold, the former things have come to pass, and new things do I declare; before they spring forth, I tell you of them.

9 Sing unto the Lord a new song, and his praise from the end of the earth, you that go down to the sea and all that is therein — the isles and the inhabitants thereof. Let the wilderness and the cities thereof lift up their voice, the villages that Kedar does inhabit. Let

the inhabitants of the rock sing, let them shout from the top of the mountains. Let them give glory unto the Lord and declare his praise in the islands. The Lord shall go forth as a mighty man, he shall stir up jealousy like a man of war; he shall cry, yea, roar; he shall prevail against his enemies. I have for a long time held my peace, I have been still and restrained myself; now will I cry like a travailing woman, I will destroy and devour at once. I will make waste mountains and hills, and dry up all their herbs, and I will make the rivers islands, and I will dry up the pools. And I will bring the blind by a way that they knew not, I will lead them in paths that they have not known; I will make darkness light before them and crooked things straight. These things will I do unto them and not forsake them. They shall be turned back, they shall be greatly ashamed that trust in engraved images, that say to the molten images, You are our gods.

[10] Hear, you deaf, and look, you blind, that you may see; for I will send my servant unto you who are blind, yea, a messenger to open the eyes of the blind and unstop the ears of the deaf. And they shall be made perfect, notwithstanding their blindness, if they will listen unto the messenger, the Lord's servant. You are a people seeing many things, but you observe not, opening the ears to hear, but you hear not. The Lord is not well pleased with such a people, but for his righteousness' sake he will magnify the law and make it honorable. You are a people robbed and spoiled; your enemies, all of them, have snared you in holes, and they have hidden you in prison houses; they have taken you for a prey and none delivers, for a spoil and none says, Restore. Who among them will give ear unto you, or listen and hear you for the time to come? And who gave Jacob for a spoil and Israel to the robbers? Did not the Lord — he against whom they have sinned? For they would not walk in his ways, neither were they obedient unto his law. Therefore, he has poured upon them the fury of his anger and the strength of battle. And they have set them on fire round about, yet they knew not; and it burned them, yet they laid it not to heart.

[11] But now thus says the Lord that created you, O Jacob, and he that formed you, O Israel: Fear not, for I have redeemed you, I have called you by your name — you are mine. When you pass through the waters, I will be with you, and through the rivers, they shall not overflow you. When you walk through the fire, you shall not be burned, neither shall

the flame kindle upon you. For I am the Lord your God, the Holy One of Israel, your Savior; I gave Egypt for your ransom, Ethiopia and Seba for you. Since you were precious in my sight, you have been honorable and I have loved you; therefore will I give men for you, and people for your life. Fear not, for I am with you. I will bring your seed from the east and gather you from the west; I will say to the north, Give up—and to the south, Keep not back. Bring my sons from far, and my daughters from the ends of the earth, even everyone that is called by my name; for I have created him for my glory, I have formed him, yea, I have made him.

12 Bring forth the blind people that have eyes and the deaf that have ears. Let all the nations be gathered together and let the people be assembled. Who among them can declare this and show us former things? Let them bring forth their witnesses, that they may be justified; or let them hear, and say, It is truth. You are my witnesses, says the Lord, and my servant whom I have chosen, that you may know and believe me, and understand that I am he. Before me, there was no God formed, neither shall there be after me. I, even I am the Lord, and besides me there is no savior. I have declared, and have saved, and I have shown when there was no strange god among you. Therefore, you are my witnesses, says the Lord, that I am God. Yea, before the day was, I am he, and there is none that can deliver out of my hand. I will work, and who shall prevent it?

13 Thus says the Lord, your Redeemer, the Holy One of Israel: For your sake I have sent to Babylon and have brought down all their nobles, and the Chaldeans whose cry is in the ships. I am the Lord, your Holy One, the Creator of Israel, your King. Thus says the Lord who makes a way in the sea and a path in the mighty waters, who brings forth the chariot and horse, the army and the power (they shall lie down together, they shall not rise; they are extinct, they are quenched as a wick): Remember not the former things, neither consider the things of old. Behold, I will do a new thing; now it shall spring forth, and shall you not know it? I will even make a way in the wilderness and rivers in the desert. The beast of the field shall honor me, the dragons and the owls, because I give waters in the wilderness and rivers in the desert to give drink to my people, my chosen. This people have I formed for myself; they shall show forth my praise.

¹⁴ But you have not called upon me, O Jacob, but you have been weary of me, O Israel. You have not brought me the small cattle of your burnt offerings, neither have you honored me with your sacrifices. I have not caused you to serve with an offering, nor wearied you with incense. You have not bought me sweet cane with money, neither have you filled me with the fat of your sacrifices, but you have made me to serve with your sins, you have wearied me with your iniquities. I, even I, am he that blots out your transgressions for my own sake, and will not remember your sins. Put me in remembrance, let us plead together; you declare, that you may be justified. Your first father has sinned, and your teachers have transgressed against me. Therefore, I have profaned the princes of the sanctuary, and have given Jacob to the curse and Israel to reproaches.

¹⁵ Yet now hear, O Jacob my servant, and Israel whom I have chosen; thus says the Lord that made you and formed you from the womb, who will help you: Fear not, O Jacob my servant, and you, Jeshurun, whom I have chosen; for I will pour water upon him that is thirsty, and floods upon the dry ground. I will pour my spirit upon your seed, and my blessing upon your offspring, and they shall spring up as among the grass, as willows by the water courses. One shall say, I am the Lord's — and another shall call himself by the name of Jacob, and another shall subscribe with his hand unto the Lord, and surname himself by the name of Israel.

¹⁶ Thus says the Lord, the King of Israel and his redeemer, the Lord of Hosts: I am the first and I am the last, and besides me there is no God. And who, as I, shall call and shall declare it, and set it in order for me, since I appointed the ancient people? And the things that are coming, and shall come, let them show unto them. Fear not, neither be afraid; have not I told you from that time, and have declared it? You are even my witnesses. Is there a God besides me? Yea, there is no God; I know not any. They that make an engraved image are all of them vanity, and their delectable things shall not profit, and they are their own witnesses; they see not, nor know, that they may be ashamed. Who has formed a god or molten an engraved image that is profitable for nothing? Behold, all his fellows shall be ashamed, and the workmen; they are of men. Let them all be gathered together, let them stand up; yet they shall fear and they shall be ashamed together.

The smith with the tongs both works in the coals and fashions it with hammers, and works it with the strength of his arms. Yea, he is hungry and his strength fails, he drinks no water and is faint. The carpenter stretches out his rule, he marks it out with a line, he fits it with planes; and he marks it out with the compass, and makes it after the figure of a man, according to the beauty of a man, that it may remain in the house. He hews down cedars and takes the cypress and the oak, which he strengthens for himself among the trees of the forest; he plants an ash, and the rain does nourish it. Then shall it be for a man to burn, for he will take thereof and warm himself; yea, he kindles it and bakes bread. Yea, he makes a god and worships it, he makes it an engraved image and falls down before it. He burns part thereof in the fire, with part thereof he eats flesh, he roasts roast and is satisfied; yea, he warms himself and says, Aha, I am warm, I have seen the fire. And the residue thereof he makes a god, even his engraved image; he falls down unto it, and worships it, and prays unto it, and says, Deliver me, for you are my god. They have not known nor understood, for he has shut their eyes that they cannot see, and their hearts that they cannot understand. And none considers in his heart, neither is there knowledge nor understanding to say, I have burned part of it in the fire, yea, also I have baked bread upon the coals thereof; I have roasted flesh and eaten it. And shall I make the residue thereof an abomination? Shall I fall down to the stock of a tree? He feeds on ashes; a deceived heart has turned him aside, that he cannot deliver his soul, nor say, Is there not a lie in my right hand? Remember these, O Jacob and Israel, for you are my servant, I have formed you. You are my servant, O Israel, you shall not be forgotten of me. I have blotted out as a thick cloud your transgressions, and as a cloud your sins; return unto me, for I have redeemed you.

17 Sing, O you heavens, for the Lord has done it; shout, you lower parts of the earth. Break forth into singing, you mountains, O forest, and every tree therein. For the Lord has redeemed Jacob and glorified himself in Israel. Thus says the Lord, your Redeemer and he that formed you from the womb: I am the Lord that makes all things, that stretches forth the heavens alone, that spreads abroad the earth by myself, that frustrates the tokens of the liars and makes diviners mad, that turns wise men backward and makes their knowledge foolish,

that confirms the word of his servant and performs the counsel of his messengers, that says to Jerusalem, You shall be inhabited — and to the cities of Judah, You shall be built, and I will raise up the decayed places thereof; that says to the deep, Be dry, and I will dry up your rivers; that says of Cyrus, He is my shepherd and shall perform all my pleasure; even saying to Jerusalem, You shall be built — and to the temple, Your foundation shall be laid.

[18] Thus says the Lord to his anointed, to Cyrus, whose right hand I have held to subdue nations before him (and I will disarm the loins of kings to open before him the two leaved gates, and the gates shall not be shut): I will go before you and make the crooked places straight, I will break in pieces the gates of brass and cut asunder the bars of iron, and I will give you the treasures of darkness and hidden riches of secret places, that you may know that I, the Lord, who call you by your name, am the God of Israel. For Jacob my servant's sake, and Israel my elect, I have even called you by your name. I have surnamed you, though you have not known me. I am the Lord and there is none else, there is no God besides me. I girded you, though you have not known me, that they may know from the rising of the sun and from the west that there is none besides me. I am the Lord and there is none else. I form the light and create darkness, I make peace and create evil. I the Lord do all these things. Drop down you heavens from above, and let the skies pour down righteousness; let the earth open and let them bring forth salvation, and let righteousness spring up together; I the Lord have created it. Woe unto him that quarrels with his Maker. Let the potsherd quarrel with the potsherds of the earth. Shall the clay say to him that fashions it, What are you making? Or your work, He has no hands? Woe unto him that says unto his father, What have you begotten? Or to the woman, What have you brought forth? Thus says the Lord, the Holy One of Israel and his Maker: Ask me of things to come concerning my sons, and concerning the work of my hands, you command me. I have made the earth and created man upon it. I, even my hands, have stretched out the heavens, and all their host have I commanded. I have raised him up in righteousness and I will direct all his ways; he shall build my city and he shall let go my captives, not for price nor reward, says the Lord of Hosts. Thus says the Lord: The labor of Egypt, and merchandise of Ethiopia, and of the Sabeans, men

of stature, shall come over unto you, and they shall be yours; they shall come after you, in chains they shall come over and they shall fall down unto you. They shall make supplication unto you, saying, Surely God is in you, and there is none else, there is no God. Truly you are a God that hides yourself, O God of Israel, the Savior. They shall be ashamed and also confounded, all of them; they shall go to confusion together that are makers of idols. But Israel shall be saved in the Lord with an everlasting salvation; you shall not be ashamed nor confounded, worlds without end.

19 For thus says the Lord that created the heavens, God himself that formed the earth and made it (he has established it, he created it not in vain, he formed it to be inhabited): I am the Lord, and there is none else. I have not spoken in secret, in a dark place of the earth. I said not unto the seed of Jacob, You seek me in vain. I the Lord speak righteousness, I declare things that are right. Assemble yourselves and come, draw near together, you that are escaped of the nations. They have no knowledge that set up the wood of their engraved image, and pray unto a god that cannot save. Speak, and bring them near, yea, let them take counsel together. Who has declared this from ancient time? Who has told it from that time? Have not I the Lord? And there is no God else besides me — a just God and a Savior, there is none besides me. Look unto me and be saved, all the ends of the earth, for I am God and there is none else. I have sworn by myself, the word is gone out of my mouth in righteousness and shall not return, that unto me every knee shall bow, every tongue shall swear. Surely shall one say, In the Lord have I righteousness and strength — even to him shall men come, and all that are incensed against him shall be ashamed. In the Lord shall all the seed of Israel be justified and shall glory.

20 Bel bows down, Nebo stoops, their idols were upon the beasts and upon the cattle. Your carriages were heavily loaded, they are a burden to the weary beast. They stoop, they bow down together; they could not deliver the burden, but themselves have gone into captivity.

21 Listen to me, O house of Jacob, and all the remnant of the house of Israel who are borne by me from the belly, who are carried from the womb; and even to your old age I am he, and even to graying hairs will I carry you; I have made and I will bear, even I will carry and will deliver you. To whom will you liken me, and make me equal and

compare me, that we may be alike? They lavish gold out of the bag, and weigh silver in the balance, and hire a goldsmith, and he makes it a god; they fall down, yea, they worship. They bear him upon the shoulder, they carry him and set him in his place, and he stands; from his place shall he not remove. Yea, they shall cry unto him. Yet can he not answer, nor save him out of his trouble. Remember this and show yourselves men; bring it again to mind, O you transgressors. Remember the former things of old, for I am God and there is none else; I am God and there is none like me, declaring the end from the beginning, and from ancient times the things that are not yet done, saying, My counsel shall stand and I will do all my pleasure — calling a ravenous bird from the east, the man that executes my counsel from a far country. Yea, I have spoken it, I will also bring it to pass; I have purposed it, I will also do it. Listen to me, you stout-hearted that are far from righteousness. I bring near my righteousness, it shall not be far off, and my salvation shall not delay; and I will place salvation in Zion for Israel, my glory.

16 Come down and sit in the dust, O virgin daughter of Babylon, sit on the ground; there is no throne, O daughter of the Chaldeans, for you shall no more be called tender and delicate. Take the millstones and grind meal; uncover your locks, make bare the leg, uncover the thigh, pass over the rivers. Your nakedness shall be uncovered, yea, your shame shall be seen; I will take vengeance and I will not meet you as a man. As for our redeemer, the Lord of Hosts is his name, the Holy One of Israel. Sit silent and go into darkness, O daughter of the Chaldeans, for you shall no more be called the lady of kingdoms. I was angry with my people; I have polluted my inheritance and given them into your hand. You did show them no mercy; upon the elder have you very heavily laid your yoke. And you said, I shall be a lady for ever — so that you did not lay these things to your heart, neither did remember the latter end of it. Therefore, hear now this, you that are given to pleasures, that dwell carelessly, that say in your heart, I am, and none else besides me; I shall not sit as a widow, neither shall I know the loss of children. But these two things shall come to you in a moment, in one day: the loss of children and widowhood. They shall come upon you in their perfection, for the multitude of your

sorceries and for the great abundance of your enchantments, for you have trusted in your wickedness; you have said, None sees me. Your wisdom and your knowledge, it has perverted you; and you have said in your heart, I am, and none else besides me. Therefore shall evil come upon you, you shall not know from where it rises; and mischief shall fall upon you, you shall not be able to put it off; and desolation shall come upon you suddenly, which you shall not know. Stand now with your enchantments and with the multitude of your sorceries wherein you have labored from your youth — if it so be you shall be able to profit, if it so be you may prevail. You are wearied in the multitude of your counsels. Let now the astrologers, the stargazers, the monthly forecasters stand up and save you from these things that shall come upon you. Behold, they shall be as stubble, the fire shall burn them, they shall not deliver themselves from the power of the flame; there shall not be a coal to warm at, nor fire to sit before it. Thus shall they be unto you — with whom you have labored, even your merchants, from your youth: they shall wander, everyone to his quarter; none shall save you.

17 Hear this, O house of Jacob, who are called by the name of Israel and have come forth out of the waters of Judah, who swear by the name of the Lord and make mention of the God of Israel, but not in truth nor in righteousness. For they call themselves of the holy city, and prop themselves upon the God of Israel — the Lord of Hosts is his name. I have declared the former things from the beginning; and they went forth out of my mouth, and I showed them. I did them suddenly and they came to pass. Because I knew that you are obstinate, and your neck is an iron sinew, and your brow brass, I have, even from the beginning, declared it to you; before it came to pass, I showed it to you, lest you should say, My idol has done them, and my engraved image and my molten image has commanded them. You have heard, see all this; and will not you declare it? I have shown you new things from this time, even hidden things, and you did not know them. They are created now, and not from the beginning, even before the day when you heard them not, lest you should say, Behold, I knew them. Yea, you heard not, yea, you knew not; yea, from that time that your ear was not opened. For I knew that you would deal very treacherously

and were called a transgressor from the womb. For my name's sake will I defer my anger, and for my praise will I refrain for you, that I cut you not off. Behold, I have refined you, but not with silver; I have chosen you in the furnace of affliction. For my own sake — even for my own sake — will I do it; for how should my name be polluted? And I will not give my glory unto another.

2 Listen unto me, O Jacob, and Israel my called: I am he; I am the First, I also am the Last. My hand also has laid the foundation of the earth, and my right hand has spanned the heavens; when I call unto them, they stand up together. All of you, assemble yourselves and hear: Who among them has declared these things? The Lord has loved him. He will do his pleasure on Babylon, and his arm shall be on the Chaldeans. I, even I, have spoken; yea, I have called him; I have brought him, and he shall make his way prosperous.

3 Come near unto me, hear this. I have not spoken in secret from the beginning; from the time that it was, there am I; and now the Lord God and his spirit has sent me. Thus says the Lord, your Redeemer, the Holy One of Israel: I am the Lord your God who teaches you to profit, who leads you by the way that you should go. Oh that you had listened to my commandments; then would your peace have been as a river and your righteousness as the waves of the sea. Your seed also would have been as the sand, and the offspring of your body like the gravel thereof. His name should not have been cut off nor destroyed from before me.

4 Go forth out of Babylon, flee from the Chaldeans; with a voice of singing declare, tell this, utter it even to the end of the earth, say, The Lord has redeemed his servant Jacob and they thirsted not; when he led them through the deserts, he caused the waters to flow out of the rock for them; he cleaved the rock also and the waters gushed out. There is no peace, says the Lord, unto the wicked.

5 Listen, O isles, unto me, and listen you people from far. The Lord has called me from the womb; from the belly of my mother has he made mention of my name. And he has made my mouth like a sharp sword; in the shadow of his hand has he hidden me and made me a polished shaft; in his quiver has he hidden me and said unto me, You are my servant, O Israel, in whom I will be glorified. Then I said, I

have labored in vain, I have spent my strength for naught and in vain;
yet surely my judgment is with the Lord, and my work with my God.

⁶And now says the Lord that formed me from the womb to be his
servant to bring Jacob again to him — though Israel is not gathered,
yet shall I be glorious in the eyes of the Lord, and my God shall be
my strength — and he said, It is a light thing that you should be my
servant to raise up the tribes of Jacob and to restore the preserved of
Israel. I will also give you for a light to the gentiles, that you may be my
salvation unto the end of the earth. Thus says the Lord, the Redeemer
of Israel and his Holy One, to him whom man despises, to him whom
the nation abhors, to a servant of rulers: Kings shall see and arise,
princes also shall worship, because of the Lord that is faithful and the
Holy One of Israel, and he shall choose you. Thus says the Lord: In an
acceptable time have I heard you, and in a day of salvation have I helped
you. And I will preserve you and give you for a covenant of the people,
to establish the earth, to cause to inherit the desolate heritages, that
you may say to the prisoners, Go forth — to them that are in darkness,
Show yourselves. They shall feed in the ways, and their pastures shall
be in all high places. They shall not hunger nor thirst, neither shall the
heat nor sun smite them; for he that has mercy on them shall lead them,
even by the springs of water shall he guide them. And I will make all
my mountains a way, and my highways shall be exalted. Behold, these
shall come from far, and behold, these from the north, and from the
west, and these from the land of Sinim.

⁷ Sing, O heavens, and be joyful, O earth, and break forth into singing,
O mountains; for the Lord has comforted his people and will have
mercy upon his afflicted. But Zion said, The Lord has forsaken me,
and my Lord has forgotten me. Can a woman forget her sucking child,
that she should not have compassion on the son of her womb? Yea,
they may forget, yet will I not forget you. Behold, I have engraved you
upon the palms of my hands; your walls are continually before me.
Your children shall make haste, your destroyers and they that made
you waste shall go forth of you.

⁸Lift up your eyes round about and behold, all these gather
themselves together and come to you. As I live, says the Lord, you
shall surely clothe yourself with them all, as with an ornament, and
bind them on you as a bride does. For your waste and your desolate

places, and the land of your destruction shall even now be too narrow by reason of the inhabitants. And they that swallowed you up shall be far away. The children whom you shall have, after you have lost the other, shall say again in your ears, The place is too confined for me; give place to me that I may dwell. Then shall you say in your heart, Who has begotten me these, seeing I have lost my children and am desolate, a captive, and removing to and fro? And who has brought up these? Behold, I was left alone; these, where had they been? Thus says the Lord: Behold, I will lift up my hand to the gentiles and set up my standard to the people. And they shall bring your sons in their arms, and your daughters shall be carried upon their shoulders. And kings shall be your nursing fathers, and their queens your nursing mothers. They shall bow down to you with their faces toward the earth and lick up the dust of your feet; and you shall know that I am the Lord, for they shall not be ashamed that wait for me. Shall the prey be taken from the mighty, or the lawful captive delivered? But thus says the Lord: Even the captives of the mighty shall be taken away and the prey of the terrible shall be delivered; for the mighty God shall deliver his covenant people. For thus says the Lord: I will contend with them that contends with you and I will save your children. And I will feed them that oppress you with their own flesh, and they shall be drunk with their own blood as with sweet wine. And all flesh shall know that I the Lord am your Savior and your Redeemer, the Mighty One of Jacob.

9 Yea, for thus says the Lord: Have I put you away? Or have I cast you off for ever? For thus says the Lord: Where is the bill of your Mother's divorcement? To whom have I put you away? Or to which of my creditors have I sold you? Yea, to whom have I sold you? Behold, for your iniquities have you sold yourselves, and for your transgressions is your Mother put away. Wherefore, when I came, there was no man; when I called, yea, there was none to answer. O house of Israel, is my hand shortened at all that it cannot redeem? Or have I no power to deliver? Behold, at my rebuke I dry up the sea. I make the rivers a wilderness and their fish to stink because the waters are dried up, and they die because of thirst. I clothe the heavens with blackness and I make sackcloth their covering.

18 The Lord God has given me the tongue of the learned, that I should know how to speak a word in season unto you, O house of Israel, when you are weary. He wakens morning by morning; he wakens my ear to hear as the learned. The Lord God has opened my ear, and I was not rebellious, neither turned away back. I gave my back to the smiters and my cheeks to them that plucked off the hair. I hid not my face from shame and spitting. For the Lord God will help me, therefore shall I not be confounded. Therefore have I set my face like a flint, and I know that I shall not be ashamed. And the Lord is near, and he justifies me. Who will contend with me? Let us stand together. Who is my adversary? Let him come near me and I will smite him with the strength of my mouth. For the Lord God will help me. And all they who shall condemn me, behold, all they shall wax old as a garment, and the moth shall eat them up. Who is among you that fears the Lord, that obeys the voice of his servant, that walks in darkness and has no light? Let him trust in the name of the Lord and rely upon his God. Behold, all you that kindle fire, that encompass yourselves about with sparks, walk in the light of your fire and in the sparks which you have kindled. This shall you have of my hand: you shall lie down in sorrow.

2 Listen unto me, you that follow after righteousness. You that seek the Lord, look unto the rock from which you were hewn, and to the hole of the pit from which you are dug. Look unto Abraham, your father, and unto Sarah that bore you; for I called him alone, and blessed him, and increased him. For the Lord shall comfort Zion; he will comfort all her waste places, and he will make her wilderness like Eden and her desert like the garden of the Lord. Joy and gladness shall be found therein, thanksgiving and the voice of melody. Listen unto me, my people, and give ear unto me, O my nation, for a law shall proceed from me and I will make my judgment to rest for a light of the people. My righteousness is near, my salvation is gone forth, and my arms shall judge the people. The isles shall wait upon me, and on my arm shall they trust. Lift up your eyes to the heavens and look upon the earth beneath, for the heavens shall vanish away like smoke, and the earth shall wax old like a garment, and they that dwell therein shall die in like manner. But my salvation shall be for ever, and my righteousness shall not be abolished. Listen unto me, you that know righteousness, the people in whose heart I have written my law. Fear

not the reproach of men, neither be afraid of their revilings. For the moth shall eat them up like a garment and the worm shall eat them like wool. But my righteousness shall be for ever, and my salvation from generation to generation.

3 Awake, awake, put on strength, O arm of the Lord. Awake as in the ancient days, in the generations of old. Are you not it that has cut Rahab and wounded the dragon? Are you not it which has dried the sea, the waters of the great deep, that has made the depths of the sea a way for the ransomed to pass over? Therefore, the redeemed of the Lord shall return and come with singing unto Zion, and everlasting joy and holiness shall be upon their head. They shall obtain gladness and joy; sorrow and mourning shall flee away. I am he, yea, I am he that comforts you.

4 Behold, who are you, that you should be afraid of a man that shall die and of the son of man who shall be made as grass, and forget the Lord your Maker that has stretched forth the heavens and laid the foundations of the earth, and have feared continually every day because of the fury of the oppressor, as if he were ready to destroy? And where is the fury of the oppressor? The captive exile hastens that he may be released and that he should not die in the pit, nor that his bread should fail. But I am the Lord your God that divided the sea, whose waves roared; the Lord of Hosts is his name. And I have put my words in your mouth and I have covered you in the shadow of my hand, that I may plant the heavens and lay the foundations of the earth, and say unto Zion, Behold, you are my people.

5 Awake, awake, stand up, O Jerusalem, who have drunk at the hand of the Lord the cup of his fury; you have drunk the dregs of the cup of trembling wrung out — and none to guide her, among all the sons she has brought forth, neither that takes her by the hand, of all the sons she has brought up. These two sons have come unto you. Who shall be sorry for you — your desolation and destruction, and the famine and the sword? And by whom shall I comfort you? Your sons have fainted, save these two; they lie at the head of all the streets, as a wild bull in a net. They are full of the fury of the Lord, the rebuke of your God.

6 Therefore, hear now this, you afflicted, and drunk but not with wine. Thus says your Lord — the Lord and your God that pleads the cause of his people: Behold, I have taken out of your hand the cup of

trembling, even the dregs of the cup of my fury; you shall no more drink it again. But I will put it into the hand of them that afflict you, who have said to your soul, Bow down that we may go over — and you have laid your body as the ground and as the street to them that went over.

⁷ Awake, awake, put on your strength, O Zion. Put on your beautiful garments, O Jerusalem, the holy city. For henceforth there shall no more come into you the uncircumcised and the unclean. Shake yourself from the dust. Arise, sit down, O Jerusalem. Free yourself from the bands of your neck, O captive daughter of Zion. For thus says the Lord: You have sold yourselves for naught, and you shall be redeemed without money. For thus says the Lord: My people went down before into Egypt, to sojourn there, and the Assyrian oppressed them without cause. Now therefore what have I here, says the Lord, that my people is taken away for naught? They that rule over them make them to howl, says the Lord, and my name continually every day is blasphemed. Therefore, my people shall know my name, yea, in that day they shall know that I am he that does speak. Behold, it is I.

⁸ And then shall they say, How beautiful upon the mountains are the feet of him that brings good tidings unto them, that publishes peace, that brings good tidings unto them of good, that publishes salvation, that says unto Zion, Your God reigns! Your watchmen shall lift up the voice; with the voice together shall they sing, for they shall see eye to eye when the Lord shall bring again Zion. Break forth into joy, sing together you waste places of Jerusalem, for the Lord has comforted his people, he has redeemed Jerusalem. The Lord has made bare his holy arm in the eyes of all the nations, and all the ends of the earth shall see the salvation of our God. Depart, depart, go out from there, touch no unclean thing; go out of her midst, be clean, you that bear the vessels of the Lord. For you shall not go out with haste, nor go by flight; for the Lord will go before you, and the God of Israel will be your rear guard.

19 Behold, my servant shall deal prudently, he shall be exalted and extolled, and be very high. As many were astonished at you, his visage was so marred, more than any man, and his form more than the sons of men. So shall he gather many nations; the kings shall shut their mouths at him, for that which had not been told to them shall they see, and that which they had not heard shall they consider.

2 Who has believed our report? And to whom is the arm of the Lord revealed? For he shall grow up before him as a tender plant, and as a root out of a dry ground. He has no form nor comeliness, and when we shall see him, there is no beauty that we should desire him. He is despised and rejected of men — a man of sorrows and acquainted with grief. And we hid, as it were, our faces from him. He was despised and we esteemed him not. Surely he has borne our griefs and carried our sorrows, yet we did esteem him stricken, smitten of God, and afflicted. But he was wounded for our transgressions, he was bruised for our iniquities; the chastisement of our peace was upon him, and with his stripes we are healed. All we, like sheep, have gone astray — we have turned every one to his own way; and the Lord has laid on him the iniquity of us all. He was oppressed and he was afflicted, yet he opened not his mouth; he is brought as a lamb to the slaughter; and as a sheep before her shearers is dumb, so he opens not his mouth. He was taken from prison and from judgment. And who shall declare his generation? For he was cut off out of the land of the living; for the transgression of my people was he stricken. And he made his grave with the wicked, and with the rich in his death. Because he had done no violence, neither was any deceit in his mouth; yet it pleased the Lord to bruise him; he has put him to grief.

3 When you shall make his soul an offering for sin, he shall see his seed; he shall prolong his days, and the pleasure of the Lord shall prosper in his hand. He shall see of the travail of his soul and shall be satisfied; by his knowledge shall my righteous Servant justify many, for he shall bear their iniquities. Therefore will I divide him a portion with the great, and he shall divide the spoil with the strong — because he has poured out his soul unto death, and he was numbered with the transgressors, and he bore the sin of many, and made intercession for the transgressors.

4 Sing, O barren, you that did not bear; break forth into singing and cry aloud, you that did not travail with child; for more are the children of the desolate than the children of the married wife, says the Lord. Enlarge the place of your tent and let them stretch forth the curtains of your habitations; spare not, lengthen your cords and strengthen

your stakes, for you shall break forth on the right hand and on the left, and your seed shall inherit the gentiles and make the desolate cities to be inhabited. Fear not, for you shall not be ashamed, neither be confounded, for you shall not be put to shame; for you shall forget the shame of your youth and shall not remember the reproach of your widowhood anymore. For your Maker, your husband, the Lord of Hosts is his name; and your Redeemer, the Holy One of Israel, the God of the whole earth shall he be called. For the Lord has called you as a woman forsaken and grieved in spirit, and a wife of youth when you were refused, says your God. For a small moment have I forsaken you, but with great mercies will I gather you. In a little wrath I hid my face from you for a moment, but with everlasting kindness will I have mercy on you, says the Lord your Redeemer. For this, the waters of Noah unto me, for as I have sworn that the waters of Noah should no more go over the earth, so have I sworn that I would not be angry with you nor rebuke you. For the mountains shall depart and the hills be removed, but my kindness shall not depart from you, neither shall the covenant of my peace be removed, says the Lord that has mercy on you.

⁵ O you afflicted, tossed with tempest and not comforted, behold, I will lay your stones with fair colors and lay your foundations with sapphires. And I will make your windows of agates, and your gates of carbuncles, and all your borders of pleasant stones. And all your children shall be taught of the Lord, and great shall be the peace of your children. In righteousness shall you be established; you shall be far from oppression, for you shall not fear, and from terror, for it shall not come near you. Behold, they shall surely gather together against you, not by me; whoever shall gather together against you shall fall for your sake. Behold, I have created the smith that blows the coals in the fire and that brings forth an instrument for his work, and I have created the waster to destroy. No weapon that is formed against you shall prosper, and every tongue that shall rise against you in judgment you shall condemn. This is the heritage of the servants of the Lord, and their righteousness is of me, says the Lord.

20 Ho, everyone that thirsts, come to the waters; and he that has no money, come, buy, and eat; yea, come buy wine and milk without money and without price. Why do you spend money for

that which is not bread? And your labor for that which satisfies not? Listen diligently unto me and eat that which is good, and let your soul delight itself in fatness. Incline your ear and come unto me; hear, and your soul shall live, and I will make an everlasting covenant with you, even the sure mercies of David. Behold, I have given him for a witness to the people, a leader and commander to the people. Behold, you shall call a nation that you know not, and nations that knew not you shall run unto you because of the Lord your God, and for the Holy One of Israel; for he has glorified you.

2 Seek the Lord while he may be found, call upon him while he is near. Let the wicked forsake his way and the unrighteous man his thoughts; and let him return unto the Lord and he will have mercy upon him, and to our God, for he will abundantly pardon. For my thoughts are not your thoughts, neither are your ways my ways, says the Lord. For as the heavens are higher than the earth, so are my ways higher than your ways, and my thoughts than your thoughts. For as the rain comes down and the snow from heaven, and returns not there but waters the earth, and makes it bring forth and bud that it may give seed to the sower and bread to the eater, so shall my word be that goes forth out of my mouth. It shall not return unto me void, but it shall accomplish that which I please, and it shall prosper in the thing to which I sent it. For you shall go out with joy and be led forth with peace; the mountains and the hills shall break forth before you into singing, and all the trees of the field shall clap their hands. Instead of the thorn shall come up the fir tree, and instead of the brier shall come up the myrtle tree; and it shall be to the Lord for a name, for an everlasting sign that shall not be cut off.

3 Thus says the Lord: Keep judgment and do justice, for my salvation is near to come and my righteousness to be revealed. Blessed is the man that does this and the son of man that lays hold on it, that keeps the Sabbath from polluting it and keeps his hand from doing any evil. Neither let the son of the stranger that has joined himself to the Lord speak, saying, The Lord has utterly separated me from his people. Neither let the eunuch say, Behold, I am a dry tree. For thus says the Lord: Unto the eunuchs that keep my Sabbaths, and choose the things that please me, and take hold of my covenant, even unto them will I give in my house and within my walls a place and a name

better than of sons and of daughters. I will give them an everlasting name that shall not be cut off. Also, the sons of the stranger that join themselves to the Lord, to serve him and to love the name of the Lord, to be his servants, every one that keeps the Sabbath from polluting it and takes hold of my covenant, even them will I bring to my holy mountain and make them joyful in my house of prayer. Their burnt offerings and their sacrifices shall be accepted upon my altar, for my house shall be called a house of prayer for all people. The Lord God who gathers the outcasts of Israel says, Yet will I gather others to him, besides those that are gathered unto him.

⁴All you beasts of the field, come to devour, yea, all you beasts in the forest. His watchmen are blind, they are all ignorant. They are all dumb dogs, they cannot bark; sleeping, lying down, loving to slumber. Yea, they are greedy dogs which can never have enough, and they are shepherds that cannot understand. They all look to their own way, every one for his gain, from his quarter. Come, say they, I will fetch wine and we will fill ourselves with strong drink, and tomorrow shall be as this day, and much more abundant.

⁵The righteous perishes, and no man lays it to heart; and merciful men are taken away, none considering that the righteous is taken away from the evil to come. He shall enter into peace; they shall rest in their beds, each one walking in his uprightness.

⁶But draw near here, you sons of the sorceress, the seed of the adulterer and the whore. Against whom do you sport yourselves? Against whom do you make a wide mouth and draw out the tongue? Are you not children of transgression, a seed of falsehood? Inflaming yourselves with idols under every green tree, slaying the children in the valleys under the clefts of the rocks? Among the smooth stones of the stream is your portion; they, they are your lot. Even to them have you poured a drink offering, you have offered a meal offering. Should I receive comfort in these? Upon a lofty and high mountain have you set your bed; even there you went up to offer sacrifice. Behind the doors also and the doorposts have you set up your remembrance, for you have revealed yourself to another than me and have gone up; you have enlarged your bed and made a covenant with them, you loved their bed where you saw it. And you went to the king with ointment and did increase your perfumes, and did send your messengers far off, and

did debase yourself even unto hell. You are wearied in the greatness of your way; yet you said not, There is no hope. You have found the life of your hand, therefore you were not grieved. And of whom have you been afraid, or feared, that you have lied and have not remembered me, nor laid it to your heart? Have not I held my peace even of old, and you fear me not? I will declare your righteousness and your works, for they shall not profit you. When you cry, let your companies deliver you, but the wind shall carry them all away; vanity shall take them. But he that puts his trust in me shall possess the land, and shall inherit my holy mountain, and shall say, Cast up, cast up, prepare the way, take up the stumbling block out of the way of my people. For thus says the high and lofty One that inhabits eternity, whose name is holy: I dwell in the high and holy place with him also that is of a contrite and humble spirit, to revive the spirit of the humble and to revive the heart of the contrite ones. For I will not contend for ever, neither will I be always angry, for the spirit should fail before me, and the souls which I have made. For the iniquity of his covetousness was I angry, and smote him. I hid myself and was angry, and he went on frowardly in the way of his heart. I have seen his ways and will heal him. I will lead him also, and restore comforts unto him and to his mourners. I create the fruit of the lips. Peace, peace to him that is far off and to him that is near, says the Lord, and I will heal him. But the wicked are like the troubled sea when it cannot rest, whose waters cast up mire and dirt. There is no peace, says my God, to the wicked.

7 Cry aloud, spare not, lift up your voice like a trumpet, and show my people their transgression and the house of Jacob their sins. Yet they seek me daily and delight to know my ways, as a nation that did righteousness and forsook not the ordinance of their God. They ask of me the ordinances of justice, they take delight in approaching to God. Why have we fasted, say they, and you see not? Why have we afflicted our soul and you take no knowledge? Behold, in the day of your fast, you find pleasure and exact all your labors. Behold, you fast for strife and debate, and to smite with the fist of wickedness. You shall not fast as you do this day to make your voice to be heard on high. Is it such a fast that I have chosen? A day for a man to afflict his soul? Is it to bow down his head as a bulrush, and to spread sackcloth and ashes under him? Will you call this a fast and an acceptable day to the Lord? Is not

this the fast that I have chosen: to remove the bands of wickedness, to undo the heavy burdens, and to let the oppressed go free, and that you break every yoke? Is it not to deal your bread to the hungry, and that you bring the poor that are cast out to your house? When you see the naked, that you cover him, and that you hide not yourself from your own flesh? Then shall your light break forth as the morning, and your health shall spring forth speedily, and your righteousness shall go before you; the glory of the Lord shall be your rear guard. Then shall you call and the Lord shall answer, you shall cry and he shall say, Here I am. If you take away from your midst the yoke, the putting forth of the finger, and speaking vanity, and if you draw out your soul to the hungry, and satisfy the afflicted soul, then shall your light rise in obscurity and your darkness be as the noonday. And the Lord shall guide you continually, and satisfy your soul in drought, and make fat your bones; and you shall be like a watered garden, and like a spring of water whose waters fail not. And they that shall be of you shall build the old waste places. You shall raise up the foundations of many generations, and you shall be called the repairer of the breach, the restorer of paths to dwell in. If you turn away your foot from the Sabbath — from doing your pleasure on my holy day — and call the Sabbath a delight, the holy of the Lord honorable, and shall honor him, not doing your own ways, nor finding your own pleasure, nor speaking your own words, then shall you delight yourself in the Lord. And I will cause you to ride upon the high places of the earth, and feed you with the heritage of Jacob your father; for the mouth of the Lord has spoken it.

21 Behold, the Lord's hand is not shortened, that it cannot save, neither his ear heavy, that it cannot hear. But your iniquities have separated between you and your God, and your sins have hidden his face from you, that he will not hear. For your hands are defiled with blood, and your fingers with iniquity; your lips have spoken lies, your tongue has muttered perverseness. None calls for justice, nor any pleads for truth; they trust in vanity and speak lies, they conceive mischief and bring forth iniquity. They hatch cockatrice' eggs and weave the spider's web. He that eats of their eggs dies, and that which is crushed breaks out into a viper. Their webs shall not become

garments, neither shall they cover themselves with their works; their works are works of iniquity, and the act of violence is in their hands. Their feet run to evil, and they make haste to shed innocent blood; their thoughts are thoughts of iniquity, wasting and destruction are in their paths. The way of peace they know not, and there is no judgment in their goings. They have made them crooked paths; whoever goes therein shall not know peace.

2 Therefore is judgment far from us, neither does justice overtake us. We wait for light, but behold obscurity — for brightness, but we walk in darkness. We grope for the wall like the blind and we grope as if we had no eyes. We stumble at noonday as in the night; we are in desolate places as dead men. We roar all like bears, and mourn severely like doves. We look for judgment, but there is none — for salvation, but it is far off from us. For our transgressions are multiplied before you and our sins testify against us, for our transgressions are with us. And as for our iniquities, we know them: in transgressing and lying against the Lord, and departing away from our God, speaking oppression and revolt, conceiving and uttering from the heart words of falsehood. And judgment is turned away backward, and justice stands afar off; for truth is fallen in the street and equity cannot enter. Yea, truth fails, and he that departs from evil makes himself a prey. And the Lord saw it, and it displeased him that there was no judgment. And he saw that there was no man, and wondered that there was no intercessor. Therefore, his arm brought salvation unto him, and his righteousness, it sustained him. For he put on righteousness as a breastplate, and a helmet of salvation upon his head; and he put on the garments of vengeance for clothing, and was clad with zeal as a cloak. According to their deeds, accordingly he will repay, fury to his adversaries, recompense to his enemies; to the islands he will repay recompense. So shall they fear the name of the Lord from the west, and his glory from the rising of the sun. When the enemy shall come in like a flood, the spirit of the Lord shall lift up a standard against him. And the Redeemer shall come to Zion, and unto them that turn from transgression in Jacob, says the Lord. As for me, this is my covenant with them, says the Lord: my spirit that is upon you and my words which I have put in your mouth shall not depart out of your mouth,

nor out of the mouth of your seed, nor out of the mouth of your seed's seed, says the Lord, from henceforth and for ever.

22 Arise, shine; for your light has come, and the glory of the Lord is risen upon you. For behold, the darkness shall cover the earth, and gross darkness the people, but the Lord shall arise upon you and his glory shall be seen upon you. And the gentiles shall come to your light, and kings to the brightness of your rising. Lift up your eyes round about and see: all they gather themselves together, they come to you. Your sons shall come from far and your daughters shall be nursed at your side. Then you shall see and flow together, and your heart shall fear and be enlarged, because the abundance of the sea shall be converted unto you, the forces of the gentiles shall come unto you. The multitude of camels shall cover you, the dromedaries of Midian and Ephah, all they from Sheba shall come; they shall bring gold and incense, and they shall show forth the praises of the Lord. All the flocks of Kedar shall be gathered together unto you, the rams of Nebaioth shall minister unto you; they shall come up with acceptance on my altar, and I will glorify the house of my glory. Who are these that fly as a cloud, and as the doves to their windows? Surely the isles shall wait for me, and the ships of Tarshish first, to bring your sons from far, their silver and their gold with them, unto the name of the Lord your God, and to the Holy One of Israel, because he has glorified you. And the sons of strangers shall build up your walls, and their kings shall minister unto you; for in my wrath I smote you, but in my favor have I had mercy on you. Therefore, your gates shall be open continually; they shall not be shut day nor night, that men may bring unto you the forces of the gentiles, and that their kings may be brought. For the nation and kingdom that will not serve you shall perish, yea, those nations shall be utterly wasted. The glory of Lebanon shall come unto you — the fir tree, the pine tree, and the box together — to beautify the place of my sanctuary; and I will make the place of my feet glorious. The sons also of them that afflicted you shall come bending unto you, and all they that despised you shall bow themselves down at the soles of your feet; and they shall call you the city of the Lord, the Zion of the Holy One of Israel. Whereas you have been forsaken and hated, so that no man went through you, I will make you an eternal excellence, a joy

of many generations. You shall also suck the milk of the gentiles and shall suck the breast of kings, and you shall know that I the Lord am your Savior and your Redeemer, the Mighty One of Jacob. For brass I will bring gold, and for iron I will bring silver, and for wood, brass, and for stones, iron. I will also make your officers peace, and your oppressors righteousness. Violence shall no more be heard in your land, wasting nor destruction within your borders; but you shall call your walls Salvation and your gates Praise. The sun shall be no more your light by day, neither for brightness shall the moon give light unto you, but the Lord shall be unto you an everlasting light, and your God your glory. Your sun shall no more go down, neither shall your moon withdraw itself, for the Lord shall be your everlasting light, and the days of your mourning shall be ended. Your people also shall be all righteous. They shall inherit the land for ever, the branch of my planting, the work of my hands, that I may be glorified. A little one shall become a thousand, and a small one a strong nation; I the Lord will hasten it in my time.

23 The spirit of the Lord God is upon me, because the Lord has anointed me to preach good tidings unto the meek; he has sent me to bind up the brokenhearted, to proclaim liberty to the captives, and the opening of the prison to them that are bound; to proclaim the acceptable year of the Lord and the day of vengeance of our God; to comfort all that mourn; to appoint unto them that mourn in Zion, to give unto them beauty for ashes, the oil of joy for mourning, the garment of praise for the spirit of heaviness, that they might be called trees of righteousness, the planting of the Lord, that he might be glorified. And they shall build the old wastes, they shall raise up the former desolations, and they shall repair the waste cities, the desolations of many generations. And strangers shall stand and feed your flocks, and the sons of the foreigner shall be your plowmen and your vinedressers. But you shall be named the priests of the Lord, men shall call you the ministers of our God; you shall eat the riches of the gentiles, and in their glory shall you boast yourselves. For your shame, you shall have double, and for confusion, they shall rejoice in their portion; therefore, in their land they shall possess the double. Everlasting joy shall be unto them. For I the Lord love judgment, I

hate robbery for burnt offering; and I will direct their work in truth, and I will make an everlasting covenant with them. And their seed shall be known among the gentiles, and their offspring among the people; all that see them shall acknowledge them, that they are the seed which the Lord has blessed. I will greatly rejoice in the Lord, my soul shall be joyful in my God; for he has clothed me with the garments of salvation, he has covered me with the robe of righteousness, as a bridegroom adorns himself with ornaments and as a bride adorns herself with her jewels. For as the earth brings forth her bud, and as the garden causes the things that are sown in it to spring forth, so the Lord God will cause righteousness and praise to spring forth before all the nations.

24 For Zion's sake will I not hold my peace, and for Jerusalem's sake I will not rest, until the righteousness thereof go forth as brightness and the salvation thereof as a lamp that burns. And the gentiles shall see your righteousness, and all kings your glory; and you shall be called by a new name, which the mouth of the Lord shall name. You shall also be a crown of glory in the hand of the Lord, and a royal diadem in the hand of your God. You shall no more be termed Forsaken, neither shall your land anymore be termed Desolate, but you shall be called Delightful, and your land Union; for the Lord delights in you, and your land shall be married. For as a young man marries a virgin, so shall your God marry you; and as the bridegroom rejoices over the bride, so shall your God rejoice over you. I have set watchmen upon your walls, O Jerusalem, who shall never hold their peace, day nor night. You that make mention of the Lord, keep not silence, and give him no rest until he establish and until he make Jerusalem a praise in the earth. The Lord has sworn by his right hand and by the arm of his strength, Surely I will no more give your grain to be food for your enemies, and the sons of the stranger shall not drink your wine for which you have labored. But they that have gathered it shall eat it and praise the Lord, and they that have brought it together shall drink it in the courts of my holiness. Go through, go through the gates, prepare the way of the people. Cast up, cast up the highway, gather out the stones. Lift up a standard for the people. Behold, the Lord has proclaimed unto the end of the

world, Say to the daughter of Zion, Behold, your salvation comes; behold, his reward is with him and his work before him. And they shall call them the holy people, the redeemed of the Lord; and you shall be called sought-out, a city not forsaken.

2 Who is this that comes from Edom, with dyed garments from Bozrah? This who is glorious in his apparel, traveling in the greatness of his strength? I, that speak in righteousness, mighty to save. Why are you red in your apparel, and your garments like him that treads in the winevat? I have trodden the winepress alone, and of the people there was none with me; for I will tread them in my anger and trample them in my fury, and their blood shall be sprinkled upon my garments, and I will stain all my raiment. For the day of vengeance is in my heart, and the year of my redeemed has come. And I looked and there was none to help, and I wondered that there was none to uphold; therefore, my own arm brought salvation unto me, and my fury, it upheld me. And I will tread down the people in my anger and make them drunk in my fury, and I will bring down their strength to the earth.

3 I will mention the loving kindnesses of the Lord and the praises of the Lord, according to all that the Lord has bestowed on us and the great goodness toward the house of Israel which he has bestowed on them, according to his mercies and according to the multitude of his loving kindnesses. For he said, Surely they are my people, children that will not lie; so he was their Savior. In all their affliction, he was afflicted, and the angel of his presence saved them. In his love and in his pity he redeemed them, and he bore them and carried them all the days of old. But they rebelled and vexed his holy spirit. Therefore, he was turned to be their enemy and he fought against them. Then he remembered the days of old, Moses and his people, saying, Where is he that brought them up out of the sea with the shepherd of his flock? Where is he that put his holy spirit within him? That led them by the right hand of Moses with his glorious arm, dividing the water before them, to make himself an everlasting name? That led them through the deep as a horse in the wilderness, that they should not stumble? As a beast goes down into the valley, the spirit of the Lord caused him to rest; so did you lead your people, to make yourself a glorious name.

4 Look down from Heaven and behold from the habitation of your holiness and of your glory. Where is your zeal and your strength, the

sounding of your heart and of your mercies toward me? Are they restrained? Doubtless you are our father, though Abraham is ignorant of us and Israel acknowledge us not. You, O Lord, are our father, our redeemer; your name is from everlasting. O Lord, why have you suffered us to err from your ways and to harden our heart from your fear? Return, for your servants' sake, the tribes of your inheritance. The people of your holiness have possessed it but a little while; our adversaries have trodden down your sanctuary. We are yours; you never bore rule over them, they were not called by your name.

5 Oh that you would rend the heavens, that you would come down, that the mountains might flow down at your presence — as when the melting fire burns, the fire causes the waters to boil — to make your name known to your adversaries, that the nations may tremble at your presence. When you did terrible things which we looked not for, you came down, the mountains flowed down at your presence. For since the beginning of the world, men have not heard, nor perceived by the ear, neither has the eye seen, O God, besides you, what he has prepared for him that waits for him. You meet him that works righteousness, and rejoice him that remembers you in your ways. In righteousness there is continuance, and such shall be saved, but we have sinned, we are all as an unclean thing. And all our righteousnesses are as filthy rags, and we all do fade as a leaf; and our iniquities, like the wind, have taken us away. And there is none that calls upon your name, that stirs up himself to take hold of you, for you have hidden your face from us and have consumed us because of our iniquities. But now, O Lord, you are our father; we are the clay and you our potter, and we all are the work of your hand. Be not exceedingly angry, O Lord, neither remember iniquity for ever. Behold, see, we implore you, we are all your people. Your holy cities are a wilderness, Zion is a wilderness, Jerusalem a desolation. Our holy and our beautiful house where our fathers praised you is burned up with fire, and all our pleasant things are laid waste. Will you restrain yourself for these things, O Lord? Will you hold your peace and afflict us exceedingly?

6 I am found of them who seek after me, I give unto all them that ask of me. I am not found of them that sought me not, or that inquires not after me. I said unto my servant, Behold me, look upon me; I will send you unto a nation that are not called by my name. For I have

spread out my hands all the day to a people who walks not in my ways, and their works are evil and not good, and they walk after their own thoughts; a people that provokes me to anger continually to my face; that sacrifices in gardens and burns incense upon altars of brick; who remain among the graves and lodge in the monuments; who eat swine's flesh, and broth of abominable beasts, and pollute their vessels; who say, Stand by yourself, come not near to me, for I am holier than you. These are a smoke in my nose, a fire that burns all the day. Behold, it is written before me: I will not keep silence, but will recompense — even recompense into their bosom — your iniquities and the iniquities of your fathers together, says the Lord, who have burned incense upon the mountains and blasphemed me upon the hills. Therefore will I measure their former work into their bosom.

7 Thus says the Lord: As the new wine is found in the cluster, and one says, Destroy it not, for a blessing is in it — so will I do for my servants' sakes, that I may not destroy them all. And I will bring forth a seed out of Jacob, and out of Judah an inheritor of my mountains; and my elect shall inherit it and my servants shall dwell there. And Sharon shall be a fold of flocks, and the valley of Achor a place for the herds to lie down in, for my people that have sought me.

8 But you are they that forsake the Lord, that forget my holy mountain, that prepare a table for that troop and that furnish the drink offering unto that number. Therefore will I number you to the sword, and you shall all bow down to the slaughter. Because when I called, you did not answer; when I spoke, you did not hear, but did evil before my eyes and did choose that wherein I delighted not. Therefore, thus says the Lord God: Behold, my servants shall eat, but you shall be hungry; behold, my servants shall drink, but you shall be thirsty. Behold, my servants shall rejoice, but you shall be ashamed; behold, my servants shall sing for joy of heart, but you shall cry for sorrow of heart and shall howl for vexation of spirit. And you shall leave your name for a curse unto my chosen, for the Lord God shall slay you and call his servants by another name, that he who blesses himself in the earth shall bless himself in the God of truth, and he that swears in the earth shall swear by the God of truth, because the former troubles are forgotten and because they are hidden from my eyes.

⁹ For behold, I create new heavens and a new earth, and the former shall not be remembered nor come into mind. But be glad and rejoice for ever in that which I create; for behold, I create Jerusalem a rejoicing and her people a joy. And I will rejoice in Jerusalem and joy in my people, and the voice of weeping shall be no more heard in her, nor the voice of crying. In those days, there shall be no more from there an infant of days, nor an old man that has not filled his day; for the child shall not die, but shall live to be a hundred years old. But the sinner living to be a hundred years old shall be accursed. And they shall build houses and inhabit them, and they shall plant vineyards and eat the fruit of them. They shall not build and another inhabit, they shall not plant and another eat; for as the days of a tree are the days of my people, and my elect shall long enjoy the work of their hands. They shall not labor in vain, nor bring forth for trouble; for they are the seed of the blessed of the Lord, and their offspring with them. And it shall come to pass that before they call, I will answer, and while they are yet speaking, I will hear. The wolf and the lamb shall feed together, and the lion shall eat straw like the bullock, and dust shall be the serpent's food. They shall not hurt nor destroy in all my holy mountain, says the Lord.

25 Thus says the Lord: The heaven is my throne and the earth is my footstool. Where is the house that you build unto me? And where is the place of my rest? For all those things has my hand made, and all those things have been, says the Lord. But to this man will I look, even to him that is poor and of a contrite spirit, and trembles at my word. He that kills an ox is as if he slew a man, he that sacrifices a lamb as if he cut off a dog's neck, he that offers an offering as if he offered swine's blood, he that burns incense as if he blessed an idol. Yea, they have chosen their own ways, and their souls delight in their abominations. I also will choose their delusions, and will bring their fears upon them. Because when I called, none did answer; when I spoke, they did not hear, but they did evil before my eyes and chose that in which I delighted not.

² Hear the word of the Lord, you that tremble at his word: Your brethren that hated you, that cast you out for my name's sake, said, Let the Lord be glorified. But he shall appear to your joy, and they shall

be ashamed. A voice of noise from the city, a voice from the temple, a voice of the Lord that renders recompense to his enemies. Before she travailed, she brought forth; before her pain came, she was delivered of a son. Who has heard such a thing? Who has seen such things? Shall the earth be made to bring forth in one day? Or shall a nation be born at once? For as soon as Zion travailed, she brought forth her children. Shall I bring to the birth and not cause to bring forth? — says the Lord. Shall I cause to bring forth and shut the womb? — says your God. Rejoice with Jerusalem and be glad with her, all you that love her; rejoice for joy with her, all you that mourn for her, that you may suck and be satisfied with the breasts of her consolations; that you may milk out and be delighted with the abundance of her glory. For thus says the Lord: Behold, I will extend peace to her like a river, and the glory of the gentiles like a flowing stream. Then shall you suck, you shall be borne upon her sides and be rocked upon her knees. As one whom his mother comforts, so will I comfort you; and you shall be comforted in Jerusalem. And when you see this, your heart shall rejoice, and your bones shall flourish like an herb; and the hand of the Lord shall be known toward his servants, and his indignation toward his enemies. For behold, the Lord will come with fire and with his chariots like a whirlwind, to render his anger with fury and his rebuke with flames of fire. For by fire and by his sword will the Lord plead with all flesh, and the slain of the Lord shall be many. They that sanctify themselves and purify themselves in the gardens behind one tree in the center, eating swine's flesh, and the abomination, and the mouse, shall be consumed together, says the Lord; for I know their works and their thoughts. It shall come that I will gather all nations and tongues, and they shall come and see my glory. And I will set a sign among them, and I will send those that escape of them unto the nations — to Tarshish, Pul, and Lud (that draw the bow), to Tubal, and Javan, to the isles afar off — that have not heard my fame, neither have seen my glory; and they shall declare my glory among the gentiles. And they shall bring all your brethren for an offering unto the Lord out of all nations — upon horses, and in chariots, and in litters, and upon mules, and upon swift beasts — to my holy mountain Jerusalem, says the Lord, as the children of Israel bring an offering in a clean vessel into the house of the Lord. And I will also take of them for priests and for Levites, says the Lord. For as the new heavens and the new earth which I will make shall remain before me, says the Lord, so shall your seed and your name remain. And it shall come to pass that from one new moon to another, and from one Sabbath to another, shall all flesh come to worship before me, says the Lord. And they shall go forth and look upon the carcasses of the men that have transgressed against me, for their worm shall not die, neither shall their fire be quenched; and they shall be abhorrent unto all flesh.

THE BOOK OF THE PROPHET JEREMIAH

The words of Jeremiah the son of Hilkiah, of the priests that were in Anathoth in the land of Benjamin, to whom the word of the Lord came in the days of Josiah the son of Amon, king of Judah, in the thirteenth year of his reign. It came also in the days of Jehoiakim the son of Josiah, king of Judah, unto the end of the eleventh year of Zedekiah the son of Josiah, king of Judah, unto the carrying away of Jerusalem captive in the fifth month.

THEN the word of the Lord came unto me, saying, Before I formed you in the belly I knew you, and before you came forth out of the womb I sanctified you, and I ordained you a prophet unto the nations. Then said I, Ah, Lord God, behold, I cannot speak, for I am a child. But the Lord said unto me, Say not, I am a child—for you shall go to all that I shall send you, and whatever I command you, you shall speak. Be not afraid of their faces, for I am with you to deliver you, says the Lord. Then the Lord put forth his hand and touched my mouth. And the Lord said unto me, Behold, I have put my words in your mouth. See, I have this day set you over the nations and over the kingdoms, to root out, and to pull down, and to destroy, and to throw down, to build, and to plant.

2 Moreover, the word of the Lord came unto me, saying, Jeremiah, what do you see? And I said, I see a rod of an almond tree. Then said the Lord unto me, You have seen well, for I will hasten my word to perform it. And the word of the Lord came unto me the second time, saying, What do you see? And I said, I see a boiling pot, and the face thereof is toward the north. Then the Lord said unto me, Out of the north an evil shall break forth upon all the inhabitants of the land. For I will call all the families of the kingdoms of the north, says the Lord, and they

shall come and they shall set every one his throne at the entering of the gates of Jerusalem, and against all the walls thereof round about, and against all the cities of Judah. And I will utter my judgments against them touching all their wickedness, who have forsaken me, and have burned incense unto other gods, and worshipped the works of their own hands. Therefore, gird up your loins and arise and speak unto them all that I command you; be not dismayed at their faces, lest I confound you before them. For behold, I have made you this day a fortified city, and an iron pillar, and brazen walls against the whole land, against the kings of Judah, against the princes thereof, against the priests thereof, and against the people of the land. And they shall fight against you, but they shall not prevail against you, for I am with you, says the Lord, to deliver you.

3 Moreover, the word of the Lord came to me, saying, Go and cry in the ears of Jerusalem, saying, Thus says the Lord: I remember you, the kindness of your youth, the love of your espousals, when you went after me in the wilderness in a land that was not sowed. Israel was holiness unto the Lord and the firstfruits of his increase. All that devour him shall offend, evil shall come upon them, says the Lord.

4 Hear the word of the Lord, O house of Jacob, and all the families of the house of Israel, thus says the Lord: What iniquity have your fathers found in me that they have gone far from me, and have walked after vanity, and have become vain? Neither said they, Where is the Lord that brought us up out of the land of Egypt, that led us through the wilderness, through a land of deserts and of pits, through a land of drought and of the shadow of death, through a land that no man passed through and where no man dwelled? And I brought you into a plentiful country to eat the fruit thereof and the goodness thereof, but when you entered, you defiled my land and made my heritage an abomination. The priests said not, Where is the Lord? And they that handle the law knew me not. The shepherds also transgressed against me, and the prophets prophesied by Baal and walked after things that do not profit. Wherefore, I will yet plead with you, says the Lord, and with your children's children will I plead.

5 For pass over the coasts of Kittim and see, and send unto Kedar and consider diligently, and see if there be such a thing: has a nation changed their gods, which are yet no gods? But my people have changed

their glory for that which does not profit. Be astonished, O you heavens, at this, and be horribly afraid; be very desolate, says the Lord. For my people have committed two evils: they have forsaken me, the fountain of living waters, and hewed them out cisterns, broken cisterns that can hold no water.

6 Is Israel a servant? Is he a homeborn slave? Why is he spoiled? The young lions roared upon him and yelled, and they made his land waste. His cities are burned without inhabitant. Also, the children of Noph and Tahpanhes have broken the crown of your head. Have you not procured this unto yourself, in that you have forsaken the Lord your God when he led you by the way? And now what have you to do in the way of Egypt, to drink the waters of Shihor? Or what have you to do in the way of Assyria, to drink the waters of the river?

7 Your own wickedness shall correct you and your backslidings shall reprove you. Know therefore and see that it is an evil thing, and bitter, that you have forsaken the Lord your God and that my fear is not in you, says the Lord God of Hosts. For of old time I have broken your yoke and burst your bands, and you said, I will not transgress — when upon every high hill and under every green tree you wander, playing the harlot. Yet I had planted you a noble vine, wholly a right seed. How then are you turned into the degenerate plant of a strange vine unto me? For though you wash with natron and take much soap, yet your iniquity is marked before me, says the Lord God. How can you say, I am not polluted, I have not gone after the Baalim? See your way in the valley, know what you have done. You are a swift dromedary traversing her ways, a wild ass used to the wilderness that snuffs up the wind at her pleasure; in her heat, who can turn her away? All they that seek her will weary themselves, in her month they shall not find her. Withhold your foot from being unshod and your throat from thirst; but you said, There is no hope, no, for I have loved strangers and after them will I go. As the thief is ashamed when he is found, so is the house of Israel ashamed — they, their kings, their princes, and their priests, and their prophets; saying to a stock, You are my father — and to a stone, You have brought me forth. For they have turned their back unto me and not their face, but in the time of their trouble they will say, Arise and save us. But where are your gods that you have made yourself? Let them arise, if they can save you in the time of your trouble; for according to

the number of your cities are your gods, O Judah. Why will you plead with me? You all have transgressed against me, says the Lord. In vain have I smitten your children; they received no correction. Your own sword has devoured your prophets like a destroying lion.

8 O generation, see the word of the Lord: Have I been a wilderness unto Israel? A land of darkness? Why do my people say, We are lords, we will come no more unto you? Can a virgin forget her ornaments? Or a bride her attire? Yet my people have forgotten me, days without number. Why do you embellish your way to seek love? Thus have you also taught the wicked ones your ways. Also, in your skirts is found the blood of the souls of the poor innocents; I have not found it by secret search, but upon all these. Yet you say, Because I am innocent, surely his anger shall turn from me. Behold, I will plead with you because you say, I have not sinned. Why do you go about so much to change your way? You also shall be ashamed of Egypt as you were ashamed of Assyria. Yea, you shall go forth from him and your hands upon your head, for the Lord has rejected your confidences and you shall not prosper in them.

9 They say, If a man divorce his wife and she go from him and become another man's, shall he return unto her again? Shall not that land be greatly polluted? But you have played the harlot with many lovers, yet return again to me, says the Lord. Lift up your eyes unto the high places and see where you have not been lain with. In the ways have you sat for them, as the Arabian in the wilderness, and you have polluted the land with your whoredoms and with your wickedness. Therefore, the showers have been withheld and there has been no spring rain. And you had a whore's forehead, yet you refused to be ashamed. Will you not from this time cry unto me, My father, you are the guide of my youth? Will he reserve his anger for ever? Will he keep it to the end? Behold, you have spoken and done evil things as you could.

2 The Lord said also unto me in the days of Josiah the king, Have you seen that which backsliding Israel has done? She is gone up upon every high mountain and under every green tree and there has played the harlot. And I said after she had done all these things, Turn unto me. But she returned not. And her treacherous sister Judah saw it. And I saw, when for all the causes whereby backsliding Israel committed

adultery, I had put her away and given her a bill of divorce, yet her treacherous sister Judah feared not, but went and played the harlot also. And it came to pass through the lightness of her whoredom that she defiled the land and committed adultery with stones and with stocks. And yet for all this, her treacherous sister Judah has not turned unto me with her whole heart, but feignedly, says the Lord. And the Lord said unto me, The backsliding Israel has justified herself more than treacherous Judah.

² Go and proclaim these words toward the north, and say, Return, you backsliding Israel, says the Lord, and I will not cause my anger to fall upon you. For I am merciful, says the Lord, and I will not keep anger for ever. Only acknowledge your iniquity — that you have transgressed against the Lord your God, and have scattered your ways to the strangers under every green tree, and you have not obeyed my voice, says the Lord.

³ Turn, O backsliding children, says the Lord, for I am married unto you. And I will take you one of a city and two of a family and I will bring you to Zion. And I will give you shepherds according to my heart, who shall feed you with knowledge and understanding. And it shall come to pass, when you have multiplied and increased in the land in those days, says the Lord, they shall say no more, The ark of the covenant of the Lord — neither shall it come to mind, neither shall they remember it, neither shall they visit it, neither shall that be done anymore. At that time they shall call Jerusalem the throne of the Lord and all the nations shall be gathered unto it, to the name of the Lord, to Jerusalem; neither shall they walk anymore after the imagination of their evil heart. In those days, the house of Judah shall walk with the house of Israel, and they shall come together out of the land of the north to the land that I have given for an inheritance unto your fathers.

⁴ But I said, How shall I put you among the children and give you a pleasant land, a goodly heritage of the hosts of nations? And I said, You shall call me, My father — and shall not turn away from me. Surely as a wife treacherously departs from her husband, so have you dealt treacherously with me, O house of Israel, says the Lord. A voice was heard upon the high places, weeping and supplications of the children of Israel, for they have perverted their way and they have forgotten the Lord their God. Return, you backsliding children, and I will heal

your backslidings. Behold, we come unto you, for you are the Lord our God. Truly in vain is salvation hoped for from the hills and from the multitude of mountains; truly in the Lord our God is the salvation of Israel. For shame has devoured the labor of our fathers from our youth, their flocks and their herds, their sons and their daughters. We lie down in our shame and our confusion covers us, for we have sinned against the Lord our God, we and our fathers, from our youth even unto this day, and have not obeyed the voice of the Lord our God.

5 If you will return O Israel, says the Lord, return unto me; and if you will put away your abominations out of my sight, then shall you not remove. And you shall swear, The Lord lives in truth, in judgment, and in righteousness — and the nations shall bless themselves in him, and in him shall they glory. For thus says the Lord to the men of Judah and Jerusalem: Break up your fallow ground and sow not among thorns. Circumcise yourselves to the Lord and take away the foreskins of your heart, you men of Judah and inhabitants of Jerusalem, lest my fury come forth like fire and burn, that none can quench it, because of the evil of your doings.

6 Declare in Judah and publish in Jerusalem, and say, Blow the trumpet in the land, cry, gather together and say, Assemble yourselves and let us go into the fortified cities. Set up the standard toward Zion; retire, stay not, for I will bring evil from the north and a great destruction. The lion has come up from his thicket and the destroyer of the gentiles is on his way. He is gone forth from his place to make your land desolate and your cities shall be laid waste, without an inhabitant. For this, gird yourself with sackcloth, lament and howl, for the fierce anger of the Lord is not turned back from us. And it shall come to pass at that day, says the Lord, that the heart of the king shall perish, and the heart of the princes and the priests shall be astonished, and the prophets shall wonder. Then said I, Ah, Lord God, surely you have greatly deceived this people and Jerusalem, saying, You shall have peace — whereas the sword reaches unto the soul.

7 At that time shall it be said to this people and to Jerusalem, A dry wind of the high places in the wilderness, toward the daughter of my people — not to winnow, nor to cleanse — even a full wind from those places shall come unto me; now also will I give sentence against them. Behold, he shall come up as clouds and his chariots shall be as a

whirlwind, his horses are swifter than eagles. Woe unto us, for we are spoiled. O Jerusalem, wash your heart from wickedness, that you may be saved. How long shall your vain thoughts lodge within you? For a voice declares from Dan and publishes affliction from Mount Ephraim. Make mention to the nations, behold, publish against Jerusalem that watchers come from a far country and give out their voice against the cities of Judah. As keepers of a field are they against her round about, because she has been rebellious against me, says the Lord. Your way and your doings have procured these things unto you; this is your wickedness, because it is bitter, because it reaches unto your heart.

3 My bowels, my bowels — I am pained at my very heart, my heart makes a noise in me. I cannot hold my peace because you have heard, O my soul, the sound of the trumpet, the alarm of war. Destruction upon destruction is cried, for the whole land is spoiled; suddenly are my tents spoiled, and my curtains in a moment. How long shall I see the standard and hear the sound of the trumpet? For my people is foolish, they have not known me; they are senseless children and they have no understanding; they are wise to do evil, but to do good they have no knowledge. I beheld the earth, and behold, it was empty and desolate; and the heavens, and they had no light. I beheld the mountains, and behold, they trembled, and all the hills moved lightly. I beheld, and behold, there was no man, and all the birds of the heavens were fled. I beheld, and behold, the fruitful place was a wilderness, and all the cities thereof were broken down at the presence of the Lord and by his fierce anger.

2 For thus has the Lord said: The whole land shall be desolate, yet will I not make a full end. For this shall the earth mourn and the heavens above be black: because I have spoken it, I have purposed it, and will not repent, neither will I turn back from it. The whole city shall flee for the noise of the horsemen and bowmen, they shall go into thickets and climb up upon the rocks; every city shall be forsaken and not a man dwell therein. And when you are spoiled, what will you do? Though you clothe yourself with crimson, though you adorn yourself with ornaments of gold, though you rend your face with painting, in vain shall you make yourself fair; your lovers will despise you, they will seek your life. For I have heard a voice as of a woman in travail, and

the anguish as of her that brings forth her first child, the voice of the daughter of Zion that bewails herself, that spreads her hands, saying, Woe is me now, for my soul is wearied because of murderers.

3 Run to and fro through the streets of Jerusalem and see now, and know, and seek in the broad places thereof, if you can find a man, if there is any that executes judgment, that seeks the truth, and I will pardon it. And though they say, The Lord lives — surely they swear falsely.

4 O Lord, are not your eyes upon the truth? You have stricken them, but they have not grieved; you have consumed them, but they have refused to receive correction; they have made their faces harder than a rock, they have refused to return. Therefore, I said, Surely these are poor; they are foolish, for they know not the way of the Lord, nor the judgment of their God. I will get myself unto the great men and will speak unto them, for they have known the way of the Lord and the judgment of their God; but these have altogether broken the yoke and burst the bonds. Wherefore, a lion out of the forest shall slay them and a wolf of the evenings shall spoil them, a leopard shall watch over their cities; everyone that goes out from there shall be torn in pieces because their transgressions are many and their backslidings are increased. How shall I pardon you for this? Your children have forsaken me and sworn by them that are no gods. When I had fed them to the full, they then committed adultery and assembled themselves by troops in the harlots' houses. They were as fed horses in the morning, everyone neighed after his neighbor's wife. Shall I not visit for these things? — says the Lord. And shall not my soul be avenged on such a nation as this?

5 Go up upon her walls and destroy, but make not a full end; take away her battlements, for they are not the Lord's. For the house of Israel and the house of Judah have dealt very treacherously against me, says the Lord. They have lied about the Lord and said, It is not he, neither shall evil come upon us, neither shall we see sword nor famine. And the prophets shall become wind, and the word is not in them; thus shall it be done unto them. Wherefore, the Lord God of Hosts declares: Because you speak this word, behold, I will make my words in your mouth fire, and this people wood, and it shall devour them. I will bring a nation upon you from far, O house of Israel, says

the Lord. It is a mighty nation, it is an ancient nation, a nation whose language you know not, neither understand what they say. Their quiver is as an open sepulcher, they are all mighty men. And they shall eat up your harvest and your bread which your sons and your daughters should eat; they shall eat up your flocks and your herds; they shall eat up your vines and your fig trees; they shall impoverish your fortified cities wherein you trusted with the sword. Nevertheless, in those days, says the Lord, I will not make a full end with you.

6 And it shall come to pass, when you shall say, Why does the Lord our God do all these things unto us? — then shall you answer them, Like you have forsaken me and served strange gods in your land, so shall you serve strangers in a land that is not yours. Declare this in the house of Jacob and publish it in Judah, saying, Hear now this, O foolish people and without understanding, who have eyes and see not, who have ears and hear not. Do you not fear me? — says the Lord. Will you not tremble at my presence — who have placed the sand for the bound of the sea by a perpetual decree that it cannot pass it? And though the waves thereof toss themselves, yet can they not prevail; though they roar, yet can they not pass over it. But this people has a revolting and a rebellious heart, they are revolted and gone. Neither say they in their heart, Let us now fear the Lord our God that gives rain, both the autumn and the spring in his season; he reserves unto us the appointed weeks of the harvest. Your iniquities have turned away these things and your sins have withheld good things from you. For among my people are found wicked men; they lay wait as he that sets snares, they set a trap, they catch men. As a cage is full of birds, so are their houses full of deceit; therefore, they have become great and have grown rich. They have grown fat, they shine, yea, they surpass the deeds of the wicked. They judge not the cause, the cause of the fatherless, yet they prosper, and the right of the needy do they not judge. Shall I not visit for these things? — says the Lord. Shall not my soul be avenged on such a nation as this?

7 A wonderful and horrible thing is committed in the land: the prophets prophesy falsely, and the priests bear rule by their means, and my people love to have it so. And what will you do in the end thereof?

8 O you children of Benjamin, gather yourselves to flee out of the midst of Jerusalem, and blow the trumpet in Tekoa, and set up a sign

of fire in Bethhaccerem; for evil appears out of the north, and great destruction. I have likened the daughter of Zion to a comely and delicate woman. The shepherds with their flocks shall come unto her, they shall pitch their tents against her round about, they shall feed every one in his place. Prepare war against her, arise and let us go up at noon. Woe unto us, for the day goes away, for the shadows of the evening are stretched out. Arise and let us go by night, and let us destroy her palaces. For thus has the Lord of Hosts said: Hew down trees and cast a mount against Jerusalem. This is the city to be visited, she is full of oppression in her midst. As a fountain casts out her waters, so she casts out her wickedness. Violence and spoil is heard in her, before me continually is grief and wounds. Be instructed, O Jerusalem, lest my soul depart from you, lest I make you desolate, a land not inhabited.

⁹ Thus says the Lord of Hosts: They shall thoroughly glean the remnant of Israel as a vine; turn back your hand as a grape-gatherer into the baskets. To whom shall I speak and give warning, that they may hear? Behold, their ear is uncircumcised and they cannot listen; behold, the word of the Lord is unto them a reproach, they have no delight in it. Therefore, I am full of the fury of the Lord, I am weary with holding in. I will pour it out upon the children abroad and upon the assembly of young men together; for even the husband with the wife shall be taken, the aged with him that is full of days. And their houses shall be turned unto others with their fields and wives together, for I will stretch out my hand upon the inhabitants of the land, says the Lord. For from the least of them even unto the greatest of them, everyone is given to covetousness, and from the prophet even unto the priest, everyone deals falsely. They have healed also the hurt of the daughter of my people slightly, saying, Peace, peace — when there is no peace. Were they ashamed when they had committed abomination? Nay, they were not at all ashamed, neither could they blush. Therefore, they shall fall among them that fall; at the time that I visit them, they shall be cast down, says the Lord. Thus says the Lord: Stand in the ways and see, and ask for the old paths where is the good way, and walk therein, and you shall find rest for your souls. But they said, We will not walk therein. Also, I set watchmen over you, saying, Listen to the sound of the trumpet. But they said, We will not listen.

¹⁰ Therefore, hear, you nations, and know, O congregation, what is among them. Hear, O earth, behold, I will bring evil upon this people, even the fruit of their thoughts, because they have not listened unto my words, nor to my law, but rejected it. To what purpose comes there to me incense from Sheba, and the sweet cane from a far country? Your burnt offerings are not acceptable, nor your sacrifices sweet unto me. Therefore, thus says the Lord: Behold, I will lay stumbling blocks before this people, and the fathers and the sons together shall fall upon them, the neighbor and his friend shall perish. Thus says the Lord: Behold, a people comes from the north country, and a great nation shall be raised from the sides of the earth. They shall lay hold on bow and spear, they are cruel and have no mercy, their voice roars like the sea, and they ride upon horses set in array as men for war against you, O daughter of Zion. We have heard the fame thereof, our hands wax feeble, anguish has taken hold of us, and pain as of a woman in travail. Go not forth into the field nor walk by the way, for the sword of the enemy and fear is on every side. O daughter of my people, gird yourself with sackcloth and wallow yourself in ashes, make yourself mourn as for an only son, a most bitter lamentation, for the spoiler shall suddenly come upon us. I have set you for a tower and a fortress among my people, that you may know and try their way. They are all grievous revolters, walking with slanders. They are brass and iron, they are all corrupters. The bellows are burned, the lead is consumed of the fire; the founder melts in vain, for the wicked are not plucked away. Reprobate silver shall men call them because the Lord has rejected them.

4 The word that came to Jeremiah from the Lord, saying, Stand in the gate of the Lord's house and proclaim there this word, and say, Hear the word of the Lord, all you of Judah that enter in at these gates to worship the Lord. Thus says the Lord of Hosts, the God of Israel: Amend your ways and your doings, and I will cause you to dwell in this place. Trust not in lying words, saying, The temple of the Lord, the temple of the Lord, the temple of the Lord are these. For if you thoroughly amend your ways and your doings, if you thoroughly execute judgment between a man and his neighbor, if you oppress not the stranger, the fatherless, and the widow, and shed not innocent blood in this place, neither walk after other gods to your hurt, then

will I cause you to dwell in this place, in the land that I gave to your fathers, for ever and ever.

2 Behold, you trust in lying words that cannot profit. Will you steal, murder, and commit adultery, and swear falsely, and burn incense unto Baal, and walk after other gods whom you know not, and come and stand before me in this house which is called by my name, and say, We are delivered to do all these abominations? Has this house which is called by my name become a den of robbers in your eyes? Behold, even I have seen it, says the Lord. But go now unto my place which was in Shiloh, where I set my name at the first, and see what I did to it for the wickedness of my people Israel. And now because you have done all these works, says the Lord, and I spoke unto you, rising up early and speaking but you heard not, and I called you but you answered not, therefore will I do unto this house which is called by my name, wherein you trust, and unto the place which I gave to you and to your fathers, as I have done to Shiloh. And I will cast you out of my sight as I have cast out all your brethren, even the whole seed of Ephraim. Therefore, pray not for this people, neither lift up cry nor prayer for them, neither make intercession to me, for I will not hear you. Do you not see what they do in the cities of Judah and in the streets of Jerusalem? The children gather wood, and the fathers kindle the fire, and the women knead their dough, to make cakes to the queen of Heaven and to pour out drink offerings unto other gods, that they may provoke me to anger. Do they provoke me to anger? — says the Lord. Do they not provoke themselves to the confusion of their own faces? Therefore, thus says the Lord: Behold, my anger and my fury shall be poured out upon this place — upon man and upon beast, and upon the trees of the field, and upon the fruit of the ground; and it shall burn and shall not be quenched.

3 Thus says the Lord of Hosts, the God of Israel: Put your burnt offerings unto your sacrifices and eat flesh. For I spoke not unto your fathers nor commanded them in the day that I brought them out of the land of Egypt concerning burnt offerings or sacrifices, but this thing I commanded them, saying, Obey my voice and I will be your God, and you shall be my people, and walk in all the ways that I have commanded you, that it may be well unto you. But they listened not, nor inclined their ear, but walked in the counsels and in the imagination of their

evil heart, and went backward and not forward. Since the day that your fathers came forth out of the land of Egypt unto this day, I have even sent unto you all my servants the prophets, daily rising up early and sending them. Yet they listened not unto me, nor inclined their ear, but hardened their neck; they did worse than their fathers. Therefore, you shall speak all these words unto them, but they will not listen to you; you shall also call unto them, but they will not answer you. But you shall say unto them, This is a nation that obeys not the voice of the Lord their God, nor receives correction; truth is perished and is cut off from their mouth.

4 Cut off your hair, O Jerusalem, and cast it away, and take up a lamentation on high places; for the Lord has rejected and forsaken the generation of his wrath. For the children of Judah have done evil in my sight, says the Lord, they have set their abominations in the house which is called by my name, to pollute it. And they have built the high places of Topheth, which is in the valley of the son of Hinnom, to burn their sons and their daughters in the fire which I commanded them not, neither came it into my heart. Therefore, behold, the days come, says the Lord, that it shall no more be called Topheth, nor the valley of the son of Hinnom, but the valley of slaughter; for they shall bury in Topheth until there is no place. And the carcasses of this people shall be food for the fowls of the heaven and for the beasts of the earth, and none shall frighten them away. Then will I cause to cease from the cities of Judah and from the streets of Jerusalem the voice of mirth and the voice of gladness, the voice of the bridegroom and the voice of the bride, for the land shall be desolate.

5 At that time, says the Lord, they shall bring out the bones of the kings of Judah, and the bones of his princes, and the bones of the priests, and the bones of the prophets, and the bones of the inhabitants of Jerusalem out of their graves. And they shall spread them before the sun and the moon and all the host of heaven, whom they have loved and whom they have served, and after whom they have walked, and whom they have sought, and whom they have worshipped. They shall not be gathered, nor be buried; they shall be for dung upon the face of the earth. And death shall be chosen rather than life by all the residue of them that remain of this evil family, who remain in all the places where I have driven them, says the Lord of Hosts.

6 Moreover, you shall say unto them, Thus says the Lord: Shall they fall, and not arise? Shall he turn away and not return? Why then is this people of Jerusalem slid back by a perpetual backsliding? They hold fast to deceit, they refuse to return. I listened and heard, but they spoke not aright; no man repents him of his wickedness, saying, What have I done? Everyone turned to his own course, as the horse rushes into the battle. Yea, the stork in the heavens knows her appointed times, and the turtledove, and the crane and the swallow observe the time of their coming, but my people know not the judgment of the Lord.

7 How do you say, We are wise and the law of the Lord is with us? Behold, certainly in vain he made it, the pen of the scribes is in vain. The wise men are ashamed, they are dismayed and taken. Behold, they have rejected the word of the Lord, and what wisdom is in them? Therefore will I give their wives unto others, and their fields to them that shall inherit them; for everyone from the least even unto the greatest is given to covetousness, from the prophet even unto the priest, everyone deals falsely. For they have healed the hurt of the daughter of my people slightly, saying, Peace, peace — when there is no peace. Were they ashamed when they had committed abomination? Nay, they were not at all ashamed, neither could they blush. Therefore shall they fall among them that fall, in the time of their visitation they shall be cast down, says the Lord. I will surely consume them, says the Lord. There shall be no grapes on the vine, nor figs on the fig tree, and the leaf shall fade, and the things that I have given them shall pass away from them.

8 Why do we sit still? Assemble yourselves and let us enter into the fortified cities, and let us be silent there; for the Lord our God has put us to silence and given us water of gall to drink, because we have sinned against the Lord. We looked for peace, but no good came, and for a time of health, and behold — trouble. The snorting of his horses was heard from Dan, the whole land trembled at the sound of the neighing of his strong ones, for they have come and have devoured the land and all that is in it, the city and those that dwell therein. For behold, I will send serpents, cockatrices among you, which will not be charmed, and they shall bite you, says the Lord.

9 When I would comfort myself against sorrow, my heart is faint in me. Behold the voice of the cry of the daughter of my people because of them that dwell in a far country: Is not the Lord in Zion? Is not her

king in her? Why have they provoked me to anger with their engraved images and with strange vanities? The harvest is past, the summer is ended, and we are not saved. For the hurt of the daughter of my people am I hurt; I am black, astonishment has taken hold on me. Is there no balm in Gilead? Is there no physician there? Why then is not the health of the daughter of my people recovered?

10 Oh that my head were waters and my eyes a fountain of tears, that I might weep day and night for the slain of the daughter of my people. Oh that I had in the wilderness a lodging place of wayfaring men, that I might leave my people and go from them. For they are all adulterers, an assembly of treacherous men. And they bend their tongue like their bow for lies, but they are not valiant for the truth upon the earth; for they proceed from evil to evil and they know not me, says the Lord. Take heed everyone of his neighbor and trust not in any brother, for every brother will utterly supplant and every neighbor will walk with slanders. And they will deceive everyone his neighbor and will not speak the truth, they have taught their tongue to speak lies and weary themselves to commit iniquity. Your habitation is in the midst of deceit, through deceit they refuse to know me, says the Lord. Therefore, thus says the Lord of Hosts: Behold, I will melt them and try them, for how shall I do for the daughter of my people? Their tongue is as an arrow shot out, it speaks deceit; one speaks peaceably to his neighbor with his mouth, but in heart he lays his wait. Shall I not visit them for these things? — says the Lord. Shall not my soul be avenged on such a nation as this?

11 For the mountains will I take up a weeping and wailing, and for the habitations of the wilderness a lamentation, because they are burned up so that none can pass through them, neither can men hear the voice of the cattle. Both the fowl of the heavens and the beast are fled, they have gone. And I will make Jerusalem heaps and a den of dragons, and I will make the cities of Judah desolate without an inhabitant. Who is the wise man that may understand this? And who is he to whom the mouth of the Lord has spoken, that he may declare it? For the land perishes and is burned up like a wilderness, that none passes through. And the Lord says, Because they have forsaken my law which I set before them, and have not obeyed my voice, neither walked therein, but have walked after the imagination of their own heart, and

after the Baalim, which their fathers taught them, therefore, thus says the Lord of Hosts, the God of Israel: Behold, I will feed them, even this people, with wormwood, and give them water of gall to drink. I will scatter them also among the heathen whom neither they nor their fathers have known, and I will send a sword after them until I have consumed them.

12 Thus says the Lord of Hosts: Consider and call for the mourning women, that they may come, and send for skilled women, that they may come; and let them make haste and take up a wailing for us, that our eyes may run down with tears and our eyelids gush out with waters. For a voice of wailing is heard out of Zion, How are we spoiled! We are greatly confounded because we have forsaken the land, because our dwellings have cast us out. Yet hear the word of the Lord, O you women, and let your ear receive the word of his mouth, and teach your daughters wailing and everyone her neighbor lamentation. For death has come up into our windows and is entered into our palaces, to cut off the children from outside and the young men from the streets. Speak, Thus says the Lord: Even the carcasses of men shall fall as dung upon the open field, and as the handful after the harvestman, and none shall gather them.

13 Thus says the Lord: Let not the wise man glory in his wisdom, neither let the mighty man glory in his might; let not the rich man glory in his riches. But let him that glories glory in this: that he understands and knows me, that I am the Lord who exercises loving kindness, judgment, and righteousness in the earth, for in these things I delight, says the Lord. Behold, the days come, says the Lord, that I will punish all them who are circumcised with the uncircumcised — Egypt, and Judah, and Edom, and the children of Ammon, and Moab, and all that are in the utmost corners that dwell in the wilderness, for all these nations are uncircumcised, and all the house of Israel are uncircumcised in the heart.

14 Hear the word which the Lord speaks unto you, O house of Israel; thus says the Lord: Learn not the way of the heathen and be not dismayed at the signs of heaven, for the heathen are dismayed at them, for the customs of the people are vain. For one cuts a tree out of the forest, the work of the hands of the workman with the axe. They adorn it with silver and with gold, they fasten it with nails and with

hammers that it move not. They are upright as the palm tree, but speak not; they must be borne because they cannot go. Be not afraid of them, for they cannot do evil, neither also is it in them to do good.

¹⁵ Forasmuch as there is none like unto you, O Lord, you are great and your name is great in might. Who would not fear you, O king of nations? For to you does it appertain, forasmuch as among all the wise men of the nations and in all their kingdoms, there is none like unto you. But they are altogether brutish and foolish, the stock is a doctrine of vanities. Silver spread into plates is brought from Tarshish, and gold from Uphaz, the work of the workman and of the hands of the founder; blue and purple is their clothing, they are all the work of skilled men. But the Lord is the true God, he is the living God and an everlasting king. At his wrath the earth shall tremble and the nations shall not be able to endure his indignation.

¹⁶ Thus shall you say unto them: The gods that have not made the heavens and the earth, even they shall perish from the earth and from under these heavens. He has made the earth by his power, he has established the world by his wisdom, and has stretched out the heavens by his discretion. When he utters his voice, there is a multitude of waters in the heavens, and he causes the vapors to ascend from the ends of the earth. He makes lightnings with rain and brings forth the wind out of his treasuries. Every man is brutish in his knowledge, every founder is confounded by the engraved image; for his molten image is falsehood and there is no breath in them. They are vanity and the work of errors. In the time of their visitation, they shall perish. The portion of Jacob is not like them, for he is the former of all things, and Israel is the rod of his inheritance. The Lord of Hosts is his name.

¹⁷ Gather up your wares out of the land, O inhabitant of the fortress, for thus says the Lord: Behold, I will sling out the inhabitants of the land at this once and will distress them, that they may find it so. Woe is me for my hurt, my wound is grievous. But I said, Truly this is a grief, and I must bear it. My tabernacle is spoiled and all my cords are broken, my children have gone forth of me and they are not, there is none to stretch forth my tent anymore and to set up my curtains. For the shepherds have become brutish and have not sought the Lord; therefore, they shall not prosper, and all their flocks shall be scattered. Behold, the noise of the report has come and a great commotion out

of the north country, to make the cities of Judah desolate and a den of dragons.

18 O Lord, I know that the way of man is not in himself, it is not in man that walks to direct his steps. O Lord, correct me — but with judgment, not in your anger, lest you bring me to nothing. Pour out your fury upon the heathen that know you not, and upon the families that call not on your name; for they have eaten up Jacob, and devoured him, and consumed him, and have made his habitation desolate.

5 The word that came to Jeremiah from the Lord, saying, Hear the words of this covenant, and speak unto the men of Judah and to the inhabitants of Jerusalem, and say unto them, Thus says the Lord God of Israel: Cursed be the man that obeys not the words of this covenant which I commanded your fathers in the day that I brought them forth out of the land of Egypt, from the iron furnace, saying, Obey my voice and do them, according to all which I command you. So shall you be my people and I will be your God, that I may perform the oath which I have sworn unto your fathers — to give them a land flowing with milk and honey, as it is this day. Then I answered and said, So be it, O Lord. Then the Lord said unto me, Proclaim all these words in the cities of Judah and in the streets of Jerusalem, saying, Hear the words of this covenant and do them. For I earnestly protested unto your fathers in the day that I brought them up out of the land of Egypt, even unto this day, rising early and protesting, saying, Obey my voice. Yet they obeyed not, nor inclined their ear, but walked everyone in the imagination of their evil heart. Therefore, I will bring upon them all the words of this covenant which I commanded them to do but they did them not. And the Lord said unto me, A conspiracy is found among the men of Judah and among the inhabitants of Jerusalem. They are turned back to the iniquities of their forefathers, who refused to hear my words, and they went after other gods to serve them; the house of Israel and the house of Judah have broken my covenant which I made with their fathers. Therefore, thus says the Lord: Behold, I will bring evil upon them which they shall not be able to escape, and though they shall cry unto me, I will not listen unto them. Then shall the cities of Judah and inhabitants of Jerusalem go and cry unto the gods unto whom they offer incense, but they shall not save them at all in the time of their

trouble. For according to the number of your cities were your gods, O Judah, and according to the number of the streets of Jerusalem have you set up altars to that shameful thing, even altars to burn incense unto Baal. Therefore, pray not for this people, neither lift up a cry or prayer for them, for I will not hear them in the time that they cry unto me for their trouble.

2 What has my beloved to do in my house, seeing she has wrought lewdness with many and the holy flesh is passed from you? When you do evil, then you rejoice. The Lord called your name a green olive tree, fair, and of goodly fruit; with the noise of a great tumult he has kindled fire upon it, and the branches of it are broken. For the Lord of Hosts that planted you has pronounced evil against you, for the evil of the house of Israel and of the house of Judah, which they have done against themselves to provoke me to anger in offering incense unto Baal. And the Lord has given me knowledge of it and I know it; then you showed me their doings. But I was like a lamb or an ox that is brought to the slaughter, and I knew not that they had devised devices against me, saying, Let us destroy the tree with the fruit thereof, and let us cut him off from the land of the living, that his name may be no more remembered. But, O Lord of Hosts who judges righteously, who tries the reins and the heart, let me see your vengeance on them, for unto you have I revealed my cause.

3 Therefore, thus says the Lord of the men of Anathoth — who seek your life, saying, Prophesy not in the name of the Lord, that you die not by our hand — therefore, thus says the Lord of Hosts: Behold, I will punish them; the young men shall die by the sword, their sons and their daughters shall die by famine. And there shall be no remnant of them, for I will bring evil upon the men of Anathoth, even the year of their visitation.

4 Righteous are you, O Lord, when I plead with you; yet let me talk with you of your judgments. Why does the way of the wicked prosper? Why are they all happy that deal very treacherously? You have planted them, yea, they have taken root; they grow, yea, they bring forth fruit. You are near in their mouth and far from their reins. But you, O Lord, know me, you have seen me and tried my heart toward you. Pull them out like sheep for the slaughter and prepare them for the day of slaughter. How long shall the land mourn and the herbs

of every field wither for the wickedness of them that dwell therein? The beasts are consumed, and the birds, because they said, He shall not see our latter end.

5 If you have run with the foot soldiers and they have wearied you, then how can you contend with horses? And if in the land of peace, wherein you trusted, they wearied you, then how will you do in the swelling of Jordan? For even your brethren and the house of your father, even they have dealt treacherously with you, yea, they have called a multitude after you. Believe them not, though they speak fair words unto you.

6 I have forsaken my house, I have left my heritage; I have given the dearly beloved of my soul into the hand of her enemies. My heritage is unto me as a lion in the forest: it cries out against me; therefore have I hated it. My heritage is unto me as a speckled bird, the birds round about are against her. Come, assemble all the beasts of the field, come to devour. Many shepherds have destroyed my vineyard, they have trodden my portion underfoot, they have made my pleasant portion a desolate wilderness. They have made it desolate, and being desolate, it mourns unto me. The whole land is made desolate because no man lays it to heart. The spoilers have come upon all high places through the wilderness. For the sword of the Lord shall devour from the one end of the land even to the other end of the land; no flesh shall have peace. They have sown wheat, but shall reap thorns; they have put themselves to pain, but shall not profit. And they shall be ashamed of your revenues because of the fierce anger of the Lord.

7 Thus says the Lord: Concerning all my evil neighbors that touch the inheritance which I have caused my people Israel to inherit, behold, I will pluck them out of their land, and pluck out the house of Judah from among them. And it shall come to pass, after I have plucked them out, I will return and have compassion on them, and will bring them again, every man to his heritage and every man to his land. And it shall come to pass, if they will diligently learn the ways of my people, to swear, by my name, The lord lives — as they taught my people to swear by Baal — then shall they be built in the midst of my people. But if they will not obey, I will utterly pluck up and destroy that nation, says the Lord.

8 Thus says the Lord unto me: Go and get yourself a linen girdle and put it upon your loins, and put it not in water. So I got a girdle according to the word of the Lord and put it on my loins. And the word of the Lord came unto me the second time, saying, Take the girdle that you have gotten, which is upon your loins, and arise; go to Euphrates and hide it there in a hole of the rock. So I went and hid it by Euphrates, as the Lord commanded me. And it came to pass after many days that the Lord said unto me, Arise, go to Euphrates and take the girdle from there, which I commanded you to hide there. Then I went to Euphrates and dug and took the girdle from the place where I had hidden it; and behold, the girdle was marred, it was profitable for nothing. Then the word of the Lord came unto me, saying, Thus says the Lord: After this manner will I mar the pride of Judah and the great pride of Jerusalem. This evil people who refuse to hear my words, who walk in the imagination of their heart and walk after other gods, to serve them and to worship them, shall even be as this girdle which is good for nothing. For as the girdle cleaves to the loins of a man, so have I caused to cleave unto me the whole house of Israel and the whole house of Judah, says the Lord, that they might be unto me for a people, and for a name, and for a praise, and for a glory; but they would not hear.

9 Therefore, you shall speak unto them this word: Thus says the Lord God of Israel: Every bottle shall be filled with wine, and they shall say unto you, Do we not certainly know that every bottle shall be filled with wine? Then shall you say unto them, Thus says the Lord: Behold, I will fill all the inhabitants of this land — even the kings that sit upon David's throne, and the priests, and the prophets, and all the inhabitants of Jerusalem — with drunkenness. And I will dash them one against another, even the fathers and the sons together, says the Lord. I will not pity, nor spare, nor have mercy, but destroy them. Hear and give ear. Be not proud, for the Lord has spoken. Give glory to the Lord your God before he cause darkness and before your feet stumble upon the dark mountains, and while you look for light he turn it into the shadow of death and make it gross darkness.

10 But if you will not hear it, my soul shall weep in secret places for your pride, and my eyes shall weep bitterly and run down with tears because the Lord's flock is carried away captive. Say unto the king and

to the queen, Humble yourselves, sit down, for your principalities shall come down, even the crown of your glory. The cities of the south shall be shut up and none shall open them; Judah shall be carried away captive, all of it; it shall be wholly carried away captive. Lift up your eyes and behold them that come from the north. Where is the flock that was given you — your beautiful flock? What will you say when he shall punish you? For you have taught them to be captains and as chief over you. Shall not sorrows take you as a woman in travail? And if you say in your heart, Why come these things upon me? — for the greatness of your iniquity are your skirts uncovered and your heels made bare. Can the Ethiopian change his skin, or the leopard his spots? Then may you also do good that are accustomed to do evil. Therefore will I scatter them as the stubble that passes away by the wind of the wilderness. This is your lot, the portion of your measures from me, says the Lord, because you have forgotten me and trusted in falsehood. Therefore will I strip bare your skirts upon your face, that your shame may appear. I have seen your adulteries and your neighings, the lewdness of your whoredom and your abominations on the hills in the fields. Woe unto you, O Jerusalem. Will you not be made clean? When shall it once be?

The word of the Lord that came to Jeremiah concerning the dearth.

6 Judah mourns and the gates thereof languish, they are black unto the ground, and the cry of Jerusalem is gone up. And their nobles have sent their little ones to the waters; they came to the pits and found no water, they returned with their vessels empty. They were ashamed and confounded, and covered their heads. Because the ground is chapped, for there was no rain in the earth, the plowmen were ashamed, they covered their heads. Yea, the hind also calved in the field and forsook it, because there was no grass. And the wild asses did stand in the high places, they snuffed up the wind like dragons, their eyes did fail because there was no grass.

2 O Lord, though our iniquities testify against us, do it for your name's sake; for our backslidings are many, we have sinned against you. O the hope of Israel, the Savior thereof in time of trouble, why should you be as a stranger in the land and as a wayfaring man that turns aside to stay for a night? Why should you be as a man astonished, as a mighty man that cannot save? Yet you, O Lord, are in our midst and

we are called by your name; leave us not. Thus says the Lord unto this people: Thus have they loved to wander, they have not restrained their feet; therefore, the Lord does not accept them, he will now remember their iniquity and visit their sins. Then said the Lord unto me, Pray not for this people for their good. When they fast, I will not hear their cry, and when they offer burnt offering and meal offering, I will not accept them, but I will consume them by the sword, and by the famine, and by the pestilence.

³ Then said I, Ah, Lord God. Behold, the prophets say unto them, You shall not see the sword, neither shall you have famine, but I will give you assured peace in this place. Then the Lord said unto me, The prophets prophesy lies in my name. I sent them not, neither have I commanded them, neither spoke unto them. They prophesy unto you a false vision and divination, and a thing of naught, and the deceit of their heart. Therefore, thus says the Lord concerning the prophets that prophesy in my name (and I sent them not, yet they say, Sword and famine shall not be in this land): By sword and famine shall those prophets be consumed. And the people to whom they prophesy shall be cast out in the streets of Jerusalem because of the famine and the sword, and they shall have none to bury them — them, their wives, nor their sons, nor their daughters; for I will pour their wickedness upon them. Therefore, you shall say this word unto them: Let my eyes run down with tears night and day, and let them not cease, for the virgin daughter of my people is broken with a great breach, with a very grievous blow. If I go forth into the field, then behold the slain with the sword. And if I enter into the city, then behold them that are sick with famine. Yea, both the prophet and the priest go about into a land that they know not.

⁴ Have you utterly rejected Judah? Has your soul loathed Zion? Why have you smitten us and there is no healing for us? We looked for peace and there is no good, and for the time of healing, and behold trouble. We acknowledge, O Lord, our wickedness, and the iniquity of our fathers, for we have sinned against you. Do not abhor us for your name's sake, do not disgrace the throne of your glory; remember, break not your covenant with us. Are there any among the vanities of the gentiles that can cause rain? Or can the heavens give showers? Are

not you he, O Lord our God? Therefore, we will wait upon you, for you have made all these things.

⁵ Then said the Lord unto me, Though Moses and Samuel stood before me, yet my mind could not be toward this people. Cast them out of my sight and let them go forth. And it shall come to pass, if they say unto you, Where shall we go forth? — then you shall tell them, Thus says the Lord: Such as are for death, to death, and such as are for the sword, to the sword, and such as are for the famine, to the famine, and such as are for the captivity, to the captivity. And I will appoint over them four kinds, says the Lord: the sword to slay, and the dogs to tear, and the fowls of the heaven and the beasts of the earth to devour and destroy. And I will cause them to be removed into all kingdoms of the earth because of Manasseh the son of Hezekiah, king of Judah, for that which he did in Jerusalem. For who shall have pity upon you, O Jerusalem? Or who shall bemoan you? Or who shall go aside to ask how you are doing? You have forsaken me, says the Lord, you have gone backward; therefore will I stretch out my hand against you and destroy you. I am weary with repenting. And I will winnow them with a winnowing shovel in the gates of the land, I will bereave them of children, I will destroy my people since they return not from their ways. Their widows are increased to me above the sand of the seas, I have brought upon them — against the mother of the young men — a spoiler at noonday. I have caused him to fall upon it suddenly, and terrors upon the city. She that has borne seven languishes, she has given up the ghost; her sun has gone down while it was yet day, she has been ashamed and confounded. And the residue of them will I deliver to the sword before their enemies, says the Lord.

⁶ Woe is me, my mother, that you have borne me, a man of strife and a man of contention to the whole earth. I have neither lent on usury, nor have men lent to me on usury, yet every one of them does curse me. The Lord said, Truly it shall be well with your remnant, truly I will cause the enemy to treat you well in the time of evil and in the time of affliction. Shall iron break — the northern iron — and the steel? Your substance and your treasures will I give to the spoil without price, and that for all your sins, even in all your borders. And I will make you to pass with your enemies into a land which you know not, for a fire is kindled in my anger which shall burn upon you.

7 O Lord, you know, remember me and visit me, and avenge me of my persecutors. Take me not away in your long-suffering, know that for your sake I have suffered rebuke. Your words were found and I did eat them, and your word was unto me the joy and rejoicing of my heart, for I am called by your name, O Lord God of Hosts. I sat not in the assembly of the mockers, nor rejoiced; I sat alone because of your hand, for you have filled me with indignation. Why is my pain perpetual and my wound incurable, which refuses to be healed? Will you be altogether unto me as a liar and as waters that fail?

8 Therefore, thus says the Lord: If you return, then will I bring you again and you shall stand before me; and if you take forth the precious from the vile, you shall be as my mouth. Let them return unto you, but return not unto them. And I will make you unto this people a fortified brazen wall; and they shall fight against you, but they shall not prevail against you, for I am with you, to save you and to deliver you, says the Lord. And I will deliver you out of the hand of the wicked and I will redeem you out of the hand of the terrible.

9 The word of the Lord came also unto me, saying, You shall not take a wife, neither shall you have sons or daughters in this place. For thus says the Lord concerning the sons and concerning the daughters that are born in this place, and concerning their mothers that bore them, and concerning their fathers that begot them in this land: They shall die of grievous deaths, they shall not be lamented, neither shall they be buried, but they shall be as dung upon the face of the earth; and they shall be consumed by the sword and by famine, and their carcasses shall be food for the fowls of heaven and for the beasts of the earth. For thus says the Lord: Enter not into the house of mourning, neither go to lament nor bemoan them, for I have taken away my peace from this people, says the Lord, even loving kindness and mercies. Both the great and the small shall die in this land; they shall not be buried, neither shall men lament for them, nor cut themselves, nor make themselves bald for them. Neither shall men tear themselves for them in mourning, to comfort them for the dead, neither shall men give them the cup of consolation to drink for their father or for their mother. You shall not also go into the house of feasting, to sit with them to eat and to drink. For thus says the Lord of Hosts, the God of Israel: Behold, I will cause to cease out of this place, in your eyes and in your days, the

voice of mirth and the voice of gladness, the voice of the bridegroom and the voice of the bride. And it shall come to pass, when you shall show this people all these words and they shall say unto you, Why has the Lord pronounced all this great evil against us? — or, What is our iniquity? — or, What is our sin that we have committed against the Lord our God? — then shall you say unto them, Because your fathers have forsaken me, says the Lord, and have walked after other gods, and have served them and have worshipped them, and have forsaken me and have not kept my law. And you have done worse than your fathers, for behold, you walk every one after the imagination of his evil heart, that they may not listen unto me. Therefore will I cast you out of this land into a land that you know not, neither you nor your fathers, and there shall you serve other gods day and night, where I will not show you favor.

10 Therefore, behold, the days come, says the Lord, that it shall no more be said, The Lord lives that brought up the children of Israel out of the land of Egypt — but, The Lord lives that brought up the children of Israel from the land of the north, and from all the lands to which he had driven them; and I will bring them again into their land that I gave unto their fathers. Behold, I will send for many fishers, says the Lord, and they shall fish them, and after will I send for many hunters, and they shall hunt them from every mountain, and from every hill, and out of the holes of the rocks. For my eyes are upon all their ways, they are not hidden from my face, neither is their iniquity hidden from my eyes. And first I will recompense their iniquity and their sin double, because they have defiled my land, they have filled my inheritance with the carcasses of their detestable and abominable things. O Lord, my strength, and my fortress, and my refuge in the day of affliction, the gentiles shall come unto you from the ends of the earth and shall say, Surely our fathers have inherited lies, vanity and things wherein there is no profit. Shall a man make gods unto himself? And they are no gods. Therefore, behold, I will this once cause them to know, I will cause them to know my hand and my might, and they shall know that my name is The Lord.

11 The sin of Judah is written with a pen of iron and with the point of a diamond, it is engraved upon the tablet of their heart and upon the horns of your altars, while their children remember their altars and

their groves by the green trees upon the high hills. O my mountain in the field, I will give your substance and all your treasures to the spoil, and your high places for sin, throughout all your borders. And you, even yourself, shall discontinue from your heritage that I gave you. And I will cause you to serve your enemies in the land which you know not, for you have kindled a fire in my anger which shall burn for ever.

12 Thus says the Lord: Cursed be the man that trusts in man and makes flesh his arm, and whose heart departs from the Lord. For he shall be like the bush in the desert and shall not see when good comes, but shall inhabit the parched places in the wilderness, in a salt land and not inhabited. Blessed is the man that trusts in the Lord and whose hope the Lord is, for he shall be as a tree planted by the waters and that spreads out her roots by the river, and shall not see when heat comes, but her leaf shall be green and shall not be anxious in the year of drought, neither shall cease from yielding fruit.

13 The heart is deceitful above all things and desperately wicked; who can know it? I the Lord search the heart, I try the reins, even to give every man according to his ways and according to the fruit of his doings. As the partridge sits on eggs and hatches them not, so he that gets riches and not by right shall leave them in the middle of his days, and at his end shall be a fool.

7 A glorious high throne from the beginning is the place of our sanctuary. O Lord, the hope of Israel, all that forsake you shall be ashamed, and they that depart from me shall be written in the earth, because they have forsaken the Lord, the fountain of living waters. Heal me, O Lord, and I shall be healed; save me and I shall be saved, for you are my praise. Behold, they say unto me, Where is the word of the Lord? Let it come now. As for me, I have not hastened from being a shepherd to follow you, neither have I desired the woeful day. You know that which came out of my lips was right before you. Be not a terror unto me, you are my hope in the day of evil. Let them be confounded that persecute me, but let not me be confounded; let them be dismayed, but let not me be dismayed; bring upon them the day of evil and destroy them with double destruction.

2 Thus said the Lord unto me: Go and stand in the gate of the children of the people whereby the kings of Judah come in and by which they

go out, and in all the gates of Jerusalem, and say unto them, Hear the word of the Lord, you kings of Judah, and all Judah, and all the inhabitants of Jerusalem that enter in by these gates; thus says the Lord: Take heed to yourselves and bear no burden on the Sabbath day, nor bring it in by the gates of Jerusalem, neither carry forth a burden out of your houses on the Sabbath day, neither do any work, but hallow the Sabbath day as I commanded your fathers. But they obeyed not, neither inclined their ear, but made their neck stiff, that they might not hear nor receive instruction. And it shall come to pass, if you diligently listen unto me, says the Lord, to bring in no burden through the gates of this city on the Sabbath day, but hallow the Sabbath day to do no work therein, then shall there enter into the gates of this city kings and princes sitting upon the throne of David, riding in chariots and on horses, they and their princes, the men of Judah and the inhabitants of Jerusalem; and this city shall remain for ever. And they shall come from the cities of Judah, and from the places about Jerusalem, and from the land of Benjamin, and from the plain, and from the mountains, and from the south, bringing burnt offerings, and sacrifices, and meal offerings, and incense, and bringing sacrifices of praise unto the house of the Lord. But if you will not listen unto me, to hallow the Sabbath day and not to bear a burden, even entering in at the gates of Jerusalem on the Sabbath day, then will I kindle a fire in the gates thereof, and it shall devour the palaces of Jerusalem and it shall not be quenched.

8 The word which came to Jeremiah from the Lord, saying, Arise, and go down to the potter's house, and there I will cause you to hear my words. Then I went down to the potter's house, and behold, he wrought a work on the wheels. And the vessel that he made of clay was marred in the hand of the potter, so he made it again, another vessel as seemed good to the potter to make it. Then the word of the Lord came to me, saying, O house of Israel, cannot I do with you as this potter? — says the Lord. Behold, as the clay is in the potter's hand, so are you in my hand, O house of Israel. At what moment I shall speak concerning a nation and concerning a kingdom, to pluck up and to pull down and to destroy it, if that nation against whom I have pronounced turn from their evil, I will withhold the evil that I thought to do unto

them. And at what moment I shall speak concerning a nation and concerning a kingdom, to build and to plant it, if it do evil in my sight, that it obey not my voice, then I will withhold the good with which I said I would benefit them.

2 Now therefore go to speak to the men of Judah and to the inhabitants of Jerusalem, saying, Thus says the Lord: Behold, I frame evil against you and devise a device against you. Return now, everyone from his evil way, and make your ways and your doings good. And they said, There is no hope, but we will walk after our own devices and we will everyone do the imagination of his evil heart. Therefore, thus says the Lord: Ask now among the heathen, Who has heard such things? The virgin of Israel has done a very horrible thing. Will you not leave the snow of the fields of Lebanon? Shall not the cold, flowing waters that come from another place, from the rock, be forsaken? Because my people has forgotten me, they have burned incense to vanity, and they have caused them to stumble in their ways from the ancient paths — to walk in paths, in a way not cast up — to make their land desolate and a perpetual hissing. Everyone that passes thereby shall be astonished and wag his head. I will scatter them as with an east wind before the enemy, I will show them the back and not the face in the day of their calamity.

3 Then said they, Come and let us devise devices against Jeremiah, for the law shall not perish from the priest, nor counsel from the wise, nor the word from the prophet. Come and let us smite him with the tongue, and let us not give heed to any of his words. Give heed to me, O Lord, and listen to the voice of them that contend with me. Shall evil be recompensed for good? For they have dug a pit for my soul. Remember that I stood before you to speak good for them, and to turn away your wrath from them. Therefore, deliver up their children to the famine, and pour out their blood by the force of the sword, and let their wives be bereaved of their children and be widows, and let their men be put to death. Let their young men be slain by the sword in battle. Let a cry be heard from their houses when you shall bring a troop suddenly upon them. For they have dug a pit to take me, and hidden snares for my feet. Yet, Lord, you know all their counsel against me to slay me; forgive not their iniquity, neither blot out their sin from your sight, but let them be overthrown before you; deal thus with them in the time of your anger.

⁴ Thus says the Lord: Go and get a potter's earthen bottle, and take of the elders of the people and of the elders of the priests, and go forth unto the valley of the son of Hinnom, which is by the entry of the east gate, and proclaim there the words that I shall tell you; and say, Hear the word of the Lord, O kings of Judah and inhabitants of Jerusalem, thus says the Lord of Hosts, the God of Israel: Behold, I will bring evil upon this place, which whoever hears, his ears shall tingle because they have forsaken me, and have estranged this place, and have burned incense in it unto other gods whom neither they nor their fathers have known, nor the kings of Judah, and have filled this place with the blood of innocents. They have built also the high places of Baal, to burn their sons with fire for burnt offerings unto Baal, which I commanded not, nor spoke it, neither came it into my mind. Therefore, behold, the days come, says the Lord, that this place shall no more be called Topheth, nor the valley of the son of Hinnom, but the valley of slaughter. And I will make void the counsel of Judah and Jerusalem in this place, and I will cause them to fall by the sword before their enemies and by the hands of them that seek their lives. And their carcasses will I give to be food for the fowls of the heaven and for the beasts of the earth. And I will make this city desolate and a hissing, everyone that passes thereby shall be astonished and hiss because of all the plagues thereof. And I will cause them to eat the flesh of their sons and the flesh of their daughters, and they shall eat everyone the flesh of his friend in the siege and confinement with which their enemies and they that seek their lives shall oppress them. Then shall you break the bottle in the sight of the men that go with you, and shall say unto them, Thus says the Lord of Hosts: Even so will I break this people and this city, as one breaks a potter's vessel that cannot be made whole again; and they shall bury them in Topheth until there be no place to bury. Thus will I do unto this place, says the Lord, and to the inhabitants thereof, and even make this city as Topheth. And the houses of Jerusalem and the houses of the kings of Judah shall be defiled as the place of Topheth, because of all the houses upon whose roofs they have burned incense unto all the host of heaven and have poured out drink offerings unto other gods.

⁵ Then came Jeremiah from Topheth, where the Lord had sent him to prophesy, and he stood in the court of the Lord's house and said to

all the people, Thus says the Lord of Hosts, the God of Israel: Behold, I will bring upon this city and upon all her towns all the evil that I have pronounced against it, because they have hardened their necks that they might not hear my words.

6 Now Pashur the son of Immer the priest, who was also chief governor in the house of the Lord, heard that Jeremiah prophesied these things. Then Pashur smote Jeremiah the prophet and put him in the stocks that were in the high gate of Benjamin, which was by the house of the Lord. And it came to pass on the next day that Pashur brought forth Jeremiah out of the stocks. Then said Jeremiah unto him, The Lord has not called your name Pashur, but Magormissabib, for thus says the Lord: Behold, I will make you a terror to yourself and to all your friends, and they shall fall by the sword of their enemies, and your eyes shall behold it. And I will give all Judah into the hand of the king of Babylon, and he shall carry them captive into Babylon and shall slay them with the sword. Moreover, I will deliver all the strength of this city, and all the labors thereof, and all the precious things thereof; and all the treasures of the kings of Judah will I give into the hand of their enemies, who shall spoil them and take them and carry them to Babylon. And you, Pashur, and all that dwell in your house, shall go into captivity; and you shall come to Babylon, and there you shall die and shall be buried there, you and all your friends to whom you have prophesied lies.

7 O Lord, you have deceived me, and I was deceived; you are stronger than I and have prevailed. I am in derision daily, everyone mocks me, for since I spoke, I cried out, I cried, Violence and spoil! — because the word of the Lord was made a reproach unto me and a derision daily, then I said, I will not make mention of him, nor speak anymore in his name. But his word was in my heart as a burning fire shut up in my bones, and I was weary with restraining, and I could not withhold. For I heard the defaming of many, fear on every side. Report, say they, and we will report it. All my close friends watched for my halting, saying, Perhaps he will be enticed and we shall prevail against him, and we shall take our revenge on him. But the Lord is with me as a mighty terrible one; therefore, my persecutors shall stumble and they shall not prevail. They shall be greatly ashamed for they shall not prosper, their everlasting confusion shall never be forgotten. But, O Lord of

Hosts that tries the righteous and sees the reins and the heart, let me
see your vengeance on them; for unto you have I opened my cause.
Sing unto the Lord, praise the Lord, for he has delivered the soul of
the poor from the hand of evildoers.

8 Cursed be the day wherein I was born, let not the day wherein my
mother bore me be blessed. Cursed be the man who brought tidings to
my father, saying, A son is born unto you — making him very glad. And
let that man be as the cities which the Lord overthrew and repented not,
and let him hear the cry in the morning and the shouting at noontime,
because he slew me not from the womb, or that my mother might have
been my grave, and her womb to be always great with me. Why came
I forth out of the womb to see labor and sorrow, that my days should
be consumed with shame?

9 The word which came unto Jeremiah from the Lord, when king
Zedekiah sent unto him Pashur the son of Malchijah, and Zephaniah
the son of Maaseiah the priest, saying, Inquire, I pray, of the Lord for
us, for Nebuchadnezzar king of Babylon makes war against us, if it so
be that the Lord will deal with us according to all his wondrous works,
that he may go up from us. Then said Jeremiah unto them, Thus shall
you say to Zedekiah: Thus says the Lord God of Israel: Behold, I will
turn back the weapons of war that are in your hands, with which you
fight against the king of Babylon and against the Chaldeans who
besiege you outside the walls, and I will assemble them into the midst
of this city. And I myself will fight against you with an outstretched
hand and with a strong arm, even in anger, and in fury, and in great
wrath. And I will smite the inhabitants of this city, both man and
beast — they shall die of a great pestilence. And afterward, says the
Lord, I will deliver Zedekiah king of Judah, and his servants, and the
people, and such as are left in this city — from the pestilence, from the
sword and from the famine — into the hand of Nebuchadnezzar king
of Babylon, and into the hand of their enemies, and into the hand of
those who seek their life. And he shall smite them with the edge of
the sword; he shall not spare them, neither have pity nor have mercy.

10 And unto this people you shall say, Thus says the Lord: Behold, I set
before you the way of life and the way of death. He that abides in this
city shall die by the sword, and by the famine, and by the pestilence;
but he that goes out and falls to the Chaldeans that besiege you, he

shall live, and his life shall be unto him for a prey. For I have set my face against this city for evil and not for good, says the Lord; it shall be given into the hand of the king of Babylon, and he shall burn it with fire.

11 And touching the house of the king of Judah, say, Hear the word of the Lord, O house of David, thus says the Lord: Execute judgment in the morning and deliver him who is spoiled out of the hand of the oppressor, lest my fury go out like fire and burn, that none can quench it, because of the evil of your doings. Behold, I am against you, O inhabitant of the valley and rock of the plain, says the Lord, who say, Who shall come down against us? Or who shall enter into our habitations? But I will punish you according to the fruit of your doings, says the Lord, and I will kindle a fire in the forest thereof, and it shall devour all things round about it.

12 Thus says the Lord: Go down to the house of the king of Judah and speak there this word, and say, Hear the word of the Lord, O king of Judah who sits upon the throne of David — you, and your servants, and your people that enter in by these gates. Thus says the Lord: Execute judgment and righteousness, and deliver the spoiled out of the hand of the oppressor, and do no wrong; do no violence to the stranger, the fatherless, nor the widow, neither shed innocent blood in this place. For if you do this thing indeed, then shall there enter in by the gates of this house kings sitting upon the throne of David, riding in chariots and on horses — he, and his servants, and his people. But if you will not hear these words, I swear by myself, says the Lord, that this house shall become a desolation. For thus says the Lord unto the king's house of Judah: You are Gilead unto me and the head of Lebanon, yet surely I will make you a wilderness and cities which are uninhabited. And I will prepare destroyers against you, everyone with his weapons, and they shall cut down your choice cedars and cast them into the fire. And many nations shall pass by this city, and they shall say every man to his neighbor, Why has the Lord done thus unto this great city? Then they shall answer, Because they have forsaken the covenant of the Lord their God, and worshipped other gods and served them.

13 Weep not for the dead, neither bemoan him, but weep bitterly for him that goes away, for he shall return no more nor see his native country. For thus says the Lord touching Shallum the son of Josiah, king of Judah, who reigned instead of Josiah his father, who went

forth out of this place: He shall not return there anymore, but he shall die in the place to which they have led him captive and shall see this land no more.

14 Woe unto him that builds his house by unrighteousness and his chambers by wrong; that uses his neighbor's service without wages and gives him not for his work; that says, I will build myself a wide house and large chambers — and cuts himself out windows, and it is paneled with cedar and painted with vermilion. Shall you reign because you close yourself in cedar? Did not your father eat and drink, and do judgment and justice, and then it was well with him? He judged the cause of the poor and needy, then it was well with him. Was not this to know me? — says the Lord. But your eyes and your heart are not but for your covetousness, and to shed innocent blood, and for oppression and for violence, to do it. Therefore, thus says the Lord concerning Jehoiakim the son of Josiah, king of Judah: They shall not lament for him, saying, Ah my brother! — or, Ah sister! They shall not lament for him, saying, Ah lord! — or, Ah his glory! He shall be buried with the burial of an ass, drawn and cast forth beyond the gates of Jerusalem. Go up to Lebanon and cry, and lift up your voice in Bashan and cry from the passages, for all your lovers are destroyed. I spoke unto you in your prosperity, but you said, I will not hear. This has been your manner from your youth: that you obeyed not my voice. The wind shall eat up all your shepherds, and your lovers shall go into captivity; surely then shall you be ashamed and confounded for all your wickedness. O inhabitant of Lebanon that make your nest in the cedars, how gracious shall you be when pangs come upon you, the pain as of a woman in travail.

15 As I live, says the Lord, though Coniah the son of Jehoiakim, king of Judah, was the signet upon my right hand, yet would I pluck you from there; and I will give you into the hand of them that seek your life and into the hand of them whose face you fear, even into the hand of Nebuchadnezzar king of Babylon and into the hand of the Chaldeans. And I will cast you out, and your mother that bore you, into another country where you were not born, and there shall you die. But to the land unto which they desire to return, there shall they not return. Is this man Coniah a despised broken idol? Is he a vessel wherein is no pleasure? Why are they cast out, he and his seed, and are cast into a

land which they know not? O earth, earth, earth, hear the word of the Lord. Thus says the Lord: Write this man childless, a man that shall not prosper in his days; for no man of his seed shall prosper sitting upon the throne of David and ruling anymore in Judah.

16 Woe be unto the shepherds that destroy and scatter the sheep of my pasture, says the Lord. Therefore, thus says the Lord God of Israel against the shepherds that feed my people: You have scattered my flock and driven them away, and have not visited them. Behold, I will visit upon you the evil of your doings, says the Lord. And I will gather the remnant of my flock out of all countries to which I have driven them, and will bring them again to their folds, and they shall be fruitful and increase. And I will set up shepherds over them who shall feed them, and they shall fear no more, nor be dismayed, neither shall they be lacking, says the Lord.

17 Behold, the days come, says the Lord, that I will raise unto David a righteous branch, and a king shall reign and prosper, and shall execute judgment and justice in the earth. In his days Judah shall be saved and Israel shall dwell safely; and this is his name whereby he shall be called: THE LORD OUR RIGHTEOUSNESS. Therefore, behold, the days come, says the Lord, that they shall no more say, The Lord lives who brought up the children of Israel out of the land of Egypt—but, The Lord lives who brought up and who led the seed of the house of Israel out of the north country, and from all countries to which I had driven them. And they shall dwell in their own land.

18 My heart within me is broken because of the prophets; all my bones shake, I am like a drunk man and like a man whom wine has overcome, because of the Lord and because of the words of his holiness. For the land is full of adulterers; for because of swearing, the land mourns, the pleasant places of the wilderness are dried up; and their course is evil and their force is not right. For both prophet and priest are corrupt, yea, in my house have I found their wickedness, says the Lord. Wherefore, their way shall be unto them as slippery ways in the darkness, they shall be driven on and fall therein; for I will bring evil upon them, even the year of their visitation, says the Lord. And I have seen folly in the prophets of Samaria: they prophesied in Baal and caused my people Israel to err. I have seen also in the prophets of Jerusalem a horrible thing: they commit adultery, and walk in lies,

they strengthen also the hands of evildoers, that none does return from his wickedness. They are all of them unto me as Sodom, and the inhabitants thereof as Gomorrah.

¹⁹ Therefore, thus says the Lord of Hosts concerning the prophets: Behold, I will feed them with wormwood and make them drink the water of gall, for from the prophets of Jerusalem is pollution gone forth into all the land. Thus says the Lord of Hosts: Listen not unto the words of the prophets that prophesy unto you; they make you vain, they speak a vision of their own heart and not out of the mouth of the Lord. They say still unto them that despise me, The Lord has said you shall have peace — and they say unto everyone that walks after the imagination of his own heart, No evil shall come upon you. For who has stood in the counsel of the Lord and has perceived and heard his word? Who has marked his word and heard it? Behold, a whirlwind of the Lord is gone forth in fury, even a grievous whirlwind; it shall fall grievously upon the head of the wicked. The anger of the Lord shall not return until he has executed and until he has performed the thoughts of his heart; in the latter days you shall consider it perfectly. I have not sent these prophets, yet they ran; I have not spoken to them, yet they prophesied. But if they had stood in my counsel and had caused my people to hear my words, then they should have turned them from their evil way and from the evil of their doings. Am I a God at hand, says the Lord, and not a God afar off? Can any hide himself in secret places that I shall not see him? — says the Lord. Do not I fill heaven and earth? — says the Lord. I have heard what the prophets said that prophesy lies in my name, saying, I have dreamed, I have dreamed. How long shall this be in the heart of the prophets that prophesy lies? Yea, they are prophets of the deceit of their own heart, who think to cause my people to forget my name by their dreams which they tell, every man to his neighbor, as their fathers have forgotten my name for Baal. The prophet who has a dream, let him tell a dream, and he who has my word, let him speak my word faithfully. What is the chaff to the wheat? — says the Lord. Is not my word like a fire? — says the Lord. And like a hammer that breaks the rock in pieces? Therefore, behold, I am against the prophets, says the Lord, who steal my words, every one from his neighbor. Behold, I am against the prophets, says the Lord, who use their tongues and say, He says. Behold, I am against

them that prophesy false dreams, says the Lord, and do tell them, and cause my people to err by their lies and by their lightness. Yet I sent them not, nor commanded them; therefore, they shall not profit this people at all, says the Lord.

20 And when this people, or the prophet, or a priest shall ask you, saying, What is the burden of the Lord? — you shall then say unto them, What burden? I will even forsake you, says the Lord. And as for the prophet, and the priest, and the people who shall say, The burden of the Lord — I will even punish that man and his house. Thus shall you say, everyone to his neighbor and everyone to his brother: What has the Lord answered? — and, What has the Lord spoken? And the burden of the Lord shall you mention no more, for every man's word shall be his burden; for you have perverted the words of the living God, of the Lord of Hosts, our God. Thus shall you say to the prophet: What has the Lord answered you? — and, What has the Lord spoken? But since you say, The burden of the Lord, therefore thus says the Lord: Because you say this word — The burden of the Lord — and I have sent unto you, saying, You shall not say, The burden of the Lord, therefore behold, I, even I, will utterly forget you, and I will forsake you and the city that I gave you and your fathers, and cast you out of my presence. And I will bring an everlasting reproach upon you and a perpetual shame which shall not be forgotten.

21 The Lord showed me, and behold, two baskets of figs were set before the temple of the Lord, after Nebuchadnezzar king of Babylon had carried away captive Jeconiah the son of Jehoiakim, king of Judah, and the princes of Judah, with the carpenters and smiths from Jerusalem, and had brought them to Babylon. One basket had very good figs, even like the figs that are first ripe, and the other basket had very bad figs which could not be eaten, they were so bad. Then said the Lord unto me, What do you see, Jeremiah? And I said, Figs, the good figs very good, and the evil very evil, that cannot be eaten they are so evil. Again the word of the Lord came unto me, saying, Thus says the Lord, the God of Israel: Like these good figs, so will I acknowledge them that are carried away captive of Judah, whom I have sent out of this place into the land of the Chaldeans for their good. For I will set my eyes upon them for good, and I will bring them again to this land, and I will build them and not pull them down, and I will plant them

and not pluck them up. And I will give them a heart to know me, that I am the Lord; and they shall be my people and I will be their God, for they shall return unto me with their whole heart. And as the evil figs which cannot be eaten they are so evil, surely thus says the Lord: So will I give Zedekiah the king of Judah and his princes, and the residue of Jerusalem that remain in this land, and them that dwell in the land of Egypt. And I will deliver them to be removed into all the kingdoms of the earth for their hurt, to be a reproach and a proverb, a taunt and a curse, in all places to which I shall drive them. And I will send the sword, the famine, and the pestilence among them, until they are consumed from off the land that I gave unto them and to their fathers.

9 The word that came to Jeremiah concerning all the people of Judah in the fourth year of Jehoiakim the son of Josiah, king of Judah, that was the first year of Nebuchadnezzar king of Babylon, which Jeremiah the prophet spoke unto all the people of Judah and to all the inhabitants of Jerusalem, saying, From the thirteenth year of Josiah the son of Amon, king of Judah, even unto this day that is the twenty-third year, the word of the Lord has come unto me and I have spoken unto you, rising early and speaking; but you have not listened. And the Lord has sent unto you all his servants the prophets, rising early and sending them; but you have not listened, nor inclined your ear to hear. They said, Turn again now everyone from his evil way and from the evil of your doings, and dwell in the land that the Lord has given unto you and to your fathers for ever and ever, and go not after other gods — to serve them and to worship them — and provoke me not to anger with the works of your hands, and I will do you no harm. Yet you have not listened unto me, says the Lord, that you might provoke me to anger with the works of your hands, to your own harm.

2 Therefore, thus says the Lord: Because you have not heard my words, behold, I will send and take all the families of the north, says the Lord, and Nebuchadnezzar the king of Babylon, my servant, and will bring them against this land, and against the inhabitants thereof, and against all these nations round about, and will utterly destroy them and make them an astonishment, and a hissing, and perpetual desolations. Moreover, I will take from them the voice of mirth and the voice of gladness, the voice of the bridegroom and the voice of the bride,

the sound of the millstones and the light of the candle. And this whole land shall be a desolation and an astonishment, and these nations shall serve the king of Babylon seventy years. And it shall come to pass, when seventy years are accomplished, that I will punish the king of Babylon and that nation, says the Lord, for their iniquity, and the land of the Chaldeans, and will make it perpetual desolations. And I will bring upon that land all my words which I have pronounced against it, even all that is written in this book which Jeremiah has prophesied against all the nations. For many nations and great kings shall serve themselves of them also, and I will recompense them according to their deeds and according to the works of their own hands.

3 For thus says the Lord God of Israel unto me: Take the wine cup of this fury at my hand, and cause all the nations to whom I send you to drink it. And they shall drink and be moved, and be mad because of the sword that I will send among them. Then took I the cup at the Lord's hand, and made all the nations to drink, unto whom the Lord had sent me: Jerusalem and the cities of Judah, and the kings thereof and the princes thereof, to make them a desolation, an astonishment, a hissing, and a curse, as it is this day; Pharaoh king of Egypt and his servants, and his princes, and all his people; and all the mingled people; and all the kings of the land of Uz; and all the kings of the land of the Philistines, and Ashkelon, and Azzah, and Ekron, and the remnant of Ashdod; Edom, and Moab, and the children of Ammon; and all the kings of Tyre, and all the kings of Sidon; and the kings of the isles which are beyond the sea; Dedan, and Tema, and Buz, and all that are in the utmost corners; and all the kings of Arabia; and all the kings of the mingled people that dwell in the desert; and all the kings of Zimri; and all the kings of Elam; and all the kings of the Medes; and all the kings of the north, far and near, one with another; and all the kingdoms of the world which are upon the face of the earth; and the king of Sheshach shall drink after them. Therefore, you shall say unto them, Thus says the Lord of Hosts, the God of Israel: Drink, and be drunk, and spew, and fall, and rise no more, because of the sword which I will send among you. And it shall be, if they refuse to take the cup at your hand to drink, then shall you say unto them, Thus says the Lord of Hosts: You shall certainly drink. For behold, I begin to bring evil on the city which is called by my name, and should you be

utterly unpunished? You shall not be unpunished, for I will call for a sword upon all the inhabitants of the earth, says the Lord of Hosts.

⁴ Therefore, prophesy against them all these words and say unto them, The Lord shall roar from on high and utter his voice from his holy habitation; he shall mightily roar upon his habitation, he shall give a shout as they that tread the grapes, against all the inhabitants of the earth. A noise shall come even to the ends of the earth, for the Lord has a controversy with the nations. He will plead with all flesh, he will give the wicked to the sword, says the Lord. Thus says the Lord of Hosts: Behold, evil shall go forth from nation to nation, and a great whirlwind shall be raised up from the ends of the earth. And the slain of the Lord shall be at that day from one end of the earth even unto the other end of the earth. They shall not be lamented, neither gathered, nor buried; they shall be dung upon the ground. Howl, you shepherds, and cry and wallow yourselves in the ashes, you principal of the flock; for the days of your slaughter and of your dispersions are accomplished, and you shall fall like a pleasant vessel. And the shepherds shall have no way to flee, nor the principal of the flock to escape; a voice of the cry of the shepherds and a howling of the principal of the flock shall be heard, for the Lord has spoiled their pasture. And the peaceable habitations are cut down because of the fierce anger of the Lord. He has forsaken his cover as the lion, for their land is desolate because of the fierceness of the oppressor and because of his fierce anger.

10 In the beginning of the reign of Jehoiakim the son of Josiah, king of Judah, came this word from the Lord, saying, Thus says the Lord: Stand in the court of the Lord's house and speak unto all the cities of Judah which come to worship in the Lord's house all the words that I command you to speak unto them; diminish not a word. If it so be they will listen, and turn every man from his evil way, and repent, I will turn away the evil which I purpose to do unto them because of the evil of their doings. And you shall say unto them, Thus says the Lord: If you will not listen to me, to walk in my law which I have set before you, to listen to the words of my servants the prophets whom I sent unto you, commanding them to rise up early and sending them, then will I make this house like Shiloh and will

make this city a curse to all the nations of the earth; for you have not listened unto my servants the prophets.

2 So the priests, and the prophets, and all the people heard Jeremiah speaking these words in the house of the Lord. Now it came to pass, when Jeremiah had made an end of speaking all that the Lord had commanded him to speak unto all the people, that the priests, and the prophets, and all the people took him, saying, You shall surely die. Why have you prophesied in the name of the Lord, saying, This house shall be like Shiloh and this city shall be desolate without an inhabitant? And all the people were gathered against Jeremiah in the house of the Lord. When the princes of Judah heard these things, then they came up from the king's house unto the house of the Lord and sat down in the entry of the new gate of the Lord's house. Then spoke the priests and the prophets unto the princes and to all the people, saying, This man is worthy to die, for he has prophesied against this city, as you have heard with your ears. Then spoke Jeremiah unto all the princes and to all the people, saying, The Lord sent me to prophesy against this house and against this city all the words that you have heard. Therefore now, amend your ways and your doings, and obey the voice of the Lord your God and repent, and the Lord will turn away the evil that he has pronounced against you. As for me, behold, I am in your hand; do with me as seems good and meet unto you. But know for certain that if you put me to death, you shall surely bring innocent blood upon yourselves, and upon this city, and upon the inhabitants thereof, for truly the Lord has sent me unto you to speak all these words in your ears.

3 Then said the princes and all the people unto the priests and to the prophets, This man is not worthy to die, for he has spoken to us in the name of the Lord our God. Then rose up certain of the elders of the land, and spoke to all the assembly of the people, saying, Micah the Morasthite prophesied in the days of Hezekiah king of Judah and spoke to all the people of Judah, saying, Thus says the Lord of Hosts: Zion shall be plowed like a field and Jerusalem shall become heaps and the mountain of the house of the Lord as the high places of a forest. Did Hezekiah king of Judah and all Judah put him at all to death? Did he not fear the Lord, and implored the Lord and repented, and the Lord turned away the evil which he had pronounced against

them? Thus, by putting Jeremiah to death, we might procure great evil against our souls.

⁴ But there was a man among the priests rose up and said that Uriah the son of Shemaiah of Kiriath-Jearim prophesied in the name of the Lord, who also prophesied against this city and against this land according to all the words of Jeremiah. And when Jehoiakim the king, with all his mighty men and all the princes, heard his words, the king sought to put him to death. But when Uriah heard it, he was afraid, and fled, and went into Egypt; and Jehoiakim the king sent men into Egypt, namely Elnathan the son of Achbor and certain men with him into Egypt; and they fetched forth Uriah out of Egypt and brought him unto Jehoiakim the king, who slew him with the sword and cast his dead body into the graves of the common people. Nevertheless, the hand of Ahikam the son of Shaphan was with Jeremiah, that they should not give him into the hand of the people to put him to death.

⁵ In the beginning of the reign of Jehoiakim the son of Josiah, king of Judah, came this word unto Jeremiah from the Lord, saying, Thus says the Lord to me: Make yourself bonds and yokes and put them upon your neck, and send them to the king of Edom, and to the king of Moab, and to the king of the Ammonites, and to the king of Tyre, and to the king of Sidon, by the hand of the messengers who come to Jerusalem, unto Zedekiah king of Judah, and command them to say unto their masters, Thus says the Lord of Hosts, the God of Israel: Thus shall you say unto your masters: I have made the earth, the man and the beast that are upon the ground, by my great power and by my outstretched arm, and have given it unto whom it seemed meet unto me. And now have I given all these lands into the hand of Nebuchadnezzar the king of Babylon, my servant, and the beasts of the field have I given him also to serve him. And all nations shall serve him, and his son, and his son's son, until the very time of their end come; and after that, many nations and great kings shall serve themselves of them. And it shall come to pass that the nation and kingdom which will not serve the same Nebuchadnezzar, the king of Babylon, and that will not put their neck under the yoke of the king of Babylon, that nation will I punish, says the Lord, with the sword, and with the famine, and with the pestilence, until I have consumed them by his hand. Therefore, listen not to your prophets, nor to your diviners, nor to your dreamers, nor

to your enchanters, nor to your sorcerers, who speak unto you saying,
You shall not serve the king of Babylon—for they prophesy a lie unto
you to remove you far from your land, and that I should drive you out
and you should perish. But the nations that bring their neck under the
yoke of the king of Babylon and serve him, those will I let remain still
in their own land, says the Lord, and they shall till it and dwell therein.

⁶ I spoke also to Zedekiah king of Judah according to all these words,
saying, Bring your necks under the yoke of the king of Babylon, and
serve him and his people, and live. Why will you die, you and your
people, by the sword, by the famine, and by the pestilence, as the
Lord has spoken against the nation that will not serve the king of
Babylon? Therefore, listen not unto the words of the prophets that
speak unto you saying, You shall not serve the king of Babylon—for
they prophesy a lie unto you. For I have not sent them, says the Lord,
yet they prophesy a lie in my name, that I might drive you out and
that you might perish, you and the prophets that prophesy unto you.

⁷ Also, I spoke to the priests and to all this people, saying, Thus says
the Lord: Listen not to the words of your prophets that prophesy unto
you saying, Behold, the vessels of the Lord's house shall now shortly be
brought again from Babylon—for they prophesy a lie unto you. Listen
not unto them, serve the king of Babylon and live. Why should this city
be laid waste? But if they are prophets, and if the word of the Lord is
with them, let them now make intercession to the Lord of Hosts that
the vessels which are left in the house of the Lord and in the house
of the king of Judah and at Jerusalem go not to Babylon. For thus
says the Lord of Hosts concerning the pillars, and concerning the sea,
and concerning the bases, and concerning the residue of the vessels
that remain in this city—which Nebuchadnezzar king of Babylon
took not when he carried away captive Jeconiah the son of Jehoiakim,
king of Judah, from Jerusalem to Babylon, and all the nobles of Judah
and Jerusalem—yea, thus says the Lord of Hosts, the God of Israel,
concerning the vessels that remain in the house of the Lord, and in
the house of the king of Judah and of Jerusalem: They shall be carried
to Babylon and there shall they be until the day that I visit them, says
the Lord; then will I bring them up and restore them to this place.

⁸ And it came to pass the same year, in the beginning of the reign of
Zedekiah king of Judah, in the fourth year and in the fifth month that

Hananiah the son of Azzur, the prophet, who was of Gibeon, spoke unto me in the house of the Lord, in the presence of the priests and of all the people, saying, Thus speaks the Lord of Hosts, the God of Israel, saying: I have broken the yoke of the king of Babylon. Within two full years will I bring again into this place all the vessels of the Lord's house that Nebuchadnezzar king of Babylon took away from this place and carried them to Babylon. And I will bring again to this place Jeconiah the son of Jehoiakim, king of Judah, with all the captives of Judah that went into Babylon, says the Lord, for I will break the yoke of the king of Babylon. Then the prophet Jeremiah said unto the prophet Hananiah, in the presence of the priests and in the presence of all the people that stood in the house of the Lord, even the prophet Jeremiah said, Amen. The Lord do so, the Lord perform your words which you have prophesied, to bring again the vessels of the Lord's house and all that is carried away captive, from Babylon into this place. Nevertheless, hear now this word that I speak in your ears and in the ears of all the people: The prophets that have been before me and before you of old prophesied both against many countries and against great kingdoms — of war, and of evil, and of pestilence. The prophet who prophesies of peace, when the word of the prophet shall come to pass, then shall the prophet be known, that the Lord has truly sent him. Then Hananiah the prophet took the yoke from off the prophet Jeremiah's neck and broke it. And Hananiah spoke in the presence of all the people, saying, Thus says the Lord: Even so will I break the yoke of Nebuchadnezzar king of Babylon from the neck of all nations within the space of two full years. And the prophet Jeremiah went his way.

9 Then the word of the Lord came unto Jeremiah the prophet, after Hananiah the prophet had broken the yoke from off the neck of the prophet Jeremiah, saying, Go and tell Hananiah, saying, Thus says the Lord: You have broken the yokes of wood, but you shall make for them yokes of iron. For thus says the Lord of Hosts, the God of Israel: I have put a yoke of iron upon the neck of all these nations, that they may serve Nebuchadnezzar king of Babylon, and they shall serve him; and I have given him the beasts of the field also. Then said the prophet Jeremiah unto Hananiah the prophet, Hear now, Hananiah, The Lord has not sent you, but you make this people to trust in a lie. Therefore, thus says the Lord: Behold, I will cast you from off the face

of the earth; this year you shall die because you have taught rebellion against the Lord. So Hananiah the prophet died the same year in the seventh month.

11 Now these are the words of the letter that Jeremiah the prophet sent from Jerusalem unto the residue of the elders who were carried away captives, and to the priests, and to the prophets, and to all the people whom Nebuchadnezzar had carried away captive from Jerusalem to Babylon (after Jeconiah the king, and the queen, and the eunuchs, the princes of Judah and Jerusalem, and the carpenters, and the smiths were departed from Jerusalem), by the hand of Elasah the son of Shaphan and Gemariah the son of Hilkiah (whom Zedekiah king of Judah sent unto Babylon, to Nebuchadnezzar king of Babylon), saying, Thus says the Lord of Hosts, the God of Israel, unto all that are carried away captives, whom I have caused to be carried away from Jerusalem unto Babylon: Build houses and dwell in them, and plant gardens and eat the fruit of them; take wives and beget sons and daughters, and take wives for your sons and give your daughters to husbands, that they may bear sons and daughters, that you may be increased there and not diminished. And seek the peace of the city where I have caused you to be carried away captives, and pray unto the Lord for it; for in the peace thereof shall you have peace. For thus says the Lord of Hosts, the God of Israel: Let not your prophets and your diviners that are in your midst deceive you, neither listen to your dreams which you cause to be dreamed. For they prophesy falsely unto you in my name; I have not sent them, says the Lord. For thus says the Lord: that after seventy years are accomplished at Babylon, I will visit you and perform my good word toward you in causing you to return to this place. For I know the thoughts that I think toward you, says the Lord — thoughts of peace and not of evil, to give you an expected end. Then shall you call upon me, and you shall go and pray unto me, and I will listen unto you. And you shall seek me and find me when you shall search for me with all your heart. And I will be found of you, says the Lord. And I will turn away your captivity, and I will gather you from all the nations and from all the places to which I have driven you, says the Lord, and I will bring you again into the place from which I caused you to be carried away captive.

² Because you have said, The Lord has raised us up prophets in Babylon — know that thus says the Lord; of the king that sits upon the throne of David, and of all the people that dwell in this city, and of your brethren that are not gone forth with you into captivity, thus says the Lord of Hosts: Behold, I will send upon them the sword, the famine, and the pestilence, and will make them like vile figs that cannot be eaten they are so evil. And I will persecute them with the sword, with famine, and with pestilence, and will deliver them to be removed to all the kingdoms of the earth — to be a curse, and an astonishment, and a hissing, and a reproach among all the nations to which I have driven them, because they have not listened to my words, says the Lord, which I sent unto them by my servants the prophets, commanding them to rise early and sending them. But you would not hear, says the Lord. Hear therefore the word of the Lord, all you of the captivity whom I have sent from Jerusalem to Babylon; thus says the Lord of Hosts, the God of Israel, of Ahab the son of Kolaiah and of Zedekiah the son of Maaseiah, who prophesy a lie unto you in my name: Behold, I will deliver them into the hand of Nebuchadnezzar king of Babylon and he shall slay them before your eyes, and of them shall be taken up a curse by all the captives of Judah who are in Babylon, saying, The Lord make you like Zedekiah and like Ahab, whom the king of Babylon roasted in the fire because they have committed villany in Israel, and have committed adultery with their neighbors' wives, and have spoken lying words in my name which I have not commanded them. Even I know and am a witness, says the Lord.

³ Thus shall you also speak to Shemaiah the Nehelamite, saying, Thus speaks the Lord of Hosts, the God of Israel, saying: Because you have sent letters in your name unto all the people that are at Jerusalem, and to Zephaniah the son of Maaseiah, the priest, and to all the priests, saying, The Lord has made you priest in the stead of Jehoiada the priest, that you should be officers in the house of the Lord for every man that is mad and makes himself a prophet, that you should put him in prison and in the stocks. Now therefore why have you not reproved Jeremiah of Anathoth, who makes himself a prophet to you? For thus he sent unto us in Babylon, saying, This captivity is long, build houses and dwell in them, and plant gardens and eat the fruit of them. And Zephaniah the priest read this letter in the ears of Jeremiah the prophet.

Then came the word of the Lord unto Jeremiah, saying, Send to all them of the captivity, saying, Thus says the Lord concerning Shemaiah the Nehelamite: Because Shemaiah has prophesied unto you and I sent him not, and he caused you to trust in a lie, therefore thus says the Lord: Behold, I will punish Shemaiah the Nehelamite and his seed; he shall not have a man to dwell among this people, neither shall he behold the good that I will do for my people, says the Lord, because he has taught rebellion against the Lord.

12 The word that came to Jeremiah from the Lord, saying, Thus speaks the Lord God of Israel, saying: Write all the words that I have spoken unto you in a book. For behold, the days come, says the Lord, that I will bring again the captives of my people Israel and Judah, says the Lord, and I will cause them to return to the land that I gave to their fathers, and they shall possess it. And these are the words that the Lord spoke concerning Israel and concerning Judah.

2 For thus says the Lord: We have heard a voice of trembling, of fear and not of peace. Ask now and see whether a man does travail with child. Why do I see every man with his hands on his loins as a woman in travail, and all faces are turned into paleness? Alas, for that day is great so that none is like it. It is even the time of Jacob's trouble, but he shall be saved out of it. For it shall come to pass in that day, says the Lord of Hosts, that I will break his yoke from off your neck, and will burst your bonds, and strangers shall no more serve themselves of him. But they shall serve the Lord their God, and David, their king whom I will raise up unto them.

3 Therefore, fear not, O my servant Jacob, says the Lord, neither be dismayed, O Israel. For I will save you from afar, and your seed from the land of their captivity. And Jacob shall return, and shall be in rest and be quiet, and none shall make him afraid. For I am with you, says the Lord, to save you. Though I make a full end of all nations where I have scattered you, yet will I not make a full end of you; but I will correct you in measure, and will not leave you altogether unpunished. For thus says the Lord: Your bruise is not incurable, although your wounds are grievous. Is there none to plead your cause that you may be bound up? Have you no healing medicines? Have all your lovers forgotten you? Do they not seek you? For I have wounded you with

the wound of an enemy, with the chastisement of a cruel one, for the multitude of your iniquity, because your sins are increased. Why do you cry for your affliction? Is your sorrow incurable? It was for the multitude of your iniquities and because your sins are increased I have done these things unto you. But all they that devour you shall be devoured. And all your adversaries, every one of them, shall go into captivity. And they that spoil you shall be a spoil. And all that prey upon you will I give for a prey. For I will restore health unto you and I will heal you of your wounds, says the Lord, because they called you an outcast, saying, This is Zion whom no man seeks after.

4 Thus says the Lord: Behold, I will bring again the captives of Jacob's tents and have mercy on his dwelling places. And the city shall be built upon her own heap and the palace shall remain after the manner thereof. And out of them shall proceed thanksgiving and the voice of them that make merry. And I will multiply them and they shall not be few. I will also glorify them and they shall not be small. Their children also shall be as before, and their congregation shall be established before me, and I will punish all that oppress them. And their nobles shall be of themselves and their governor shall proceed from the midst of them. And I will cause him to draw near and he shall approach unto me, for who is this that engaged his heart to approach unto me? — says the Lord. And you shall be my people and I will be your God. Behold, the whirlwind of the Lord goes forth with fury, a continuing whirlwind. It shall fall with pain upon the head of the wicked. The fierce anger of the Lord shall not return until he has done it and until he has performed the intents of his heart. In the latter days you shall consider it.

5 At the same time, says the Lord, will I be the God of all the families of Israel, and they shall be my people. Thus says the Lord: The people who were left of the sword found grace in the wilderness — even Israel, when I went to cause him to rest. The Lord has appeared of old unto me, saying, Yea, I have loved you with an everlasting love. Therefore, with loving kindness have I drawn you. Again I will build you and you shall be built, O virgin of Israel. You shall again be adorned with your tambourines and shall go forth in the dances of them that make merry. You shall yet plant vines upon the mountains of Samaria. The planters shall plant and shall eat them as common things. For there

shall be a day that the watchmen upon the mount Ephraim shall cry, Arise and let us go up to Zion, unto the Lord our God. For thus says the Lord: Sing with gladness for Jacob and shout among the chief of the nations. Publish praise and say, O Lord, save your people, the remnant of Israel. Behold, I will bring them from the north country and gather them from the ends of the earth, and with them the blind and the lame, the woman with child and her that travails with child together. A great company shall return there. They shall come with weeping, and with supplications will I lead them. I will cause them to walk by the rivers of waters in a straight way wherein they shall not stumble. For I am a father to Israel, and Ephraim is my firstborn.

6 Hear the word of the Lord, O you nations, and declare it in the isles afar off, and say: He that scattered Israel will gather him and keep him as a shepherd does his flock. For the Lord has redeemed Jacob and ransomed him from the hand of him that was stronger than he. Therefore, they shall come and sing in the height of Zion and shall flow together to the goodness of the Lord: for wheat, and for wine, and for oil, and for the young of the flock and of the herd. And their soul shall be as a watered garden, and they shall not sorrow anymore at all. Then shall the virgin rejoice in the dance, both young men and old together. For I will turn their mourning into joy, and will comfort them, and make them rejoice from their sorrow. And I will satiate the soul of the priests with fatness and my people shall be satisfied with my goodness, says the Lord.

7 Thus says the Lord: A voice was heard in Ramah, lamentation and bitter weeping. Rachel, weeping for her children, refused to be comforted for her children because they were not. Thus says the Lord: Restrain your voice from weeping and your eyes from tears, for your work shall be rewarded, says the Lord, and they shall come again from the land of the enemy. And there is hope in your end, says the Lord, that your children shall come again to their own border. I have surely heard Ephraim bemoaning himself thus: You have chastised me, and I was chastised as a bullock unaccustomed to the yoke. Turn me, and I shall be turned, for you are the Lord my God. Surely after I was turned, I repented; and after I was instructed, I smote upon my thigh. I was ashamed, yea, even confounded, because I did bear the reproach of my youth.

8 Is Ephraim my dear son? Is he a pleasant child? For since I spoke against him, I do earnestly remember him still. Therefore, my heart is troubled for him. I will surely have mercy upon him, says the Lord. Set up waymarks, make high heaps; set your heart toward the highway, even the way which you went. Return again, O virgin of Israel, return again to these your cities. How long will you go about, O you backsliding daughter? For the Lord has created a new thing in the earth: a woman shall encompass a man. Thus says the Lord of Hosts, the God of Israel: As yet, they shall use this speech in the land of Judah and in the cities thereof when I shall bring again their captives: The Lord bless you, O habitation of justice and mountain of holiness. And there shall dwell in Judah itself, and in all the cities thereof together, husbandmen and they that go forth with flocks. For I have satiated the weary soul and I have replenished every sorrowful soul. Upon this I awoke and beheld, and my sleep was sweet unto me.

9 Behold, the days come, says the Lord, that I will sow the house of Israel and the house of Judah with the seed of man and with the seed of beast. And it shall come to pass that as I have watched over them to pluck up, and to break down, and to throw down, and to destroy, and to afflict, so will I watch over them to build and to plant, says the Lord. In those days, they shall say no more, The fathers have eaten a sour grape, and the children's teeth are set on edge — but everyone shall die for his own iniquity. Every man that eats the sour grape, his teeth shall be set on edge. Behold, the days come, says the Lord, that I will make a new covenant with the house of Israel and with the house of Judah — not according to the covenant that I made with their fathers in the day that I took them by the hand to bring them out of the land of Egypt (which my covenant they broke, although I was a husband unto them, says the Lord), but this shall be the covenant that I will make with the house of Israel: after those days, says the Lord, I will put my law in their inward parts, and write it in their hearts, and will be their God and they shall be my people. And they shall teach no more every man his neighbor and every man his brother, saying, Know the Lord — for they shall all know me, from the least of them unto the greatest of them, says the Lord. For I will forgive their iniquity and I will remember their sin no more.

¹⁰ Thus says the Lord, who gives the sun for a light by day, and the ordinances of the moon and of the stars for a light by night, who divides the sea when the waves thereof roar — the Lord of Hosts is his name: If those ordinances depart from before me, says the Lord, then the seed of Israel also shall cease from being a nation before me for ever. Thus says the Lord: If heaven above can be measured and the foundations of the earth searched out beneath, I will also cast off all the seed of Israel for all that they have done, says the Lord. Behold, the days come, says the Lord, that the city shall be built to the Lord from the tower of Hananel unto the gate of the corner. And the measuring line shall yet go forth straight before it upon the hill Gareb and shall turn to Goah. And the whole valley of the dead bodies and of the ashes, and all the fields unto the brook of Kidron, unto the corner of the horse gate toward the east, shall be holy unto the Lord. It shall not be plucked up nor thrown down anymore for ever.

13 The word that came to Jeremiah from the Lord in the tenth year of Zedekiah king of Judah, which was the eighteenth year of Nebuchadnezzar. For then the king of Babylon's army besieged Jerusalem, and Jeremiah the prophet was shut up in the court of the prison which was in the king of Judah's house. For Zedekiah king of Judah had shut him up, saying, Why do you prophesy and say, Thus says the Lord: Behold, I will give this city into the hand of the king of Babylon and he shall take it, and Zedekiah king of Judah shall not escape out of the hand of the Chaldeans, but shall surely be delivered into the hand of the king of Babylon and shall speak with him mouth to mouth, and his eyes shall behold his eyes. And he shall lead Zedekiah to Babylon, and there shall he be until I visit him, says the Lord. Though you fight with the Chaldeans, you shall not prosper.

² And Jeremiah said, The word of the Lord came unto me, saying, Behold, Hanamel, the son of Shallum your uncle, shall come unto you, saying, Buy my field that is in Anathoth, for the right of redemption is yours to buy it. So Hanamel, my uncle's son, came to me in the court of the prison according to the word of the Lord, and said unto me, Buy my field, I pray you, that is in Anathoth, which is in the country of Benjamin, for the right of inheritance is yours and the redemption is yours. Buy it for yourself. Then I knew that this was the word of the

Lord, and I bought the field of Hanamel, my uncle's son, that was in Anathoth, and weighed him the money, even seventeen shekels of silver. And I subscribed the evidence and sealed it, and took witnesses, and weighed him the money in the balances. So I took the evidence of the purchase, both that which was sealed according to the law and custom, and that which was open. And I gave the evidence of the purchase unto Baruch the son of Neriah, the son of Maaseiah, in the sight of Hanamel, my uncle's son, and in the presence of the witnesses that subscribed the book of the purchase before all the Jews that sat in the court of the prison. And I charged Baruch before them, saying, Thus says the Lord of Hosts, the God of Israel: Take these evidences, this evidence of the purchase, both which is sealed and this evidence which is open, and put them in an earthen vessel, that they may continue many days. For thus says the Lord of Hosts, the God of Israel: Houses and fields and vineyards shall be possessed again in this land.

3 Now when I had delivered the evidence of the purchase unto Baruch the son of Neriah, I prayed unto the Lord, saying, Ah, Lord God, behold, you have made the heaven and the earth by your great power and stretched out arm, and there is nothing too hard for you. You show loving kindness unto thousands and recompense the iniquity of the fathers into the bosom of their children after them. The Great, the Mighty God, the Lord of Hosts is his name — great in counsel and mighty in work, for your eyes are open upon all the ways of the sons of men, to give everyone according to his ways and according to the fruit of his doings; who have set signs and wonders in the land of Egypt, even unto this day, and in Israel, and among other men; and have made you a name as at this day; and have brought forth your people Israel out of the land of Egypt with signs, and with wonders, and with a strong hand, and with a stretched out arm, and with great terror; and have given them this land which you did swear to their fathers to give them — a land flowing with milk and honey. And they came in and possessed it, but they obeyed not your voice, neither walked in your law. They have done nothing of all that you commanded them to do. Therefore, you have caused all this evil to come upon them. Behold the mounts, they have come unto the city to take it. And the city is given into the hand of the Chaldeans that fight against it, because of the sword, and of the famine, and of the pestilence. And what you have

spoken has come to pass. And behold, you see it. And you have said unto me, O Lord God, Buy the field for money and take witnesses, for the city is given into the hand of the Chaldeans.

4 Then came the word of the Lord unto Jeremiah, saying, Behold, I am the Lord, the God of all flesh. Is there anything too hard for me? Therefore, thus says the Lord: Behold, I will give this city into the hand of the Chaldeans and into the hand of Nebuchadnezzar king of Babylon, and he shall take it. And the Chaldeans that fight against this city shall come and set fire on this city, and burn it with the houses, upon whose roofs they have offered incense unto Baal and poured out drink offerings unto other gods, to provoke me to anger. For the children of Israel and the children of Judah have only done evil before me from their youth. For the children of Israel have only provoked me to anger with the work of their hands, says the Lord. For this city has been to me as a provocation of my anger and of my fury, from the day that they built it even unto this day, that I should remove it from before my face because of all the evil of the children of Israel and of the children of Judah which they have done to provoke me to anger — they, their kings, their princes, their priests, and their prophets, and the men of Judah, and the inhabitants of Jerusalem. And they have turned unto me the back and not the face. Though I taught them, rising up early and teaching them, yet they have not listened to receive instruction, but they set their abominations in the house which is called by my name, to defile it. And they built the high places of Baal which are in the valley of the son of Hinnom, to cause their sons and their daughters to pass through the fire unto Molech, which I commanded them not; neither came it into my mind that they should do this abomination, to cause Judah to sin.

5 And now therefore thus says the Lord the God of Israel, concerning this city of which you say, It shall be delivered into the hand of the king of Babylon by the sword, and by the famine, and by the pestilence: Behold, I will gather them out of all countries to which I have driven them — in my anger, and in my fury, and in great wrath — and I will bring them again unto this place, and I will cause them to dwell safely, and they shall be my people and I will be their God. And I will give them one heart and one way, that they may fear me for ever, for the good of them and of their children after them. And I will make an

everlasting covenant with them that I will not turn away from them to do them good, but I will put my fear in their hearts, that they shall not depart from me. Yea, I will rejoice over them to do them good, and I will plant them in this land assuredly with my whole heart and with my whole soul. For thus says the Lord: As I have brought all this great evil upon this people, so will I bring upon them all the good that I have promised them. And fields shall be bought in this land whereof you say, It is desolate without man or beast, it is given into the hand of the Chaldeans. Men shall buy fields for money, and subscribe evidences, and seal them, and take witnesses in the land of Benjamin, and in the places about Jerusalem, and in the cities of Judah, and in the cities of the mountains, and in the cities of the valley, and in the cities of the south; for I will cause their captivity to turn back, says the Lord.

⁶ Moreover, the word of the Lord came unto Jeremiah the second time, while he was yet shut up in the court of the prison, saying, Thus says the Lord, the maker thereof, the Lord that formed it to establish it — The Lord is his name: Call unto me and I will answer you and show you great and mighty things which you know not. For thus says the Lord, the God of Israel, concerning the houses of this city and concerning the houses of the kings of Judah which are thrown down by the mounts and by the sword: They come to fight with the Chaldeans, but it is to fill them with the dead bodies of men whom I have slain in my anger and in my fury, and for all whose wickedness I have hidden my face from this city. Behold, I will bring it health and cure, and I will cure them, and will reveal unto them the abundance of peace and truth. And I will cause the captivity of Judah and the captivity of Israel to turn back, and will build them as at the first. And I will cleanse them from all their iniquity whereby they have sinned against me, and I will pardon all their iniquities whereby they have sinned and whereby they have transgressed against me. And it shall be to me a name of joy, a praise and an honor before all the nations of the earth who shall hear all the good that I do unto them. And they shall fear and tremble for all the goodness and for all the prosperity that I procure unto it.

⁷ Thus says the Lord: Again there shall be heard in this place — which you say shall be desolate, without man and without beast, even in the cities of Judah and in the streets of Jerusalem that are desolate without

man, and without inhabitant, and without beast — the voice of joy and the voice of gladness, the voice of the bridegroom and the voice of the bride, the voice of them that shall say, Praise the Lord of Hosts, for the Lord is good, for his mercy endures for ever unto them that shall bring the sacrifice of praise into the house of the Lord. For I will cause to turn back the captivity of the land as at the first, says the Lord.

⁸ Thus says the Lord of Hosts: Again in this place which is desolate, without man and without beast, and in all the cities thereof, shall be a habitation of shepherds causing their flocks to lie down. In the cities of the mountains, in the cities of the vale, and in the cities of the south, and in the land of Benjamin, and in the places about Jerusalem, and in the cities of Judah shall the flocks pass again under the hands of him that tells them, says the Lord.

⁹ Behold, the days come, says the Lord, that I will perform that good thing which I have promised unto the house of Israel and to the house of Judah. In those days and at that time will I cause the branch of righteousness to grow up unto David, and he shall execute judgment and righteousness in the land. In those days shall Judah be saved, and Jerusalem shall dwell safely. And this is the name by which she shall be called: the Lord our Righteousness. For thus says the Lord: David shall never lack a man to sit upon the throne of the house of Israel, neither shall the priests the Levites lack a man before me to offer burnt offerings, and to kindle meal offerings, and to do sacrifice continually.

¹⁰ And the word of the Lord came unto Jeremiah, saying, Thus says the Lord: If you can break my covenant of the day and my covenant of the night, and that there should not be day and night in their season, then may also my covenant be broken with David my servant, that he should not have a son to reign upon his throne, and with the Levites the priests, my ministers. As the host of heaven cannot be numbered, neither the sand of the sea measured, so will I multiply the seed of David my servant and the Levites that minister unto me. Moreover, the word of the Lord came to Jeremiah, saying, Do you not consider what this people have spoken? — saying, The two families whom the Lord has chosen, he has even cast them off. Thus they have despised my people, that they should be no more a nation before them. Thus says the Lord: If my covenant be not with day and night, and if I have not appointed the ordinances of heaven and earth, then will I cast

away the seed of Jacob, and David my servant, so that I will not take any of his seed to be rulers over the seed of Abraham, Isaac, and Jacob. For I will cause their captivity to turn back and have mercy on them.

14 The word which came unto Jeremiah from the Lord when Nebuchadnezzar king of Babylon, and all his army, and all the kingdoms of the earth of his dominion, and all the people fought against Jerusalem and against all the cities thereof, saying, Thus says the Lord, the God of Israel: Go and speak to Zedekiah king of Judah, and tell him, Thus says the Lord: Behold, I will give this city into the hand of the king of Babylon, and he shall burn it with fire. And you shall not escape out of his hand, but shall surely be taken and delivered into his hand. And your eyes shall behold the eyes of the king of Babylon, and he shall speak with you mouth to mouth. And you shall go to Babylon. Yet hear the word of the Lord, O Zedekiah king of Judah. Thus says the Lord of you: You shall not die by the sword, but you shall die in peace. And with the burnings of your fathers, the former kings who were before you, so shall they burn odors for you. And they will lament you, saying, Ah lord! For I have pronounced the word, says the Lord. Then Jeremiah the prophet spoke all these words unto Zedekiah king of Judah in Jerusalem when the king of Babylon's army fought against Jerusalem, and against all the cities of Judah that were left — against Lachish and against Azekah, for these fortified cities remained of the cities of Judah.

2 This is the word that came unto Jeremiah from the Lord after the king, Zedekiah, had made a covenant with all the people who were at Jerusalem, to proclaim liberty unto them: that every man should let his manservant, and every man his maidservant, being a Hebrew or a Hebrewess, go free, that none should serve himself of them, namely of a Jew — his brother. Now when all the princes and all the people who had entered into the covenant heard that everyone should let his manservant, and everyone his maidservant, go free, that none should serve themselves of them anymore, then they obeyed and let them go. But afterward, they turned and caused the servants and the handmaids whom they had let go free to return, and brought them into subjection for servants and for handmaids.

³ Therefore, the word of the Lord came to Jeremiah from the Lord, saying, Thus says the Lord, the God of Israel: I made a covenant with your fathers in the day that I brought them forth out of the land of Egypt, out of the house of bondmen, saying, At the end of seven years, let go every man his brother a Hebrew who has been sold unto you; and when he has served you six years, you shall let him go free from you. But your fathers listened not unto me, neither inclined their ear. But you were now turned and had done right in my sight in proclaiming liberty, every man to his neighbor, and you had made a covenant before me in the house which is called by my name. But you turned and polluted my name, and caused every man his servant and every man his handmaid, whom you had set at liberty at their pleasure, to return, and brought them into subjection, to be unto you for servants and for handmaids.

⁴ Therefore, thus says the Lord: You have not listened unto me in proclaiming liberty, everyone to his brother and every man to his neighbor. Behold, I proclaim a liberty for you, says the Lord, to the sword, to the pestilence, and to the famine. And I will make you to be removed into all the kingdoms of the earth. And I will give the men that have transgressed my covenant, who have not performed the words of the covenant which they had made before me, when they cut the calf in two and passed between the parts thereof — the princes of Judah, and the princes of Jerusalem, the eunuchs, and the priests, and all the people of the land who passed between the parts of the calf — I will even give them into the hand of their enemies and into the hand of them that seek their life. And their dead bodies shall be for food unto the fowls of the heaven and to the beasts of the earth. And Zedekiah king of Judah and his princes will I give into the hand of their enemies, and into the hand of them that seek their life, and into the hand of the king of Babylon's army who have gone up from you. Behold, I will command, says the Lord, and cause them to return to this city; and they shall fight against it, and take it, and burn it with fire. And I will make the cities of Judah a desolation without an inhabitant.

⁵ The word which came unto Jeremiah from the Lord in the days of Jehoiakim the son of Josiah, king of Judah, saying, Go unto the house of the Rechabites and speak unto them, and bring them into the house of the Lord, into one of the chambers, and give them wine to drink.

Then I took Jaazaniah the son of Jeremiah, the son of Habazziniah, and his brethren, and all his sons, and the whole house of the Rechabites, and I brought them into the house of the Lord, into the chamber of the sons of Hanan the son of Igdaliah, a man of God, which was by the chamber of the princes, which was above the chamber of Maaseiah the son of Shallum, the keeper of the door. And I set before the sons of the house of the Rechabites pots full of wine, and cups, and I said unto them, Drink wine. But they said, We will drink no wine, for Jonadab the son of Rechab our father commanded us, saying, You shall drink no wine, neither you nor your sons for ever. Neither shall you build house, nor sow seed, nor plant vineyard, nor have any, but all your days you shall dwell in tents, that you may live many days in the land where you are strangers. Thus have we obeyed the voice of Jonadab the son of Rechab our father in all that he has charged us, to drink no wine all our days — we, our wives, our sons, nor our daughters — nor to build houses for us to dwell in. Neither have we vineyard, nor field, nor seed, but we have dwelled in tents and have obeyed and done according to all that Jonadab our father commanded us. But it came to pass, when Nebuchadnezzar king of Babylon came up into the land, that we said, Come, and let us go to Jerusalem, for fear of the army of the Chaldeans and for fear of the army of the Syrians. So we dwell at Jerusalem.

6 Then came the word of the Lord unto Jeremiah, saying, Thus says the Lord of Hosts, the God of Israel: Go and tell the men of Judah and the inhabitants of Jerusalem, Will you not receive instruction to listen to my words? — says the Lord. The words of Jonadab the son of Rechab that he commanded his sons, not to drink wine, are performed. For unto this day they drink none, but obey their father's commandment. Notwithstanding, I have spoken unto you, commanding you to rise early and speaking to you, but you listened not unto me. I have sent also unto you all my servants the prophets, commanding them to rise up early and sending them, saying, Return now every man from his evil way, and amend your doings, and go not after other gods to serve them; and you shall dwell in the land which I have given to you and to your fathers. But you have not inclined your ear nor listened unto me. Because the sons of Jonadab the son of Rechab have performed the commandment of their father which he commanded them, but this people has not listened unto me, therefore, thus says the Lord God of

Hosts, the God of Israel: Behold, I will bring upon Judah and upon all the inhabitants of Jerusalem all the evil that I have pronounced against them, because I have spoken unto them but they have not heard, and I have called unto them but they have not answered.

7 And Jeremiah said unto the house of the Rechabites, Thus says the Lord of Hosts, the God of Israel: Because you have obeyed the commandment of Jonadab your father, and kept all his precepts, and done according unto all that he has commanded you, therefore thus says the Lord of Hosts, the God of Israel: Jonadab the son of Rechab shall not lack a man to stand before me for ever.

15 And it came to pass in the fourth year of Jehoiakim the son of Josiah, king of Judah, that this word came unto Jeremiah from the Lord, saying: Take a scroll and write therein all the words that I have spoken unto you against Israel, and against Judah, and against all the nations, from the day I spoke unto you, from the days of Josiah, even unto this day. It may be that the house of Judah will hear all the evil which I purpose to do unto them, that they may return every man from his evil way, that I may forgive their iniquity and their sin.

2 Then Jeremiah called Baruch the son of Neriah, and Baruch wrote, from the mouth of Jeremiah, all the words of the Lord which he had spoken unto him, upon a scroll. And Jeremiah commanded Baruch, saying, I am shut up. I cannot go into the house of the Lord; therefore, you go, and read in the scroll which you have written from my mouth the words of the Lord in the ears of the people in the Lord's house upon the fasting day. And also, you shall read them in the ears of all Judah that come out of their cities. It may be they will present their supplication before the Lord and will return everyone from his evil way, for great is the anger and the fury that the Lord has pronounced against this people. And Baruch the son of Neriah did according to all that Jeremiah the prophet commanded him, reading in the book the words of the Lord in the Lord's house.

3 And it came to pass in the fifth year of Jehoiakim the son of Josiah, king of Judah, in the ninth month, that they proclaimed a fast before the Lord to all the people in Jerusalem, and to all the people that came from the cities of Judah unto Jerusalem. Then read Baruch in the book the words of Jeremiah, in the house of the Lord, in the chamber of

Gemariah the son of Shaphan, the scribe, in the higher court, at the entry of the new gate of the Lord's house, in the ears of all the people.

⁴When Michaiah the son of Gemariah, the son of Shaphan, had heard out of the book all the words of the Lord, then he went down into the king's house, into the scribe's chamber, and behold, all the princes sat there, even Elishama the scribe, and Delaiah the son of Shemaiah, and Elnathan the son of Achbor, and Gemariah the son of Shaphan, and Zedekiah the son of Hananiah, and all the princes. Then Michaiah declared unto them all the words that he had heard when Baruch read the book in the ears of the people. Therefore, all the princes sent Jehudi the son of Nethaniah, the son of Shelemiah, the son of Cushi, unto Baruch, saying, Take in your hand the scroll wherein you have read in the ears of the people, and come. So Baruch the son of Neriah took the scroll in his hand and came unto them. And they said unto him, Sit down now and read it in our ears. So Baruch read it in their ears. Now it came to pass, when they had heard all the words, they were afraid both one and other, and said unto Baruch, We will surely tell the king of all these words. And they asked Baruch, saying, Tell us now, How did you write all these words at his mouth? Then Baruch answered them, He pronounced all these words unto me with his mouth and I wrote them with ink in the book. Then said the princes unto Baruch, Go, hide, you and Jeremiah, and let no man know where you are.

⁵And they went in to the king, into the court, but they laid up the scroll in the chamber of Elishama the scribe, and told all the words in the ears of the king. So the king sent Jehudi to fetch the scroll, and he took it out of Elishama the scribe's chamber. And Jehudi read it in the ears of the king and in the ears of all the princes who stood beside the king. Now the king sat in the winter house in the ninth month, and there was a fire on the hearth burning before him. And it came to pass that when Jehudi had read three or four leaves, he cut it with the penknife and cast it into the fire that was on the hearth, until all the scroll was consumed in the fire that was on the hearth. Yet they were not afraid nor rent their garments — neither the king, nor any of his servants that heard all these words. Nevertheless, Elnathan and Delaiah and Gemariah had made intercession to the king that he would not burn the scroll, but he would not hear them. But the king

commanded Jerahmeel the son of Hammelech, and Seraiah the son of Azriel, and Shelemiah the son of Abdeel to take Baruch the scribe and Jeremiah the prophet; but the Lord hid them.

6 Then the word of the Lord came to Jeremiah, after the king had burned the scroll and the words which Baruch wrote at the mouth of Jeremiah, saying, Take again another scroll and write in it all the former words that were in the first scroll which Jehoiakim the king of Judah has burned. And you shall say to Jehoiakim king of Judah, Thus says the Lord: You have burned this scroll, saying, Why have you written therein, saying the king of Babylon shall certainly come and destroy this land, and shall cause to cease from there man and beast? Therefore, thus says the Lord unto Jehoiakim king of Judah: He shall have none to sit upon the throne of David, and his dead body shall be cast out in the day to the heat and in the night to the frost. And I will punish him, and his seed, and his servants, for their iniquity. And I will bring upon them, and upon the inhabitants of Jerusalem, and upon the men of Judah all the evil that I have pronounced against them, but they listened not.

7 Then took Jeremiah another scroll, and gave it to Baruch the scribe, the son of Neriah, who wrote therein from the mouth of Jeremiah all the words of the book which Jehoiakim king of Judah had burned in the fire. And there were added besides unto them many like words.

8 And king Zedekiah the son of Josiah reigned instead of Coniah the son of Jehoiakim, whom Nebuchadnezzar king of Babylon made king in the land of Judah. But neither he, nor his servants, nor the people of the land did listen unto the words of the Lord which he spoke by the prophet Jeremiah.

9 And Zedekiah the king sent Jehucal the son of Shelemiah, and Zephaniah the son of Maaseiah, the priest, to the prophet Jeremiah, saying, Pray now unto the Lord our God for us. Now Jeremiah came in and went out among the people, for they had not put him into prison. Then Pharaoh's army had come forth out of Egypt, and when the Chaldeans that besieged Jerusalem heard tidings of them, they departed from Jerusalem.

10 Then came the word of the Lord unto the prophet Jeremiah, saying, Thus says the Lord, the God of Israel: Thus shall you say to the king of Judah that sent you unto me to inquire of me: Behold, Pharaoh's

army which has come forth to help you shall return to Egypt, into their own land. And the Chaldeans shall come again and fight against this city, and take it, and burn it with fire. Thus says the Lord: Deceive not yourselves, saying, The Chaldeans shall surely depart from us — for they shall not depart. For though you had smitten the whole army of the Chaldeans that fight against you, and there remained but wounded men among them, yet should they rise up every man in his tent and burn this city with fire.

11 And it came to pass that when the army of the Chaldeans was broken up from Jerusalem for fear of Pharaoh's army, then Jeremiah went forth out of Jerusalem to go into the land of Benjamin, to separate himself there in the midst of the people. And when he was in the gate of Benjamin, a captain of the guard was there whose name was Irijah the son of Shelemiah, the son of Hananiah. And he took Jeremiah the prophet, saying, You fall away to the Chaldeans. Then said Jeremiah, It is false, I fall not away to the Chaldeans. But he listened not to him, so Irijah took Jeremiah and brought him to the princes. Wherefore, the princes were angry with Jeremiah and smote him, and put him in prison in the house of Jonathan the scribe — for they had made that the prison. And Jeremiah was entered into the dungeon and into the cells, and he remained there many days.

12 Then Zedekiah the king sent and took him out. And the king asked him secretly in his house, and said, Is there any word from the Lord? And Jeremiah said, There is; for, said he, you shall be delivered into the hand of the king of Babylon. Moreover, Jeremiah said unto king Zedekiah, What have I offended against you, or against your servants, or against this people, that you have put me in prison? Where are now your prophets who prophesied unto you, saying, The king of Babylon shall not come against you, nor against this land? Therefore, hear now, I pray you, O my lord the king. Let my supplication, I pray you, be accepted before you, that you cause me not to return to the house of Jonathan the scribe, lest I die there. Then Zedekiah the king commanded that they should commit Jeremiah into the court of the prison, and that they should give him daily a piece of bread out of the bakers' street, until all the bread in the city was spent. Thus, Jeremiah remained in the court of the prison.

¹³ Then Shephatiah the son of Mattan, and Gedaliah the son of Pashur, and Jucal the son of Shelemiah, and Pashur the son of Malchijah heard the words that Jeremiah had spoken unto all the people, saying, Thus says the Lord: He that remains in this city shall die by the sword, by the famine, and by the pestilence. But he that goes forth to the Chaldeans shall live, for he shall have his life for a prey, and shall live. Thus says the Lord: This city shall surely be given into the hand of the king of Babylon's army, which shall take it. Therefore, the princes said unto the king, We implore you, let this man be put to death. For thus he weakens the hands of the men of war that remain in this city, and the hands of all the people, in speaking such words unto them. For this man seeks not the welfare of this people, but the hurt. Then Zedekiah the king said, Behold, he is in your hand, for the king is not he that can do anything against you. Then they took Jeremiah and cast him into the dungeon of Malchijah the son of Hammelech that was in the court of the prison. And they let down Jeremiah with cords. And in the dungeon there was no water, but mire, so Jeremiah sunk in the mire.

¹⁴ Now when Ebedmelech the Ethiopian, one of the eunuchs who was in the king's house, heard that they had put Jeremiah in the dungeon — the king then sitting in the gate of Benjamin — Ebedmelech went forth out of the king's house and spoke to the king, saying, My lord the king, these men have done evil in all that they have done to Jeremiah the prophet whom they have cast into the dungeon, and he is likely to die for hunger in the place where he is, for there is no more bread in the city. Then the king commanded Ebedmelech the Ethiopian, saying, Take from here thirty men with you and take up Jeremiah the prophet out of the dungeon before he die. So Ebedmelech took the men with him and went into the house of the king, under the treasury, and took from there old cast clothes and old rotten rags, and let them down by cords into the dungeon, to Jeremiah. And Ebedmelech the Ethiopian said unto Jeremiah, Put now these old cast clothes and rotten rags under your armpits under the cords. And Jeremiah did so. So they drew up Jeremiah with cords and took him up out of the dungeon, and Jeremiah remained in the court of the prison. Then Zedekiah the king sent and took Jeremiah the prophet unto him, into the third entry that is in the house of the Lord. And the king said unto Jeremiah, I will ask you a thing; hide nothing from me. Then Jeremiah said unto Zedekiah,

If I declare it unto you, will you not surely put me to death? And if I give you counsel, will you not listen unto me? So Zedekiah the king swore secretly unto Jeremiah, saying, As the Lord lives that made us this soul, I will not put you to death, neither will I give you into the hand of these men that seek your life.

[15] Then said Jeremiah unto Zedekiah, Thus says the Lord, the God of Hosts, the God of Israel: If you will assuredly go forth unto the king of Babylon's princes, then your soul shall live and this city shall not be burned with fire, and you shall live, and your house. But if you will not go forth to the king of Babylon's princes, then shall this city be given into the hand of the Chaldeans, and they shall burn it with fire, and you shall not escape out of their hand. And Zedekiah the king said unto Jeremiah, I am afraid of the Jews that are fallen to the Chaldeans, lest they deliver me into their hand and they mock me. But Jeremiah said, They shall not deliver you. Obey, I implore you, the voice of the Lord which I speak unto you, so it shall be well unto you and your soul shall live. But if you refuse to go forth, this is the word that the Lord has shown me: And behold, all the women that are left in the king of Judah's house shall be brought forth to the king of Babylon's princes, and those women shall say, Your friends have set you on and have prevailed against you. Your feet are sunk in the mire and they are turned away back. So they shall bring out all your wives and your children to the Chaldeans, and you shall not escape out of their hand, but shall be taken by the hand of the king of Babylon. And you shall cause this city to be burned with fire.

[16] Then said Zedekiah unto Jeremiah, Let no man know of these words and you shall not die. But if the princes hear that I have talked with you, and they come unto you and say unto you, Declare unto us now what you have said unto the king, hide it not from us and we will not put you to death — also what the king said unto you — then you shall say unto them, I presented my supplication before the king that he would not cause me to return to Jonathan's house, to die there. Then came all the princes unto Jeremiah and asked him, and he told them according to all these words that the king had commanded. So they left off speaking with him, for the matter was not perceived. So Jeremiah remained in the court of the prison until the day that Jerusalem was taken, and he was there when Jerusalem was taken.

17 In the ninth year of Zedekiah king of Judah, in the tenth month, came Nebuchadnezzar king of Babylon and all his army against Jerusalem, and they besieged it. And in the eleventh year of Zedekiah, in the fourth month, the ninth day of the month, the city was broken up. And all the princes of the king of Babylon came in and sat in the middle gate, even Nergalsharezer, Samgarnebo, Sarsekim chief of the eunuchs, Nergalsharezer chief of the magi, with all the residue of the princes of the king of Babylon. And it came to pass that when Zedekiah the king of Judah saw them, and all the men of war, then they fled and went forth out of the city by night, by the way of the king's garden, by the gate between the two walls; and he went out the way of the plain. But the Chaldeans' army pursued after them and overtook Zedekiah in the plains of Jericho. And when they had taken him, they brought him up to Nebuchadnezzar king of Babylon, to Riblah in the land of Hamath, where he gave judgment upon him. Then the king of Babylon slew the sons of Zedekiah in Riblah before his eyes. Also, the king of Babylon slew all the nobles of Judah. Moreover, he put out Zedekiah's eyes and bound him with chains to carry him to Babylon. And the Chaldeans burned the king's house and the houses of the people with fire, and broke down the walls of Jerusalem. Then Nebuzaradan the captain of the guard carried away captive into Babylon the remnant of the people that remained in the city, and those that fell away, that fell to him, with the rest of the people that remained. But Nebuzaradan the captain of the guard left of the poor of the people, who had nothing, in the land of Judah, and gave them vineyards and fields at the same time.

18 Now Nebuchadnezzar king of Babylon gave charge concerning Jeremiah to Nebuzaradan the captain of the guard, saying, Take him and look well to him, and do him no harm, but do unto him even as he shall say unto you. So Nebuzaradan the captain of the guard sent, and Nebushazban chief of the eunuchs, and Nergalsharezer chief of the magi, and all the king of Babylon's princes, even they sent and took Jeremiah out of the court of the prison and committed him unto Gedaliah the son of Ahikam, the son of Shaphan, that he should carry him home. So he dwelled among the people.

16 Now the word of the Lord came unto Jeremiah while he was shut up in the court of the prison, saying, Go and speak to

Ebedmelech the Ethiopian, saying, Thus says the Lord of Hosts, the God of Israel: Behold, I will bring my words upon this city for evil and not for good, and they shall be accomplished in that day before you. But I will deliver you in that day, says the Lord, and you shall not be given into the hand of the men of whom you are afraid, for I will surely deliver you. And you shall not fall by the sword, but your life shall be for a prey unto you, because you have put your trust in me, says the Lord.

2 The word that came to Jeremiah from the Lord, after Nebuzaradan the captain of the guard had let him go from Ramah, when he had taken him being bound in chains among all that were carried away captive of Jerusalem and Judah who were carried away captive unto Babylon. And the captain of the guard took Jeremiah and said unto him, The Lord your God has pronounced this evil upon this place. Now the Lord has brought it and done according as he has said, because you have sinned against the Lord and have not obeyed his voice. Therefore, this thing has come upon you. And now behold, I release you this day from the chains which were upon your hand. If it seem good unto you to come with me into Babylon, come, and I will look well unto you. But if it seem ill unto you to come with me into Babylon, decline. Behold, all the land is before you — where it seems good and convenient for you to go, there go. Now, while he was not yet gone back, he said, Go back also to Gedaliah the son of Ahikam, the son of Shaphan, whom the king of Babylon has made governor over the cities of Judah, and dwell with him among the people. Or go wherever it seems proper unto you to go. So the captain of the guard gave him provisions and a reward and let him go. Then went Jeremiah unto Gedaliah the son of Ahikam, to Mizpah, and dwelled with him among the people that were left in the land.

3 Now when all the captains of the forces who were in the fields, even they and their men, heard that the king of Babylon had made Gedaliah the son of Ahikam governor in the land, and had committed unto him men, and women, and children, and of the poor of the land, of them that were not carried away captive to Babylon, then they came to Gedaliah, to Mizpah — even Ishmael the son of Nethaniah; and Johanan and Jonathan, the sons of Kareah; and Seraiah the son of Tanhumeth; and the sons of Ephai the Netophathite; and Jezaniah

the son of a Maachathite — they and their men. And Gedaliah the son of Ahikam, the son of Shaphan, swore unto them and to their men, saying, Fear not to serve the Chaldeans. Dwell in the land and serve the king of Babylon, and it shall be well with you. As for me, behold, I will dwell at Mizpah to serve the Chaldeans who will come unto us. But you, gather wine, and summer fruits, and oil, and put them in your vessels, and dwell in your cities that you have taken. Likewise, when all the Jews that were in Moab, and among the Ammonites, and in Edom, and that were in all the countries heard that the king of Babylon had left a remnant of Judah, and that he had set over them Gedaliah the son of Ahikam, the son of Shaphan, even all the Jews returned out of all places to which they were driven and came to the land of Judah, to Gedaliah, unto Mizpah, and gathered wine and summer fruits very much.

4 Moreover, Johanan the son of Kareah and all the captains of the forces that were in the fields came to Gedaliah, to Mizpah, and said unto him, Do you certainly know that Baalis the king of the Ammonites has sent Ishmael the son of Nethaniah to slay you? But Gedaliah the son of Ahikam believed them not. Then Johanan the son of Kareah spoke to Gedaliah in Mizpah secretly, saying, Let me go, I pray you, and I will slay Ishmael the son of Nethaniah, and no man shall know it. Why should he slay you, that all the Jews who are gathered unto you should be scattered and the remnant in Judah perish? But Gedaliah the son of Ahikam said unto Johanan the son of Kareah, You shall not do this thing, for you speak falsely of Ishmael.

5 Now it came to pass in the seventh month that Ishmael the son of Nethaniah, the son of Elishama, of the royal seed, and the princes of the king, even ten men with him, came unto Gedaliah the son of Ahikam, to Mizpah. And there they did eat bread together in Mizpah. Then arose Ishmael the son of Nethaniah, and the ten men that were with him, and smote Gedaliah the son of Ahikam, the son of Shaphan, with the sword, and slew him whom the king of Babylon had made governor over the land. Ishmael also slew all the Jews that were with him, even with Gedaliah at Mizpah, and the Chaldeans that were found there, and the men of war.

6 And it came to pass the second day after he had slain Gedaliah — and no man knew it — that there came certain from Shechem, from Shiloh,

and from Samaria, even eighty men having their beards shaven and their clothes rent, and having cut themselves, with offerings and incense in their hand, to bring them to the house of the Lord. And Ishmael the son of Nethaniah went forth from Mizpah to meet them, weeping all along as he went. And it came to pass as he met them, he said unto them, Come to Gedaliah the son of Ahikam. And it was so, when they came into the midst of the city, that Ishmael the son of Nethaniah slew them and cast them into the midst of the pit, he and the men that were with him. But ten men were found among them that said unto Ishmael, Slay us not, for we have treasures in the field of wheat, and of barley, and of oil, and of honey. So he refrained and slew them not among their brethren.

7 Now the pit, wherein Ishmael had cast all the dead bodies of the men whom he had slain because of Gedaliah, was it which Asa the king had made for fear of Baasha king of Israel. And Ishmael the son of Nethaniah filled it with them that were slain. Then Ishmael carried away captive all the residue of the people that were in Mizpah, even the king's daughters and all the people that remained in Mizpah whom Nebuzaradan the captain of the guard had committed to Gedaliah the son of Ahikam. And Ishmael the son of Nethaniah carried them away captive and departed to go over to the Ammonites.

8 But when Johanan the son of Kareah, and all the captains of the forces that were with him, heard of all the evil that Ishmael the son of Nethaniah had done, then they took all the men and went to fight with Ishmael the son of Nethaniah, and found him by the great waters that are in Gibeon. Now it came to pass that when all the people who were with Ishmael saw Johanan the son of Kareah, and all the captains of the forces that were with him, then they were glad. So all the people that Ishmael had carried away captive from Mizpah cast about, and returned and went unto Johanan the son of Kareah. But Ishmael the son of Nethaniah escaped from Johanan with eight men and went to the Ammonites. Then took Johanan the son of Kareah, and all the captains of the forces that were with him, all the remnant of the people whom he had recovered from Ishmael the son of Nethaniah, from Mizpah, after he had slain Gedaliah the son of Ahikam — even mighty men of war, and the women, and the children, and the eunuchs whom he had brought again from Gibeon. And they departed and dwelled in

the habitation of Chimham which is by Bethlehem, to go to enter into Egypt because of the Chaldeans; for they were afraid of them, because Ishmael the son of Nethaniah had slain Gedaliah the son of Ahikam, whom the king of Babylon made governor in the land.

9 Then all the captains of the forces, and Johanan the son of Kareah, and Jezaniah the son of Hoshaiah, and all the people from the least even unto the greatest came near and said unto Jeremiah the prophet, Let, we implore you, our supplication be accepted before you, and pray for us unto the Lord your God, even for all this remnant (for we are left but a few of many, as your eyes do behold us), that the Lord your God may show us the way wherein we may walk and the thing that we may do. Then Jeremiah the prophet said unto them, I have heard you. Behold, I will pray unto the Lord your God according to your words. And it shall come to pass that whatever thing the Lord shall answer you, I will declare it unto you. I will keep nothing back from you. Then they said to Jeremiah, The Lord be a true and faithful witness between us if we do not even according to all things for which the Lord your God shall send you to us. Whether it be good or whether it be evil, we will obey the voice of the Lord our God to whom we send you, that it may be well with us when we obey the voice of the Lord our God.

10 And it came to pass after ten days that the word of the Lord came unto Jeremiah. Then he called Johanan the son of Kareah, and all the captains of the forces who were with him, and all the people from the least even to the greatest, and said unto them, Thus says the Lord, the God of Israel, unto whom you sent me to present your supplication before him: If you will still abide in this land, then will I build you and not pull down. And I will plant you and not pluck up, and I will turn away the evil that I have done unto you. Be not afraid of the king of Babylon, of whom you are afraid. Be not afraid of him, says the Lord, for I am with you to save you and to deliver you from his hand. And I will show mercies unto you, that he may have mercy upon you and cause you to return to your own land. But if you say, We will not dwell in this land, neither obey the voice of the Lord your God — saying, No, but we will go into the land of Egypt, where we shall see no war, nor hear the sound of the trumpet, nor have hunger for lack of bread, and there will we dwell — and now therefore hear the word of the Lord, you remnant of Judah, thus says the Lord of Hosts, the God of Israel:

If you wholly set your faces to enter into Egypt and go to sojourn there, then it shall come to pass that the sword which you feared shall overtake you there in the land of Egypt, and the famine whereof you were afraid shall follow close after you there in Egypt, and there you shall die. So shall it be with all the men that set their faces to go into Egypt to sojourn there: they shall die by the sword, by the famine, and by the pestilence, and none of them shall remain or escape from the evil that I will bring upon them. For thus says the Lord of Hosts, the God of Israel: As my anger and my fury has been poured forth upon the inhabitants of Jerusalem, so shall my fury be poured forth upon you when you shall enter into Egypt. And you shall be an execration, and an astonishment, and a curse, and a reproach, and you shall see this place no more. The Lord has said concerning you, O remnant of Judah, Go not into Egypt. Know certainly that I have admonished you this day. For you went astray in your hearts when you sent me unto the Lord your God, saying, Pray for us unto the Lord our God, and according unto all that the Lord our God shall say, so declare unto us and we will do it. And now I have this day declared it to you, that you have not obeyed the voice of the Lord your God, nor anything for which he has sent me unto you. Now therefore know certainly that you shall die by the sword, by the famine, and by the pestilence, in the place where you desire to go and to sojourn.

¹¹ And it came to pass that when Jeremiah had made an end of speaking unto all the people all the words of the Lord their God, for which the Lord their God had sent him to them, even all these words, then spoke Azariah the son of Hoshaiah, and Johanan the son of Kareah, and all the proud men, saying unto Jeremiah, You speak falsely. The Lord our God has not sent you to say, Go not into Egypt to sojourn there. But Baruch the son of Neriah sets you on against us in order to deliver us into the hand of the Chaldeans, that they might put us to death and carry us away captives into Babylon. So Johanan the son of Kareah, and all the captains of the forces, and all the people obeyed not the voice of the Lord, to dwell in the land of Judah. But Johanan the son of Kareah and all the captains of the forces took all the remnant of Judah, that were returned from all nations to which they had been driven to dwell in the land of Judah — even men, and women, and children, and the king's daughters, and every person that

Nebuzaradan the captain of the guard had left with Gedaliah the son of Ahikam, the son of Shaphan, and Jeremiah the prophet, and Baruch the son of Neriah. So they came into the land of Egypt, for they obeyed not the voice of the Lord; thus came they even to Tahpanhes.

12 Then came the word of the Lord unto Jeremiah in Tahpanhes, saying, Take great stones in your hand and hide them in the clay in the brick kiln which is at the entry of Pharaoh's house in Tahpanhes, in the sight of the men of Judah, and say unto them, Thus says the Lord of Hosts, the God of Israel: Behold, I will send and take Nebuchadnezzar the king of Babylon, my servant, and will set his throne upon these stones that I have hidden. And he shall spread his royal pavilion over them. And when he comes, he shall smite the land of Egypt and deliver such as are for death to death, and such as are for captivity to captivity, and such as are for the sword to the sword. And I will kindle a fire in the houses of the gods of Egypt and he shall burn them and carry them away captives. And he shall array himself with the land of Egypt as a shepherd puts on his garment. And he shall go forth from there in peace. He shall break also the images of Bethshemesh that is in the land of Egypt, and the houses of the gods of the Egyptians shall he burn with fire.

13 The word that came to Jeremiah concerning all the Jews who dwell in the land of Egypt, who dwell at Migdol, and at Tahpanhes, and at Noph, and in the country of Pathros, saying, Thus says the Lord of Hosts, the God of Israel: You have seen all the evil that I have brought upon Jerusalem and upon all the cities of Judah. And behold, this day they are a desolation and no man dwells therein, because of their wickedness which they have committed to provoke me to anger, in that they went to burn incense, and to serve other gods whom they knew not — neither they, you, nor your fathers. Nevertheless, I sent unto you all my servants the prophets, commanding them to rise early and sending them, saying, Oh, do not this abominable thing that I hate. But they listened not, nor inclined their ear to turn from their wickedness, to burn no incense unto other gods. Wherefore, my fury and my anger was poured forth, and was kindled in the cities of Judah and in the streets of Jerusalem. And they are wasted and desolate, as at this day. Therefore now, thus says the Lord, the God of Hosts, the God of Israel: Why do you commit this great evil against your souls, to

cut off from you man and woman, child and suckling, out of Judah? To leave you none to remain, in that you provoke me unto wrath with the works of your hands, burning incense unto other gods in the land of Egypt where you have gone to dwell, that you might cut yourselves off and that you might be a curse and a reproach among all the nations of the earth? Have you forgotten the wickedness of your fathers, and the wickedness of the kings of Judah, and the wickedness of their wives, and your own wickedness, and the wickedness of your wives which they have committed in the land of Judah and in the streets of Jerusalem? They are not humbled even unto this day, neither have they feared nor walked in my law nor in my statutes that I set before you and before your fathers.

14 Therefore, thus says the Lord of Hosts, the God of Israel: Behold, I will set my face against you for evil and to cut off all Judah. And I will take the remnant of Judah that have set their faces to go into the land of Egypt, to sojourn there, and they shall all be consumed and fall in the land of Egypt. They shall even be consumed by the sword and by the famine. They shall die, from the least even unto the greatest, by the sword and by the famine. And they shall be an execration, and an astonishment, and a curse, and a reproach. For I will punish them that dwell in the land of Egypt as I have punished Jerusalem — by the sword, by the famine, and by the pestilence — so that none of the remnant of Judah who have gone into the land of Egypt, to sojourn there, shall escape or remain that they should return into the land of Judah to which they have a desire to return, to dwell there. For none shall return but such as shall escape.

15 Then all the men who knew that their wives had burned incense unto other gods, and all the women that stood by — a great multitude — even all the people that dwelled in the land of Egypt, in Pathros, answered Jeremiah, saying, As for the word that you have spoken unto us in the name of the Lord, we will not listen unto you, but we will certainly do whatever thing goes forth out of our own mouth, to burn incense unto the queen of Heaven and to pour out drink offerings unto her as we have done — we and our fathers, our kings and our princes, in the cities of Judah and in the streets of Jerusalem. For then had we plenty of provisions, and were well, and saw no evil. But since we left off to burn incense to the queen of Heaven

and to pour out drink offerings unto her, we have lacked all things and have been consumed by the sword and by the famine. And when we burned incense to the queen of Heaven and poured out drink offerings unto her, did we make her cakes to worship her and pour out drink offerings unto her without our men? Then Jeremiah said unto all the people — to the men, and to the women, and to all the people who had given him that answer — saying, The incense that you burned in the cities of Judah and in the streets of Jerusalem, you and your fathers, your kings and your princes, and the people of the land, did not the Lord remember them and came it not into his mind? So that the Lord could no longer bear because of the evil of your doings and because of the abominations which you have committed? Therefore is your land a desolation, and an astonishment, and a curse, without an inhabitant, as at this day. Because you have burned incense, and because you have sinned against the Lord, and have not obeyed the voice of the Lord, nor walked in his law, nor in his statutes, nor in his testimonies, therefore this evil is happened unto you, as at this day. Moreover, Jeremiah said unto all the people and to all the women, Hear the word of the Lord, all Judah that are in the land of Egypt; thus says the Lord of Hosts, the God of Israel, saying: You and your wives have both spoken with your mouths and fulfilled with your hand, saying, We will surely perform our vows that we have vowed, to burn incense to the queen of Heaven and to pour out drink offerings unto her. You will surely accomplish your vows and surely perform your vows. Therefore hear the word of the Lord, all Judah that dwell in the land of Egypt: Behold, I have sworn by my great name, says the Lord, that my name shall no more be named in the mouth of any man of Judah in all the land of Egypt, saying, The Lord God lives. Behold, I will watch over them for evil and not for good. And all the men of Judah that are in the land of Egypt shall be consumed by the sword and by the famine until there is an end of them. Yet a small number that escape the sword shall return out of the land of Egypt into the land of Judah. And all the remnant of Judah that have gone into the land of Egypt to sojourn there shall know whose words shall stand — mine or theirs. And this shall be a sign unto you, says the Lord, that I will punish you in this place, that you may know that my words shall surely stand against you for evil. Thus says the Lord: Behold, I will give Pharaoh Hophra, king of Egypt, into the hand of his enemies and into the hand of them that seek his life, as I gave Zedekiah king of Judah into the hand of Nebuchadnezzar king of Babylon, his enemy, and that sought his life.

17 The word that Jeremiah the prophet spoke unto Baruch the son of Neriah, when he had written these words in a book at the mouth of Jeremiah, in the fourth year of Jehoiakim the son of Josiah, king of Judah, saying, Thus says the Lord, the God of Israel, unto you, O Baruch: You did say, Woe is me now, for the Lord has added grief to my sorrow. I fainted in my sighing and I find no rest. Thus shall you say unto him: The Lord says thus: Behold, that which I have built will I break down, and that which I have planted I will pluck up, even this whole land. And do you seek great things for yourself? Seek them not, for behold, I will bring evil upon all flesh, says the Lord. But your life will I give unto you for a prey in all places where you go.

2 The word of the Lord which came to Jeremiah the prophet against the gentiles, against Egypt, against the army of Pharaoh Necho, king of Egypt, which was by the river Euphrates in Carchemish, which Nebuchadnezzar king of Babylon smote in the fourth year of Jehoiakim the son of Josiah, king of Judah: Order the buckler and shield and draw near to battle. Harness the horses and get up, you horsemen, and stand forth with your helmets. Polish the spears and put on the brigandines. Why have I seen them dismayed and turned away back? And their mighty ones are beaten down, and are fled quickly, and look not back, for fear was round about, says the Lord. Let not the swift flee away nor the mighty man escape. They shall stumble and fall toward the north by the river Euphrates. Who is this that comes up as a flood, whose waters are moved as the rivers? Egypt rises up like a flood and his waters are moved like the rivers. And he says, I will go up and will cover the earth, I will destroy the city and the inhabitants thereof. Come up, you horses, and rage, you chariots. And let the mighty men come forth — the Ethiopians and the Libyans that handle the shield, and the Lydians that handle and bend the bow. For this is the day of the Lord God of Hosts, a day of vengeance, that he may avenge him of his adversaries. And the sword shall devour and it shall be satiated and made drunk with their blood, for the Lord God of Hosts has a sacrifice in the north country by the river Euphrates. Go up into Gilead

and take balm, O virgin, the daughter of Egypt. In vain shall you use many medicines, for you shall not be cured. The nations have heard of your shame and your cry has filled the land, for the mighty man has stumbled against the mighty and they are fallen both together.

³ The word that the Lord spoke to Jeremiah the prophet, how Nebuchadnezzar king of Babylon should come and smite the land of Egypt: Declare in Egypt, and publish in Migdol, and publish in Noph and in Tahpanhes. Say, Stand fast and prepare yourself, for the sword shall devour round about you. Why are your valiant men swept away? They stood not, because the Lord did drive them. He made many to fall, yea, one fell upon another. And they said, Arise and let us go again to our own people and to the land of our nativity, from the oppressing sword. They did cry there, Pharaoh king of Egypt is but a noise, he has passed the time appointed. As I live, says the King, whose name is the Lord of Hosts, surely as Tabor is among the mountains and as Carmel by the sea, so shall he come. O you daughter dwelling in Egypt, furnish yourself to go into captivity, for Noph shall be waste and desolate, without an inhabitant. Egypt is like a very fair heifer, but destruction comes; it comes out of the north. Also, her hired men are in her midst like fattened bullocks, for they also are turned back and are fled away together. They did not stand because the day of their calamity had come upon them, and the time of their visitation. The voice thereof shall go like a serpent, for they shall march with an army and come against her with axes as hewers of wood. They shall cut down her forest, says the Lord, though it cannot be searched, because they are more than the grasshoppers and are innumerable. The daughter of Egypt shall be confounded; she shall be delivered into the hand of the people of the north.

⁴ The Lord of Hosts, the God of Israel, says, Behold, I will punish the multitude of No, and Pharaoh, and Egypt, with their gods and their kings — even Pharaoh and all them that trust in him. And I will deliver them into the hand of those that seek their lives, and into the hand of Nebuchadnezzar king of Babylon, and into the hand of his servants. And afterward it shall be inhabited as in the days of old, says the Lord. But fear not, O my servant Jacob, and be not dismayed, O Israel; for behold, I will save you from afar off, and your seed from the land of their captivity. And Jacob shall return and be in rest and at ease, and

none shall make him afraid. Fear not, O Jacob my servant, says the Lord, for I am with you. For I will make a full end of all the nations to which I have driven you. But I will not make a full end of you, but correct you in measure; yet will I not leave you wholly unpunished.

5 The word of the Lord that came to Jeremiah the prophet against the Philistines, before Pharaoh smote Gaza. Thus says the Lord: Behold, waters rise up out of the north, and shall be an overflowing flood, and shall overflow the land and all that is therein — the city and them that dwell therein. Then the men shall cry and all the inhabitants of the land shall howl. At the noise of the stamping of the hooves of his strong horses, at the rushing of his chariots, and at the rumbling of his wheels, the fathers shall not look back to their children for feebleness of hands, because of the day that comes to spoil all the Philistines and to cut off from Tyre and Sidon every helper that remains. For the Lord will spoil the Philistines, the remnant of the country of Caphtor. Baldness has come upon Gaza; Ashkelon is cut off with the remnant of their valley. How long will you cut yourself? O you sword of the Lord, how long will it be before you are quiet? Put up yourself into your scabbard, rest and be still. How can it be quiet, seeing the Lord has given it a charge against Ashkelon and against the seashore? There has he appointed it.

6 Against Moab, thus says the Lord of Hosts, the God of Israel: Woe unto Nebo, for it is spoiled. Kiriathaim is confounded and taken. Misgab is confounded and dismayed. There shall be no more praise of Moab; in Heshbon they have devised evil against it: Come, and let us cut it off from being a nation. Also, you shall be cut down, O Madmen, the sword shall pursue you. A voice of crying shall be from Horonaim, Spoiling and great destruction! Moab is destroyed, her little ones have caused a cry to be heard. For in the ascent of Luhith, continual weeping shall go up. For in the descent of Horonaim, the enemies have heard a cry of destruction: Flee, save your lives, and be like the juniper in the wilderness! For, because you have trusted in your works and in your treasures, you shall also be taken. And Chemosh shall go forth into captivity, with his priests and his princes together. And the spoiler shall come upon every city, and no city shall escape. The valley also shall perish, and the plain shall be destroyed, as the Lord has spoken. Give wings unto Moab, that it may flee and get away; for the cities thereof shall be desolate, without any to dwell therein. Cursed be he

that does the work of the Lord deceitfully, and cursed be he that keeps back his sword from blood.

7 Moab has been at ease from his youth, and he has settled on his lees, and has not been emptied from vessel to vessel; neither has he gone into captivity. Therefore his taste remained in him and his scent is not changed. Therefore, behold, the days come, says the Lord, that I will send unto him wanderers that shall cause him to wander, and shall empty his vessels, and break their bottles. And Moab shall be ashamed of Chemosh as the house of Israel was ashamed of Beth-el their confidence. How can you say, We are mighty and strong men for the war? Moab is spoiled and gone up out of her cities, and his chosen young men have gone down to the slaughter, says the King, whose name is the Lord of Hosts.

8 The calamity of Moab is near to come, and his affliction hastens fast. All you that are about him bemoan him. And all you that know his name say, How is the strong staff broken, and the beautiful rod! You, daughter, that do inhabit Dibon, come down from your glory and sit in thirst. For the spoiler of Moab shall come upon you, and he shall destroy your strongholds. O inhabitant of Aroer, stand by the way and watch. Ask him that flees and her that escapes, and say, What is done? Moab is confounded, for it is broken down. Howl and cry, tell it in Arnon, that Moab is spoiled. And judgment has come upon the plain country — upon Holon, and upon Jahzah, and upon Mephaath, and upon Dibon, and upon Nebo, and upon Bethdiblathaim, and upon Kiriathaim, and upon Bethgamul, and upon Bethmeon, and upon Kerioth, and upon Bozrah, and upon all the cities of the land of Moab, far or near. The horn of Moab is cut off and his arm is broken, says the Lord. Make him drunk, for he magnified himself against the Lord. Moab also shall wallow in his vomit, and he also shall be in derision. For was not Israel a derision unto you? Was he found among thieves? For since you spoke of him, you skipped for joy.

9 O you that dwell in Moab, leave the cities and dwell in the rock, and be like the dove that makes her nest in the sides of the hole's mouth. We have heard the pride of Moab (he is exceedingly proud), his loftiness, and his arrogance, and his pride, and the haughtiness of his heart. I know his wrath, says the Lord, but it shall not be so. His lies shall not so effect it. Therefore will I howl for Moab, and I will cry

out for all Moab. My heart shall mourn for the men of Kirhareseth. O vine of Sibmah, I will weep for you with the weeping of Jazer. Your plants have gone over the sea, they reach even to the sea of Jazer. The spoiler is fallen upon your summer fruits and upon your vintage, and joy and gladness is taken from the plentiful field and from the land of Moab. And I have caused wine to fail from the winepresses, none shall tread with shouting; their shouting shall be no shouting. From the cry of Heshbon even unto Elealeh, and even unto Jahaz have they uttered their voice, from Zoar even unto Horonaim, as a heifer of three years old. For the waters also of Nimrim shall be desolate. Moreover, I will cause to cease in Moab, says the Lord, him that offers in the high places and him that burns incense to his gods. Therefore, my heart shall sound for Moab like pipes, and my heart shall sound like pipes for the men of Kirhareseth, because the riches that he has gotten are perished; for every head shall be bald and every beard clipped. Upon all the hands shall be cuttings, and upon the loins — sackcloth. There shall be lamentation generally upon all the housetops of Moab and in the streets thereof, for I have broken Moab like a vessel, wherein is no pleasure, says the Lord.

10 They shall howl, saying, How is it broken down! How has Moab turned the back with shame! So shall Moab be a derision and a dismaying to all them about him. For thus says the Lord: Behold, he shall fly as an eagle and shall spread his wings over Moab. Kerioth is taken, and the strongholds are surprised, and the mighty men's hearts in Moab at that day shall be as the heart of a woman in her pangs. And Moab shall be destroyed from being a people because he has magnified himself against the Lord. Fear, and the pit, and the snare shall be upon you, O inhabitant of Moab, says the Lord. He that flees from the fear shall fall into the pit, and he that gets up out of the pit shall be taken in the snare; for I will bring upon it, even upon Moab, the year of their visitation, says the Lord. They that fled stood under the shadow of Heshbon because of the force, but a fire shall come forth out of Heshbon, and a flame from the midst of Sihon, and shall devour the corner of Moab and the crown of the head of the tumultuous ones. Woe be unto you, O Moab. The people of Chemosh perishes, for your sons are taken captives and your daughters captives. Yet will I bring

again the captives of Moab in the latter days, says the Lord. Thus far is the judgment of Moab.

¹¹ Concerning the Ammonites, thus says the Lord: Has Israel no sons? Has he no heir? Why then does their king inherit Gad, and his people dwell in his cities? Therefore, behold, the days come, says the Lord, that I will cause an alarm of war to be heard in Rabbah of the Ammonites. And it shall be a desolate heap, and her daughters shall be burned with fire. Then shall Israel be heir unto them that were his heirs, says the Lord. Howl, O Heshbon, for Ai is spoiled. Cry, you daughters of Rabbah, gird yourselves with sackcloth, lament and run to and fro by the hedges. For their king shall go into captivity, and his priests and his princes together. Why do you glory in the valleys, your flowing valley, O backsliding daughter that trusted in her treasures, saying, Who shall come unto me? Behold, I will bring a fear upon you, says the Lord God of Hosts, from all those that are about you. And you shall be driven out, every man right forth, and none shall gather up him that wanders. And afterward I will bring again the captives of the children of Ammon, says the Lord.

¹² Concerning Edom, thus says the Lord of Hosts: Is wisdom no more in Teman? Is counsel perished from the prudent? Is their wisdom vanished? Flee, turn back, dwell deep, O inhabitants of Dedan, for I will bring the calamity of Esau upon him the time that I will visit him. If grape gatherers come to you, would they not leave some gleaning grapes? If thieves by night, they will destroy until they have enough. But I have made Esau bare. I have uncovered his secret places and he shall not be able to hide himself. His seed is spoiled, and his brethren, and his neighbors; and he is not. Leave your fatherless children, I will preserve them alive, and let your widows trust in me.

¹³ For thus says the Lord: Behold, they whose judgment was not to drink of the cup have assuredly drunk. And are you he that shall altogether go unpunished? You shall not go unpunished, but you shall surely drink of it. For I have sworn by myself, says the Lord, that Bozrah shall become a desolation, a reproach, a waste, and a curse, and all the cities thereof shall be perpetual wastes. I have heard a rumor from the Lord, and an ambassador is sent unto the heathen, saying, Gather yourselves together and come against her, and rise up to the battle, for behold, I will make you small among the heathen and

despised among men. Your terror has deceived you, and the pride of your heart, O you that dwell in the clefts of the rock, that hold the height of the hill. Though you should make your nest as high as the eagle, I will bring you down from there, says the Lord.

14 Also, Edom shall be a desolation. Everyone that goes by it shall be astonished and shall hiss at all the plagues thereof. As in the overthrow of Sodom and Gomorrah and the neighbor cities thereof, says the Lord, no man shall abide there, neither shall a son of man dwell in it. Behold, he shall come up like a lion from the swelling of Jordan against the habitation of the strong, but I will suddenly make him run away from her. And who is a chosen man that I may appoint over her? For who is like me? And who will appoint me the time? And who is that shepherd that will stand before me? Therefore, hear the counsel of the Lord that he has taken against Edom, and his purposes that he has purposed against the inhabitants of Teman: Surely the least of the flock shall draw them out, surely he shall make their habitations desolate with them. The earth is moved at the noise of their fall. At the cry, the noise thereof was heard in the Red Sea. Behold, he shall come up and fly as the eagle and spread his wings over Bozrah. And at that day shall the heart of the mighty men of Edom be as the heart of a woman in her pangs.

15 Concerning Damascus: Hamath is confounded, and Arpad, for they have heard evil tidings. They are faint-hearted. There is sorrow on the sea; it cannot be quiet. Damascus is waxed feeble and turns herself to flee, and fear has seized on her. Anguish and sorrows have taken her as a woman in travail. How is the city of praise not left, the city of my joy? Therefore, her young men shall fall in her streets and all the men of war shall be cut off in that day, says the Lord of Hosts. And I will kindle a fire in the wall of Damascus, and it shall consume the palaces of Benhadad.

16 Concerning Kedar and concerning the kingdoms of Hazor, which Nebuchadnezzar king of Babylon shall smite, thus says the Lord: Arise, go up to Kedar, and spoil the men of the east. Their tents and their flocks shall they take away. They shall take to themselves their curtains, and all their vessels, and their camels. And they shall cry unto them, Fear is on every side! Flee, go far off! Dwell deep, O you inhabitants of Hazor, says the Lord, for Nebuchadnezzar king of Babylon has taken

counsel against you and has conceived a purpose against you. Arise, go up unto the wealthy nation that dwells without care, says the Lord, who have neither gates nor bars, who dwell alone. And their camels shall be a booty and the multitude of their cattle a spoil. And I will scatter into all winds them that are in the utmost corners. And I will bring their calamity from all sides thereof, says the Lord. And Hazor shall be a dwelling for dragons and a desolation for ever. There shall no man abide there, nor any son of man dwell in it.

18 The word of the Lord that came to Jeremiah the prophet against Elam in the beginning of the reign of Zedekiah king of Judah, saying, Thus says the Lord of Hosts: Behold, I will break the bow of Elam, the chief of their might. And upon Elam will I bring the four winds from the four quarters of heaven, and will scatter them toward all those winds. And there shall be no nation to which the outcasts of Elam shall not come. For I will cause Elam to be dismayed before their enemies and before them that seek their life. And I will bring evil upon them, even my fierce anger, says the Lord. And I will send the sword after them until I have consumed them. And I will set my throne in Elam and will destroy from there the king and the princes, says the Lord. But it shall come to pass in the latter days that I will bring again the captives of Elam, says the Lord.

2 The word that the Lord spoke against Babylon and against the land of the Chaldeans by Jeremiah the prophet: Declare among the nations, and publish and set up a standard; publish, and conceal not. Say, Babylon is taken, Bel is confounded, Merodach is broken in pieces. Her idols are confounded, her images are broken in pieces. For out of the north there comes up a nation against her which shall make her land desolate, and none shall dwell therein. They shall remove, they shall depart, both man and beast. In those days and in that time, says the Lord, the children of Israel shall come, they and the children of Judah together, going and weeping. They shall go and seek the Lord their God. They shall ask the way to Zion with their faces toward it, saying, Come, and let us join ourselves to the Lord in a perpetual covenant that shall not be forgotten. My people have been lost sheep, their shepherds have caused them to go astray. They have turned them away on the mountains, they have gone from mountain to hill. They

have forgotten their resting place. All that found them have devoured them. And their adversaries said, We offend not, because they have sinned against the Lord, the habitation of justice, even the Lord, the hope of their fathers.

³ Remove out of the midst of Babylon and go forth out of the land of the Chaldeans, and be as the he-goats before the flocks. For behold, I will raise and cause to come up against Babylon an assembly of great nations from the north country. And they shall set themselves in array against her; from there she shall be taken. Their arrows shall be as of a mighty expert man, none shall return in vain. And Chaldea shall be a spoil. All that spoil her shall be satisfied, says the Lord, because you were glad, because you rejoiced, O you destroyers of my heritage, because you are grown fat as the heifer at grass and bellow as bulls. Your mother shall be severely confounded, she that bore you shall be ashamed. Behold, the rearmost of the nations shall be a wilderness, a dry land and a desert. Because of the wrath of the Lord, it shall not be inhabited, but it shall be wholly desolate. Everyone that goes by Babylon shall be astonished and hiss at all her plagues. Put yourselves in array against Babylon round about. All you that bend the bow, shoot at her, spare no arrows, for she has sinned against the Lord. Shout against her round about. She has given her hand. Her foundations are fallen, her walls are thrown down, for it is the vengeance of the Lord. Take vengeance upon her; as she has done, do unto her. Cut off the sower from Babylon and him that handles the sickle in the time of harvest. For fear of the oppressing sword, they shall turn everyone to his people and they shall flee everyone to his own land.

⁴ Israel is a scattered sheep, the lions have driven him away. First, the king of Assyria has devoured him, and last, this Nebuchadnezzar king of Babylon has broken his bones. Therefore thus says the Lord of Hosts, the God of Israel: Behold, I will punish the king of Babylon and his land as I have punished the king of Assyria. And I will bring Israel again to his habitation, and he shall feed on Carmel and Bashan, and his soul shall be satisfied upon Mount Ephraim and Gilead. In those days and in that time, says the Lord, the iniquity of Israel shall be sought for, and there shall be none, and the sins of Judah, and they shall not be found; for I will pardon them whom I reserve. Go up against the land of Merathaim, even against it and against the inhabitants

of Pekod. Waste and utterly destroy after them, says the Lord, and do according to all that I have commanded you. A sound of battle is in the land and of great destruction. How is the hammer of the whole earth cut asunder and broken! How is Babylon become a desolation among the nations! I have laid a snare for you and you are also taken, O Babylon, and you were not aware. You are found and also caught, because you have fought against the Lord. The Lord has opened his armory and has brought forth the weapons of his indignation, for this is the work of the Lord God of Hosts in the land of the Chaldeans. Come against her from the utmost border, open her storehouses. Cast her up as heaps and destroy her utterly, let nothing of her be left. Slay all her bullocks, let them go down to the slaughter. Woe unto them, for their day has come, the time of their visitation, the voice of them that flee and escape out of the land of Babylon to declare in Zion the vengeance of the Lord our God, the vengeance of his temple. Call together the archers against Babylon. All you that bend the bow, camp against it round about. Let none thereof escape. Recompense her according to her work. According to all that she has done, do unto her, for she has been proud against the Lord, against the Holy One of Israel.

5 Therefore shall her young men fall in the streets and all her men of war shall be cut off in that day, says the Lord. Behold, I am against you, O you most proud, says the Lord God of Hosts, for your day has come, the time that I will visit you. And the most proud shall stumble and fall, and none shall raise him up. And I will kindle a fire in his cities and it shall devour all round about him.

6 Thus says the Lord of Hosts: The children of Israel and the children of Judah were oppressed together. And all that took them captives held them fast; they refused to let them go. Their Redeemer is strong; the Lord of Hosts is his name. He shall thoroughly plead their cause, that he may give rest to the land and disquiet the inhabitants of Babylon.

7 A sword is upon the Chaldeans, says the Lord, and upon the inhabitants of Babylon, and upon her princes, and upon her wise men. A sword is upon the liars, and they shall become fools. A sword is upon her mighty men and they shall be dismayed. A sword is upon their horses, and upon their chariots, and upon all the mingled people that are in her midst, and they shall become as women. A sword is upon her treasures and they shall be robbed. A drought is upon her waters

and they shall be dried up. For it is the land of engraved images, and they are mad over their idols. Therefore, the wild beasts of the desert with the wild beasts of the islands shall dwell there, and the owls shall dwell therein. And it shall be no more inhabited for ever, neither shall it be dwelled in from generation to generation. As God overthrew Sodom and Gomorrah and the neighbor cities thereof, says the Lord, so shall no man abide there, neither shall any son of man dwell therein.

8 Behold, a people shall come from the north, and a great nation and many kings shall be raised up from the ends of the earth. They shall hold the bow and the lance. They are cruel and will not show mercy. Their voice shall roar like the sea and they shall ride upon horses, everyone put in array like a man to the battle against you, O daughter of Babylon. The king of Babylon has heard the report of them and his hands waxed feeble. Anguish took hold of him, and pangs as of a woman in travail.

9 Behold, he shall come up like a lion from the swelling of Jordan unto the habitation of the strong, but I will make them suddenly run away from her. And who is a chosen man that I may appoint over her? For who is like me? And who will appoint me the time? And who is that shepherd that will stand before me? Therefore, hear the counsel of the Lord that he has taken against Babylon, and his purposes that he has purposed against the land of the Chaldeans. Surely the least of the flock shall draw them out. Surely he shall make their habitation desolate with them. At the noise of the taking of Babylon, the earth is moved and the cry is heard among the nations.

10 Thus says the Lord: Behold, I will raise up against Babylon, and against them that dwell in the midst of them that rise up against me, a destroying wind, and will send unto Babylon winnowers that shall winnow her, and shall empty her land. For in the day of trouble, they shall be against her round about. Against him that bends, let the archer bend his bow, and against him that lifts himself up in his brigandine. And spare not her young men — destroy utterly all her host. Thus, the slain shall fall in the land of the Chaldeans, and they that are thrust through in her streets. For Israel has not been forsaken, nor Judah, of his God, of the Lord of Hosts, though their land was filled with sin against the Holy One of Israel. Flee out of the midst of Babylon and deliver every man his soul. Be not cut off in her iniquity, for this is the

time of the Lord's vengeance. He will render unto her a recompense. Babylon has been a golden cup in the Lord's hand that made all the earth drunk. The nations have drunk of her wine, therefore the nations are mad. Babylon is suddenly fallen and destroyed. Howl for her, take balm for her pain, if it so be she may be healed.

11 We would have healed Babylon, but she is not healed. Forsake her and let us go everyone into his own country. For her judgment reaches unto heaven and is lifted up even to the skies. The Lord has brought forth our righteousness. Come, and let us declare in Zion the work of the Lord our God.

12 Make bright the arrows, gather the shields. The Lord has raised up the spirit of the kings of the Medes. For his device is against Babylon, to destroy it, because it is the vengeance of the Lord, the vengeance of his temple. Set up the standard upon the walls of Babylon, make the watch strong. Set up the watchmen, prepare the ambushes, for the Lord has both devised and done that which he spoke against the inhabitants of Babylon. O you that dwell upon many waters, abundant in treasures, your end has come, and the measure of your covetousness. The Lord of Hosts has sworn by himself, saying, Surely I will fill you with men as with caterpillars, and they shall lift up a shout against you.

13 He has made the earth by his power, he has established the world by his wisdom and has stretched out the heaven by his understanding. When he utters his voice, there is a multitude of waters in the heavens, and he causes the vapors to ascend from the ends of the earth. He makes lightnings with rain and brings forth the wind out of his treasuries. Every man is brutish by his knowledge. Every founder is confounded by the engraved image, for his molten image is falsehood and there is no breath in them. They are vanity, the work of errors. In the time of their visitation, they shall perish. The portion of Jacob is not like them, for he is the former of all things, and Israel is the rod of his inheritance — the Lord of Hosts is his name.

14 You are my battle-ax and weapons of war, for with you will I break in pieces the nations, and with you will I destroy kingdoms. And with you will I break in pieces the horse and his rider, and with you will I break in pieces the chariot and his rider. With you also will I break in pieces man and woman, and with you will I break in pieces old and young, and with you will I break in pieces the young man and the

virgin. I will also break in pieces with you the shepherd and his flock, and with you will I break in pieces the husbandman and his yoke of oxen, and with you will I break in pieces captains and rulers. And I will render unto Babylon and to all the inhabitants of Chaldea all their evil that they have done in Zion in your sight, says the Lord. Behold, I am against you, O destroying mountain, says the Lord which destroys all the earth, and I will stretch out my hand upon you and roll you down from the rocks, and will make you a burnt mountain. And they shall not take of you a stone for a corner, nor a stone for foundations, but you shall be desolate for ever, says the Lord.

[15] Set up a standard in the land, blow the trumpet among the nations. Prepare the nations against her, call together against her the kingdoms of Ararat, Minni, and Ashkenaz. Appoint a captain against her, cause the horses to come up as the rough caterpillars. Prepare against her the nations with the kings of the Medes, the captains thereof, and all the rulers thereof, and all the land of his dominion. And the land shall tremble and sorrow, for every purpose of the Lord shall be performed against Babylon, to make the land of Babylon a desolation without an inhabitant. The mighty men of Babylon have refused to fight, they have remained in their holds. Their might has failed, they became as women. They have burned her dwelling places, her bars are broken. One courier shall run to meet another, and one messenger to meet another, to show the king of Babylon that his city is taken at one end, and that the passages are stopped, and the reeds they have burned with fire, and the men of war are frightened. For thus says the Lord of Hosts, the God of Israel: The daughter of Babylon is like a threshing floor. It is time to thresh her. Yet a little while, and the time of her harvest shall come. Nebuchadnezzar the king of Babylon has devoured me, he has crushed me, he has made me an empty vessel, he has swallowed me up like a dragon, he has filled his belly with my delicacies, he has cast me out. The violence done to me and to my flesh be upon Babylon, shall the inhabitant of Zion say. And my blood upon the inhabitants of Chaldea, shall Jerusalem say.

[16] Therefore, thus says the Lord: Behold, I will plead your cause and take vengeance for you. And I will dry up her sea and make her springs dry. And Babylon shall become heaps, a dwelling place for dragons, an astonishment and a hissing, without an inhabitant. They shall roar

together like lions, they shall yell as lions' whelps. In their heat I will make their feasts and I will make them drunk, that they may rejoice and sleep a perpetual sleep and not wake, says the Lord. I will bring them down like lambs to the slaughter, like rams with he-goats. How is Sheshach taken, and how is the praise of the whole earth surprised! How is Babylon become an astonishment among the nations! The sea has come up upon Babylon, she is covered with the multitude of the waves thereof. Her cities are a desolation, a dry land and a wilderness, a land wherein no man dwells, neither does any son of man pass thereby. And I will punish Bel in Babylon, and I will bring forth out of his mouth that which he has swallowed up. And the nations shall not flow together anymore unto him. Yea, the wall of Babylon shall fall.

¹⁷ My people, go out of her midst and deliver every man his soul from the fierce anger of the Lord. And lest your heart faint and you fear for the rumor that shall be heard in the land—a rumor shall both come one year, and after that, in another year shall come a rumor, and violence in the land, ruler against ruler—therefore behold, the days come that I will do judgment upon the engraved images of Babylon. And her whole land shall be confounded and all her slain shall fall in her midst. Then the heaven and the earth and all that is therein shall sing for Babylon, for the spoilers shall come unto her from the north, says the Lord.

¹⁸ As Babylon has caused the slain of Israel to fall, so at Babylon shall fall the slain of all the earth. You that have escaped the sword, go away, stand not still. Remember the Lord afar off and let Jerusalem come into your mind. We are confounded because we have heard reproach; shame has covered our faces, for strangers have come into the sanctuaries of the Lord's house. Wherefore, behold, the days come, says the Lord, that I will do judgment upon her engraved images, and through all her land the wounded shall groan. Though Babylon should mount up to heaven, and though she should fortify the height of her strength, yet from me shall spoilers come unto her, says the Lord. A sound of a cry comes from Babylon, and great destruction from the land of the Chaldeans, because the Lord has spoiled Babylon and destroyed out of her the great voice. When her waves do roar like great waters, a noise of their voice is uttered, because the spoiler has come upon her, even upon Babylon, and her mighty men are taken. Every one of their bows

is broken, for the Lord God of recompenses shall surely repay. And I will make drunk her princes and her wise men, her captains, and her rulers, and her mighty men. And they shall sleep a perpetual sleep and not wake, says the King, whose name is the Lord of Hosts. Thus says the Lord of Hosts: The broad walls of Babylon shall be utterly broken and her high gates shall be burned with fire. And the people shall labor in vain, and the folk in the fire, and they shall be weary.

19 The word which Jeremiah the prophet commanded Seraiah the son of Neriah, the son of Maaseiah, when he went with Zedekiah the king of Judah into Babylon in the fourth year of his reign; and this Seraiah was a quiet prince. So Jeremiah wrote in a book all the evil that should come upon Babylon, even all these words that are written against Babylon. And Jeremiah said to Seraiah, When you come to Babylon, and shall see and shall read all these words, then shall you say, O Lord, you have spoken against this place, to cut it off that none shall remain in it, neither man nor beast, but that it shall be desolate for ever. And it shall be, when you have made an end of reading this book, that you shall bind a stone to it and cast it into the middle of Euphrates. And you shall say, Thus shall Babylon sink and shall not rise from the evil that I will bring upon her, and they shall be weary. Thus far are the words of Jeremiah.

2 Zedekiah was twenty-one years old when he began to reign, and he reigned eleven years in Jerusalem. And his mother's name was Hamutal, the daughter of Jeremiah of Libnah. And he did that which was evil in the eyes of the Lord, according to all that Jehoiakim had done. For through the anger of the Lord it came to pass in Jerusalem and Judah, until he had cast them out from his presence, that Zedekiah rebelled against the king of Babylon. And it came to pass in the ninth year of his reign, in the tenth month, in the tenth day of the month, that Nebuchadnezzar king of Babylon came, he and all his army, against Jerusalem, and pitched against it, and built forts against it round about. So the city was besieged unto the eleventh year of king Zedekiah. And in the fourth month, in the ninth day of the month, the famine was severe in the city so that there was no bread for the people of the land. Then the city was broken up, and all the men of war fled and went forth out of the city by night, by the way of the gate between the two walls

which was by the king's garden (now the Chaldeans were by the city round about). And they went by the way of the plain. But the army of the Chaldeans pursued after the king and overtook Zedekiah in the plains of Jericho, and all his army was scattered from him. Then they took the king and carried him up unto the king of Babylon, to Riblah in the land of Hamath, where he gave judgment upon him. And the king of Babylon slew the sons of Zedekiah before his eyes. He slew also all the princes of Judah in Riblah. Then he put out the eyes of Zedekiah, and the king of Babylon bound him in chains and carried him to Babylon, and put him in prison until the day of his death.

3 Now in the fifth month, in the tenth day of the month, which was the nineteenth year of Nebuchadnezzar king of Babylon, Nebuzaradan, captain of the guard who served the king of Babylon, came into Jerusalem and burned the house of the Lord, and the king's house, and all the houses of Jerusalem; and all the houses of the great men burned he with fire. And all the army of the Chaldeans that were with the captain of the guard broke down all the walls of Jerusalem round about. Then Nebuzaradan the captain of the guard carried away captive certain of the poor of the people, and the residue of the people that remained in the city, and those that fell away, that fell to the king of Babylon, and the rest of the multitude. But Nebuzaradan the captain of the guard left certain of the poor of the land for vinedressers and for husbandmen.

4 Also, the pillars of brass that were in the house of the Lord, and the bases, and the brazen sea that was in the house of the Lord, the Chaldeans broke and carried all the brass of them to Babylon. The cauldrons also, and the shovels, and the snuffers, and the bowls, and the spoons, and all the vessels of brass with which they ministered, took they away. And the basins, and the fire pans, and the bowls, and the cauldrons, and the candlesticks, and the spoons, and the cups — that which was of gold, in gold, and that which was of silver, in silver — the captain of the guard took away. The two pillars, one sea, and twelve brazen bulls that were under the bases, which king Solomon had made in the house of the Lord, the brass of all these vessels was without weight. And concerning the pillars, the height of one pillar was eighteen cubits, and a fillet of twelve cubits did encompass it. And the thickness thereof was four fingers — it was hollow. And a chapiter

of brass was upon it. And the height of one chapiter was five cubits, with network and pomegranates upon the chapiters round about, all of brass. The second pillar also, and the pomegranates were like unto these. And there were ninety-six pomegranates on a side, and all the pomegranates upon the network were a hundred round about.

5 And the captain of the guard took Seraiah the chief priest, and Zephaniah the second priest, and the three keepers of the door. He took also out of the city a eunuch who had the charge of the men of war, and seven men of them that were near the king's person who were found in the city, and the principal scribe of the host who mustered the people of the land, and sixty men of the people of the land that were found in the midst of the city. So Nebuzaradan the captain of the guard took them and brought them to the king of Babylon, to Riblah. And the king of Babylon smote them and put them to death in Riblah in the land of Hamath. Thus Judah was carried away captive out of his own land.

6 This is the people whom Nebuchadnezzar carried away captive: in the seventh year, three thousand twenty-three Jews; in the eighteenth year of Nebuchadnezzar he carried away captive from Jerusalem eight hundred thirty-two people; in the twenty-third year of Nebuchadnezzar, Nebuzaradan the captain of the guard carried away captive of the Jews seven hundred forty-five people. All the people were four thousand six hundred.

7 And it came to pass in the thirty-seventh year of the captivity of Jehoiachin king of Judah, in the twelfth month, in the twenty-fifth day of the month, that Evilmerodach king of Babylon, in the first year of his reign, lifted up the head of Jehoiachin king of Judah and brought him forth out of prison, and spoke kindly unto him, and set his throne above the throne of the kings that were with him in Babylon, and changed his prison garments. And he did continually eat bread before him all the days of his life. And for his diet, there was a continual diet given him of the king of Babylon, every day a portion until the day of his death, all the days of his life.

THE LAMENTATIONS OF JEREMIAH

How does the city sit solitary that was full of people! How is she become as a widow! She that was great among the nations, and princess among the provinces, how is she become tributary! She weeps severely in the night, and her tears are on her cheeks. Among all her lovers she has none to comfort her, all her friends have dealt treacherously with her, they are become her enemies. Judah is gone into captivity because of affliction and because of great servitude. She dwells among the heathen, she finds no rest, all her persecutors overtook her in the straits.

2 The ways of Zion do mourn because none come to the solemn feasts. All her gates are desolate, her priests sigh, her virgins are afflicted, and she is in bitterness. Her adversaries are the chief, her enemies prosper, for the Lord has afflicted her for the multitude of her transgressions. Her children have gone into captivity before the enemy. And from the daughter of Zion all her beauty is departed. Her princes are become like harts that find no pasture, and they have gone without strength before the pursuer.

3 Jerusalem remembered in the days of her affliction and of her miseries all her pleasant things that she had in the days of old, when her people fell into the hand of the enemy, and none did help her — the adversaries saw her, and did mock at her Sabbaths. Jerusalem has grievously sinned, therefore she is removed. All that honored her despise her because they have seen her nakedness; yea, she sighs and turns backward. Her filthiness is in her skirts; she remembers not her latter end. Therefore, she came down wonderfully, she had no comforter. O Lord, behold my affliction, for the enemy has magnified himself. The adversary has spread out his hand upon all her pleasant things, for she has seen that the heathen entered into her sanctuary, whom you did command that they should not enter into your congregation.

4 All her people sigh, they seek bread, they have given their pleasant things for food to relieve the soul. See, O Lord, and consider, for I am become vile. Is it nothing to you, all you that pass by? Behold and see if there is any sorrow like unto my sorrow which is done unto me, with which the Lord has afflicted me in the day of his fierce anger. From

above has he sent fire into my bones and it prevails against them; he has spread a net for my feet, he has turned me back. He has made me desolate and faint all the day. The yoke of my transgressions is bound by his hand, they are wreathed and come up upon my neck. He has made my strength to fall; the Lord has delivered me into their hands from whom I am not able to rise up. The Lord has trodden underfoot all my mighty men in my midst. He has called an assembly against me to crush my young men. The Lord has trodden the virgin, the daughter of Judah, as in a winepress. For these things I weep. My eye, my eye runs down with water because the comforter that should relieve my soul is far from me. My children are desolate because the enemy prevailed. Zion spreads forth her hands and there is none to comfort her. The Lord has commanded, concerning Jacob, that his adversaries should be round about him; Jerusalem is as a menstruous woman among them.

5 The Lord is righteous, for I have rebelled against his commandment. Hear, I pray you, all people, and behold my sorrow; my virgins and my young men have gone into captivity. I called for my lovers, but they deceived me. My priests and my elders gave up the ghost in the city while they sought their food to relieve their souls. Behold, O Lord, for I am in distress. My inward parts are troubled, my heart is turned within me, for I have grievously rebelled. Abroad, the sword bereaves; at home, there is as death. They have heard that I sigh; there is none to comfort me. All my enemies have heard of my trouble, they are glad that you have done it. You will bring the day that you have called, and they shall be like unto me. Let all their wickedness come before you, and do unto them as you have done unto me for all my transgressions, for my sighs are many and my heart is faint.

6 How has the Lord covered the daughter of Zion with a cloud in his anger, and cast down from Heaven unto the earth the beauty of Israel, and remembered not his footstool in the day of his anger! The Lord has swallowed up all the habitations of Jacob and has not pitied. He has thrown down in his wrath the strongholds of the daughter of Judah, he has brought them down to the ground. He has polluted the kingdom and the princes thereof.

7 He has cut off in his fierce anger all the horn of Israel. He has drawn back his right hand from before the enemy, and he burned against Jacob like a flaming fire which devours round about. He has bent his

bow like an enemy. He stood with his right hand as an adversary and slew all that were pleasant to the eye in the tabernacle of the daughter of Zion. He poured out his fury like fire. The Lord was as an enemy; he has swallowed up Israel, he has swallowed up all her palaces. He has destroyed his strongholds, and has increased in the daughter of Judah mourning and lamentation. And he has violently taken away his tabernacle, as if it were of a garden. He has destroyed his places of the assembly.

⁸ The Lord has caused the solemn feasts and Sabbaths to be forgotten in Zion, and has despised in the indignation of his anger the king and the priest. The Lord has cast off his altar, he has abhorred his sanctuary, he has given up into the hand of the enemy the walls of her palaces; they have made a noise in the house of the Lord as in the day of a solemn feast. The Lord has purposed to destroy the wall of the daughter of Zion — he has stretched out a line, he has not withdrawn his hand from destroying — therefore, he made the rampart and the wall to lament; they languished together. Her gates are sunk into the ground; he has destroyed and broken her bars. Her king and her princes are among the gentiles, the law is no more, her prophets also find no vision from the Lord. The elders of the daughter of Zion sit upon the ground and keep silence, they have cast up dust upon their heads, they have girded themselves with sackcloth. The virgins of Jerusalem hang down their heads to the ground. My eyes do fail with tears, my heart is troubled, my liver is poured upon the earth for the destruction of the daughter of my people, because the children and the sucklings swoon in the streets of the city. They say to their mothers, Where is grain and wine? — when they swooned as the wounded in the streets of the city, when their soul was poured out into their mothers' bosom. What thing shall I take to witness for you? What thing shall I liken to you, O daughter of Jerusalem? What shall I equate to you, that I may comfort you, O virgin daughter of Zion? For your breach is great like the sea. Who can heal you?

⁹ Your prophets have seen vain and foolish things for you, and they have not uncovered your iniquity to turn away your captivity, but have seen for you false burdens and causes of banishment. All that pass by clap their hands at you, they hiss and wag their head at the daughter of Jerusalem, saying, Is this the city that men call the perfection of

beauty, the joy of the whole earth? All your enemies have opened their mouth against you, they hiss and gnash the teeth, they say, We have swallowed her up. Certainly this is the day that we looked for; we have found, we have seen it.

¹⁰ The Lord has done that which he had devised, he has fulfilled his word that he had commanded in the days of old. He has thrown down and has not pitied, and he has caused your enemy to rejoice over you; he has set up the horn of your adversaries. Their heart cried unto the Lord. O wall of the daughter of Zion, let tears run down like a river, day and night. Give yourself no rest, let not the apple of your eye cease. Arise, cry out in the night, in the beginning of the watches pour out your heart like water before the face of the Lord. Lift up your hands toward him for the life of your young children that faint for hunger in the top of every street. Behold, O Lord, and consider to whom you have done this. Shall the women eat their fruit and children of a span long? Shall the priest and the prophet be slain in the sanctuary of the Lord? The young and the old lie on the ground in the streets, my virgins and my young men are fallen by the sword. You have slain them in the day of your anger, you have killed and not pitied. You have called as in a solemn day my terrors round about, so that in the day of the Lord's anger, none escaped nor remained. Those that I have swaddled and brought up has my enemy consumed.

¹¹ I am the man that has seen affliction by the rod of his wrath. He has led me and brought me into darkness, but not into light. Surely against me is he turned; he turns his hand against me all the day. My flesh and my skin has he made old, he has broken my bones. He has built against me, and encompassed me with gall and travail. He has set me in dark places, as they that are dead of old. He has hedged me about that I cannot get out; he has made my chain heavy. Also, when I cry and shout, he shuts out my prayer. He has enclosed my ways with hewn stone, he has made my paths crooked. He was unto me as a bear lying in wait, and as a lion in secret places. He has turned aside my ways and pulled me in pieces; he has made me desolate. He has bent his bow and set me as a mark for the arrow, he has caused the arrows of his quiver to enter into my reins. I was a derision to all my people, and their song all the day. He has filled me with bitterness, he has made me drunk with wormwood. He has also broken my teeth with gravel

stones, he has covered me with ashes. And you have removed my soul far off from peace; I forgot prosperity. And I said, My strength and my hope is perished from the Lord.

¹² Remembering my affliction and my misery, the wormwood and the gall, my soul has them still in remembrance and is humbled in me. This I recall to my mind, therefore have I hope: It is of the Lord's mercies that we are not consumed, because his compassions fail not. They are new every morning; great is your faithfulness. The Lord is my portion, says my soul, therefore will I hope in him. The Lord is good unto them that wait for him, to the soul that seeks him. It is good that a man should both hope and quietly wait for the salvation of the Lord. It is good for a man that he bear the yoke in his youth. He sits alone and keeps silence because he has borne it upon him. He puts his mouth in the dust if it so be there may be hope. He gives his cheek to him that smites him, he is filled full with reproach. For the Lord will not cast off for ever, but though he cause grief, yet will he have compassion according to the multitude of his mercies. For he does not afflict willingly nor grieve the children of men. To crush under his feet all the prisoners of the earth, to turn aside the right of a man before the face of the Most High, to subvert a man in his cause, the Lord approves not.

¹³ Who is he that says and it comes to pass, when the Lord commands it not? Out of the mouth of the Most High proceeds not evil and good? Why does a living man complain, a man for the punishment of his sins? Let us search and try our ways, and turn again to the Lord. Let us lift up our heart with our hands unto God in the heavens. We have transgressed and have rebelled, you have not pardoned. You have covered with anger and persecuted us, you have slain, you have not pitied. You have covered yourself with a cloud, that our prayer should not pass through. You have made us as the offscouring and refuse in the midst of the people. All our enemies have opened their mouths against us. Fear and a snare has come upon us, desolation and destruction. My eye runs down with rivers of water for the destruction of the daughter of my people. My eye trickles down and ceases not, without any intermission, until the Lord look down and behold from Heaven. My eye affects my heart because of all the daughters of my city. My enemies chased me intensely, like a bird, without cause. They

have cut off my life in the dungeon and cast a stone upon me. Waters flowed over my head; then I said, I am cut off.

¹⁴ I called upon your name, O Lord, out of the low dungeon. You have heard my voice; hide not your ear at my breathing, at my cry. You drew near in the day that I called upon you; you said, Fear not. O Lord, you have pled the causes of my soul, you have redeemed my life. O Lord, you have seen my wrong; judge my cause. You have seen all their vengeance and all their imaginations against me. You have heard their reproach, O Lord, and all their imaginations against me, the lips of those that rose up against me and their device against me all the day. Behold their sitting down and their rising up; I am their music. Render unto them a recompense, O Lord, according to the work of their hands. Give them sorrow of heart, your curse unto them. Persecute and destroy them in anger from under the heavens of the Lord.

¹⁵ How is the gold become dim! How is the most fine gold changed! The stones of the sanctuary are poured out in the top of every street. The precious sons of Zion, comparable to fine gold, how are they esteemed as earthen pitchers, the work of the hands of the potter! Even the sea monsters draw out the breast, they give suck to their young ones; the daughter of my people has become cruel, like the ostriches in the wilderness. The tongue of the sucking child cleaves to the roof of his mouth for thirst; the young children ask bread and no man breaks it unto them. They that did feed delicately are desolate in the streets, they that were brought up in scarlet embrace dunghills.

¹⁶ For the punishment of the iniquity of the daughter of my people is greater than the punishment of the sin of Sodom, that was overthrown as in a moment and no hands stayed on her. Her Nazarites were purer than snow, they were whiter than milk, they were more ruddy in body than rubies, their polishing was of sapphire. Their visage is blacker than a coal, they are not known in the streets, their skin cleaves to their bones, it is withered, it is become like a stick. They that are slain with the sword are better than they that are slain with hunger, for these waste away, stricken through for lack of the fruits of the field. The hands of the pitiful women have boiled their own children, they were their food in the destruction of the daughter of my people.

¹⁷ The Lord has accomplished his fury, he has poured out his fierce anger and has kindled a fire in Zion, and it has devoured the

foundations thereof. The kings of the earth and all the inhabitants of the world would not have believed that the adversary and the enemy should have entered into the gates of Jerusalem. For the sins of her prophets and the iniquities of her priests that have shed the blood of the just in her midst, they have wandered as blind men in the streets; they have polluted themselves with blood, so that men could not touch their garments. They cried unto them, Depart, it is unclean; depart, depart, touch not! When they fled away and wandered, they said among the heathen, They shall no more sojourn there. The anger of the Lord has divided them, he will no more regard them. They respected not the persons of the priests, they favored not the elders.

18 As for us, our eyes as yet failed for our vain help; in our watching, we have watched for a nation that could not save us. They hunt our steps, that we cannot go in our streets; our end is near, our days are fulfilled, for our end has come. Our persecutors are swifter than the eagles of the heaven, they pursued us upon the mountains, they laid wait for us in the wilderness. The breath of our nostrils, the anointed of the Lord was taken in their pits, of whom we said, Under his shadow we shall live among the heathen.

19 Rejoice and be glad, O daughter of Edom that dwells in the land of Uz; the cup also shall pass through unto you. You shall be drunk and shall make yourself naked. The punishment of your iniquity is accomplished, O daughter of Zion; he will no more carry you away into captivity. He will visit your iniquity, O daughter of Edom, he will reveal your sins.

20 Remember, O Lord, what has come upon us, consider and behold our reproach. Our inheritance is turned to strangers, our houses to foreigners. We are orphans and fatherless, our mothers are as widows. We have drunk our water for money, our wood is sold unto us. Our necks are under persecution, we labor and have no rest. We have given the hand to the Egyptians and to the Assyrians to be satisfied with bread. Our fathers have sinned, and are not, and we have borne their iniquities. Servants have ruled over us; there is none that does deliver us out of their hand. We got our bread with the peril of our lives because of the sword of the wilderness. Our skin was black like an oven because of the terrible famine. They violated the women in Zion and the maids in the cities of Judah. Princes are hung up by their

hand, the faces of elders were not honored. They took the young men to grind, and the children fell under the wood. The elders have ceased from the gate, the young men from their music. The joy of our heart is ceased, our dance is turned into mourning. The crown is fallen from our head; woe unto us, that we have sinned. For this our heart is faint, for these things our eyes are dim. Because of the mountain of Zion, which is desolate, the foxes walk upon it.

21 You, O Lord, remain for ever, your throne from generation to generation. Why do you forget us for ever and forsake us for so long a time? Turn us unto you, O Lord, and we shall be turned; renew our days as of old. But you have utterly rejected us, you are very angry against us.

THE BOOK OF THE PROPHET EZEKIEL

Now it came to pass in the thirtieth year, in the fourth month, in the fifth day of the month, as I was among the captives by the river of Chebar, that the Heavens were opened and I saw visions of God. In the fifth day of the month, which was the fifth year of king Jehoiachin's captivity, the word of the Lord came expressly unto Ezekiel the priest, the son of Buzi, in the land of the Chaldeans by the river Chebar; and the hand of the Lord was there upon him.

2 And I looked, and behold, a whirlwind came out of the north, a great cloud, and a fire enfolding itself, and a brightness was about it, and out of the midst thereof, as the color of amber, out of the midst of the fire. Also, out of the midst thereof came the likeness of four living creatures, and this was their appearance: they had the likeness of a man, and every one had four faces, and every one had four wings. And their feet were straight feet, and the sole of their feet was like the sole of a calf's foot, and they sparkled like the color of burnished brass. And they had the hands of a man under their wings on their four sides, and they four had their faces and their wings. Their wings were joined one to another, they turned not when they went, they went every one straight forward. As for the likeness of their faces, they four had the face of a man, and the face of a lion on the right side, and they four had the face of an ox on the left side; they four also had the face of an eagle. Thus were their faces. And their wings were stretched upward; two wings of every one were joined one to another, and two covered their

bodies. And they went every one straight forward — where the spirit was to go, they went, and they turned not when they went.

3 As for the likeness of the living creatures, their appearance was like burning coals of fire, and like the appearance of lamps — it went up and down among the living creatures; and the fire was bright, and out of the fire went forth lightning. And the living creatures ran and returned as the appearance of a flash of lightning.

4 Now as I beheld the living creatures, behold, one wheel upon the earth by the living creatures, with his four faces, the appearance of the wheels and their work was like unto the color of a beryl, and they four had one likeness. And their appearance and their work was like a wheel in the middle of a wheel. When they went, they went upon their four sides, and they turned not when they went. As for their rings, they were so high that they were dreadful, and their rings were full of eyes round about them four. And when the living creatures went, the wheels went by them; and when the living creatures were lifted up from the earth, the wheels were lifted up. Wherever the spirit was to go, they went, there was their spirit to go; and the wheels were lifted up alongside them, for the spirit of the living creature was in the wheels. When those went, these went; and when those stood, these stood; and when those were lifted up from the earth, the wheels were lifted up alongside them, for the spirit of the living creature was in the wheels.

5 And the likeness of the firmament upon the heads of the living creature was as the color of the terrible crystal, stretched forth over their heads above. And under the firmament were their wings straight, the one toward the other; every one had two which covered on this side, and every one had two which covered on that side their bodies. And when they went, I heard the noise of their wings like the noise of great waters, as the voice of the Almighty, the voice of speech as the noise of a host. When they stood, they let down their wings; and there was a voice from the firmament that was over their heads when they stood and had let down their wings.

6 And above the firmament that was over their heads was the likeness of a throne, as the appearance of a sapphire stone; and upon the likeness of the throne was the likeness as the appearance of a man above upon it. And I saw as the color of amber, as the appearance of fire round about within it, from the appearance of his loins even

upward. And from the appearance of his loins even downward I saw, as it were, the appearance of fire; and it had brightness round about. As the appearance of the bow that is in the cloud in the day of rain, so was the appearance of the brightness round about. This was the appearance of the likeness of the glory of the Lord. And when I saw it, I fell upon my face.

7 And I heard a voice of one that spoke, and he said unto me, Son of man, stand upon your feet and I will speak unto you. And the spirit entered into me when he spoke unto me and set me upon my feet, that I heard him that spoke unto me. And he said unto me, Son of man, I send you to the children of Israel, to a rebellious nation that has rebelled against me. They and their fathers have transgressed against me, even unto this very day, for they are impudent children, and stiff-hearted. I do send you unto them, and you shall say unto them, Thus says the Lord God. And they, whether they will hear or whether they will refuse — for they are a rebellious house — yet shall know that there has been a prophet among them. And you, son of man, be not afraid of them, neither be afraid of their words, though briers and thorns are with you and you do dwell among scorpions. Be not afraid of their words, nor be dismayed at their looks, though they are a rebellious house. And you shall speak my words unto them, whether they will hear or whether they will refuse, for they are most rebellious. But you, son of man, hear what I say unto you: Be not rebellious like that rebellious house; open your mouth and eat that I give you.

8 And when I looked, behold, a hand was sent unto me, and behold, a scroll was therein. And he spread it before me, and it was written within and without, and there were written therein lamentations, and mourning, and woe. Moreover, he said unto me, Son of man, eat that you find; eat this scroll, and go speak unto the house of Israel. So I opened my mouth and he caused me to eat that scroll. And he said unto me, Son of man, cause your belly to eat, and fill your bowels with this scroll that I give you. Then did I eat it, and it was in my mouth as honey for sweetness.

9 And he said unto me, Son of man, go, get yourself unto the house of Israel and speak with my words unto them. For you are not sent to a people of a strange speech and of a hard language, but to the house of Israel, not to many people of a strange speech and of a hard language

whose words you cannot understand. Surely, had I sent you to them, they would have listened unto you. But the house of Israel will not listen unto you for they will not listen unto me, for all the house of Israel are impudent and hard-hearted. Behold, I have made your face strong against their faces, and your forehead strong against their foreheads. As a diamond harder than flint have I made your forehead. Fear them not, neither be dismayed at their looks, though they are a rebellious house. Moreover, he said unto me, Son of man, all my words that I shall speak unto you, receive in your heart and hear with your ears. And go, get yourself to them of the captivity, unto the children of your people, and speak unto them and tell them, Thus says the Lord God — whether they will hear or whether they will refuse.

10 Then the spirit took me up, and I heard behind me a voice of a great rushing, saying, Blessed be the glory of the Lord from his place. I heard also the noise of the wings of the living creatures that touched one another, and the noise of the wheels beside them, and a noise of a great rushing. So the spirit lifted me up and took me away, and I went in bitterness, in the heat of my spirit, but the hand of the Lord was strong upon me.

11 Then I came to them of the captivity at Telabib, that dwelled by the river of Chebar, and I sat where they sat, and remained there astonished among them seven days. And it came to pass at the end of seven days that the word of the Lord came unto me, saying, Son of man, I have made you a watchman unto the house of Israel, therefore hear the word at my mouth and give them warning from me. When I say unto the wicked, You shall surely die — and you give him not warning, nor speak to warn the wicked from his wicked way to save his life, the same wicked man shall die in his iniquity, but his blood will I require at your hand. Yet if you warn the wicked and he turn not from his wickedness, nor from his wicked way, he shall die in his iniquity, but you have delivered your soul. Again, when a righteous man does turn from his righteousness and commit iniquity, and I lay a stumbling block before him, he shall die because you have not given him warning. He shall die in his sin and his righteousness which he has done shall not be remembered, but his blood will I require at your hand. Nevertheless, if you warn the righteous man that the righteous

sin not, and he does not sin, he shall surely live because he is warned, and you have delivered your soul.

12 And the hand of the Lord was there upon me, and he said unto me, Arise, go forth into the plain and I will there talk with you. Then I arose and went forth into the plain. And behold, the glory of the Lord stood there, as the glory which I saw by the river of Chebar, and I fell on my face. Then the spirit entered into me and set me upon my feet, and spoke with me and said unto me, Go, shut yourself within your house. But you, O son of man, behold, they shall put bands upon you and shall bind you with them, and you shall not go out among them. And I will make your tongue cleave to the roof of your mouth, that you shall be dumb and shall not be to them a reprover, for they are a rebellious house. But when I speak with you, I will open your mouth, and you shall say unto them, Thus says the Lord God. He that hears, let him hear, and he that refuses, let him refuse, for they are a rebellious house.

13 You also, son of man, take a tile and lay it before you, and portray upon it the city, even Jerusalem; and lay siege against it, and build a fort against it, and cast a mount against it. Set the camp also against it, and set battering rams against it round about. Moreover, take unto yourself an iron pan, and set it for a wall of iron between you and the city, and set your face against it; and it shall be besieged, and you shall lay siege against it. This shall be a sign to the house of Israel.

14 Lie also upon your left side, and lay the iniquity of the house of Israel upon it; according to the number of the days that you shall lie upon it, you shall bear their iniquity. For I have laid upon you the years of their iniquity, according to the number of the days — three hundred ninety days. So shall you bear the iniquity of the house of Israel.

15 And when you have accomplished them, lie again on your right side, and you shall bear the iniquity of the house of Judah forty days; I have appointed you each day for a year. Therefore, you shall set your face toward the siege of Jerusalem, and your arm shall be uncovered, and you shall prophesy against it. And behold, I will lay bands upon you, and you shall not turn from one side to another until you have ended the days of your siege.

16 Take also unto yourself wheat, and barley, and beans, and lentils, and millet, and spelt, and put them in one vessel, and make for yourself

bread thereof, according to the number of the days that you shall lie upon your side — three hundred ninety days shall you eat thereof. And your food which you shall eat shall be by weight twenty shekels a day; from time to time shall you eat it. You shall drink also water by measure, the sixth part of a hin; from time to time shall you drink. And you shall eat it as barley cakes, and you shall bake it with dung that comes out of man, in their sight. And the Lord said, Even thus shall the children of Israel eat their defiled bread among the gentiles, where I will drive them.

17 Then said I, Ah Lord God, behold, my soul has not been polluted, for from my youth up even until now have I not eaten of that which dies of itself, or is torn in pieces, neither came there abominable flesh into my mouth. Then he said unto me, See, I have given you cow's dung for man's dung, and you shall prepare your bread with it. Moreover, he said unto me, Son of man, behold, I will break the support of bread in Jerusalem, and they shall eat bread by weight and with care, and they shall drink water by measure and with astonishment, that they may lack bread and water, and be astonished one with another, and consume away for their iniquity.

18 And you, son of man, take a sharp knife, take a barber's razor, and cause it to pass upon your head and upon your beard; then take balances to weigh and divide the hair. You shall burn with fire a third part in the midst of the city when the days of the siege are fulfilled, and you shall take a third part and smite about it with a knife, and a third part you shall scatter in the wind, and I will draw out a sword after them. You shall also take thereof a few in number and bind them in your skirts. Then take of them again, and cast them into the midst of the fire, and burn them in the fire, for thereof shall a fire come forth into all the house of Israel.

19 Thus says the Lord God: This is Jerusalem. I have set it in the midst of the nations and countries that are round about her. And she has changed my judgments into wickedness more than the nations, and my statutes more than the countries that are round about her; for they have refused my judgments and my statutes, they have not walked in them.

20 Therefore, thus says the Lord God: Because you multiplied more than the nations that are round about you, and have not walked in

my statutes, neither have kept my judgments, neither have done according to the judgments of the nations that are round about you, therefore, thus says the Lord God: Behold, I, even I, am against you, and will execute judgments in your midst in the sight of the nations. And I will do in you that which I have not done, and unto which I will not do anymore the like, because of all your abominations.

21 Therefore, the fathers shall eat the sons in your midst, and the sons shall eat their fathers; and I will execute judgments in you, and the whole remnant of you will I scatter into all the winds. Wherefore, as I live, says the Lord God, surely because you have defiled my sanctuary with all your detestable things and with all your abominations, therefore will I also diminish you, neither shall my eye spare, neither will I have any pity. A third part of you shall die with the pestilence, and with famine shall they be consumed in your midst; and a third part shall fall by the sword round about you; and I will scatter a third part into all the winds, and I will draw out a sword after them. Thus shall my anger be accomplished, and I will cause my fury to rest upon them, and I will be comforted, and they shall know that I the Lord have spoken it in my zeal when I have accomplished my fury in them.

22 Moreover, I will make you waste and a reproach among the nations that are round about you, in the sight of all that pass by. So it shall be a reproach and a taunt, an instruction and an astonishment unto the nations that are round about you, when I shall execute judgments in you in anger, and in fury, and in furious rebukes. I the Lord have spoken it. When I shall send upon them the evil arrows of famine which shall be for their destruction, and which I will send to destroy you, and I will increase the famine upon you and will break your support of bread, so will I send upon you famine and evil beasts, and they shall bereave you, and pestilence and blood shall pass through you, and I will bring the sword upon you. I the Lord have spoken it.

2 And the word of the Lord came unto me, saying, Son of man, set your face toward the mountains of Israel and prophesy against them, and say, You mountains of Israel, hear the word of the Lord God; thus says the Lord God to the mountains and to the hills, to the rivers and to the valleys: Behold, I, even I, will bring a sword upon you, and I will destroy your high places. And your altars shall be desolate

and your images shall be broken, and I will cast down your slain men before your idols. And I will lay the dead carcasses of the children of Israel before their idols, and I will scatter your bones round about your altars. In all your dwelling places, the cities shall be laid waste and the high places shall be desolate, that your altars may be laid waste and made desolate, and your idols may be broken and cease, and your images may be cut down, and your works may be abolished; and the slain shall fall in your midst, and you shall know that I am the Lord.

2 Yet will I leave a remnant, that you may have some that shall escape the sword among the nations when you shall be scattered through the countries. And they that escape of you shall remember me among the nations to which they shall be carried captives, because I am broken with their whorish heart which has departed from me, and with their eyes which go whoring after their idols; and they shall loathe themselves for the evils which they have committed in all their abominations. And they shall know that I am the Lord, and that I have not said in vain that I would do this evil unto them.

3 Thus says the Lord God: Smite with your hand and stamp with your foot, and say, Alas — for all the evil abominations of the house of Israel; for they shall fall by the sword, by the famine, and by the pestilence. He that is far off shall die of the pestilence, and he that is near shall fall by the sword, and he that remains and is besieged shall die by the famine; thus will I accomplish my fury upon them. Then shall you know that I am the Lord, when their slain men shall be among their idols, round about their altars upon every high hill, in all the tops of the mountains, and under every green tree, and under every thick oak, the place where they did offer sweet savor to all their idols. So will I stretch out my hand upon them and make the land desolate, yea, more desolate than the wilderness toward Diblath, in all their habitations; and they shall know that I am the Lord.

4 Moreover, the word of the Lord came unto me, saying, Also, you son of man, thus says the Lord God unto the land of Israel: An end, the end has come upon the four corners of the land. Now has the end come upon you, and I will send my anger upon you, and will judge you according to your ways, and will recompense upon you all your abominations. And my eye shall not spare you, neither will I have pity,

but I will recompense your ways upon you, and your abominations shall be in your midst; and you shall know that I am the Lord.

5 Thus says the Lord God: An evil, an only evil, behold, has come. An end has come, the end has come, it watches for you; behold, it has come. The morning has come unto you, O you that dwell in the land. The time has come, the day of trouble is near, and not the sounding again of the mountains. Now will I shortly pour out my fury upon you and accomplish my anger upon you, and I will judge you according to your ways and will recompense you for all your abominations. And my eye shall not spare, neither will I have pity. I will recompense you according to your ways and your abominations that are in your midst, and you shall know that I am the Lord that smites. Behold the day, behold, it has come. The morning is gone forth, the rod has blossomed, pride has budded. Violence is risen up into a rod of wickedness, none of them shall remain, nor of their multitude, nor of any of theirs; neither shall there be wailing for them. The time has come, the day draws near. Let not the buyer rejoice nor the seller mourn, for wrath is upon all the multitude thereof; for the seller shall not return to that which is sold, although they were yet alive. For the vision is touching the whole multitude thereof which shall not return, neither shall any strengthen himself in the iniquity of his life.

6 They have blown the trumpet, even to make all ready, but none goes to the battle, for my wrath is upon all the multitude thereof. The sword is without, and the pestilence and the famine within. He that is in the field shall die with the sword; and he that is in the city, famine and pestilence shall devour him. But they that escape of them shall escape and shall be on the mountains like doves of the valleys, all of them mourning, everyone for his iniquity. All hands shall be feeble, and all knees shall be weak as water. They shall also gird themselves with sackcloth, and horror shall cover them, and shame shall be upon all faces and baldness upon all their heads. They shall cast their silver in the streets and their gold shall be removed. Their silver and their gold shall not be able to deliver them in the day of the wrath of the Lord. They shall not satisfy their souls, neither fill their bowels, because it is the stumbling block of their iniquity.

7 As for the beauty of his ornament, he set it in majesty, but they made the images of their abominations and of their detestable things

therein; therefore, I have set it far from them. And I will give it into the hands of the strangers for a prey, and to the wicked of the earth for a spoil, and they shall pollute it. My face will I turn also from them, and they shall pollute my secret place, for the robbers shall enter into it and defile it. Make a chain, for the land is full of bloody crimes and the city is full of violence. Wherefore, I will bring the worst of the heathen and they shall possess their houses. I will also make the pomp of the strong to cease, and their holy places shall be defiled. Destruction comes and they shall seek peace, and there shall be none. Mischief shall come upon mischief, and rumor shall be upon rumor.

8 Then shall they seek a vision of the prophet, but the law shall perish from the priest and counsel from the elders. The king shall mourn and the prince shall be clothed with desolation, and the hands of the people of the land shall be troubled. I will do unto them after their way, and according to their deserts will I judge them; and they shall know that I am the Lord.

3 And it came to pass in the sixth year, in the sixth month, in the fifth day of the month, as I sat in my house and the elders of Judah sat before me, that the hand of the Lord God fell there upon me. Then I beheld, and behold, a likeness as the appearance of fire: from the appearance of his loins even downward, fire, and from his loins even upward, as the appearance of brightness as the color of amber. And he put forth the form of a hand, and took me by a lock of my head, and the spirit lifted me up between the earth and the heaven and brought me in the visions of God to Jerusalem, to the door of the inner gate that looks toward the north, where was the seat of the image of jealousy which provokes to jealousy. And behold, the glory of the God of Israel was there, according to the vision that I saw in the plain.

2 Then said he unto me, Son of man, lift up your eyes now the way toward the north. So I lifted up my eyes the way toward the north, and behold, northward at the gate of the altar, this image of jealousy in the entry. He said furthermore unto me, Son of man, do you see what they do—even the great abominations that the house of Israel commits here, that I should go far off from my sanctuary? But turn yet again and you shall see greater abominations.

3 And he brought me to the door of the court, and when I looked, behold, a hole in the wall. Then said he unto me, Son of man, dig now in the wall. And when I had dug in the wall, behold, a door. And he said unto me, Go in and behold the wicked abominations that they do here.

4 So I went in and saw, and behold, every form of creeping things and abominable beasts, and all the idols of the house of Israel, portrayed upon the wall round about. And there stood before them seventy men of the elders of the house of Israel, and in the midst of them stood Jaazaniah the son of Shaphan, with every man his censer in his hand, and a thick cloud of incense went up. Then said he unto me, Son of man, have you seen what the elders of the house of Israel do in the dark — every man in the chambers of his imagery? For they say, The Lord sees us not, the Lord has forsaken the earth. He said also unto me, Turn yet again and you shall see greater abominations that they do.

5 Then he brought me to the door of the gate of the Lord's house which was toward the north, and behold, there sat women weeping for Tammuz. Then said he unto me, Have you seen this, O son of man? Turn yet again and you shall see greater abominations than these.

6 And he brought me into the inner court of the Lord's house, and behold, at the door of the temple of the Lord, between the porch and the altar, were about twenty-five men with their backs toward the temple of the Lord and their faces toward the east; and they worshipped the sun toward the east. Then he said unto me, Have you seen this, O son of man? Is it a light thing to the house of Judah that they commit the abominations which they commit here? For they have filled the land with violence, and have returned to provoke me to anger, and behold, they put the branch to their nose. Therefore will I also deal in fury. My eye shall not spare, neither will I have pity, and though they cry in my ears with a loud voice, yet will I not hear them.

7 He cried also in my ears with a loud voice, saying, Cause them that have charge over the city to draw near, even every man with his destroying weapon in his hand! And behold, six men came from the way of the higher gate which lies toward the north, and every man a slaughter weapon in his hand — and one man among them was clothed with linen, with a writer's inkwell by his side — and they went in and stood beside the brazen altar. And the glory of the God of Israel was gone up from the cherub, whereupon he was, to the threshold of the

house. And he called to the man clothed with linen who had the writer's inkwell by his side, and the Lord said unto him, Go through the midst of the city, through the midst of Jerusalem, and set a mark upon the foreheads of the men that sigh and that cry for all the abominations that are done in the midst thereof. And to the others he said in my hearing, Go after him through the city, and smite. Let not your eye spare, neither have pity. Slay utterly old and young, both virgins, and little children, and women, but come not near any man upon whom is the mark; and begin at my sanctuary. Then they began at the old men who were before the house. And he said unto them, Defile the house, and fill the courts with the slain; go forth. And they went forth and slew in the city.

8 And it came to pass, while they were slaying them and I was left, that I fell upon my face and cried, and said, Ah Lord God, will you destroy all the residue of Israel in your pouring out of your fury upon Jerusalem? Then said he unto me, The iniquity of the house of Israel and Judah is exceedingly great, and the land is full of blood, and the city full of perverseness; for they say, The Lord has forsaken the earth and the Lord sees not. And as for me also, my eye shall not spare, neither will I have pity, but I will recompense their way upon their head. And behold, the man clothed with linen, who had the inkwell by his side, reported the matter, saying, I have done as you have commanded me.

9 Then I looked, and behold, in the firmament that was above the head of the cherubim, there appeared over them, as it were, a sapphire stone, as the appearance of the likeness of a throne. And he spoke unto the man clothed with linen and said, Go in between the wheels, even under the cherub, and fill your hand with coals of fire from between the cherubim and scatter them over the city. And he went in, in my sight. Now the cherubim stood on the right side of the house when the man went in, and the cloud filled the inner court. Then the glory of the Lord went up from the cherub and stood over the threshold of the house, and the house was filled with the cloud, and the court was full of the brightness of the Lord's glory. And the sound of the cherubim's wings was heard even to the outer court, as the voice of the Almighty God when he speaks.

10 And it came to pass that when he had commanded the man clothed with linen, saying, Take fire from between the wheels, from between

the cherubim — then he went in and stood beside the wheels. And one cherub stretched forth his hand from between the cherubim unto the fire that was between the cherubim, and took thereof, and put it into the hands of him that was clothed with linen, who took it and went out.

11 And there appeared in the cherubim the form of a man's hand under their wings. And when I looked, behold, the four wheels by the cherubim — one wheel by one cherub and another wheel by another cherub, and the appearance of the wheels was as the color of a beryl stone. And as for their appearances, they four had one likeness, as if a wheel had been in the middle of a wheel. When they went, they went upon their four sides. They turned not as they went, but to the place where the head looked, they followed it; they turned not as they went. And their whole body, and their backs, and their hands, and their wings, and the wheels were full of eyes round about, even the wheels that they four had.

12 As for the wheels, it was cried unto them in my hearing, O wheel! And every one had four faces: the first face was the face of a cherub, and the second face was the face of a man, and the third the face of a lion, and the fourth the face of an eagle. And the cherubim were lifted up. This is the living creature that I saw by the river of Chebar.

13 And when the cherubim went, the wheels went by them; and when the cherubim lifted up their wings to mount up from the earth, the same wheels also turned not from beside them. When they stood, these stood; and when they were lifted up, these lifted up themselves also; for the spirit of the living creature was in them.

14 Then the glory of the Lord departed from off the threshold of the house and stood over the cherubim. And the cherubim lifted up their wings and mounted up from the earth in my sight. When they went out, the wheels also were beside them. And every one stood at the door of the east gate of the Lord's house, and the glory of the God of Israel was over them above. This is the living creature that I saw under the God of Israel by the river of Chebar, and I knew that they were the cherubim. Every one had four faces apiece, and every one four wings, and the likeness of the hands of a man was under their wings. And the likeness of their faces was the same faces which I saw by the river of Chebar; their appearances and themselves, they went every one straight forward.

¹⁵ Moreover, the spirit lifted me up and brought me unto the east gate of the Lord's house which looks eastward. And behold, at the door of the gate, twenty-five men, among whom I saw Jaazaniah the son of Azzur, and Pelatiah the son of Benaiah, princes of the people. Then said he unto me, Son of man, these are the men that devise mischief and give wicked counsel in this city, who say, It is not near, let us build houses, this city is the cauldron and we are the flesh.

¹⁶ Therefore, prophesy against them; prophesy, O son of man. And the spirit of the Lord fell upon me and said unto me, Speak, Thus says the Lord: Thus have you said, O house of Israel, for I know the things that come into your mind, every one of them. You have multiplied your slain in this city, and you have filled the streets thereof with the slain. Therefore, thus says the Lord God: Your slain whom you have laid in the midst of it, they are the flesh and this city is the cauldron, but I will bring you forth out of the midst of it. You have feared the sword, and I will bring a sword upon you, says the Lord God. And I will bring you out of the midst thereof and deliver you into the hands of strangers, and will execute judgments among you. You shall fall by the sword. I will judge you in the border of Israel, and you shall know that I am the Lord. This city shall not be your cauldron, neither shall you be the flesh in the midst thereof, but I will judge you in the border of Israel. And you shall know that I am the Lord, for you have not walked in my statutes, neither executed my judgments, but have done after the manners of the heathen that are round about you.

¹⁷ And it came to pass, when I prophesied, that Pelatiah the son of Benaiah died. Then I fell down upon my face and cried with a loud voice, and said, Ah Lord God, will you make a full end of the remnant of Israel? Again the word of the Lord came unto me, saying, Son of man, your brethren — even your brethren the men of your kindred, and all the house of Israel wholly — are they unto whom the inhabitants of Jerusalem have said, Go far from the Lord; unto us is this land given in possession.

¹⁸ Therefore, say, Thus says the Lord God: Although I have cast them far off among the heathen, and although I have scattered them among the countries, yet will I be to them as a little sanctuary in the countries where they shall come. Therefore, say, Thus says the Lord God: I will even gather you from the people, and assemble you out of the countries

where you have been scattered, and I will give you the land of Israel. And they shall come there, and they shall take away all the detestable things thereof, and all the abominations thereof from there. And I will give them one heart, and I will put a new spirit within you, and I will take the stony heart out of their flesh and will give them a heart of flesh, that they may walk in my statutes, and keep my ordinances, and do them. And they shall be my people, and I will be their God. But as for them whose heart walks after the heart of their detestable things and their abominations, I will recompense their way upon their own heads, says the Lord God.

19 Then did the cherubim lift up their wings, and the wheels beside them, and the glory of the God of Israel was over them above. And the glory of the Lord went up from the midst of the city and stood upon the mountain which is on the east side of the city. Afterward, the spirit took me up and brought me in a vision by the spirit of God into Chaldea, to them of the captivity. So the vision that I had seen went up from me. Then I spoke unto them of the captivity all the things that the Lord had shown me.

4 The word of the Lord also came unto me, saying, Son of man, you dwell in the midst of a rebellious house, who have eyes to see, and see not; they have ears to hear, and hear not; for they are a rebellious house.

2 Therefore, you son of man, prepare stuff for removing, and remove by day in their sight; and you shall remove from your place to another place in their sight. It may be they will consider, though they be a rebellious house. Then shall you bring forth your stuff by day in their sight, as stuff for removing, and you shall go forth at evening in their sight, as they that go forth into captivity. Dig through the wall in their sight, and carry out thereby. In their sight shall you bear it upon your shoulders and carry it forth in the twilight. You shall cover your face that you see not the ground, for I have set you for a sign unto the house of Israel.

3 And I did so as I was commanded. I brought forth my stuff by day, as stuff for captivity, and in the evening I dug through the wall with my hand. I brought it forth in the twilight and I bore it upon my shoulder in their sight.

4 And in the morning came the word of the Lord unto me, saying, Son of man, has not the house of Israel, the rebellious house, said unto you, What are you doing? Say unto them, Thus says the Lord God: This burden concerns the prince in Jerusalem, and all the house of Israel that are among them. Say, I am your sign. As I have done, so shall it be done unto them — they shall remove and go into captivity. And the prince that is among them shall bear upon his shoulder in the twilight and shall go forth; they shall dig through the wall to carry out thereby. He shall cover his face, that he see not the ground with his eyes. My net also will I spread upon him, and he shall be taken in my snare, and I will bring him to Babylon, to the land of the Chaldeans. Yet shall he not see it, though he shall die there. And I will scatter toward every wind all that are about him to help him, and all his bands, and I will draw out the sword after them. And they shall know that I am the Lord when I shall scatter them among the nations and disperse them in the countries. But I will leave a few men of them from the sword, from the famine, and from the pestilence, that they may declare all their abominations among the heathen where they come; and they shall know that I am the Lord.

5 Moreover, the word of the Lord came to me, saying, Son of man, eat your bread with quaking, and drink your water with trembling and with anxiousness, and say unto the people of the land, Thus says the Lord God of the inhabitants of Jerusalem and of the land of Israel: They shall eat their bread with anxiousness and drink their water with astonishment, that her land may be desolate from all that is therein because of the violence of all them that dwell therein. And the cities that are inhabited shall be laid waste, and the land shall be desolate, and you shall know that I am the Lord.

5 And the word of the Lord came unto me, saying, Son of man, what is that proverb that you have in the land of Israel, saying, The days are prolonged and every vision fails? Tell them, therefore, Thus says the Lord God: I will make this proverb to cease, and they shall no more use it as a proverb in Israel. But say unto them, The days are at hand, and the fulfillment of every vision. For there shall be no more any vain vision nor flattering divination within the house of Israel. For I am the Lord. I will speak, and the word that I shall speak shall come to pass. It

shall be no more prolonged, for in your days, O rebellious house, will I say the word and will perform it, says the Lord God.

2 Again the word of the Lord came to me, saying, Son of man, behold, they of the house of Israel say, The vision that he sees is for many days to come, and he prophesies of the times that are far off. Therefore, say unto them, Thus says the Lord God: There shall none of my words be prolonged anymore, but the word which I have spoken shall be done, says the Lord God.

3 And the word of the Lord came unto me, saying, Son of man, prophesy against the prophets of Israel that prophesy, and say unto them that prophesy out of their own hearts, Hear the word of the Lord; thus says the Lord God: Woe unto the foolish prophets that follow their own spirit and have seen nothing. O Israel, your prophets are like the foxes in the deserts. You have not gone up into the gaps, neither made up the hedge for the house of Israel to stand in the battle in the day of the Lord. They have seen vanity and lying divination, saying, The Lord says — and the Lord has not sent them; and they have made others to hope that they would confirm the word. Have you not seen a vain vision, and have you not spoken a lying divination, whereas you say, The Lord says it — albeit I have not spoken?

4 Therefore, thus says the Lord God: Because you have spoken vanity and seen lies, therefore behold, I am against you, says the Lord God. And my hand shall be upon the prophets that see vanity and that divine lies. They shall not be in the assembly of my people, neither shall they be written in the writing of the house of Israel, neither shall they enter into the land of Israel; and you shall know that I am the Lord God. Because, even because they have seduced my people, saying, Peace — and there was no peace, and one built up a wall, and behold, others plastered it with untempered mortar, say unto them who plaster it with untempered mortar, that it shall fall. There shall be an overflowing shower, and you, O great hailstones, shall fall, and a stormy wind shall rend it. Behold, when the wall is fallen shall it not be said unto you, Where is the plaster with which you have plastered it?

5 Therefore, thus says the Lord God: I will even rend it with a stormy wind in my fury, and there shall be an overflowing shower in my anger, and great hailstones in my fury to consume it. So will I break down the wall that you have plastered with untempered mortar, and bring it

down to the ground, so that the foundation thereof shall be uncovered. And it shall fall, and you shall be consumed in the midst thereof; and you shall know that I am the Lord. Thus will I accomplish my wrath upon the wall and upon them that have plastered it with untempered mortar, and will say unto you, The wall is no more, neither they that plastered it—namely the prophets of Israel who prophesy concerning Jerusalem and who see visions of peace for her, and there is no peace, says the Lord God.

6 Likewise, you son of man, set your face against the daughters of your people who prophesy out of their own heart, and prophesy against them, and say, Thus says the Lord God: Woe to the women that sew pillows to all armholes, and make kerchiefs upon the head of every stature to hunt souls. Will you hunt the souls of my people and will you save the souls alive that come unto you? And will you pollute me among my people for handfuls of barley and for pieces of bread? To slay the souls that should not die and to save the souls alive that should not live, by your lying to my people that hear your lies?

7 Wherefore, thus says the Lord God: Behold, I am against your pillows with which you there hunt the souls to make them fly; and I will tear them from your arms and will let the souls go, even the souls that you hunt to make them fly. Your kerchiefs also will I tear, and deliver my people out of your hand, and they shall be no more in your hand to be hunted; and you shall know that I am the Lord. Because with lies you have made the heart of the righteous sad whom I have not made sad, and strengthened the hands of the wicked that he should not return from his wicked way, by promising him life, therefore you shall see no more vanity nor divine divinations; for I will deliver my people out of your hand, and you shall know that I am the Lord.

8 Then certain of the elders of Israel came unto me and sat before me. And the word of the Lord came unto me, saying, Son of man, these men have set up their idols in their heart and put the stumbling block of their iniquity before their face. Should I be inquired of at all by them? Therefore, speak unto them, and say unto them, Thus says the Lord God: Every man of the house of Israel that sets up his idols in his heart, and puts the stumbling block of his iniquity before his face, and comes to the prophet, I the Lord will answer him that comes according to the multitude of his idols, that I may take the house of Israel in

their own heart, because they are all estranged from me through their idols. Therefore, say unto the house of Israel, Thus says the Lord God: Repent, and turn yourselves from your idols, and turn away your faces from all your abominations; for everyone of the house of Israel, or of the stranger that sojourns in Israel, who separates himself from me, and sets up his idols in his heart, and puts the stumbling block of his iniquity before his face, and comes to a prophet to inquire of him concerning me, I the Lord will answer him by myself. And I will set my face against that man and will make him a sign and a proverb, and I will cut him off from the midst of my people, and you shall know that I am the Lord.

9 And if the prophet is deceived when he has spoken a thing, I, the Lord, have not deceived that prophet; therefore, I will stretch out my hand upon him and will destroy him from the midst of my people Israel, and they shall bear the punishment of their iniquity. The punishment of the prophet shall be even as the punishment of him that seeks unto him, that the house of Israel may go no more astray from me, neither be polluted anymore with all their transgressions, but that they may be my people and I may be their God, says the Lord God.

10 The word of the Lord came again to me, saying, Son of man, when the land sins against me by trespassing grievously, then will I stretch out my hand upon it, and will break the support of the bread thereof, and will send famine upon it, and will cut off man and beast from it. Though these three men — Noah, Daniel, and Job — were in it, they should deliver but their own souls by their righteousness, says the Lord God. If I cause noxious beasts to pass through the land, and they spoil it so that it be desolate, that no man may pass through because of the beasts, though these three men were in it, as I live, says the Lord God, they shall deliver neither sons nor daughters — they only shall be delivered; but the land shall be desolate. Or if I bring a sword upon that land and say, Sword, go through the land so that I cut off man and beast from it, though these three men were in it, as I live, says the Lord God, they shall deliver neither sons nor daughters, but they only shall be delivered themselves. Or if I send a pestilence into that land and pour out my fury upon it in blood, to cut off from it man and beast, though Noah, Daniel, and Job were in it, as I live, says the

Lord God, they shall deliver neither son nor daughter; they shall but deliver their own souls by their righteousness.

11 For thus says the Lord God: How much more when I send my four severe judgments upon Jerusalem — the sword, and the famine, and the noxious beast, and the pestilence — to cut off from it man and beast? Yet behold, therein shall be left a remnant that shall be brought forth, both sons and daughters. Behold, they shall come forth unto you, and you shall see their way and their doings, and you shall be comforted concerning the evil that I have brought upon Jerusalem, even concerning all that I have brought upon it. And they shall comfort you when you see their ways and their doings, and you shall know that I have not done without cause all that I have done in it, says the Lord God.

6 And the word of the Lord came unto me, saying, Son of man, What is the vine tree more than any tree, or than a branch which is among the trees of the forest? Shall wood be taken thereof to do any work? Or will men take a pin of it to hang any vessel thereon? Behold, it is cast into the fire for fuel; the fire devours both the ends of it, and the middle of it is burned. Is it meet for any work? Behold, when it was whole, it was meet for no work; how much less shall it be meet yet for any work when the fire has devoured it and it is burned.

2 Therefore, thus says the Lord God: As the vine tree among the trees of the forest which I have given to the fire for fuel, so will I give the inhabitants of Jerusalem. And I will set my face against them; they shall go out from one fire and another fire shall devour them. And you shall know that I am the Lord when I set my face against them. And I will make the land desolate because they have committed a trespass, says the Lord God.

3 Again the word of the Lord came unto me, saying, Son of man, cause Jerusalem to know her abominations, and say, Thus says the Lord God unto Jerusalem: Your birth and your nativity is of the land of Canaan; your father was an Amorite and your mother a Hittite. And as for your nativity, in the day you were born, your navel was not cut, neither were you washed in water to cleanse you. You were not salted at all, nor swaddled at all. No eye pitied you to do any of these unto

you, to have compassion upon you, but you were cast out in the open field, to the loathing of your person, in the day that you were born.

4 And when I passed by you and saw you polluted in your own blood, I said unto you when you were in your blood, Live. Yea, I said unto you when you were in your blood, Live. I have caused you to multiply as the bud of the field, and you have increased and grown great, and you have come to excellent ornaments; your breasts are fashioned and your hair is grown, whereas you were naked and bare.

5 Now when I passed by you and looked upon you, behold, your time was the time of love; and I spread my skirt over you and covered your nakedness. Yea, I swore unto you and entered into a covenant with you, says the Lord God, and you became mine. Then I washed you with water, yea, I thoroughly washed away your blood from you, and I anointed you with oil. I clothed you also with embroidered work, and shod you with badgers' skin, and I girded you about with fine linen, and I covered you with silk. I adorned you also with ornaments, and I put bracelets upon your hands and a chain on your neck. And I put a jewel on your forehead, and earrings in your ears, and a beautiful crown upon your head. Thus were you adorned with gold and silver, and your raiment was of fine linen, and silk, and embroidered work. You did eat fine flour, and honey, and oil, and you were exceedingly beautiful, and you did prosper into a kingdom. And your renown went forth among the heathen for your beauty, for it was perfect through my comeliness which I had put upon you, says the Lord God.

6 But you did trust in your own beauty, and played the harlot because of your renown, and poured out your fornications on everyone that passed by — his it was. And of your garments you did take and adorned your high places with diverse colors, and played the harlot thereupon; the like things shall not come, neither shall it be so. You have also taken your fair jewels of my gold and of my silver which I had given you, and made to yourself images of men, and did commit whoredom with them, and took your embroidered garments and covered them, and you have set my oil and my incense before them. My food also which I gave you — fine flour, and oil, and honey with which I fed you — you have even set it before them for a sweet savor; and thus it was, says the Lord God. Moreover, you have taken your sons and your daughters whom you have borne unto me, and these have you sacrificed unto

them to be devoured. Is this of your whoredoms a small matter — that you have slain my children, and delivered them, to cause them to pass through the fire for them? And in all your abominations and your whoredoms you have not remembered the days of your youth, when you were naked and bare, and were polluted in your blood.

7 And it came to pass after all your wickedness — woe, woe unto you, says the Lord God — that you have also built unto you an eminent place, and have made you a high place in every street. You have built your high place at every head of the way, and have made your beauty to be abhorred, and have opened your feet to everyone that passed by, and multiplied your whoredoms. You have also committed fornication with the Egyptians, your neighbors great of flesh, and have increased your whoredoms, to provoke me to anger. Behold, therefore I have stretched out my hand over you, and have diminished your ordinary food, and delivered you unto the will of them that hate you, the daughters of the Philistines, who are ashamed of your lewd way. You have played the whore also with the Assyrians because you were insatiable, yea, you have played the harlot with them, and yet could not be satisfied. You have moreover multiplied your fornication in the land of Canaan unto Chaldea, and yet you were not satisfied herewith.

8 How weak is your heart, says the Lord God, seeing you do all these things, the work of an imperious whorish woman, in that you build your eminent place in the head of every way, and make your high place in every street, and have not been as a harlot — in that you scorn hire — but as a wife that commits adultery, who takes strangers instead of her husband! They give gifts to all whores, but you give your gifts to all your lovers and hire them, that they may come unto you on every side for your whoredom. And the contrary is in you from other women in your whoredoms, whereas none follow you to commit whoredoms, and in that you give a reward and no reward is given unto you; therefore, you are contrary.

9 Wherefore, O harlot, hear the word of the Lord. Thus says the Lord God: Because your filthiness was poured out and your nakedness uncovered through your whoredoms with your lovers, and with all the idols of your abominations, and by the blood of your children which you did give unto them, behold, therefore I will gather all your lovers with whom you have taken pleasure, and all them that

you have loved, with all them that you have hated; I will even gather them round about against you, and will uncover your nakedness unto them, that they may see all your nakedness. And I will judge you as women that break wedlock and shed blood are judged, and I will give you blood in fury and jealousy. And I will also give you into their hand, and they shall throw down your eminent place and shall break down your high places. They shall strip you also of your clothes, and shall take your fair jewels, and leave you naked and bare. They shall also bring up a company against you, and they shall stone you with stones and thrust you through with their swords. And they shall burn your houses with fire and execute judgments upon you in the sight of many women. And I will cause you to cease from playing the harlot, and you also shall give no hire anymore. So will I make my fury toward you to rest, and my jealousy shall depart from you, and I will be quiet and will be no more angry. Because you have not remembered the days of your youth but have fretted me in all these things, behold, therefore I also will recompense your way upon your head, says the Lord God, and you shall not commit this lewdness above all your abominations.

10 Behold, everyone that uses proverbs shall use this proverb against you, saying: As is the mother, so is her daughter. You are your mother's daughter, that loathes her husband and her children; and you are the sister of your sisters, who loathed their husbands and their children. Your mother was a Hittite and your father an Amorite. And your elder sister is Samaria, she and her daughters that dwell at your left hand; and your younger sister that dwells at your right hand is Sodom, and her daughters. Yet have you not walked after their ways, nor done after their abominations? But as if that were a very little thing, you were corrupted more than they in all your ways.

11 As I live, says the Lord God, Sodom your sister has not done — she nor her daughters — as you have done, you and your daughters. Behold, this was the iniquity of your sister Sodom: pride, fullness of bread, and abundance of idleness was in her and in her daughters, neither did she strengthen the hand of the poor and needy. And they were haughty, and committed abomination before me; therefore, I took them away as I saw good.

12 Neither has Samaria committed half of your sins, but you have multiplied your abominations more than they, and have justified your

sisters in all your abominations which you have done. You also, who have judged your sisters, bear your own shame for your sins that you have committed more abominable than they. They are more righteous than you. Yea, be confounded also, and bear your shame, in that you have justified your sisters.

13 When I shall bring again their captives — the captives of Sodom and her daughters, and the captives of Samaria and her daughters — then will I bring again the captivity of your captives in the midst of them, that you may bear your own shame and may be confounded in all that you have done, in that you are a comfort unto them. When your sisters, Sodom and her daughters, shall return to their former estate, and Samaria and her daughters shall return to their former estate, then you and your daughters shall return to your former estate. For your sister Sodom was not mentioned by your mouth in the day of your pride, before your wickedness was revealed, as at the time of your reproach of the daughters of Syria and all that are round about her, the daughters of the Philistines, who despise you round about. You have borne your lewdness and your abominations, says the Lord.

14 For thus says the Lord God: I will even deal with you as you have done, who have despised the oath in breaking the covenant. Nevertheless, I will remember my covenant with you in the days of your youth, and I will establish unto you an everlasting covenant. Then you shall remember your ways and be ashamed when you shall receive your sisters, your elder and your younger; and I will give them unto you for daughters, but not by your covenant. And I will establish my covenant with you, and you shall know that I am the Lord, that you may remember and be confounded, and never open your mouth anymore because of your shame when I am pacified toward you for all that you have done, says the Lord God.

7 And the word of the Lord came unto me, saying, Son of man, put forth a riddle and speak a parable unto the house of Israel, and say, Thus says the Lord God: A great eagle with great wings, long-winged, full of feathers which had diverse colors, came unto Lebanon and took the highest branch of the cedar. He cropped off the top of his young twigs, and carried it into a land of commerce; he set it in a city of merchants. He took also of the seed of the land and planted it

in a fruitful field; he placed it by great waters, and set it as a willow tree. And it grew and became a spreading vine of low stature, whose branches turned toward him, and the roots thereof were under him; so it became a vine, and brought forth branches and shot forth sprigs.

2 There was also another great eagle with great wings and many feathers, and behold, this vine did bend her roots toward him, and shot forth her branches toward him, that he might water it by the furrows of her plantation. It was planted in a good soil by great waters, that it might bring forth branches and that it might bear fruit, that it might be a goodly vine.

3 Say, Thus says the Lord God: Shall it prosper? Shall he not pull up the roots thereof and cut off the fruit thereof, that it wither? It shall wither in all the leaves of her spring, even without great power or many people to pluck it up by the roots thereof. Yea, behold, being planted, shall it prosper? Shall it not utterly wither when the east wind touches it? It shall wither in the furrows where it grew.

4 Moreover, the word of the Lord came unto me, saying, Say now to the rebellious house, Do you not know what these things mean? Tell them, Behold, the king of Babylon has come to Jerusalem, and has taken the king thereof and the princes thereof, and led them with him to Babylon, and has taken of the king's seed and made a covenant with him, and has taken an oath of him. He has also taken the mighty of the land, that the kingdom might be base, that it might not lift itself up, but that by keeping of his covenant, it might stand. But he rebelled against him in sending his ambassadors into Egypt, that they might give him horses and much people. Shall he prosper? Shall he escape that does such things? Or shall he break the covenant and be delivered?

5 As I live, says the Lord God, surely in the place where the king dwells that made him king, whose oath he despised and whose covenant he broke, even with him in the midst of Babylon he shall die. Neither shall Pharaoh with his mighty army and great company make for him in the war by casting up mounts and building forts to cut off many people. Seeing he despised the oath by breaking the covenant, when behold, he had given his hand, and has done all these things, he shall not escape.

6 Therefore, thus says the Lord God: As I live, surely my oath that he has despised and my covenant that he has broken, even it will I

recompense upon his own head. And I will spread my net upon him and he shall be taken in my snare; and I will bring him to Babylon, and will plead with him there for his trespass that he has trespassed against me. And all his fugitives with all his bands shall fall by the sword, and they that remain shall be scattered toward all winds; and you shall know that I the Lord have spoken it.

7 Thus says the Lord God: I will also take of the highest branch of the high cedar and will set it. I will crop off from the top of his young twigs a tender one, and will plant it upon a high mountain, and eminent. In the mountain of the height of Israel will I plant it, and it shall bring forth boughs and bear fruit, and be a goodly cedar, and under it shall dwell all fowl of every wing; in the shadow of the branches thereof shall they dwell. And all the trees of the field shall know that I the Lord have brought down the high tree, have exalted the low tree, have dried up the green tree, and have made the dry tree to flourish. I the Lord have spoken and have done it.

8 The word of the Lord came unto me again, saying, What do you mean, that you use this proverb concerning the land of Israel, saying, The fathers have eaten sour grapes and the children's teeth are set on edge? As I live, says the Lord God, you shall not have occasion anymore to use this proverb in Israel. Behold, all souls are mine; as the soul of the father, so also the soul of the son is mine. The soul that sins, it shall die.

2 But if a man is just and does that which is lawful and right, and has not eaten upon the mountains, neither has lifted up his eyes to the idols of the house of Israel, neither has defiled his neighbor's wife, neither has come near to a menstruous woman, and has not oppressed any, but has restored to the debtor his pledge, has spoiled none by violence, has given his bread to the hungry, and has covered the naked with a garment, he that has not given forth upon usury neither has taken any increase, that has withdrawn his hand from iniquity, has executed true judgment between man and man, has walked in my statutes, and has kept my judgments, to deal truly — he is just. He shall surely live, says the Lord God.

3 If he beget a son that is a robber, a shedder of blood, and that does the like to any one of these things, and that does not any of those duties,

but even has eaten upon the mountains, and defiled his neighbor's wife, has oppressed the poor and needy, has spoiled by violence, has not restored the pledge, and has lifted up his eyes to the idols, has committed abomination, has given forth upon usury, and has taken increase — shall he then live? He shall not live. He has done all these abominations, he shall surely die, his blood shall be upon him.

4 Now behold, if he beget a son that sees all his father's sins which he has done, and considers and does not such like — that has not eaten upon the mountains, neither has lifted up his eyes to the idols of the house of Israel, has not defiled his neighbor's wife, neither has oppressed any, has not withheld the pledge, neither has spoiled by violence, but has given his bread to the hungry, and has covered the naked with a garment, that has taken off his hand from the poor, that has not received usury nor increase, has executed my judgments, has walked in my statutes — he shall not die for the iniquity of his father; he shall surely live. As for his father, because he cruelly oppressed, spoiled his brother by violence, and did that which is not good among his people, behold, even he shall die in his iniquity.

5 Yet say you, Why does not the son bear the iniquity of the father? When the son has done that which is lawful and right, and has kept all my statutes and has done them, he shall surely live. The soul that sins, it shall die. The son shall not bear the iniquity of the father, neither shall the father bear the iniquity of the son; the righteousness of the righteous shall be upon him, and the wickedness of the wicked shall be upon him. But if the wicked will turn from all his sins that he has committed, and keep all my statutes, and do that which is lawful and right, he shall surely live — he shall not die. All his transgressions that he has committed, they shall not be mentioned unto him; in his righteousness that he has done, he shall live.

6 Have I any pleasure at all that the wicked should die? — says the Lord God, and not that he should return from his ways and live? But when the righteous turns away from his righteousness, and commits iniquity, and does according to all the abominations that the wicked man does, shall he live? All his righteousness that he has done shall not be mentioned. In his trespass that he has trespassed, and in his sin that he has sinned, in them shall he die.

7 Yet you say, The way of the Lord is not equal. Hear now, O house of Israel, is not my way equal? Are not your ways unequal? When a righteous man turns away from his righteousness, and commits iniquity and dies in them, for his iniquity that he has done shall he die. Again, when the wicked man turns away from his wickedness that he has committed, and does that which is lawful and right, he shall save his soul alive. Because he considers and turns away from all his transgressions that he has committed, he shall surely live—he shall not die. Yet says the house of Israel, The way of the Lord is not equal. O house of Israel, are not my ways equal? Are not your ways unequal?

8 Therefore, I will judge you, O house of Israel, everyone according to his ways, says the Lord God. Repent and turn yourselves from all your transgressions, so iniquity shall not be your ruin. Cast away from you all your transgressions whereby you have transgressed, and make yourself a new heart and a new spirit; for why will you die, O house of Israel? For I have no pleasure in the death of him that dies, says the Lord God; wherefore, turn and live.

9 Moreover, take up a lamentation for the princes of Israel and say, What is your mother? A lioness. She lay down among lions, she nourished her whelps among young lions, and she brought up one of her whelps—it became a young lion and it learned to catch the prey. It devoured men. The nations also heard of him. He was taken in their pit, and they brought him with chains unto the land of Egypt. Now when she saw that she had waited and her hope was lost, then she took another of her whelps and made him a young lion. And he went up and down among the lions, he became a young lion, and learned to catch the prey and devoured men. And he knew their desolate palaces, and he laid waste their cities; and the land was desolate, and the fullness thereof, by the noise of his roaring. Then the nations set against him on every side from the provinces, and spread their net over him; he was taken in their pit. And they put him in confinement, in chains, and brought him to the king of Babylon. They brought him into holds, that his voice should no more be heard upon the mountains of Israel.

10 Your mother is like a vine planted by the waters. She was fruitful and full of branches by reason of many waters, and she had strong rods for the scepters of them that bore rule, and her stature was exalted among the thick branches, and she appeared in her height with the

multitude of her branches. But she was plucked up in fury, she was cast down to the ground, and the east wind dried up her fruit. Her strong rods were broken and withered, the fire consumed them, and now she is planted in the wilderness, in a dry and thirsty ground. And fire is gone out of a rod of her branches, which has devoured her fruit so that she has no strong rod to be a scepter to rule. This is a lamentation, and shall be for a lamentation.

9 And it came to pass in the seventh year, in the fifth month, the tenth day of the month, that certain of the elders of Israel came to inquire of the Lord, and sat before me. Then came the word of the Lord unto me, saying, Son of man, speak unto the elders of Israel, and say unto them, Thus says the Lord God: Have you come to inquire of me? As I live, says the Lord God, I will not be inquired of by you. Will you judge them, son of man? Will you judge them? Cause them to know the abominations of their fathers, and say unto them, Thus says the Lord God: In the day when I chose Israel, and lifted up my hand unto the seed of the house of Jacob, and made myself known unto them in the land of Egypt—when I lifted up my hand unto them, saying, I am the Lord your God—in the day that I lifted up my hand unto them to bring them forth of the land of Egypt into a land that I had searched out for them, flowing with milk and honey, which is the glory of all lands, then said I unto them, Cast away every man the abominations of his eyes, and do not defile yourselves with the idols of Egypt. I am the Lord your God. But they rebelled against me, and would not listen unto me. They did not every man cast away the abominations of their eyes, neither did they forsake the idols of Egypt.

2 Then I said, I will pour out my fury upon them to accomplish my anger against them in the midst of the land of Egypt. But I worked for my name's sake, that it should not be polluted before the heathen—among whom they were, in whose sight I made myself known unto them in bringing them forth out of the land of Egypt. Wherefore, I caused them to go forth out of the land of Egypt and brought them into the wilderness. And I gave them my statutes, and showed them my judgments—which if a man do, he shall even live in them. Moreover also, I gave them my Sabbaths to be a sign between me and them, that they might know that I am the Lord that sanctify

them. But the house of Israel rebelled against me in the wilderness, they walked not in my statutes, and they despised my judgments — which if a man do, he shall even live in them; and my Sabbaths they greatly polluted.

3 Then I said I would pour out my fury upon them in the wilderness, to consume them. But I worked for my name's sake, that it should not be polluted before the heathen in whose sight I brought them out. Yet also I lifted up my hand unto them in the wilderness, that I would not bring them into the land which I had given them, flowing with milk and honey, which is the glory of all lands, because they despised my judgments and walked not in my statutes, but polluted my Sabbaths; for their heart went after their idols.

4 Nevertheless, my eye spared them from destroying them, neither did I make an end of them in the wilderness. But I said unto their children in the wilderness, Walk not in the statutes of your fathers, neither observe their judgments, nor defile yourselves with their idols. I am the Lord your God. Walk in my statutes, and keep my judgments and do them, and hallow my Sabbaths, and they shall be a sign between me and you, that you may know that I am the Lord your God. Notwithstanding, the children rebelled against me. They walked not in my statutes, neither kept my judgments to do them — which if a man do, he shall even live in them. They polluted my Sabbaths.

5 Then I said I would pour out my fury upon them, to accomplish my anger against them in the wilderness. Nevertheless, I withdrew my hand, and worked for my name's sake, that it should not be polluted in the sight of the heathen in whose sight I brought them forth. I lifted up my hand unto them also in the wilderness, that I would scatter them among the heathen and disperse them through the countries, because they had not executed my judgments, but had despised my statutes and had polluted my Sabbaths, and their eyes were after their fathers' idols. Wherefore, I gave them also statutes that were not good, and judgments whereby they should not live, and I polluted them in their own gifts, in that they caused to pass through the fire all that opens the womb, that I might make them desolate, to the end that they might know that I am the Lord.

6 Therefore, son of man, speak unto the house of Israel, and say unto them, Thus says the Lord God: Yet in this your fathers have blasphemed

me, in that they have committed a trespass against me; for when I had brought them into the land, for which I lifted up my hand to give it to them, then they saw every high hill, and all the thick trees, and they offered there their sacrifices, and there they presented the provocation of their offering. There also they made their sweet savor, and poured out there their drink offerings. Then I said unto them, What is the high place unto which you go? And the name thereof is called Bamah unto this day.

7 Wherefore, say unto the house of Israel, thus says the Lord God: You are polluted after the manner of your fathers and you commit whoredom after their abominations; for when you offer your gifts, when you make your sons to pass through the fire, you pollute yourselves with all your idols, even unto this day. And shall I be inquired of by you, O house of Israel? As I live, says the Lord God, I will not be inquired of by you. And that which comes into your mind shall not be at all — that you say, We will be as the heathen, as the families of the countries, to serve wood and stone.

8 As I live, says the Lord God, surely with a mighty hand, and with a stretched out arm, and with fury poured out will I rule over you. And I will bring you out from the people, and will gather you out of the countries wherein you are scattered with a mighty hand, and with a stretched out arm, and with fury poured out. And I will bring you into the wilderness of the people, and there will I plead with you face to face — as I pled with your fathers in the wilderness of the land of Egypt, so will I plead with you, says the Lord God. And I will cause you to pass under the rod, and I will bring you into the bond of the covenant, and I will purge out from among you the rebels and them that transgress against me. I will bring them forth out of the country where they sojourn, and they shall not enter into the land of Israel, and you shall know that I am the Lord.

9 As for you, O house of Israel, thus says the Lord God: Go, serve everyone his idols, and hereafter also, if you will not listen unto me; but pollute my holy name no more with your gifts and with your idols. For in my holy mountain, in the mountain of the height of Israel, says the Lord God, there shall all the house of Israel, all of them in the land, serve me. There will I accept them, and there will I require your offerings and the firstfruits of your offerings, with all your holy

things. I will accept you with your sweet savor when I bring you out
from the people and gather you out of the countries wherein you have
been scattered, and I will be sanctified in you before the heathen. And
you shall know that I am the Lord when I shall bring you into the land
of Israel, into the country for which I lifted up my hand to give it to
your fathers. And there shall you remember your ways and all your
doings wherein you have been defiled, and you shall loathe yourselves
in your own sight for all your evils that you have committed. And you
shall know that I am the Lord when I have worked with you for my
name's sake — not according to your wicked ways, nor according to
your corrupt doings, O you house of Israel, says the Lord God.

10 Moreover, the word of the Lord came unto me, saying, Son of man,
set your face toward the south, and drop your word toward the south,
and prophesy against the forest of the south field. And say to the forest
of the south, Hear the word of the Lord; thus says the Lord God: Behold,
I will kindle a fire in you, and it shall devour every green tree in you,
and every dry tree. The flaming flame shall not be quenched, and all
faces from the south to the north shall be burned therein. And all
flesh shall see that I the Lord have kindled it; it shall not be quenched.

11 Then I said, Ah Lord God, they say of me, Does he not speak
parables?

10 And the word of the Lord came unto me, saying, Son of man,
set your face toward Jerusalem, and drop your word toward
the holy places, and prophesy against the land of Israel, and say to
the land of Israel, Thus says the Lord: Behold, I am against you, and
will draw forth my sword out of his sheath, and will cut off from you
the righteous and the wicked. Seeing then that I will cut off from you
the righteous and the wicked, therefore shall my sword go forth out
of his sheath against all flesh from the south to the north, that all
flesh may know that I the Lord have drawn forth my sword out of
his sheath; it shall not return anymore.

2 Sigh therefore, you son of man, with the breaking of your loins and
with bitterness, sigh before their eyes. And it shall be, when they say
unto you, Why do you sigh? — that you shall answer, For the tidings,
because it comes, and every heart shall melt, and all hands shall be

feeble, and every spirit shall faint, and all knees shall be weak as water. Behold, it comes and shall be brought to pass, says the Lord God.

³ Again the word of the Lord came unto me, saying, Son of man, prophesy and say, Thus says the Lord; say, A sword, a sword is sharpened and also polished. It is sharpened to make a severe slaughter, it is polished that it may glitter. Should we then make mirth? It despises the rod of my son, as every tree, and he has given it to be polished, that it may be handled. This sword is sharpened and it is polished, to give it into the hand of the slayer. Cry and howl, son of man, for it shall be upon my people, it shall be upon all the princes of Israel; terrors by reason of the sword shall be upon my people. Smite therefore upon your thigh, because it is a trial. And what if the sword despise even the rod? It shall be no more, says the Lord God. You, therefore, son of man, prophesy, and smite your hands together, and let the sword be doubled the third time — the sword of the slain. It is the sword of the great men that are slain, which enters into their private chambers. I have set the point of the sword against all their gates, that their heart may faint and their ruins be multiplied. Ah, it is made bright, it is wrapped up for the slaughter. Go one way or another, either on the right hand or on the left, wherever your face is set. I will also smite my hands together, and I will cause my fury to rest. I the Lord have said it.

⁴ The word of the Lord came unto me again, saying, Also, you son of man, appoint two ways that the sword of the king of Babylon may come — both shall come forth out of one land. And choose a place, choose it at the head of the way to the city. Appoint a way that the sword may come to Rabbah of the Ammonites, and to Judah in Jerusalem the fortified. For the king of Babylon stood at the parting of the way, at the head of the two ways, to use divination: he made his arrows bright, he consulted with images, he looked in the liver. At his right hand was the divination for Jerusalem — to appoint captains, to open the mouth in the slaughter, to lift up the voice with shouting, to appoint battering rams against the gates, to cast a mount, and to build a fort. And it shall be unto them as a false divination in their sight, to them that have sworn oaths, but he will call to remembrance the iniquity, that they may be taken.

⁵ Therefore, thus says the Lord God: Because you have made your iniquity to be remembered, in that your transgressions are revealed so

that in all your doings your sins do appear — because, I say, you have come to remembrance — you shall be taken with the hand. And you, profane wicked prince of Israel, whose day has come when iniquity shall have an end, thus says the Lord God: Remove the diadem and take off the crown, this shall not be the same. Exalt him that is low, and abase him that is high. I will overturn, overturn, overturn it, and it shall be no more until he come whose right it is, and I will give it to him.

⁶And you, son of man, prophesy and say, Thus says the Lord God concerning the Ammonites and concerning their reproach; even say: The sword, the sword is drawn, for the slaughter it is polished, to consume because of the glittering — while they see vanity unto you, while they divine a lie unto you, to bring you upon the necks of them that are slain of the wicked, whose day has come when their iniquity shall have an end. Shall I cause it to return into his sheath? I will judge you in the place where you were created, in the land of your nativity. And I will pour out my indignation upon you, I will blow against you in the fire of my wrath, and deliver you into the hand of brutish men, and skillful to destroy. You shall be for fuel to the fire, your blood shall be in the midst of the land, you shall be no more remembered, for I the Lord have spoken it.

⁷ Moreover, the word of the Lord came unto me, saying, Now, you son of man, will you judge? Will you judge the bloody city? Yea, you shall show her all her abominations. Then say, Thus says the Lord God: The city sheds blood in its midst, that her time may come, and makes idols against herself, to defile herself. You have become guilty in your blood that you have shed, and have defiled yourself in your idols which you have made; and you have caused your days to draw near, and have come even unto your years. Therefore have I made you a reproach unto the heathen and a mocking to all countries. Those that are near and those that are far from you shall mock you, who are infamous and much vexed.

⁸ Behold the princes of Israel, every one were in you to their power to shed blood. In you have they set light by father and mother, in your midst have they dealt by oppression with the stranger, in you have they vexed the fatherless and the widow. You have despised my holy things and have profaned my Sabbaths. In you are men that carry tales to shed blood, and in you they eat upon the mountains; in

your midst they commit lewdness, in you have they uncovered their fathers' nakedness, in you have they violated her that was set apart for uncleanness. And one has committed abomination with his neighbor's wife, and another has lewdly defiled his daughter-in-law, and another in you has violated his sister, his father's daughter. In you have they taken bribes to shed blood, you have taken usury and increase, and you have greedily gained of your neighbors by extortion, and have forgotten me, says the Lord God.

9 Behold, therefore, I have smitten my hand at your dishonest gain which you have made, and at your blood which has been in your midst. Can your heart endure or can your hands be strong in the days that I shall deal with you? I the Lord have spoken it and will do it. And I will scatter you among the heathen, and disperse you in the countries, and will consume your filthiness out of you. And you shall take your inheritance in yourself in the sight of the heathen, and you shall know that I am the Lord.

10 And the word of the Lord came unto me, saying, Son of man, the house of Israel has to me become dross; they all are brass, and tin, and iron, and lead within the furnace; they are even the dross of silver. Therefore, thus says the Lord God: Because you have all become dross, behold therefore, I will gather you within Jerusalem. As they gather silver, and brass, and iron, and lead, and tin within the furnace to blow the fire upon it, to melt it, so will I gather you in my anger and in my fury, and I will leave you there and melt you. Yea, I will gather you and blow upon you in the fire of my wrath, and you shall be melted within. As silver is melted within the furnace, so shall you be melted within, and you shall know that I the Lord have poured out my fury upon you.

11 And the word of the Lord came unto me, saying, Son of man, say unto her, You are the land that is not cleansed, nor rained upon in the day of indignation. There is a conspiracy of her prophets in the midst thereof, like a roaring lion ravening the prey. They have devoured souls, they have taken the treasure and precious things, they have made her many widows in the midst thereof. Her priests have violated my law and have profaned my holy things, they have put no difference between the holy and common, neither have they shown difference between the unclean and the clean, and have hidden their eyes from my Sabbaths, and I am profaned among them.

12 Her princes in the midst thereof are like wolves ravening the prey, to shed blood and to destroy souls, to get dishonest gain. And her prophets have plastered them with untempered mortar, seeing vanity and divining lies unto them, saying, Thus says the Lord God — when the Lord has not spoken. The people of the land have used oppression and exercised robbery, and have vexed the poor and needy, yea, they have oppressed the stranger wrongfully. And I sought for a man among them that should make up the hedge, and stand in the gap before me for the land, that I should not destroy it, but I found none. Therefore have I poured out my indignation upon them, I have consumed them with the fire of my wrath; their own way have I recompensed upon their heads, says the Lord God.

11 The word of the Lord came again unto me, saying, Son of man, there were two women, the daughters of one mother. And they committed whoredoms in Egypt, they committed whoredoms in their youth; there were their breasts pressed, and there they bruised the teats of their virginity. And the names of them were Oholah the elder, and Oholibah her sister, and they were mine; and they bore sons and daughters. Thus were their names: Samaria is Oholah, and Jerusalem Oholibah.

2 And Oholah played the harlot when she was mine, and she doted on her lovers — on the Assyrians her neighbors, who were clothed with blue, captains and rulers, all of them desirable young men, horsemen riding upon horses. Thus she committed her whoredoms with them, with all them that were the chosen men of Assyria, and with all on whom she doted. With all their idols she defiled herself, neither left she her whoredoms brought from Egypt; for in her youth they lay with her, and they bruised the breasts of her virginity and poured their whoredom upon her. Wherefore, I have delivered her into the hand of her lovers, into the hand of the Assyrians upon whom she doted. These exposed her nakedness, they took her sons and her daughters and slew her with the sword; and she became famous among women, for they had executed judgment upon her.

3 And when her sister Oholibah saw this, she was more corrupt in her inordinate love than she, and in her whoredoms, more than her sister in her whoredoms. She doted upon the Assyrians her neighbors,

captains and rulers clothed most gorgeously, horsemen riding upon horses, all of them desirable young men. Then I saw that she was defiled, that they took both one way, and that she increased her whoredoms. For when she saw men portrayed upon the wall, the images of the Chaldeans portrayed with vermilion, girded with girdles upon their loins, exceeding in dyed attire upon their heads, all of them princes to look to after the manner of the Babylonians of Chaldea, the land of their nativity — and as soon as she saw them with her eyes, she doted upon them and sent messengers unto them, into Chaldea. And the Babylonians came to her, into the bed of love; and they defiled her with their whoredom, and she was polluted with them, and her mind was alienated from me by them. So she revealed her whoredoms and exposed her nakedness. Then my mind was alienated from her like my mind was alienated from her sister. Yet she multiplied her whoredoms, in calling to remembrance the days of her youth wherein she had played the harlot in the land of Egypt; for she doted upon their paramours, whose flesh is as the flesh of asses, and whose emission is like the emission of horses. Thus you called to remembrance the lewdness of your youth, in bruising your teats by the Egyptians for the breasts of your youth.

⁴ Therefore, O Oholibah, thus says the Lord God: Behold, I will raise up your lovers against you, by whom your mind is alienated from me, and I will bring them against you on every side: the Babylonians, and all the Chaldeans, Pekod, and Shoa, and Koa, and all the Assyrians with them — all of them desirable young men, captains and rulers, great lords and renowned, all of them riding upon horses. And they shall come against you with chariots, wagons, and wheels, and with an assembly of people which shall set against you buckler, and shield, and helmet round about. And I will set judgment before them, and they shall judge you according to their judgments. And I will set my jealousy against you, and they shall deal furiously with you. They shall take away your nose and your ears, and your remnant shall fall by the sword. They shall take your sons and your daughters, and your residue shall be devoured by the fire. They shall also strip you out of your clothes and take away your fair jewels. Thus will I make your lewdness to cease from you, and your whoredom brought from the

land of Egypt, so that you shall not lift up your eyes unto them nor remember Egypt anymore.

⁵ For thus says the Lord God: Behold, I will deliver you into the hand of them whom you hate, into the hand of them by whom your mind is alienated. And they shall deal with you hatefully, and shall take away all your labor, and shall leave you naked and bare; and the nakedness of your whoredoms shall be exposed, both your lewdness and your whoredoms. I will do these things unto you because you have gone whoring after the heathen, and because you are polluted with their idols. You have walked in the way of your sister, therefore will I give her cup into your hand. Thus says the Lord God: You shall drink of your sister's cup deep and large, you shall be laughed to scorn and had in derision — it contains much — you shall be filled with drunkenness and sorrow, with the cup of astonishment and desolation, with the cup of your sister Samaria. You shall even drink it and suck it out, and you shall break the shards thereof, and pluck off your own breasts; for I have spoken it, says the Lord God. Therefore, thus says the Lord God: Because you have forgotten me and cast me behind your back, therefore bear also your lewdness and your whoredoms.

⁶ The Lord said moreover unto me, Son of man, will you judge Oholah and Oholibah? Yea, declare unto them their abominations, that they have committed adultery, and blood is in their hands, and with their idols have they committed adultery, and have also caused their sons whom they bore unto me to pass for them through the fire, to devour them. Moreover, this they have done unto me: they have defiled my sanctuary in the same day, and have profaned my Sabbaths; for when they had slain their children to their idols, then they came the same day into my sanctuary to profane it, and behold, thus have they done in the midst of my house.

⁷ And furthermore, that you have sent for men to come from far, unto whom a messenger was sent; and behold, they came, for whom you did wash yourself, painted your eyes and adorned yourself with ornaments, and sat upon a stately bed, and a table prepared before it, whereupon you have set my incense and my oil. And a voice of a multitude being at ease was with her, and with the men of the common sort were brought Sabeans from the wilderness, who put bracelets upon their hands and beautiful crowns upon their heads. Then said I

unto her that was old in adulteries, Will they now commit whoredoms with her, and she with them? Yet they went in unto her: as they go in unto a woman that plays the harlot, so went they in unto Oholah and unto Oholibah, the lewd women.

⁸ And the righteous men, they shall judge them after the manner of adulteresses and after the manner of women that shed blood, because they are adulteresses and blood is in their hands. For thus says the Lord God: I will bring up a company upon them, and will give them to be removed and spoiled. And the company shall stone them with stones, and dispatch them with their swords. They shall slay their sons and their daughters, and burn up their houses with fire. Thus will I cause lewdness to cease out of the land, that all women may be taught not to do after your lewdness. And they shall recompense your lewdness upon you, and you shall bear the sins of your idols, and you shall know that I am the Lord God.

12 Again in the ninth year, in the tenth month, in the tenth day of the month, the word of the Lord came unto me, saying, Son of man, write the name of the day, even of this same day; the king of Babylon set himself against Jerusalem this same day. And utter a parable unto the rebellious house, and say unto them, Thus says the Lord God: Set on a pot, set it on, and also pour water into it. Gather the pieces thereof into it, even every good piece, the thigh and the shoulder; fill it with the choice bones. Take the choice of the flock, and burn also the bones under it, and make it boil well, and let them boil the bones of it therein.

² Wherefore, thus says the Lord God: Woe to the bloody city, to the pot whose scum is therein, and whose scum is not gone out of it. Bring it out piece by piece, let no lot fall upon it, for her blood is in her midst, she set it upon the top of a rock. She poured it not upon the ground, to cover it with dust. That it might cause fury to come up to take vengeance, I have set her blood upon the top of a rock, that it should not be covered. Therefore, thus says the Lord God: Woe to the bloody city. I will even make the pile for fire great. Heap on wood, kindle the fire, consume the flesh and spice it well, and let the bones be burned. Then set it empty upon the coals thereof, that the brass of it may be hot and may burn, and that the filthiness of it may be molten in it, that

the scum of it may be consumed. She has wearied herself with lies, and her great scum went not forth out of her; her scum shall be in the fire. In your filthiness is lewdness. Because I have purged you and you were not purged, you shall not be purged from your filthiness anymore until I have caused my fury to rest upon you. I the Lord have spoken it — it shall come to pass, and I will do it. I will not go back, neither will I spare, neither will I repent. According to your ways and according to your doings shall they judge you, says the Lord God.

³ Also, the word of the Lord came unto me, saying, Son of man, behold, I take away from you the desire of your eyes with a stroke, yet neither shall you mourn nor weep, neither shall your tears run down. Refuse to cry, make no mourning for the dead, bind the attire of your head upon you, and put on your shoes upon your feet, and cover not your lips, and eat not the bread of men. So I spoke unto the people in the morning, and at evening my wife died, and I did in the morning as I was commanded.

⁴ And the people said unto me, Will you not tell us what these things are to us that you do so? Then I answered them, The word of the Lord came unto me, saying, Speak unto the house of Israel, Thus says the Lord God: Behold, I will profane my sanctuary, the excellence of your strength, the desire of your eyes, and that which your soul pities; and your sons and your daughters whom you have left shall fall by the sword. And you shall do as I have done: you shall not cover your lips, nor eat the bread of men. And your headdressings shall be upon your heads, and your shoes upon your feet; you shall not mourn nor weep, but you shall waste away for your iniquities, and mourn one toward another. Thus Ezekiel is unto you a sign; according to all that he has done shall you do, and when this comes, you shall know that I am the Lord God.

⁵ Also, you son of man, shall it not be in the day when I take from them their strength, the joy of their glory, the desire of their eyes, and that whereupon they set their minds, their sons and their daughters, that he that escapes in that day shall come unto you, to cause you to hear it with your ears? In that day shall your mouth be opened to him who is escaped, and you shall speak and be no more dumb; and you shall be a sign unto them, and they shall know that I am the Lord.

13 The word of the Lord came again unto me, saying, Son of man, set your face against the Ammonites, and prophesy against them, and say unto the Ammonites, Hear the word of the Lord God; thus says the Lord God: Because you said, Aha — against my sanctuary when it was profaned, and against the land of Israel when it was desolate, and against the house of Judah when they went into captivity, behold, therefore I will deliver you to the men of the east for a possession; and they shall set their palaces in you, and make their dwellings in you. They shall eat your fruit and they shall drink your milk. And I will make Rabbah a stable for camels, and the Ammonites a resting place for flocks; and you shall know that I am the Lord.

2 For thus says the Lord God: Because you have clapped your hands, and stamped with the feet, and rejoiced in heart with all your spite against the land of Israel, behold, therefore I will stretch out my hand upon you, and will deliver you for a spoil to the heathen, and I will cut you off from the people, and I will cause you to perish out of the countries. I will destroy you, and you shall know that I am the Lord.

3 Thus says the Lord God: Because Moab and Seir do say, Behold, the house of Judah is like unto all the heathen — therefore, behold, I will open the side of Moab from the cities, from his cities which are on his frontiers, the glory of the country — Bethjeshimoth, Baal-Meon, and Kiriathaim — unto the men of the east with the Ammonites, and will give them in possession, that the Ammonites may not be remembered among the nations. And I will execute judgments upon Moab, and they shall know that I am the Lord.

4 Thus says the Lord God: Because Edom has dealt against the house of Judah by taking vengeance, and has greatly offended, and avenged himself upon them, therefore thus says the Lord God: I will also stretch out my hand upon Edom, and will cut off man and beast from it, and I will make it desolate from Teman, and they of Dedan shall fall by the sword. And I will lay my vengeance upon Edom by the hand of my people Israel, and they shall do in Edom according to my anger and according to my fury, and they shall know my vengeance, says the Lord God.

5 Thus says the Lord God: Because the Philistines have dealt by revenge, and have taken vengeance with a spiteful heart, to destroy

it for the old hatred, therefore thus says the Lord God: Behold, I will stretch out my hand upon the Philistines, and I will cut off the Cherethites, and destroy the remnant of the sea coast. And I will execute great vengeance upon them with furious rebukes, and they shall know that I am the Lord when I shall lay my vengeance upon them.

14 And it came to pass in the eleventh year, in the first day of the month, that the word of the Lord came unto me, saying, Son of man, because Tyre has said against Jerusalem, Aha, she is broken that was the gates of the people, she is turned unto me, I shall be replenished, now she is laid waste — therefore thus says the Lord God: Behold, I am against you, O Tyre, and will cause many nations to come up against you as the sea causes his waves to come up. And they shall destroy the walls of Tyre and break down her towers. I will also scrape her dust from her and make her like the top of a rock. It shall be a place for the spreading of nets in the midst of the sea, for I have spoken it, says the Lord God, and it shall become a spoil to the nations. And her daughters which are in the field shall be slain by the sword, and they shall know that I am the Lord.

2 For thus says the Lord God: Behold, I will bring upon Tyre Nebuchadnezzar king of Babylon, a king of kings from the north, with horses, and with chariots, and with horsemen, and companies, and many people. He shall slay with the sword your daughters in the field, and he shall make a fort against you, and cast a mount against you, and lift up the buckler against you. And he shall set engines of war against your walls, and with his axes he shall break down your towers. By reason of the abundance of his horses, their dust shall cover you. Your walls shall shake at the noise of the horsemen, and of the wheels, and of the chariots when he shall enter into your gates, as men enter into a city wherein is made a breach. With the hooves of his horses shall he tread down all your streets. He shall slay your people by the sword, and your strong garrisons shall go down to the ground. And they shall make a spoil of your riches and make a prey of your merchandise, and they shall break down your walls and destroy your pleasant houses, and they shall lay your stones and your timber and your dust in the midst of the water. And I will cause the noise

of your songs to cease, and the sound of your harps shall be no more heard. And I will make you like the top of a rock, you shall be a place to spread nets upon. You shall be built no more, for I the Lord have spoken it, says the Lord God.

3 Thus says the Lord God to Tyre: Shall not the isles shake at the sound of your fall, when the wounded cry, when the slaughter is made in your midst? Then all the princes of the sea shall come down from their thrones, and lay away their robes, and put off their embroidered garments. They shall clothe themselves with trembling. They shall sit upon the ground and shall tremble at every moment and be astonished at you. And they shall take up a lamentation for you, and say to you, How you are destroyed, that was inhabited of seafaring men, the renowned city which was strong in the sea, she and her inhabitants which cause their terror to be on all that inhabit it! Now shall the isles tremble in the day of your fall. Yea, the isles that are in the sea shall be troubled at your departure.

4 For thus says the Lord God: When I shall make you a desolate city, like the cities that are not inhabited, when I shall bring up the deep upon you and great waters shall cover you, when I shall bring you down with them that descend into the pit, with the people of old time, and shall set you in the low parts of the earth, in places desolate of old with them that go down to the pit, that you be not inhabited, and I shall set glory in the land of the living, I will make you a terror and you shall be no more. Though you will be sought for, yet shall you never be found again, says the Lord God.

5 The word of the Lord came again unto me, saying, Now, you son of man, take up a lamentation for Tyre, and say unto Tyre, O you that are situated at the entry of the sea, who are a merchant of the people for many coasts, thus says the Lord God: O Tyre, you have said, I am of perfect beauty. Your borders are in the midst of the seas; your builders have perfected your beauty. They have made all your ship boards of fir trees of Senir. They have taken cedars from Lebanon to make masts for you. Of the oaks of Bashan have they made your oars. The company of the Ashurites have made your benches of ivory brought out of the coasts of Kittim. Fine linen with embroidered work from Egypt was that which you spread forth to be your sail. Blue and purple from the coasts of Elishah was that which covered you.

⁶ The inhabitants of Sidon and Arvad were your mariners. Your wise men, O Tyre, that were in you, were your pilots. The elders of Gebal and the wise men thereof were in you your caulkers. All the ships of the sea with their mariners were in you to trade your merchandise.

⁷ They of Persia and of Lud and of Put were in your army, your men of war. They hung the shield and helmet in you. They set forth your comeliness. The men of Arvad with your army were upon your walls round about, and the Gammadim were in your towers. They hung their shields upon your walls round about. They have made your beauty perfect.

⁸ Tarshish was your merchant by reason of the multitude of all kind of riches. With silver, iron, tin, and lead they traded in your wares. Javan, Tubal, and Meshech, they were your merchants; they traded men and vessels of brass in your market. They of the house of Togarmah traded in your wares, with horses and horsemen and mules. The men of Dedan were your merchants. Many coasts were the merchandise of your hand. They brought you for a present horns of ivory, and ebony. Syria was your merchant by reason of the multitude of the wares of your making. They traded in your wares with emeralds, purple, and embroidered work, and fine linen, and coral, and agate. Judah and the land of Israel, they were your merchants. They traded in your market wheat of Minnith and Pannag, and honey, and oil, and balm. Damascus was your merchant in the multitude of the wares of your making, for the multitude of all riches, in the wine of Helbon and white wool. Dan also, and Javan, going to and fro, traded in your wares: bright iron, cassia, and calamus were in your market. Dedan was your merchant in precious clothes for chariots. Arabia and all the princes of Kedar, they traded with you in lambs and rams and goats; in these were they your merchants. The merchants of Sheba and Raamah, they were your merchants, they traded in your wares with chief of all spices, and with all precious stones and gold. Haran, and Canneh, and Eden, the merchants of Sheba, Assyria, and Chilmad were your merchants; these were your merchants in all sorts of things: in blue clothes and embroidered work, and in chests of rich apparel, bound with cords and made of cedar, among your merchandise.

⁹ The ships of Tarshish did sing of you in your market, and you were replenished and made very glorious in the midst of the seas.

Your rowers have brought you into great waters. The east wind has broken you in the midst of the seas. Your riches and your wares, your merchandise, your mariners, and your pilots, your caulkers, and the traders of your merchandise, and all your men of war that are in you, and in all your company which is in your midst shall fall into the midst of the seas in the day of your ruin. The suburbs shall shake at the sound of the cry of your pilots, and all that handle the oar, the mariners, and all the pilots of the sea shall come down from their ships. They shall stand upon the land and shall cause their voice to be heard against you, and shall cry bitterly, and shall cast up dust upon their heads. They shall wallow themselves in the ashes, and they shall make themselves utterly bald for you, and gird themselves with sackcloth, and they shall weep for you with bitterness of heart and bitter wailing. And in their wailing they shall take up a lamentation for you and lament over you, saying, What city is like Tyre, like the destroyed in the midst of the sea? When your wares went forth out of the seas, you filled many people. You did enrich the kings of the earth with the multitude of your riches and of your merchandise. In the time when you shall be broken by the seas, in the depths of the waters your merchandise and all your company in your midst shall fall. All the inhabitants of the isles shall be astonished at you, and their kings shall be sorely afraid. They shall be troubled in their countenance. The merchants among the people shall hiss at you. You shall be a terror, and never shall be anymore.

¹⁰ The word of the Lord came again unto me, saying, Son of man, say unto the prince of Tyre, Thus says the Lord God: Because your heart is lifted up and you have said, I am a God, I sit in the seat of God in the midst of the seas — yet you are a man and not God; though you set your heart as the heart of God. Behold, you are wiser than Daniel; there is no secret that they can hide from you. With your wisdom and with your understanding you have gotten yourself riches, and have gotten gold and silver into your treasuries. By your great wisdom and by your commerce have you increased your riches, and your heart is lifted up because of your riches. Therefore, thus says the Lord God: Because you have set your heart as the heart of God, behold, therefore I will bring strangers upon you, the terrible of the nations. And they shall draw their swords against the beauty of your wisdom, and they

shall defile your brightness. They shall bring you down to the pit, and you shall die the deaths of them that are slain in the midst of the seas. Will you yet say before him that slays you, I am God? But you shall be a man and no God in the hand of him that slays you. You shall die the deaths of the uncircumcised by the hand of strangers, for I have spoken it, says the Lord God.

11 Moreover, the word of the Lord came unto me, saying, Son of man, take up a lamentation upon the king of Tyre, and say unto him, Thus says the Lord God: You seal up the sum, full of wisdom and perfect in beauty. You have been in Eden, the garden of God. Every precious stone was your covering: the sardius, topaz, and the diamond, the beryl, the onyx, and the jasper, the sapphire, the emerald, and the carbuncle, and gold. The workmanship of your tambourines and of your pipes was prepared in you in the day that you were created. You are the anointed cherub that covers, and I have set you so. You were upon the holy mountain of God. You have walked up and down in the midst of the stones of fire. You were perfect in your ways from the day that you were created until iniquity was found in you.

12 By the multitude of your merchandise they have filled your midst with violence, and you have sinned. Therefore, I will cast you as defiled out of the mountain of God, and I will destroy you, O covering cherub, from the midst of the stones of fire. Your heart was lifted up because of your beauty. You have corrupted your wisdom by reason of your brightness. I will cast you to the ground. I will lay you before kings, that they may behold you. You have defiled your sanctuaries by the multitude of your iniquities, by the iniquity of your commerce. Therefore will I bring forth a fire from your midst; it shall devour you. And I will bring you to ashes upon the earth in the sight of all them that behold you. All they that know you among the people shall be astonished at you. You shall be a terror, and never shall you be anymore.

13 Again the word of the Lord came unto me, saying, Son of man, set your face against Sidon, and prophesy against it and say, Thus says the Lord God: Behold, I am against you, O Sidon, and I will be glorified in your midst. And they shall know that I am the Lord when I shall have executed judgments in her, and shall be sanctified in her; for I will send into her pestilence, and blood into her streets, and the wounded shall be judged in her midst by the sword upon her on every

side. And they shall know that I am the Lord. And there shall be no more a pricking brier unto the house of Israel, nor any grieving thorn of all that are round about them that despised them. And they shall know that I am the Lord God.

14 Thus says the Lord God: When I shall have gathered the house of Israel from the people among whom they are scattered, and shall be sanctified in them in the sight of the heathen, then shall they dwell in their land that I have given to my servant Jacob. And they shall dwell safely therein, and shall build houses and plant vineyards. Yea, they shall dwell with confidence when I have executed judgments upon all those that despise them round about them. And they shall know that I am the Lord their God.

15 In the tenth year, in the tenth month, in the twelfth day of the month, the word of the Lord came unto me, saying, Son of man, set your face against Pharaoh, king of Egypt, and prophesy against him and against all Egypt. Speak, and say, Thus says the Lord God: Behold, I am against you, Pharaoh, king of Egypt, the great dragon that lies in the midst of his rivers, which has said, My river is my own, and I have made it for myself. But I will put hooks in your jaws, and I will cause the fish of your rivers to stick unto your scales, and I will bring you up out of the midst of your rivers, and all the fish of your rivers shall stick unto your scales. And I will leave you thrown into the wilderness, you and all the fish of your rivers. You shall fall upon the open fields. You shall not be brought together nor gathered. I have given you for food to the beasts of the field and to the fowls of the heaven. And all the inhabitants of Egypt shall know that I am the Lord, because they have been a staff of reed to the house of Israel. When they took hold of you by your hand, you did break and rend all their shoulder. And when they leaned upon you, you broke and made all their loins to be at a stand.

2 Therefore, thus says the Lord God: Behold, I will bring a sword upon you and cut off man and beast out of you. And the land of Egypt shall be desolate and waste, and they shall know that I am the Lord. Because he has said, The river is mine and I have made it—behold therefore, I am against you and against your rivers, and I will make the land of Egypt utterly waste and desolate, from the tower of Syene

even unto the border of Ethiopia. No foot of man shall pass through it, nor foot of beast shall pass through it, neither shall it be inhabited forty years. And I will make the land of Egypt desolate in the midst of the countries that are desolate, and her cities among the cities that are laid waste shall be desolate forty years. And I will scatter the Egyptians among the nations and will disperse them through the countries.

³ Yet thus says the Lord God: At the end of forty years will I gather the Egyptians from the people to whom they were scattered, and I will bring again the captives of Egypt and will cause them to return into the land of Pathros, into the land of their habitation; and they shall be there a base kingdom. It shall be the basest of the kingdoms, neither shall it exalt itself anymore above the nations, for I will diminish them that they shall no more rule over the nations. And it shall be no more the confidence of the house of Israel which brings their iniquity to remembrance when they shall look after them, but they shall know that I am the Lord God.

⁴ And it came to pass in the twenty-seventh year, in the first month, in the first day of the month, the word of the Lord came unto me, saying, Son of man, Nebuchadnezzar king of Babylon caused his army to serve a great service against Tyre. Every head was made bald and every shoulder was chafed, yet he had no wages, nor his army, for Tyre, for the service that he had served against it. Therefore, thus says the Lord God: Behold, I will give the land of Egypt unto Nebuchadnezzar king of Babylon, and he shall take her multitude, and take her spoil, and take her prey; and it shall be the wages for his army. I have given him the land of Egypt for his labor by which he served against it, because they worked for me, says the Lord God. In that day will I cause the horn of the house of Israel to bud forth, and I will give you the opening of the mouth in the midst of them, and they shall know that I am the Lord.

⁵ The word of the Lord came again unto me, saying, Son of man, prophesy and say, Thus says the Lord God: Howl, Woe for the day! For the day is near, even the day of the Lord is near, a cloudy day. It shall be the time of the heathen. And the sword shall come upon Egypt, and great pain shall be in Ethiopia when the slain shall fall in Egypt; and they shall take away her multitude, and her foundations shall be broken down. Ethiopia, and Libya, and Lydia, and all the mingled

people, and Chub, and the men of the land that is in league shall fall with them by the sword.

⁶ Thus says the Lord: They also that uphold Egypt shall fall, and the pride of her power shall come down. From the tower of Syene shall they fall in it by the sword, says the Lord God. And they shall be desolate in the midst of the countries that are desolate, and her cities shall be in the midst of the cities that are wasted. And they shall know that I am the Lord when I have set a fire in Egypt, and when all her helpers shall be destroyed. In that day shall messengers go forth from me in ships to make the careless Ethiopians afraid, and great pain shall come upon them as in the day of Egypt, for behold, it comes.

⁷ Thus says the Lord God: I will also make the multitude of Egypt to cease by the hand of Nebuchadnezzar king of Babylon. He and his people with him, the terrible of the nations, shall be brought to destroy the land, and they shall draw their swords against Egypt and fill the land with the slain. And I will make the rivers dry and sell the land into the hand of the wicked. And I will make the land waste, and all that is therein, by the hand of strangers. I the Lord have spoken it.

⁸ Thus says the Lord God: I will also destroy the idols, and I will cause their images to cease out of Noph; and there shall be no more a prince of the land of Egypt, and I will put a fear in the land of Egypt. And I will make Pathros desolate, and will set fire in Zoan, and will execute judgments in No. And I will pour my fury upon Sin, the strength of Egypt, and I will cut off the multitude of No. And I will set fire in Egypt. Sin shall have great pain, and No shall be rent asunder, and Noph shall have distresses daily. The young men of Aven and of Pibeseth shall fall by the sword, and these cities shall go into captivity. At Tahpanhes also, the day shall be darkened when I shall break there the yokes of Egypt, and the pomp of her strength shall cease in her. As for her, a cloud shall cover her, and her daughters shall go into captivity. Thus will I execute judgments in Egypt, and they shall know that I am the Lord.

⁹ And it came to pass in the eleventh year, in the first month, in the seventh day of the month, that the word of the Lord came unto me, saying, Son of man, I have broken the arm of Pharaoh, king of Egypt, and behold, it shall not be bound up to be healed, to put a dressing to bind it, to make it strong to hold the sword. Therefore, thus says the Lord God: Behold, I am against Pharaoh, king of Egypt, and will break

his arms — the strong and that which was broken — and I will cause the sword to fall out of his hand. And I will scatter the Egyptians among the nations and will disperse them through the countries. And I will strengthen the arms of the king of Babylon and put my sword in his hand. But I will break Pharaoh's arms, and he shall groan before him with the groanings of a mortally wounded man. But I will strengthen the arms of the king of Babylon, and the arms of Pharaoh shall fall down. And they shall know that I am the Lord when I shall put my sword into the hand of the king of Babylon and he shall stretch it out upon the land of Egypt. And I will scatter the Egyptians among the nations and disperse them among the countries, and they shall know that I am the Lord.

10 And it came to pass in the eleventh year, in the third month, in the first day of the month, that the word of the Lord came unto me, saying, Son of man, speak unto Pharaoh, king of Egypt, and to his multitude, Who are you like in your greatness? Behold, the Assyrian was a cedar in Lebanon, with fair branches, and with a shadowing shroud, and of a high stature; and his top was among the thick boughs. The waters made him great, the deep set him up on high with her rivers running round about his plants, and sent out her little rivers unto all the trees of the field. Therefore, his height was exalted above all the trees of the field, and his boughs were multiplied, and his branches became long because of the multitude of waters when he shot forth. All the fowls of heaven made their nests in his boughs, and under his branches did all the beasts of the field bring forth their young, and under his shadow dwelled all great nations. Thus was he fair in his greatness, in the length of his branches — for his root was by great waters. The cedars in the garden of God could not hide him. The fir trees were not like his boughs, and the chestnut trees were not like his branches, nor any tree in the garden of God was like unto him in his beauty. I have made him fair by the multitude of his branches so that all the trees of Eden that were in the garden of God envied him.

11 Therefore, thus says the Lord God: Because you have lifted up yourself in height, and he has shot up his top among the thick boughs, and his heart is lifted up in his height, I have therefore delivered him into the hand of the mighty one of the heathen; he shall surely deal with him. I have driven him out for his wickedness, and strangers — the

terrible of the nations — have cut him off and have left him. Upon the mountains and in all the valleys his branches are fallen, and his boughs are broken by all the rivers of the land, and all the people of the earth are gone down from his shadow and have left him. Upon his ruin shall all the fowls of the heaven remain, and all the beasts of the field shall be upon his branches, to the end that none of all the trees by the waters exalt themselves for their height, neither shoot up their top among the thick boughs, neither their trees stand up in their height, all that drink water. For they are all delivered unto death, to the depths of the earth, in the midst of the children of men, with them that go down to the pit.

12 Thus says the Lord God: In the day when he went down to the grave, I caused a mourning. I covered the deep for him, and I restrained the floods thereof, and the great waters were held back. And I caused Lebanon to mourn for him, and all the trees of the field withered for him. I made the nations to shake at the sound of his fall when I cast him down to hell with them that descend into the pit. And all the trees of Eden, the choice and best of Lebanon, all that drink water, shall be comforted in the depths of the earth. They also went down into hell with him, unto them that are slain with the sword, and they that were his arm, that dwelled under his shadow in the midst of the heathen. To whom are you thus like in glory and in greatness among the trees of Eden? Yet shall you be brought down with the trees of Eden unto the depths of the earth. You shall lie in the midst of the uncircumcised, with them that are slain by the sword. This is Pharaoh and all his multitude, says the Lord God.

13 And it came to pass in the twelfth year, in the twelfth month, in the first day of the month, that the word of the Lord came unto me, saying, Son of man, take up a lamentation for Pharaoh, king of Egypt, and say unto him, You are like a young lion of the nations, and you are as a whale in the seas; and you came forth with your rivers and troubled the waters with your feet, and fouled their rivers. Thus says the Lord God: I will therefore spread out my net over you with a company of many people, and they shall bring you up in my net. Then will I leave you upon the land, I will cast you forth upon the open field, and will cause all the fowls of the heaven to remain upon you; and I will fill the beasts of the whole earth with you. And I will lay your flesh upon

the mountains and fill the valleys with your height. I will also water with your blood the land wherein you swim, even to the mountains, and the rivers shall be full of you. And when I shall put you out, I will cover the heaven and make the stars thereof dark. I will cover the sun with a cloud and the moon shall not give her light. All the bright lights of heaven will I make dark over you, and set darkness upon your land, says the Lord God.

14 I will also vex the hearts of many people when I shall bring your destruction among the nations into the countries which you have not known. Yea, I will make many people appalled at you, and their kings shall be horribly afraid for you when I shall brandish my sword before them. And they shall tremble at every moment, every man for his own life, in the day of your fall.

15 For thus says the Lord God: The sword of the king of Babylon shall come upon you. By the swords of the mighty will I cause your multitude to fall — the terrible of the nations — all of them. And they shall spoil the pomp of Egypt, and all the multitude thereof shall be destroyed. I will destroy also all the beasts thereof from beside the great waters, neither shall the foot of man trouble them anymore, nor the hooves of beasts trouble them. Then will I make their waters deep and cause their rivers to run like oil, says the Lord God. When I shall make the land of Egypt desolate, and the country shall be destitute of that whereof it was full, when I shall smite all them that dwell therein, then shall they know that I am the Lord.

16 This is the lamentation with which they shall lament her. The daughters of the nations shall lament her, they shall lament for her, even for Egypt and for all her multitude, says the Lord God.

17 It came to pass also in the twelfth year, in the fifteenth day of the month, that the word of the Lord came unto me, saying, Son of man, wail for the multitude of Egypt and cast them down, even her and the daughters of the famous nations, unto the depths of the earth with them that go down into the pit. Who do you pass in beauty? Go down and be laid with the uncircumcised. They shall fall in the midst of them that are slain by the sword; she is delivered to the sword. Draw her and all her multitudes. The strong among the mighty shall speak to him out of the midst of hell with them that help him: They are gone down, they lie uncircumcised, slain by the sword.

¹⁸ Assyria is there, and all her company. His graves are about him, all of them slain, fallen by the sword, whose graves are set in the sides of the pit; and her company is round about her grave, all of them slain, fallen by the sword, which caused terror in the land of the living.

¹⁹ There is Elam and all her multitude round about her grave, all of them slain, fallen by the sword, which have gone down uncircumcised into the depths of the earth, which caused their terror in the land of the living. Yet have they borne their shame with them that go down to the pit. They have set her a bed in the midst of the slain with all her multitude. Her graves are round about him, all of them uncircumcised, slain by the sword. Though their terror was caused in the land of the living, yet have they borne their shame with them that go down to the pit. He is put in the midst of them that are slain.

²⁰ There is Meshech, Tubal, and all her multitude. Her graves are round about him, all of them uncircumcised, slain by the sword, though they caused their terror in the land of the living. And they shall not lie with the mighty that are fallen of the uncircumcised, which have gone down to hell with their weapons of war. And they have laid their swords under their heads, but their iniquities shall be upon their bones, though they were the terror of the mighty in the land of the living. Yea, you shall be broken in the midst of the uncircumcised and shall lie with them that are slain with the sword.

²¹ There is Edom, her kings and all her princes, who with their might are laid by them that were slain by the sword. They shall lie with the uncircumcised, and with them that go down to the pit.

²² There are the princes of the north, all of them, and all the Sidonians, who are gone down with the slain. With their terror they are ashamed of their might, and they lie uncircumcised with them that are slain by the sword, and bear their shame with them that go down to the pit.

²³ Pharaoh shall see them and shall be comforted over all his multitude, even Pharaoh and all his army slain by the sword, says the Lord God, for I have caused my terror in the land of the living, and he shall be laid in the midst of the uncircumcised with them that are slain with the sword, even Pharaoh and all his multitude, says the Lord God.

16 Again the word of the Lord came unto me, saying, Son of man, speak to the children of your people, and say unto them, When I bring the sword upon a land, if the people of the land take a man of their borders and set him for their watchman, if, when he sees the sword come upon the land, he blows the trumpet and warns the people, then whoever hears the sound of the trumpet and takes not warning, if the sword come and take him away, his blood shall be upon his own head. He heard the sound of the trumpet and took not warning; his blood shall be upon him. But he that takes warning shall deliver his soul.

2 But if the watchman sees the sword come and blows not the trumpet, and the people are not warned, if the sword come and take any person from among them, he is taken away in his iniquity, but his blood will I require at the watchman's hand.

3 So you, O son of man, I have set you a watchman unto the house of Israel; therefore, you shall hear the word at my mouth and warn them from me. When I say unto the wicked, O wicked man, you shall surely die — if you do not speak to warn the wicked from his way, that wicked man shall die in his iniquity, but his blood will I require at your hand. Nevertheless, if you warn the wicked of his way, to turn from it, if he does not turn from his way, he shall die in his iniquity, but you have delivered your soul.

4 Therefore, O you son of man, speak unto the house of Israel, Thus you speak — saying, If our transgressions and our sins are upon us and we waste away in them, how should we then live? Say unto them, As I live, says the Lord God, I have no pleasure in the death of the wicked, but that the wicked turn from his way and live. Turn, turn from your evil ways, for why will you die, O house of Israel?

5 Therefore, you son of man, say unto the children of your people, The righteousness of the righteous shall not deliver him in the day of his transgression. As for the wickedness of the wicked, he shall not fall thereby in the day that he turns from his wickedness. Neither shall the righteous be able to live for his righteousness in the day that he sins. When I shall say to the righteous that he shall surely live, if he trust to his own righteousness and commit iniquity, all his righteousness shall not be remembered, but for his iniquity that he has committed — he shall die for it. Again, when I say unto the wicked, You shall surely

die — if he turns from his sin and does that which is lawful and right, if the wicked restore the pledge, give again that he had robbed, walk in the statutes of life without committing iniquity — he shall surely live; he shall not die. None of his sins that he has committed shall be mentioned unto him. He has done that which is lawful and right, he shall surely live.

6 Yet the children of your people say, The way of the Lord is not equal. But as for them, their way is not equal. When the righteous turns from his righteousness and commits iniquity, he shall even die thereby. But if the wicked turn from his wickedness and do that which is lawful and right, he shall live thereby. Yet you say, The way of the Lord is not equal. O house of Israel, I will judge you, everyone after his ways.

17 And it came to pass in the twelfth year of our captivity, in the tenth month, in the fifth day of the month, that one who had escaped out of Jerusalem came unto me, saying, The city is smitten.

2 Now the hand of the Lord was upon me in the evening — before he that was escaped came — and had opened my mouth, until he came to me in the morning. And my mouth was opened, and I was no more dumb. Then the word of the Lord came unto me, saying, Son of man, they that inhabit those wastes of the land of Israel speak, saying, Abraham was one and he inherited the land, but we are many; the land is given to us for inheritance. Wherefore, say unto them, Thus says the Lord God: You eat with the blood, and lift up your eyes toward your idols, and shed blood — and shall you possess the land? You stand upon your sword, you work abomination, and you defile everyone his neighbor's wife — and shall you possess the land?

3 Say thus unto them, Thus says the Lord God: As I live, surely they that are in the wastes shall fall by the sword, and him that is in the open field will I give to the beasts to be devoured, and they that are in the forts and in the caves shall die of the pestilence. For I will lay the land most desolate, and the pomp of her strength shall cease. And the mountains of Israel shall be desolate, that none shall pass through. Then shall they know that I am the Lord, when I have laid the land most desolate because of all their abominations which they have committed.

4 Also, you son of man, the children of your people still are talking against you by the walls, and in the doors of the houses, and speak one

to another, everyone to his brother, saying, Come, I pray you, and hear what is the word that comes forth from the Lord. And they come unto you as the people come, and they sit before you as my people, and they hear your words — but they will not do them. For with their mouth they show much love, but their heart goes after their covetousness. And behold, you are unto them as a very lovely song of one that has a pleasant voice and can play well on an instrument; for they hear your words, but they do them not. And when this comes to pass — behold, it will come — then shall they know that a prophet has been among them.

5 And the word of the Lord came unto me, saying, Son of man, prophesy against the shepherds of Israel, prophesy and say unto them, Thus says the Lord God unto the shepherds: Woe be to the shepherds of Israel that do feed themselves. Should not the shepherds feed the flocks? You eat the fat and you clothe yourself with the wool. You kill them that are fed, but you feed not the flock. The diseased have you not strengthened, neither have you healed that which was sick, neither have you bound up that which was broken, neither have you brought again that which was driven away, neither have you sought that which was lost; but with force and with cruelty have you ruled them. And they were scattered because there is no shepherd, and they became food to all the beasts of the field when they were scattered. My sheep wandered through all the mountains and upon every high hill, yea, my flock was scattered upon all the face of the earth, and none did search or seek after them.

6 Therefore, you shepherds, hear the word of the Lord. As I live, says the Lord God, surely because my flock became a prey, and my flock became food to every beast of the field, because there was no shepherd, neither did my shepherds search for my flock, but the shepherds fed themselves and fed not my flock, therefore, O you shepherds, hear the word of the Lord. Thus says the Lord God: Behold, I am against the shepherds, and I will require my flock at their hand, and cause them to cease from feeding the flock; neither shall the shepherds feed themselves anymore, for I will deliver my flock from their mouth, that they may not be food for them.

7 For thus says the Lord God: Behold, I, even I, will both search my sheep and seek them out. As a shepherd seeks out his flock in the day that he is among his sheep that are scattered, so will I seek out my

sheep, and will deliver them out of all places where they have been scattered in the cloudy and dark day. And I will bring them out from the people, and gather them from the countries, and will bring them to their own land, and feed them upon the mountains of Israel by the rivers, and in all the inhabited places of the country. I will feed them in a good pasture, and upon the high mountains of Israel shall their fold be. There shall they lie in a good fold, and in a fat pasture shall they feed upon the mountains of Israel. I will feed my flock and I will cause them to lie down, says the Lord God. I will seek that which was lost, and bring again that which was driven away, and will bind up that which was broken, and will strengthen that which was sick. But I will destroy the fat and the strong, I will feed them with judgment.

8 And as for you, O my flock, thus says the Lord God: Behold, I judge between cattle and cattle, between the rams and the he-goats. Does it seem a small thing unto you to have eaten up the good pasture, but you must tread down with your feet the residue of your pastures? And to have drunk of the deep waters, but you must foul the residue with your feet? And as for my flock, they eat that which you have trodden with your feet, and they drink that which you have fouled with your feet.

9 Therefore, thus says the Lord God unto them: Behold, I, even I, will judge between the fat cattle and between the lean cattle. Because you have thrust with side and with shoulder, and pushed all the diseased with your horns, until you have scattered them abroad, therefore will I save my flock, and they shall no more be a prey. And I will judge between cattle and cattle.

10 And I will set up one shepherd over them and he shall feed them, even my servant David. He shall feed them and he shall be their shepherd. And I the Lord will be their God, and my servant David a prince among them. I the Lord have spoken it.

11 And I will make with them a covenant of peace, and will cause the evil beasts to cease out of the land; and they shall dwell safely in the wilderness and sleep in the woods. And I will make them and the places round about my hill a blessing, and I will cause the shower to come down in his season. There shall be showers of blessing. And the tree of the field shall yield her fruit, and the earth shall yield her increase, and they shall be safe in their land, and shall know that I am the Lord when I have broken the bands of their yoke and delivered them out

of the hand of those that served themselves of them. And they shall no more be a prey to the heathen, neither shall the beast of the land devour them, but they shall dwell safely, and none shall make them afraid. And I will raise up for them a plant of renown, and they shall be no more consumed with hunger in the land, neither bear the shame of the heathen anymore. Thus shall they know that I, the Lord their God, am with them, and that they, even the house of Israel, are my people, says the Lord God. And you, my flock, the flock of my pasture, are men; and I am your God, says the Lord God.

18 Moreover, the word of the Lord came unto me, saying, Son of man, set your face against Mount Seir and prophesy against it. And say unto it, Thus says the Lord God: Behold, O Mount Seir, I am against you, and I will stretch out my hand against you, and I will make you most desolate. I will lay your cities waste and you shall be desolate, and you shall know that I am the Lord.

2 Because you have had a perpetual hatred, and have shed the blood of the children of Israel by the force of the sword in the time of their calamity, in the time that their iniquity had an end, therefore as I live, says the Lord God, I will prepare you unto blood, and blood shall pursue you; since you have not hated blood, even blood shall pursue you. Thus will I make Mount Seir most desolate, and cut off from it him that passes out and him that returns. And I will fill his mountains with his slain men. In your hills, and in your valleys, and in all your rivers shall they fall that are slain with the sword. I will make you perpetual desolations and your cities shall not return. And you shall know that I am the Lord.

3 Because you have said, These two nations and these two countries shall be mine and we will possess it — whereas the Lord was there, therefore, as I live, says the Lord God, I will even do according to your anger and according to your envy which you have used out of your hatred against them, and I will make myself known among them when I have judged you. And you shall know that I am the Lord, and that I have heard all your blasphemies which you have spoken against the mountains of Israel, saying, They are laid desolate, they are given to us to consume. Thus with your mouth you have boasted against me and have multiplied your words against me; I have heard them. Thus says

the Lord God: When the whole earth rejoices, I will make you desolate. As you did rejoice at the inheritance of the house of Israel because it was desolate, so will I do unto you. You shall be desolate, O Mount Seir and all Idumea, even all of it. And they shall know that I am the Lord.

4 Also, you son of man, prophesy unto the mountains of Israel, and say, You mountains of Israel, hear the word of the Lord. Thus says the Lord God: Because the enemy has said against you, Aha, even the ancient high places are ours in possession — therefore prophesy and say, Thus says the Lord God: Because they have made you desolate and swallowed you up on every side, that you might be a possession unto the residue of the heathen, and you are taken up in the lips of talkers, and are an infamy of the people, therefore, you mountains of Israel, hear the word of the Lord God. Thus says the Lord God to the mountains and to the hills, to the rivers and to the valleys, to the desolate wastes and to the cities that are forsaken, which became a prey and derision to the residue of the heathen that are round about; therefore, thus says the Lord God: Surely in the fire of my jealousy have I spoken against the residue of the heathen and against all Idumea, which have appointed my land into their possession, with the joy of all their heart, with spiteful minds, to cast it out for a prey.

5 Prophesy therefore concerning the land of Israel, and say unto the mountains and to the hills, to the rivers and to the valleys, Thus says the Lord God: Behold, I have spoken in my jealousy and in my fury because you have borne the shame of the heathen. Therefore, thus says the Lord God: I have lifted up my hand; surely the heathen that are about you, they shall bear their shame. But you, O mountains of Israel, you shall shoot forth your branches and yield your fruit to my people of Israel, for they are at hand to come. For behold, I am for you, and I will turn unto you, and you shall be tilled and sown. And I will multiply men upon you, all the house of Israel, even all of it. And the cities shall be inhabited and the wastes shall be built. And I will multiply upon you man and beast, and they shall increase and bring fruit. And I will settle you after your old estates, and will do better unto you than at your beginnings. And you shall know that I am the Lord. Yea, I will cause men to walk upon you, even my people Israel, and they shall possess you, and you shall be their inheritance; and you shall no more henceforth bereave them of men.

⁶ Thus says the Lord God: Because they say unto you, You land, devour up men and have bereaved your nations — therefore you shall devour men no more, neither bereave your nations anymore, says the Lord God. Neither will I cause men to hear in you the shame of the heathen anymore, neither shall you bear the reproach of the people anymore, neither shall you cause your nations to fall anymore, says the Lord God.

⁷ Moreover, the word of the Lord came unto me, saying, Son of man, when the house of Israel dwelled in their own land, they defiled it by their own way and by their doings. Their way was before me as the uncleanness of a removed woman. Wherefore, I poured my fury upon them for the blood that they had shed upon the land, and for their idols with which they had polluted it. And I scattered them among the heathen and they were dispersed through the countries. According to their way and according to their doings I judged them. And when they entered unto the heathen where they went, they profaned my holy name when they said to them, These are the people of the Lord and are gone forth out of his land.

⁸ But I had pity for my holy name, which the house of Israel had profaned among the heathen where they went. Therefore, say unto the house of Israel, Thus says the Lord God: I do not do this for your sakes, O house of Israel, but for my holy name's sake, which you have profaned among the heathen where you went. And I will sanctify my great name, which was profaned among the heathen, which you have profaned in the midst of them; and the heathen shall know that I am the Lord, says the Lord God, when I shall be sanctified in you before their eyes.

⁹ For I will take you from among the heathen, and gather you out of all countries, and will bring you into your own land. Then will I sprinkle clean water upon you and you shall be clean from all your filthiness; and from all your idols will I cleanse you. A new heart also will I give you, and a new spirit will I put within you, and I will take away the stony heart out of your flesh and I will give you a heart of flesh. And I will put my spirit within you and cause you to walk in my statutes, and you shall keep my judgments and do them. And you shall dwell in the land that I gave to your fathers, and you shall be my people and I will be your God. I will also save you from all your uncleanness, and I

will call for the grain and will increase it, and lay no famine upon you. And I will multiply the fruit of the tree and the increase of the field, that you shall receive no more reproach of famine among the heathen. Then shall you remember your own evil ways, and your doings that were not good, and shall loathe yourselves in your own sight for your iniquities and for your abominations. Not for your sakes do I do this, says the Lord God, be it known unto you; be ashamed and confounded for your own ways, O house of Israel.

10 Thus says the Lord God: In the day that I shall have cleansed you from all your iniquities, I will also cause you to dwell in the cities, and the wastes shall be built. And the desolate land shall be tilled, whereas it lay desolate in the sight of all that passed by. And they shall say, This land that was desolate has become like the Garden of Eden, and the waste and desolate and ruined cities have become fortified and are inhabited. Then the heathen that are left round about you shall know that I the Lord build the ruined places and plant that which was desolate. I the Lord have spoken it, and I will do it.

11 Thus says the Lord God: I will yet for this be inquired of by the house of Israel, to do it for them. I will increase them with men like a flock. As the holy flock, as the flock of Jerusalem in her solemn feasts, so shall the waste cities be filled with flocks of men. And they shall know that I am the Lord.

19 The hand of the Lord was upon me and carried me out in the spirit of the Lord, and set me down in the middle of the valley which was full of bones, and caused me to pass by them round about. And behold, there were very many in the open valley, and behold, they were very dry. And he said unto me, Son of man, can these bones live? And I answered, O Lord God, you know. Again he said unto me, Prophesy upon these bones, and say unto them, O you dry bones, hear the word of the Lord. Thus says the Lord God unto these bones: Behold, I will cause breath to enter into you and you shall live. And I will lay sinews upon you, and will bring up flesh upon you, and cover you with skin, and put breath in you, and you shall live. And you shall know that I am the Lord.

2 So I prophesied as I was commanded. And as I prophesied, there was a noise, and behold, a shaking; and the bones came together, bone to

his bone. And when I beheld, behold, the sinews and the flesh came up upon them, and the skin covered them above; but there was no breath in them. Then he said unto me, Prophesy unto the wind, prophesy, son of man, and say to the wind, Thus says the Lord God: Come from the four winds, O breath, and breathe upon these slain, that they may live. So I prophesied as he commanded me, and the breath came into them, and they lived and stood up upon their feet, an exceedingly great army.

3 Then he said unto me, Son of man, these bones are the whole house of Israel. Behold, they say, Our bones are dried and our hope is lost, we are cut off for our parts. Therefore, prophesy and say unto them, Thus says the Lord God: Behold, O my people, I will open your graves, and cause you to come up out of your graves, and bring you into the land of Israel. And you shall know that I am the Lord when I have opened your graves, O my people, and brought you up out of your graves, and shall put my spirit in you. And you shall live, and I shall place you in your own land. Then shall you know that I the Lord have spoken it and performed it, says the Lord.

4 The word of the Lord came again unto me, saying, Moreover, you son of man, take one stick and write upon it: For Judah, and for the children of Israel his companions. Then take another stick and write upon it: For Joseph, the stick of Ephraim, and for all the house of Israel his companions. And join them one to another, into one stick, and they shall become one in your hand. And when the children of your people shall speak unto you, saying, Will you not show us what you mean by these? Say unto them, Thus says the Lord God: Behold, I will take the stick of Joseph which is in the hand of Ephraim, and the tribes of Israel his fellows, and will put them with him, even with the stick of Judah, and make them one stick; and they shall be one in my hand. And the sticks on which you write shall be in your hand before their eyes.

5 And say unto them, Thus says the Lord God: Behold, I will take the children of Israel from among the heathen where they are gone, and will gather them on every side and bring them into their own land. And I will make them one nation in the land upon the mountains of Israel, and one king shall be king to them all. And they shall be no more two nations, neither shall they be divided into two kingdoms anymore at all. Neither shall they defile themselves anymore with their idols, nor with their detestable things, nor with any of their

transgressions, but I will save them out of all their dwelling places wherein they have sinned, and will cleanse them. So shall they be my people and I will be their God.

6 And David my servant shall be king over them, and they all shall have one shepherd. They shall also walk in my judgments, and observe my statutes, and do them. And they shall dwell in the land that I have given unto Jacob my servant, wherein your fathers have dwelled. And they shall dwell therein — even they, and their children, and their children's children for ever. And my servant David shall be their prince for ever.

7 Moreover, I will make a covenant of peace with them. It shall be an everlasting covenant with them. And I will place them, and multiply them, and will set my sanctuary in the midst of them for ever. My tabernacle also shall be with them, yea, I will be their God and they shall be my people. And the heathen shall know that I the Lord do sanctify Israel when my sanctuary shall be in the midst of them for ever.

20 And the word of the Lord came unto me, saying, Son of man, set your face against Gog, the land of Magog, the chief prince of Meshech and Tubal, and prophesy against him. And say, Thus says the Lord God: Behold, I am against you, O Gog, the chief prince of Meshech and Tubal. And I will turn you back and put hooks into your jaws, and I will bring you forth and all your army, horses and horsemen, all of them clothed with all sorts of armor, even a great company with bucklers and shields, all of them handling swords — Persia, Ethiopia, and Libya with them, all of them with shield and helmet — Gomer and all his bands, the house of Togarmah of the north quarters and all his bands, and many people with you.

2 Be prepared and prepare for yourself, you and all your company that are assembled unto you, and be a guard unto them. After many days, you shall be visited. In the latter years, you shall come into the land that is brought back from the sword and is gathered out of many people, against the mountains of Israel, which have been always waste. But it is brought forth out of the nations, and they shall dwell safely — all of them. You shall ascend and come like a storm, you shall be like a cloud to cover the land, you and all your bands, and many people with you.

³ Thus says the Lord God: It shall also come to pass that at the same time shall things come into your mind, and you shall think an evil thought. And you shall say, I will go up to the land of unwalled villages, I will go to them that are at rest, that dwell safely, all of them dwelling without walls and having neither bars nor gates, to take a spoil and to take a prey — to turn your hand upon the desolate places that are now inhabited, and upon the people that are gathered out of the nations, who have gotten cattle and goods, that dwell in the midst of the land. Sheba, and Dedan, and the merchants of Tarshish, with all the young lions thereof, shall say unto you, Are you come to take a spoil? Have you gathered your company to take a prey? To carry away silver and gold, to take away cattle and goods, to take a great spoil?

⁴ Therefore, son of man, prophesy and say unto Gog, Thus says the Lord God: In that day when my people of Israel dwells safely, shall you not know it? And you shall come from your place out of the north parts — you, and many people with you, all of them riding upon horses, a great company and a mighty army — and you shall come up against my people of Israel as a cloud to cover the land. It shall be in the latter days. And I will bring you against my land, that the heathen may know me when I shall be sanctified in you, O Gog, before their eyes.

⁵ Thus says the Lord God: Are you he of whom I have spoken in old time by my servants, the prophets of Israel? Who prophesied in those days many years that I would bring you against them? And it shall come to pass at the same time when Gog shall come against the land of Israel, says the Lord God, that my fury shall come up in my face; for in my jealousy and in the fire of my wrath have I spoken.

⁶ Surely in that day, there shall be a great shaking in the land of Israel, so that the fishes of the sea, and the fowls of the heaven, and the beasts of the field, and all creeping things that creep upon the earth, and all the men that are upon the face of the earth shall shake at my presence; and the mountains shall be thrown down, and the steep places shall fall, and every wall shall fall to the ground. And I will call for a sword against him throughout all my mountains, says the Lord God. Every man's sword shall be against his brother. And I will plead against him with pestilence and with blood, and I will rain upon him, and upon his bands, and upon the many people that are with him, an overflowing rain and great hailstones, fire and brimstone. Thus will

I magnify myself and sanctify myself, and I will be known in the eyes of many nations, and they shall know that I am the Lord.

7 Therefore, you son of man, prophesy against Gog and say, Thus says the Lord God: Behold, I am against you, O Gog, the chief prince of Meshech and Tubal. And I will turn you back and leave but the sixth part of you, and will cause you to come up from the north parts, and will bring you upon the mountains of Israel. And I will smite your bow out of your left hand and will cause your arrows to fall out of your right hand. You shall fall upon the mountains of Israel—you, and all your bands, and the people that is with you. I will give you unto the ravenous birds of every sort, and to the beasts of the field to be devoured. You shall fall upon the open field, for I have spoken it, says the Lord God. And I will send a fire on Magog, and among them that dwell carelessly in the isles, and they shall know that I am the Lord.

8 So will I make my holy name known in the midst of my people Israel, and I will not let them pollute my holy name anymore; and the heathen shall know that I am the Lord, the Holy One in Israel. Behold, it has come and it is done, says the Lord God; this is the day whereof I have spoken.

9 And they that dwell in the cities of Israel shall go forth and shall set on fire and burn the weapons, both the shields and the bucklers, the bows and the arrows, and the handstaves and the spears; and they shall burn them with fire seven years, so that they shall take no wood out of the field neither cut down any out of the forests, for they shall burn the weapons with fire. And they shall spoil those that spoiled them, and rob those that robbed them, says the Lord God.

10 And it shall come to pass in that day that I will give unto Gog a place there of graves in Israel, the valley of the travelers on the east of the sea, and it shall stop the noses of the travelers. And there they shall bury Gog and all his multitude. And they shall call it the valley of Hamon-Gog. And seven months shall the house of Israel be burying them, that they may cleanse the land. Yea, all the people of the land shall bury them, and it shall be to them a renown the day that I shall be glorified, says the Lord God. And they shall sever out men of continual employment passing through the land, to bury with the travelers those that remain upon the face of the earth, to cleanse it; after the end of seven months shall they search. And the travelers that pass through

the land, when any sees a man's bone, then shall he set up a sign by it until the buriers have buried it in the valley of Hamon-Gog. And also the name of the city shall be Hamonah. Thus shall they cleanse the land.

11 And you, son of man, thus says the Lord God: Speak unto every feathered fowl and to every beast of the field, Assemble yourselves and come, gather yourselves on every side to my sacrifice that I do sacrifice for you, even a great sacrifice upon the mountains of Israel, that you may eat flesh and drink blood. You shall eat the flesh of the mighty and drink the blood of the princes of the earth, of rams, of lambs, and of goats, of bullocks—all of them fatlings of Bashan. And you shall eat fat until you are full and drink blood until you are drunk of my sacrifice which I have sacrificed for you. Thus you shall be filled at my table with horses and chariots, with mighty men and with all men of war, says the Lord God.

12 And I will set my glory among the heathen, and all the heathen shall see my judgment that I have executed and my hand that I have laid upon them. So the house of Israel shall know that I am the Lord their God, from that day and forward. And the heathen shall know that the house of Israel went into captivity for their iniquity, because they trespassed against me; therefore, I hid my face from them and gave them into the hand of their enemies so fell they all by the sword. According to their uncleanness and according to their transgressions have I done unto them and hid my face from them.

13 Therefore, thus says the Lord God: Now will I bring again the captives of Jacob and have mercy upon the whole house of Israel, and will be jealous for my holy name, after they have borne their shame and all their trespasses whereby they have trespassed against me when they dwelled safely in their land and none made them afraid. When I have brought them again from the people, and gathered them out of their enemies' lands, and am sanctified in them in the sight of many nations, then shall they know that I am the Lord their God who caused them to be led into captivity among the heathen. But I have gathered them unto their own land, and have left none of them anymore there, neither will I hide my face anymore from them; for I have poured out my spirit upon the house of Israel, says the Lord God.

21 In the twenty-fifth year of our captivity, in the beginning of the year, in the tenth day of the month, in the fourteenth year after the city was smitten, in the selfsame day, the hand of the Lord was upon me and brought me there. In the visions of God he brought me into the land of Israel and set me upon a very high mountain by which was as the frame of a city on the south, and he brought me there.

2 And behold, there was a man whose appearance was like the appearance of brass, with a line of flax in his hand and a measuring reed, and he stood in the gate. And the man said unto me, Son of man, behold with your eyes, and hear with your ears, and set your heart upon all that I shall show you. For the intent that I might show them unto you are you brought here. Declare all that you see to the house of Israel.

3 And behold, a wall on the outside of the house round about, and in the man's hand a measuring reed of six cubits long, by the cubit and a hand breadth. So he measured the breadth of the building, one reed, and the height, one reed. Then came he unto the gate which looks toward the east, and went up the stairs thereof, and measured the threshold of the gate, which was one reed broad, and the other threshold of the gate, which was one reed broad.

4 And every little chamber was one reed long and one reed broad, and between the little chambers were five cubits. And the threshold of the gate by the porch of the gate within was one reed. He measured also the porch of the gate within, one reed. Then he measured the porch of the gate, eight cubits, and the posts thereof, two cubits. And the porch of the gate was inward.

5 And the little chambers of the gate eastward were three on this side and three on that side. They three were of one measure, and the posts had one measure on this side and on that side. And he measured the breadth of the entry of the gate, ten cubits, and the length of the gate, thirteen cubits. The space also before the little chambers was one cubit on this side, and the space was one cubit on that side. And the little chambers were six cubits on this side and six cubits on that side. He measured then the gate from the roof of one little chamber to the roof of another; the breadth was twenty-five cubits, door against door.

6 He made also posts of sixty cubits, even unto the post of the court round about the gate. And from the face of the gate of the entrance unto the face of the porch of the inner gate were fifty cubits. And there

were narrow windows to the little chambers, and to their posts within the gate round about, and likewise to the arches and windows were round about inward. And upon each post were palm trees.

7 Then he brought me into the outward court, and behold, there were chambers and a pavement made for the court round about. Thirty chambers were upon the pavement. And the pavement by the side of the gates, corresponding to the length of the gates, was the lower pavement. Then he measured the breadth from the forefront of the lower gate unto the forefront of the inner court outside, a hundred cubits eastward and northward.

8 And the gate of the outward court that looked toward the north, he measured the length thereof and the breadth thereof, and the little chambers thereof were three on this side and three on that side. And the posts thereof and the arches thereof were after the measure of the first gate: the length thereof was fifty cubits, and the breadth twenty-five cubits. And their windows and their arches and their palm trees were after the measure of the gate that looks toward the east, and they went up unto it by seven steps. And the arches thereof were before them. And the gate of the inner court was opposite the gate toward the north, and toward the east. And he measured from gate to gate a hundred cubits.

9 After that, he brought me toward the south, and behold, a gate toward the south. And he measured the posts thereof and the arches thereof according to these measures. And there were windows in it, and in the arches thereof round about like those windows; the length was fifty cubits, and the breadth twenty-five cubits. And there were seven steps to go up to it, and the arches thereof were before them. And it had palm trees, one on this side and another on that side, upon the posts thereof. And there was a gate in the inner court toward the south, and he measured from gate to gate toward the south, a hundred cubits.

10 And he brought me to the inner court by the south gate. And he measured the south gate according to these measures, and the little chambers thereof, and the posts thereof, and the arches thereof according to these measures. And there were windows in it, and in the arches thereof round about; it was fifty cubits long and twenty-five cubits broad, and the arches round about were twenty-five cubits long and five cubits broad. And the arches thereof were toward the outer

court, and palm trees were upon the posts thereof, and the ascent to it had eight steps.

¹¹ And he brought me into the inner court toward the east, and he measured the gate according to these measures, and the little chambers thereof, and the posts thereof, and the arches thereof were according to these measures. And there were windows therein, and in the arches thereof round about; it was fifty cubits long and twenty-five cubits broad. And the arches thereof were toward the outward court, and palm trees were upon the posts thereof, on this side and on that side, and the ascent to it had eight steps.

¹² And he brought me to the north gate and measured it according to these measures, the little chambers thereof, the posts thereof, and the arches thereof, and the windows to it round about; the length was fifty cubits and the breadth twenty-five cubits. And the posts thereof were toward the outer court, and palm trees were upon the posts thereof, on this side and on that side, and the ascent to it had eight steps. And the chambers and the entries thereof were by the posts of the gates where they washed the burnt offering.

¹³ And in the porch of the gate were two tables on this side and two tables on that side, to slay thereon the burnt offering, and the sin offering, and the trespass offering. And at the side outside, as one goes up to the entry of the north gate, were two tables, and on the other side, which was at the porch of the gate, were two tables. Four tables were on this side, and four tables on that side — by the side of the gate, eight tables — whereupon they slew their sacrifices. And the four tables were of hewn stone for the burnt offering, of a cubit and a half long and a cubit and a half broad and one cubit high, whereupon also they laid the instruments with which they slew the burnt offering and the sacrifice. And within were hooks, a hand broad, fastened round about; and upon the tables was the flesh of the offering.

¹⁴ And outside the inner gate were the chambers of the singers in the inner court which was at the side of the north gate, and their prospect was toward the south — one at the side of the east gate having the prospect toward the north. And he said unto me, This chamber, whose prospect is toward the south, is for the priests — the keepers of the charge of the house. And the chamber whose prospect is toward the north is for the priests — the keepers of the charge of the altar. These

are the sons of Zadok among the sons of Levi who come near to the Lord to minister unto him.

¹⁵ So he measured the court — a hundred cubits long and a hundred cubits broad, square — and the altar that was before the house. And he brought me to the porch of the house and measured each post of the porch, five cubits on this side and five cubits on that side. And the breadth of the gate was three cubits on this side and three cubits on that side. The length of the porch was twenty cubits, and the breadth eleven cubits. And he brought me by the steps whereby they went up to it, and there were pillars by the posts, one on this side and another on that side.

¹⁶ Afterward, he brought me to the temple and measured the posts, six cubits broad on the one side and six cubits broad on the other side, which was the breadth of the tabernacle. And the breadth of the door was ten cubits, and the sides of the door were five cubits on the one side and five cubits on the other side. And he measured the length thereof, forty cubits, and the breadth, twenty cubits. Then went he inward and measured the post of the door, two cubits, and the door, six cubits, and the breadth of the door, seven cubits. So he measured the length thereof, twenty cubits, and the breadth, twenty cubits, before the temple. And he said unto me, This is the most holy place.

¹⁷ After, he measured the wall of the house, six cubits; and the breadth of every side chamber, four cubits, round about the house on every side. And the side chambers were three, one over another and thirty in order, and they entered into the wall which was of the house for the side chambers round about, that they might have hold; but they had not hold in the wall of the house. And there was an enlarging and a winding about still upward to the side chambers, for the winding about of the house went still upward round about the house. Therefore, the breadth of the house was still upward and so increased from the lowest chamber to the highest by the middle.

¹⁸ I saw also the height of the house round about. The foundations of the side chambers were a full reed of six great cubits. The thickness of the wall which was for the side chamber outside was five cubits, and that which was left was the place of the side chambers that were within. And between the chambers was the width of twenty cubits round about the house on every side. And the doors of the side chambers

were toward the place that was left, one door toward the north and another door toward the south, and the breadth of the place that was left was five cubits round about.

19 Now the building that was before the separate place, at the end toward the west, was seventy cubits broad, and the wall of the building was five cubits thick round about, and the length thereof ninety cubits. So he measured the house, a hundred cubits long, and the separate place and the building with the walls thereof, a hundred cubits long; also, the breadth of the face of the house and of the separate place toward the east, a hundred cubits. And he measured the length of the building facing the separate place which was behind it, and the galleries thereof on the one side and on the other side, a hundred cubits.

20 With the inner temple and the porches of the court, the thresholds and the narrow windows and the galleries round about on their three stories, opposite the door, paneled with wood round about and from the ground up to the windows (and the windows were covered), to that above the door, even unto the inner house and outside, and by all the wall round about, within and without, by measure; and it was made with cherubim and palm trees, so that a palm tree was between a cherub and a cherub. And every cherub had two faces, so that the face of a man was toward the palm tree on the one side, and the face of a young lion toward the palm tree on the other side; it was made through all the house round about. From the ground unto above the door were cherubim and palm trees made, and on the wall of the temple.

21 The doorposts of the temple were squared, and the face of the sanctuary, the appearance of the one as the appearance of the other. The altar of wood was three cubits high and the length thereof two cubits, and the corners thereof, and the length thereof, and the walls thereof were of wood. And he said unto me, This is the table that is before the Lord.

22 And the temple and the sanctuary had two doors. And the doors had two leaves apiece, two turning leaves: two leaves for the one door and two leaves for the other door. And there were made on them, on the doors of the temple, cherubim and palm trees like were made upon the walls; and there were thick planks upon the face of the porch outside. And there were narrow windows, and palm trees on the one

side and on the other side, on the sides of the porch and upon the side chambers of the house, and thick planks.

23 Then he brought me forth into the outer court, the way toward the north. And he brought me into the chamber that was opposite the separate place and which was before the building toward the north. Before the length of a hundred cubits was the north door, and the breadth was fifty cubits. Opposite the twenty cubits which were for the inner court, and opposite the pavement which was for the outer court, was gallery against gallery in three stories. And before the chambers was a walk of ten cubits breadth inward, a way of one cubit, and their doors toward the north. Now the upper chambers were shorter, for the galleries were higher than these—than the lower and than the middlemost of the building—for they were in three stories, but had not pillars as the pillars of the courts. Therefore, the building was narrowed more than the lowest and the middlemost from the ground. And the wall that was outside, opposite the chambers toward the outer court, on the forepart of the chambers, the length thereof was fifty cubits. For the length of the chambers that were in the outer court was fifty cubits, and behold, before the temple were a hundred cubits. And from under these chambers was the entry on the east side, as one goes into them from the outer court.

24 The chambers were in the thickness of the wall of the court toward the east, opposite the separate place and opposite the building. And the way before them was like the appearance of the chambers which were toward the north, as long as they and as broad as they, and all their exits were both according to their fashions and according to their doors. And according to the doors of the chambers that were toward the south was a door in the head of the way, even the way directly before the wall toward the east, as one enters into them.

25 Then said he unto me, The north chambers and the south chambers which are before the separate place, they are holy chambers where the priests that approach unto the Lord shall eat the most holy things. There shall they lay the most holy things, and the meal offering, and the sin offering, and the trespass offering; for the place is holy. When the priests enter therein, then shall they not go out of the holy place into the outer court, but there they shall lay their garments wherein

they minister, for they are holy, and shall put on other garments, and shall approach to those things which are for the people.

²⁶ Now when he had made an end of measuring the inner house, he brought me forth toward the gate whose prospect is toward the east and measured it round about. He measured the east side with the measuring reed, five hundred reeds with the measuring reed round about. He measured the north side, five hundred reeds with the measuring reed round about. He measured the south side, five hundred reeds with the measuring reed. He turned about to the west side and measured five hundred reeds with the measuring reed. He measured it by the four sides. It had a wall round about, five hundred reeds long and five hundred broad, to make a separation between the sanctuary and the common place.

²⁷ Afterward, he brought me to the gate, even the gate that looks toward the east. And behold, the glory of the God of Israel came from the way of the east, and his voice was like a noise of many waters, and the earth shined with his glory. And it was according to the appearance of the vision which I saw, even according to the vision that I saw when I came to destroy the city. And the visions were like the vision that I saw by the river Chebar. And I fell upon my face, and the glory of the Lord came into the house by the way of the gate whose prospect is toward the east. So the spirit took me up and brought me into the inner court, and behold, the glory of the Lord filled the house.

²⁸ And I heard him speaking unto me out of the house (and the man stood by me), and he said unto me, Son of man, the place of my throne, and the place of the soles of my feet where I will dwell in the midst of the children of Israel for ever, and my holy name, shall the house of Israel no more defile — neither they nor their kings — by their whoredom, nor by the carcasses of their kings in their high places. In their setting of their threshold by my thresholds, and their doorpost by my doorposts, and the wall between me and them, they have even defiled my holy name by their abominations that they have committed; wherefore, I have consumed them in my anger. Now let them put away their whoredom and the carcasses of their kings far from me, and I will dwell in the midst of them for ever.

²⁹ You son of man, show the house to the house of Israel, that they may be ashamed of their iniquities. And let them measure the pattern,

and if they are ashamed of all that they have done, show them the form of the house and the fashion thereof, and the exits thereof, and the entrances thereof, and all the forms thereof, and all the ordinances thereof, and all the forms thereof, and all the laws thereof; and write it in their sight, that they may keep the whole form thereof, and all the ordinances thereof, and do them.

30 This is the law of the house: upon the top of the mountain, the whole limit thereof round about shall be most holy. Behold, this is the law of the house.

31 And these are the measures of the altar after the cubits (the cubit is a cubit and a hand breadth): even the bottom shall be a cubit and the breadth a cubit, and the border thereof by the edge thereof round about shall be a span; and this shall be the higher place of the altar. And from the bottom upon the ground even to the lower ledge shall be two cubits, and the breadth one cubit; and from the lesser ledge even to the greater ledge shall be four cubits, and the breadth one cubit. So the altar shall be four cubits. And from the altar and upward shall be four horns. And the altar shall be twelve cubits long, twelve broad, square in the four squares thereof. And the ledge shall be fourteen cubits long and fourteen broad in the four squares thereof; and the border about it shall be half a cubit, and the bottom thereof shall be a cubit about, and his stairs shall look toward the east.

32 And he said unto me, Son of man, thus says the Lord God: These are the ordinances of the altar, in the day when they shall make it to offer burnt offerings thereon and to sprinkle blood thereon. And you shall give to the priests — the Levites that are of the seed of Zadok who approach unto me to minister unto me, says the Lord God — a young bullock for a sin offering. And you shall take of the blood thereof and put it on the four horns of it, and on the four corners of the ledge, and upon the border round about. Thus shall you cleanse and purge it. You shall take the bullock also of the sin offering, and he shall burn it in the appointed place of the house outside the sanctuary.

33 And on the second day, you shall offer a kid of the goats without blemish for a sin offering, and they shall cleanse the altar as they did cleanse it with the bullock. When you have made an end of cleansing it, you shall offer a young bullock without blemish and a ram out of the flock without blemish. And you shall offer them before the Lord,

and the priests shall cast salt upon them, and they shall offer them up for a burnt offering unto the Lord.

34 Seven days shall you prepare every day a goat for a sin offering; they shall also prepare a young bullock and a ram out of the flock without blemish. Seven days shall they purge the altar and purify it, and they shall consecrate themselves. And when these days are expired, it shall be that upon the eighth day and so forward the priests shall make your burnt offerings upon the altar and your peace offerings, and I will accept you, says the Lord God.

35 Then he brought me back the way of the gate of the outward sanctuary which looks toward the east, and it was shut. Then said the Lord unto me, This gate shall be shut, it shall not be opened and no man shall enter in by it, because the Lord, the God of Israel, has entered in by it; therefore, it shall be shut. It is for the prince — the prince, he shall sit in it to eat bread before the Lord. He shall enter by the way of the porch of that gate, and shall go out by the way of the same.

36 Then he brought me the way of the north gate before the house, and I looked, and behold, the glory of the Lord filled the house of the Lord; and I fell upon my face. And the Lord said unto me, Son of man, mark well, and behold with your eyes, and hear with your ears all that I say unto you concerning all the ordinances of the house of the Lord, and all the laws thereof. And mark well the entering in of the house with every exit of the sanctuary. And you shall say to the rebellious, even to the house of Israel, Thus says the Lord God: O you house of Israel, let it suffice you of all your abominations, in that you have brought into my sanctuary strangers, uncircumcised in heart and uncircumcised in flesh, to be in my sanctuary, to pollute it, even my house, when you offer my bread, the fat and the blood; and they have broken my covenant because of all your abominations. And you have not kept the charge of my holy things, but you have set keepers of my charge in my sanctuary for yourselves. Thus says the Lord God: No stranger, uncircumcised in heart nor uncircumcised in flesh, shall enter into my sanctuary, of any stranger that is among the children of Israel.

37 And the Levites that are gone away far from me, when Israel went astray, who went astray away from me after their idols, they shall even bear their iniquity. Yet they shall be ministers in my sanctuary, having charge at the gates of the house and ministering to the house. They

shall slay the burnt offering and the sacrifice for the people, and they shall stand before them to minister unto them. Because they ministered unto them before their idols, and caused the house of Israel to fall into iniquity, therefore have I lifted up my hand against them, says the Lord God, and they shall bear their iniquity. And they shall not come near unto me to do the office of a priest unto me, nor to come near to any of my holy things in the most holy place, but they shall bear their shame and their abominations which they have committed. But I will make them keepers of the charge of the house, for all the service thereof and for all that shall be done therein.

38 But the priests the Levites — the sons of Zadok that kept the charge of my sanctuary when the children of Israel went astray from me — they shall come near to me to minister unto me, and they shall stand before me to offer unto me the fat and the blood, says the Lord God. They shall enter into my sanctuary, and they shall come near to my table to minister unto me, and they shall keep my charge.

39 And it shall come to pass that when they enter in at the gates of the inner court, they shall be clothed with linen garments, and no wool shall come upon them while they minister in the gates of the inner court and within. They shall have linen caps upon their heads and shall have linen breeches upon their loins; they shall not gird themselves with anything that causes sweat. And when they go forth into the outer court, even into the outer court to the people, they shall put off their garments wherein they ministered and lay them in the holy chambers, and they shall put on other garments; and they shall not sanctify the people with their garments.

40 Neither shall they shave their heads, nor suffer their locks to grow long. They shall only trim their heads. Neither shall any priest drink wine when they enter into the inner court. Neither shall they take for their wives a widow, nor her that is divorced, but they shall take virgins of the seed of the house of Israel, or a widow that had a priest before. And they shall teach my people the difference between the holy and common, and cause them to discern between the unclean and the clean.

41 And in controversy they shall stand in judgment, and they shall judge it according to my judgments. And they shall keep my laws and my statutes in all my assemblies, and they shall hallow my Sabbaths. And they shall come at no dead person to defile themselves; but for

father, or for mother, or for son, or for daughter, for brother, or for sister that has had no husband, they may defile themselves. And after he is cleansed, they shall reckon unto him seven days. And in the day that he goes into the sanctuary, unto the inner court to minister in the sanctuary, he shall offer his sin offering, says the Lord God.

⁴²And it shall be unto them for an inheritance — I am their inheritance. And you shall give them no possession in Israel — I am their possession. They shall eat the meal offering, and the sin offering, and the trespass offering, and every dedicated thing in Israel shall be theirs. And the first of all the firstfruits of all things, and every offering of all, of every sort of your offerings, shall be the priests'. You shall also give unto the priest the first of your dough, that he may cause the blessing to rest in your house. The priests shall not eat of anything that is dead of itself, or torn, whether it be fowl or beast.

⁴³ Moreover, when you shall divide by lot the land for inheritance, you shall offer an offering unto the Lord, a holy portion of the land. The length shall be the length of twenty-five thousand reeds, and the breadth shall be ten thousand. This shall be holy in all the borders thereof round about. Of this, there shall be for the sanctuary five hundred in length with five hundred in breadth, square round about, and fifty cubits round about for the suburbs thereof. And of this measure shall you measure the length of twenty-five thousand and the breadth of ten thousand, and in it shall be the sanctuary and the most holy place. The holy portion of the land shall be for the priests, the ministers of the sanctuary, who shall come near to minister unto the Lord. And it shall be a place for their houses and a holy place for the sanctuary. And the twenty-five thousand of length and the ten thousand of breadth shall also the Levites, the ministers of the house, have for themselves for a possession, for twenty chambers.

⁴⁴And you shall appoint the possession of the city five thousand broad and twenty-five thousand long, alongside the offering of the holy portion. It shall be for the whole house of Israel.

⁴⁵And a portion shall be for the prince, on the one side and on the other side of the offering of the holy portion and of the possession of the city, before the offering of the holy portion and before the possession of the city, from the west side, westward, and from the east side, eastward. And the length shall be corresponding to one of the

portions from the west border unto the east border. In the land shall be his possession in Israel. And my princes shall no more oppress my people, and the rest of the land shall they give to the house of Israel according to their tribes.

⁴⁶ Thus says the Lord God: Let it suffice you, O princes of Israel, remove violence and spoil, and execute judgment and justice. Take away your exactions from my people, says the Lord God. You shall have just balances, and a just ephah, and a just bath. The ephah and the bath shall be of one measure, that the bath may contain the tenth part of a homer, and the ephah the tenth part of a homer. The measure thereof shall be after the homer. And the shekel shall be twenty gerahs; twenty shekels, twenty-five shekels, fifteen shekels shall be your maneh.

⁴⁷ This is the offering that you shall offer: the sixth part of an ephah of a homer of wheat, and you shall give the sixth part of an ephah of a homer of barley. Concerning the ordinance of oil, the bath of oil, you shall offer the tenth part of a bath out of the cor (which is a homer of ten baths, for ten baths are a homer). And one lamb out of the flock, out of two hundred, out of the fat pastures of Israel, for a meal offering, and for a burnt offering, and for peace offerings, to make reconciliation for them, says the Lord God. All the people of the land shall give this offering for the prince in Israel. And it shall be the prince's part to give burnt offerings, and meal offerings, and drink offerings in the feasts, and in the new moons, and in the Sabbaths. In all solemnities of the house of Israel, he shall prepare the sin offering, and the meal offering, and the burnt offering, and the peace offerings, to make reconciliation for the house of Israel.

⁴⁸ Thus says the Lord God: In the first month, in the first day of the month, you shall take a young bullock without blemish and cleanse the sanctuary. And the priest shall take of the blood of the sin offering and put it upon the doorposts of the house, and upon the four corners of the ledge of the altar, and upon the posts of the gate of the inner court. And so you shall do the seventh day of the month, for everyone that errs and for him that is simple. So shall you reconcile the house.

⁴⁹ In the first month, in the fourteenth day of the month, you shall have the Passover, a feast of seven days. Unleavened bread shall be eaten. And upon that day shall the prince prepare for himself and for all the people of the land a bullock for a sin offering. And seven

days of the feast he shall prepare a burnt offering to the Lord, seven bullocks and seven rams without blemish daily, the seven days, and a kid of the goats daily for a sin offering. And he shall prepare a meal offering of an ephah for a bullock, and an ephah for a ram, and a hin of oil for an ephah.

50 In the seventh month, in the fifteenth day of the month shall he do the like in the feast of the seven days, according to the sin offering, according to the burnt offering, and according to the meal offering, and according to the oil.

51 Thus says the Lord God: The gate of the inner court that looks toward the east shall be shut the six working days, but on the Sabbath it shall be opened, and in the day of the new moon it shall be opened. And the prince shall enter by the way of the porch of that gate outside, and shall stand by the post of the gate. And the priests shall prepare his burnt offering and his peace offerings, and he shall worship at the threshold of the gate. Then he shall go forth, but the gate shall not be shut until the evening. Likewise, the people of the land shall worship at the door of this gate before the Lord in the Sabbaths and in the new moons. And the burnt offering that the prince shall offer unto the Lord in the Sabbath day shall be six lambs without blemish and a ram without blemish. And the meal offering shall be an ephah for a ram, and the meal offering for the lambs as he shall be able to give, and a hin of oil to an ephah. And in the day of the new moon, it shall be a young bullock without blemish, and six lambs and a ram — they shall be without blemish. And he shall prepare a meal offering, an ephah for a bullock and an ephah for a ram, and for the lambs according as his hand shall attain unto, and a hin of oil to an ephah. And when the prince shall enter, he shall go in by the way of the porch of that gate, and he shall go forth by the way thereof.

52 But when the people of the land shall come before the Lord in the solemn feasts, he that enters in by the way of the north gate to worship shall go out by the way of the south gate. And he that enters by the way of the south gate shall go forth by the way of the north gate. He shall not return by the way of the gate whereby he came in, but shall go forth opposite it. And the prince in the midst of them, when they go in shall go in, and when they go forth shall go forth. And in the feasts and in the solemnities, the meal offering shall be an ephah to a

bullock and an ephah to a ram, and to the lambs as he is able to give, and a hin of oil to an ephah.

53 Now when the prince shall prepare a voluntary burnt offering or peace offerings voluntarily unto the Lord, one shall then open him the gate that looks toward the east, and he shall prepare his burnt offering and his peace offerings as he did on the Sabbath day. Then he shall go forth, and after his going forth, one shall shut the gate.

54 You shall daily prepare a burnt offering unto the Lord of a lamb of the first year without blemish; you shall prepare it every morning. And you shall prepare a meal offering for it every morning, the sixth part of an ephah and the third part of a hin of oil, to temper with the fine flour — a meal offering continually by a perpetual ordinance unto the Lord. Thus shall they prepare the lamb, and the meal offering, and the oil every morning for a continual burnt offering.

55 Thus says the Lord God: If the prince give a gift unto any of his sons, the inheritance thereof shall be his sons', it shall be their possession by inheritance. But if he give a gift of his inheritance to one of his servants, then it shall be his to the year of liberty; after, it shall return to the prince. But his inheritance shall be his sons' for them. Moreover, the prince shall not take of the people's inheritance by oppression, to thrust them out of their possession, but he shall give his sons inheritance out of his own possession, that my people be not scattered every man from his possession.

56 After, he brought me through the entry which was at the side of the gate, into the holy chambers of the priests which looked toward the north; and behold, there was a place on the two sides westward. Then said he unto me, This is the place where the priests shall boil the trespass offering and the sin offering, where they shall bake the meal offering, that they bear them not out into the outer court, to sanctify the people.

57 Then he brought me forth into the outer court, and caused me to pass by the four corners of the court; and behold, in every corner of the court, there was a court. In the four corners of the court, there were courts joined of forty cubits long and thirty broad; these four corners were of one measure. And there was a row of building round about in them, round about them four, and it was made with boiling places under the rows round about. Then said he unto me, These are

the places of them that boil, where the ministers of the house shall boil the sacrifice of the people.

⁵⁸ Afterward, he brought me again unto the door of the house, and behold, waters issued out from under the threshold of the house eastward — for the forefront of the house stood toward the east — and the waters came down from under, from the right side of the house at the south side of the altar. Then he brought me out of the way of the gate northward, and led me about the way outside unto the outer gate by the way that looks eastward; and behold, there ran out waters on the right side.

⁵⁹ And when the man that had the line in his hand went forth eastward, he measured a thousand cubits, and he brought me through the waters (the waters were to the ankles). Again he measured a thousand, and brought me through the waters (the waters were to the knees). Again he measured a thousand, and brought me through (the waters were to the loins). Afterward he measured a thousand, and it was a river that I could not pass over, for the waters were risen, waters to swim in, a river that could not be passed over. And he said unto me, Son of man, have you seen this?

⁶⁰ Then he brought me and caused me to return to the brink of the river. Now when I had returned, behold, at the bank of the river were very many trees on the one side and on the other. Then said he unto me, These waters issue out toward the east country, and go down into the desert, and go into the sea — which, being brought forth into the sea, the waters shall be healed. And it shall come to pass that everything that lives, which moves, wherever the rivers shall come, shall live. And there shall be a very great multitude of fish because these waters shall come there, for they shall be healed. And everything shall live where the river comes. And it shall come to pass that the fishers shall stand upon it from Engedi even unto Eneglaim. They shall be a place to spread forth nets; their fish shall be according to their kinds, as the fish of the great sea, exceedingly many. But the miry places thereof and the marshes thereof shall not be healed; they shall be given to salt.

⁶¹ And by the river, upon the bank thereof, on this side and on that side, shall grow all trees for food — whose leaf shall not fade, neither shall the fruit thereof be consumed. It shall bring forth new fruit according to his months, because their waters they issued out of the

sanctuary; and the fruit thereof shall be for food, and the leaf thereof for medicine.

62 Thus says the Lord God: This shall be the border whereby you shall inherit the land, according to the twelve tribes of Israel—Joseph shall have two portions, and you shall inherit it, one as well as another—concerning which I lifted up my hand to give it unto your fathers; and this land shall fall unto you for inheritance.

63 And this shall be the border of the land: toward the north side, from the great sea, the way of Hethlon as men go to Zedad, Hamath, Berothah, Sibraim (which is between the border of Damascus and the border of Hamath), Hazar-Hatticon (which is by the border of Hauran). And the border from the sea shall be Hazar-Enan, the border of Damascus, and the north northward, and the border of Hamath. And this is the north side.

64 And the east side you shall measure from Hauran, and from Damascus, and from Gilead, and from the land of Israel by Jordan, from the border unto the east sea. And this is the east side.

65 And the south side southward, from Tamar even to the waters of strife in Kadesh, the river to the great sea. And this is the south side southward.

66 The west side also shall be the great sea from the border, until a man come opposite Hamath. This is the west side.

67 So shall you divide this land unto you, according to the tribes of Israel. And it shall come to pass that you shall divide it by lot for an inheritance unto you, and to the strangers that sojourn among you who shall beget children among you, and they shall be unto you as born in the country among the children of Israel. They shall have inheritance with you among the tribes of Israel. And it shall come to pass that in what tribe the stranger sojourns, there shall you give him his inheritance, says the Lord God.

68 Now these are the names of the tribes: from the north end to the border of the way of Hethlon as one goes to Hamath, Hazar-Enan, the border of Damascus northward to the border of Hamath—for these are his sides east and west—a portion for Dan. And by the border of Dan, from the east side unto the west side, a portion for Asher. And by the border of Asher, from the east side even unto the west side, a portion for Naphtali. And by the border of Naphtali, from the east side unto

the west side, a portion for Manasseh. And by the border of Manasseh, from the east side unto the west side, a portion for Ephraim. And by the border of Ephraim, from the east side even unto the west side, a portion for Reuben. And by the border of Reuben, from the east side unto the west side, a portion for Judah. And by the border of Judah, from the east side unto the west side, shall be the offering which you shall offer of twenty-five thousand reeds in breadth, and in length as one of the other parts, from the east side unto the west side; and the sanctuary shall be in the center of it.

69 The offering that you shall offer unto the Lord shall be of twenty-five thousand in length, and of ten thousand in breadth. And for them, even for the priests, shall be this holy offering: toward the north twenty-five thousand in length, and toward the west ten thousand in breadth, and toward the east ten thousand in breadth, and toward the south twenty-five thousand in length; and the sanctuary of the Lord shall be in the center thereof. It shall be for the priests that are sanctified of the sons of Zadok who have kept my charge, who went not astray when the children of Israel went astray as the Levites went astray. And this offering of the land that is offered shall be unto them a thing most holy, by the border of the Levites.

70 And alongside the border of the priests, the Levites shall have twenty-five thousand in length and ten thousand in breadth. All the length shall be twenty-five thousand and the breadth ten thousand. And they shall not sell of it, neither exchange, nor alienate the firstfruits of the land, for it is holy unto the Lord.

71 And what remains, the five thousand in the breadth by the twenty-five thousand, shall be a common place for the city, for dwelling and for suburbs; and the city shall be in the middle thereof. And these shall be the measures thereof: the north side, four thousand five hundred, and the south side, four thousand five hundred, and on the east side, four thousand five hundred, and the west side, four thousand five hundred.

72 And the suburbs of the city shall be toward the north, two hundred fifty, and toward the south, two hundred fifty, and toward the east, two hundred fifty, and toward the west, two hundred fifty. And the residue in length alongside the offering of the holy portion shall be ten thousand eastward and ten thousand westward, and it shall be alongside the offering of the holy portion; and the increase thereof

shall be for food unto them that serve the city. And they that serve the city shall serve it out of all the tribes of Israel. All the offering shall be twenty-five thousand by twenty-five thousand. You shall offer the holy offering square with the possession of the city.

73 And the residue shall be for the prince, on the one side and on the other of the holy offering and of the possession of the city — alongside the twenty-five thousand of the offering, toward the east border, and westward alongside the twenty-five thousand, toward the west border, alongside the portions for the prince. And it shall be the holy offering, and the sanctuary of the house shall be in the center thereof. Moreover, from the possession of the Levites and from the possession of the city, being in the center of that which is the prince's, between the border of Judah and the border of Benjamin, shall be for the prince.

74 As for the rest of the tribes, from the east side unto the west side, Benjamin shall have a portion. And by the border of Benjamin, from the east side unto the west side, Simeon shall have a portion. And by the border of Simeon, from the east side unto the west side, Issachar a portion. And by the border of Issachar, from the east side unto the west side, Zebulun a portion. And by the border of Zebulun, from the east side unto the west side, Gad a portion. And by the border of Gad, at the south side southward, the border shall be even from Tamar unto the waters of strife in Kadesh, and to the river toward the great sea.

75 This is the land which you shall divide by lot unto the tribes of Israel for inheritance, and these are their portions, says the Lord God.

76 And these are the exits of the city. On the north side, four thousand five hundred measures (and the gates of the city shall be after the names of the tribes of Israel), three gates northward: one gate of Reuben, one gate of Judah, one gate of Levi. And at the east side, four thousand five hundred, and three gates: and one gate of Joseph, one gate of Benjamin, one gate of Dan. And at the south side, four thousand five hundred measures, and three gates: one gate of Simeon, one gate of Issachar, one gate of Zebulun. At the west side, four thousand five hundred, with their three gates: one gate of Gad, one gate of Asher, one gate of Naphtali.

77 It was round about eighteen thousand measures, and the name of the city from that day shall be called holy, for the Lord shall be there.

THE BOOK OF DANIEL

IN the third year of the reign of Jehoiakim king of Judah, Nebuchadnezzar king of Babylon came unto Jerusalem and besieged it. And the Lord gave Jehoiakim king of Judah into his hand, with part of the vessels of the house of God, which he carried into the land of Shinar to the house of his god. And he brought the vessels into the treasure house of his god.

2 And the king spoke unto Ashpenaz, the master of his eunuchs, that he should bring certain of the children of Israel, and of the king's seed, and of the princes — children in whom was no blemish, but well-favored and skillful in all wisdom, and proficient in knowledge, and understanding science, and such as had ability in them to stand in the king's palace, and whom they might teach the learning and the tongue of the Chaldeans. And the king appointed them a daily provision of the king's food and of the wine which he drank, so nourishing them three years, that at the end thereof they might stand before the king. Now among these were, of the children of Judah: Daniel, Hananiah, Mishael, and Azariah, unto whom the prince of the eunuchs gave names; for he gave unto Daniel the name of Belteshazzar; and to Hananiah, of Shadrach; and to Mishael, of Meshach; and to Azariah, of Abednego.

3 But Daniel purposed in his heart that he would not defile himself with the portion of the king's food, nor with the wine which he drank; therefore, he requested of the prince of the eunuchs that he might not defile himself. Now God had brought Daniel into favor and tender love with the prince of the eunuchs, and the prince of the eunuchs said unto Daniel, I fear my lord the king, who has appointed your food and your drink. For why should he see your faces looking worse than the children who are of your sort? Then shall you make me endanger my head to the king. Then said Daniel to Melzar — whom the prince of the eunuchs had set over Daniel, Hananiah, Mishael, and Azariah — Prove your servants, I implore you, ten days, and let them give us pulse to eat and water to drink. Then let our countenances be looked upon before you, and the countenance of the children that eat of the portion of the king's food, and as you see, deal with your servants. So he consented to them in this matter and proved them ten days. And at the end of ten days, their countenances appeared fairer and fatter in flesh than all

the children who did eat the portion of the king's food. Thus Melzar took away the portion of their food and the wine that they should drink, and gave them pulse.

⁴As for these four children, God gave them knowledge and skill in all learning and wisdom, and Daniel had understanding in all visions and dreams. Now at the end of the days that the king had said he should bring them in, the prince of the eunuchs brought them in before Nebuchadnezzar, and the king spoke with them. And among them all was found none like Daniel, Hananiah, Mishael, and Azariah; therefore stood they before the king. And in all matters of wisdom and understanding that the king inquired of them, he found them ten times better than all the magicians and astrologers that were in all his realm. And Daniel continued even unto the first year of king Cyrus.

2 And in the second year of the reign of Nebuchadnezzar, Nebuchadnezzar dreamed dreams by which his spirit was troubled, and his sleep broke from him. Then the king commanded to call the magicians, and the astrologers, and the sorcerers, and the Chaldeans, in order to show the king his dreams. So they came and stood before the king, and the king said unto them, I have dreamed a dream, and my spirit was troubled to know the dream. Then spoke the Chaldeans to the king in Syriac, O king, live for ever. Tell your servants the dream and we will show the interpretation. The king answered and said to the Chaldeans, The thing is gone from me. If you will not make known unto me the dream, with the interpretation thereof, you shall be cut in pieces and your houses shall be made a dunghill. But if you show the dream and the interpretation thereof, you shall receive of me gifts and rewards and great honor; therefore, show me the dream and the interpretation thereof. They answered again and said, Let the king tell his servants the dream and we will show the interpretation of it. The king answered and said, I know of certainty that you would gain the time, because you see the thing is gone from me. But if you will not make known unto me the dream, there is but one decree for you, for you have prepared lying and corrupt words to speak before me until the time is changed. Therefore, tell me the dream and I shall know that you can show me the interpretation thereof. The Chaldeans answered before the king, and said, There is not a man upon the earth that can

show the king's matter, therefore there is no king, lord, nor ruler that asked such things at any magician, or astrologer, or Chaldean. And it is a rare thing that the king requires, and there is no other that can show it before the king except the gods, whose dwelling is not with flesh. For this cause, the king was angry and very furious, and commanded to destroy all the wise men of Babylon.

2 And the decree went forth that the wise men should be slain, and they sought Daniel and his fellows to be slain. Then Daniel answered with counsel and wisdom to Arioch, the captain of the king's guard, who was gone forth to slay the wise men of Babylon. He answered and said to Arioch the king's captain, Why is the decree so hasty from the king? Then Arioch made the thing known to Daniel. Then Daniel went in and desired of the king that he would give him time, and that he would show the king the interpretation. Then Daniel went to his house and made the thing known to Hananiah, Mishael, and Azariah, his companions, that they would desire mercies of the God of Heaven concerning this secret, that Daniel and his fellows should not perish with the rest of the wise men of Babylon.

3 Then was the secret revealed unto Daniel in a night vision. Then Daniel blessed the God of Heaven. Daniel answered and said, Blessed be the name of God for ever and ever, for wisdom and might are his. And he changes the times and the seasons, he removes kings and sets up kings, he gives wisdom unto the wise and knowledge to them that know understanding. He reveals the deep and secret things, he knows what is in the darkness, and the light dwells with him. I thank you and praise you, O you God of my fathers, who have given me wisdom and might, and have made known unto me now what we desired of you; for you have now made known unto us the king's matter.

4 Therefore, Daniel went in unto Arioch, whom the king had ordained to destroy the wise men of Babylon. He went and said thus unto him: Destroy not the wise men of Babylon. Bring me in before the king and I will show unto the king the interpretation.

5 Then Arioch brought in Daniel before the king in haste and said thus unto him: I have found a man of the captives of Judah that will make known unto the king the interpretation. The king answered and said to Daniel — whose name was Belteshazzar — Are you able to make known unto me the dream which I have seen and the interpretation

thereof? Daniel answered in the presence of the king and said, The secret which the king has demanded cannot the wise men, the astrologers, the magicians, the fortune-tellers show unto the king. But there is a God in Heaven that reveals secrets, and makes known to the king Nebuchadnezzar what shall be in the latter days. Your dream, and the visions of your head upon your bed, are these. As for you, O king, your thoughts came into your mind upon your bed, what should come to pass hereafter. And he that reveals secrets makes known to you what shall come to pass. But as for me, this secret is not revealed to me for any wisdom that I have more than any living, but for their sakes that shall make known the interpretation to the king, and that you might know the thoughts of your heart.

6 You, O king, saw and beheld a great image. This great image, whose brightness was excellent, stood before you, and the form thereof was terrible. This image's head was of fine gold, his breast and his arms of silver, his belly and his thighs of brass, his legs of iron, his feet, part of iron and part of clay. You saw until a stone was cut out without hands, which smote the image upon his feet that were of iron and clay and broke them to pieces. Then was the iron, the clay, the brass, the silver, and the gold broken to pieces together, and became like the chaff of the summer threshing floors, and the wind carried them away, that no place was found for them. And the stone that smote the image became a great mountain and filled the whole earth.

7 This is the dream, and we will tell the interpretation thereof before the king. You, O king, are a king of kings, for the God of Heaven has given you a kingdom, power, and strength, and glory. And wheresoever the children of men dwell, the beasts of the field and the fowls of the heaven has he given into your hand, and has made you ruler over them all. You are this head of gold. And after you shall arise another kingdom inferior to you, and another third kingdom of brass, which shall bear rule over all the earth. And the fourth kingdom shall be strong as iron, forasmuch as iron breaks in pieces and subdues all things, and as iron that breaks all these shall it break in pieces and bruise. And whereas you saw the feet and toes, part of potters' clay and part of iron, the kingdom shall be divided, but there shall be in it of the strength of the iron, forasmuch as you saw the iron mixed with miry clay. And as the toes of the feet were part of iron and part of clay, so the kingdom

shall be partly strong and partly broken. And whereas you saw iron mixed with miry clay, they shall mingle themselves with the seed of men, but they shall not cleave one to another, even as iron is not mixed with clay. And in the days of these kings shall the God of Heaven set up a kingdom which shall never be destroyed. And the kingdom shall not be left to other people, but it shall break in pieces and consume all these kingdoms, and it shall stand for ever. Forasmuch as you saw that the stone was cut out of the mountain without hands, and that it broke in pieces the iron, the brass, the clay, the silver, and the gold, the great God has made known to the king what shall come to pass hereafter. And the dream is certain, and the interpretation thereof sure.

8 Then the king Nebuchadnezzar fell upon his face and worshipped Daniel, and commanded that they should offer an offering and sweet odors unto him. The king answered unto Daniel and said, Truly it is that your God is a God of gods, and a Lord of kings, and a revealer of secrets, seeing you could reveal this secret. Then the king made Daniel a great man, and gave him many great gifts, and made him ruler over the whole province of Babylon and chief of the governors over all the wise men of Babylon. Then Daniel requested of the king, and he set Shadrach, Meshach, and Abednego over the affairs of the province of Babylon; but Daniel sat in the gate of the king.

3 Nebuchadnezzar the king made an image of gold whose height was sixty cubits and the breadth thereof six cubits. He set it up in the plain of Dura, in the province of Babylon. Then Nebuchadnezzar the king sent to gather together the princes, the governors, and the captains, the judges, the treasurers, the counselors, the sheriffs, and all the rulers of the provinces, to come to the dedication of the image which Nebuchadnezzar the king had set up. Then the princes, the governors, and captains, the judges, the treasurers, the counselors, the sheriffs, and all the rulers of the provinces were gathered together unto the dedication of the image that Nebuchadnezzar the king had set up, and they stood before the image that Nebuchadnezzar had set up. Then a herald cried aloud, To you it is commanded, O people, nations, and languages, that when you hear the sound of the horn, flute, harp, lyre, psaltery, dulcimer, and all kinds of music, you fall down and worship the golden image that Nebuchadnezzar the king

has set up! And whoever falls not down and worships shall the same hour be cast into the midst of a burning fiery furnace. Therefore, at that time, when all the people heard the sound of the horn, flute, harp, lyre, psaltery, and all kinds of music, all the people, the nations, and the languages fell down and worshipped the golden image that Nebuchadnezzar the king had set up.

2 Wherefore, at that time, certain Chaldeans came near and accused the Jews. They spoke and said to the king Nebuchadnezzar, O king, live for ever. You, O king, have made a decree that every man that shall hear the sound of the horn, flute, harp, lyre, psaltery, and dulcimer, and all kinds of music, shall fall down and worship the golden image; and whoever falls not down and worships, that he should be cast into the midst of a burning fiery furnace. There are certain Jews whom you have set over the affairs of the province of Babylon: Shadrach, Meshach, and Abednego. These men, O king, have not regarded you; they serve not your gods, nor worship the golden image which you have set up.

3 Then Nebuchadnezzar in his rage and fury commanded to bring Shadrach, Meshach, and Abednego. Then they brought these men before the king. Nebuchadnezzar spoke and said unto them, Is it true, O Shadrach, Meshach, and Abednego, do not you serve my gods, nor worship the golden image which I have set up? Now if you are ready, that when you hear the sound of the horn, flute, harp, lyre, psaltery, and dulcimer, and all kinds of music, you fall down and worship the image which I have made, well. But if you worship not, you shall be cast the same hour into the midst of a burning fiery furnace. And who is that god that shall deliver you out of my hands? Shadrach, Meshach, and Abednego answered and said to the king, O Nebuchadnezzar, we are not anxious to answer you in this matter. If it be so, our God whom we serve is able to deliver us from the burning fiery furnace, and he will deliver us out of your hand, O king. But if not, be it known unto you, O king, that we will not serve your gods, nor worship the golden image which you have set up.

4 Then was Nebuchadnezzar full of fury, and the form of his visage was changed against Shadrach, Meshach, and Abednego. Therefore he spoke, and commanded that they should heat the furnace seven times more than it was accustomed to be heated. And he commanded the most mighty men that were in his army to bind Shadrach, Meshach,

and Abednego, and to cast them into the burning fiery furnace. Then these men were bound in their coats, their trousers, and their hats, and their other garments, and were cast into the midst of the burning fiery furnace. Therefore, because the king's commandment was urgent and the furnace exceedingly hot, the flame of the fire slew those men that took up Shadrach, Meshach, and Abednego. And these three men, Shadrach, Meshach, and Abednego, fell down bound into the midst of the burning fiery furnace.

5 Then Nebuchadnezzar the king was astonished, and rose up in haste and spoke, and said unto his counselors, Did not we cast three men bound into the midst of the fire? They answered and said unto the king, True, O king. He answered and said, Look, I see four men loose, walking in the midst of the fire, and they have no hurt; and the form of the fourth is like the son of god. Then Nebuchadnezzar came near to the mouth of the burning fiery furnace and spoke, and said, Shadrach, Meshach, and Abednego, you servants of the Most High God, come forth and come here. Then Shadrach, Meshach, and Abednego came forth of the midst of the fire. And the princes, governors, and captains, and the king's counselors, being gathered together, saw these men upon whose bodies the fire had no power, nor was a hair of their head singed, neither were their coats changed, nor had the smell of fire passed on them. Then Nebuchadnezzar spoke, and said, Blessed be the God of Shadrach, Meshach, and Abednego, who has sent his angel and delivered his servants that trusted in him, and have changed the king's word and yielded their bodies that they might not serve nor worship any god except their own God. Therefore, I make a decree that every people, nation, and language which speak anything amiss against the God of Shadrach, Meshach, and Abednego shall be cut in pieces, and their houses shall be made a dunghill, because there is no other God that can deliver after this sort. Then the king promoted Shadrach, Meshach, and Abednego in the province of Babylon.

4 Nebuchadnezzar the king, unto all people, nations, and languages that dwell in all the earth: Peace be multiplied unto you. I thought it good to show the signs and wonders that the high God has wrought toward me. How great are his signs, and how mighty are his wonders!

His kingdom is an everlasting kingdom, and his dominion is from generation to generation.

2 I, Nebuchadnezzar, was at rest in my house and flourishing in my palace. I saw a dream which made me afraid, and the thoughts upon my bed and the visions of my head troubled me. Therefore made I a decree to bring in all the wise men of Babylon before me, that they might make known unto me the interpretation of the dream. Then came in the magicians, the astrologers, the Chaldeans, and the fortune-tellers, and I told the dream before them, but they did not make known unto me the interpretation thereof.

3 But at the last Daniel came in before me, whose name was Belteshazzar according to the name of my god, and in whom is the spirit of the holy gods. And before him I told the dream, saying, O Belteshazzar, master of the magicians, because I know that the spirit of the holy gods is in you, and no secret troubles you, tell me the visions of my dream that I have seen and the interpretation thereof.

4 Thus were the visions of my head in my bed: I saw, and behold, a tree in the middle of the earth, and the height thereof was great. The tree grew and was strong, and the height thereof reached unto heaven, and the sight thereof to the end of all the earth. The leaves thereof were fair, and the fruit thereof much, and in it was food for all. The beasts of the field had shadow under it, and the fowls of the heaven dwelled in the boughs thereof, and all flesh was fed of it. I saw in the visions of my head upon my bed, and behold, a watcher and a holy one came down from Heaven. He cried aloud and said thus: Hew down the tree and cut off his branches, shake off his leaves and scatter his fruit; let the beasts get away from under it, and the fowls from his branches! Nevertheless, leave the stump of his roots in the earth, even with a band of iron and brass, in the tender grass of the field; and let it be wet with the dew of heaven, and let his portion be with the beasts in the grass of the earth. Let his heart be changed from man's, and let a beast's heart be given unto him, and let seven times pass over him. This matter is by the decree of the watchers, and the demand by the word of the holy ones, to the intent that the living may know that the Most High rules in the kingdom of men, and gives it to whomever he will, and sets up over it the basest of men.

⁵This dream, I, king Nebuchadnezzar, have seen. Now you, O Belteshazzar, declare the interpretation thereof, forasmuch as all the wise men of my kingdom are not able to make known unto me the interpretation, but you are able, for the spirit of the holy gods is in you.

⁶Then Daniel, whose name was Belteshazzar, was astonished for one hour, and his thoughts troubled him. The king spoke and said, Belteshazzar, let not the dream or the interpretation thereof trouble you. Belteshazzar answered and said, My lord, the dream is to them that hate you, and the interpretation thereof to your enemies. The tree that you saw, which grew and was strong, whose height reached unto the heaven and the sight thereof to all the earth, whose leaves were fair and the fruit thereof much, and in it was food for all, under which the beasts of the field dwelled, and upon whose branches the fowls of the heaven had their habitation — it is you, O king, that are grown and become strong; for your greatness is grown and reaches unto heaven, and your dominion to the end of the earth.

⁷And whereas the king saw a watcher and a holy one coming down from Heaven and saying, Hew the tree down and destroy it, yet leave the stump of the roots thereof in the earth, even with a band of iron and brass in the tender grass of the field, and let it be wet with the dew of heaven, and let his portion be with the beasts of the field until seven times pass over him — this is the interpretation, O king, and this is the decree of the Most High which has come upon my lord the king: that they shall drive you from men, and your dwelling shall be with the beasts of the field; and they shall make you eat grass as oxen, and they shall wet you with the dew of heaven, and seven times shall pass over you until you know that the Most High rules in the kingdom of men and gives it to whomever he will. And whereas they commanded to leave the stump of the tree roots, your kingdom shall be sure unto you, after you shall have known that the heavens do rule.

⁸Wherefore, O king, let my counsel be acceptable unto you, and break off your sins by righteousness and your iniquities by showing mercy to the poor, if it may be a lengthening of your tranquility.

⁹All this came upon the king Nebuchadnezzar. At the end of twelve months, he walked in the palace of the kingdom of Babylon. The king spoke and said, Is not this great Babylon, that I have built for the house of the kingdom by the might of my power and for the honor of my

majesty? While the word was in the king's mouth, there fell a voice
from Heaven, saying, O king Nebuchadnezzar, to you it is spoken, The
kingdom is departed from you, and they shall drive you from men, and
your dwelling shall be with the beasts of the field. They shall make
you to eat grass as oxen, and seven times shall pass over you, until
you know that the Most High rules in the kingdom of men and gives
it to whomever he will. The same hour was the thing fulfilled upon
Nebuchadnezzar. And he was driven from men and did eat grass as
oxen, and his body was wet with the dew of heaven, until his hairs
were grown like eagles' feathers and his nails like birds' claws.

10 And at the end of the days I, Nebuchadnezzar, lifted up my eyes
unto Heaven, and my understanding returned unto me, and I blessed
the Most High, and I praised and honored him that lives for ever,
whose dominion is an everlasting dominion, and his kingdom is
from generation to generation. And all the inhabitants of the earth
are reputed as nothing, and he does according to his will in the army
of Heaven and among the inhabitants of the earth, and none can stop
his hand or say unto him, What are you doing? At the same time, my
reason returned unto me, and for the glory of my kingdom, my honor
and brightness returned unto me, and my counselors and my lords
sought unto me, and I was established in my kingdom and excellent
majesty was added unto me. Now I, Nebuchadnezzar, praise and extol
and honor the King of Heaven, all whose works are truth, and his ways
judgment; and those that walk in pride, he is able to abase.

5 Belshazzar the king made a great feast to a thousand of his lords,
and drank wine before the thousand. Belshazzar, while he tasted
the wine, commanded to bring the golden and silver vessels which
his father Nebuchadnezzar had taken out of the temple which was in
Jerusalem, that the king and his princes, his wives, and his concubines
might drink therein. Then they brought the golden vessels that were
taken out of the temple of the House of God which was at Jerusalem,
and the king and his princes, his wives, and his concubines drank in
them. They drank wine and praised the gods of gold and of silver, of
brass, of iron, of wood, and of stone.

2 In the same hour came forth fingers of a man's hand, and wrote
opposite the candlestick, upon the plaster of the wall of the king's

palace; and the king saw the part of the hand that wrote. Then the king's countenance was changed and his thoughts troubled him, so that the joints of his loins were loosened and his knees smote one against another. The king cried aloud to bring in the astrologers, the Chaldeans, and the fortune-tellers. And the king spoke and said to the wise men of Babylon, Whoever shall read this writing and show me the interpretation thereof shall be clothed with scarlet, and have a chain of gold about his neck, and shall be the third ruler in the kingdom. Then came in all the king's wise men, but they could not read the writing nor make known to the king the interpretation thereof. Then was king Belshazzar greatly troubled, and his countenance was changed in him, and his lords were astonished.

3 Now the queen, by reason of the words of the king and his lords, came into the banquet house. And the queen spoke and said, O king, live for ever; let not your thoughts trouble you, nor let your countenance be changed. There is a man in your kingdom in whom is the spirit of the holy gods. And in the days of your father, light and understanding and wisdom like the wisdom of the gods was found in him, whom the king, Nebuchadnezzar your father — the king, I say, your father — made master of the magicians, astrologers, Chaldeans, and fortune-tellers. Forasmuch as an excellent spirit, and knowledge, and understanding, interpreting of dreams, and showing of hard sentences, and dissolving of doubts were found in the same Daniel — whom the king named Belteshazzar — now let Daniel be called, and he will show the interpretation.

4 Then was Daniel brought in before the king. And the king spoke and said unto Daniel, Are you that Daniel who are of the children of the captivity of Judah, whom the king my father brought out of Jewry? I have even heard of you, that the spirit of the gods is in you, and that light and understanding and excellent wisdom is found in you. And now the wise men, the astrologers, have been brought in before me, that they should read this writing and make known unto me the interpretation thereof; but they could not show the interpretation of the thing. And I have heard of you, that you can make interpretations and dissolve doubts. Now if you can read the writing and make known to me the interpretation thereof, you shall be clothed with scarlet and

have a chain of gold about your neck, and shall be the third ruler in the kingdom.

5 Then Daniel answered and said before the king, Let your gifts be to yourself and give your rewards to another; yet I will read the writing unto the king and make known to him the interpretation.

6 O you king, the Most High God gave Nebuchadnezzar your father a kingdom, and majesty, and glory, and honor. And for the majesty that he gave him, all people, nations, and languages trembled and feared before him; whom he wished, he slew; and whom he wished, he kept alive; and whom he wished, he set up; and whom he wished, he put down. But when his heart was lifted up and his mind hardened in pride, he was deposed from his kingly throne, and they took his glory from him, and he was driven from the sons of men, and his heart was made like the beasts, and his dwelling was with the wild asses. They fed him with grass like oxen and his body was wet with the dew of heaven until he knew that the Most High God ruled in the kingdom of men, and that he appoints over it whomever he will.

7 And you, his son, O Belshazzar, have not humbled your heart, though you knew all this, but have lifted up yourself against the Lord of Heaven. And they have brought the vessels of his house before you, and you and your lords, your wives, and your concubines have drunk wine in them. And you have praised the gods of silver and gold, of brass, iron, wood, and stone, which see not, nor hear, nor know. And the God in whose hand your breath is, and whose are all your ways, you have not glorified.

8 Then was the part of the hand sent from him and this writing was written, and this is the writing that was written: MENE, MENE, TEKEL, UPHARSIN. This is the interpretation of the thing: MENE —God has numbered your kingdom and finished it; tekel —you are weighed in the balances and are found lacking; upharsin —your kingdom is divided and given to the Medes and Persians.

9 Then commanded Belshazzar, and they clothed Daniel with scarlet and put a chain of gold about his neck, and made a proclamation concerning him, that he should be the third ruler in the kingdom. In that night was Belshazzar the king of the Chaldeans slain, and Darius the Median took the kingdom, being about sixty-two years old.

6 It pleased Darius to set over the kingdom a hundred twenty princes who should be over the whole kingdom, and over these, three presidents — of whom Daniel was first — that the princes might give accounts unto them and the king should have no damage. Then this Daniel was preferred above the presidents and princes because an excellent spirit was in him, and the king thought to set him over the whole realm.

2 Then the presidents and princes sought to find accusation against Daniel concerning the kingdom; but they could find no accusation nor fault, forasmuch as he was faithful, neither was there any error or fault found in him. Then said these men, We shall not find any accusation against this Daniel except we find it against him concerning the law of his God. Then these presidents and princes assembled together to the king and said thus unto him: King Darius, live for ever. All the presidents of the kingdom, the governors, and the princes, the counselors, and the captains have consulted together to establish a royal statute and to make a firm decree, that whoever shall ask a petition of any god or man for thirty days — save of you, O king — he shall be cast into the den of lions. Now, O king, establish the decree and sign the writing that it be not changed, according to the law of the Medes and Persians, which alters not. Wherefore, king Darius signed the writing and the decree.

3 Now when Daniel knew that the writing was signed, he went into his house; and his windows being open in his chamber toward Jerusalem, he kneeled upon his knees three times a day and prayed, and gave thanks before his God as he did before. Then these men assembled and found Daniel praying and making supplication before his God.

4 Then they came near and spoke before the king concerning the king's decree, Have you not signed a decree that every man that shall ask a petition of any god or man within thirty days, save of you, O king, shall be cast into the den of lions? The king answered and said, The thing is true, according to the law of the Medes and Persians, which alters not. Then they answered and said before the king, That Daniel who is of the children of the captivity of Judah regards not you, O king, nor the decree that you have signed, but makes his petition three times a day. Then the king, when he heard these words, was severely

displeased with himself, and set his heart on Daniel to deliver him; and he labored until the going down of the sun to deliver him.

5 Then these men assembled unto the king and said unto the king, Know, O king, that the law of the Medes and Persians is that no decree nor statute which the king establishes may be changed. Then the king commanded, and they brought Daniel and cast him into the den of lions. Now the king spoke and said unto Daniel, Your God whom you serve continually, he will deliver you. And a stone was brought, and laid upon the mouth of the den; and the king sealed it with his own signet and with the signet of his lords, that the purpose might not be changed concerning Daniel.

6 Then the king went to his palace and passed the night fasting, neither were instruments of music brought before him, and his sleep went from him. Then the king arose very early in the morning and went in haste unto the den of lions. And when he came to the den, he cried with a lamentable voice unto Daniel; and the king spoke and said to Daniel, O Daniel, servant of the living God, is your God, whom you serve continually, able to deliver you from the lions? Then said Daniel unto the king, O king, live for ever. My God has sent his angel and has shut the lions' mouths, that they have not hurt me, forasmuch as before him innocence was found in me; and also before you, O king, have I done no hurt. Then was the king exceedingly glad for him, and commanded that they should take Daniel up out of the den. So Daniel was taken up out of the den, and no manner of hurt was found upon him because he believed in his God.

7 And the king commanded, and they brought those men who had accused Daniel, and they cast them into the den of lions — them, their children, and their wives — and the lions had the mastery of them, and broke all their bones in pieces or ever they came at the bottom of the den.

8 Then king Darius wrote unto all people, nations, and languages that dwell in all the earth: Peace be multiplied unto you. I make a decree that in every dominion of my kingdom, men tremble and fear before the God of Daniel — for he is the living God, and steadfast for ever, and his kingdom that which shall not be destroyed. And his dominion shall be even unto the end. He delivers and rescues, and he

works signs and wonders in heaven and in earth, who has delivered Daniel from the power of the lions.

⁹ So this Daniel prospered in the reign of Darius and in the reign of Cyrus the Persian.

7 In the first year of Belshazzar king of Babylon, Daniel had a dream and visions of his head upon his bed. Then he wrote the dream, and told the sum of the matters. Daniel spoke and said, I saw in my vision by night, and behold, the four winds of the heaven strove upon the great sea. And four great beasts came up from the sea, diverse one from another. The first was like a lion and had eagle's wings. I beheld until the wings thereof were plucked, and it was lifted up from the earth and made to stand upon the feet as a man, and a man's heart was given to it. And behold, another beast, a second like unto a bear, and it raised up itself on one side, and it had three ribs in the mouth of it, between the teeth of it. And they said thus unto it: Arise, devour much flesh. After this, I beheld and saw another, like a leopard which had upon the back of it four wings of a fowl. The beast had also four heads, and dominion was given to it. After this, I saw in the night visions, and behold, a fourth beast, dreadful and terrible and exceedingly strong, and it had great iron teeth. It devoured, and broke in pieces, and stamped the residue with the feet of it, and it was diverse from all the beasts that were before it, and it had ten horns. I considered the horns, and behold, there came up among them another little horn, before whom there were three of the first horns plucked up by the roots. And behold, in this horn were eyes like the eyes of man, and a mouth speaking great things.

² I beheld until the thrones were cast down and the Ancient of Days did sit, whose garment was white as snow, and the hair of his head like the pure wool; his throne was like the fiery flame, and his wheels as burning fire. A fiery stream issued and came forth from before him. Thousand thousands ministered unto him, and ten thousand times ten thousand stood before him. The judgment was set and the books were opened.

³ I beheld then, because of the voice of the great words which the horn spoke, I beheld even until the beast was slain, and his body destroyed and given to the burning flame. As concerning the rest of

the beasts, they had their dominion taken away; yet their lives were prolonged for a season and time.

4 I saw in the night visions, and behold, one like the Son of Man came with the clouds of Heaven, and came to the Ancient of Days, and they brought him near before him. And there was given him dominion, and glory, and a kingdom, that all people, nations, and languages should serve him. His dominion is an everlasting dominion which shall not pass away, and his kingdom that which shall not be destroyed.

5 I, Daniel, was grieved in my spirit in the midst of my body, and the visions of my head troubled me. I came near unto one of them that stood by and asked him the truth of all this. So he told me and made me know the interpretation of the things.

6 These great beasts, which are four, are four kings who shall arise out of the earth; but the saints of the Most High shall take the kingdom and possess the kingdom for ever, even for ever and ever.

7 Then I desired to know the truth of the fourth beast, which was diverse from all the others, exceedingly dreadful, whose teeth were of iron and his nails of brass; which devoured, broke in pieces, and stamped the residue with his feet; and of the ten horns that were in his head, and of the other which came up and before whom three fell, even of that horn that had eyes and a mouth that spoke very great things, whose look was more stout than his fellows. I beheld, and the same horn made war with the saints, and prevailed against them until the Ancient of Days came, and judgment was given to the saints of the Most High, and the time came that the saints possessed the kingdom.

8 Thus he said: The fourth beast shall be the fourth kingdom upon earth, which shall be diverse from all kingdoms and shall devour the whole earth, and shall tread it down and break it in pieces. And the ten horns out of this kingdom are ten kings that shall arise. And another shall rise after them, and he shall be diverse from the first, and he shall subdue three kings. And he shall speak great words against the Most High, and shall wear out the saints of the Most High, and think to change times and laws. And they shall be given into his hand until a time, and times, and the dividing of time. But the judgment shall sit and they shall take away his dominion, to consume and to destroy it unto the end. And the kingdom, and dominion, and the greatness of the kingdom under the whole heaven shall be given to the people

of the saints of the Most High, whose kingdom is an everlasting kingdom; and all dominions shall serve and obey him. Hitherto is the end of the matter.

9 As for me, Daniel, my thoughts much troubled me and my countenance changed in me; but I kept the matter in my heart.

8 In the third year of the reign of king Belshazzar, a vision appeared unto me — even unto me, Daniel — after that which appeared unto me at the first. And I saw in a vision, and it came to pass when I saw, that I was at Shushan in the palace, which is in the province of Elam. And I saw in a vision, and I was by the river of Ulai. Then I lifted up my eyes and saw, and behold, there stood before the river a ram which had two horns. And the two horns were high, but one was higher than the other, and the higher came up last. I saw the ram pushing westward, and northward, and southward, so that no beasts might stand before him; neither was there any that could deliver out of his hand. But he did according to his will and became great.

2 And as I was considering, behold, a he-goat came from the west, on the face of the whole earth, and touched not the ground. And the goat had a notable horn between his eyes. And he came to the ram that had two horns which I had seen standing before the river, and ran unto him in the fury of his power. And I saw him come close unto the ram, and he was moved with anger against him, and smote the ram, and broke his two horns. And there was no power in the ram to stand before him, but he cast him down to the ground and stamped upon him; and there was none that could deliver the ram out of his hand. Therefore, the he-goat waxed very great.

3 And when he was strong, the great horn was broken, and for it came up four notable ones, toward the four winds of heaven. And out of one of them came forth a little horn which waxed exceedingly great toward the south, and toward the east, and toward the pleasant land. And it waxed great, even to the host of heaven, and it cast down some of the host and of the stars to the ground, and stamped upon them. Yea, he magnified himself even to the prince of the host. And by him the daily sacrifice was taken away, and the place of his sanctuary was cast down. And a host was given to him against the daily sacrifice by

reason of transgression, and it cast down the truth to the ground, and it practiced and prospered.

4 Then I heard one saint speaking, and another saint said unto that certain saint who spoke, How long shall be the vision concerning the daily sacrifice, and the transgression of desolation, to give both the sanctuary and the host to be trodden underfoot? And he said unto me, Unto two thousand three hundred days; then shall the sanctuary be cleansed.

5 And it came to pass when I, even I Daniel, had seen the vision and sought for the meaning, then behold, there stood before me as the appearance of a man. And I heard a man's voice between the banks of Ulai, which called and said, Gabriel, make this man to understand the vision. So he came near where I stood. And when he came, I was afraid and fell upon my face; but he said unto me, Understand, O son of man, for at the time of the end shall be the vision. Now as he was speaking with me, I was in a deep sleep on my face toward the ground, but he touched me and set me upright. And he said, Behold, I will make you know what shall be in the last end of the indignation; for at the time appointed, the end shall be.

6 The ram which you saw having two horns are the kings of Media and Persia. And the rough goat is the king of Greece, and the great horn that is between his eyes is the first king. Now that being broken, whereas four stood up for it, four kingdoms shall stand up out of the nation, but not in his power. And in the latter time of their kingdom, when the transgressors have come to the full, a king of fierce countenance and understanding dark sentences shall stand up. And his power shall be mighty, but not by his own power, and he shall destroy wonderfully, and shall prosper and practice, and shall destroy the mighty and the holy people. And through his policy also he shall cause craft to prosper in his hand, and he shall magnify himself in his heart, and by peace shall destroy many. He shall also stand up against the Prince of princes, but he shall be broken without hand. And the vision of the evening and the morning which was told is true. Wherefore, shut up the vision, for it shall be for many days.

7 And I, Daniel, fainted, and was sick certain days. Afterward, I rose up and did the king's business, and I was astonished at the vision, but none understood it.

9 In the first year of Darius — the son of Ahasuerus, of the seed of the Medes, who was made king over the realm of the Chaldeans — in the first year of his reign, I, Daniel, understood by books the number of the years whereof the word of the Lord came to Jeremiah the prophet, that he would accomplish seventy years in the desolations of Jerusalem. And I set my face unto the Lord God, to seek by prayer and supplications, with fasting and sackcloth and ashes. And I prayed unto the Lord my God, and made my confession and said, O Lord, the great and dreadful God keeping the covenant and mercy to them that love him and to them that keep his commandments, we have sinned and have committed iniquity, and have done wickedly and have rebelled, even by departing from your precepts and from your judgments. Neither have we listened unto your servants the prophets, who spoke in your name to our kings, our princes, and our fathers, and to all the people of the land.

2 O Lord, righteousness belongs unto you, but unto us confusion of faces, as at this day — to the men of Judah, and to the inhabitants of Jerusalem, and unto all Israel that are near and that are far off, through all the countries to which you have driven them because of their trespass that they have trespassed against you. O Lord, to us belongs confusion of face — to our kings, to our princes, and to our fathers — because we have sinned against you. To the Lord our God belong mercies and forgivenesses, though we have rebelled against him. Neither have we obeyed the voice of the Lord our God, to walk in his laws which he set before us by his servants the prophets. Yea, all Israel have transgressed your law, even by departing that they might not obey your voice. Therefore, the curse is poured upon us and the oath that is written in the law of Moses the servant of God, because we have sinned against him. And he has confirmed his words which he spoke against us, and against our judges that judged us, by bringing upon us a great evil; for under the whole heaven has not been done as has been done upon Jerusalem. As it is written in the law of Moses, all this evil has come upon us; yet we made not our prayer before the Lord our God, that we might turn from our iniquities and understand your truth. Therefore has the Lord watched upon the evil and brought it upon us, for the Lord our God is righteous in all his works which he does, for we obeyed not his voice.

3 And now, O Lord our God, that have brought your people forth out of the land of Egypt with a mighty hand, and have gotten you renown as at this day, we have sinned; we have done wickedly. O Lord, according to all your righteousness, I implore you, let your anger and your fury be turned away from your city Jerusalem, your holy mountain; because for our sins, and for the iniquities of our fathers, Jerusalem and your people are become a reproach to all that are about us. Now therefore, O our God, hear the prayer of your servant and his supplications, and cause your face to shine upon your sanctuary that is desolate, for the Lord's sake. O my God, incline your ear and hear, open your eyes and behold our desolations and the city which is called by your name, for we do not present our supplications before you for our righteousnesses, but for your great mercies. O Lord, hear; O Lord, forgive; O Lord, listen and do. Defer not, for your own sake, O my God, for your city and your people are called by your name.

4 And while I was speaking, and praying, and confessing my sin and the sin of my people Israel, and presenting my supplication before the Lord my God for the holy mountain of my God — yea, while I was speaking in prayer, even the man Gabriel whom I had seen in the vision at the beginning, being caused to fly swiftly, touched me about the time of the evening offering. And he informed me, and talked with me, and said, O Daniel, I have now come forth to give you skill and understanding. At the beginning of your supplications, the commandment came forth, and I have come to show you; for you are greatly beloved. Therefore, understand the matter and consider the vision.

5 Seventy weeks are determined upon your people and upon your holy city, to finish the transgression, and to make an end of sins, and to make reconciliation for iniquity, and to bring in everlasting righteousness, and to seal up the vision and prophecy, and to anoint the most holy. Know therefore and understand that from the going forth of the commandment to restore and to build Jerusalem unto the Messiah, the Prince, shall be seven weeks and sixty-two weeks. The street shall be built again, and the wall, even in troublous times. And after sixty-two weeks shall Messiah be cut off, but not for himself. And the people of the prince that shall come shall destroy the city and the sanctuary, and the end thereof shall be with a flood; and unto the end of

the war, desolations are determined. And he shall confirm the covenant with many for one week. And in the middle of the week, he shall cause the sacrifice and the offering to cease. And for the overspreading of abominations he shall make it desolate, even until the consummation and that determined shall be poured upon the desolate.

10 In the third year of Cyrus king of Persia, a thing was revealed unto Daniel — whose name was called Belteshazzar — and the thing was true, but the time appointed was long; and he understood the thing, and had understanding of the vision. In those days, I, Daniel, was mourning three full weeks. I ate no pleasant bread, neither came flesh nor wine in my mouth, neither did I anoint myself at all, until three whole weeks were fulfilled.

2 And in the twenty-fourth day of the first month, as I was by the side of the great river which is Hiddekel, then I lifted up my eyes and looked, and behold, a certain man clothed in linen, whose loins were girded with fine gold of Uphaz. His body also was like the beryl, and his face as the appearance of lightning, and his eyes as lamps of fire, and his arms and his feet like in color to polished brass, and the voice of his words like the voice of a multitude. And I, Daniel, alone saw the vision; for the men that were with me saw not the vision, but a great quaking fell upon them, so that they fled to hide themselves. Therefore, I was left alone and saw this great vision. And there remained no strength in me, for my comeliness was turned in me into corruption, and I retained no strength. Yet I heard the voice of his words. And when I heard the voice of his words, then was I in a deep sleep on my face, and my face toward the ground.

3 And behold, a hand touched me, which set me upon my knees and upon the palms of my hands. And he said unto me, O Daniel, a man greatly beloved, understand the words that I speak unto you and stand upright, for unto you am I now sent. And when he had spoken this word unto me, I stood trembling. Then said he unto me, Fear not, Daniel, for from the first day that you did set your heart to understand, and to chasten yourself before your God, your words were heard; and I have come for your words. But the prince of the kingdom of Persia withstood me twenty-one days. But behold, Michael, one of the chief princes, came to help me, and I remained there with the kings of Persia.

Now I have come to make you understand what shall befall your people in the latter days, for yet the vision is for many days.

4 And when he had spoken such words unto me, I set my face toward the ground and I became dumb. And behold, one like the similitude of the sons of men touched my lips. Then I opened my mouth and spoke, and said unto him that stood before me, O my lord, by the vision my sorrows are turned upon me and I have retained no strength. For how can the servant of this my lord talk with this my lord? For as for me, immediately there remained no strength in me, neither is there breath left in me.

5 Then there came again and touched me one like the appearance of a man, and he strengthened me and said, O man greatly beloved, fear not. Peace be unto you; be strong, yea, be strong. And when he had spoken unto me, I was strengthened, and said, Let my lord speak, for you have strengthened me. Then said he, Do you know why I come unto you? And now will I return to fight with the prince of Persia, and when I am gone forth, behold, the prince of Greece shall come. But I will show you that which is noted in the scripture of truth, and there is none that holds with me in these things but Michael, your prince. Also I, in the first year of Darius the Mede, even I stood to confirm and to strengthen him.

6 And now I will show you the truth. Behold, there shall stand up yet three kings in Persia, and the fourth shall be far richer than they all; and by his strength through his riches, he shall stir up all against the realm of Greece. And a mighty king shall stand up that shall rule with great dominion and do according to his will. And when he shall stand up, his kingdom shall be broken, and shall be divided toward the four winds of heaven and not to his posterity, nor according to his dominion which he ruled; for his kingdom shall be plucked up, even for others besides those.

7 And the king of the south shall be strong, and one of his princes — and he shall be strong above him and have dominion; his dominion shall be a great dominion. And in the end of years, they shall join themselves together, for the king's daughter of the south shall come to the king of the north to make an agreement. But she shall not retain the power of the arm, neither shall he stand, nor his arm, but she shall be given up, and they that brought her, and he that begot

her, and he that strengthened her in these times. But out of a branch of her roots shall one stand up in his estate, which shall come with an army and shall enter into the fortress of the king of the north, and shall deal against them, and shall prevail, and shall also carry captives into Egypt — their gods, with their princes, and with their precious vessels of silver and of gold. And he shall continue more years than the king of the north. So the king of the south shall come into his kingdom, and shall return into his own land.

8 But his sons shall be stirred up and shall assemble a multitude of great forces, and one shall certainly come, and overflow, and pass through. Then shall he return and be stirred up, even to his fortress. And the king of the south shall be moved with anger, and shall come forth and fight with him, even with the king of the north; and he shall set forth a great multitude, but the multitude shall be given into his hand. And when he has taken away the multitude, his heart shall be lifted up, and he shall cast down many ten thousands, but he shall not be strengthened by it; for the king of the north shall return and shall set forth a multitude greater than the former, and shall certainly come after certain years with a great army and with much riches.

9 And in those times, there shall many stand up against the king of the south; also the robbers of your people shall exalt themselves to establish the vision, but they shall fall. So the king of the north shall come and cast up a mount, and take the most fortified cities. And the arms of the south shall not withstand, neither his chosen people, neither shall there be any strength to withstand. But he that comes against him shall do according to his own will, and none shall stand before him, and he shall stand in the glorious land which by his hand shall be consumed. He shall also set his face to enter with the strength of his whole kingdom, and upright ones with him. Thus shall he do, and he shall give him the daughter of women, corrupting her; but she shall not stand on his side, neither be for him.

10 After this shall he turn his face unto the isles and shall take many, but a prince for his own behalf shall cause the reproach offered by him to cease; without his own reproach, he shall cause it to turn upon him. Then he shall turn his face toward the fort of his own land, but he shall stumble, and fall, and not be found. Then shall stand up in his estate

a raiser of taxes in the glory of the kingdom, but within few days he shall be destroyed — neither in anger nor in battle.

11 And in his estate shall stand up a vile person, to whom they shall not give the honor of the kingdom, but he shall come in peaceably and obtain the kingdom by flatteries. And with the arms of a flood shall they be overflowed from before him and shall be broken — yea, also the prince of the covenant. And after the league made with him, he shall work deceitfully, for he shall come up and shall become strong with a small people. He shall enter peaceably even upon the fattest places of the province, and he shall do that which his fathers have not done, nor his fathers' fathers: he shall scatter among them the prey, and spoil, and riches; yea, and he shall devise plans against the strongholds, even for a time.

12 And he shall stir up his power and his courage against the king of the south with a great army, and the king of the south shall be stirred up to battle with a very great and mighty army; but he shall not stand, for they shall devise plans against him. Yea, they that feed of the portion of his food shall destroy him, and his army shall overflow, and many shall fall down slain. And both these kings' hearts shall be to do mischief, and they shall speak lies at one table; but it shall not prosper, for yet the end shall be at the time appointed. Then shall he return into his land with great riches, and his heart shall be against the holy covenant, and he shall do exploits and return to his own land.

13 At the time appointed, he shall return and come toward the south, but it shall not be as the former or as the latter, for the ships of Kittim shall come against him. Therefore, he shall be grieved and return, and have indignation against the holy covenant. So shall he do: he shall even return and have intelligence with them that forsake the holy covenant. And arms shall stand on his part, and they shall pollute the sanctuary of strength and shall take away the daily sacrifice, and they shall place the abomination that makes desolate. And such as do wickedly against the covenant shall he corrupt by flatteries, but the people that do know their God shall be strong and do exploits. And they that understand among the people shall instruct many, yet they shall fall by the sword and by flame, by captivity and by spoil, many days.

14 Now when they shall fall, they shall be helped with a little help, but many shall cleave to them with flatteries. And some of them of

understanding shall fall, to try them, and to purge, and to make them white, even to the time of the end, because it is yet for a time appointed.

15 And the king shall do according to his will, and he shall exalt himself and magnify himself above every god, and shall speak marvelous things against the God of gods, and shall prosper until the indignation be accomplished; for that which is determined shall be done. Neither shall he regard the God of his fathers, nor the desire of women, nor regard any god, for he shall magnify himself above all. But in his estate shall he honor the God of forces, and a god whom his fathers knew not shall he honor with gold, and silver, and with precious stones, and pleasant things. Thus shall he do in the most strongholds with a strange god whom he shall acknowledge and increase with glory. And he shall cause them to rule over many, and shall divide the land for gain.

16 And at the time of the end shall the king of the south push at him, and the king of the north shall come against him like a whirlwind, with chariots, and with horsemen, and with many ships. And he shall enter into the countries and shall overflow and pass over. He shall enter also into the glorious land and many countries shall be overthrown, but these shall escape out of his hand — even Edom, and Moab, and the chief of the children of Ammon. He shall stretch forth his hand also upon the countries and the land of Egypt shall not escape, but he shall have power over the treasures of gold and of silver, and over all the precious things of Egypt; and the Libyans and the Ethiopians shall be at his steps.

17 But tidings out of the east and out of the north shall trouble him; therefore, he shall go forth with great fury to destroy, and utterly to make away many. And he shall plant the tabernacles of his palace between the seas in the glorious holy mountain; yet he shall come to his end, and none shall help him.

18 And at that time shall Michael stand up, the great prince who stands for the children of your people. And there shall be a time of trouble, such as never was since there was a nation even to that same time. And at that time, your people shall be delivered, everyone that shall be found written in the book. And many of them that sleep in the dust of the earth shall awake; some to everlasting life, and some to shame and everlasting contempt. And they that are wise shall

shine as the brightness of the firmament, and they that turn many to righteousness as the stars for ever and ever. But you, O Daniel, shut up the words and seal the book, even to the time of the end; many shall run to and fro, and knowledge shall be increased.

¹⁹ Then I, Daniel, looked, and behold, there stood other two — the one on this side of the bank of the river and the other on that side of the bank of the river. And one said to the man clothed in linen — who was upon the waters of the river — How long shall it be to the end of these wonders? And I heard the man clothed in linen who was upon the waters of the river, when he held up his right hand and his left hand unto Heaven, and swore by him that lives for ever that it shall be for a time, times, and a half. And when he shall have accomplished to scatter the power of the holy people, all these things shall be finished.

²⁰ And I heard, but I understood not. Then said I, O my Lord, what shall be the end of these things? And he said, Go your way, Daniel, for the words are closed up and sealed until the time of the end. Many shall be purified, and made white, and tried; but the wicked shall do wickedly. And none of the wicked shall understand, but the wise shall understand. And from the time that the daily sacrifice shall be taken away, and the abomination that makes desolate set up, there shall be a thousand two hundred ninety days. Blessed is he that waits, and comes to the thousand three hundred thirty-five days. But go your way until the end be, for you shall rest, and stand in your lot at the end of the days.

HOSEA

The word of the Lord that came unto Hosea the son of Beeri, in the days of Uzziah, Jotham, Ahaz, and Hezekiah — kings of Judah — and in the days of Jeroboam the son of Joash, king of Israel. The beginning of the word of the Lord by Hosea.

AND the Lord said to Hosea, Go, take unto you a wife of whoredoms and children of whoredoms, for the land has committed great whoredom, departing from the Lord. So he went and took Gomer the daughter of Diblaim, who conceived and bore him a son. And the Lord said unto him, Call his name Jezreel, for yet a little while and I will avenge the blood of Jezreel upon the house of Jehu, and will cause to cease the kingdom of the house of Israel. And it shall come to pass at that day that I will break the bow of Israel in the valley of Jezreel.

2 And she conceived again and bore a daughter. And God said unto him, Call her name Loruhamah, for I will no more have mercy upon the house of Israel, but I will utterly take them away. But I will have mercy upon the house of Judah, and will save them by the Lord their God, and will not save them by bow, nor by sword, nor by battle, by horses, nor by horsemen.

3 Now when she had weaned Loruhamah, she conceived and bore a son. Then said God, Call his name Loammi, for you are not my people, and I will not be your God. Yet the number of the children of Israel shall be as the sand of the sea, which cannot be measured nor numbered. And it shall come to pass that in the place where it was said unto them, You are not my people — there it shall be said unto them, You are the sons of the living God. Then shall the children of Judah and the children of Israel be gathered together and appoint themselves one head, and they shall come up out of the land, for great shall be the day of Jezreel.

4 Say unto your brethren, Ammi — and to your sisters, Ruhamah. Plead with your mother, plead; for she is not my wife, neither am I her husband. Let her therefore put away her whoredoms out of her sight, and her adulteries from between her breasts, lest I strip her naked and set her as in the day that she was born, and make her as a wilderness, and set her like a dry land, and slay her with thirst.

5 And I will not have mercy upon her children, for they are the children of whoredoms; for their mother has played the harlot, she that conceived them has done shamefully, for she said, I will go after my lovers that give me my bread and my water, my wool and my flax, my oil and my drink. Therefore, behold, I will hedge up your way with thorns and make a wall, that she shall not find her paths. And she shall follow after her lovers, but she shall not overtake them; and she shall seek them, but shall not find them.

6 Then shall she say, I will go and return to my first husband, for then was it better with me than now — for she did not know that I gave her grain, and wine, and oil, and multiplied her silver and gold, which they prepared for Baal. Therefore will I return and take away my grain in the time thereof, and my wine in the season thereof, and will recover my wool and my flax given to cover her nakedness. And now will I

reveal her lewdness in the sight of her lovers, and none shall deliver her out of my hand. I will also cause all her mirth to cease; her feast days, her new moons, and her sabbaths, and all her solemn feasts. And I will destroy her vines and her fig trees whereof she has said, These are my rewards that my lovers have given me, and I will make them a forest, and the beasts of the field shall eat them. And I will visit upon her the days of the Baalim wherein she burned incense to them, and she adorned herself with her earrings and her jewels, and she went after her lovers and forgot me, says the Lord.

7 Therefore, behold, I will allure her and bring her into the wilderness, and speak comfortingly unto her. And I will give her her vineyards from there, and the valley of Achor for a door of hope. And she shall sing there, as in the days of her youth and as in the day when she came up out of the land of Egypt.

8 And it shall be at that day, says the Lord, that you shall call me Ishi, and shall call me no more Baali—for I will take away the names of the Baalim out of her mouth, and they shall no more be remembered by their name. And in that day will I make a covenant for them with the beasts of the field, and with the fowls of heaven, and with the creeping things of the ground. And I will break the bow and the sword and the battle out of the earth, and will make them to lie down safely. And I will betroth you unto me for ever; yea, I will betroth you unto me in righteousness, and in judgment, and in loving kindness, and in mercies. I will even betroth you unto me in faithfulness, and you shall know the Lord.

9 And it shall come to pass in that day, I will hear, says the Lord, I will hear the heavens, and they shall hear the earth, and the earth shall hear the grain, and the wine, and the oil, and they shall hear Jezreel. And I will sow her unto me in the earth, and I will have mercy upon her that had not obtained mercy, and I will say to them who were not my people, You are my people—and they shall say, You are my God.

10 Then said the Lord unto me, Go yet, love a woman beloved of her friend, yet an adulteress, according to the love of the Lord toward the children of Israel who look to other gods and love flagons of wine. So I bought her to me for fifteen pieces of silver, and for a homer of barley, and a half homer of barley. And I said unto her, You shall abide for me many days, you shall not play the harlot, and you shall not be

for another man; so will I also be for you. For the children of Israel shall abide many days without a king, and without a prince, and without a sacrifice, and without an image, and without an ephod, and without idols. Afterward shall the children of Israel return and seek the Lord their God, and David their king, and shall fear the Lord and his goodness in the latter days.

2 Hear the word of the Lord, you children of Israel, for the Lord has a controversy with the inhabitants of the land, because there is no truth, nor mercy, nor knowledge of God in the land. By swearing, and lying, and killing, and stealing, and committing adultery they break out, and bloodshed touches bloodshed. Therefore shall the land mourn, and everyone that dwells therein shall languish with the beasts of the field and with the fowls of heaven; yea, the fishes of the sea also shall be taken away. Yet let no man quarrel, nor reprove another, for your people are as they that quarrel with the priest. Therefore shall you fall in the day, and the prophet also shall fall with you in the night, and I will destroy your mother. My people are destroyed for lack of knowledge.

2 Because you have rejected knowledge, I will also reject you, that you shall be no priest to me. Seeing you have forgotten the law of your God, I will also forget your children. As they were increased, so they sinned against me; therefore will I change their glory into shame. They eat up the sin of my people and they set their heart on their iniquity. And there shall be, like people, like priest; and I will punish them for their ways and reward them their doings, for they shall eat and not have enough, they shall commit whoredom and shall not increase, because they have left off to take heed to the Lord. Whoredom and wine and new wine take away the heart. My people ask counsel at their stocks, and their staff declares unto them, for the spirit of whoredoms has caused them to err and they have gone whoring from under their God. They sacrifice upon the tops of the mountains and burn incense upon the hills, under oaks and poplars and elms, because the shadow thereof is good. Therefore, your daughters shall commit whoredom and your spouses shall commit adultery. I will not punish your daughters when they commit whoredom, nor your spouses when they commit adultery, for they themselves are separated with whores and they sacrifice with harlots. Therefore the people that does not understand shall fall.

3 Though you, Israel, play the harlot, yet let not Judah offend; and come not unto Gilgal, neither go up to Bethaven, nor swear, The Lord lives — for Israel slides back as a backsliding heifer. Now the Lord will feed them as a lamb in a large place. Ephraim is joined to idols, let him alone. Their drink is sour, they have committed whoredom continually, her rulers dearly love shame. The wind has bound her up in her wings, and they shall be ashamed because of their sacrifices.

4 Hear this, O priests, and listen, you house of Israel, and give ear, O house of the king; for judgment is toward you because you have been a snare on Mizpah and a net spread upon Tabor. And the revolters are deep in slaughter, though I have been a rebuker of them all. I know Ephraim, and Israel is not hidden from me; for now, O Ephraim, you commit whoredom, and Israel is defiled. They will not frame their doings to turn unto their God, for the spirit of whoredoms is in the midst of them, and they have not known the Lord. And the pride of Israel does testify to his face; therefore shall Israel and Ephraim fall in their iniquity. Judah also shall fall with them. They shall go with their flocks and with their herds to seek the Lord, but they shall not find him; he has withdrawn himself from them. They have dealt treacherously against the Lord, for they have begotten strange children. Now shall a month devour them with their portions.

5 Blow the horn in Gibeah and the trumpet in Ramah; cry aloud at Bethaven, After you, O Benjamin! Ephraim shall be desolate in the day of rebuke. Among the tribes of Israel have I made known that which shall surely be. The princes of Judah were like them that remove the bound; therefore, I will pour out my wrath upon them like water. Ephraim is oppressed and broken in judgment because he willingly walked after the commandment. Therefore will I be unto Ephraim as a moth, and to the house of Judah as rottenness.

6 When Ephraim saw his sickness, and Judah saw his wound, then went Ephraim to the Assyrian and sent to king Jareb; yet could he not heal you, nor cure you of your wound. For I will be unto Ephraim as a lion, and as a young lion to the house of Judah. I, even I, will tear and go away; I will take away and none shall rescue him. I will go and return to my place until they acknowledge their offense and seek my face; in their affliction they will seek me early.

7 Come, and let us return unto the Lord, for he has torn and he will heal us, he has smitten and he will bind us up. After two days will he revive us. In the third day he will raise us up and we shall live in his sight. Then shall we know, if we follow on to know the Lord; his going forth is prepared as the morning, and he shall come unto us as the rain, as the spring and autumn rain unto the earth.

8 O Ephraim, what shall I do unto you? O Judah, what shall I do unto you? For your goodness is as a morning cloud, and as the early dew it goes away. Therefore have I hewn them by the prophets; I have slain them by the words of my mouth, and your judgments are as the light that goes forth. For I desired mercy and not sacrifice, and the knowledge of God more than burnt offerings. But they, like men, have transgressed the covenant; there have they dealt treacherously against me.

9 Gilead is a city of them that work iniquity, and is polluted with blood. And as troops of robbers wait for a man, so the company of priests murder in the way by consent, for they commit lewdness. I have seen a horrible thing in the house of Israel, there is the whoredom of Ephraim; Israel is defiled. Also, O Judah, he has set a harvest for you when I returned the captives of my people.

10 When I would have healed Israel, then the iniquity of Ephraim was uncovered and the wickedness of Samaria; for they commit falsehood, and the thief comes in, and the troop of robbers spoils outside. And they consider not in their hearts that I remember all their wickedness. Now their own doings have beset them about; they are before my face. They make the king glad with their wickedness, and the princes with their lies. They are all adulterers, as an oven heated by the baker who ceases from raising after he has kneaded the dough until it be leavened. In the day of our king, the princes have made him sick with bottles of wine; he stretched out his hand with scorners. For they have made ready their heart like an oven while they lie in wait, their baker sleeps all the night; in the morning, it burns as a flaming fire. They are all hot as an oven and have devoured their judges. All their kings are fallen, there is none among them that calls unto me.

11 Ephraim, he has mixed himself among the people; Ephraim is a cake not turned. Strangers have devoured his strength and he knows it not; yea, gray hairs are here and there upon him, yet he knows not.

And the pride of Israel testifies to his face, and they do not return to the Lord their God, nor seek him for all this.

12 Ephraim also is like a silly dove without heart. They call to Egypt, they go to Assyria. When they shall go, I will spread my net upon them, I will bring them down as the fowls of the heaven, I will chastise them as their congregation has heard. Woe unto them, for they have fled from me; destruction unto them, because they have transgressed against me. Though I have redeemed them, yet they have spoken lies against me, and they have not cried unto me with their heart when they howled upon their beds. They assemble themselves for grain and wine, and they rebel against me. Though I have bound and strengthened their arms, yet do they imagine mischief against me. They return, but not to the Most High; they are like a deceitful bow. Their princes shall fall by the sword for the rage of their tongue; this shall be their derision in the land of Egypt.

13 Set the trumpet to your mouth. He shall come as an eagle against the house of the Lord, because they have transgressed my covenant and trespassed against my law. Israel shall cry unto me, My God, we know you. Israel has cast off the thing that is good; the enemy shall pursue him. They have set up kings, but not by me; they have made princes, and I knew it not; of their silver and their gold have they made them idols, that they may be cut off.

14 Your calf, O Samaria, has cast you off; my anger is kindled against them. How long will it be before they attain to innocence? For from Israel was it also — the workman made it, therefore it is not God. But the calf of Samaria shall be broken in pieces. For they have sown the wind, and they shall reap the whirlwind. It has no stalk, the bud shall yield no meal. If it so be it yield, the strangers shall swallow it up.

15 Israel is swallowed up, now shall they be among the gentiles as a vessel wherein is no pleasure. For they are gone up to Assyria — a wild ass alone by himself. Ephraim has hired lovers. Yea, though they have hired among the nations, now will I gather them, and they shall sorrow a little for the burden of the king of princes. Because Ephraim has made many altars to sin, altars shall be unto him to sin.

16 I have written to him the great things of my law, but they were counted as a strange thing. They sacrifice flesh for the sacrifices of my offerings, and eat it; but the Lord accepts them not. Now will he

remember their iniquity and visit their sins. They shall return to Egypt. For Israel has forgotten his Maker and builds temples, and Judah has multiplied fortified cities; but I will send a fire upon his cities, and it shall devour the palaces thereof.

17 Rejoice not, O Israel, for joy as other people; for you have gone whoring from your God, you have loved a reward upon every grain floor. The floor and the winepress shall not feed them, and the new wine shall fail in her. They shall not dwell in the Lord's land, but Ephraim shall return to Egypt and they shall eat unclean things in Assyria. They shall not offer wine offerings to the Lord, neither shall they be pleasing unto him. Their sacrifices shall be unto them as the bread of mourners. All that eat thereof shall be polluted, for their bread for their soul shall not come into the house of the Lord.

18 What will you do in the solemn day, and in the day of the feast of the Lord? For behold, they are gone because of destruction. Egypt shall gather them up, Memphis shall bury them. The pleasant places for their silver — nettles shall possess them, thorns shall be in their tabernacles.

19 The days of visitation have come, the days of recompense have come. Israel shall know it. The prophet is a fool, the spiritual man is mad, for the multitude of your iniquity and the great hatred. The watchman of Ephraim was with my God, but the prophet is a snare of a fowler in all his ways, and hatred in the house of his God. They have deeply corrupted themselves, as in the days of Gibeah; therefore, he will remember their iniquity, he will visit their sins.

20 I found Israel like grapes in the wilderness, I saw your fathers as the first ripe in the fig tree at her first time. But they went to Baal-Peor and separated themselves unto that shame, and their abominations were according as they loved.

21 As for Ephraim, their glory shall fly away like a bird — from the birth, and from the womb, and from the conception. Though they bring up their children, yet will I bereave them, that there shall not be a man left. Yea, woe also to them when I depart from them. Ephraim, as I saw Tyre, is planted in a pleasant place; but Ephraim shall bring forth his children to the murderer.

22 Give them, O Lord — what will you give? Give them a miscarrying womb and dry breasts. All their wickedness is in Gilgal, for there I hated them. For the wickedness of their doings I will drive them out

of my house, I will love them no more; all their princes are revolters.
Ephraim is smitten, their root is dried up, they shall bear no fruit; yea,
though they bring forth, yet will I slay even the beloved fruit of their
womb. My God will cast them away because they did not listen unto
him, and they shall be wanderers among the nations.

23 Israel is an empty vine, he brings forth fruit unto himself;
according to the multitude of his fruit he has increased the altars,
according to the goodness of his land they have made goodly images.
Their heart is divided, now shall they be found faulty. He shall break
down their altars, he shall spoil their images. For now they shall say,
We have no king because we feared not the Lord; what then should a
king do to us? They have spoken words, swearing falsely in making
a covenant; thus, judgment springs up as hemlock in the furrows of
the field.

24 The inhabitants of Samaria shall fear because of the calves of
Bethaven, for the people thereof shall mourn over it, and the priests
thereof that rejoiced on it, for the glory thereof, because it is departed
from it. It shall be also carried unto Assyria for a present to king Jareb.

25 Ephraim shall receive shame, and Israel shall be ashamed of his
own counsel. As for Samaria, her king is cut off as the foam upon the
water. The high places also of Aven, the sin of Israel, shall be destroyed.
The thorn and the thistle shall come up on their altars, and they shall
say to the mountains, Cover us — and to the hills, Fall on us.

26 O Israel, you have sinned from the days of Gibeah. There they
stood; the battle in Gibeah against the children of iniquity did not
overtake them. It is in my desire that I should chastise them, and the
people shall be gathered against them when they shall bind themselves
in their two furrows. And Ephraim is as a heifer that is taught and loves
to tread out the grain, but I passed over upon her fair neck. I will make
Ephraim to ride; Judah shall plow, and Jacob shall break his clods.

27 Sow to yourselves in righteousness, reap in mercy, break up your
fallow ground, for it is time to seek the Lord until he come and rain
righteousness upon you. You have plowed wickedness, you have reaped
iniquity, you have eaten the fruit of lies because you did trust in your
way, in the multitude of your mighty men. Therefore shall a tumult
arise among your people and all your fortresses shall be spoiled, as
Shalman spoiled Betharbel in the day of battle — the mother was dashed

in pieces upon her children. So shall Beth-el do unto you because of your great wickedness. In a morning shall the king of Israel utterly be cut off.

28 When Israel was a child, then I loved him, and called my son out of Egypt. As they called them, so they went from them. They sacrificed unto the Baalim, and burned incense to engraved images. I taught Ephraim also to go, taking them by their arms, but they knew not that I healed them. I drew them with cords of a man, with bands of love, and I was to them as they that take off the yoke on their jaws, and I laid food unto them.

29 He shall not return into the land of Egypt, but the Assyrian shall be his king, because they refused to return. And the sword shall abide on his cities, and shall consume his branches, and devour them because of their own counsels. And my people are bent to backsliding from me. Though they called them to the Most High, none at all would exalt him.

30 How shall I give you up, Ephraim? How shall I deliver you, Israel? How shall I make you as Admah? How shall I set you as Zeboiim? My heart is turned toward you and my mercies are extended to gather you. I will not execute the fierceness of my anger, I will not return to destroy Ephraim, for I am God and not man — the Holy One in your midst — and I will enter into the city. They shall walk after the Lord, he shall roar like a lion. When he shall roar, then the children shall tremble from the west. They shall tremble as a bird out of Egypt and as a dove out of the land of Assyria. And I will place them in their houses, says the Lord. Ephraim encompasses me about with lies, and the house of Israel with deceit, but Judah yet rules with God and is faithful with the saints. Ephraim feeds on wind and follows after the east wind, he daily increases lies and desolation. And they do make a covenant with the Assyrians, and oil is carried into Egypt.

31 The Lord has also a controversy with Judah, and will punish Jacob according to his ways; according to his doings will he recompense him. He took his brother by the heel in the womb, and by his strength he had power with God. Yea, he had power over the angel and prevailed, he wept and made supplication unto him. He found him in Beth-el, and there he spoke with us, even the Lord God of Hosts; the Lord is his memorial. Therefore, turn to your God, keep mercy and judgment, and wait on your God continually.

³² He is a merchant, the balances of deceit are in his hand, he loves to oppress. And Ephraim said, Yet I have become rich, I have found me out substance, in all my labors they shall find no iniquity in me that were sin. And I that am the Lord your God from the land of Egypt will yet make you to dwell in tabernacles, as in the days of the solemn feast. I have also spoken by the prophets, and I have multiplied visions, and used similitudes by the ministry of the prophets.

³³ Is there iniquity in Gilead? Surely they are vanity. They sacrifice bullocks in Gilgal, yea, their altars are as heaps in the furrows of the fields. And Jacob fled into the country of Syria, and Israel served for a wife, and for a wife he kept sheep. And by a prophet the Lord brought Israel out of Egypt, and by a prophet was he preserved.

³⁴ Ephraim provoked him to anger most bitterly, therefore shall he leave his blood upon him, and his reproach shall his Lord return unto him. When Ephraim spoke trembling, he exalted himself in Israel; but when he offended in Baal, he died. And now they sin more and more, and have made themselves molten images of their silver, and idols according to their own understanding — all of it the work of the craftsmen. They say of them, Let the men that sacrifice kiss the calves. Therefore, they shall be as the morning cloud, and as the early dew that passes away, as the chaff that is driven with the whirlwind out of the floor, and as the smoke out of the chimney.

³⁵ Yet I am the Lord your God from the land of Egypt, and you shall know no god but me, for there is no savior besides me. I did know you in the wilderness, in the land of great drought. According to their pasture, so were they filled. They were filled and their heart was exalted, therefore they have forgotten me. Therefore, I will be unto them as a lion, as a leopard by the way will I observe them. I will meet them as a bear that is bereaved of her whelps, and will rend the casing of their heart, and there will I devour them like a lion; the wild beast shall tear them.

³⁶ O Israel, you have destroyed yourself, but in me is your help. I will be your king. Where is any other that may save you in all your cities, and your judges of whom you said, Give me a king and princes? I gave you a king in my anger, and took him away in my wrath.

³⁷ The iniquity of Ephraim is bound up, his sin is hidden. The sorrows of a travailing woman shall come upon him. He is an unwise

son, for he should not stay long in the place of the breaking forth of children. I will ransom them from the power of the grave, I will redeem them from death.

38 O death, I will be your plagues; O grave, I will be your destruction. Repentance shall be hidden from my eyes. Though he is fruitful among his brethren, an east wind shall come, the wind of the Lord shall come up from the wilderness, and his spring shall become dry, and his fountain shall be dried up. He shall spoil the treasure of all pleasant vessels. Samaria shall become desolate, for she has rebelled against her God. They shall fall by the sword, their infants shall be dashed in pieces, and their women with child shall be ripped up.

39 O Israel, return unto the Lord your God, for you have fallen by your iniquity. Take with you words and turn to the Lord; say unto him, Take away all iniquity and receive us graciously, so will we render the calves of our lips. Assyria shall not save us, we will not ride upon horses, neither will we say anymore to the work of our hands, You are our gods—for in you the fatherless finds mercy.

40 I will heal their backsliding, I will love them freely, for my anger is turned away from him. I will be as the dew unto Israel, he shall grow as the lily, and cast forth his roots as Lebanon. His branches shall spread, and his beauty shall be as the olive tree, and his smell as Lebanon. They that dwell under his shadow shall return, they shall revive as the grain and grow as the vine. The scent thereof shall be as the wine of Lebanon. Ephraim shall say, What have I to do anymore with idols? I have heard him, and observed him; I am like a green fir tree. From me is your fruit found. Who is wise, and he shall understand these things, prudent, and he shall know them? For the ways of the Lord are right and the just shall walk in them, but the transgressors shall fall therein.

JOEL

The word of the Lord that came to Joel the son of Pethuel.

HEAR this, you old men, and give ear, all you inhabitants of the land. Has this been in your days, or even in the days of your fathers? Tell your children of it, and let your children tell their children, and their children another generation. That which the palmerworm has left has the locust eaten, and that which the locust has left has the cankerworm eaten, and that which the cankerworm has left has the caterpillar eaten.

2 Awake, you drunkards, and weep and howl, all you drinkers of wine, because of the new wine; for it is cut off from your mouth. For a nation has come up upon my land, strong and without number, whose teeth are as the teeth of a lion, and he has the fangs of a great lion. He has laid my vine waste and barked my fig tree; he has stripped it bare and cast it away; the branches thereof are made white.

3 Lament like a virgin girded with sackcloth for the husband of her youth. The meal offering and the drink offering is cut off from the house of the Lord; the priests, the Lord's ministers, mourn. The field is wasted, the land mourns, for the grain is wasted. The new wine is dried up, the oil languishes. Be ashamed, O you husbandmen, howl, O you vinedressers, for the wheat and for the barley; because the harvest of the field is perished, the vine is dried up and the fig tree languishes; the pomegranate tree, the palm tree also, and the apple tree — even all the trees of the field are withered, because joy is withered away from the sons of men.

4 Gird yourselves and lament, you priests; howl, you ministers of the altar. Come, lie all night in sackcloth, you ministers of my God, for the meal offering and the drink offering is withheld from the house of your God. Sanctify a fast, call a solemn assembly, gather the elders and all the inhabitants of the land into the house of the Lord your God, and cry unto the Lord, Alas for the day, for the day of the Lord is at hand, and as a destruction from the Almighty shall it come! Is not the food cut off before our eyes? Yea, joy and gladness from the house of our God?

5 The seed is rotten under their clods, the stores are laid desolate, the barns are broken down, for the grain is withered. How do the beasts groan! The herds of cattle are perplexed because they have no pasture; yea, the flocks of sheep are made desolate. O Lord, to you will I cry, for the fire has devoured the pastures of the wilderness, and the flame has burned all the trees of the field. The beasts of the field cry also unto you, for the rivers of waters are dried up, and the fire has devoured the pastures of the wilderness.

6 Blow the trumpet in Zion, and sound an alarm in my holy mountain. Let all the inhabitants of the land tremble, for the day

of the Lord comes, for it is near at hand — a day of darkness and of gloominess, a day of clouds and of thick darkness.

7 As the morning spread upon the mountains, a great people, and a strong — there has not been ever the like, neither shall be anymore after it, even to the years of many generations. A fire devours before them, and behind them a flame burns; the land is as the Garden of Eden before them, and behind them a desolate wilderness. Yea, and nothing shall escape them. The appearance of them is as the appearance of horses, and as horsemen, so shall they run. Like the noise of chariots on the tops of mountains shall they leap, like the noise of a flame of fire that devours the stubble, as a strong people set in battle array. Before their face the people shall be much pained; all faces shall gather blackness. They shall run like mighty men, they shall climb the wall like men of war, and they shall march everyone on his ways, and they shall not break their ranks. Neither shall one thrust another, they shall walk everyone in his path; and when they fall upon the sword, they shall not be wounded. They shall run to and fro in the city, they shall run upon the wall, they shall climb up upon the houses, they shall enter in at the windows like a thief. The earth shall quake before them, the heavens shall tremble. The sun and the moon shall be dark, and the stars shall withdraw their shining. And the Lord shall utter his voice before his army, for his camp is very great, for he is strong that executes his word. For the day of the Lord is great and very terrible, and who can endure it?

8 Therefore also now, says the Lord, turn even to me with all your heart, and with fasting, and with weeping, and with mourning; and rend your heart and not your garments, and repent and turn unto the Lord your God, for he is gracious and merciful, slow to anger and of great kindness, and he will turn away the evil from you. Therefore, repent, and who knows but he will return and leave a blessing behind him, that you may offer a meal offering and a drink offering unto the Lord your God?

9 Blow the trumpet in Zion, sanctify a fast, call a solemn assembly, gather the people, sanctify the congregation, assemble the elders, gather the children and those that suck the breasts. Let the bridegroom go forth of his chamber, and the bride out of her closet. Let the priests, the ministers of the Lord, weep between the porch and the altar, and

let them say, Spare your people, O Lord, and give not your heritage to reproach, that the heathen should rule over them. Why should they say among the people, Where is their God?

¹⁰ Then will the Lord be jealous for his land, and pity his people. Yea, the Lord will answer and say unto his people, Behold, I will send you grain, and wine, and oil, and you shall be satisfied with them. And I will no more make you a reproach among the heathen, but I will remove far off from you the northern army, and will drive him into a land barren and desolate, with his face toward the east sea and his rear part toward the utmost sea; and his stink shall come up, and his ill savor shall come up — because he has done great things.

¹¹ Fear not, O land, be glad and rejoice, for the Lord will do great things. Be not afraid, you beasts of the field, for the pastures of the wilderness do spring, for the tree bears her fruit, the fig tree and the vine do yield their strength. Be glad then, you children of Zion, and rejoice in the Lord your God, for he has given you the autumn rain moderately, and he will cause to come down for you the rain, the autumn rain and the spring rain in the first month. And the floors shall be full of wheat, and the vats shall overflow with wine and oil. And I will restore to you the years that the locust has eaten, the cankerworm, and the caterpillar, and the palmerworm, my great army which I sent among you. And you shall eat in plenty and be satisfied, and praise the name of the Lord your God that has dealt wondrously with you; and my people shall never be ashamed. And you shall know that I am in the midst of Israel, and that I am the Lord your God, and none else; and my people shall never be ashamed.

¹² And it shall come to pass afterward that I will pour out my spirit upon all flesh, and your sons and your daughters shall prophesy, your old men shall dream dreams, your young men shall see visions. And also upon the servants and upon the handmaids in those days will I pour out my spirit. And I will show wonders in the heavens and in the earth — blood, and fire, and pillars of smoke. The sun shall be turned into darkness and the moon into blood before the great and the terrible day of the Lord come. And it shall come to pass that whoever shall call on the name of the Lord shall be delivered, for in Mount Zion and in Jerusalem shall be deliverance, as the Lord has said, and in the remnant whom the Lord shall call.

¹³ For behold, in those days and in that time, when I shall bring again the captives of Judah and Jerusalem, I will also gather all nations and will bring them down into the valley of Jehoshaphat, and will plead with them there, for my people and for my heritage Israel, whom they have scattered among the nations and parted my land. And they have cast lots for my people, and have given a boy for a harlot, and sold a girl for wine that they might drink. Yea, and what have you to do with me, O Tyre and Sidon, and all the borders of Palestine? Will you render me a recompense? And if you recompense me, swiftly and speedily will I return your recompense upon your own head, because you have taken my silver and my gold, and have carried into your temples my goodly pleasant things. The children also of Judah and the children of Jerusalem have you sold unto the Greeks, that you might remove them far from their border. Behold, I will rouse them out of the place where you have sold them and will return your recompense upon your own head. And I will sell your sons and your daughters into the hand of the children of Judah, and they shall sell them to the Sabeans, to a people far off, for the Lord has spoken it.

¹⁴ Proclaim this among the gentiles: Prepare war, wake up the mighty men, let all the men of war draw near, let them come up. Beat your plowshares into swords and your pruning hooks into spears, let the weak say, I am strong. Assemble yourselves and come, all you heathen, and gather yourselves together round about.

¹⁵ There cause your mighty ones to come down, O Lord. Let the heathen be wakened and come up to the valley of Jehoshaphat, for there will I sit to judge all the heathen round about. Put in the sickle, for the harvest is ripe. Come, go down, for the press is full, the vats overflow, for their wickedness is great. Multitudes, multitudes in the valley of decision, for the day of the Lord is near in the valley of decision. The sun and the moon shall be darkened, and the stars shall withdraw their shining. The Lord also shall roar out of Zion and utter his voice from Jerusalem, and the heavens and the earth shall shake; but the Lord will be the hope of his people and the strength of the children of Israel.

¹⁶ So shall you know that I am the Lord your God dwelling in Zion, my holy mountain. Then shall Jerusalem be holy, and there shall no strangers pass through her anymore. And it shall come to pass in that

day that the mountains shall drop down new wine, and the hills shall flow with milk, and all the rivers of Judah shall flow with waters, and a fountain shall come forth of the house of the Lord and shall water the valley of Shittim. Egypt shall be a desolation, and Edom shall be a desolate wilderness for the violence against the children of Judah, because they have shed innocent blood in their land. But Judah shall dwell for ever, and Jerusalem from generation to generation, for I will cleanse their blood that I have not cleansed; for the Lord dwells in Zion.

AMOS

The words of Amos, who was among the herdsmen of Tekoa, which he saw concerning Israel in the days of Uzziah king of Judah, and in the days of Jeroboam the son of Joash, king of Israel, two years before the earthquake.

AND he said, The Lord will roar from Zion and utter his voice from Jerusalem, and the habitations of the shepherds shall mourn and the top of Carmel shall wither. Thus says the Lord: For three transgressions of Damascus and for four, I will not turn away the punishment thereof, because they have threshed Gilead with threshing instruments of iron. But I will send a fire into the house of Hazael which shall devour the palaces of Benhadad. I will break also the bar of Damascus and cut off the inhabitant from the plain of Aven, and him that holds the scepter from the house of Eden. And the people of Syria shall go into captivity unto Kir, says the Lord.

2 Thus says the Lord: For three transgressions of Gaza and for four, I will not turn away the punishment thereof, because they carried away captive the whole captivity to deliver them up to Edom. But I will send a fire on the wall of Gaza, which shall devour the palaces thereof. And I will cut off the inhabitant from Ashdod, and him that holds the scepter from Ashkelon. And I will turn my hand against Ekron, and the remnant of the Philistines shall perish, says the Lord God.

3 Thus says the Lord: For three transgressions of Tyre and for four, I will not turn away the punishment thereof, because they delivered up the whole captivity to Edom and remembered not the brotherly covenant. But I will send a fire on the wall of Tyre which shall devour the palaces thereof.

⁴ Thus says the Lord: For three transgressions of Edom and for four, I will not turn away the punishment thereof, because he did pursue his brother with the sword and did cast off all pity. And his anger did tear perpetually, and he kept his wrath for ever. But I will send a fire upon Teman, which shall devour the palaces of Bozrah.

⁵ Thus says the Lord: For three transgressions of the children of Ammon and for four, I will not turn away the punishment thereof, because they have ripped up the women with child of Gilead, that they might enlarge their border. But I will kindle a fire in the wall of Rabbah, and it shall devour the palaces thereof with shouting in the day of battle, with a tempest in the day of the whirlwind. And their king shall go into captivity, he and his princes together, says the Lord.

⁶ Thus says the Lord: For three transgressions of Moab and for four, I will not turn away the punishment thereof, because he burned the bones of the king of Edom into lime. But I will send a fire upon Moab, and it shall devour the palaces of Kerioth. And Moab shall die with tumult, with shouting, and with the sound of the trumpet. And I will cut off the judge from the midst thereof and will slay all the princes thereof with him, says the Lord.

⁷ Thus says the Lord: For three transgressions of Judah and for four, I will not turn away the punishment thereof, because they have despised the law of the Lord and have not kept his commandments, and their lies caused them to err, after which their fathers have walked. But I will send a fire upon Judah, and it shall devour the palaces of Jerusalem.

⁸ Thus says the Lord: For three transgressions of Israel and for four, I will not turn away the punishment thereof, because they sold the righteous for silver and the poor for a pair of shoes, that pant after the dust of the earth on the head of the poor, and turn aside the way of the meek. And a man and his father will go in unto the same maid to profane my holy name, and they lay themselves down upon clothes laid to pledge by every altar. And they drink the wine of the condemned in the house of their god. Yet destroyed I the Amorite before them, whose height was like the height of the cedars, and he was strong as the oaks. Yet I destroyed his fruit from above and his roots from beneath. Also, I brought you up from the land of Egypt and led you forty years through the wilderness to possess the land of the Amorite. And I raised up of your sons for prophets and of your young men

for Nazarites. Is it not even thus, O you children of Israel? — says the Lord. But you gave the Nazarites wine to drink, and commanded the prophets, saying, Prophesy not. Behold, I am pressed under you as a cart is pressed that is full of sheaves. Therefore, the flight shall perish from the swift, and the strong shall not strengthen his force. Neither shall the mighty deliver himself, neither shall he stand that handles the bow. And he that is swift of foot shall not deliver himself, neither shall he that rides the horse deliver himself. And he that is courageous among the mighty shall flee away naked in that day, says the Lord.

⁹ Hear this word that the Lord has spoken against you, O children of Israel, against the whole family which I brought up from the land of Egypt, saying, You only have I known of all the families of the earth, therefore I will punish you for all your iniquities. Can two walk together except they are agreed? Will a lion roar in the forest when he has no prey? Will a young lion cry out of his den if he has taken nothing? Can a bird fall in a snare upon the earth where no trap is for him? Shall one take up a snare from the earth and have taken nothing at all? Shall a trumpet be blown in the city and the people not be afraid? Shall there be evil in a city and the Lord has not known it? Surely the Lord God will do nothing until he reveals the secret unto his servants the prophets. The lion has roared. Who will not fear? The Lord God has spoken. Who can but prophesy?

¹⁰ Publish in the palaces at Ashdod and in the palaces in the land of Egypt, and say, Assemble yourselves upon the mountains of Samaria, and behold the great tumults in the midst thereof, and the oppressed in the midst thereof. For they know not to do right, says the Lord, who store up violence and robbery in their palaces. Therefore, thus says the Lord God: An adversary there shall be even round about the land, and he shall bring down your strength from you, and your palaces shall be spoiled. Thus says the Lord: As the shepherd takes out of the mouth of the lion two legs or a piece of an ear, so shall the children of Israel be taken out that dwell in Samaria in the corner of a bed and in Damascus in a couch. Hear and testify in the house of Jacob, says the Lord God, the God of Hosts, that in the day that I shall visit the transgressions of Israel upon him, I will also visit the altars of Beth-el. And the horns of the altar shall be cut off and fall to the ground. And I will smite the

winter house with the summer house. And the houses of ivory shall perish, and the great houses shall have an end, says the Lord.

11 Hear this word, you cattle of Bashan that are in the mountain of Samaria, which oppress the poor, which crush the needy, which say to their masters, Bring and let us drink. The Lord God has sworn by his holiness that, behold, the days shall come upon you that he will take you away with hooks, and your posterity with fishhooks. And you shall go out at the breaches, everyone before his enemy, and you shall be cast out of your palaces, says the Lord.

12 Come to Beth-el and transgress; at Gilgal multiply transgression. And bring your sacrifices every morning, and your tithes after three years, and offer a sacrifice of thanksgiving with leaven, and proclaim and publish the free offerings. For thus do you, O you children of Israel, says the Lord God. Therefore, I also have given you cleanness of teeth in all your cities and lack of bread in all your places. Yet have you not returned unto me, says the Lord. And also I have withheld the rain from you when there were yet three months to the harvest. And I caused it to rain upon one city and caused it not to rain upon another city. One piece was rained upon, and the piece whereupon it rained not withered. So two or three cities wandered unto one city to drink water, but they were not satisfied. Yet have you not returned unto me, says the Lord. I have smitten you with blasting and mildew. When your gardens, and your vineyards, and your fig trees, and your olive trees increased, the palmerworm devoured them. Yet have you not returned unto me, says the Lord. I have sent among you the pestilence after the manner of Egypt. Your young men have I slain with the sword and have taken away your horses. And I have made the stink of your camps to come up unto your nostrils. Yet have you not returned unto me, says the Lord. I have overthrown some of you, as God overthrew Sodom and Gomorrah, and you were as a firebrand plucked out of the burning. Yet have you not returned unto me, says the Lord. Therefore, thus will I do unto you, O Israel, and because I will do this unto you, prepare to meet your God, O Israel. For behold, he that forms the mountains, and creates the wind, and declares unto man what is his thought, that makes the morning darkness, and treads upon the high places of the earth — The Lord, the God of Hosts, is his name.

¹³ Hear this word which I take up against you, even a lamentation, O house of Israel. The virgin of Israel is fallen, she shall no more rise. He is forsaken upon her land, there is none to raise her up. For thus says the Lord God: The city that went out by a thousand shall leave a hundred, and that which went forth by a hundred shall leave ten to the house of Israel.

¹⁴ For thus says the Lord unto the house of Israel: Seek me, and you shall live. But seek not Beth-el, nor enter into Gilgal, and pass not to Beersheba. For Gilgal shall surely go into captivity, and Beth-el shall come to naught. Seek the Lord and you shall live, lest he break out like fire in the house of Joseph and devour it, and there be none to quench it in Beth-el. You who turn judgment to wormwood and leave off righteousness in the earth, seek him that makes the seven stars and Orion, and turns the shadow of death into the morning, and makes the day dark with night, that calls for the waters of the sea, and pours them out upon the face of the earth. The Lord is his name that strengthens the spoiled against the strong, so that the spoiled shall come against the fortress. They hate him that rebukes in the gate and they abhor him that speaks uprightly. Forasmuch therefore as your treading is upon the poor and you take from him burdens of wheat, you have built houses of hewn stone, but you shall not dwell in them. You have planted pleasant vineyards, but you shall not drink wine of them. For I know your various transgressions and your mighty sins. They afflict the just, they take a bribe, and they turn aside the poor in the gate from their right. Therefore, the prudent shall keep silence in that time, for it is an evil time. Seek good and not evil, that you may live. And so the Lord, the God of Hosts, shall be with you as you have spoken. Hate the evil, and love the good, and establish judgment in the gate. It may be that the Lord God of Hosts will be gracious unto the remnant of Joseph.

¹⁵ Therefore, the Lord, the God of Hosts, the Lord says thus: Wailing shall be in all streets, and they shall say in all the highways, Alas, alas. And they shall call the husbandman to mourning, and such as are skillful of lamentation to wailing. And in all vineyards shall be wailing, for I will pass through you, says the Lord. Woe unto you that desire the day of the Lord. To what end is it for you? The day of the Lord is darkness and not light, as if a man did flee from a lion and a bear met

him, or went into the house and leaned his hand on the wall and a serpent bit him. Shall not the day of the Lord be darkness and not light? Even very dark and no brightness in it?

¹⁶ I hate, I despise your feast days, and I will not smell in your solemn assemblies. Though you offer me burnt offerings and your meal offerings, I will not accept them, neither will I regard the peace offerings of your fat beasts. Take away from me the noise of your songs, for I will not hear the melody of your viols. But let judgment run down as waters, and righteousness as a mighty stream. Have you offered unto me sacrifices and offerings in the wilderness forty years, O house of Israel? But you have borne the tabernacle of your Moloch and Chiun your images, the star of your god, which you made to yourselves. Therefore will I cause you to go into captivity beyond Damascus, says the Lord, whose name is The God of Hosts.

¹⁷ Woe to them that are at ease in Zion and trust in the mountain of Samaria, which are named chief of the nations, to whom the house of Israel came. Pass unto Calneh and see; and from there go to Hamath the great. Then go down to Gath of the Philistines. Are they better than these kingdoms? Or their border greater than your border? You that put far away the evil day and cause the seat of violence to come near, that lie upon beds of ivory, and stretch themselves upon their couches, and eat the lambs out of the flock and the calves out of the midst of the stall, that chant to the sound of the viol and invent to themselves instruments of music like David, that drink wine in bowls and anoint themselves with the chief ointments. But they are not grieved for the affliction of Joseph.

¹⁸ Therefore, now shall they go captive with the first that go captive, and the banquet of them that stretched themselves shall be removed. The Lord God has sworn by himself, says the Lord the God of Hosts, I abhor the excellence of Jacob and hate his palaces; therefore will I deliver up the city with all that is therein. And it shall come to pass, if there remain ten men in one house, that they shall die. And a man's uncle shall take him up, and he that burns him, to bring out the bones out of the house, and shall say unto him that is by the sides of the house, Is there yet any with you? And he shall say, No. Then shall he say, Hold your tongue, for we may not make mention of the name of

the Lord. For behold, the Lord commands and he will smite the great house with breaches and the little house with clefts.

19 Shall horses run upon the rock? Will one plow there with oxen? For you have turned judgment into gall, and the fruit of righteousness into hemlock. You who rejoice in a thing of naught, who say, Have we not taken to us horns by our own strength? But behold, I will raise up against you a nation, O house of Israel, says the Lord the God of Hosts, and they shall afflict you from the entering in of Hamath unto the river of the wilderness.

20 Thus has the Lord God showed unto me: and behold, he formed grasshoppers in the beginning of the shooting up of the latter growth, and behold, it was the latter growth after the king's mowings. And it came to pass that when they had made an end of eating the grass of the land, then I said, O Lord God, forgive, I implore you. By whom shall Jacob arise? For he is small. And the Lord said concerning Jacob, Jacob shall repent for this; therefore, I will not utterly destroy him, says the Lord.

21 Thus has the Lord God showed unto me: and behold, the Lord God called to contend by fire, and it devoured the great deep and did eat up a part. Then said I, O Lord God, cease, I implore you. By whom shall Jacob arise? For he is small. And the Lord said concerning Jacob, Jacob shall repent of his wickedness; therefore, I will not utterly destroy him, says the Lord God.

22 Thus he showed me: and behold, the Lord stood upon a wall made by a plumbline, with a plumbline in his hand. And the Lord said unto me, Amos, what do you see? And I said, A plumbline. Then said the Lord, Behold, I will set a plumbline in the midst of my people Israel. I will not again pass by them anymore. And the high places of Isaac shall be desolate, and the sanctuaries of Israel shall be laid waste. And I will rise against the house of Jeroboam with the sword.

23 Then Amaziah the priest of Beth-el sent to Jeroboam king of Israel, saying, Amos has conspired against you in the midst of the house of Israel. The land is not able to bear all his words. For thus Amos says: Jeroboam shall die by the sword, and Israel shall surely be led away captive out of their own land.

24 Also, Amaziah said unto Amos, O you seer, go, flee away into the land of Judah, and there eat bread, and prophesy there. But prophesy

not again anymore at Beth-el, for it is the king's chapel and it is the king's court. Then answered Amos, and said to Amaziah, I was no prophet, neither was I a prophet's son, but I was a herdsman and a gatherer of sycamore fruit. And the Lord took me as I followed the flock, and the Lord said unto me, Go prophesy unto my people Israel. Now therefore hear the word of the Lord. You say, Prophesy not against Israel, and drop not your word against the house of Isaac. Therefore, thus says the Lord: Your wife shall be a harlot in the city, and your sons and your daughters shall fall by the sword. And your land shall be divided by line, and you shall die in a polluted land. And Israel shall surely go into captivity out of his land.

25 Thus has the Lord God showed unto me: and behold, a basket of summer fruit. And he said, Amos, what do you see? And I said, A basket of summer fruit. Then said the Lord unto me, The end has come upon my people of Israel. I will not again pass by them anymore. And the songs of the temple shall be howlings in that day, says the Lord God. There shall be many dead bodies in every place. They shall cast them forth with silence.

26 Hear this, O you that swallow up the needy, even to make the poor of the land to fail, saying, When will the new moon be gone, that we may sell grain? And the Sabbath, that we may set forth wheat? — making the ephah small and the shekel great, and falsifying the balances by deceit, that we may buy the poor for silver and the needy for a pair of shoes, yea, and sell the refuse of the wheat. The Lord has sworn by the excellence of Jacob, Surely I will never forget any of their works. Shall not the land tremble for this, and everyone mourn that dwells therein? And it shall rise up wholly as a flood, and it shall be cast out and drowned, as by the flood of Egypt. And it shall come to pass in that day, says the Lord God, that I will cause the sun to go down at noon, and I will darken the earth in the clear day. And I will turn your feasts into mourning and all your songs into lamentation. And I will bring up sackcloth upon all loins and baldness upon every head. And I will make it as the mourning of an only son, and the end thereof as a bitter day.

27 Behold, the days come, says the Lord God, that I will send a famine in the land — not a famine of bread, nor a thirst for water, but of hearing the words of the Lord. And they shall wander from sea to sea, and from

the north even to the east. They shall run to and fro to seek the word of the Lord and shall not find it. In that day shall the fair virgins and young men faint for thirst; they that swear by the sin of Samaria and say, Your god, O Dan, lives — and, The manner of Beersheba lives — even they shall fall and never rise up again.

28 I saw the Lord standing upon the altar, and he said, Smite the lintel of the door, that the doorposts may shake, and cut them in the head, all of them. And I will slay the last of them with the sword. He that flees of them shall not flee away, and he that escapes of them shall not be delivered. Though they dig into hell, from there shall my hand take them. Though they climb up to Heaven, from there will I bring them down. And though they hide themselves in the top of Carmel, I will search and take them out from there. And though they be hidden from my sight in the bottom of the sea, from there will I command the serpent, and he shall bite them. And though they go into captivity before their enemies, from there will I command the sword and it shall slay them. And I will set my eyes upon them for evil and not for good.

29 And the Lord God of Hosts is he that touches the land and it shall melt, and all that dwell therein shall mourn. And it shall rise up wholly like a flood and shall be drowned, as by the flood of Egypt. It is he that builds his stories in the heaven and has founded his troop in the earth, he that calls for the waters of the sea and pours them out upon the face of the earth. The Lord is his name.

30 Are you not as children of the Ethiopians unto me, O children of Israel? — says the Lord. Have not I brought up Israel out of the land of Egypt? And the Philistines from Caphtor? And the Syrians from Kir? Behold, the eyes of the Lord God are upon the sinful kingdom, and I will destroy it from off the face of the earth — saving that I will not utterly destroy the house of Jacob, says the Lord. For behold, I will command, and I will sift the house of Israel among all nations like grain is sifted in a sieve. Yet shall not the least grain fall upon the earth. All the sinners of my people shall die by the sword who say, The evil shall not overtake nor prevent us.

31 In that day will I raise up the tabernacle of David that is fallen and close up the breaches thereof. And I will raise up his ruins, and I will build it as in the days of old, that they may possess the remnant of Edom and of all the heathen which are called by my name, says

the Lord that does this. Behold, the days come, says the Lord, that the plowman shall overtake the reaper, and the treader of grapes him that sows seed. And the mountains shall drop sweet wine, and all the hills shall melt. And I will bring again the captives of my people of Israel, and they shall build the waste cities and inhabit them. And they shall plant vineyards and drink the wine thereof. They shall also make gardens and eat the fruit of them. And I will plant them upon their land, and they shall no more be pulled up out of their land which I have given them, says the Lord your God.

OBADIAH

The vision of Obadiah.

THUS says the Lord God concerning Edom: We have heard a rumor from the Lord, and an ambassador is sent among the heathen, Arise, and let us rise up against her in battle. Behold, I have made you small among the heathen; you are greatly despised. The pride of your heart has deceived you, you that dwell in the clefts of the rock, whose habitation is high, that says in his heart, Who shall bring me down to the ground? Though you exalt yourself as the eagle, and though you set your nest among the stars, from there will I bring you down, says the Lord. If thieves came to you, if robbers by night — how are you cut off! — would they not have stolen until they had enough? If the grape gatherers came to you, would they not leave some grapes? How are the things of Esau searched out, how are his hidden things sought up! All the men of your confederacy have brought you even to the border. The men that were at peace with you have deceived you and prevailed against you. They that eat your bread have laid a wound under you — there is no understanding in him. Shall I not in that day, says the Lord, even destroy the wise men out of Edom, and understanding out of the mount of Esau? And your mighty men, O Teman, shall be dismayed, to the end that everyone of the mount of Esau may be cut off by slaughter.

2 For your violence against your brother Jacob, shame shall cover you and you shall be cut off for ever. In the day that you stood on the other side, in the day that the strangers carried away captive his forces, and foreigners entered into his gates and cast lots upon Jerusalem, even

you were as one of them. But you should not have looked on the day of your brother in the day that he became a stranger. Neither should you have rejoiced over the children of Judah in the day of their destruction. Neither should you have spoken proudly in the day of distress. You should not have entered into the gate of my people in the day of their calamity. Yea, you should not have looked on their affliction in the day of their calamity, nor have laid hands on their substance in the day of their calamity. Neither should you have stood in the crossway to cut off those of his that did escape. Neither should you have delivered up those of his that did remain in the day of distress. For the day of the Lord is near upon all the heathen. As you have done, it shall be done unto you. Your reward shall return upon your own head. For as you have drunk upon my holy mountain, so shall all the heathen drink continually — yea, they shall drink, and they shall swallow down, and they shall be as though they had not been.

3 But upon Mount Zion shall be deliverance, and there shall be holiness. And the house of Jacob shall possess their possessions. And the house of Jacob shall be a fire, and the house of Joseph a flame, and the house of Esau for stubble, and they shall kindle in them and devour them. And there shall not be any remaining of the house of Esau, for the Lord has spoken it. And they of the south shall possess the mount of Esau, and they of the plain, the Philistines. And they shall possess the fields of Ephraim and the fields of Samaria. And Benjamin shall possess Gilead, and the captives of this host of the children of Israel that of the Canaanites, even unto Zarephath. And the captives of Jerusalem which are in Sepharad shall possess the cities of the south. And saviors shall come up on Mount Zion to judge the mount of Esau, and the kingdom shall be the Lord's.

JONAH

Now the word of the Lord came unto Jonah the son of Amittai, saying, Arise, go to Nineveh, that great city, and cry against it, for their wickedness has come up before me. But Jonah rose up to flee unto Tarshish from the presence of the Lord, and went down to Joppa. And he found a ship going to Tarshish, so he paid the fare thereof and went down into it, to go with them unto Tarshish from the presence of the Lord.

2 But the Lord sent out a great wind into the sea, and there was a mighty tempest in the sea, so that the ship was like to be broken. Then the mariners were afraid, and cried every man unto his god, and cast forth the wares that were in the ship into the sea, to lighten it of them. But Jonah was gone down into the sides of the ship, and he lay and was fast asleep. So the shipmaster came to him and said unto him, What do you mean, O sleeper? Arise, call upon your god, if it so be that god will think upon us, that we perish not.

3 And they said everyone to his fellow, Come and let us cast lots, that we may know for whose cause this evil is upon us. So they cast lots, and the lot fell upon Jonah. Then said they unto him, Tell us, we pray you, for whose cause this evil is upon us? What is your occupation and where do you come from? What is your country and of what people are you? And he said unto them, I am a Hebrew and I fear the Lord, the God of Heaven, who has made the sea and the dry land. Then were the men exceedingly afraid, and said unto him, Why have you done this? For the men knew that he fled from the presence of the Lord, because he had told them. Then said they unto him, What shall we do unto you that the sea may be calm unto us? For the sea raged and was tempestuous. And he said unto them, Take me up and cast me forth into the sea; so shall the sea be calm unto you. For I know that for my sake this great tempest is upon you.

4 Nevertheless, the men rowed hard to bring it to the land, but they could not; for the sea raged and was tempestuous against them. Wherefore, they cried unto the Lord and said, We implore you, O Lord, we implore you, let us not perish for this man's life, and lay not upon us innocent blood. For you, O Lord, have done as it pleased you. So they took up Jonah and cast him forth into the sea. And the sea ceased from her raging. Then the men feared the Lord exceedingly, and offered a sacrifice unto the Lord and made vows.

5 Now the Lord had prepared a great fish to swallow up Jonah, and Jonah was in the belly of the fish three days and three nights. Then Jonah prayed unto the Lord his God out of the fish's belly and said, I cried by reason of my affliction unto the Lord, and he heard me. Out of the belly of hell cried I, and you heard my voice. For you had cast

me into the deep, in the midst of the seas, and the floods encompassed me about. All your billows and your waves passed over me. Then I said, I am cast out of your sight. Yet I will look again toward your holy temple. The waters encompassed me about, even to the soul; the depths closed me round about. The weeds were wrapped about my head. I went down to the bottoms of the mountains. The Earth with her bars was about me for ever. Yet have you brought up my life from corruption, O Lord my God. When my soul fainted within me, I remembered the Lord, and my prayer came in unto you, into your holy temple. They that observe lying vanities forsake their own mercy. But I will sacrifice unto you with the voice of thanksgiving. I will pay that that I have vowed. Salvation is of the Lord. And the Lord spoke unto the fish, and it vomited out Jonah upon the dry land.

⁶ And the word of the Lord came unto Jonah the second time, saying, Arise, go unto Nineveh, that great city, and preach unto it the preaching that I bid you. So Jonah arose and went unto Nineveh according to the word of the Lord. Now Nineveh was an exceedingly great city of three days' journey. And Jonah began to enter into the city a day's journey, and he cried and said, Yet forty days and Nineveh shall be overthrown.

⁷ So the people of Nineveh believed God, and proclaimed a fast, and put on sackcloth — from the greatest of them even to the least of them. For word came unto the king of Nineveh, and he arose from his throne, and he laid his robe from himself, and covered himself with sackcloth, and sat in ashes. And he caused it to be proclaimed and published through Nineveh by the decree of the king and his nobles, saying, Let neither man nor beast, herd nor flock, taste anything. Let them not feed nor drink water, but let man and beast be covered with sackcloth and cry mightily unto God. Yea, let them turn every one from his evil way and from the violence that is in their hands. Who can tell, if we will repent and turn unto God, but he will turn away from us his fierce anger, that we perish not?

⁸ And God saw their works, that they turned from their evil way and repented. And God turned away the evil that he had said he would bring upon them.

⁹ But it displeased Jonah exceedingly, and he was very angry. And he prayed unto the Lord and said, I pray you, O Lord, was not this my saying when I was yet in my country? Therefore, I fled before unto

Tarshish; for I knew that you are a gracious God, and merciful, slow to anger and of great kindness, and you turn away the evil. Therefore now, O Lord, take, I implore you, my life from me, for it is better for me to die than to live. Then said the Lord, Do you do well to be angry?

¹⁰ So Jonah went out of the city and sat on the east side of the city, and there made him a booth, and sat under it in the shadow until he might see what would become of the city. And the Lord God prepared a gourd and made it to come up over Jonah, that it might be a shadow over his head to deliver him from his grief. So Jonah was exceedingly glad of the gourd. But God prepared a worm when the morning rose the next day, and it smote the gourd, that it withered. And it came to pass when the sun did arise that God prepared a vehement east wind, and the sun beat upon the head of Jonah, that he fainted and wished in himself to die, and said, It is better for me to die than to live.

¹¹ And God said to Jonah, Do you do well to be angry for the gourd? And he said, I do well to be angry, even unto death. Then said the Lord, You have had pity on the gourd for which you have not labored, neither made it grow, which came up in a night and perished in a night. And should not I spare Nineveh, that great city, wherein are more than one hundred twenty thousand people that cannot discern between their right hand and their left hand, and also much cattle?

MICAH

The word of the Lord that came to Micah the Morasthite in the days of Jotham, Ahaz, and Hezekiah, kings of Judah, which he saw concerning Samaria and Jerusalem.

HEAR, all you people. Listen, O earth, and all that therein is. And let the Lord God be witness against you, the Lord from his holy temple. For behold, the Lord comes forth out of his place, and will come down and tread upon the high places of the earth. And the mountains shall be molten under him, and the valleys shall be cleft, as wax before the fire and as the waters that are poured down a steep place. For the transgression of Jacob is all this, and for the sins of the house of Israel. What is the transgression of Jacob? Is it not Samaria? And what are the high places of Judah? Are they not Jerusalem? Therefore, I will make Samaria as a heap of the field and as plantings of a vineyard. And I will pour down the stones thereof into the valley, and I will uncover the foundations thereof. And all the engraved images thereof shall be beaten to pieces. And all the hires thereof shall be burned with the fire. And all the idols thereof will I lay desolate. For she gathered it of the hire of a harlot, and they shall return to the hire of a harlot. Therefore, I will wail and howl, I will go stripped and naked. I will make a wailing like the dragons and mourning as the owls. For her wound is incurable, for it has come unto Judah; he has come unto the gate of my people, even to Jerusalem.

2 Declare it not at Gath. Weep not at all. In the house of Aphrah, roll yourself in the dust. Pass on your way, you inhabitant of Saphir, having your shame naked. The inhabitant of Zaanan came not forth in the mourning of Bethezel. He shall receive of you his standing. For the inhabitant of Maroth waited anxiously for good, but evil came down from the Lord unto the gate of Jerusalem. O you inhabitant of Lachish, bind the chariot to the swift beast. She is the beginning of the sin to the daughter of Zion, for the transgressions of Israel were found in you. Therefore shall you give presents to Moresheth-Gath. The houses of Achzib shall be a lie to the kings of Israel. Yet will I bring an heir unto you, O inhabitant of Mareshah. He shall come unto Adullam, the glory of Israel. Make yourself bald and shave yourself for your delicate children. Enlarge your baldness as the eagle, for they are gone into captivity from you.

3 Woe to them that devise iniquity and work evil upon their beds. When the morning is light, they practice it because it is in the power of their hand. And they covet fields and take them by violence, and houses, and take them away. So they oppress a man and his house, even a man and his heritage. Therefore, thus says the Lord: Behold, against this family do I devise an evil from which you shall not remove your necks. Neither shall you go haughtily, for this time is evil.

4 In that day shall one take up a parable against you and lament with a doleful lamentation, and say, We are utterly spoiled; he has changed the portion of my people. How has he removed it from me! Turning away, he has divided our fields. Therefore, you shall have none that shall cast a cord by lot in the congregation of the Lord. Prophesy not, say they to them that prophesy. They shall not prophesy to them, that they shall not take shame.

⁵ O you that are named the house of Jacob, is the spirit of the Lord restricted? Are these his doings? Do not my words do good to him that walks uprightly? Even of late my people is risen up as an enemy. You pull off the robe with the garment from them that pass by securely as men averse from war. The women of my people have you cast out from their pleasant houses. From their children have you taken away my glory for ever. Arise and depart, for this is not your rest. Because it is polluted, it shall destroy you, even with a severe destruction. If a man walking in the spirit and falsehood do lie, saying, I will prophesy unto you of wine and of strong drink — he shall even be the prophet of this people.

⁶ I will surely assemble, O Jacob, all of you. I will surely gather the remnant of Israel. I will put them together as the sheep of Bozrah, as the flock in the midst of their fold. They shall make great noise by reason of the multitude of men. The breaker has come up before them; they have broken up, and have passed through the gate, and are gone out by it. And their king shall pass before them, and the Lord on the head of them.

⁷ And I said, Hear, I pray you, O heads of Jacob and you princes of the house of Israel, is it not for you to know judgment? Who hate the good, and love the evil; who pluck off their skin from off them, and their flesh from off their bones; who also eat the flesh of my people, and flay their skin from off them. And they break their bones and chop them in pieces as for the pot, and as flesh within the cauldron. Then shall they cry unto the Lord, but he will not hear them. He will even hide his face from them at that time, as they have behaved themselves ill in their doings.

⁸ Thus says the Lord: Concerning the prophets that make my people err, that bite with their teeth and cry, Peace — and he that puts not into their mouths, they even prepare war against him — therefore, night shall be unto you, that you shall not have a vision. And it shall be dark unto you, that you shall not divine. And the sun shall go down over the prophets, and the day shall be dark over them. Then shall the seers be ashamed and the diviners confounded. Yea, they shall all cover their lips, for there is no answer of God. But truly I am full of power by the spirit of the Lord, and of judgment, and of might, to declare unto Jacob his transgression and to Israel his sin. Hear this, I

pray you, you heads of the house of Jacob and princes of the house of Israel, that abhor judgment and pervert all equity. They build up Zion with blood and Jerusalem with iniquity. The heads thereof judge for reward, and the priests thereof teach for hire, and the prophets thereof divine for money. Yet will they lean upon the Lord and say, Is not the Lord among us? No evil can come upon us. Therefore shall Zion for your sake be plowed as a field, and Jerusalem shall become heaps, and the mountain of the house as the high places of the forest.

9 But in the last days, it shall come to pass that the mountain of the house of the Lord shall be established in the top of the mountains, and it shall be exalted above the hills, and people shall flow unto it. And many nations shall come and say, Come, and let us go up to the mountain of the Lord and to the house of the God of Jacob; and he will teach us of his ways, and we will walk in his paths. For the law shall go forth of Zion and the word of the Lord from Jerusalem. And he shall judge among many people and rebuke strong nations afar off. And they shall beat their swords into plowshares and their spears into pruning hooks. Nation shall not lift up a sword against nation, neither shall they learn war anymore, but they shall sit every man under his vine and under his fig tree, and none shall make them afraid. For the mouth of the Lord of Hosts has spoken it. For all people will walk everyone in the name of his god, and we will walk in the name of the Lord our God for ever and ever. In that day, says the Lord, will I assemble her that halts, and I will gather her that is driven out, and her that I have afflicted. And I will make her that halted a remnant, and her that was cast far off a strong nation. And the Lord shall reign over them in Mount Zion from henceforth, even for ever. And you, O tower of the flock, the stronghold of the daughter of Zion, unto you shall it come, even the first dominion. The kingdom shall come to the daughter of Jerusalem.

10 Now why do you cry out aloud? Is there no king in you? Is your counselor perished? For pangs have taken you as a woman in travail. Be in pain and labor to bring forth, O daughter of Zion, like a woman in travail. For now shall you go forth out of the city, and you shall dwell in the field. And you shall go even to Babylon. There shall you be delivered. There the Lord shall redeem you from the hand of your enemies. Now also many nations are gathered against you, that say,

Let her be defiled, and let our eye look upon Zion. But they know not the thoughts of the Lord, neither understand they his counsel. For he shall gather them as the sheaves into the floor. Arise and thresh, O daughter of Zion, for I will make your horn iron, and I will make your hooves brass, and you shall beat in pieces many people. And I will consecrate their gain unto the Lord and their substance unto the Lord of the whole earth.

11 Now gather yourself in troops, O daughter of troops. He has laid siege against us. They shall smite the judge of Israel with a rod upon the cheek. But you, Bethlehem, Ephrathah, though you be little among the thousands of Judah, yet out of you shall he come forth unto me that is to be ruler in Israel, whose goings forth have been from of old, from everlasting. Therefore will he give them up until the time that she which travails has brought forth. Then the remnant of his brethren shall return unto the children of Israel. And he shall stand and feed in the strength of the Lord, in the majesty of the name of the Lord his God. And they shall abide, for now shall he be great unto the ends of the earth. And this man shall be the peace when the Assyrian shall come into our land and when he shall tread in our palaces. Then shall we raise against him seven shepherds and eight principal men, and they shall waste the land of Assyria with the sword and the land of Nimrod in the entrances thereof. Thus shall he deliver us from the Assyrian when he comes into our land and when he treads within our borders.

12 And the remnant of Jacob shall be in the midst of many people as a dew from the Lord, as the showers upon the grass that tarries not for man nor waits for the sons of men. And the remnant of Jacob shall be among the gentiles, in the midst of many people, as a lion among the beasts of the forest, as a young lion among the flocks of sheep — who, if he go through, both treads down and tears in pieces, and none can deliver. Your hand shall be lifted up upon your adversaries, and all your enemies shall be cut off.

13 And it shall come to pass in that day, says the Lord, that I will cut off your horses out of your midst, and I will destroy your chariots. And I will cut off the cities of your land and throw down all your strongholds. And I will cut off witchcrafts out of your hand. And you shall have no more fortune-tellers. Your engraved images also will I cut off and your standing images out of your midst. And you shall no more worship

the work of your hands. And I will pluck up your groves out of your midst. So will I destroy your cities. And I will execute vengeance in anger and fury upon the heathen, such as they have not heard.

14 Hear now what the Lord says: Arise, contend before the mountains and let the hills hear your voice. Hear, O mountains, the Lord's controversy, and you strong foundations of the earth. For the Lord has a controversy with his people, and he will plead with Israel. O my people, what have I done unto you? And wherein have I wearied you? Testify against me. For I brought you up out of the land of Egypt and redeemed you out of the house of servants. And I sent before you Moses, Aaron, and Miriam. O my people, remember now what Balak king of Moab consulted, and what Balaam the son of Beor answered him, from Shittim unto Gilgal, that you may know the righteousness of the Lord. With what shall I come before the Lord and bow myself before the high God? Shall I come before him with burnt offerings, with calves of a year old? Will the Lord be pleased with thousands of rams or with ten thousands of rivers of oil? Shall I give my firstborn for my transgression, the fruit of my body for the sin of my soul? He has shown you, O man, what is good. And what does the Lord require of you? But to do justly, and to love mercy, and to walk humbly with your God.

15 The Lord's voice cries unto the city, and the man of wisdom shall see your name. Hear the rod and who has appointed it. Are there yet the treasures of wickedness in the house of the wicked, and the scant measure that is abominable? Shall I count them pure with the wicked balances and with the bag of deceitful weights? For the rich men thereof are full of violence, and the inhabitants thereof have spoken lies, and their tongue is deceitful in their mouth. Therefore also will I make you sick in smiting you, in making you desolate because of your sins. You shall eat, but not be satisfied. And your casting down shall be in your midst. And you shall take hold, but shall not deliver; and that which you deliver will I give up to the sword. You shall sow, but you shall not reap. You shall tread the olives, but you shall not anoint yourself with oil, and sweet wine, but shall not drink wine. For the statutes of Omri are kept, and all the works of the house of Ahab, and you walk in their counsels, that I should make you a desolation

and the inhabitants thereof a hissing. Therefore, you shall bear the reproach of my people.

16 Woe is me, for I am as when they have gathered the summer fruits, as the grape gleanings of the vintage; there is no cluster to eat. My soul desired the first ripe fruit. The good man is perished out of the earth, and there is none upright among men. They all lie in wait for blood. They hunt every man his brother with a net, that they may do evil with both hands earnestly. The prince asks and the judge asks for a reward. And the great man, he utters his mischievous desire, so they wrap it up. The best of them is as a brier. The most upright is sharper than a thorn hedge. The day of your watchmen and your visitation comes. Now shall be their perplexity. Trust not in a friend. Put not confidence in a guide. Keep the doors of your mouth from her that lies in your bosom. For the son dishonors the father, the daughter rises up against her mother, the daughter-in-law against her mother-in-law. A man's enemies are the men of his own house. Therefore, I will look unto the Lord, I will wait for the God of my salvation. My God will hear me.

17 Rejoice not against me, O my enemy. When I fall, I shall arise. When I sit in darkness, the Lord shall be a light unto me. I will bear the indignation of the Lord because I have sinned against him, until he plead my cause and execute judgment for me. He will bring me forth to the light and I shall behold his righteousness. Then she that is my enemy shall see it, and shame shall cover her which said unto me, Where is the Lord your God? My eyes shall behold her. Now shall she be trodden down as the mire of the streets. In the day that your walls are to be built, in that day shall the decree be far removed. In that day also, he shall come even to you from Assyria, and from the fortified cities, and from the fortress even to the river, and from sea to sea, and from mountain to mountain. Notwithstanding, the land shall be desolate because of them that dwell therein, for the fruit of their doings. Feed your people with your rod, the flock of your heritage which dwell solitarily in the wood, in the midst of Carmel. Let them feed in Bashan and Gilead as in the days of old. According to the days of your coming out of the land of Egypt will I show unto him marvelous things. The nations shall see and be confounded at all their might. They shall lay their hand upon their mouth. Their ears shall be deaf. They shall lick the dust like a serpent. They shall move

out of their holes like worms of the earth. They shall be afraid of the Lord our God and shall fear because of you.

¹⁸ Who is a God like unto you that pardons iniquity, and passes by the transgression of the remnant of his heritage? He retains not his anger for ever because he delights in mercy. He will turn again. He will have compassion upon us. He will subdue our iniquities. And you will cast all their sins into the depths of the sea. You will perform the truth to Jacob and the mercy to Abraham, which you have sworn unto our fathers from the days of old.

NAHUM

The burden of Nineveh; the book of the vision of Nahum the Elkoshite.

God is jealous, and the Lord avenges; the Lord avenges and is furious. The Lord will take vengeance on his adversaries, and he reserves wrath for his enemies. The Lord is slow to anger and great in power, and will not at all acquit the wicked. The Lord has his way in the whirlwind and in the storm, and the clouds are the dust of his feet. He rebukes the sea and makes it dry, and dries up all the rivers. Bashan languishes, and Carmel, and the flower of Lebanon languishes. The mountains quake at him and the hills melt, and the earth is burned at his presence, yea, the world and all that dwell therein. Who can stand before his indignation? And who can stand in the fierceness of his anger? His fury is poured out like fire, and the rocks are thrown down by him. The Lord is good, a stronghold in the day of trouble, and he knows them that trust in him. But with an overrunning flood he will make an utter end of the place thereof, and darkness shall pursue his enemies.

² What do you imagine against the Lord? He will make an utter end. Affliction shall not rise up the second time. For while they are folded as thorns, and while they are drunk as drunkards, they shall be devoured as stubble fully dry. There is one come out of you that imagines evil against the Lord, a wicked counselor. Thus says the Lord: Though they are quiet, and likewise many, yet thus shall they be cut down when he shall pass through. Though I have afflicted you, I will afflict you no more. For now will I break his yoke from off you and will burst your bonds asunder. And the Lord has given a commandment concerning

you, that no more of your name be sown. Out of the house of your gods will I cut off the engraved image and the molten image. I will make your grave, for you are vile.

3 Behold upon the mountains the feet of him that brings good tidings, that publishes peace. O Judah, keep your solemn feasts, perform your vows, for the wicked shall no more pass through you — he is utterly cut off. He that dashes in pieces has come up before your face. Keep the stronghold, watch the way. Make your loins strong, fortify your power mightily.

4 For the Lord has turned away the excellence of Jacob as the excellence of Israel, for the emptiers have emptied them out and marred their vine branches. The shield of his mighty men is made red; the valiant men are in scarlet. The chariots shall be with flaming torches in the day of his preparation, and the fir trees shall be terribly shaken. The chariots shall rage in the streets, they shall jostle one against another in the broad ways. They shall seem like torches, they shall run like the lightnings. He shall recount his worthies — they shall stumble in their walk, they shall make haste to the wall thereof, and the defense shall be prepared. The gates of the rivers shall be opened and the palace shall be dissolved. And Huzzab shall be led away captive, she shall be brought up and her maids shall lead her as with the voice of doves, beating upon their breasts. But Nineveh is of old like a pool of water, yet they shall flee away. Stand, stand! — shall they cry, but none shall look back. Take the spoil of silver, take the spoil of gold. For there is no end of the store and glory out of all the pleasant furniture. She is empty, and void, and waste. And the heart melts, and the knees smite together, and much pain is in all loins, and the faces of them all gather blackness. Where is the dwelling of the lions, and the feeding place of the young lions? Where the lion, even the old lion, walked, and the lion's whelp, and none made them afraid? The lion did tear in pieces enough for his whelps, and strangled for his lionesses, and filled his holes with prey and his dens with plunder. Behold, I am against you, says the Lord of Hosts, and I will burn her chariots in the smoke. And the sword shall devour your young lions. And I will cut off your prey from the earth, and the voice of your messengers shall no more be heard.

5 Woe to the bloody city, it is all full of lies and robbery, the prey departs not. The noise of a whip, and the noise of the rattling of the wheels, and of the galloping horses, and of the jumping chariots, the horseman lifts up both the bright sword and the glittering spear, and there is a multitude of slain and a great number of carcasses. And there is no end of their corpses. They stumble upon their corpses because of the multitude of the whoredoms of the well-favored harlot, the mistress of witchcrafts that sells nations through her whoredoms and families through her witchcrafts.

6 Behold, I am against you, says the Lord of Hosts, and I will uncover your skirts upon your face. And I will show the nations your nakedness and the kingdoms your shame. And I will cast abominable filth upon you and make you vile, and will set you as a spectacle. And it shall come to pass that all they that look upon you shall flee from you and say, Nineveh is laid waste. Who will bemoan her? From where shall I seek comforters for you?

7 Are you better than populous No that was situated among the rivers, that had the waters round about it, whose rampart was the sea and her wall was from the sea? Ethiopia and Egypt were her strength, and it was infinite; Put and Lubim were your helpers. Yet was she carried away, she went into captivity. Her young children also were dashed in pieces at the top of all the streets. And they cast lots for her honorable men, and all her great men were bound in chains. You also shall be drunk; you shall be hidden. You also shall seek strength because of the enemy. All your strongholds shall be like fig trees with the first ripe figs; if they are shaken, they shall even fall into the mouth of the eater.

8 Behold, your people in your midst are women. The gates of your land shall be set wide open unto your enemies. The fire shall devour your bars. Draw waters for the siege, fortify your strongholds. Go into clay, and tread the mortar; make strong the brickkiln. There shall the fire devour you. The sword shall cut you off; it shall eat you up like the cankerworm. Make yourself many as the cankerworm; make yourself many as the locusts. You have multiplied your merchants above the stars of heaven. The cankerworm spoils and flies away. Your crowned are as the locusts, and your captains as the great grasshoppers — which camp in the hedges in the cold day, but when the sun arises they flee away, and their place is not known where they are.

⁹ Your shepherds slumber, O king of Assyria. Your nobles shall dwell in the dust. Your people is scattered upon the mountains, and no man gathers them. There is no healing of your bruise, your wound is grievous. All that hear the report of you shall clap the hands over you. For upon whom has not your wickedness passed continually?

HABAKKUK

The burden which Habakkuk the prophet did see.

O LORD, how long shall I cry and you will not hear, even cry out unto you of violence and you will not save? Why do you show me iniquity and cause me to behold grievance? For spoiling and violence are before me, and there are that raise up strife and contention. Therefore, the law is slacked, and judgment does never go forth. For the wicked does turn the righteous, therefore wrong judgment proceeds.

² Behold among the heathen, and regard and wonder marvelously. For I will work a work in your days which you will not believe, though it be told to you. For behold, I raise up the Chaldeans, that bitter and hasty nation, which shall march through the breadth of the land to possess the dwelling places that are not theirs. They are terrible and dreadful. Their judgment and their dignity shall proceed of themselves. Their horses also are swifter than the leopards and are more fierce than the evening wolves. And their horsemen shall spread themselves, and their horsemen shall come from far. They shall fly as the eagle that hastens to eat. They shall come all for violence, their faces shall swallow up as the east wind, and they shall gather the captives as the sand. And they shall scoff at the kings, and the princes shall be a scorn unto them. They shall deride every stronghold, for they shall heap dust and take it. Then shall his mind change, and he shall pass over and offend, imputing this his power unto his god.

³ Are you not from everlasting, O Lord my God, my Holy One? We shall not die. O Lord, you have ordained them for judgment, and, O mighty God, you have established them for correction. You are of purer eyes than to behold evil, and cannot look on iniquity. Why do you look upon them that deal treacherously and hold your tongue when the wicked devours the man that is more righteous than he? And

makes men as the fishes of the sea, as the creeping things that have no ruler over them? They take up all of them with the fishhook. They catch them in their net and gather them in their drag; therefore, they rejoice and are glad. Therefore, they sacrifice unto their net and burn incense unto their drag, because by them their portion is fat and their food plenteous. Shall they therefore empty their net and not spare continually to slay the nations?

4 I will stand upon my watch and set myself upon the tower, and will watch to see what he will say unto me, and what I shall answer when I am reproved.

5 And the Lord answered me, and said, Write the vision and make it plain upon plates, that he may run that reads it. For the vision is yet for an appointed time, but at the end it shall speak and not lie. Though it delay, wait for it, because it will surely come — it will not fail. Behold, his soul which is lifted up is not upright in him. But the just shall live by his faith.

6 Yea also, because he transgresses by wine, he is a proud man, neither keeps at home, who enlarges his desire as hell and is as death, and cannot be satisfied, but gathers unto himself all nations and heaps unto himself all people. Shall not all these take up a parable against him and a taunting proverb against him, and say, Woe to him that increases that which is not his. How long? And to him that loads himself with thick clay, Shall they not rise up suddenly that shall bite you, and awake that shall vex you? And you shall be for prey unto them. Because you have spoiled many nations, all the remnant of the people shall spoil you — because of men's blood, and for the violence of the land, of the city, and of all that dwell therein.

7 Woe to him that covets an evil covetousness to his house, that he may set his nest on high, that he may be delivered from the power of evil. You have consulted shame to your house by cutting off many people, and have sinned against your soul. For the stone shall cry out of the wall and the beam out of the timber shall answer it.

8 Woe to him that builds a town with blood and establishes a city by iniquity. Behold, is it not of the Lord of Hosts that the people shall labor in the very fire, and the people shall weary themselves for very vanity? For the earth shall be filled with the knowledge of the glory of the Lord, as the waters cover the sea.

⁹ Woe unto him that gives his neighbor drink, that puts your bottle to him and makes him drunk also, that you may look on their nakedness. You are filled with shame for glory. Drink also, and let your foreskin be uncovered. The cup of the Lord's right hand shall be turned unto you, and shameful spewing shall be on your glory. For the violence of Lebanon shall cover you, and the spoil of beasts, which made them afraid because of men's blood, and for the violence of the land, of the city, and of all that dwell therein.

¹⁰ What profits the engraved image, that the maker thereof has engraved it — the molten image and a teacher of lies — that the maker of his work trusts therein to make dumb idols? Woe unto him that says to the wood, Awake — to the dumb stone, Arise, it shall teach. Behold, it is laid over with gold and silver, and there is no breath at all in the midst of it. But the Lord is in his holy temple. Let all the earth keep silence before him.

A prayer of Habakkuk the prophet upon Shigionoth.

2 O Lord, I have heard your speech and was afraid. O Lord, revive your work in the midst of the years, in the midst of the years make known. In wrath, remember mercy.

² God came from Teman, and the Holy One from Mount Paran. Selah. His glory covered the heavens, and the earth was full of his praise. And his brightness was as the light. He had horns coming out of his hand, and there was the hiding of his power. Before him went the pestilence, and burning coals went forth at his feet. He stood and measured the earth. He beheld and drove asunder the nations. And the everlasting mountains were scattered. The perpetual hills did bow. His ways are everlasting. I saw the tents of Cushan in affliction, and the curtains of the land of Midian did tremble. Was the Lord displeased against the rivers? Was your anger against the rivers? Was your wrath against the sea, that you did ride upon your horses and your chariots of salvation? Your bow was made quite naked, according to the oaths of the tribes, even your word. Selah. You did cleave the earth with rivers. The mountains saw you, and they trembled. The overflowing of the water passed by. The deep uttered his voice and lifted up his hands on high. The sun and moon stood still in their habitation. At the light of your arrows they went, and at the shining of your glittering spear.

You did march through the land in indignation. You did thresh the heathen in anger. You went forth for the salvation of your people, even for salvation with your anointed. You wounded the head out of the house of the wicked by exposing the foundation unto the neck. Selah. You did strike through with his staves the head of his villages. They came out as a whirlwind to scatter me. Their rejoicing was as to devour the poor secretly. You did walk through the sea with your horses, through the heap of great waters.

3 When I heard, my belly trembled. My lips quivered at the voice. Rottenness entered into my bones, and I trembled in myself, that I might rest in the day of trouble. When he comes up unto the people, he will invade them with his troops.

4 Although the fig tree shall not blossom, neither shall fruit be in the vines. The labor of the olive shall fail, and the fields shall yield no food. The flock shall be cut off from the fold, and there shall be no herd in the stalls. Yet I will rejoice in the Lord. I will joy in the God of my salvation. The Lord God is my strength, and he will make my feet like hinds' feet, and he will make me to walk upon my high places. To the chief singer on my stringed instruments.

ZEPHANIAH

THE word of the Lord which came unto Zephaniah the son of Cushi, the son of Gedaliah, the son of Amariah, the son of Hezekiah, in the days of Josiah the son of Amon, king of Judah: I will utterly consume all things from off the land, says the Lord. I will consume man and beast. I will consume the fowls of the heaven, and the fishes of the sea, and the stumbling blocks with the wicked. And I will cut off man from off the land, says the Lord. I will also stretch out my hand upon Judah and upon all the inhabitants of Jerusalem. And I will cut off the remnant of Baal from this place, and the name of the Chemarim with the priests, and them that worship the host of heaven upon the housetops, and them that worship and that swear by the Lord, and that swear by Milcom, and them that are turned back from the Lord, and those that have not sought the Lord, nor inquired for him.

2 Hold your peace at the presence of the Lord God, for the day of the Lord is at hand. For the Lord has prepared a sacrifice; he has bid his

guests. And it shall come to pass in the day of the Lord's sacrifice that I will punish the princes, and the king's children, and all such as are clothed with strange apparel. In the same day also will I punish all those that leap on the threshold, who fill their masters' houses with violence and deceit.

³ And it shall come to pass in that day, says the Lord, that there shall be the noise of a cry from the fish gate, and a howling from the second, and a great crashing from the hills. Howl, you inhabitants of Maktesh, for all the merchant people are cut down. All they that bear silver are cut off.

⁴ And it shall come to pass at that time that I will search Jerusalem with candles and punish the men that are settled on their lees — that say in their heart, The Lord will not do good, neither will he do evil. Therefore, their goods shall become a prey and their houses a desolation. They shall also build houses, but not inhabit them. And they shall plant vineyards, but not drink the wine thereof.

⁵ The great day of the Lord is near; it is near and hastens greatly, even the voice of the day of the Lord. The mighty man shall cry there bitterly. That day is a day of wrath, a day of trouble and distress, a day of devastation and desolation, a day of darkness and gloominess, a day of clouds and thick darkness, a day of the trumpet and alarm, against the fortified cities and against the high towers. And I will bring distress upon men, that they shall walk like blind men, because they have sinned against the Lord. And their blood shall be poured out as dust and their flesh as the dung. Neither their silver nor their gold shall be able to deliver them in the day of the Lord's wrath, but the whole land shall be devoured by the fire of his jealousy. For he shall make even a speedy riddance of all them that dwell in the land.

⁶ Gather yourselves together, yea, gather together, O nation not desired, before the decree bring forth, before the day pass as the chaff, before the fierce anger of the Lord come upon you, before the day of the Lord's anger come upon you. Seek the Lord, all you meek of the earth who have wrought his judgment. Seek righteousness, seek meekness. It may be you shall be hidden in the day of the Lord's anger.

⁷ For Gaza shall be forsaken and Ashkelon a desolation. They shall drive out Ashdod at the noonday, and Ekron shall be rooted up. Woe unto the inhabitants of the sea coast, the nation of the Cherethites. The

word of the Lord is against you, O Canaan, the land of the Philistines; I will even destroy you, that there shall be no inhabitant. And the sea coast shall be dwellings and cottages for shepherds and folds for flocks. And the coast shall be for the remnant of the house of Judah, they shall feed thereupon. In the houses of Ashkelon shall they lie down in the evening, for the Lord their God shall visit them and turn away their captivity.

8 I have heard the reproach of Moab, and the revilings of the children of Ammon, whereby they have reproached my people and magnified themselves against their border. Therefore, as I live, says the Lord of Hosts, the God of Israel, surely Moab shall be as Sodom, and the children of Ammon as Gomorrah — even the breeding of nettles, and salt pits, and a perpetual desolation. The residue of my people shall spoil them, and the remnant of my people shall possess them. This shall they have for their pride, because they have reproached and magnified themselves against the people of the Lord of Hosts. The Lord will be terrible unto them, for he will famish all the gods of the earth. And men shall worship him, everyone from his place, even all the isles of the heathen.

9 You Ethiopians also, you shall be slain by my sword. And he will stretch out his hand against the north and destroy Assyria, and will make Nineveh a desolation, and dry like a wilderness, and flocks shall lie down in her midst, all the beasts of the nations. Both the cormorant and the bittern shall lodge in the upper lintels of it; their voice shall sing in the windows. Desolation shall be in the thresholds, for he shall uncover the cedar work. This is the rejoicing city that dwelled carelessly, that said in her heart, I am, and there is none besides me. How is she become a desolation, a place for beasts to lie down in! Everyone that passes by her shall hiss and wag his hand.

10 Woe to her that is filthy and polluted, to the oppressing city. She obeyed not the voice, she received not correction. She trusted not in the Lord, she drew not near to her God. Her princes within her are roaring lions, her judges are evening wolves. They gnaw not the bones until the next day. Her prophets are light and treacherous people, her priests have polluted the sanctuary. They have done violence to the law. The just Lord is in the midst thereof. He will not do iniquity. Every morning does he bring his judgment to light. He fails not, but the

unjust knows no shame. I have cut off the nations, their towers are desolate. I made their streets waste, that none passes by. Their cities are destroyed, so that there is no man, that there is no inhabitant. I said, Surely you will fear me, you will receive instruction. So their dwelling should not be cut off; however, I punished them. But they rose early and corrupted all their doings.

11 Therefore, wait upon me, says the Lord, until the day that I rise up to the prey. For my determination is to gather the nations, that I may assemble the kingdoms, to pour upon them my indignation, even all my fierce anger. For all the earth shall be devoured with the fire of my jealousy. For then will I turn to the people a pure language, that they may all call upon the name of the Lord, to serve him with one consent. From beyond the rivers of Ethiopia, my suppliants, even the daughter of my dispersed, shall bring my offering. In that day, shall you not be ashamed for all your doings wherein you have transgressed against me? For then I will take away out of your midst them that rejoice in your pride, and you shall no more be haughty, because of my holy mountain. I will also leave in your midst an afflicted and poor people, and they shall trust in the name of the Lord. The remnant of Israel shall not do iniquity, nor speak lies, neither shall a deceitful tongue be found in their mouth. For they shall feed and lie down, and none shall make them afraid.

12 Sing, O daughter of Zion. Shout, O Israel. Be glad and rejoice with all the heart, O daughter of Jerusalem. The Lord has taken away your judgments. He has cast out your enemy. The king of Israel, even the Lord, is in your midst. You shall not see evil anymore. In that day, it shall be said to Jerusalem, Fear not — and to Zion, Let not your hands be slack. The Lord your God in your midst is mighty. He will save. He will rejoice over you with joy. He will rest in his love. He will joy over you with singing. I will gather them that are sorrowful for the solemn assembly, who are of you to whom the reproach of it was a burden. Behold, at that time I will undo all that afflict you. And I will save her that halts, and gather her that was driven out. And I will get them praise and fame in every land where they have been put to shame. At that time will I bring you again, even in the time that I gather you. For I will make you a name and a praise among all people of the earth when I turn back your captivity before your eyes, says the Lord.

HAGGAI

IN the second year of Darius the king, in the sixth month, in the first day of the month, came the word of the Lord by Haggai the prophet, unto Zerubbabel the son of Shealtiel, governor of Judah, and to Joshua the son of Jehozadak, the high priest, saying, Thus speaks the Lord of Hosts, saying: This people say, The time has not come, the time that the Lord's house should be built. Then came the word of the Lord by Haggai the prophet, saying, Is it time for you, O you, to dwell in your paneled houses and this house lie waste? Now therefore thus says the Lord of Hosts: Consider your ways. You have sown much and bring in little. You eat, but you have not enough. You drink, but you are not filled with drink. You clothe yourself, but there is none warm. And he that earns wages earns wages to put it into a bag with holes.

2 Thus says the Lord of Hosts: Consider your ways. Go up to the mountain, and bring wood, and build the house. And I will take pleasure in it and I will be glorified, says the Lord. You looked for much, and behold, it came to little. And when you brought it home, I did blow upon it. Why? — says the Lord of Hosts: Because of my house that is waste, and you run every man unto his own house. Therefore, the heaven over you is halted from dew and the earth is halted from fruit. And I called for a drought upon the land, and upon the mountains, and upon the grain, and upon the new wine, and upon the oil, and upon that which the ground brings forth, and upon men, and upon cattle, and upon all the labor of the hands.

3 Then Zerubbabel the son of Shealtiel, and Joshua the son of Jehozadak, the high priest, with all the remnant of the people, obeyed the voice of the Lord their God, and the words of Haggai the prophet, as the Lord their God had sent him. And the people did fear before the Lord. Then spoke Haggai the Lord's messenger in the Lord's message unto the people, saying, I am with you, says the Lord. And the Lord stirred up the spirit of Zerubbabel the son of Shealtiel, governor of Judah, and the spirit of Joshua the son of Jehozadak, the high priest, and the spirit of all the remnant of the people. And they came and did work in the house of the Lord of Hosts, their God, in the twenty-fourth day of the sixth month, in the second year of Darius the king.

⁴ In the seventh month, in the twenty-first day of the month, came the word of the Lord by the prophet Haggai, saying, Speak now to Zerubbabel the son of Shealtiel, governor of Judah, and to Joshua the son of Jehozadak, the high priest, and to the residue of the people, saying, Who is left among you that saw this house in her first glory? And how do you see it now? Is it not in your eyes in comparison of it as nothing? Yet now be strong, O Zerubbabel, says the Lord, and be strong, O Joshua son of Jehozadak, the high priest. And be strong, all you people of the land, says the Lord, and work. For I am with you, says the Lord of Hosts. According to the word that I covenanted with you when you came out of Egypt, so my spirit remains among you. Fear not, for thus says the Lord of Hosts: Yet once, it is a little while, and I will shake the heavens, and the earth, and the sea, and the dry land. And I will shake all nations. And the desire of all nations shall come. And I will fill this house with glory, says the Lord of Hosts. The silver is mine, and the gold is mine, says the Lord of Hosts. The glory of this latter house shall be greater than of the former, says the Lord of Hosts. And in this place will I give peace, says the Lord of Hosts.

⁵ In the twenty-fourth day of the ninth month, in the second year of Darius, came the word of the Lord by Haggai the prophet, saying, Thus says the Lord of Hosts: Ask now the priests concerning the law, saying, If one bear holy flesh in the skirt of his garment, and with his skirt do touch bread, or stew, or wine, or oil, or any food, shall it be holy? And the priests answered and said, No. Then said Haggai, If one that is unclean by a dead body touch any of these, shall it be unclean? And the priests answered and said, It shall be unclean. Then answered Haggai, and said, So is this people, and so is this nation before me, says the Lord, and so is every work of their hands. And that which they offer there is unclean. And now, I pray you, consider from this day and upward: from before a stone was laid upon a stone in the temple of the Lord, since those days were when one came to a heap of twenty measures, there were but ten; when one came to the winevat in order to draw out fifty vessels out of the press, there were but twenty. I smote you with blasting, and with mildew, and with hail in all the labors of your hands; yet you turned not to me, says the Lord. Consider now from this day and upward — from the twenty-fourth day of the ninth month, even from the day that the foundation of the Lord's temple was

laid, consider it—Is the seed yet in the barn? Yea, as yet the vine, and the fig tree, and the pomegranate, and the olive tree has not brought forth. From this day will I bless you.

6 And again the word of the Lord came unto Haggai, in the twenty-fourth day of the month, saying, Speak to Zerubbabel, governor of Judah, saying, I will shake the heavens and the earth, and I will overthrow the throne of kingdoms, and I will destroy the strength of the kingdoms of the heathen. And I will overthrow the chariots and those that ride in them, and the horses and their riders shall come down, every one by the sword of his brother. In that day, says the Lord of Hosts, will I take you, O Zerubbabel my servant, the son of Shealtiel, says the Lord, and will make you as a signet. For I have chosen you, says the Lord of Hosts.

ZECHARIAH

In the eighth month, in the second year of Darius, came the word of the Lord unto Zechariah the son of Berechiah, the son of Iddo the prophet, saying, The Lord has been sorely displeased with your fathers. Therefore, say unto them, Thus says the Lord of Hosts: Turn unto me, says the Lord of Hosts, and I will turn unto you, says the Lord of Hosts. Be not as your fathers unto whom the former prophets have cried, saying, Thus says the Lord of Hosts: Turn now from your evil ways and from your evil doings—but they did not hear, nor listen unto me, says the Lord. Your fathers, where are they? And the prophets, do they live for ever? But my words and my statutes which I commanded my servants the prophets, did they not take hold of your fathers? And they returned and said, Like the Lord of Hosts thought to do unto us, according to our ways and according to our doings, so has he dealt with us.

2 Upon the twenty-fourth day of the eleventh month, which is the month Sebat, in the second year of Darius, came the word of the Lord unto Zechariah the son of Berechiah, the son of Iddo the prophet, saying, I saw by night, and behold, a man riding upon a red horse, and he stood among the myrtle trees that were in the bottom. And behind him were there red horses, speckled, and white. Then said I, O my lord, what are these? And the angel that talked with me said unto me, I will

show you what these are. And the man that stood among the myrtle trees answered and said, These are they whom the Lord has sent to walk to and fro through the earth. And they answered the angel of the Lord that stood among the myrtle trees, and said, We have walked to and fro through the earth, and behold, all the earth sits still and is at rest. Then the angel of the Lord answered and said, O Lord of Hosts, how long will you not have mercy on Jerusalem and on the cities of Judah, against which you have had indignation these seventy years? And the Lord answered the angel that talked with me with good words and comforting words.

3 So the angel that spoke with me said unto me, Cry, saying, Thus says the Lord of Hosts: I am jealous for Jerusalem and for Zion with a great jealousy. And I am very sorely displeased with the heathen that are at ease. For I was but a little displeased, and they helped forward the affliction. Therefore, thus says the Lord: I am returned to Jerusalem with mercies, my house shall be built in it, says the Lord of Hosts, and a line shall be stretched forth upon Jerusalem. Cry yet, saying, Thus says the Lord of Hosts: My cities through prosperity shall yet be spread abroad. And the Lord shall yet comfort Zion, and shall yet choose Jerusalem.

4 Then lifted I up my eyes, and saw, and behold, four horns. And I said unto the angel that talked with me, What are these? And he answered me, These are the horns which have scattered Judah, Israel, and Jerusalem. And the Lord showed me four carpenters. Then said I, What do these come to do? And he spoke, saying, These are the horns which have scattered Judah, so that no man did lift up his head, but these have come to frighten them, to cast out the horns of the gentiles, which lifted up their horn over the land of Judah to scatter it.

5 I lifted up my eyes again and looked, and behold, a man with a measuring line in his hand. Then said I, Where are you going? And he said unto me, To measure Jerusalem, to see what is the breadth thereof and what is the length thereof. And behold, the angel that talked with me went forth, and another angel went out to meet him, and said unto him, Run, speak to this young man, saying, Jerusalem shall be inhabited as towns without walls for the multitude of men and cattle therein. For I, says the Lord, will be unto her a wall of fire round about, and will be the glory in her midst.

⁶ Ho, ho, come forth, and flee from the land of the north, says the Lord. For I have spread you abroad as the four winds of the heaven, says the Lord. Deliver yourself, O Zion, that dwells with the daughter of Babylon. For thus says the Lord of Hosts: After the glory has he sent me unto the nations which spoiled you — for he that touches you touches the apple of his eye — for behold, I will shake my hand upon them, and they shall be a spoil to their servants. And you shall know that the Lord of Hosts has sent me.

⁷ Sing and rejoice, O daughter of Zion, for behold, I come, and I will dwell in your midst, says the Lord. And many nations shall be joined to the Lord in that day and shall be my people. And I will dwell in your midst, and you shall know that the Lord of Hosts has sent me unto you. And the Lord shall inherit Judah, his portion in the holy land, and shall choose Jerusalem again. Be silent, O all flesh, before the Lord, for he is raised up out of his holy habitation.

⁸ And he showed me Joshua the high priest standing before the angel of the Lord, and Satan standing at his right hand to resist him. And the Lord said unto Satan, The Lord rebuke you, O Satan, even the Lord that has chosen Jerusalem rebuke you. Is not this a brand plucked out of the fire? Now Joshua was clothed with filthy garments and stood before the angel. And he answered and spoke unto those that stood before him, saying, Take away the filthy garments from him. And unto him he said, Behold, I have caused your iniquity to pass from you, and I will clothe you with change of raiment. And I said, Let them set a fair miter upon his head. So they set a fair miter upon his head and clothed him with garments. And the angel of the Lord stood by. And the angel of the Lord protested unto Joshua, saying, Thus says the Lord of Hosts: If you will walk in my ways and if you will keep my charge, then you shall also judge my house and shall also keep my courts. And I will give you places to walk among these that stand by. Hear now, O Joshua the high priest, you and your fellows that sit before you, for they are men wondered at. For behold, I will bring forth my servant the Branch. For behold the stone that I have laid before Joshua; upon one stone shall be seven eyes. Behold, I will engrave the engraving thereof, says the Lord of Hosts, and I will remove the iniquity of that land in one day. In that day, says the Lord of Hosts, shall you call every man his neighbor under the vine and under the fig tree.

9 And the angel that talked with me came again and woke me, as a man that is awakened out of his sleep, and said unto me, What do you see? And I said, I have looked, and behold a candlestick all of gold with a bowl upon the top of it, and his seven lamps thereon, and seven pipes to the seven lamps which are upon the top thereof; and two olive trees by it, one upon the right side of the bowl and the other upon the left side thereof. So I answered and spoke to the angel that talked with me, saying, What are these, my lord? Then the angel that talked with me answered and said unto me, Do you not know what these are? And I said, No, my lord.

10 Then he answered and spoke unto me, saying, This is the word of the Lord unto Zerubbabel, saying, Not by might nor by power, but by my spirit, says the Lord of Hosts. Who are you, O great mountain? Before Zerubbabel you shall become a plain. And he shall bring forth the headstone thereof with shoutings, crying, Grace, grace unto it! Moreover, the word of the Lord came unto me, saying, The hands of Zerubbabel have laid the foundation of this house; his hands shall also finish it. And you shall know that the Lord of Hosts has sent me unto you. For who has despised the day of small things? For they shall rejoice, and shall see the plummet in the hand of Zerubbabel with those seven. They are the servants of the Lord which run to and fro through the whole earth.

11 Then I answered and said unto him, What are these two olive trees, upon the right side of the candlestick and upon the left side thereof? And I answered again and said unto him, What are these two olive branches which, through the two golden pipes, empty the golden oil out of themselves? And he answered me and said, Do you not know what these are? And I said, No, my lord. Then said he, These are the two anointed ones that stand before the Lord of the whole earth.

12 Then I turned and lifted up my eyes and looked, and behold, a flying scroll. And he said unto me, What do you see? And I answered, I see a flying scroll. The length thereof is twenty cubits, and the breadth thereof ten cubits. Then said he unto me, This is the curse that goes forth over the face of the whole earth; for everyone that steals shall be cut off, as on this side according to it, and everyone that swears shall be cut off, as on that side according to it. I will bring it forth, says the Lord of Hosts, and it shall enter into the house of the thief and into

the house of him that swears falsely by my name. And it shall remain in the midst of his house, and shall consume it with the timber thereof and the stones thereof.

13 Then the angel that talked with me went forth, and said unto me, Lift up now your eyes, and see what is this that goes forth. And I said, What is it? And he said, This is an ephah that goes forth. He said moreover, This is their resemblance through all the earth. And behold, there was lifted up a talent of lead, and this is a woman that sits in the midst of the ephah. And he said, This is wickedness. And he cast it into the midst of the ephah, and he cast the weight of lead upon the mouth thereof. Then lifted I up my eyes and looked, and behold, there came out two women, and the wind was in their wings — for they had wings like the wings of a stork. And they lifted up the ephah between the earth and the heaven. Then said I to the angel that talked with me, Where do these bear the ephah? And he said unto me, To build it a house in the land of Shinar. And it shall be established and set there upon her own base.

14 And I turned and lifted up my eyes and looked, and behold, there came four chariots out from between two mountains; and the mountains were mountains of brass. In the first chariot were red horses, and in the second chariot black horses, and in the third chariot white horses, and in the fourth chariot grizzled and bay horses. Then I answered and said unto the angel that talked with me, What are these, my lord? And the angel answered and said unto me, These are the four servants of the heavens, which go forth from standing before the Lord of all the earth. The black horses which are therein go forth unto the north country, and the white go forth after them, and the grizzled go forth toward the south country. And the bay went forth and sought to go, that they might walk to and fro through the earth, and he said, Depart from here, walk to and fro through the earth. So they walked to and fro through the earth. Then cried he unto me, and spoke unto me, saying, Behold, these that go toward the north country have quieted my spirit in the north country.

15 And the word of the Lord came unto me, saying, Take of them of the captivity, even of Heldai, of Tobijah, and of Jedaiah, who have come from Babylon, and come the same day, and go into the house of Josiah the son of Zephaniah. Then take silver and gold and make

crowns, and set them upon the head of Joshua the son of Jehozadak, the high priest. And speak unto him, saying, Thus speaks the Lord of Hosts, saying: Behold the man whose name is The Branch. And he shall grow up out of his place, and he shall build the temple of the Lord. Even he shall build the temple of the Lord. And he shall bear the glory and shall sit and rule upon his throne. And he shall be a priest upon his throne. And the counsel of peace shall be between them both. And the crowns shall be to Helem, and to Tobijah, and to Jedaiah, and to Hen the son of Zephaniah, for a memorial in the temple of the Lord. And they that are far off shall come and build in the temple of the Lord. And you shall know that the Lord of Hosts has sent me unto you. And this shall come to pass if you will diligently obey the voice of the Lord your God.

16 And it came to pass, in the fourth year of king Darius, that the word of the Lord came unto Zechariah in the fourth day of the ninth month, even in Chislev, when they had sent unto the house of God Sharezer, and Regemmelech, and their men, to pray before the Lord and to speak unto the priests which were in the house of the Lord of Hosts, and to the prophets, saying, Should I weep in the fifth month, separating myself, as I have done these so many years?

17 Then came the word of the Lord of Hosts unto me, saying, Speak unto all the people of the land, and to the priests, saying, When you fasted and mourned in the fifth and seventh month, even those seventy years, did you at all fast unto me, even to me? And when you did eat and when you did drink, did not you eat for yourselves and drink for yourselves? Should you not hear the words which the Lord has cried by the former prophets when Jerusalem was inhabited and in prosperity, and the cities thereof round about her, when men inhabited the south and the plain?

18 And the word of the Lord came unto Zechariah, saying, Thus speaks the Lord of Hosts, saying: Execute true judgment, and show mercy and compassions, every man to his brother. And oppress not the widow nor the fatherless, the stranger nor the poor. And let none of you imagine evil against his brother in your heart. But they refused to listen, and pulled away the shoulder, and stopped their ears, that they should not hear. Yea, they made their hearts as a diamond, lest they should hear the law and the words which the Lord of Hosts has

sent in his spirit by the former prophets. Therefore came a great wrath from the Lord of Hosts. Therefore, it has come to pass that as he cried and they would not hear, so they cried and I would not hear, says the Lord of Hosts. But I scattered them with a whirlwind among all the nations whom they knew not. Thus the land was desolate after them, that no man passed through nor returned. For they laid the pleasant land desolate.

19 Again the word of the Lord of Hosts came to me, saying, Thus says the Lord of Hosts: I was jealous for Zion with great jealousy, and I was jealous for her with great fury. Thus says the Lord: I am returned unto Zion and will dwell in the midst of Jerusalem. And Jerusalem shall be called a city of truth, and the mountain of the Lord of Hosts, the holy mountain. Thus says the Lord of Hosts: There shall yet old men and old women dwell in the streets of Jerusalem, and every man with his staff in his hand for very age. And the streets of the city shall be full of boys and girls playing in the streets thereof. Thus says the Lord of Hosts: If it is marvelous in the eyes of the remnant of this people in these days, should it also be marvelous in my eyes? — says the Lord of Hosts.

20 Thus says the Lord of Hosts: Behold, I will gather my people from the east country and from the west country. And I will bring them, and they shall dwell in the midst of Jerusalem. And they shall be my people and I will be their God, in truth and in righteousness.

21 Thus says the Lord of Hosts: Let your hands be strong, you that hear in these days these words by the mouth of the prophets, which were in the day that the foundation of the house of the Lord of Hosts was laid, that the temple might be built. For before these days, there was no hire for man, nor any hire for beast, neither was there any peace to him that went out or came in, because of the affliction; for I set all men everyone against his neighbor. But now I will not be unto the residue of this people as in the former days, says the Lord of Hosts. For the seed shall be prosperous, the vine shall give her fruit, and the ground shall give her increase, and the heavens shall give their dew. And I will cause the remnant of this people to possess all these things. And it shall come to pass that as you were a curse among the heathen, O house of Judah and house of Israel, so will I gather you, and you shall be a blessing. Fear not, but let your hands be strong. For thus says the Lord of Hosts: As I thought to punish you when your fathers

provoked me to wrath, says the Lord of Hosts, and I repented not, so again have I thought in these days to do well unto Jerusalem and to the house of Judah. Fear not. These are the things that you shall do: speak every man the truth to his neighbor, execute the judgment of truth and peace in your gates, and let none of you imagine evil in your hearts against his neighbor, and love no false oath. For all these are things that I hate, says the Lord.

22 And the word of the Lord of Hosts came unto me, saying, Thus says the Lord of Hosts: The fast of the fourth month, and the fast of the fifth, and the fast of the seventh, and the fast of the tenth shall be to the house of Judah joy, and gladness, and cheerful feasts. Therefore, love the truth and peace.

23 Thus says the Lord of Hosts: It shall yet come to pass that there shall come people and the inhabitants of many cities. And the inhabitants of one city shall go to another, saying, Let us go speedily to pray before the Lord, and to seek the Lord of Hosts; I will go also. Yea, many people and strong nations shall come to seek the Lord of Hosts in Jerusalem and to pray before the Lord.

24 Thus says the Lord of Hosts: In those days, it shall come to pass that ten men shall take hold out of all languages of the nations, even shall take hold of the skirt of him that is a Jew, saying, We will go with you, for we have heard that God is with you.

25 The burden of the word of the Lord in the land of Hadrach; and Damascus shall be the rest thereof, when the eyes of man, as of all the tribes of Israel, shall be toward the Lord; and Hamath also shall border thereby; Tyre and Sidon, though it is very wise. And Tyre did build herself a stronghold, and heaped up silver as the dust, and fine gold as the mire of the streets. Behold, the Lord will cast her out and he will smite her power in the sea, and she shall be devoured with fire. Ashkelon shall see it and fear. Gaza also shall see it and be very sorrowful; and Ekron, for her expectation, shall be ashamed. And the king shall perish from Gaza, and Ashkelon shall not be inhabited. And a bastard shall dwell in Ashdod, and I will cut off the pride of the Philistines. And I will take away his blood out of his mouth, and his abominations from between his teeth. But he that remains, even he shall be for our God; and he shall be as a governor in Judah, and Ekron as a Jebusite. And I will encamp about my house because of the

army, because of him that passes by, and because of him that returns. And no oppressor shall pass through them anymore, for now have I seen with my eyes.

26 Rejoice greatly, O daughter of Zion. Shout, O daughter of Jerusalem. Behold, your King comes unto you. He is just, and having salvation, lowly, and riding upon an ass, and upon a colt, the foal of an ass. And I will cut off the chariot from Ephraim and the horse from Jerusalem, and the battle bow shall be cut off. And he shall speak peace unto the heathen. And his dominion shall be from sea even to sea, and from the river even to the ends of the earth. As for you also, by the blood of your covenant I have sent forth your prisoners out of the pit wherein is no water. Turn to the stronghold, you prisoners of hope. Even today do I declare that I will render double unto you, when I have bent Judah for me, filled the bow with Ephraim, and raised up your sons, O Zion, against your sons, O Greece, and made you as the sword of a mighty man. And the Lord shall be seen over them, and his arrow shall go forth as the lightning, and the Lord God shall blow the trumpet and shall go with whirlwinds of the south. The Lord of Hosts shall defend them, and they shall devour, and subdue with sling stones. And they shall drink and make a noise as through wine. And they shall be filled like bowls, and as the corners of the altar. And the Lord their God shall save them in that day as the flock of his people. For they shall be as the stones of a crown, lifted up as an ensign upon his land. For how great is his goodness and how great is his beauty! Grain shall make the young men cheerful, and new wine the virgins.

27 Ask of the Lord rain in the time of the spring rain. So the Lord shall make bright clouds and give them showers of rain, to everyone grass in the field. For the idols have spoken vanity, and the diviners have seen a lie and have told false dreams. They comfort in vain. Therefore, they went their way as a flock. They were troubled because there was no shepherd.

28 My anger was kindled against the shepherds, and I punished the goats. For the Lord of Hosts has visited his flock, the house of Judah, and has made them as his goodly horse in the battle. Out of him came forth the corner, out of him the nail, out of him the battle bow, out of him every oppressor together. And they shall be as mighty men, who tread down their enemies in the mire of the streets in the battle. And

they shall fight because the Lord is with them, and the riders on horses shall be confounded. And I will strengthen the house of Judah, and I will save the house of Joseph, and I will bring them again, to place them. For I have mercy upon them. And they shall be as though I had not cast them off, for I am the Lord their God and will hear them.

29 And they of Ephraim shall be like a mighty man, and their heart shall rejoice as through wine. Yea, their children shall see it and be glad. Their heart shall rejoice in the Lord. I will hiss for them and gather them, for I have redeemed them, and they shall increase as they have increased. And I will sow them among the people, and they shall remember me in far countries. And they shall live with their children and turn again. I will bring them again also out of the land of Egypt and gather them out of Assyria, and I will bring them into the land of Gilead and Lebanon, and place shall not be found for them. And he shall pass through the sea with affliction and shall smite the waves in the sea, and all the depths of the river shall dry up. And the pride of Assyria shall be brought down, and the scepter of Egypt shall depart away. And I will strengthen them in the Lord, and they shall walk up and down in his name, says the Lord.

30 Open your doors, O Lebanon, that the fire may devour your cedars. Howl, fir tree, for the cedar is fallen, because the mighty are spoiled. Howl, O you oaks of Bashan, for the forest of the vintage has come down. There is a voice of the howling of the shepherds, for their glory is spoiled, a voice of the roaring of young lions, for the pride of Jordan is spoiled. Thus says the Lord my God: Feed the flock of the slaughter, whose possessors slay them and hold themselves not guilty. And they that sell them say, Blessed be the Lord, for I am rich. And their own shepherds pity them not. For I will no more pity the inhabitants of the land, says the Lord, but behold, I will deliver the men, every one into his neighbor's hand and into the hand of his king. And they shall smite the land, and out of their hand I will not deliver them.

31 And I will feed the flock of slaughter, even you, O poor of the flock. And I took unto me two staves — the one I called Beauty, and the other I called Bands; and I fed the flock. Three shepherds also I cut off in one month. And my soul loathed them, and their soul also abhorred me. Then said I, I will not feed you. That which dies, let it die. And that which is to be cut off, let it be cut off. And let the rest eat everyone the

flesh of another. And I took my staff, even Beauty, and cut it asunder, that I might break my covenant which I had made with all the people. And it was broken in that day. And so the poor of the flock that waited upon me knew that it was the word of the Lord. And I said unto them, If you think good, give me my price, and if not, refuse. So they weighed for my price thirty pieces of silver. And the Lord said unto me, Cast it unto the potter—a goodly price that I was priced at of them. And I took the thirty pieces of silver and cast them to the potter in the house of the Lord. Then I cut asunder my other staff, even Bands, that I might break the brotherhood between Judah and Israel.

32 And the Lord said unto me, Take unto you yet the instruments of a foolish shepherd. For behold, I will raise up a shepherd in the land which shall not visit those that are cut off, neither shall seek the young one, nor heal that which is broken, nor feed that which stands still, but he shall eat the flesh of the fat and tear their claws in pieces. Woe to the idol shepherd that leaves the flock. The sword shall be upon his arm and upon his right eye. His arm shall be entirely dried up, and his right eye shall be utterly darkened.

33 The burden of the word of the Lord for Israel, says the Lord who stretches forth the heavens, and lays the foundation of the earth, and forms the spirit of man within him: Behold, I will make Jerusalem a cup of trembling unto all the people round about, when they shall be in the siege both against Judah and against Jerusalem. And in that day will I make Jerusalem a burdensome stone for all people. All that burden themselves with it shall be cut in pieces, though all the people of the earth be gathered together against it. In that day, says the Lord, I will smite every horse with astonishment and his rider with madness. And I will open my eyes upon the house of Judah and will smite every horse of the people with blindness. And the governors of Judah shall say in their heart, The inhabitants of Jerusalem shall be my strength in the Lord of Hosts, their God.

34 In that day will I make the governors of Judah like a hearth of fire among the wood, and like a torch of fire in a sheaf. And they shall devour all the people round about, on the right hand and on the left. And Jerusalem shall be inhabited again in her own place, even in Jerusalem. The Lord also shall save the tents of Judah first, that the glory of the house of David and the glory of the inhabitants of

Jerusalem do not magnify themselves against Judah. In that day shall the Lord defend the inhabitants of Jerusalem. And he that is feeble among them at that day shall be as David. And the house of David shall be as God, as the angel of the Lord before them. And it shall come to pass in that day that I will seek to destroy all the nations that come against Jerusalem.

35 And I will pour upon the house of David and upon the inhabitants of Jerusalem the spirit of grace and of supplications. And they shall look upon me whom they have pierced, and they shall mourn for him as one mourns for his only son, and shall be in bitterness for him as one that is in bitterness for his firstborn. In that day shall there be a great mourning in Jerusalem, as the mourning of Hadadrimmon in the valley of Megiddo. And the land shall mourn, every family apart. The family of the house of David apart and their wives apart, the family of the house of Nathan apart and their wives apart, the family of the house of Levi apart and their wives apart, the family of Shimei apart and their wives apart—all the families that remain, every family apart and their wives apart.

36 In that day, there shall be a fountain opened to the house of David and to the inhabitants of Jerusalem, for sin and for uncleanness. And it shall come to pass in that day, says the Lord of Hosts, that I will cut off the names of the idols out of the land, and they shall no more be remembered. And also I will cause the prophets and the unclean spirit to pass out of the land. And it shall come to pass that when any shall yet prophesy, then his father and his mother that begot him shall say unto him, You shall not live, for you speak lies in the name of the Lord. And his father and his mother that begot him shall thrust him through when he prophesies. And it shall come to pass in that day that the prophets shall be ashamed every one of his vision when he has prophesied, neither shall they wear a rough garment to deceive. But he shall say, I am no prophet, I am a husbandman, for man taught me to keep cattle from my youth. And one shall say unto him, What are these wounds in your hands? Then he shall answer, Those with which I was wounded in the house of my friends.

37 Awake, O sword, against my shepherd, and against the man that is my fellow, says the Lord of Hosts. Smite the shepherd and the sheep shall be scattered, and I will turn my hand upon the little ones. And it

shall come to pass that in all the land, says the Lord, two parts therein shall be cut off and die, but the third shall be left therein. And I will bring the third part through the fire, and will refine them as silver is refined, and will try them as gold is tried. They shall call on my name, and I will hear them. I will say, It is my people — and they shall say, The Lord is my God.

38 Behold, the day of the Lord comes, and your spoil shall be divided in your midst. For I will gather all nations against Jerusalem to battle, and the city shall be taken, and the houses rifled, and the women violated. And half of the city shall go forth into captivity, and the residue of the people shall not be cut off from the city. Then shall the Lord go forth and fight against those nations as when he fought in the day of battle. And his feet shall stand in that day upon the Mount of Olives, which is before Jerusalem on the east; and the Mount of Olives shall cleave in the middle thereof toward the east and toward the west, and there shall be a very great valley. And half of the mountain shall remove toward the north and half of it toward the south. And you shall flee to the valley of the mountains, for the valley of the mountains shall reach unto Azel. Yea, you shall flee like you fled from before the earthquake in the days of Uzziah king of Judah. And the Lord my God shall come, and all the saints with you.

39 And it shall come to pass in that day that the light shall not be clear nor dark, but it shall be one day which shall be known to the Lord, not day nor night; but it shall come to pass that at evening time it shall be light. And it shall be in that day that living waters shall go out from Jerusalem, half of them toward the eastern sea and half of them toward the western sea. In summer and in winter shall it be. And the Lord shall be king over all the earth. In that day shall there be one Lord, and his name one. All the land shall be turned as a plain, from Geba to Rimmon south of Jerusalem. And it shall be lifted up and inhabited in her place, from Benjamin's gate unto the place of the first gate, unto the corner gate, and from the tower of Hananel unto the king's winepresses. And men shall dwell in it, and there shall be no more utter destruction, but Jerusalem shall be safely inhabited.

40 And this shall be the plague with which the Lord will smite all the people that have fought against Jerusalem: their flesh shall consume away while they stand upon their feet, and their eyes shall consume

away in their holes, and their tongue shall consume away in their mouth. And it shall come to pass in that day that a great tumult from the Lord shall be among them. And they shall lay hold everyone on the hand of his neighbor, and his hand shall rise up against the hand of his neighbor. And Judah also shall fight at Jerusalem. And the wealth of all the heathen round about shall be gathered together — gold, and silver, and apparel in great abundance. And so shall be the plague of the horse, of the mule, of the camel, and of the ass, and of all the beasts that shall be in these tents, as this plague.

41 And it shall come to pass that everyone that is left of all the nations which came against Jerusalem shall even go up from year to year to worship the King, the Lord of Hosts, and to keep the Feast of Tabernacles. And it shall be that whoever will not come up of all the families of the earth unto Jerusalem to worship the King, the Lord of Hosts, even upon them shall be no rain. And if the family of Egypt go not up and come not, that have no rain, there shall be the plague by which the Lord will smite the heathen that come not up to keep the Feast of Tabernacles. This shall be the punishment of Egypt and the punishment of all nations that come not up to keep the Feast of Tabernacles.

42 In that day shall there be upon the bells of the horses, holiness unto the lord. And the pots in the Lord's house shall be like the bowls before the altar. Yea, every pot in Jerusalem and in Judah shall be holiness unto the Lord of Hosts, and all they that sacrifice shall come and take of them and boil therein. And in that day, there shall be no more the Canaanite in the house of the Lord of Hosts.

MALACHI

The burden of the word of the Lord to Israel by Malachi.

I HAVE loved you, says the Lord. Yet you say, Wherein have you loved us? Was not Esau Jacob's brother? — says the Lord. Yet I loved Jacob, and I hated Esau and laid his mountains and his heritage waste for the dragons of the wilderness. Whereas Edom says, We are impoverished, but we will return and build the desolate places — thus says the Lord of Hosts: They shall build, but I will throw down, and they shall call them the Region of Wickedness, and the people against whom the

Lord has indignation for ever. And your eyes shall see, and you shall say, The Lord will be magnified from the border of Israel.

2 A son honors his father, and a servant his master. If then I am a father, where is my honor? And if I am a master, where is my fear?—says the Lord of Hosts unto you, O priests, that despise my name. And you say, Wherein have we despised your name? You offer polluted bread upon my altar, and you say, Wherein have we polluted you? In that you say, The table of the Lord is contemptible. And if you offer the blind for sacrifice, is it not evil? And if you offer the lame and sick, is it not evil? Offer it now unto your governor. Will he be pleased with you or respect your person?—says the Lord of Hosts. And now, I pray you, implore God that he will be gracious unto us. This has been by your means, will he regard your persons?—says the Lord of Hosts. Who is there even among you that would shut the doors for naught? Neither do you kindle fire on my altar for naught. I have no pleasure in you, says the Lord of Hosts, neither will I accept an offering at your hand. For from the rising of the sun even unto the going down of the same, my name shall be great among the gentiles. And in every place, incense shall be offered unto my name, and a pure offering, for my name shall be great among the heathen, says the Lord of Hosts. But you have profaned it, in that you say, The table of the Lord is polluted, and the fruit thereof, even his food, is contemptible. You said also, Behold, what a weariness is it—and you have sniffed at it, says the Lord of Hosts. And you brought that which was torn, and the lame, and the sick—thus you brought an offering. Should I accept this of your hand?—says the Lord. But cursed be the deceiver which has in his flock a male, and vows, and sacrifices unto the Lord a corrupt thing; for I am a great king, says the Lord of Hosts, and my name is dreadful among the heathen.

3 And now, O you priests, this commandment is for you. If you will not hear and if you will not lay it to heart, to give glory unto my name, says the Lord of Hosts, I will even send a curse upon you, and I will curse your blessings. Yea, I have cursed them already, because you do not lay it to heart. Behold, I will corrupt your seed and spread dung upon your faces, even the dung of your solemn feasts, and one shall take you away with it. And you shall know that I have sent this commandment unto you, that my covenant might be with Levi, says

the Lord of Hosts. My covenant was with him of life and peace, and I gave them to him for the fear with which he feared me and was afraid before my name. The law of truth was in his mouth and iniquity was not found in his lips. He walked with me in peace and equity, and did turn many away from iniquity. For the priest's lips should keep knowledge, and they should seek the law at his mouth, for he is the messenger of the Lord of Hosts. But you are departed out of the way, you have caused many to stumble at the law, you have corrupted the covenant of Levi, says the Lord of Hosts. Therefore have I also made you contemptible and base before all the people, according as you have not kept my ways but have been partial in the law.

4 Have we not all one father? Has not one God created us? Why do we deal treacherously every man against his brother by profaning the covenant of our fathers? Judah has dealt treacherously, and an abomination is committed in Israel and in Jerusalem; for Judah has profaned the holiness of the Lord which he loved and has married the daughter of a strange god. The Lord will cut off the man that does this, the master and the scholar out of the tabernacles of Jacob, and him that offers an offering unto the Lord of Hosts. And this have you done again: covering the altar of the Lord with tears, with weeping and with crying out, insomuch that he regards not the offering anymore, or receives it with goodwill at your hand. Yet you say, Why? Because the Lord has been witness between you and the wife of your youth, against whom you have dealt treacherously. Yet is she your companion and the wife of your covenant. And did not he make one? Yet had he the residue of the spirit. And why one? That he might seek a godly seed. Therefore, take heed to your spirit, and let none deal treacherously against the wife of his youth. For the Lord, the God of Israel, says that he hates divorce, for one covers violence with his garment, says the Lord of Hosts. Therefore, take heed to your spirit, that you deal not treacherously.

5 You have wearied the Lord with your words. Yet you say, Wherein have we wearied him? When you say, Everyone that does evil is good in the sight of the Lord, and he delights in them — or, Where is the God of judgment?

6 Behold, I will send my messenger, and he shall prepare the way before me. And the Lord whom you seek shall suddenly come to his

temple, even the messenger of the covenant whom you delight in. Behold, he shall come, says the Lord of Hosts. But who may endure the day of his coming? And who shall stand when he appears? For he is like a refiner's fire and like fullers' soap. And he shall sit as a refiner and purifier of silver, and he shall purify the sons of Levi and purge them as gold and silver, that they may offer unto the Lord an offering in righteousness. Then shall the offering of Judah and Jerusalem be pleasant unto the Lord, as in the days of old and as in former years. And I will come near to you to judgment, and I will be a swift witness against the sorcerers, and against the adulterers, and against false swearers; and against those that oppress the hired hand in his wages, the widow, and the fatherless; and that turn aside the stranger from his right, and fear not me, says the Lord of Hosts. For I am the Lord, I change not; therefore, you sons of Jacob are not consumed.

7 Even from the days of your fathers you are gone away from my ordinances and have not kept them. Return unto me and I will return unto you, says the Lord of Hosts. But you said, Wherein shall we return? Will a man rob God? Yet you have robbed me. But you say, Wherein have we robbed you? In tithes and offerings. You are cursed with a curse, for you have robbed me, even this whole nation. Bring you all the tithes into the storehouse, that there may be food in my house, and prove me now herewith, says the Lord of Hosts, if I will not open you the windows of heaven and pour you out a blessing that there shall not be room enough to receive it. And I will rebuke the devourer for your sakes, and he shall not destroy the fruits of your ground, neither shall your vine cast her fruit before the time in the field, says the Lord of Hosts. And all nations shall call you blessed, for you shall be a delightsome land, says the Lord of Hosts.

8 Your words have been stout against me, says the Lord. Yet you say, What have we spoken so much against you? You have said, It is vain to serve God, and what profit is it that we have kept his ordinance and that we have walked mournfully before the Lord of Hosts? And now we call the proud happy. Yea, they that work wickedness are set up; yea, they that test God are even delivered.

9 Then they that feared the Lord spoke often one to another, and the Lord listened and heard it, and a book of remembrance was written before him for them that feared the Lord and that thought upon his

name. And they shall be mine, says the Lord of Hosts, in that day when I make up my jewels. And I will spare them as a man spares his own son that serves him. Then shall you return and discern between the righteous and the wicked, between him that serves God and him that serves him not.

¹⁰ For behold, the day comes that shall burn as an oven; and all the proud, yea, and all that do wickedly shall be stubble. And the day that comes shall burn them up, says the Lord of Hosts, that it shall leave them neither root nor branch. But unto you that fear my name shall the Sun of Righteousness arise with healing in his wings, and you shall go forth and grow up as calves of the stall. And you shall tread down the wicked, for they shall be ashes under the soles of your feet in the day that I shall do this, says the Lord of Hosts.

¹¹ Remember the law of Moses my servant, which I commanded unto him in Horeb for all Israel, with the statutes and judgments.

¹² Behold, I will send you Elijah the prophet before the coming of the great and dreadful day of the Lord. And he shall seal the heart of the Fathers to the children and the heart of the children to their Fathers, lest I come and smite the earth with a curse.

APPENDIX

Correlation of the Restoration Edition of the Old Testament
to Standard Bible Divisions

When references span multiple chapters, smaller-sized numbers refer to paragraph numbers.

RE	KJV/NIV/RSV	RE	KJV/NIV/RSV
GEN 1	–	LEV 1	LEV 1–6:8
GEN 2	GEN 1–3	LEV 2	LEV 6:9–10
GEN 3	GEN 4–5	LEV 3	LEV 11
GEN 4	–	LEV 4	LEV 12–14
GEN 5	GEN 6–9	LEV 5	LEV 15
GEN 6	GEN 10–11	LEV 6	LEV 16
GEN 7	GEN 12–20	LEV 7	LEV 17–18:5
GEN 8	GEN 21–25:18	LEV 8	LEV 18:6–30
GEN 9	GEN 25:19–35	LEV 9	LEV 19–20
GEN 10	GEN 36	LEV 10	LEV 21–22
GEN 11	GEN 37–46:7	LEV 11	LEV 23–24:9
GEN 12	GEN 46:8–50	LEV 12	LEV 24:10–23
EXO 1	EXO 1–2	LEV 13	LEV 25–26
EXO 2	EXO 3–4	LEV 14	LEV 27
EXO 3	EXO 5	NUM 1	NUM 1–3:4
EXO 4	EXO 6–7	NUM 2	NUM 3:5–4
EXO 5	EXO 8	NUM 3	NUM 5
EXO 6	EXO 9	NUM 4	NUM 6
EXO 7	EXO 10	NUM 5	NUM 7:1–88
EXO 8	EXO 11–13	NUM 6	NUM 7:89–8
EXO 9	EXO 14–15:21	NUM 7	NUM 9–12
EXO 10	EXO 15:22–17	NUM 8	NUM 13–15
EXO 11	EXO 18	NUM 9	NUM 16–19
EXO 12	EXO 19–20	NUM 10	NUM 20–24
EXO 13	EXO 21–24	NUM 11	NUM 25–27:11
EXO 14	EXO 25–27	NUM 12	NUM 27:12–30
EXO 15	EXO 28–29:37	NUM 13	NUM 31–36
EXO 16	EXO 29:38–31	DEUT 1	DEUT 1–3
EXO 17	EXO 32–33:6	DEUT 2	DEUT 2–6:9
EXO 18	EXO 33:7–34:28	DEUT 3	DEUT 6:10–11:17
EXO 19	EXO 34:29–39	DEUT 4	DEUT 11:18–13
EXO 20	EXO 40	DEUT 5	DEUT 14–17:13

Correlation of the Restoration Edition of the Old Testament to Standard Bible Divisions

When references span multiple chapters, smaller-sized numbers refer to paragraph numbers.

RE	KJV/NIV/RSV	RE	KJV/NIV/RSV
DEUT 6	DEUT 17:14–20	2 SAM 3	2 SAM 9–10
DEUT 7	DEUT 21–26	2 SAM 4	2 SAM 11–12:25
DEUT 8	DEUT 27–29:1	2 SAM 5	2 SAM 12:25–15:6
DEUT 9	DEUT 29:2–34	2 SAM 6	2 SAM 15:7–16:14
JOSH 1	JOSH 1–5	2 SAM 7	2 SAM 16:15–18:18
JOSH 2	JOSH 6–12	2 SAM 8	2 SAM 18:19–20
JOSH 3	JOSH 13–21	2 SAM 9	2 SAM 21
JOSH 4	JOSH 22	2 SAM 10	2 SAM 22
JOSH 5	JOSH 23–24	2 SAM 11	2 SAM 23
JUDG 1	JUDG 1–3:6	2 SAM 12	2 SAM 24
JUDG 2	JUDG 3:7–5	1 KGS 1	1 KGS 1
JUDG 3	JUDG 6–8:32	1 KGS 2	1 KGS 2–11
JUDG 4	JUDG 8:33–10:5	1 KGS 3	1 KGS 12–16
JUDG 5	JUDG 10:6–12	1 KGS 4	1 KGS 17–22
JUDG 6	JUDG 13–16	2 KGS 1	2 KGS 1–2
JUDG 7	JUDG 17–18	2 KGS 2	2 KGS 3–9
JUDG 8	JUDG 19–21	2 KGS 3	2 KGS 10
RUTH 1	RUTH 1	2 KGS 4	2 KGS 11–13
RUTH 2	RUTH 2	2 KGS 5	2 KGS 14–17
RUTH 3	RUTH 3–4	2 KGS 6	2 KGS 18–20
1 SAM 1	1 SAM 1–2:11	2 KGS 7	2 KGS 21–23
1 SAM 2	1 SAM 2:12–4:1	2 KGS 8	2 KGS 24–25
1 SAM 3	1 SAM 4:1–7	1 CHR 1	1 CHR 1–2:1
1 SAM 4	1 SAM 8–10	1 CHR 2	1 CHR 2:2–4:23
1 SAM 5	1 SAM 11–12	1 CHR 3	1 CHR 4:24–5
1 SAM 6	1 SAM 13–14	1 CHR 4	1 CHR 6
1 SAM 7	1 SAM 15–16	1 CHR 5	1 CHR 7
1 SAM 8	1 SAM 17–19:7	1 CHR 6	1 CHR 8–10
1 SAM 9	1 SAM 19:8–24	1 CHR 7	1 CHR 11–12
1 SAM 10	1 SAM 25–27:7	1 CHR 8	1 CHR 13–16
1 SAM 11	1 SAM 27:8–28	1 CHR 9	1 CHR 17–20
1 SAM 12	1 SAM 29–31	1 CHR 10	1 CHR 21–22
2 SAM 1	2 SAM 1–5:5	1 CHR 11	1 CHR 23–27
2 SAM 2	2 SAM 5:5–8	1 CHR 12	1 CHR 28–29
		2 CHR 1	2 CHR 1–5:1

Correlation of the Restoration Edition of the Old Testament
to Standard Bible Divisions

When references span multiple chapters, smaller-sized numbers refer to paragraph numbers.

RE	KJV/NIV/RSV	RE	KJV/NIV/RSV
2 CHR 2	2 CHR 5:2–7	PSALMS	PSALMS
2 CHR 3	2 CHR 8–9	PROV 1	PROV 1–9
2 CHR 4	2 CHR 10–12	PROV 2	PROV 10–22:16
2 CHR 5	2 CHR 13–14:1	PROV 3	PROV 22:17–24
2 CHR 6	2 CHR 14:2–16	PROV 4	PROV 25–29
2 CHR 7	2 CHR 17–20	PROV 5	PROV 30
2 CHR 8	2 CHR 21–22:1	PROV 6	PROV 31
2 CHR 9	2 CHR 22:1–5	ECCL 1	ECCL 1:1–3
2 CHR 10	2 CHR 23	ECCL 2	ECCL 1:4–9
2 CHR 11	2 CHR 24	ECCL 3	ECCL 1:10–14
2 CHR 12	2 CHR 25	ECCL 4	ECCL 1:15–18
2 CHR 13	2 CHR 26	ECCL 5	ECCL 1:19–23
2 CHR 14	2 CHR 27	ECCL 6	ECCL 1:24–26
2 CHR 15	2 CHR 28	ECCL 7	ECCL 1:27–32
2 CHR 16	2 CHR 29–32	ECCL 8	ECCL 1:32–36
2 CHR 17	2 CHR 33	ECCL 9	ECCL 1:37–41
2 CHR 18	2 CHR 34–35	ECCL 10	ECCL 1:42–52
2 CHR 19	2 CHR 36	ECCL 11	ECCL 1:53–57
EZRA 1	EZRA 1–6	ECCL 12	ECCL 1:58–60
EZRA 2	EZRA 7–10	ISA 1	ISA 1–5
NEH 1	NEH 1–2:8	ISA 2	ISA 6
NEH 2	NEH 2:9–13	ISA 3	ISA 7–8
ESTR	ESTR 1–10	ISA 4	ISA 9–10:19
JOB 1	JOB 1	ISA 5	ISA 10:20–12
JOB 2	JOB 2–3	ISA 6	ISA 13–23
JOB 3	JOB 4–7	ISA 7	ISA 24–27
JOB 4	JOB 8–10	ISA 8	ISA 28–29:10
JOB 5	JOB 11–14	ISA 9	ISA 29:11–30:26
JOB 6	JOB 15–17	ISA 10	ISA 30:26–31
JOB 7	JOB 18–19	ISA 11	ISA 32–33
JOB 8	JOB 20–21	ISA 12	ISA 34–35
JOB 9	JOB 22–24	ISA 13	36–40:2
JOB 10	JOB 25–31	ISA 14	ISA 40:3–31
JOB 11	JOB 32–37	ISA 15	ISA 41–46
JOB 12	JOB 38–42:6	ISA 16	ISA 47
JOB 13	JOB 42:7–17	ISA 17	ISA 48–50:3

Correlation of the Restoration Edition of the Old Testament to Standard Bible Divisions

When references span multiple chapters, smaller-sized numbers refer to paragraph numbers.

RE	KJV/NIV/RSV	RE	KJV/NIV/RSV
ISA 18	ISA 50:4–52:12	EZEK 9	EZEK 20
ISA 19	ISA 52:13–54	EZEK 10	EZEK 21–22
ISA 20	ISA 55–58	EZEK 11	EZEK 23
ISA 21	ISA 59	EZEK 12	EZEK 24
ISA 22	ISA 60	EZEK 13	EZEK 25
ISA 23	ISA 61	EZEK 14	EZEK 26–28
ISA 24	ISA 62–65	EZEK 15	EZEK 29–32
ISA 25	ISA 66	EZEK 16	EZEK 33:1–20
JER 1	JER 1–3:5	EZEK 17	EZEK 33:21–34
JER 2	JER 3:6–4:18	EZEK 18	EZEK 35–36
JER 3	JER 4:19–6	EZEK 19	EZEK 37
JER 4	JER 7–10	EZEK 20	EZEK 38–39
JER 5	JER 11–13	EZEK 21	EZEK 40–48
JER 6	JER 14–17:11	DAN 1	DAN 1
JER 7	JER 17:12–27	DAN 2	DAN 2
JER 8	JER 18–24	DAN 3	DAN 3
JER 9	JER 25	DAN 4	DAN 4
JER 10	JER 26–28	DAN 5	DAN 5
JER 11	JER 29	DAN 6	DAN 6
JER 12	JER 30–31	DAN 7	DAN 7
JER 13	JER 32–33	DAN 8	DAN 8
JER 14	JER 34–35	DAN 9	DAN 9
JER 15	JER 36–39:14	DAN 10	DAN 10–12
JER 16	JER 39:15–44	HOSEA 1	HOSEA 1–3
JER 17	JER 45–49	HOSEA 2	HOSEA 4–14
JER 18	JER 50–51	JOEL	JOEL 1–3
JER 19	JER 52	AMOS	AMOS 1–9
LAM	LAM 1–5	OBADIAH	OBADIAH
EZEK 1	EZEK 1–5	JONAH	JONAH 1–4
EZEK 2	EZEK 6–7	MICAH	MICAH 1–7
EZEK 3	EZEK 8–11	NAHUM	NAHUM 1–3
EZEK 4	EZEK 12:1–20	HAB 1	HAB
EZEK 5	EZEK 12:21–14	HAB 2	HAB
EZEK 6	EZEK 15–16	ZEPH	ZEPH 1–3
EZEK 7	EZEK 17	HAG	HAG 1–2
EZEK 8	EZEK 18–19	ZECH	ZECH 1–14
		MAL	MAL 1–4

Correlation of Standard Bible Divisions to the Restoration Edition of the Old Testament

KJV/NIV/RSV	RE	KJV/NIV/RSV	RE
–	GEN 1	GEN 34	GEN 9:50–51
GEN 1	GEN 2:1–8	GEN 35	GEN 9:52–59
GEN 2	GEN 2:8–14	GEN 36	GEN 10
GEN 3	GEN 2:15–20	GEN 37	GEN 11:1–10
GEN 4	GEN 3:1–14	GEN 38	GEN 11:11–13
GEN 5	GEN 3:15–23	GEN 39	GEN 11:14–16
–	GEN 4	GEN 40	GEN 11:17–20
GEN 6	GEN 5:1–12	GEN 41	GEN 11:21–27
GEN 7	GEN 5:13–16	GEN 42	GEN 11:28–32
GEN 8	GEN 5:17–21	GEN 43	GEN 11:33–34
GEN 9	GEN 5:21–24	GEN 44	GEN 11:35–38
GEN 10	GEN 6:1–5	GEN 45	GEN 11:39–42
GEN 11	GEN 6:6–8	GEN 46	GEN 11:43–12:7
GEN 12	GEN 7:1–5	GEN 47	GEN 12:8–16
GEN 13	GEN 7:6–13	GEN 48	GEN 12:17–18
GEN 14	GEN 7:12–22	GEN 49	GEN 12:19–32
GEN 15	GEN 7:23–25	GEN 50	GEN 12:33–43
GEN 16	GEN 7:26–28	EXO 1	EXO 1:1–3
GEN 17	GEN 7:29–35	EXO 2	EXO 1:4–2:1
GEN 18	GEN 7:36–40	EXO 3	EXO 2:2–5
GEN 19	GEN 7:41–46	EXO 4	EXO 2:6–11
GEN 20	GEN 7:47–48	EXO 5	EXO 3
GEN 21	GEN 8:1–4	EXO 6	EXO 4:1–9
GEN 22	GEN 8:5–8	EXO 7	EXO 4:10–12
GEN 23	GEN 8:9–10	EXO 8	EXO 5
GEN 24	GEN 8:11–18	EXO 9	EXO 6
GEN 25	GEN 8:19–9:3	EXO 10	EXO 7
GEN 26	GEN 9:4–11	EXO 11	EXO 8:1
GEN 27	GEN 9:12–17	EXO 12	EXO 8:2–7
GEN 28	GEN 9:18–21	EXO 13	EXO 8:8–10
GEN 29	GEN 9:22–26	EXO 14	EXO 9:1–4
GEN 30	GEN 9:27–30	EXO 15	EXO 9:5–10:1
GEN 31	GEN 9:31–38	EXO 16	EXO 10:2–8
GEN 32	GEN 9:39–44	EXO 17	EXO 10:9–10
GEN 33	GEN 9:45–49	EXO 18	EXO 11

Correlation of Standard Bible Divisions to the Restoration Edition of the Old Testament

KJV/NIV/RSV	RE	KJV/NIV/RSV	RE
EXO 19	EXO 12:1–3	LEV 14	LEV 4:15–21
EXO 20	EXO 12:4–15	LEV 15	LEV 5
EXO 21	EXO 13:1–3	LEV 16	LEV 6
EXO 22	EXO 13:4–16	LEV 17	LEV 7:1–3
EXO 23	EXO 13:17–23	LEV 18	LEV 7:4–8:3
EXO 24	EXO 13:24–26	LEV 19	LEV 9:1–15
EXO 25	EXO 14:1–3	LEV 20	LEV 9:16–21
EXO 26	EXO 14:4–7	LEV 21	LEV 10:1–3
EXO 27	EXO 14:8–10	LEV 22	LEV 10:4–8
EXO 28	EXO 15:1–6	LEV 23	LEV 11:1–11
EXO 29	EXO 15:7–16:1	LEV 24	LEV 11:12–12:3
EXO 30	EXO 16:2–6	LEV 25	LEV 13:1–7
EXO 31	EXO 16:7–8	LEV 26	LEV 13:8–16
EXO 32	EXO 17:1–9	LEV 27	LEV 14
EXO 33	EXO 17:10–18:4	NUM 1	NUM 1:1–16
EXO 34	EXO 18:5–19:1	NUM 2	NUM 1:17–22
EXO 35	EXO 19:2–6	NUM 3	NUM 1:23–2:9
EXO 36	EXO 19:7–12	NUM 4	NUM 2:10–18
EXO 37	EXO 19:13–17	NUM 5	NUM 3
EXO 38	EXO 19:18–22	NUM 6	NUM 4
EXO 39	EXO 19:23–27	NUM 7	NUM 5–6:1
EXO 40	EXO 20	NUM 8	NUM 6:2–5
LEV 1	LEV 1:1–3	NUM 9	NUM 7:1–3
LEV 2	LEV 1:4–7	NUM 10	NUM 7:4–10
LEV 3	LEV 1:8–10	NUM 11	NUM 7:11–20
LEV 4	LEV 1:11–5	NUM 12	NUM 7:21–23
LEV 5	LEV 1:16–20	NUM 13	NUM 8:1–5
LEV 6	LEV 1:21–2:4	NUM 14	NUM 8:6–13
LEV 7	LEV 2:5–10	NUM 15	NUM 8:14–18
LEV 8	LEV 2:11–8	NUM 16	NUM 9:1–10
LEV 9	LEV 2:19–24	NUM 17	NUM 9:11–12
LEV 10	LEV 2:25–29	NUM 18	NUM 9:13–16
LEV 11	LEV 3	NUM 19	NUM 9:17–20
LEV 12	LEV 4:1–2	NUM 20	NUM 10:1–5
LEV 13	LEV 4:3–14	NUM 21	NUM 10:6–13

Correlation of Standard Bible Divisions to the
Restoration Edition of the Old Testament

KJV/NIV/RSV	RE	KJV/NIV/RSV	RE
NUM 22	NUM 10:14–20	DEUT 21	DEUT 7:1–5
NUM 23	NUM 10:20–25	DEUT 22	DEUT 7:6–9
NUM 24	NUM 10:26–34	DEUT 23	DEUT 7:10–12
NUM 25	NUM 11:1–3	DEUT 24	DEUT 7:13–22
NUM 26	NUM 11:4–17	DEUT 25	DEUT 7:23–28
NUM 27	NUM 11:18–12:3	DEUT 26	DEUT 7:29–31
NUM 28	NUM 12:4–7	DEUT 27	DEUT 8:1–3
NUM 29	NUM 12:8–18	DEUT 28	DEUT 8:4–13
NUM 30	NUM 12:19–23	DEUT 29	DEUT 8:14–9:3
NUM 31	NUM 13:1–8	DEUT 30	DEUT 9:4–7
NUM 32	NUM 13:9–14	DEUT 31	DEUT 9:8–14
NUM 33	NUM 13:15–20	DEUT 32	DEUT 9:14–21
NUM 34	NUM 13:21–25	DEUT 33	DEUT 9:22–33
NUM 35	NUM 13:26–33	DEUT 34	DEUT 9:34–35
NUM 36	NUM 13:34–36	JOSH 1	JOSH 1:1–3
DEUT 1	DEUT 1:1–4	JOSH 2	JOSH 1:4–7
DEUT 2	DEUT 1:5–9	JOSH 3	JOSH 1:8–10
DEUT 3	DEUT 1:10–14	JOSH 4	JOSH 1:11–13
DEUT 4	DEUT 2:1–8	JOSH 5	JOSH 1:14–17
DEUT 5	DEUT 2:9–12	JOSH 6	JOSH 2:1–5
DEUT 6	DEUT 2:13–3:3	JOSH 7	JOSH 2:6–10
DEUT 7	DEUT 3:4–7	JOSH 8	JOSH 2:11–14
DEUT 8	DEUT 3:8–9	JOSH 9	JOSH 2:15–16
DEUT 9	DEUT 3:10–15	JOSH 10	JOSH 2:17–23
DEUT 10	DEUT 3:16–19	JOSH 11	JOSH 2:24–26
DEUT 11	DEUT 3:20–4:2	JOSH 12	JOSH 2:27–28
DEUT 12	DEUT 4:3–1	JOSH 13	JOSH 3:1
DEUT 13	DEUT 4:11–13	JOSH 14	JOSH 3:2–7
DEUT 14	DEUT 5:1–5	JOSH 15	JOSH 3:8–10
DEUT 15	DEUT 5:6–8	JOSH 16	JOSH 3:11
DEUT 16	DEUT 5:9–13	JOSH 17	JOSH 3:12–14
DEUT 17	DEUT 5:14–6:1	JOSH 18	JOSH 3:15–16
DEUT 18	DEUT 6:2–4	JOSH 19	JOSH 3:17–23
DEUT 19	DEUT 6:5–10	JOSH 20	JOSH 3:24
DEUT 20	DEUT 6:11–14	JOSH 21	JOSH 3:25–30

Correlation of Standard Bible Divisions to the Restoration Edition of the Old Testament

KJV/NIV/RSV	RE	KJV/NIV/RSV	RE
JOSH 22	JOSH 4	1 SAM 8	1 SAM 4:1–4
JOSH 23	JOSH 5:1–2	1 SAM 9	1 SAM 4:5–13
JOSH 24	JOSH 5:3–6	1 SAM 10	1 SAM 4:1–22
JUDG 1	JUDG 1:1–3	1 SAM 11	1 SAM 5:1–5
JUDG 2	JUDG 1:3–6	1 SAM 12	1 SAM 5:6–12
JUDG 3	JUDG 1:7–2:3	1 SAM 13	1 SAM 6:1–6
JUDG 4	JUDG 2:3–7	1 SAM 14	1 SAM 6:7–7:2
JUDG 5	JUDG 2:8–2:17	1 SAM 15	1 SAM 7:2–13
JUDG 6	JUDG 3:1–5	1 SAM 16	1 SAM 7:14–21
JUDG 7	JUDG 3:6–9	1 SAM 17	1 SAM 8:1–18
JUDG 8	JUDG 3:10–4:1	1 SAM 18	1 SAM 8:19–28
JUDG 9	JUDG 4:2–6	1 SAM 19	1 SAM 8:29–9:5
JUDG 10	JUDG 4:7–5:3	1 SAM 20	1 SAM 9:6–15
JUDG 11	JUDG 5:4–6	1 SAM 21	1 SAM 9:16–19
JUDG 12	JUDG 5:7–10	1 SAM 22	1 SAM 9:20–27
JUDG 13	JUDG 6:1–3	1 SAM 23	1 SAM 9:28–35
JUDG 14	JUDG 6:3–5	1 SAM 24	1 SAM 9:36–42
JUDG 15	JUDG 6:6–8	1 SAM 25	1 SAM 10:1–15
JUDG 16	JUDG 6:9–16	1 SAM 26	1 SAM 10:16–23
JUDG 17	JUDG 7:1–2	1 SAM 27	1 SAM 10:24–11:2
JUDG 18	JUDG 7:3–7	1 SAM 28	1 SAM 11:3–11
JUDG 19	JUDG 8:1–3	1 SAM 29	1 SAM 12:1–4
JUDG 20	JUDG 8:4–7	1 SAM 30	1 SAM 12:5–14
JUDG 21	JUDG 8:8–11	1 SAM 31	1 SAM 12:15–19
RUTH 1	RUTH 1	2 SAM 1	2 SAM 1:1–7
RUTH 2	RUTH 2	2 SAM 2	2 SAM 1:8–15
RUTH 3	RUTH 3:1–3	2 SAM 3	2 SAM 1:16–26
RUTH 4	RUTH 3:4–6	2 SAM 4	2 SAM 1:27–31
1 SAM 1	1 SAM 1:1–7	2 SAM 5	2 SAM 1:32–2:6
1 SAM 2	1 SAM 1:7–2:7	2 SAM 6	2 SAM 2:7–13
1 SAM 3	1 SAM 2:8–13	2 SAM 7	2 SAM 2:14–21
1 SAM 4	1 SAM 2:13–3:7	2 SAM 8	2 SAM 2:22–27
1 SAM 5	1 SAM 3:8–11	2 SAM 9	2 SAM 3:1–4
1 SAM 6	1 SAM 3:11–19	2 SAM 10	2 SAM 3:5–11
1 SAM 7	1 SAM 3:19–24	2 SAM 11	2 SAM 4:1–11

Correlation of Standard Bible Divisions to the
Restoration Edition of the Old Testament

KJV/NIV/RSV	RE	KJV/NIV/RSV	RE
2 SAM 12	2 SAM 4:11–5:2	2 KGS 1	2 KGS 1:1–6
2 SAM 13	2 SAM 5:3–17	2 KGS 2	2 KGS 1:7–14
2 SAM 14	2 SAM 5:18–27	2 KGS 3	2 KGS 2:1–5
2 SAM 15	2 SAM 5:28–6:8	2 KGS 4	2 KGS 2:6–12
2 SAM 16	2 SAM 6:9–7:2	2 KGS 5	2 KGS 2:13–18
2 SAM 17	2 SAM 7:3–11	2 KGS 6	2 KGS 2:19–25
2 SAM 18	2 SAM 7:12–8:4	2 KGS 7	2 KGS 2:26–32
2 SAM 19	2 SAM 8:5–16	2 KGS 8	2 KGS 2:33–40
2 SAM 20	2 SAM 8:17–26	2 KGS 9	2 KGS 2:41–8
2 SAM 21	2 SAM 9	2 KGS 10	2 KGS 3
2 SAM 22	2 SAM 10	2 KGS 11	2 KGS 4:1–5
2 SAM 23	2 SAM 11	2 KGS 12	2 KGS 4:6–11
2 SAM 24	2 SAM 12	2 KGS 13	2 KGS 4:12–17
1 KGS 1	1 KGS 1	2 KGS 14	2 KGS 5:1–6
1 KGS 2	1 KGS 2:1–14	2 KGS 15	2 KGS 5:7–13
1 KGS 3	1 KGS 2:15–21	2 KGS 16	2 KGS 5:14–17
1 KGS 4	1 KGS 2:22–26	2 KGS 17	2 KGS 5:18–26
1 KGS 5	1 KGS 2:27–30	2 KGS 18	2 KGS 6:1–5
1 KGS 6	1 KGS 2:31–39	2 KGS 19	2 KGS 6:6–11
1 KGS 7	1 KGS 2:40–50	2 KGS 20	2 KGS 6:12–16
1 KGS 8	1 KGS 2:51–69	2 KGS 21	2 KGS 7:1–4
1 KGS 9	1 KGS 2:70–76	2 KGS 22	2 KGS 7:5–8
1 KGS 10	1 KGS 2:77–84	2 KGS 23	2 KGS 7:9–15
1 KGS 11	1 KGS 2:85–96	2 KGS 24	2 KGS 8:1–4
1 KGS 12	1 KGS 3:1–10	2 KGS 25	2 KGS 8:5–10
1 KGS 13	1 KGS 3:11–21	1 CHR 1	1 CHR 1:1–13
1 KGS 14	1 KGS 3:22–31	1 CHR 2	1 CHR 1:14–2:13
1 KGS 15	1 KGS 3:32–41	1 CHR 3	1 CHR 2:14–17
1 KGS 16	1 KGS 3:42–52	1 CHR 4	1 CHR 2:18–3:5
1 KGS 17	1 KGS 4:1–7	1 CHR 5	1 CHR 3:6–13
1 KGS 18	1 KGS 4:8–22	1 CHR 6	1 CHR 4
1 KGS 19	1 KGS 4:22–29	1 CHR 7	1 CHR 5
1 KGS 20	1 KGS 4:30–47	1 CHR 8	1 CHR 6:1–2
1 KGS 21	1 KGS 4:48–57	1 CHR 9	1 CHR 6:3–11
1 KGS 22	1 KGS 5:1–17	1 CHR 10	1 CHR 6:12–17

Correlation of Standard Bible Divisions to the
Restoration Edition of the Old Testament

KJV/NIV/RSV	RE	KJV/NIV/RSV	RE
1 CHR 11	1 CHR 7:1–6	2 CHR 17	2 CHR 7:1–5
1 CHR 12	1 CHR 7:7–13	2 CHR 18	2 CHR 7:6–18
1 CHR 13	1 CHR 8:1–3	2 CHR 19	2 CHR 7:19–22
1 CHR 14	1 CHR 8:4–7	2 CHR 20	2 CHR 7:23–35
1 CHR 15	1 CHR 8:8–15	2 CHR 21	2 CHR 8:1–8
1 CHR 16	1 CHR 8:16–26	2 CHR 22	2 CHR 8:8–9:5
1 CHR 17	1 CHR 9:1–8	2 CHR 23	2 CHR 10
1 CHR 18	1 CHR 9:13	2 CHR 24	2 CHR 11
1 CHR 19	1 CHR 9:14–23	2 CHR 25	2 CHR 12
1 CHR 20	1 CHR 9:24–25	2 CHR 26	2 CHR 13
1 CHR 21	1 CHR 10:1–12	2 CHR 27	2 CHR 14
1 CHR 22	1 CHR 10:13–18	2 CHR 28	2 CHR 15
1 CHR 23	1 CHR 11:1–7	2 CHR 29	2 CHR 16:1–12
1 CHR 24	1 CHR 11:8–11	2 CHR 30	2 CHR 16:13–19
1 CHR 25	1 CHR 11:12–14	2 CHR 31	2 CHR 16:20–28
1 CHR 26	1 CHR 11:15–24	2 CHR 32	2 CHR 16:29–40
1 CHR 27	1 CHR 11:15–30	2 CHR 33	2 CHR 17
1 CHR 28	1 CHR 12:1–8	2 CHR 34	2 CHR 18:1–14
1 CHR 29	1 CHR 12:9–19	2 CHR 35	2 CHR 18:15–26
2 CHR 1	2 CHR 1:1–4	2 CHR 36	2 CHR 19
2 CHR 2	2 CHR 1:5–12	EZRA 1	EZRA 1:1–2
2 CHR 3	2 CHR 1:13–18	EZRA 2	EZRA 1:3–14
2 CHR 4	2 CHR 1:19–24	EZRA 3	EZRA 1:15–17
2 CHR 5	2 CHR 1:25–2:4	EZRA 4	EZRA 1:18–22
2 CHR 6	2 CHR 2:5–19	EZRA 5	EZRA 1:23–25
2 CHR 7	2 CHR 2:20–27	EZRA 6	EZRA 1:26–30
2 CHR 8	2 CHR 3:1–6	EZRA 7	EZRA 2:1–5
2 CHR 9	2 CHR 3:7–14	EZRA 8	EZRA 2:6–12
2 CHR 10	2 CHR 4:1–6	EZRA 9	EZRA 2:13–15
2 CHR 11	2 CHR 4:7–11	EZRA 10	EZRA 2:16–21
2 CHR 12	2 CHR 4:12–18	NEH 1	NEH 1:1–3
2 CHR 13	2 CHR 5:1–6	NEH 2	NEH 1:3–2:2
2 CHR 14	2 CHR 5:7–6:5	NEH 3	NEH 2:3–6
2 CHR 15	2 CHR 6:6–10	NEH 4	NEH 2:7–11
2 CHR 16	2 CHR 6:11–14	NEH 5	NEH 2:12–14

Correlation of Standard Bible Divisions to the
Restoration Edition of the Old Testament

KJV/NIV/RSV	RE	KJV/NIV/RSV	RE
NEH 6	NEH 2:15–17	JOB 18	JOB 7:1–4
NEH 7	NEH 2:18–30	JOB 19	JOB 7:5–10
NEH 8	NEH 2:31–33	JOB 20	JOB 8:1–5
NEH 9	NEH 2:34–37	JOB 21	JOB 8:6–10
NEH 10	NEH 2:38–41	JOB 22	JOB 9:1–4
NEH 11	NEH 2:42–50	JOB 23	JOB 9:5–7
NEH 12	NEH 2:51–57	JOB 24	JOB 9:8–10
NEH 13	NEH 2:58–64	JOB 25	JOB 10:1
ESTR 1	ESTR 1:1–4	JOB 26	JOB 10:2–4
ESTR 2	ESTR 1:5–11	JOB 27	JOB 10:5–7
ESTR 3	ESTR 1:12–14	JOB 28	JOB 10:8–10
ESTR 4	ESTR 1:15–19	JOB 29	JOB 10:11–14
ESTR 5	ESTR 1:20–22	JOB 30	JOB 10:15–19
ESTR 6	ESTR 1:23–24	JOB 31	JOB 10:20–29
ESTR 7	ESTR 1:25–26	JOB 32	JOB 11:1–4
ESTR 8	ESTR 1:27–31	JOB 33	JOB 11:5–11
ESTR 9	ESTR 1:32–38	JOB 34	JOB 11:12–18
ESTR 10	ESTR 1:39	JOB 35	JOB 11:19–21
JOB 1	JOB 1	JOB 36	JOB 11:22–27
JOB 2	JOB 2:1–4	JOB 37	JOB 11:28–31
JOB 3	JOB 2:5–7	JOB 38	JOB 12:1–9
JOB 4	JOB 3:1–3	JOB 39	JOB 12:10–15
JOB 5	JOB 3:4–7	JOB 40	JOB 12:16–20
JOB 6	JOB 3:8–13	JOB 41	JOB 12:21–24
JOB 7	JOB 3:14–14	JOB 42	JOB 12:25–13:4
JOB 8	JOB 4:1–3	PSALMS	PSALMS
JOB 9	JOB 4:4–8	PROV 1	PROV 1:1–4
JOB 10	JOB 4:9–12	PROV 2	PROV 1:5–6
JOB 11	JOB 5:1–3	PROV 3	PROV 1:7–15
JOB 12	JOB 5:4–7	PROV 4	PROV 1:16–19
JOB 13	JOB 5:8–12	PROV 5	PROV 1:20–22
JOB 14	JOB 5:12–15	PROV 6	PROV 1:23–30
JOB 15	JOB 6:1–6	PROV 7	PROV 1:31–33
JOB 16	JOB 6:7–12	PROV 8	PROV 1:34–37
JOB 17	JOB 6:12–15	PROV 9	PROV 1:38–40

Correlation of Standard Bible Divisions to the
Restoration Edition of the Old Testament

KJV/NIV/RSV	RE	KJV/NIV/RSV	RE
PROV 10	PROV 2:1–32	ISA 1	ISA 1:1–4
PROV 11	PROV 2:33–63	ISA 2	ISA 1:5–8
PROV 12	PROV 2:64–91	ISA 3	ISA 1:9–10
PROV 13	PROV 2:92–116	ISA 4	ISA 1:11–12
PROV 14	PROV 2:117–151	ISA 5	ISA 1:13–20
PROV 15	PROV 2:152–184	ISA 6	ISA 2
PROV 16	PROV 2:185–217	ISA 7	ISA 3:1–3
PROV 17	PROV 2:218–245	ISA 8	ISA 3:4–7
PROV 18	PROV 2:246–269	ISA 9	ISA 4:1–4
PROV 19	PROV 2:270–298	ISA 10	ISA 4:5–5:3
PROV 20	PROV 2:299–328	ISA 11	ISA 5:4–5
PROV 21	PROV 2:329–358	ISA 12	ISA 5:6
PROV 22	PROV 2:359–3:7	ISA 13	ISA 6:1–3
PROV 23	PROV 3:8–16	ISA 14	ISA 6:4–8
PROV 24	PROV 3:17–32	ISA 15	ISA 6:9
PROV 25	PROV 4:1–23	ISA 16	ISA 6:10–11
PROV 26	PROV 4:24–47	ISA 17	ISA 6:12–13
PROV 27	PROV 4:48–69	ISA 18	ISA 6:14
PROV 28	PROV 4:70–97	ISA 19	ISA 6:15–17
PROV 29	PROV 4:98–124	ISA 20	ISA 6:18–19
PROV 30	PROV 5	ISA 21	ISA 6:20–22
PROV 31	PROV 6	ISA 22	ISA 6:23–24
ECCL 1	ECCL	ISA 23	ISA 6:25–27
ECCL 2	ECCL	ISA 24	ISA 7:1–2
ECCL 3	ECCL	ISA 25	ISA 7:3
ECCL 4	ECCL	ISA 26	ISA 7:4–5
ECCL 5	ECCL	ISA 27	ISA 7:6–7
ECCL 6	ECCL	ISA 28	ISA 8:1–5
ECCL 7	ECCL	ISA 29	ISA 8:6
ECCL 8	ECCL	ISA 30	ISA 8:7–10:1
ECCL 9	ECCL	ISA 31	ISA 10:2–4
ECCL 10	ECCL	ISA 32	ISA 11:1–2
ECCL 11	ECCL	ISA 33	ISA 11:3–5
ECCL 12	ECCL	ISA 34	ISA 12:1–3
SONG OF SOLOMON	–	ISA 35	ISA 12:4–5

Correlation of Standard Bible Divisions to the
Restoration Edition of the Old Testament

KJV/NIV/RSV	RE	KJV/NIV/RSV	RE
ISA 36	ISA 13:1–5	JER 5	JER 3:3–7
ISA 37	ISA 13:6–12	JER 6	JER 3:8–10
ISA 38	ISA 13:13–15	JER 7	JER 4:1–4
ISA 39	ISA 13:16	JER 8	JER 4:5–9
ISA 40	ISA 13:17–14:5	JER 9	JER 4:10–13
ISA 41	ISA 15:1–6	JER 10	JER 4:14–18
ISA 42	ISA 15:7–10	JER 11	JER 5:1–3
ISA 43	ISA 15:11–14	JER 12	JER 5:4–7
ISA 44	ISA 15:15–17	JER 13	JER 5:8–10
ISA 45	ISA 15:8–19	JER 14	JER 6:1–4
ISA 46	ISA 15:20–21	JER 15	JER 6:5–8
ISA 47	ISA 16	JER 16	JER 6:9–10
ISA 48	ISA 17:1–4	JER 17	JER 6:11–7:2
ISA 49	ISA 17:5–8	JER 18	JER 8:1–3
ISA 50	ISA 17:9–18:1	JER 19	JER 8:4–5
ISA 51	ISA 18:2–6	JER 20	JER 8:6–8
ISA 52	ISA 18:7–19:1	JER 21	JER 8:9–11
ISA 53	ISA 19:2–3	JER 22	JER 8:12–15
ISA 54	ISA 19:4–5	JER 23	JER 8:16–20
ISA 55	ISA 20:1–2	JER 24	JER 8:21
ISA 56	ISA 20:3–4	JER 25	JER 9:1–4
ISA 57	ISA 20:5–6	JER 26	JER 10:1–4
ISA 58	ISA 20:7	JER 27	JER 10:5–7
ISA 59	ISA 21	JER 28	JER 10:8–9
ISA 60	ISA 22	JER 29	JER 11
ISA 61	ISA 23	JER 30	JER 12:1–4
ISA 62	ISA 24:1	JER 31	JER 12:5–10
ISA 63	ISA 24:2–4	JER 32	JER 13:1–5
ISA 64	ISA 24:5	JER 33	JER 13:6–10
ISA 65	ISA 24:6–9	JER 34	JER 14:1–4
ISA 66	ISA 25	JER 35	JER 14:5–7
JER 1	JER 1:1–3	JER 36	JER 15:1–7
JER 2	JER 1:4–9	JER 37	JER 15:8–12
JER 3	JER 1:10–2:4	JER 38	JER 15:13–16
JER 4	JER 2:5–3:2	JER 39	JER 15:17–16:1

Correlation of Standard Bible Divisions to the Restoration Edition of the Old Testament

KJV/NIV/RSV	RE	KJV/NIV/RSV	RE
JER 40	JER 16:2–4	EZEK 18	EZEK 8:1–8
JER 41	JER 16:5–8	EZEK 19	EZEK 8:9–10
JER 42	JER 16:9–10	EZEK 20	EZEK 9
JER 43	JER 16:11–12	EZEK 21	EZEK 10:1–6
JER 44	JER 16:13–15	EZEK 22	EZEK 10:7–10
JER 45	JER 17:1	EZEK 23	EZEK 11
JER 46	JER 17:2–4	EZEK 24	EZEK 12
JER 47	JER 17:5	EZEK 25	EZEK 13
JER 48	JER 17:6–10	EZEK 26	EZEK 14:1–4
JER 49	JER 17:11–18:1	EZEK 27	EZEK 14:5–9
JER 50	JER 18:2–9	EZEK 28	EZEK 14:10–14
JER 51	JER 18:10–19:1	EZEK 29	EZEK 15:1–4
JER 52	JER 19:2–7	EZEK 30	EZEK 15:5–9
LAM 1	LAM 1:1–5	EZEK 31	EZEK 15:10–12
LAM 2	LAM 1:6–10	EZEK 32	EZEK 15:13–23
LAM 3	LAM 1:11–14	EZEK 33	EZEK 16:1–17:4
LAM 4	LAM 1:15–19	EZEK 34	EZEK 17:5–11
LAM 5	LAM 1:20–21	EZEK 35	EZEK 18:1–3
EZEK 1	EZEK 1:1–7	EZEK 36	EZEK 18:4–11
EZEK 2	EZEK 1:7–8	EZEK 37	EZEK 19
EZEK 3	EZEK 1:8–12	EZEK 38	EZEK 20:1–6
EZEK 4	EZEK 1:13–17	EZEK 39	EZEK 20:7–13
EZEK 5	EZEK 1:18–22	EZEK 40	EZEK 21:1–15
EZEK 6	EZEK 2:1–3	EZEK 41	EZEK 21:16–22
EZEK 7	EZEK 2:4–8	EZEK 42	EZEK 21:23–26
EZEK 8	EZEK 3:1–6	EZEK 43	EZEK 21:27–34
EZEK 9	EZEK 3:7–8	EZEK 44	EZEK 21:35–42
EZEK 10	EZEK 3:9–14	EZEK 45	EZEK 21:43–50
EZEK 11	EZEK 3:15–19	EZEK 46	EZEK 21:51–57
EZEK 12	EZEK 4:1–5:2	EZEK 47	EZEK 21:58–67
EZEK 13	EZEK 5:3–7	EZEK 48	EZEK 21:68–77
EZEK 14	EZEK 5:8–11	DAN 1	DAN 1
EZEK 15	EZEK 6:1–2	DAN 2	DAN 2
EZEK 16	EZEK 6:3–14	DAN 3	DAN 3
EZEK 17	EZEK 7	DAN 4	DAN 4

Correlation of Standard Bible Divisions to the
Restoration Edition of the Old Testament

KJV/NIV/RSV	RE	KJV/NIV/RSV	RE
DAN 5	DAN 5	JONAH 1	JONAH 1:1–5
DAN 6	DAN 6	JONAH 2	JONAH 1:5
DAN 7	DAN 7	JONAH 3	JONAH 1:6–8
DAN 8	DAN 8	JONAH 4	JONAH 1:9–11
DAN 9	DAN 9	MICAH 1	MICAH 1:1–2
DAN 10	DAN 10:1–5	MICAH 2	MICAH 1:3–6
DAN 11	DAN 10:5–17	MICAH 3	MICAH 1:7–8
DAN 12	DAN 10:18–20	MICAH 4	MICAH 1:9–10
HOSEA 1	HOSEA 1:1–4	MICAH 5	MICAH 1:11–13
HOSEA 2	HOSEA 1:5–10	MICAH 6	MICAH 1:14–15
HOSEA 3	HOSEA 1:11	MICAH 7	MICAH 1:16–18
HOSEA 4	HOSEA 2:1–3	NAHUM 1	NAHUM 1:1–3
HOSEA 5	HOSEA 2:4–6	NAHUM 2	NAHUM 1:3–4
HOSEA 6	HOSEA 2:7–9	NAHUM 3	NAHUM 1:5–9
HOSEA 7	HOSEA 2:10–12	HAB 1	HAB 1:1–3
HOSEA 8	HOSEA 2:13–16	HAB 2	HAB 1:4–10
HOSEA 9	HOSEA 2:17–22	HAB 3	HAB 2
HOSEA 10	HOSEA 2:23–27	ZEPH 1	ZEPH 1:1–5
HOSEA 11	HOSEA 2:28–30	ZEPH 2	ZEPH 1:6–9
HOSEA 12	HOSEA 2:30–34	ZEPH 3	ZEPH 1:10–12
HOSEA 13	HOSEA 2:34–38	HAG 1	HAG 1:1–3
HOSEA 14	HOSEA 2:39–40	HAG 2	HAG 1:4–6
JOEL 1	JOEL 1:1–5	ZECH 1	ZECH 1:1–4
JOEL 2	JOEL 1:6–12	ZECH 2	ZECH 1:5–7
JOEL 3	JOEL 1:13–16	ZECH 3	ZECH 1:8
AMOS 1	AMOS 1:1–5	ZECH 4	ZECH 1:9–11
AMOS 2	AMOS 1:6–8	ZECH 5	ZECH 1:12–13
AMOS 3	AMOS 1:9–10	ZECH 6	ZECH 1:14–15
AMOS 4	AMOS 1:11–12	ZECH 7	ZECH 1:16–18
AMOS 5	AMOS 1:13–16	ZECH 8	ZECH 1:19–24
AMOS 6	AMOS 1:17–19	ZECH 9	ZECH 1:25–26
AMOS 7	AMOS 1:20–24	ZECH 10	ZECH 1:27–29
AMOS 8	AMOS 1:25–27	ZECH 11	ZECH 1:30–32
AMOS 9	AMOS 1:28–31	ZECH 12	ZECH 1:33–35
OBADIAH	OBADIAH		

Correlation of Standard Bible Divisions to the Restoration Edition of the Old Testament

KJV/NIV/RSV	RE
ZECH 13	ZECH 1:36–37
ZECH 14	ZECH 1:38–42
MAL 1	MAL 1:1–2
MAL 2	MAL 1:3–5
MAL 3	MAL 1:6–9
MAL 4	MAL 1:10–12

CPSIA information can be obtained
at www.ICGtesting.com
Printed in the USA
LVHW061457180723
752687LV00009B/742

9 781951 168551